2005 Tax Angles for Special Taxpayers

CCH Editorial Staff Publication

CCH INCORPORATED
Chicago

A WoltersKluwer Company

ISBN 0-8080-1213-4

4025 W. Peterson Ave.
Chicago, IL 60646-6085
1 800 449 8114
http://tax.cchgroup.com

A WoltersKluwer Company

TAXPAYERS IN SPECIAL CLASSIFICATIONS

The Internal Revenue Code focuses on four groups of taxpayers—individuals (single, married, head of household), business entities, estates, and trusts. Individuals, however, may be in any number of special categories, such as corporate executives, professional persons, farmers, salespersons, U.S. citizens abroad, day-care center operators, clergy, and students. Provisions affecting these special categories of individual taxpayers are scattered throughout the Code.

Therefore, CCH tax law editors have culled from the Code, and coordinated in this convenient work, the provisions affecting taxpayers in a number of classifications.

The material here supplements and is an extension of the 2005 FEDERAL TAX GUIDE through paragraph references. Also, the Topical Index, Case Table, Rulings Finding List, and Code and Regulations Finding Lists of the GUIDE contain entries to the paragraphs in this work.

For later developments affecting the material contained in this work, users should consult the weekly issues of *Tax Week* and the Cumulative Indexes in Volume 1A of the 2005 GUIDE.

Please retain this material for coordination with the FEDERAL TAX GUIDE during the remainder of the 2005 reporting year.

As we go to press, there is still a chance for tax legislation coming out of a lame duck congressional session. To track late-breaking legislative developments, visit CCH's website at tax.cchgroup.com for the latest news and information.

November 2004

SPECIAL TAXPAYERS

Salespersons

Schoolteachers

Military Service Members

Residents of Community Property States

U.S. Citizens Abroad

Members of the Clergy

Older Taxpayers
Day-Care Providers

Students

Aliens

Statutory Employees

Tip Recipients and Payors

CORPORATE EXECUTIVES

Introduction

¶25,001 Tax planning for corporate executives strives both to provide compensation that is not subject to tax (e.g., tax-free fringe benefits) and to defer current compensation until a later year (e.g., incentive stock options (ISOs) or pension plan contributions) when the executive may be in a lower tax bracket.

Tax planning for executives should also be of interest to their corporate employers. If the corporation offers an attractive compensation package, one that provides a combination of high current income and tax-favored benefits, the corporation will be able to recruit and retain valuable key executives. Tax planning for corporate executives becomes even more important to corporations because executive compensation in excess of $1,000,000 is not deductible unless tied to the achievement of performance-based objectives.

Reasonableness of compensation. Corporations, particularly those that are closely held by their executives-owners, must make sure to pay reasonable compensation to those executives.

Excessive compensation. A problem that often arises with respect to compensation paid by a corporation to an executive who is also a shareholder in the corporation is the reclassification of compensation as a dividend payment because such compensation exceeds an amount that is considered reasonable compensation. The executive must report the amount received as ordinary income, regardless of whether the income is treated as compensation or a dividend. However, the corporation may not deduct a dividend payment from its gross income; it may only deduct a compensation payment.

Insufficient compensation. One problem that may arise with respect to compensation paid to executives of closely held corporations is that the executive may prefer to forgo a salary that would generate an employment tax liability, and instead receive dividends that are not subject to such liability. Particularly in the case of an S corporation that may avoid double taxation of corporate earnings, the overall tax burden to the executive and the corporation may be lessened by this course of conduct. Caution is necessary because the IRS has required such corporations and their owners to pay employment taxes on a reasonable amount of compensation for services rendered to these entities by the executives.

Capital gains. Generally, a noncorporate taxpayer's net capital gain is taxed at a maximum rate ranging from 5 to 15 percent. (Higher rates apply to certain

types of gains (e.g., gain from collectibles). As result of the low capital gains rates, an executive whose ordinary income is subject to a higher rate (e.g., 35 percent) will achieve a greater tax savings if some of that income is received in the form of long-term capital gain.

Cash v. Stock Compensation

¶25,002 Cash v. Stock Compensation. An executive who receives cash compensation is subject to ordinary income tax rates. Such rates are progressive in that they increase with increases in taxable income until they reach the maximum tax rate. A major objective of tax-conscious executives is to avoid application of the higher income tax rates on their compensation by having income deferred until a tax year when the executive may be in a lower tax bracket or by receiving current compensation in nontaxable forms. Sometimes a mere deferral of compensation is not in the executive's best interest due to the time value of money. Thus, while executives may be able to obtain a short-run tax advantage by deferring a portion of their income, in the long run they may lose economically because they do not have the use of the money (for example, for investment purposes) for a period of years. An ideal arrangement defers taxation while allowing the money to work and grow for the executive.

One effective method of reducing an executive's current income tax is to provide compensation in the form of stock bonuses (.05) or stock purchase plans (.10). If these stock plans are not "qualified" under specific standards set forth in the Internal Revenue Code, then executives will generally be taxed on the fair market value of the stock when it is transferred to them unless the property is subject to a substantial risk of forfeiture or the employee's interest is nontransferable. Once the risk of forfeiture is lifted and the employee's interest is transferable, the value of the stock at that time less any amount paid for the stock is includible in income (.15).

In the situation in which the stock is transferred under a nonqualified plan without restrictions on the executive's ownership rights, there are few tax-saving aspects that are available to the executive. Due to this lack of tax savings under nonqualified stock plans, most stock compensation plans are designed to be meet requirements imposed by the Code.

Under a qualified stock bonus or stock option plan, executives will enjoy favorable tax treatment when stock is transferred to them. Qualified stock compensation plans are an effective method of rewarding executives and yet helping them to avoid current income tax on the value of the reward. In addition, the corporate employer benefits under the stock compensation plan: an executive who is acquiring a tangible interest in the future worth of the employer will have a personal motivation in seeing that the corporation prospers.

.05 Reg. §1.401-1(b)(2)(iii).
.10 Code Sec. 421(a).
.15 Code Sec. 83(a).

Alternative Minimum Tax on Tax Preferences

¶25,003 Tax Preferences. An executive who receives certain tax breaks may become liable for the alternative minimum tax (AMT) (.05). AMT is in addition to any regularly computed income tax and is based on the taxpayer's having taken advantage of certain deductions, credits or exclusions referred to as tax preference items. Its purpose is to ensure that individuals who receive large amounts of tax preference items pay at least some income tax on the value of these items.

Awareness of AMT is important in the executive's tax planning process because its effect is to reduce the tax savings that tne executive hopes to achieve. Although AMT generally will not eliminate the tax savings that have been achieved, it is still a factor that must be contended with.

As a general rule, the alternative minimum tax imposes a 26- or 28-percent tax rate on an alternative minimum taxable income that exceeds a specified exemption amount. Lower rates are imposed on most types of capital gains. Because the minimum tax rate is below the marginal tax rate for individuals who are in the highest tax brackets, executives may still realize some tax advantage by moving income into a year in which AMT applies and out of a year in which it does not apply.

.05 Code Sec. 55 through 59.

Relocation

¶ 25,004 Moving Expense Reimbursement. A corporation that searches for executive talent may find it necessary to hire someone living a significant distance from the corporate work site. If the company is large enough, it may also find it necessary to transfer executives within the corporation from one location to another. For those reasons, it is not unusual for employers to set up a moving expense reimbursement plan (.05).

Qualified moving expenses reimbursed by an employer are excludable from an employee's gross income as a fringe benefit (.10). To the extent that it is a reimbursement of qualified moving expenses, it is not considered wages for purposes of withholding taxes (.15). A moving expense allowance that exceeds an executive's qualified moving expenses, even if it is paid for actual expenses, is subject to withholding taxes.

Allowable moving expenses are claimed as a deduction from gross income. However, no moving expense deduction is allowable in the absence of adequate documentation, and no deduction is allowed for other than what is reasonable under the circumstances. Moving expenses cannot be deducted unless two tests are met:

(1) The new main job location must be at least 50 miles farther from the executive's former home than the distance from the former job location to the former home; if the executive did not have an old job location, the new job location must be at least 50 miles from the executive's former home.

(2) Upon arriving in the general area of the new job location, an executive must be employed full time for at least 39 weeks during the 12-month period following the executive's arrival (78 weeks during a 24-month period for self-employed persons).

Even if the above tests are met, the only moving expenses that are deductible are the expenses of moving household goods and personal effects from the former to the new residence and the cost of traveling (including lodging but not meals) from the former to the new residence.

Most moving expenses are not deductible. The cost of house-hunting trips and temporary living expenses not deductible. Similarly, certain expenses associated with the sale of the former residence and the purchase or lease of the new residence are not deductible. Also, a relocated executive cannot deduct as moving expenses the cost of home improvements to help sell a home, mortgage penalties, loss on the sale of a home, or any part of the purchase price of a new home. An executive also cannot deduct losses from disposing of memberships in clubs, the cost of refitting draperies, and expenses relating to title transfer costs for vehicles or costs for obtaining a new driver's license.

Travel and transportation expenses

There is no limit on the amount of the deduction for moving expenses; there are only limits on the type of deductions allowed. If an executive has expenses relating to a sale, exchange, or purchase of a residence, the expenses may be used to reduce the amount realized on the sale of the executive's former home or may be added to the basis of the new home, but they cannot be deducted as moving expenses.

A relocated executive may deduct reasonable travel expenses from the former residence to the new residence and the expenses of moving household goods and personal effects. No fixed dollar limit is placed upon such amounts. Travel expenses include the cost of a one-way trip to the new home for the executive and the members of the executive's household. Although only a one-way trip is allowed, not all of the members of a household need travel together.

Transportation expenses can be computed either according to actual cost or, if the executive has used an automobile, at 14 cents a mile for 2004 plus parking fees and tolls. Travel expenses also include any lodging expenses incurred while traveling as well as such expenses incurred on the day of arrival. In addition, the executive may further include such expenses incurred on the day of departure if he was unable to live in the former home because the furniture had been moved out (.20).

The cost of moving household goods and personal effects includes the cost of packing and crating, insurance, in-transit storage for up to 30 consecutive days (higher amounts allowed for foreign relocations), and the actual cost of transportation. If the household goods and personal effects are transported from a place other than the former home, the deductible amount includes only the cost that would have otherwise been incurred to move them from the former home. No deduction is allowed for the transportation of furniture purchased en route.

Reporting the deduction

The moving expense deduction is calculated on Form 3903 and then claimed on Form 1040 as an above-the-line adjustment to gross income. A moving expense may be deducted by a cash-basis executive in the year in which it is reimbursed by his employer instead of the year in which paid (.25). There are two instances in which this election may be made:

(1) when the expenses are paid in a tax year preceding the tax year in which the reimbursement is received; or

(2) when the expenses are paid in the tax year immediately following the tax year in which reimbursement is received, provided that payment occurs on or before the due date of the return for the tax year in which reimbursement is received.

In determining the due date of the return, extensions of time for filing are taken into account. Once a deduction is claimed, any later reimbursement cannot be excluded from income as a fringe benefit (.30).

If the employer advances or loans money to the executive to cover moving expenses, subject to an accounting, the executive is not considered to have received a reimbursement until that accounting is made (.35).

The choice to shift moving expenses from the year of payment to the year of reimbursement is made by claiming the deduction on an original or amended return for the year of reimbursement or on a refund claim for that year.

.05 Code Sec. 217; Reg. §1.217-2.
.10 Code Sec. 132(a)(6).
.15 Code Sec. 3401(a)(15).
.20 Reg. §1.217-2(b)(4).
.25 Reg. §1.217-2(a)(2).
.30 Code Sec. 132(a)(6).
.35 Reg. §1.82-1(a)(2).

¶25,005 Mortgage Assistance. In order to assist an executive in relocating, many employers will arrange to pay part of the executive's mortgage payment on his home in the new location. These mortgage assistance payments take many forms, but the primary method involves the employer "buying down" the executive's mortgage loan.

The term "buying down" means that the employer will assist in the executive's mortgage payment for a specified period of time (e.g., one year after relocation). By this method, the employer "buys down" the executive's cost for his mortgage and helps overcome a major disadvantage of relocation, especially during periods of high mortgage interest rates.

If the employer makes its portion of the mortgage payment to an unrelated third-party lender in order to buy down the executive's mortgage loan, the employer's payment generally must be included in the executive's income as taxable wages. This is due to the fact that the buy-down or other form of mortgage assistance is treated as compensation to the executive and not as a type of tax-free fringe benefit.

However, if the employer loans money directly to an executive in order to provide mortgage assistance, or to help in the relocation process, and the loan is made either on an interest-free basis or at a below-market interest rate, the tax effect upon the executive is determined under different rules. Below-market and interest-free loans are discussed at ¶25,019.

¶25,006 Temporary Relocations. At times, executives are asked to relocate for a temporary period of one year or more, rather than permanently. Such a temporary relocation may cause the executive to maintain two households: his present home to which he expects to return, and a household in the temporary work location. Generally, living expenses incurred in the temporary work location will be considered "away from home" travel expenses that are deductible as business expenses (.05). The expenses of traveling between the taxpayer's main home and the temporary work location will also be considered to be deductible business expenses.

If the assignment is expected to last less than one year, it will be considered to be temporary. Expenses associated with an indefinite employment in the new location will not be deductible.

.05 Code Sec. 162.

Golden Parachute Payments

¶25,007 "Golden Parachute" Payments. In an effort to protect the financial interests of its executives and other key personnel, a corporation may agree to pay these employees substantial amounts above their normal compensation in the event there is a change in ownership or control of the corporation. These extra amounts have been labeled "golden parachute" payments because they allow an executive a "soft landing" after he or she has been forced to leave the employ of the corporation after a change in ownership or control. In general, a payment is to be treated as contingent on a change in ownership or control if the payment would not have been made to the disqualified individual had no change in ownership or control occurred.

Congress has viewed excessive golden parachute payments as detrimental to the interests of shareholders and also as a deterrent to corporate acquisitions. Therefore, there are restrictions that limit the use of such payments (.05). If golden parachute payments are found to be excessive, the corporation will be unable to claim a business deduction for the excess amounts. In addition, the employees who receive the excess payments will be liable for a nondeductible excise tax of 20 percent on the amount of the excess payment.

However, the following two types of corporations are generally exempt from the golden parachute provisions (.10): (1) S corporations, and (2) corporations that, immediately before the change in control, have no stock that is readily tradeable on an established securities market or elsewhere. An exemption applies to payments by the latter type of corporation only if the payments are approved, after adequate disclosure, by a shareholder vote of more than 75 percent.

These exemptions enable some corporations to provide their executives with golden parachute payments without being concerned about tax restrictions being imposed.

The IRS has issued final regulations that are generally effective on January 1, 2004 (.15). Prior to the effective date of the final regulations, taxpayers may rely on proposed regulations issued in 1989 (.20) or proposed regulations issued in February 2002 (.25).

Restrictions

Parachute payment. A parachute payment is any payment in the nature of compensation to a disqualified individual if: (1) the payment is contingent on a change in the ownership or effective control of the corporation, or in the ownership of a substantial portion of the corporation's assets, and (2) the aggregate present value (computed at 120 percent of the applicable federal rate, compounded semiannually) of such contingent payments equals or exceeds three times the base amount.

Disqualified individual. Before a payment can be a parachute payment, the payment must be made to a disqualified individual–any individual who (1) is an employee, independent contractor, or other person specified in regulations who performs personal services for the corporation and (2) is an officer, shareholder or highly compensated individual. A personal service corporation (or similar entity) is treated as an individual under this provision. A highly compensated individual is an employee (or former employee) who is among the group consisting of the highest paid one percent of individuals performing personal services for the corporation (determined on an affiliated group basis) or, if less, among the highest paid 250 employees of the corporation.

Base amount. A requirement of the parachute payment is that the total present value of the payments equals or exceeds three times an individual's base amount of compensation. The base amount is an individual's average annual compensation paid by the corporation and includible by the individual in gross income for the most recent five tax years preceding the tax year that the change in ownership or control of the corporation occurs, or the portion of this period during which the individual was an employee of or performed services for the corporation. Compensation includes items such as ordinary income from stock options, or other property includible in gross income, if the receipt of the property was considered compensation for services rendered.

.05 Code Sec. 280G and Code Sec. 4999.
.10 Code Sec. 280G(b)(5)(A).
.15 Reg. §1.280G-1, adopted August 1, 2003 by T.D. 9083.
.20 Proposed Reg. §1.280G-1, published 1989.
.25 Proposed Reg. §1.280G-1, published February 20, 2002.

Noncash Compensation-Fringe Benefits

¶25,009 Tax-Free Fringe Benefits. An executive's gross income does not, for federal tax purposes, include any fringe benefit that qualifies as a (1) no-additional-cost service; (2) qualified employee discount; (3) working-condition fringe; (4) *de minimis* fringe; (5) qualified transportation fringe; or (6) qualified moving expense reimbursement (see ¶25,004) (.05). The enumerated fringe benefits are also excluded from the wage base (and, if applicable, benefit base) for purposes of income tax withholding and related payroll taxes (i.e., FICA, FUTA and RRTA).

However, to be nontaxable, some of these fringe benefits must be provided on a nondiscriminatory basis. This means that the benefit must be provided to a broad cross section of employees and not just to executives. See "Rules for nondiscrimination," below. In other words, any fringe benefit not qualifying for exclusion as a tax-free fringe benefit and not excludable under any other Tax Code provision is taxable to the executive and includible in the executive's wages, for employment tax purposes, at the excess of its fair market value over any amount paid by the executive for the benefit (.10).

Rules for nondiscrimination

Generally, highly compensated employees defined in Code Sec. 414(q) may not exclude no-additional-cost services, qualified employee discounts, certain *de minimis* fringe benefits (specifically, employee eating facilities) or tuition reduction benefits from their gross income unless such fringe benefits are available on substantially the same basis to each person in a "group" of employees. The group, in turn, is defined under a reasonable classification set up by the employer that does not discriminate in favor of highly compensated employees. Whether a particular classification is reasonable depends on the facts and circumstances of each case. If a classification makes benefits available only to highly compensated employees, it is obviously discriminatory. However, an employer can establish a classification based on certain other factors—such as seniority, full-time v. part-time status, or job description—if the effect of such classification is nondiscriminatory.

If the nondiscrimination test is not satisfied, the fringe benefit can be excluded from wages only by those employees who receive the benefit and who are not members of the favored group.

The nondiscrimination rules do not apply to working-condition or *de minimis* fringe benefits (other than subsidized eating facilities). Thus, if an employer has valid business reasons to make business cars available only to its executives, the working-condition fringe benefit exclusion applies, even though the availability of the benefit does not satisfy the nondiscrimination rules.

No-additional-cost services

The value of no-additional-cost services, such as free standby flights to airline employees and free telephone service to phone company employees, provided by an employer to an executive (as well as to the executive's spouse and dependent children) is excluded, both for income tax and employment tax purposes. This exclusion applies only if the service is available to employees on a nondiscriminatory basis.

In addition, this exclusion applies whether the service is provided directly for no charge, at a reduced price, or through a cash rebate of all or part of the amount paid for the service (.15). However, an employer must not incur any significant additional costs in providing the service to the executive (disregarding any amounts paid by the executive for the service). In addition, the service provided to the executive must be one that is offered for sale to customers in the ordinary course of the employer's line of business in which the executive works.

For purposes of the line-of-business limitation, a single employer is treated as consisting of more than one line of business if, after aggregating businesses under common control, the products or services the employer sells to nonemployee customers fall into more than one industry group.

Qualified employee discounts

Various employee discounts provided to executives on the selling price of qualified property or services of their employer are excludable for income and employment tax purposes. Employee discounts that do not exceed (1) 20 percent of the price at which a service is offered by the employer to nonemployee customers in the ordinary course of business or (2) the gross profit percentage multiplied by the price at which the property (product) is offered to customers in the ordinary course of business are excludable if the discounts are available on a nondiscriminatory basis to all employees. The employee discount is the amount by which the price at which the property or services provided for the use of the employee by the employer is less than the price at which the property or services are offered by the employer to customers. The exclusion applies whether the qualified employee discount is provided through a reduction in price or through a cash rebate from a third party (.20). The exclusion does not apply to discounts on any employee purchases of securities, gold coins, residential or commercial real estate, or interests in mineral-producing property. For example, an employee of a brokerage house may purchase stock and receive a tax-free discount on a commission (subject to the 20-percent limitation for discounts on services). However, any discount allowed on the price of the stock itself is not eligible for the discount exclusion.

In order to qualify for the exclusion, the goods or services discounted must be offered for sale by the employer to nonemployee customers in the ordinary course of the employer's line of business in which the executive works. Consequently, where most or all of the employer's production of certain goods or services is provided to employees, these goods or services would not qualify for the exclusion.

Line-of-business limitation. In order to qualify for the exclusion, the goods or services offered either as no-additional-cost services or as qualified employee discounts must be offered for sale by the employer to nonemployee customers in the ordinary course of the employer's line of business in which the employee works (.25). Thus, an employee who does not perform substantial services in a particular line of business of the employer may not exclude the value of services or employee discounts received on property or services in that line of business. However, if an employee performs substantial services in more than one line of business, he can receive no-additional-cost services or qualified employee discounts relating to any line of business for which he performs substantial services. The line of business rule is not satisfied if the employer's products or services are sold primarily to employees of the employer, rather than to customers.

Working condition fringe benefits

The concept of a working condition fringe benefit includes many of the items employees take for granted as part of their work environment. It is probably one of the most frequently utilized fringe benefits. It encompasses such diverse items as computers, uniforms, magazine subscriptions and cars. A working condition fringe benefit is, essentially, any property or service provided to an employee to the extent that, if the employee paid for the property or service, the payment would be allowable as a business expense or depreciation deduction.

The fair market value of any property or service provided to an executive by an employer as a working condition fringe benefit is excludable for income and employment tax purposes to the extent that the costs of the property or service would be deductible by the executive as an ordinary and necessary business expense if the executive had paid for such property or service. Nondiscrimination rules do not apply except with regard to product testing programs (.30).

The following are examples of excludable working condition fringe benefits (.35):

(1) the value of the use by an executive of a company car or airplane for business purposes;

(2) subscriptions to business periodicals by an employer for an executive;

(3) fringe benefits provided by an employer for the safety of an executive (if such precautions would be considered ordinary and necessary business expenses);

(4) employer expenditures for on-the-job training or employee travel (if such expenditures meet the requirements for deduction as an ordinary and necessary business expense);

(5) the fair market value of the use of consumer goods manufactured for sale to nonemployee customers but that are provided to the executive for product testing and evaluation outside the employer's office, but only if certain conditions are met; and

(6) the fair market value of free or reduced-cost parking that is provided to an executive on, under, or near the business premises of the employer. However, a maximum of $195 for 2004 per month in "qualified parking expenses" is excludable from the executive's gross income.

(7) the value of outplacement services.

Denial of a deduction to an employer for its payment of expenses, such as travel expenses of a spouse, dependent, or other individual accompanying an employee on business travel, does not preclude those items from qualifying as working condition fringe benefits (.40)

De minimis fringe benefits

If the value of any property or service provided to an executive is so minimal that accounting for the property or service would be unreasonable or administratively impracticable, it is an excludable *de minimis* fringe benefit for income and employment tax purposes (.45). In determining whether the *de minimis* exclusion applies, the frequency with which similar fringe benefits (otherwise excludable as *de minimis* fringes) are provided by an employer to its employees is taken into account.

Examples of benefits that are excluded as *de minimis* fringes (without regard to the aggregation rule) are (1) typing of personal letters by a company secretary, (2) occasional personal use of the company copying machine, (3) occasional parties or picnics for employees, and (4) tickets that are occasionally given out for entertainment events, such as plays or baseball games.

A dining room operated by an employer for the benefit of officers is treated as a *de minimis* fringe benefit if (1) the dining room is located on or near the business premises of the employer, (2) the revenue derived from such facility normally equals or exceeds the direct operating costs of such facility, and (3) access to the dining facility is available on substantially the same terms to all employees or each member of a group of employees that is defined under a reasonable classification set up by the employer that does not discriminate in favor of highly compensated employees. If these conditions are satisfied, the excess of the value of the meals over the fees charged to executives is excluded.

Transportation fringe benefits

The value of qualified transportation fringe benefits provided to an employee is excluded from the employee's gross income and wages for income and payroll tax purposes (.50). A qualified transportation fringe includes: (1) transportation in a commuter highway vehicle if the transportation is in connection with travel between the employee's residence and place of employment, (2) a transit pass, and (3) qualified parking. For 2004, the maximum excludable amount for qualified parking is $195 per month and $100 of van pooling and transit passes per month.

Athletic facilities

An executive's gross income does not include the value of any on-premises athletic facilities provided by an employer. In order to be excluded, however, the facility must be located on the premises of, and operated by, the employer, and substantially all of the use of the facility must be by employees of the employer, their spouses, or their dependent children.

Athletic facilities that qualify for the exclusion are swimming pools, gymnasiums, tennis courts, and golf courses.

.05 Code Sec. 132.
.10 Code Sec. 61 and 83; Reg. §1.61-1(a).
.15 Reg. §1.132-2(a).
.20 Reg. §1.132-3(a)(4) and (5).
.25 Reg. §1.132-4.
.30 Reg. §1.132-5(n)(3).
.35 Reg. §1.132-5.
.40 Reg. §1.132-5(s) and 1.132-5(t).
.45 Code Sec. 132(a)(4) and Reg. §1.132-6.
.50 Code Sec. 132(f).

¶25,010 Cafeteria Plans. A cafeteria plan is an employee benefit plan under which a participant may choose between cash compensation and one or more qualified fringe benefits, such as group-term life insurance with up to $50,000 coverage, disability benefits, accident and health benefits, and certain group legal services (.05). Included under the definition of a cafeteria plan is one under which an employee may choose from among certain qualified benefits only and may not choose either cash or a taxable benefit. If a participating executive elects to receive cash compensation, a cafeteria plan can also allow a choice between the immediate receipt of cash and the deferral of the compensation through a profit-sharing plan or a stock bonus plan.

Participation in a cafeteria plan may provide important tax planning opportunities for executives because they may choose among a variety of tax-free fringe benefits. This ability to choose among various benefits not only is important in the tax planning process but also provides an executive, and any other participating employee, with an important psychological benefit in that he is taking an active part in determining his benefits.

However, an executive who is a highly compensated employee (see ¶25,009) is taxable on such benefits unless the plan is nondiscriminatory. Therefore, an employer must take care in establishing a cafeteria plan to see that it is nondiscriminatory in its operation in order to ensure tax-free benefits to participating executives. Each benefit is judged according to its own rules. For example, group-term life insurance benefits under a cafeteria plan will be required to satisfy the nondiscrimination rules applicable to group-term life insurance plans outside a cafeteria plan.

.05 Code Sec. 125.

¶25,011 Health and Accident Plans. Employer contributions to an insurance company for employee health and accident benefits are generally not taxable to employees, including officers and executives (.05). Paid benefits, whether from an insured plan or a self-insured plan, are also generally not includible in gross income. However, there are exceptions.

For example, medical benefits reimbursements are includible in gross income where an employee incurred medical expenses and took a medical expense deduction in one year and received an insurance reimbursement in a succeeding year. Similarly, they are includible in gross income if they exceed the amount of the medical costs. In such case, the excessive indemnification is includible in gross income to the extent that it is attributable to employer premiums or employer contributions. If any part of the excessive indemnification is due to employee-paid premiums, it is apportioned according to the respective amounts paid by the employer and the employee.

Nondiscrimination rules

Amounts paid to a highly compensated individual under a self-insured medical reimbursement plan that does not satisfy certain nondiscrimination requirements (.10) will be included in the income of such individual to the extent that they constitute an excess reimbursement.

Flexible spending arrangement

A flexible spending arrangement (FSA) generally is a benefit program that provides employees with coverage under which specified, incurred expenses may be reimbursed (subject to reimbursement maximums and any other reasonable conditions). They are generally beneficial to employees who expect to have medical expenses that won't be reimbursed by their regular health plan. Health FSAs can be used to pay for the costs of annual deductibles, co-payments to physicians, and other expenses not paid for by the employer's health plan. Another form of FSAs–dependent care FSAs–can be used to pay for the costs of day care, summer day camp, and for the care of a physically or mentally incapacitated dependent of any age.

.05 Code Sec. 105, 106, and 125. **.10** Code Sec. 105(h).

¶25,012 Life Insurance. An employer may provide up to $50,000 in group-term life insurance for its employees, including retired employees, during a tax year and it will not result in realizable income to them (.05). A group-term life insurance plan must meet special nondiscrimination rules in order to enable key employees to exclude from gross income the cost of the first $50,000 of employer-provided group-term life insurance. Generally, the exclusion will not be available if the group-term life insurance plan discriminates in favor of key employees as to eligibility to participate or as to type and amount of benefits available. For the definition of a key employee, see Code Sec. 416(i).

Amount included in income

If a group-term life insurance plan discriminates in favor of key employees, the cost of the first $50,000 of group-term life insurance (otherwise excludable from a key employee's income) is included in income. The cost of such insurance is the *greater* of (1) the cost under the uniform premium table that is provided by the IRS (see Reg. §1.79-3(d)(2)) or (2) the employer's actual cost in providing the insurance. Benefits provided to employees who are not key employees remain eligible for the exclusion from income for the first $50,000 of group-term life insurance.

Even if a plan is not discriminatory, an executive (and any other employee) who has employer-paid group-term life insurance coverage of over $50,000 during any part of a tax year must include in his gross income for that tax year the cost of the coverage that is in excess of $50,000. If the plan is nondiscriminatory, this cost is not based on the actual cost of the excess insurance to the employer, but, rather, on uniform premium cost rates for group-term life insurance provided by the IRS (see Reg. §1.79-3(d)(2)). However, any amount paid by the executive (for example, through payroll deductions) towards the purchase of the insurance reduces, dollar for dollar, the amount of such cost that is includible in gross income.

If a group insurance policy also provides for "permanent benefits" to an executive, the cost of the permanent benefits less the amount paid for the permanent benefits by him is includible in his income. A "permanent benefit" is defined as an economic value that extends beyond one year and includes policies that provide for paid-up insurance and cash surrender values. All or a part of the dividends under such a policy may also be includible in an employee's income, depending on whether the executive contributes toward the purchase of the permanent benefits.

Nongroup life insurance

Premiums on nongroup life insurance policies for employees are includible in the employee's gross income. Such insurance includes key-person insurance.

Split-dollar life insurance

Generally, a split-dollar life insurance arrangement can be defined as any arrangement (that is not part of a group term life insurance plan described in Code Sec. 79 between an owner of a life insurance contract and a nonowner of the contract under which either party to the arrangement pays all or part of the premiums, and one of the parties paying the premiums is entitled to recover (either conditionally or unconditionally) all or any portion of those premiums and such recovery is to be made from, or is secured by, the proceeds of the contract (.10). Split-dollar life insurance arrangments between an employer and an employee are discussed at ¶3668.

.05 Code Sec. 79; Reg. §1.79-1 and following. **.10** Reg. §1.61-22(b).

¶25,013 Recreation. An employer may maintain recreational, social, athletic or similar facilities primarily for the benefit of employees, including executives. When such facilities are offered or furnished to employees generally, the related expenditures are not considered as taxable wages if such facilities or privileges are of relatively small value and are offered or furnished by the employer merely as a means of promoting the employees' health, goodwill, contentment, or efficiency (.05).

☐ See ¶25,009 regarding the exclusion from an executive's gross income of the value of any on-premises athletic facilities provided by an employer.

.05 Reg. §31.3401(a)-1(b)(10).

¶25,015 Meals or Lodging Furnished by Employer. The value of meals or lodging furnished to an executive will usually be part of taxable wages. However, an exclusion from gross income for the value of meals and lodging is allowed if certain requirements are met (.05). In order for an executive-taxpayer to exclude the value of meals and lodging furnished to him, his spouse, or dependents by or on behalf of the employer, such meals and lodging must be furnished for the convenience of the employer and on the business premises. Additionally, in order to exclude the value of lodging, the lodging must be required as a condition of employment.

The fair market value of qualified campus housing furnished to an employee or executive of an educational institution is not included in the individual's gross income if the rent paid for the housing equals or exceeds five percent of the value of the housing. The fair market value of the housing is to be determined on an annualized basis by a qualified independent appraiser.

.05 Code Sec. 119.

¶25,016 Child and Dependent Care Services. The value of child or dependent care services provided by an employer pursuant to a written nondiscriminatory plan is not includible in the executive's gross income (.05). The exclusion does not apply to the value of services in excess of the earned income of an unmarried employee, or the earned income of the lower-earning spouse of a married employee.

The most that can be excluded from an employee's gross income for dependent care assistance payments made by an employer is $5,000 ($2,500 for a married person filing a separate return) (.10).

.05 Code Sec. 129(a)(1). **.10** Code Sec. 129(a)(2).

¶25,017 Limitations on Shareholder-Employees of S Corporations. Shareholder-employees of S corporations who own more than two percent of the outstanding stock are treated like partners in a partnership with respect to employee fringe benefits, including the following tax-favored fringe benefits (.05):

(1) amounts paid for or to certain accident and health plans,

(2) the cost of up to $50,000 of group-term life insurance on the employee's life, and

(3) the cost of meals or lodging furnished for the convenience of the employer.

Thus, the corporation cannot deduct its payment for such expenses, and the executive employee-owner generally cannot exclude such amounts from gross income.

.05 Code Sec. 1372(a) and (b).

¶25,018 Educational Assistance. A corporation may establish an educational benefit trust (EBT) to provide funds to meet college or postgraduate educational expenses of the children of certain employees, including executives. An EBT represents a deferred compensation plan because the corporate executive is not taxed on such payments until they are received by his children (.05). Although the IRS has contended that such payments cannot be currently deducted by the corporation but must be deducted in the same year that the executive includes such payments in income (.10), the U.S. Court of Appeals for the Federal Circuit ruled that such contributions may be currently deducted by the corporation if certain criteria are met (.15).

.05 Rev. Rul. 75-448, 1975-2 CB 55.

.10 *Citrus Orthopedic Medical Group, Inc.*, 72 TC 461, CCH Dec. 36,121; *R.T. Armantrout*, CA-7, 78-1 USTC ¶9232, 570 F2d 210, aff'g TC, 67 TC 996, CCH Dec. 34,314.

.15 *Greensboro Pathology Assoc.*, CA FC, 83-1 USTC ¶9112, 698 F2d 1196.

¶25,019 Below-Market and Interest-Free Loans. Many years ago, the making of below-market or interest-free loans to executives did not result in any taxable income to the executive, either as dividends, in the case of corporation-shareholder loans, or as compensation, in the case of compensation-related loans. In order to prevent tax avoidance, the Code provides that the imputed interest on below-market term loans or demand loans is treated as income or deductions according to their economic substance (.05).

(1) A term loan is a below-market loan if the amount loaned exceeds the present value of all payments due under the loan.

(2) A demand loan is a below-market loan if the interest on it is payable at a rate less than the applicable federal rate (AFR) determined daily by using the short-term AFR.

Present value is determined by discounting at the applicable federal rate. For all below-market loans, the amount treated as loaned is the amount received by the borrower.

These rules apply to any below-market loan that is (1) a gift loan, (2) a loan between a corporation and a shareholder, (3) a compensation-related loan between an employer and an employee or between an independent contractor and a person for whom the independent contractor provides services, or (4) a loan that has tax avoidance as one of its principal purposes.

Because business executives as a class are likely to be concerned with compensation-related and corporation-shareholder loans, the discussion that follows will concentrate on those types of loans.

Caution

CCH Analysts note that the Sarbanes-Oxley Act of 2002, which was signed into law July 30, 2002, amends the Securities Exchange Act to prohibit public companies from making any personal loans to their directors or executive officers (.10). However, consumer credit companies may make home improvement and consumer credit loans and issue credit cards to their directors and executive officers if it is done in the ordinary course of business on the same terms and conditions made to the general public.

Foregone interest

If a below-market loan is not a gift loan, any "foregone interest" is treated as transferred from the lender to the borrower and then retransferred to the lender as interest. As to below-market demand loans, the lender is treated as if it had transferred foregone interest to the borrower in the form of a dividend (corporation-shareholder transaction), compensation (transaction involving services), or some other payment in accordance with the substance of the transaction. Such foregone interest is includible in the borrower's income. The foregone interest that is treated as retransferred to the lender is includible in income by the lender and is deductible by the borrower to the same extent as if it were interest actually paid by the borrower. Thus, this type of interest is nondeductible personal interest expense.

With respect to any taxable period, foregone interest is defined as an amount that is equal to the excess of (1) the amount of interest that would have been payable on the loan for such taxable period if interest had accrued at the applicable federal rate and was payable annually at the time the transfer was made *over* (2) any interest payable on the loan properly allocable to such period.

Corporation-shareholder loans

A corporation-shareholder loan is any below-market loan made directly or indirectly between a corporation and any shareholder of such corporation.

Compensation-related loans

A compensation-related loan is any below-market loan made in connection with the performance of services directly or indirectly between (1) an employer and an employee, or (2) an independent contractor and a person for whom such independent contractor provides services.

For purposes of determining the timing and amount of the transfers deemed made under the provision, a compensation-related term loan is treated as a demand loan if the benefit derived by the employee from the interest arrangement is (1) nontransferable and (2) conditioned on the future performance of substantial services by the employee.

An arrangement will be treated as a compensation-related loan only if, in substance, there is a debtor-creditor relationship between the employee and the employer at the time the loan is made (.15). For example, if an employer makes a payment to an unrelated third-party lender to buy down a mortgage loan for an employee (see ¶25,005), the payment by the employer to the lender is treated as taxable compensation. To that extent, the below-market-loan rules do not apply. However, if the transaction is, in substance, a loan by the employer made with the aid of services provided by the third-party lender acting as an agent of the employer, it is a compensation-related loan.

Also, if an employee receives payment from a customer for services rendered on behalf of an employer and is permitted to retain the money for a period of time without paying interest at a rate equal to or greater than the applicable federal rate, there is generally a compensation-related loan (.20). For example, if an investment banker is permitted by an issuer to retain the proceeds from a public offering of stock or debt for a period of time without paying interest, there is a below-market loan from the issuer to the banker. To the extent the benefit is in lieu of a fee for services, the loan is a compensation-related loan.

In the case of a compensation-related loan, the deemed payment by the lender to the borrower is treated as wages for employment tax purposes. Generally, a payment must be included in gross income by the borrower even if the borrower is likely to be entitled to an offsetting deduction. In addition, even though there is no requirement that employment tax be withheld, a payment must be reported under the appropriate information-reporting provision.

Tax-avoidance loans

A below-market loan is a tax-avoidance loan if one of the principal purposes of the interest arrangement is the avoidance of any federal tax by either the borrower or the lender. Tax avoidance is a principal purpose of the interest arrangement if it is a principal factor in the decision to structure the transaction as a below-market loan, rather than a loan requiring the payment of interest at a rate that equals or exceeds the applicable federal rate and a payment by the lender to the borrower.

De minimis exception

In the case of any compensation-related or corporation-shareholder below-market loan, no interest will be imputed to either the borrower or the lender for any day on which the aggregate outstanding amount of the loan between the borrower and the lender is not in excess of $10,000. The imputed interest amount is computed on a daily basis. This exception does not apply to loans in which tax avoidance is a principal purpose.

.05 Code Sec. 7872.

.10 Act Sec. 402(a) of the Sarbanes-Oxley Act of 2002, amending Sec. 13 of the Securities Exchange Act of 1934 by adding (k).

.15 Conference Committee Report on Sec. 172, P.L. 98-369.

.20 Conference Committee Report on Sec. 172, P.L. 98-369.

Stock Options

¶25,021 Types of Stock Options. In order to nurture the entrepreneurial spirit of their employees and also provide them with a financial interest in the success of their employer, many corporations offer employees an opportunity to buy company stock, typically through stock option arrangements. A stock option is a right to purchase stock in a corporation on or before a specified date and at a given price. From the corporation's viewpoint, granting an executive a stock option gives him a personal incentive to increase the corporation's earnings and profits. From the executive's viewpoint, a stock option can be the vehicle by which he is able to defer taxation on compensation.

There are several types of statutory stock options. These include incentive stock options (ISOs) (see ¶25,022) and employee stock purchase plans (ESOPs) (see ¶25,023). In addition to granting statutory stock options, a corporation may grant an executive a stock option that does not meet the requirements of the Internal Revenue Code (i.e., a nonstatutory stock option) and is not granted favorable tax treatment. Generally, nonstatutory stock options (see ¶25,024) are taxed as ordinary income to the executive, but only when their fair market value is ascertainable.

In addition to stock options, phantom stock and stock appreciation rights may be given to an executive (see ¶25,025). The executive's compensation from such items is related to the company's increased profitability.

Securities law considerations. Stock options, stock appreciation rights, and phantom stock plans must satisfy certain federal securities laws or the executive of a corporation subject to the Security Exchange Act of 1934, generally a larger or a publicly traded corporation, may be required to return all or a portion of the compensation derived from such items under Section 16(b) of that Act. In essence, Section 16(b) requires corporate officers and directors of certain larger corporations to give back the profits from the sale and purchase or purchase and sale of the corporation's securities where the matched transactions occur within a six-month period. The grant or exercise of a stock option or similar right with a value derived from the value of any of the corporation's equity securities may be considered a prohibited purchase or sale unless the grant of the right is pursuant to a written plan that complies with certain securities law rules, and the plan is administered by a board of disinterested directors.

Caution

CCH Analysts note that the requirements imposed on incentive stock options and employee stock purchase plans are very complex and subject to change. The following discussions highlight the main points. For more detailed explanations, see ¶11,800 and following.

¶25,022 Incentive Stock Options. An incentive stock option (ISO) is usually aimed at giving key employee an opportunity to acquire stock at a "bargain price" without incurring any tax liability until the shares are sold. An executive who receives an incentive stock option is not taxed either when the option is granted or when he exercises it (.05). The executive is taxed only upon disposition of the stock acquired under the option. In order for a stock option to be considered an incentive stock option, an employee (1) must not sell or dispose of stock received under an option within two years after the option is granted, and (2) must hold the shares of stock for at least one year after they have been transferred to him.

The executive must be an employee from the date of the granting of the option until a date three months before the date of exercise of the option (except that a disabled employee may exercise an option within 12 months of leaving employment).

From the employer's point of view the most significant drawback to the use of an incentive stock option as a form of compensation is that it is not allowed as a business expense deduction either at the time the options are granted or at the time the shares are issued. The only exception to this general rule is in the event that the executive does not comply with the holding period rules mentioned above. In this case the employer may claim a business deduction for the amount that the executive must include in his gross income as ordinary income (.10).

Options do not have to be exercised in the order they were granted. Thus, if an employer's stock has declined in value, new options can be granted that will enable an executive to purchase the stock at the depressed price.

FICA and FUTA. In the past, the IRS had announced that until it issued further guidance on statutory stock options (both incentive stock options (ISOs) and options granted under employee stock purchase plans (ESPPs), it would not assess FICA or FUTA tax, or require income tax withholding, upon either the exercise of the option or the disposition of the stock acquired by an employee through the exercise of an option (.15). As a result of the the American Jobs Creation Act of 2004, and effective for stock acquired under options acquired after October 22, 2004, employment taxes do not apply to remuneration generated by the transfer of stock under an exercise of an ISO or ESPP, or because of the disposition of stock acquired under such an option (.20).

.05 Code Sec. 422.

.10 Code Sec. 421(b).

.15 Notice 2002-47, I.R.B. 2002-28.

.20 Code Sec. 3121(a), as amended by the American Jobs Creation Act of 2004 (P.L. 108-357).

¶25,023 Employee Stock Purchase Plans. Employee stock purchase plans are similar to incentive stock option plans (.05). Under an employee stock purchase plan, an executive may purchase stock for as little as 85 percent of its fair market value. Under the plan, an employee (1) must not sell or dispose of stock received under an option within two years after the option is granted, and (2) must hold the shares of stock for at least one year after they have been transferred.

Employee stock purchase plans provide a convenient method by which executives may acquire an ownership interest in their corporate employer and obtain significant tax advantages at the same time.

If the specified conditions are met, the executive incurs no tax liability on the grant or exercise of an option under these stock purchase plans. When the stock is disposed of after the required holding period, if the option price was less than 100 percent of the fair market value at the time granted, the executive realizes ordinary income to the extent of the *lesser* of (1) the amount by which the fair market value of the stock at the time the option was granted exceeded the option price or (2) the amount by which the fair market value of the stock at the time of disposition exceeded the option price. Any further gain is taxed as capital gain.

If the stock is sold before the expiration of the required holding period, the executive realizes ordinary income (compensation) to the extent of the difference between the option price and the fair market value of the stock on the date the option was exercised. To avoid this additional ordinary income, the stock must be held for the long-term capital asset holding period and the combined holding period of the stock and the option must be at least two years.

.05 Code Sec. 423.

¶25,024 Nonstatutory Stock Options. Unlike statutory stock options, which are taxable only upon the disposition of the stock acquired by exercise of the option, nonstatutory stock options are usually taxed as compensation either when the executive receives the option or when the option is exercised (.05). Whether the executive is taxed immediately upon receipt of the option depends on whether the option has a readily ascertainable fair market value at the time it is granted.

Readily ascertainable fair market value

If it is established that the option has a readily ascertainable fair market value when granted, the executive realizes income at the time of the grant to the extent of the difference between the option's fair market value and the executive's cost. Normally, the executive will have paid nothing for the option, and the value of the option usually will be the discount amount at which stock can be purchased. Therefore, this discount amount generally will be the amount taxable to the executive. The employer will be able to take a deduction for a like amount.

No readily ascertainable value

If an option has no readily ascertainable market value, the grant of the option is not the taxable event. Instead, the exercise of the option will be taxable if the executive's interest in the stock acquired pursuant to the option is not subject to a substantial risk of forfeiture. If a substantial risk of forfeiting the stock is present at the time the option is exercised, the taxation will be further postponed until the executive's interest in the stock is no longer subject to substantial risk of forfeiture.

The IRS, fully aware that an executive is likely to realize substantial tax savings if the option is taxed at the time it is granted, has set up formidable roadblocks to the establishment of any market value. The IRS requires either that the option be regularly traded on an established market or that the transaction meet the following requirements (.10):

(1) the option must be freely transferable by the optionee;

(2) the option must be exercisable immediately in full by the optionee;

(3) the stock subject to the option must be free from any restrictions affecting its market value; and

(4) the fair market value of the *option privilege* must be readily ascertainable.

The term "option privilege," in (4), above, means the opportunity to benefit, at any time during the period in which the option may be exercised, from any appreciation in the value of the subject of the option that occurs during such period and does not involve the risk of any capital. The IRS seems to emphasize that the value of the option privilege is something more than the mere spread between option price and market value of the stock at the time the option is granted.

There is no indication that the courts will impose such serious obstacles to a determination of market value, although it seems certain that freedom of transfer would be required (.15). For example, the U.S. Supreme Court ruled that an option can have no fair market value when granted simply because the option price is greater than the market value at the time when the option was granted (.20). This seems to imply that, if the option price were less than the market value, there might be no insuperable obstacle to determining market value. In this regard, the court stated, "[w]hen the option price is less than the market price of the property, it may have present value and may be found to be itself compensation for services rendered."

IRS Guidance

A recent IRS ruling provides guidance concerning the tax consequences when an employee exercises, or a corporation cancels, a nonstatutory stock option. The guidance is provided in the form of four examples that illustrate when an employee would be required to include compensation in income and when the grantor of the option would be entitled to a deduction. All the examples involve a grantor that was subsequently acquired by another corporation (.25)

.05 Code Sec. 83; *P. J. LoBue*, SCt, 56-2 USTC ¶9607, 351 U.S. 243.

.10 Reg. §1.83-7(b)(2).

.15 *H.V. McNamara*, CA-7, 54-1 USTC ¶9255, 210 F2d 505; *Stone Est.*, CA-3, 54-1 USTC ¶9209, 210 F2d 33.

.20 *J.H. Smith*, SCt, 45-1 USTC ¶9187, 324 U. S. 177, 65 SCt 591.

.25 Rev. Rul. 2003-98 I.R.B. 2003-34.

¶25,025 Stock Appreciation Rights and Phantom Stock Plans. Closely associated with stock option plans, and often offered as an alternative to, or in conjunction with, a stock option are (1) stock appreciation rights (SARs) and (2) phantom stock plans. Like a stock option plan, these two plans give an executive an incentive to enhance the performance of the corporation as measured by the value of its stock. In addition, unlike the stock option plans, both plans generally permit the executive to receive additional compensation in the form of cash if the value of the corporation's stock increases over a fixed period. This compensation is not taxed to the executive until he receives it and is not deductible by the corporation until it is paid.

Stock appreciation rights

Stock appreciation rights (SARs) are, as the name implies, the right to receive compensation based on the amount by which the corporation's stock increases over a set period of time. Generally, at the end of the fixed period, the executive is entitled to receive a cash payment equal to the value of appreciation in value of the stock. Payments received for the stock appreciation rights are includible in gross income in the year the rights are exercised (.05).

Phantom stock arrangement

Under the phantom stock arrangement, an executive receives a hypothetical number of shares in the corporation based on either the fair market value or the book value of such shares. However, no actual shares are set aside for him. His phantom stock account may also be credited with any dividends paid by the corporation. Usually, at the end of a fixed period, the executive's phantom stock account can be converted into cash, stock or a combination of both. A participant who receives phantom stock units will not include an amount in his or her gross income as a result of the award of the units. The appreciation in value of phantom stock units will not be included in the participant's gross income until the tax year in which the participant exercises (or is deemed to exercise) the phantom stock units (.10).

.05 Rev. Rul. 80-300, 1980-2 CB 165.

.10 IRS Letter Ruling 8949032, 9/8/89, CCH IRS Letter Rulings Reports.

Restricted Property

¶25,027 Restricted Property. A corporation may compensate an executive with property that is subject to certain restrictions (.05). Often, the property that is used is stock in the corporation. If the restrictions on the property, by their terms, will never lapse, such restrictions curb the executive's beneficial interest in the stock. For example, a common restriction employed is one that requires the executive to return the stock to the employer if he does not complete a specified period of employment and prohibits the employee from selling the stock in the interim. Another common type of restriction provides that the executive may not sell the stock for a specified period of time, such as a five-year period, or until retirement.

An executive who receives restricted property is taxed on the value of the property at the time of receipt unless his interest therein is subject to a substantial risk of forfeiture. In the latter case, he is taxed on the value of the property (in excess of his cost) at the time the risk of forfeiture is removed or when his interest becomes transferable (provided the rights of the transferee are not subject to a substantial risk of forfeiture).

A substantial risk of forfeiture is considered to exist when the executive's rights to the full enjoyment of the property are conditioned upon his future performance of substantial services. In other cases, the question of whether there is a substantial risk of forfeiture depends upon the facts and circumstances.

.05 Code Sec. 83.

¶25,028 Election to Be Taxed upon Receipt. An executive who receives restricted property has the option of treating it as taxable compensation in the year it is received, even though it is nontransferable and subject to a substantial risk of forfeiture (.05). If this election is made, the restricted property rules do not apply, and later appreciation in the value of the property is not treated as taxable compensation. However, if the property is later forfeited, no deduction is allowed with respect to the forfeiture. The executive must make this election not later than 30 days after the date of transfer, and the election may not be revoked except with the consent of the IRS.

Making the election. The election is made by filing two copies of a written statement with the IRS Service Center where the executive's tax return is filed. The first copy is sent to the IRS at the time of the election and the second copy is filed with the tax return for the tax year in which the property was transferred. In addition to stating that the election is being made under Code Sec. 83(b), the statement must include the following (.10): (1) name, address and taxpayer identification number; (2) description of each property for which the election is being made; (3) date (or dates) when the property was transferred, and the tax year for which such election was made; (4) nature of restriction or restrictions on the property; (5) fair market value of property (determined without considering any restriction other than one which will never lapse) at the time of transfer; (6) amount of consideration paid for the property; and (7) statement that required copies have been provided.

The person who performed the services must give a copy of the written statement to the person for whom the services were performed. If the person who performs the services and the person who receives the restricted property are not the same, a copy of the statement must be given to the one receiving the property by the one who performed the service (.15).

.05 Code Sec. 83(b).

.10 Reg. §1.83-2(e).

.15 Reg. §1.83-2(d).

Deferred Compensation Plans

¶25,030 Qualified Plans Defined. One of the fundamental ideas behind a retirement plan is to provide the employee with income after retirement as a partial substitute for current salary increases. The plan, because of its tax savings, need not cost the employer any more than a salary increase (except for the costs associated with establishing and maintaining the plan). However, the qualified plan will often yield a greater benefit to the executive than an outright increase in salary. In order to optimize the tax advantages available to both employee and employer the plan must be "qualified" (i.e., the plan must meet the requirements established by the Code and IRS regulations).

The term "deferred compensation plans" is broad enough to embrace the qualified pension, profit-sharing, stock bonus, and annuity plans governed by the Internal Revenue Code (.05). While these Code provisions, which are among the most complicated in the tax law, are not discussed in any detail here, the major tax advantages of deferred compensation plans are summarized below.

Participation

Generally, a new employee can be required to wait no more than one year to participate in a deferred compensation plan. However, participation can be delayed until an employee reaches age 21, even though this stretches the waiting period beyond one year. A plan can set a two-year waiting period if benefits are 100-percent vested at the end of that time.

Vesting

A plan may adopt one of two minimum vesting schedules:

(1) A three-to-seven-year graduated schedule under which an employee's accrued benefit will be 20-percent vested after three years' service, 40-percent vested after four years' service, 60-percent vested after five years' service, 80-percent vested after six years' service, and 100-percent vested after seven years' service; or

(2) A five-year schedule under which an employee's accrued benefit will be 100-percent vested after five years' service.

The foregoing vesting schedules apply only to the benefits derived from the employer's contributions to the plan. Benefits derived from the employee's own contributions must be 100-percent vested at all times. A plan may not defeat the vesting rules by delaying benefit accruals until after a long period of service.

Matching contributions. In the case of employer matching contributions, a faster vesting schedule applies. At a minimum, a plan must either provide that an employee acquires a 100% right to the employer's matching contributions after three years of service, or that the employee has a right to 20% of the matching contributions for each year of service beginning with the second year of service and ending with a 100% right after six years of service (.10).

Defined benefit plan v. defined contribution plan

Under a defined benefit plan, the amount of the employee's pension is established, but not the amount of the employer's contribution. Conversely, under a defined contribution plan, the amount that the employee will receive at retirement is not established, but the amount of the employer's annual contributions are established by the plan. For 2005, the basic rules for both types of plans provide:

(1) For a defined contribution plan, the maximum annual contribution for 2003 from all sources (i.e., employer, employee and forfeitures) may not exceed the *lesser* of $42,000 or 100 percent of the participant's qualified compensation for the year (.15).

(2) For a defined benefit plan, the overall annual benefit for 2005 is limited to the *lesser* of $170,000 or 100 percent of the employee's highest average compensation for any three consecutive years during which the employee was an active participant in the plan (.20).

401(k) plan

A qualified 401(k) plan, sometimes termed a "cash or deferred arrangement," is a type of retirement plan under which employer contributions to an employee trust will not be included in the income of the executive or other participating employee, merely because the employee has the option of taking the employer contribution in cash or having it paid to the trust. A 401(k) plan must be part of a qualified retirement plan. In addition, certain requirements relating to employee elections, distributions and vesting must be met.

For 2005, the maximum amount that an employee can elect to defer for any tax year under *all* 401(k) plans in which the employee participates is generally $14,000 (.25).

Catch-up contributions

Individuals who will reach at least age 50 by the end of a tax year, are able to make catch-up contributions to most types of retirement plans. However, the particular plan must permit these catch-up contributions to be made. Catch-up contributions made to "elective deferral plans" (e.g., Code Sec. 401(k)) do not have to be included in the individual's gross income, provided the amount of the catch-up contribution does not exceed the maximum allowable for the tax year. For 2005, the maximum amount of the catch-up contribution to a 401(k) plan is $4,000. This amount will reache a maximum of $5,000 in 2006. After 2006, the maximum amount is subject to an inflation adjustment. Employers are not required to include catch-up provisions in their 401(k) plans. However, if they do, the 401(k) plans must comply with the requirements imposed by the IRS. The exact amount of the allowable catch-up contribution depends upon the particular type of retirement plan, For example, for 2005 the maximum catch-up contribution to a 401(k) plan is $4,000 and to an IRA it is $500 (.30).

Funding

An employer's minimum annual contribution to a defined benefit plan must cover the total normal cost of funding the plan plus amortization of past service costs, increases in liabilities, and experience losses minus amortization of reductions in pension liabilities and experience gains.

Advantages of qualified plans

The major tax advantages of qualified plans are:

(1) contributions are deductible (within limits) when made to the plan by the employer;

(2) the plan itself is exempt from income tax on its earnings;

(3) the plan participants (employees) are not taxed until they receive distributions; and

(4) under certain circumstances, a participant may make a tax-free transfer ("rollover") of assets from one type of qualified plan to another.

When no trust is set up to administer the plan, but the employer establishes a qualified annuity plan, the employer may take deductions for the premiums and the employees will receive no income until they receive the annuity payments. However, the use of deferred annuities to fund nonqualified plans may result in income to the employer.

Lump-sum distributions

The income tax on lump-sum distributions may be computed under a favorable method (i.e., 10-year forward averaging). However, this method may only be used by employees who attained age 50 by January 1, 1986.

Tax-free "rollover"

An executive who participates in a qualified plan and who receives a lump-sum distribution from the plan may, under certain circumstances, contribute ("rollover"), on a tax-free basis, the distribution to another qualified plan or traditional IRA.

The advantage of a "rollover" is that it enables a corporate executive to defer the tax liability that would result if the entire amount of a lump-sum distribution is taxed in a one tax year. Executives are thus given greater employment flexibility because they may change jobs without fear of adverse tax consequences resulting from a lump-sum distribution.

However, when an executive receives property (e.g., stock) as part of his distribution from a plan, he must either roll over the stock into the new plan or IRA or he must sell the stock and contribute the money from such sale to the new plan or IRA. The executive may not keep the stock and rollover money equal to the fair market value of the stock (.35).

Top-heavy plans

Additional qualification requirements are imposed for defined benefit and defined contribution plans that primarily benefit an employer's key employees. These types of plans are referred to as "top-heavy plans."

The additional qualification requirements that are imposed on top-heavy plans are:

(1) alternative rapid vesting schedules,

(2) minimum amounts of nonintegrated contributions or benefits for plan participants who are not key employees,

(3) limits on the amount of a participant's compensation that may be taken into account, and

(4) further limitations on the aggregate limit on contributions and benefits for some key employees (.40).

Problems with qualified plans

Although a qualified plan from a tax standpoint is by far more favorable, for both the employer and the employee, than a nonqualified plan, there are reasons why such a plan may not be the most desirable. The main problem is that a qualified plan cannot discriminate in favor of highly paid executives, shareholders, and officers.

Another problem is that an executive who joins a corporation late in his career may not be able to participate under a qualified plan for a period of time sufficiently long to amply reward him. Finally, the corporation may simply be unable to afford to fund a qualified plan while being perfectly able to provide deferred compensation for certain favored executives. If any of these circumstances is present, the employer may wish to work out a nonqualified deferred compensation plan for its executives, either as a substitute for, or as a supplement to, a qualified plan.

Nonqualified plans

When tax advisers refer to a "deferred compensation plan" they generally have in mind the nonqualified plan—that is, a plan involving nothing more than an agreement by the employer to pay the employee something in the future. For a discussion of nonqualified plans, see ¶25,032.

SIMPLE Plans

A SIMPLE plan (savings incentive match plan for employees) is designed to encourage small employers to establish retirement plans for their employees (.45). A SIMPLE plan may take the form of an IRA or a cash or deferred 401(k) arrangement. Contributions are limited to $10,000 for 2005 and thereafter (.50). There are a number of requirements for both the employer and employee to meet.

.05 Code Sect. 401-404, 416 and 501(a).
.10 Code Sec. 411(a)(12).
.15 Code Sec. 415(c)(1).
.20 Code Sec. 415(b)(1).
.25 Code Sec. 402(g)(1).
.30 Code Sec. 414(v).
.35 Rev. Rul. 87-77, 1987-2 CB 115.
.40 Code Sec. 416.
.45 Code Sec. 408(p).
.50 Code Sec. 408(p)(2)(E).

¶25,031 Nonqualified Plans. An effective nonqualified deferred compensation plan may:

(1) be made up for one or two or a group of executives or key employees;

(2) be funded or unfunded;

(3) be established by simple contract; and

(4) provide *nonforfeitable* rights to the executive or employee (.05).

Item (4) is the most important point.

Of the types of deferred compensation plans, two are of particular interest to corporate executives. One may be referred to as a "management contract retirement plan" (see ¶25,035). The other may be designated as a "profit-sharing retirement fund" (see ¶25,036).

Amounts payable to an executive (.10) under a deferred compensation plan are not includible in gross income until received or made available. Compensation is not made available to an employee until a present interest is transferred (.15). The IRS will not give advance approval to such plans unless a substantial forfeiture provision remains in effect throughout the entire period of deferral (.20).

Note: For amounts deferred after December 31, 2004, new rules that were enacted by the Amercian Jobs Creation Act of 2004 control the tax treatment of nonqualified deferred compensation plans (.25). Basically, these new rules impose strict limits on when distributions may be made from nonqualified deferred compensation plans (.30).

.05 Rev. Rul. 60-31, 1960-1 CB 174, as modified by Rev. Rul. 64-279, 1964-2 CB 121, and Rev. Rul. 70-435, 1970-2 CB 100.

.10 Rev. Rul. 71-419, 1971-2 CB 220.

.15 *Lombard and Co.*, 38 TCM 1158, CCH Dec. 36,220(M), TC Memo. 1979-297.

.20 Rev. Proc. 71-19, 1971-1 CB 698.

.25 Code Sec. 409A, as enacted by the American Jobs Creation Act of 2004 (P.L. 108-357).

.30 Code Sec. 409A(a)(1), as enacted by the American Jobs Creation Act of 2004 (P.L. 108-357).

¶25,033 Individual Retirement Account. An executive has the option, as does any other employed taxpayer, to defer up to $4,000 of annual compensation for 2005 ($4,500 if over age 49) into a traditional IRA (.05) or Roth IRA (.10). The company can make contributions on the executive's behalf up to the maximum yearly limit. An executive can also combine personal contributions with the employer's contributions, so long as the total contributions made outside of a SEP plan (see ¶25,034) do not exceed the annual limit.

.05 Code Sec. 219(g). **.10** Code Sec. 408A.

¶25,034 Simplified Employee Pension Plans. A simplified employee pension plan (SEP) is a special kind of IRA (see ¶25,033) (.05). Employers contributing to a simplified pension plan generally are treated as if they were contributing to an employees' trust or annuity plan. From an executive's standpoint, the big advantage of a SEP over a regular IRA is that for 2005, the employee's tax may be deferred on up to the lesser of $42,000, or 25 percent of compensation received (up to a maximum of $210,000) from the contributing employer. An employee for whom an employer contributes under a SEP is allowed to take additional deductions for contributions to the IRA to the extent of the $4,000 ($4,500 if over age 49) and phaseout rules noted at ¶25,033. The amount of the SEP contribution is not included in the total amount of wages, tips, and other compensation reported on Form W-2. In the case of an executive, shareholder or owner-employee, the dollar limitation is reduced by any self-employment tax or employer FICA tax that is taken into account in determining the amount of the employer contribution.

.05 Code Sec. 402(h).

¶25,035 Management Contract Retirement Plan. This plan is adaptable to a business that wishes to provide deferred compensation benefits for executives at the management level. A separate contract of employment may be entered into with each management employee or one contract may be entered into with a group of management employees (.05).

The essential part of the contract is the restriction on the employee's right to receive currently the additional compensation; *it is not necessary to make the rights contingent or forfeitable.* Thus, although the employee's right to distributions from the reserve created in his favor is not forfeitable, in no event can he receive, or will he be entitled to, payments from the reserve until the happening of one of the specified events. Note: After December 31, 2004, such contracts will have to be comply with the requirements of new Code Sec. 409A in order to ensure that income is deferred under a nonqualified deferred compensation plan.

Contractual clause

A contractual clause reflecting this type of deferred compensation could read as follows, with details or modifications to fit the individual case:

Clause for One Executive

The compensation which X shall be entitled to receive from the Y corporation during the 5-year term of his employment contract shall be an annual salary of $100,000 plus additional compensation equal to 5% of the Y corporation's annual net profits from operations, computed as follows: [here, specify desired details].

The annual salary shall be payable in equal monthly installments on the first day of each month. The additional compensation shall be credited on the Y corporation's books to a reserve account, and will be deferred, accumulated, and paid in annual installments equal to one-fifth of the amount in the reserve as of the close of the year immediately preceding the year of first payment. Payments to X from the reserve account are to begin only upon the happening of any one of the three following events, namely:

(1) termination of employment,

(2) conversion from full-time to part-time employee status, or

(3) partial or total incapacitation.

[Follow this with provisions concerning credits and payments in the event of the executive's death, failure to fulfill duties, etc.]

Clause for Group of Executives

The compensation that the President, A, the Vice-President, B, and the Comptroller, C, shall be entitled to receive from the Y corporation during the 5-year term of this employment contract shall be as follows: to A, an annual salary of $150,000 plus additional compensation equal to 8% of the Y corporation's annual net profits from operations; to B, an annual salary of $140,000 plus additional compensation equal to 5% of the Y corporation's annual net profits from operations; and to C, an annual salary of $135,000 plus additional compensation equal to 3% of the Y corporation's annual net profits from operations. The annual salaries of each of these officers shall be payable in equal monthly installments on the first day of each month. The additional compensation of each of them shall be credited on the Y corporation's books to a reserve account, and will be deferred, accumulated, and paid in annual installments equal to one-fifth of the amount in the reserve to the credit of each of the officers as of the close of the year immediately preceding the year of the first payment. Payments which each of these officers is entitled to receive from the reserve account are to begin only upon the happening of any one of the three following events, namely,

(1) termination of employment,

(2) conversion from full-time to part-time employee status, or

(3) partial or total incapacitation.

[Follow this with provisions concerning credits and payments in the event of the officer's death, failure to fulfill duties, etc.]

Funding the deferred compensation

The additional compensation to be paid the executive is to be credited to a bookkeeping reserve. As to funding or not funding the reserve, the employer can do as it deems best. It is not necessary to fund the reserve; the deferred compensation may be paid out of current earnings when the executive reaches retirement age. If the company wishes to make doubly certain that funds will be available to pay the deferred compensation, it can create a special fund instead. The actual cash may be accumulated in a special bank account or may be invested in government securities. Earnings on the fund may be added to the fund itself or could be used by the business for its ordinary operating purposes. How the earnings on the fund are used will not affect the tax status of the deferred compensation plan.

> ***Example:*** A corporation enters into a deferred compensation agreement with a number of its key employees. To fund the plan, the corporation sets aside a

percentage of its annual profits, with which it purchases U.S. savings bonds and Treasury notes, retaining ownership. The earnings from these investments are also added to the fund. By such procedure, the employees as well as the employer-corporation are assured that there will be funds to pay the deferred compensation when the key employees reach retirement age.

The plan may also be funded by the purchase of straight life insurance or endowment policies. An additional advantage accruing from the purchase of insurance contracts is that it is thereby possible to guarantee the payment of substantial amounts to the employee's family in the event that the executive dies before reaching retirement age.

When payments are taxable—and when deductible

Under this "management contract retirement" type of deferred compensation plan, the executive will not be taxable on the additional compensation until payments are actually received. Insofar as the taxability of the employee is concerned, the forfeitability or nonforfeitability of rights under the contract is of no importance. The restrictions upon payment in the agreement prevent the payments from being constructively received when credits are made to the reserve. Because it is not intended that the amount in the reserve be held in trust for the executive, the provisions governing taxation of employees on contributions to a nonqualified employees' trust (.10) do not apply. However, when a trust is intended (and results), then the employee is taxable at the time the credits are made to the trust if the employee's rights are nonforfeitable at that time. If the employee's rights are forfeitable when credits are made to the trust, then the employee will not be taxed until the rights become nonforfeitable.

The corporation is entitled to a deduction only when payments of the deferred compensation are actually made to the employee. A deduction will not be permissible each year credits are made to the reserve. This is equally true whether employers use the cash or accrual method of accounting. If a trust is intended, then the corporation is entitled to a deduction as credits are made to the reserve when the employee's rights are nonforfeitable.

If life insurance or endowment policies are purchased, the employer should be sure it is the owner of the policy and that the proceeds are payable to the employer upon maturity or death of the employee. Then upon receipt of the proceeds the employer will in turn make the required distributions under the plan to the employee following retirement or to the employee's beneficiary. If this is not done, then the premiums for the policies will be taxable income to the employees when the employer pays them and, in effect, there will be no deferment of the additional compensation. However, the use of deferred annuities to fund nonqualified plans may result in income to the employer (see ¶25,030).

.05 Rev. Rul. 60-31, 1960-1 CB 174, as modified by Rev. Rul. 64-279, 1964-2 CB 121, and Rev. Rul. 70-435, 1970-2 CB 100.

.10 Code Sec. 402(b).

¶25,036 Profit-Sharing Retirement Funds. A nonqualified plan for sharing profits among a number of executives and key employees (.05) is also a viable method for providing executive compensation. Additional compensation for executives and key employees attributable to current services is deferred from income tax until the years following retirement or other separation from the employee of the corporation. Forfeitability of the participants' benefits need not be a condition of effective deferral of income.

Because this type of plan may involve a large number of employees rather than relatively few, it may be desirable that the plan be funded to make certain that payments will be made when they become due. The designated portion of each year's profits can be set aside and invested, with the earnings on the investments added to the fund. Also, life insurance or endowment policies can be purchased for the employees, but in the employer's name and with the employer as beneficiary. This has the additional advantage of making more readily available substantial sums to the executive's family if the executive dies before retirement.

The executives and key employees covered by the plan are not taxed on the deferred compensation until they actually receive payments following retirement. The doctrine of constructive receipt is not applicable. In addition to the usual restrictions on the employer's liability to make the payments (that is, the executive must reach a designated retirement age, cease employment, or become disabled), there are additional contingencies provided in this plan. The executive must:

(1) refrain from engaging in a competing business,

(2) be available for consultation and advice after retirement or termination of services, and

(3) retain an unencumbered interest or benefit in the plan.

Also, under this plan, an employer is not entitled to a deduction until payments of the deferred compensation are actually made. The mere setting aside of the profits of the business and crediting of each participant's share to the participant's account on the books will not entitle the employer to a deduction. This applies whether the employer uses the cash or accrual method of accounting.

If life insurance or endowment policies are purchased, the employer should be the owner of the policies and should be the one to receive the proceeds upon maturity or death of the employee. By following this procedure, the employee will not be taxable on the premiums when they are paid by the employer, although the employer will not be able to deduct the premiums. If this procedure is not followed, then the premiums constitute taxable income to the employee when paid by the employer and, consequently, the tax on the additional compensation is not deferred.

Example

The following, in simplified form, is an example of an agreement that provides for additional compensation on a deferred basis through profit-sharing and that is a plan of the nonqualified (or nonexempt) type.

PROFIT-SHARING AGREEMENT—Establishment of Plan

Corporation X does hereby establish a profit-sharing plan for the purpose of providing additional compensation on a deferred basis for current services to those officers and key employees designated from time to time by the corporation's board of directors.

Funding the Plan

In furtherance of the plan, Corporation X agrees to set aside on the last day of each annual accounting period 50 percent of its annual net profits, before federal income taxes and other taxes imposed upon income, in excess of $1,000,000.

Division of Fund

The amount of net profits so set aside by Corporation X is to be divided among the participants in the plan as designated by the board of directors in the ratio that each participant's salary, as of the last day of each annual accounting period, bears to the total of all the salaries of the participants as of the last day of each annual accounting period.

Accounting and Administration

Corporation X is to maintain in its accounting records a separate account for each participant in the plan and at the end of each annual accounting period is to credit to each participant's account the appropriate share, as determined above, of the net profits required to be set aside by Corporation X as provided herein. Each participant's account is also to be credited with the net amount, if any, realized from investing any portion of the amount in the participant's account.

Distribution of Fund

A participant's share of the net profits set aside by Corporation X each year under the plan is not to be paid currently to the participant. Payments or distributions from each participant's account are to be made annually and are to begin only when (1) the participant reaches retirement age, (2) the participant's employment with the corporation is terminated, including termination due to death, or (3) the participant becomes totally unable to perform the participant's duties, whichever event occurs first.

Moreover, Corporation X's liability to make distributions to the participants is contingent upon the participant's (1) refraining from engaging in any business competitive to that of Corporation X, (2) being available to Corporation X for consultation and advice after retirement or termination of services, unless disabled, and (3) retaining unencumbered any interest or benefit under the plan. If the participant fails to fulfill any one or more of these contingencies, Corporation X's obligations under the plan are automatically terminated as to that participant.

Amount of Annual Distribution

The annual distributions or payments to each participant are to be in an amount equal to 10 percent of the balance in the participant's account at the close of the annual accounting period immediately preceding the year of the first payment and are to continue until the participant's account is exhausted. In the event of the participant's death, either before or after payments or distributions to the participant have begun, the amount in the participant's account is to be distributed or paid to the participant's designated beneficiaries or heirs-at-law in installments computed in the same manner as if the participant were still living.

.05 Rev. Rul. 60-31, 1960-1 CB 174, as modified by Rev. Rul. 64-279, 1964-2 CB 121, and Rev. Rul. 70-435, 1970-2 CB 100.

PROFESSIONALS

Introduction

¶25,037 Persons engaged in professions make up a body of special taxpayers, although they are subject to most of the same tax rules that apply to commercial businesses.

The term "profession," in general, embraces those individuals who sell their professional services to clients and who are regulated by state certification laws. Thus, included in the professions are law, medicine, optometry, nursing, dentistry, accountancy, professional engineering, and architecture, among others. See ¶25,048.

Fees received for professional services, like other compensation received for services performed, are includible in gross income regardless of whether or not they are deductible by the payor and regardless of whether or not they are received in cash or property. Individuals engaged in a profession, like others engaged in a trade or business, are entitled to deduct all ordinary and necessary expenses incurred in the practice of their profession.

With these basic points as background, the material at ¶25,039 -¶25,073 describes the general federal income tax rules applicable in situations peculiar to professional persons, along with the means and methods that may be used to keep their income taxes at a minimum.

Limited liability companies can be taxed as partnerships for federal income tax purposes with no investor being liable for the company's debts. However, there are some issues regarding the operation of limited liability companies that have not been fully resolved. This is especially true in some states and should be considered when deciding whether to use this form of doing business.

Income

¶25,039 Income of Professionals. The professional earns income primarily by rendering a service (e.g., medical, legal, accounting or engineering). While additional income may be realized from investments as well (the rules pertaining to investment income are discussed beginning at ¶25,229), professional income itself is composed primarily of such items as fees, commissions, and split fees for referrals (.05). If a professional is a member of a partnership or a limited liability partnership that is taxed as a partnership, income consists of the distributive share of partnership income (.10).

Most states and the District of Columbia have statutes governing the incorporation of professionals for the purpose of carrying on a practice. If a professional is employed by a corporation, professional income consists of salary and dividend distributions on any shares of stock owned in the corporation.

Income from a professional practice that the taxpayer engages in individually (not as a partner) is reported in detail on separate Schedule C, "Profit or Loss From Business," Form 1040. Net profit or loss is then entered on page 1, Form 1040.

Income from partnership

If a professional practice is carried on as a partnership, then partners must report on their personal tax return, Form 1040, their share of the partnership's taxable income. Individual partners include in Part II, Schedule E, Form 1040, their share of the ordinary income (whether actually received or not) or the net loss of a partnership, the tax year of which ends within or with the partner's own tax year (.15). Other items of income, deductions, etc., to be carried to the appropriate schedules of individual return Form 1040 are shown in Schedule K of the partnership return.

Income from LLC

Under the check-the-box regulations,(.20) limited liability companies (LLCs) can be taxed as partnerships, or LLC members can elect to have the entity taxed as a corporation. The IRS does not use any separate LLC forms. All tax items are reported using either the partnership forms or the corporation forms, depending on how the LLC is classified.

Income from corporation

Income received from a corporation in the form of a salary is reported on Form 1040, 1040A or 1040EZ. The professional's W-2 form should be attached to the return. Any dividend income must be reported on Form 1040 or 1040A; Form 1040EZ cannot be used by a taxpayer with dividend income. If the professional is a member of an S corporation, income from such a corporation is reported in a manner similar to that for partnership income (.25). Similar rules regarding the treatment of salary and distributions apply to S corporations (.30).

.05 Code Sec. 61.

.10 Code Sec. 704; Reg. §1.701-1.

.15 Code Sec. 704; Reg. §1.704-1.

.20 Reg. §3201.7701-3.

.25 Code Sec. 1402(f), Rev. Rul. 56-675 1956-2 CB 459.

.30 Code Sec. 1366.

¶25,040 Estimated Tax. Estimated tax is the method used to pay tax on income that is not subject to withholding. This includes income from self-employment, interest, dividends, alimony, rent, gains from the sale of assets, and guaranteed payment from a partnership. Estimated tax also must be paid if the withholding from salary, pension, or other income is not enough.

Estimated tax is used to pay both income tax and self-employment tax, as well as other taxes. If a taxpayer does not pay enough through withholding or by making estimated tax payments, he may be charged a penalty if more than $1,000 is owed after taking withheld taxes into account. For 2005, no estimated tax is due if all three of the following conditions are met: (1) the taxpayer had no tax liability for the 2004 tax year, (2) the taxpayer was a U.S. citizen or resident for the whole year, and (3) the taxpayer's 2004 tax year covered a 12-month period. There is no tax liability for a prior year if the total tax was zero or the taxpayer did not have to file a tax return.

Married taxpayers may make joint payments of estimated tax even if they are not living together. Spouses may not make joint estimated tax payments if they are legally separated under a decree of divorce or separate maintenance. Also, spouses may not make joint payments if either spouse is a nonresident alien or if the spouses have different tax years.

Because estimated tax payments are indeed "estimated", there is a "safe harbor" for estimated taxes. If you have paid the safe-harbor amount, you are not subject to penalties even if you fall short of what you should have paid for the current year. The general safe-harbor payment is the smaller of (1) 90 percent of the total expected tax for 2005 or (2) 100 percent of the total tax shown on the 2004 return. The 2004 return must cover all 12 months.

For certain high-income taxpayers (adjusted gross income of more than $150,000, or $75,000 for a married individual filing separately) the safe harbor is the smaller of (1) 90 percent of the total expected tax for 2004, or (2) 110 percent of the total tax shown on the 2003 return (.05).

If a taxpayer files a return for the taxable year on or before January 31 of the following tax year and pays in full the amount computed on the return as payable, then there will be no penalty with respect to any underpayment of the fourth required installment for the taxable year (.10).

For calendar-year taxpayers, the estimated tax payments for 2005 are due April 15, 2005, June 15, 2005, September 15, 2005, and January 16, 2006. For fiscal-year taxpayers, payments are due the 15th day of the fourth, sixth, and ninth months of the fiscal year, and the 15th day of the first month following the end of the fiscal year. When the due date falls on a Saturday, Sunday or legal holiday, the due date is extended to the next business day.

Estimated tax payments are made by using Form 1040-ES payment vouchers.

.05 Code Sec. 6654(d)(1)(C); Reg. §1.6654-1. **.10** Code Sec. 6654(h).

¶25,041 Self-Employment Tax. The self-employment tax is in the nature of a social security tax for individuals who work for themselves.

Professionals who are either self-employed or members of a partnership must file a self-employment tax return (Schedule SE of Form 1040) if they have self-employment income of $400 or more for the tax year (.05). Guaranteed payments from a partnership to a partner are counted as self-employment income (.10).

There is a maximum wage base of $90,000 in 2005 for the old-age, survivors and disability insurance portion of the self-employment tax, computed at 12.4 percent. For 2004, the maximum wage base was $87,900. There is no cap on earnings subject to the health insurance portion of the self-employment tax, which is computed at 2.9 percent.

For purposes of computing the self-employment tax, a deduction of 7.65 percent (one-half of the self-employment tax rate) of the net earnings from self-employment is taken. This deduction is allowed only in the computation of the self-employment tax. It is not a reduction in the income tax. However, a deduction of one-half of the taxpayer's self- employment tax can be deducted from gross income.

.05 Code Sec. 6017; Reg. §1.6017-1. **.10** Reg. §1.707-1(c).

¶25,042 Accounting Periods. Some professionals work in fields where the activity is seasonal in nature. For example, an accountant's practice may be such that a disproportionate amount of the work may be performed before April 15 each year. When a business has an uneven work flow during the calendar year, a taxpayer may wish to adopt a fiscal year. In general, a fiscal year is a tax year that ends on the last day of a calendar month other than December 31 (.05). Ordinarily, a fiscal year will end at or soon after the close of the peak period (.10).

As a general rule, a taxpayer may select either a calendar or fiscal tax year the first time a return is filed. However, individuals are generally required to use a calendar year as their tax year. A taxpayer's tax year may be changed only with the prior approval of the IRS (.15). A change of annual accounting period will be approved for federal income tax purposes when the taxpayer establishes a substantial business purpose for making the change (.20). All the facts and circumstances are considered in determining whether a taxpayer has established a substantial business purpose.

Partnerships, S corporations, and personal service corporations are often required to use either the calendar tax year, or the tax year of the entity's owners, regardless of whether such tax year corresponds with the entity's accounting period (see ¶15,035).

If a partner has a different tax year from that of the partnership, the partner declares partnership income from any partnership year ending within or with the partner's tax year. Similarly, the shareholders of an S corporation are required to take into account their distributive shares of flow-through items in the tax year in which the S corporation tax year ends.

> ***Example:*** Arnold Smith reports his income for a calendar year, while the partnership of which he is a member reports its income for a fiscal year ending May 31. During the partnership tax year ending in 2005, Smith receives his distributive share of partnership income totaling $12,000. Of this amount, $7,000 is received by him between June 1 and December 31, 2004, and the remaining $5,000 is received by him between January 1 and May 31, 2005. The entire $12,000 received by Smith is includible in his taxable income for the 2005 calendar year(.25).

A partnership must use as its tax year the tax year of those partners owning a majority interest in its profits and capital. If partners owning a majority interest have different tax years, then the partnership must employ the same tax year as the one used by all of its principal partners (those with at least a five-percent interest in profits and capital). If a partnership is unable to determine a tax year under either the majority interest rule or the principal partners rule, it generally must use a calendar year or other year that results in the least amount of aggregate deferral for its partners (.30). However, it may use a different tax year if it can show that there is a business purpose for that year or it elects a different tax year under Code Sec. 444 and makes required payments to the IRS.

An S corporation generally is required to use the calendar year as its tax year unless it can show that there is a business purpose for a different tax year or it elects another tax year under Code Sec. 444.

A personal service corporation is required to use the calendar year as its tax year unless it can show that there is a business purpose for a different tax year or it elects another tax year under Code Sec. 444 and subjects itself to certain limitations on its deductions if it fails to make certain minimum distributions.

.05 Code Sec. 441(e).

.10 Rev. Proc. 74-33, 1974-2 CB 489 clarified by Rev. Proc. 87-32, 1987-2 CB 396.

.15 Code Sec. 442.

.20 Reg. §1.442-1(a).

.25 Reg. §1.706-1(a)(1).

.30 Reg. §1.706-1(b)(2).

¶25,043 Accounting Methods—Computing Taxable Income. The taxpayer engaged in the practice of a profession must maintain books and records that will facilitate a clear reflection of income (.05). The method of accounting adopted is entirely up to the professional, as long as it clearly reflects income.

Under the cash method, income items and expenses are reported as received or paid. An accrual-method taxpayer must report income when the right to receive it becomes unconditional and the amount becomes fixed (.10). Nevertheless, certain expenses such as the providing of services to or by the professional, the use of property by a professional, and the payment of workers' compensation or tort liability by a professional are not deductible until "economic performance" has occurred (.15). The economic performance rules can also affect the deduction of certain interest payments; rebates and refunds; insurance, warranty, and service contracts; and taxes. However, certain recurring items are exempt from the economic performance rule if all the other requirements for deduction under the accrual method are met.

When business transactions during the year are many and complex, the accrual method will usually permit the deduction of expenses in the year the income to which they relate is reported. However, for the vast majority of professionals, the accrual method will not necessarily result in more effective equalization of income than will the cash-receipts- and-disbursements method.

Generally, C corporations, partnerships that have one or more C corporations as partners, and tax shelters cannot use the cash method of accounting; they must adopt the accrual method (.20), as must taxpayers in a profession that involves both the sale of goods and services requiring the keeping of inventories, such as a self-employed pharmacist or an optometrist (.25). A qualifying partnership, a small business (average annual gross receipts of $5 million or less in the preceding three tax years) and an S corporation are not subject to the prohibition and may continue to use the cash method of accounting. A qualifying partnership is a partnership in which all of the partners are individuals, qualified personal service corporations, S corporations, or other qualifying partnerships (.30). In addition, an exception to the required use of the accrual method has been provided for small businesses with average annual gross receipts of $1 million or less (see ¶15,220) (.35).

.05 Code Sec. 446.

.10 Reg. §1.451-1(a); *Life Insurance Company of Georgia*, CtCls, 81-1 USTC ¶9445, 650 F2d 250.

.15 Temporary Reg. §1.7519-1T.

.20 Code Sec. 448.

.25 Rev. Rul. 74-279, 1974-1 CB 110.

.30 Temporary Reg. §1.448-1T(f)(2).

.35 Rev. Proc. 2001-10, 2001-1 CB 272.

¶25,044 Constructive Receipt of Income. Professionals using the cash method of accounting may be tempted to try to put over income earned in one tax year to the next tax year and thus postpone the payment of tax on it. For example, an attorney who reports income using the calendar year and who performs services in December might delay billing for those services until the very end of the month so that the payment for those services would not be received until January. If services were performed on December 5 and billed on December 6, for example, payment could easily have been received before the end of the year so that the payment would be included as part of the earlier year's income.

However, the "constructive receipt" rule must be kept in mind. This rule treats as taxable income any amount that is subject to the taxpayer's unqualified demand, whether or not it has actually been received in cash (.05). Thus, an attorney was taxable upon the full amount of a fee that had been earned and was unconditionally available to him during a particular year, even though at his request the payment was not made until the following year (.10).

Also, the taxpayer can control expenses to some extent by accelerating or deferring payment to another year, depending upon when it would be more advantageous to take the deduction and considering the size of the gross income against which the deduction is to be taken. The control gives the taxpayer a chance to equalize income from year to year. However, certain expenses, even though paid in the current tax year, may have to be deferred until a subsequent tax year.

.05 Reg. §1.451-2; *D.M. Goldsmith*, CtCls, 78-2 USTC ¶9804, 586 F2d 810.

.10 *J.S. Price*, 22 TCM 818, CCH Dec. 26,188(M), TC Memo. 1963-172.

¶25,045 Spreading Income Forward into Future Years. The spreading of income forward into future years is mostly a matter of arranging by contract the conditions of payment for the services to be rendered. Thus, the contract can provide either that the professional fees are to be paid over a period of years or that the payout of royalties on books, compositions, patents, etc., is to have a yearly limit.

If the contract is clear about the taxpayer's right to receive income, there should be no problem with income spreading. If the contract is vague or uncertain and the taxpayer tries to spread income over tax years, however, the IRS may use the constructive receipt doctrine to make all the income immediately taxable. If income is unreservedly subject to the taxpayer's demand and the taxpayer could have received it but chose not to do so, it is regarded as having been constructively received and is taxable as if it had been received (see ¶25,044).

¶25,046 Deferring and Shifting Income by Incorporation. Some professionals have tried to divide their incomes among members of their families by incorporating their businesses and dividing the stock among family members. Thus, after the expenses of running the professional's business have been deducted, the remainder can be distributed as corporate dividends payable directly to the family members in proportion to their ownership of the corporate stock. This device, a form of income splitting, is intended to transfer income from individuals with high marginal income rates to those with lower rates, thus saving tax on the total income earned. In recent years, with the disparities in marginal income rates being much less than in the past, this device is not as important as it once was. Nevertheless, such income-splitting continues, and is supportable when the total compensation received by the professional from the corporation is equivalent to that which the professional would have received absent the use of the corporate entity (.05).

However, when the corporate device is used to shift to others income that otherwise would have been taxed to the professional, the IRS has the power to attribute the income to the professional (.10).

.05 *D.F. Keller*, 77 TC 1014, CCH Dec. 38,401, aff'd CA-10, 83-2 USTC ¶9740, 723 F2d 58.

.10 Code Sec. 318.

¶25,047 Deferring Professional Earnings Through Pension Plan. A professional may engage in a trade or business alone, as a partner in a partnership, or as an employee of a corporation. In any of these instances, a professional may establish a pension plan. In general, pension plans may be used to defer tax on significant amounts of income because contributions to qualified pension plans are deductible as business expenses at the time they are made and earnings are not taxed to the professional until they are received upon distribution. This is also true in the case of self-employed professionals, who can set up retirement plans for their business.

Generally, there are two main types of retirement plans:

(1) The first type is the defined contribution plan (.05). For 2005, the maximum amount that may be deducted for amounts contributed to the plan is the *lesser* of $42,000 or 25 percent of compensation (.10). The computations involved in determining the maximum deduction for the self-employed owner's contribution to his own retirement plan are complex (see ¶11,350).

(2) The second type of pension plan is the defined benefit plan (.15). Under a defined benefit plan, the business owner contributes the amount necessary to produce a fixed benefit at retirement. Under this plan, the maximum amount a professional may *receive* in 2005 is the *lesser* of $170,000, or 100 percent of his average compensation for the three consecutive years in which the greatest aggregate compensation is achieved (.20).

When a professional establishes a retirement plan, the plan must also be made available to employees who have completed one year of service with not less than 1,000 hours, and who are 21 years of age or more (.25). The professional's contributions for employees are deductible as a business expense (.30).

A self-employed professional can set up a 401(k) plan, assuming the plan meets the employee coverage requirements (.35). If the professional is a sole proprietor, the professional is treated as an employee for purposes of the 401(k) rules (.40). If the professional is a partner, the partner is treated as an employee of the partnership (an owner-employee when more than 10 percent of either the capital or profits interest in the partnership is owned) (.45). If the professional has a professional corporation, then the professional is an employee of the corporation.

A 401(k) plan allows an employee to make an election between receiving current compensation or having a portion of the compensation contributed to a qualified profit-sharing or stock bonus plan. The maximum amount an employee can elect to defer in 2005 is $14,000 or $18,000 if the employee is over age 49 by the end of the year) (.50).

Employers with 100 or fewer employees who received at least $5,000 in compensation in the preceding year may adopt a retirement plan called the Savings Incentive Match Plan for Employees (SIMPLE), if they do not currently maintain another qualified plan (.55). Simplified employee pensions (SEPs) are another option that should be considered (.60). Details concerning SIMPLEs and SEPs are discussed at ¶11,470 and ¶11,500.

Another type of IRA, called a "Roth IRA", enables taxpayers to make contributions that are not currently deductible, but permits tax-free build up of interest and dividends and withdrawals from which may be tax free under certain circumstances (.65). Roth IRAs should be considered in addition to the retirement plan established for the business.

Corporate advantages

Corporate plans are favored over self-employed pension plans in several areas:

(1) A participant in a corporate plan may borrow from the plan in certain circumstances without the loan proceeds being treated as a distribution (.70). Plan loans made to sole proprietors and partners have been removed from the category of prohibited transactions (.75).

(2) Corporations can offer sick pay benefits (.80), accident and health plans (.85), group-term life insurance (.90), cafeteria plans (.95), employer-provided meals and lodging (.100), and disability insurance (.105).

There is a difference between the taxation of benefits offered by subchapter C corporations and benefits offered by S corporations. C corporations can offer

(1) the exclusion of amounts paid for or to certain accident and health plans (.110);

(2) the exclusion of the cost of up to $50,000 of group-term life insurance on an employee's life (.115); and

(3) the exclusion from income of meals or lodging furnished for the convenience of the employer (.120).

S corporations can offer these tax benefits only to shareholders owning two percent or less of the stock in the corporation without incurring tax consequences that would make such plans undesirable (.125).

Unless there are provisions to the contrary, partners are not employees of the partnership. Thus, partners generally fall into the category of sole proprietors for purposes of the fringe benefit rules. However, partnerships may provide employee benefits for non-partner employees of the firms.

☐ For a discussion of the advantages and disadvantages of the various forms of doing business that a professional may use, see ¶25,135 and following.

.05 Code Sec. 414(i).
.10 Code Sec. 402(h).
.15 Code Sec. 414(j).
.20 Code Sec. 415(b)(1) and (3).final figures not out
.25 Code Sec. 410(a)(1)(A).
.30 Code Sec. 162.
.35 Proposed Reg. §1.401(k)-1(a)(6)(i).
.40 Code Sec. 401(c)(1)(A).
.45 Code Sec. 401(c)(3).
.50 Code Sec. 402(g).
.55 Code Sec. 408(p).
.60 Code Sec. 408(k).
.65 Code Sec. 408A.
.70 Code Sec. 4975(c)(1)(B) and (d); Code Sec. 401(c)(3).
.75 Code Sec. 4975(f)(6)(B)(i)(III).
.80 Code Sec. 3402.
.85 Code Sec. 105.
.90 Code Sec. 79.
.95 Code Sec. 125.
.100 Code Sec. 119.
.105 Reg. §1.72-15.
.110 Reg. §1.105-1.
.115 Code Sec. 79.
.120 Code Sec. 119.
.125 Code Sec. 1372.

¶25,048 State Laws Aiding Formation of Professional Service Corporations and Associations. Although at one time many states prohibited associations of professionals, such as a partnership of attorneys, from incorporating, all states and the District of Columbia have now enacted laws permitting the formation of professional corporations or associations. This action has paved the way for professionals to gain tax-deferred pensions and other benefits by being held to be either corporations or associations taxable as corporations (.05). A qualifying professional corporation can elect to be taxed as an S corporation (.10).

The inclusion of certain professionals as being specifically permitted to incorporate or to form stock associations does not necessarily mean that other professionals cannot incorporate as well. The definition of what constitutes a "profession" also varies from state to state.

Professionals should consult the statutes of the state in which they practice to determine what statutory restrictions, if any, apply to the practice of their profession within the corporate form.

LLCs

Most states permit professionals to join together using the limited liability company (LLC) format. This form of doing business offers the limited liability of corporations with the flexibility of organization associated with partnerships. In addition, LLCs are not hampered by the special rules that apply to S corporations.

.05 Rev. Rul. 70-101, 1970-1 CB 278, as modified by Rev. Rul. 73-596, 1973-2 CB 424 and amplified by Rev. Rul. 70-455, 1970-2 CB 297; Rev. Rul. 77-31, 1977-1 CB 409; Rev. Rul. 82-213, 1982-2 CB 1.
.10 Code Sec. 1361.

Special Partnership Provisions

¶25,050 Partnerships and Professionals. Many professionals practice their profession as a member of a partnership. Unlike C corporations, partnerships are not subject to income tax, but are required to file Form 1065, "U.S. Partnership Return of Income," for information purposes (.05). Individual partners must take into account their distributive shares of partnership income or loss. Income reported is taxed to the individual partners, even though it is not distributed to them (.10) and even though distribution was prevented by litigation (.15).

Limited liability partnerships

Many professionals like to conduct their practices as limited liability partnerships. This is not the same as a limited partnership where some partners's risk for partnership losses do not extend beyond their contributions or an agreed amount. An LLP is a general partnership where each individual partner remains liable for his or her own malpractice, and the liabilities arising out of the wrongful acts or omissions of those over whom the partner had supervisory duties. However, upon the fulfillment of a given registration requirement, the partner is otherwise insulated from the malpractice, misdeeds, negligence, and the like, of his partners in excess of the value of the partner's interest in the partnership. In some states, this registration requirement even protects the individual partner from the partnership's general contractual obligations. Those states that provide only protection from joint and several liability are referred to as "partial shield" states. Those states that provide protection from both joint and several liability and from entity contractual liability are referred to as "full shield" states (.20).

Other forms

Many professionals have used passthrough S corporations as their preferred from of doing business. As a passthrough, the S corporation offered one-tier taxation. The professionals who set up the corporation were corporate employees. In the past, S corporations offered an opportunity for employee benefits that were not available to a partnership or sole practitioner. However, in recent years. the advantages among the various forms of doing business have been evened out.

.05 Code Sec. 701; Reg. §1.701-1.

.10 Reg. §1.702-1(a); *W.P. Neil*, CA-9, 53-1 USTC ¶9393, 205 F2d 121.

.15 *Beck Chemical Equipment Corporation*, 27 TC 840, CCH Dec. 22,265.

.20 Rev. Rul. 95-55, 1995-2 CB 313.

¶25,051 Acquisition of a Partnership Interest. In general, gain or loss is not recognized to a partner or the partnership upon the contribution of money or property, including installment obligations, to the partnership in exchange for an interest therein (.05). This is the rule for a partnership that is being formed as well as for a partnership that is already functioning (.10).

As a general rule, the basis of a contributing partner's interest in the partnership is the amount of money contributed *plus* his adjusted basis in any property contributed *plus* the amount (if any) of gain recognized to the contributing partner at the time (.15). The selling partners recognize a capital gain on the sale of their interests except with regard to unrealized receivables and inventory items that give rise to ordinary income (.20).

If the partner contributes property as whole or partial payment for his partnership interest and the property is subject to an indebtedness, or if an indebtedness of the partner is assumed by the partnership, the basis of the partner's interest must be reduced by the amount of the indebtedness assumed by the other partners. The partnership's assumption of the indebtedness is treated as a distribution of money to the partner (.25).

Existing partners are subject to taxation when a new partner is admitted to a partnership and assumes a portion of the partnership's existing liabilities and is allocated a share of the partnership's existing unrealized receivables (.30). This taxation of the existing partners can be avoided if there is an express agreement that the new partner is not assuming any share of the partnership liabilities in existence at the time of admission.

A professional who contributes unrealized receivables to the partnership for services that were performed in an individual capacity has no basis for these receivables if the professional is using the cash method of accounting. Their value, although it is credited to that partner on the books of the partnership, is not includible in the income tax basis of that partnership interest. If the professional uses the accrual method, any amounts due to the professional from customers are unrealized receivables for which the professional has a basis equal to the amounts previously reported as income.

If unrealized receivables are transferred to a partnership of professionals, the partnership agreement should state whether the other professionals who are partners are to share in the income therefrom upon their collection and, if so, should set out the extent of such sharing (.35).

Interest acquired as compensation for services

If a partnership interest is acquired for past services, the partner's basis in such interest generally is the fair market value of the interest at the time it is received (.40). The partner then recognizes ordinary income in the amount of the value of the partnership interest received. If a partnership interest is acquired for future services, the partner's basis is zero until such time as the fair market value of the interest is recognized as income. However, authorities are divided on the valuation method to be used where a partner receives only an income interest in the partnership rather than a capital interest.

.05 Code Sec. 721, 722 and 723.
.10 Code Sec. 721.
.15 Code Sec. 705 and Code Sec. 722.
.20 Code Sec. 751(a).
.25 Code Sec. 752.
.30 Reg. §1.752-3.
.35 Code Sec. 735 and Code Sec. 751.
.40 Reg. §1.721-1(b)(1).

¶25,052 Distributions from a Partnership. A partner generally recognizes gain on a partnership distribution only to the extent any money (and marketable securities treated as money) included in the distribution exceeds the adjusted basis of the partner's interest in the partnership. Any gain recognized is generally treated as capital gain from the sale of the partnership interest on the date of the distribution. If partnership property (other than marketable securities treated as money) is distributed to a partner, he generally does not recognize any gain until the sale or other disposition of the property.(.05). A partner's adjusted basis in the partnership includes the partner's distributive share of the partnership earnings for the year, less the amount actually distributed. For instance, a partner who owns a 50 percent interest in a partnership that earned $100,000 during one tax year and who withdrew $50,000 during the same year would have no change in partnership adjusted basis resulting from that year's earnings and distributions (.10).

A partner may also have to recognize gain when a distribution is made in exchange for all or part of that partner's interest in the partnership to the extent attributable to unrealized receivables of the partnership or inventory items of the partnership that have substantially appreciated in value. Also, payments made to a partner who is leaving the partnership for that partner's share of the partnership's goodwill may have to be realized as ordinary income.

A partner who contributes appreciated property to a partnership is required to include pre-contribution gain in income to the extent that the value of other property distributed by the partnership to that partner exceeds his or her adjusted basis in the partnership interest. The provision applies whether or not the contributing partner's interest in the partnership is reduced in connection with the distribution, but applies only if the distribution is made within five years after the contribution of the appreciated property (.15).

On the other hand, loss is recognized with regard to distributions only with respect to a distribution made in complete liquidation of a partnership interest and only if the distribution consists solely of money, unrealized receivables and inventory items. However, loss deductions are limited to the amount at risk (.20).

Marketable securities

Generally, a marketable security distributed to a partner is treated as money in determining whether gain is recognized on the distribution. This treatment, however, does not generally apply if that partner contributed the security to the partnership or an investment partnership made the distribution to an eligible partner.

The amount treated as money is the security's fair market value when distributed, reduced (but not below zero) by the excess (if any) of:

(1) The partner's distributive share of the gain that would be recognized had the partnership sold all its marketable securities at their fair market value immediately before the transaction resulting in the distribution, over

(2) The partner's distributive share of the gain that would be recognized had the partnership sold all such securities it still held after the distribution at the fair market value in (1) (.25).

.05 Code Sec. 731, 732 and Code Sec. 737.
.10 Code Sec. 705.
.15 Code Sec. 737.
.20 Code Sec. 465.
.25 Code Sec. 731(c).

¶25,053 Accounting Methods. The choice of accounting methods for reporting income for a partnership of professionals is made by the partnership (.05). The partnership may elect the cash or accrual method, or any other accounting method permissible under the tax law. Although restrictions apply to use of the cash method, such as partnerships with inventories, tax shelters and partnerships with a C corporation as a partner, these would not ordinarily apply to partnerships organized to carry on a profession. Thus, a cash-method professional may be a partner in an accrual method partnership. The professional reports income and expenses from the partnership for the partnership tax year ending with or during the professional's tax year (.10). The selection of such items as depreciation methods and Code Sec. 179 expense deductions is also made at the partnership level, and is not made individually by each partner.

A partnership may have a tax year other than that of all of its principal partners only if it establishes a business purpose (.15) or makes a Code Sec. 444 election.

.05 Code Sec. 6221.
.10 Code Sec. 706.
.15 Code Sec. 706.

¶25,054 Limited Liability Companies. One of the most important developments in tax law in the past few years have been the IRS's recognition of limited liability companies (LLCs). These entities, if properly qualified, are taxed like partnerships, yet offer the limited liability of corporations.

The IRS's definition of an LLC is quite simple: An LLC is an organization formed under a law that allows the limitation of the liability of all members for the organization's debts and other obligations, and which is classified as a partnership for federal tax purposes. The classification of an LLC for Code purposes is controlled by the check-the-box regulations (.05).

According to the IRS, limited liability companies combine features of both partnerships and corporations. The most notable characteristics of LLCs are: contractual freedom, two or more members (some states have authorized single-members LLCs), and limited liability for *all* investors.

Like partnerships, limited liability companies are a creation of state law. Also, like partnerships, the Code's treatment of these entities is not controlled by state law.

.05 Reg. §7701-3.

Sale of Business Including Goodwill

¶25,055 Sale of Sole Proprietorship. In the sale of a sole proprietorship, the professional is treated as having sold each asset comprising that business separately (.05). Each individual asset must be classified as capital assets, depreciable property used in the business, real property used in the business, or property held for sale to customers, such as inventory or stock in trade. The sale of capital assets results in capital gain or loss. The sale of real property or depreciable property results in gain or loss from a Code Sec. 1231 transaction. The sale of inventory results in ordinary income or loss.

The selling price of the professional's business is apportioned among the assets according to their relative *values*—not their bases in the sole proprietor's hands. Separate computations should be made with respect to each asset or asset category sold, and any gain or loss is treated in accordance with each asset's tax classification (.10).

.05 Rev. Rul. 55-79, 1955-1 CB 370.

.10 Reg. §1.1221-1(d).

¶25,056 Sale or Liquidation of Partnership Interest. The sale of a partnership interest by a professional is treated for federal income tax purposes as the sale of a capital asset (.05). The major exception to this rule is that any payments representing either unrealized accounts receivable for the sale of goods or of services to be rendered, or inventory that has substantially appreciated in value, are taxed to the professional as ordinary income. If a professional is relieved from partnership liabilities as a part of the sale or liquidation of the partner's interest, this relief from liabilities is considered income to the professional (.10).

Withdrawal from partnership

When a professional withdraws from a partnership and liquidates his or her complete interest, any payments received from the partnership are divided between (1) payments in liquidation and (2) distributive shares or guaranteed payments. Payments in liquidation are treated as partnership distributions to the partner; that is, they are not included in income unless they exceed the adjusted basis of the partnership interest (.15). As with the disposition of any partnership interest, payments in excess of adjusted basis are taxed as capital gains (see above). Partnership liquidation payments made for goodwill and unrealized receivables are treated as made in exchange for the partner's interest in partnership property, and not as a distributive share or guaranteed payment that could give rise to a deduction or its equivalent for the partnership. The new law does not apply to payments made to withdrawing general partners in a partnership in which capital is not a material income-producing factor (.20). Nor does the new law affect the deductibility of compensation paid to a retiring partner for past services.

Payments in consideration for unrealized receivables and goodwill of the partnership are treated as ordinary income (.25). If the payment represents the partner's distributive share of partnership income, it is usually taxed as ordinary income or capital gain, depending on its character in the hands of the partnership. Guaranteed payments to a professional in a partnership for services or use of capital are taxed to that partner as ordinary income (.30).

Net capital gains on property held for more than one year are generally taxed at a maximum rate of 15 percent. Ordinary income is taxed at the maximum rate of 35 percent. Thus, there is a tax-rate differential that favors structuring a transaction so that it will produce long-term capital gains wherever possible. Further, capital gains may be offset by capital losses up to any amount, and ordinary income can be used to offset up to $3,000 of capital losses ($1,500 if married and filing separately) (.35).

.05 Code Sec. 741.
.10 Code Sec. 752(b).
.15 Code Sec. 732; Reg. §1.732-1.
.20 Code Sec. 736(b)(3).
.25 Code Sec. 736(b)(2).
.30 Reg. §1.707-1(c).
.35 Code Sec. 1211(b).

¶25,057 Sale or Liquidation of Corporate Interest. If a professional owns stock in a professional corporation, the ownership interest may be disposed of in one of three ways:

(1) by selling the stock,

(2) by completely liquidating the corporation, or

(3) by having the corporation redeem the stock.

Sale of stock

A professional may dispose of stock in a professional corporation either by selling it to other shareholders in the corporation or by selling it to a party buying into the corporation. As with other stock, a professional's ownership of stock in a professional corporation generally constitutes the ownership of a capital asset. If the stock has been held for more than one year (.05), its sale will result in a long-term capital gain or loss (.10).

Liquidation of the corporation

For the professional selling shares of stock, liquidating distributions are treated as payments in exchange for stock (.15). Accordingly, liquidating distributions in excess of the value of the professional's adjusted basis in the stock are taxed to the professional at capital gain rates. This is true whether the distribution is in cash or in property. When property is distributed, gain or loss to the professional is measured against its fair market value, not its adjusted basis in the hands of the corporation. The fair market value then becomes its basis in the hands of the shareholder to the extent gain or loss has been recognized for federal income tax purposes (.20).

Generally, gain or loss is recognized by a corporation upon the liquidating distribution or sale of its assets. Thus, sales of assets pursuant to a liquidation, and the deemed sale of assets in a stock acquisition treated like an asset purchase, will give rise to gain or loss.

If an S corporation was formerly a C corporation, a tax is imposed on any unrealized gain that arose prior to the conversion (built-in gain) and that is recognized by the S corporation, through sale or distribution, within ten years after the date on which the S corporation election took effect. This does not apply to a corporation that has been an S corporation all of its tax years, including those of any predecessor (.25).

Redemption of stock

When a professional corporation redeems stock (.30), the distribution made in redemption is taxed as a capital gain to the professional whose shares are being redeemed, but only if the redemption is not in the nature of a dividend (.35). If the redemption is in the nature of a dividend, the professional is taxed as if a dividend had been received—that is, at ordinary income rates (.40). The distribution is treated as a sale of stock by a professional rather than as a dividend if one of the following tests is met (.45):

(1) the redemption is substantially disproportionate with respect to the professional shareholder;

(2) the redemption terminates the professional shareholder's entire interest in the corporation;

(3) the redemption is not substantially equivalent to a dividend; or

(4) the redemption is of stock held by a noncorporate shareholder and is made in partial liquidation of the redeeming corporation.

In this instance, of course, the professional corporation would still be in existence and would be run by the remaining shareholders.

Corporate reorganizations

If professionals who have been jointly conducting a successful professional practice as a professional corporation wish to go their separate ways, they may face problems in not recognizing gain. However, a tax-free split-up of a professional corporation can be achieved through the use of a corporate reorganization.

> ***Example:*** Two lawyers in joint practice decide to split their practice into two separate practices. Each had gross receipts and operating expenses representative of an active trade or business for each of the five years immediately preceding the split-up. The existing corporation transfers half of its assets to one of the two owners in exchange for that owner's stock and assumption of related liabilities. Pursuant to an integrated plan, that person immediately transfers all of the assets received to a new corporation in exchange for all of the new corporation's stock and its assumption of all related liabilities. (This is done because, under state law, the stock in a professional corporation could not be owned by another corporation.) The transfer is treated as a tax-free reorganization with no gain or loss recognized to either corporation upon the transfer or receipt of the assets. The basis of the assets is carried over from the existing to the new corporation, and the holding period of the assets includes the period they were held by the original corporation (.50).

.05 Code Sec. 1222.
.10 Code Sec. 1221.
.15 Code Sec. 331.
.20 Reg. §1.334-1(a).
.25 Reg. §1.1374-4.
.30 Code Sec. 317(b).
.35 Code Sec. 302.
.40 Code Sec. 301.
.45 Code Sec. 302(b).
.50 Code Sec. 355.

¶25,058 Goodwill. The goodwill of a business is its potential to realize earnings above a normal return by means of the investment in its intangible assets. Goodwill is a capital asset (.05).

Because of the many facts and circumstances in each business situation, there are a number of methods for figuring the value of goodwill when such value cannot be assigned readily. The IRS's position is that the value of goodwill must be determined using the "residual method." Under this method, the consideration paid for the business is allocated first to cash, demand deposits and similar accounts transferred in the sale. Then, the purchase price is allocated to certificates of deposit, U.S. government securities, readily marketable stock or securities, and foreign currency. Any consideration paid for the going concern that remains after all these allocations represents the value of the goodwill. An allocation is made for all other assets, tangible and intangible, including Code Sec. 197 intangibles.

For a long time, the IRS maintained that no portion of the sales price of a business was allocable to goodwill when a business was dependent solely upon the personal characteristics and professional skill of the owner. However, a number of judicial decisions indicated that, in appropriate factual circumstances, a professional practice or other business may possess salable goodwill even though its success is solely attributable to the skill, integrity and other characteristics of the owner (.10).

In cases involving the sale of an entire professional practice, the extent to which the proceeds of the sale can be allocated to goodwill will be determined on the facts rather than by whether the business is, or is not, dependent solely upon the professional skill or other personal characteristics of the owner. Likewise, the question whether there has been a partial transfer of goodwill or merely an anticipatory assignment of future earnings upon the admission of partners by a professional person to his or her practice will be treated as a question of fact (.15).

The IRS recognizes the existence of transferable goodwill in connection with the sale of a business, the success of which is not dependent solely upon the personal characteristics of the owner, even though the sale does not include a valid assignment of the exclusive use of the firm name (.20). However, no goodwill can exist in a nontransferable, personal service contract, such as a franchise dealership, if the privileges thereunder could be divested from the taxpayer-dealer under circumstances completely beyond the dealer's control. The proper valuation in such case is the net fair market value of the tangible assets (.25).

The purchase price of the assets of a trade or business is to be allocated for tax purposes using the residual method to determine the amount allocable to goodwill and the going concern. Under the residual method, the purchase price is allocated first to the assets to the extent of their fair market value, and any excess is allocated to goodwill and the going concern value (.30).

.05 Code Sec. 1221; Reg. §1.1221-1.

.10 *F.G. Masquelette*, CA-5, 57-1 USTC ¶9267, 239 F2d 322; *M.B. Karan*, CA-7, 63-2 USTC ¶9571, 319 F2d 303; *Wilmot Fleming Engineering Co.*, 65 TC 847, CCH Dec. 33,634.

.15 Rev. Rul. 64-235, 1964-2 CB 18, as modified by Rev. Rul. 70-45, 1970-1 CB 17.

.20 Rev. Rul. 70-45, 1970-1 CB 17, modifying Rev. Rul. 64-235, 1964-2 CB 18, and Rev. Rul. 60-301, 1960-2 CB 15.

.25 *F.E. Zorniger*, 62 TC 435, CCH Dec. 32,667 (Acq.).

.30 Code Sec. 1060.

¶25,059 Agreements Not to Compete. Generally, the amount of consideration paid to a professional for a covenant not to compete is ordinary income to the professional (.05). However, if the covenant not to compete is executed coincident to and as part of the contract of sale, the covenant is treated as a capital transaction, and the amount received under the covenant is not ordinary income. The Tax Court, considering the tax status of consideration received for an agreement not to compete, stated: "But where it [the agreement] accompanies the transfer of goodwill in the sale of a going business, and it is apparent that the covenant not to compete has the function primarily of assuring the purchaser the beneficial enjoyment of the goodwill that he has acquired, the covenant is regarded as nonseverable and as being in effect a contributing element to the assets transferred." The court found as a fact that the agreement was a capital asset ancillary to the transfer of goodwill and customers and held the proceeds attributable thereto taxable as a capital gain (.10). The IRS follows the Tax Court's reasoning, but it notes that this is a factual issue, not a matter of law (.15).

The cost of a covenant not to compete is amortized over 15 years (.20). It cannot be currently deducted as a business expense.

> ***Example:*** Grace Vail sells her business for $100,000. Of this amount, $7,500 is allocated to a five-year covenant not to compete. The purchaser may claim a deduction of $500 per year for fifteen years without regard to how long the covenant is in force.

.05 Rev. Rul. 69-643, 1969-2 CB 10.

.10 *A. Michaels*, 12 TC 17, CCH Dec. 16,758 (Acq.).

.15 Rev. Rul. 65-180, 1965-2 CB 279, as modified by Rev. Rul. 74-456, 1974-2 CB 65.

.20 Code Sec. 197 and *J.T. Fletcher*, 24 TCM 1489, CCH Dec. 27,589(M), TC Memo. 1965-273.

Expenses

¶25,061 Business Deductions. Individuals engaged in a profession are entitled to deduct ordinary and necessary expenses incurred in the practice of their profession. Deductible professional expenses include the cost of supplies, expense of operating and maintaining an automobile used in making professional calls, dues paid to professional societies, rent paid for office rooms, cost of fuel, light, water and telephone used in the office, the cost of hiring office assistants, and the cost of books, instruments, and equipment (when such items have a short useful life) (.05).

Persons engaged in the practice of a profession may also deduct the amounts paid for subscriptions to professional journals and the cost of information services that are purchased in connection with the performance of their professional duties. For example, lawyers and accountants may deduct the cost of federal or state tax reporters, labor law reporters, trade regulation reporters, and other law reporters.

Expenses incurred in attending business conventions have been held to be deductible by professionals (see ¶25,066). Such expenses and other business-related travel expenses are business expenses of persons engaged in the practice of a profession (.10).

Depreciable assets

The cost of certain items must be recovered through depreciation rather than by deducting the full cost in the year of payment. Office furniture is seven-year property. Most office equipment, including computers, typewriters, calculators, and copiers, is five-year property under MACRS (.15).

In the case of technical books and services that have a useful life of one year or less, including periodicals and loose-leaf reporting services that are currently purchased on an annual basis, the cost is deductible currently as a business expense. On the other hand, other additions to a library, such as bound law or medical volumes that have a more permanent value, are regarded as capital additions subject to depreciation (.20). Because books do not have a class life under the ADR system, they are classified as seven-year property under MACRS (.25).

Business form as factor

The business form may influence the deductibility of a given expenditure. For instance, if a professional's business has been incorporated, an otherwise nondeductible personal expenditure for medical, disability, or life insurance premiums for officer-shareholders may be deductible as a corporate business expense.

Information return

Any professional who, in the course of a trade or business, pays money (or other valuable consideration) worth $600 or more to another professional must report the payment on Forms 1096 (Annual Summary and Transmittal of U.S. Information Returns) and 1099-MISC (Statement for Recipients of Miscellaneous Income). This rule applies to fee splitting and referral commissions as well as to other arrangements (.30).

.05 Code Sec. 162(a); Reg. §1.162-6.

.10 Code Sec. 167(l).

.15 Code Sec. 167(m) and Code Sec. 168(e)(1); Rev. Proc. 87-56, 1987-2 CB 674, clarified and modified by Rev. Proc. 88-22, 1988-1 CB 785.

.20 *A.A. Beaudry*, CA-2, 45-2 USTC ¶9328, 150 F2d 20.

.25 Rev. Proc. 87-56, 1987-2 CB 674, clarified and modified by Rev. Proc. 88-22, 1988-1 CB 785.

.30 Rev. Rul. 85-50, 1985-1 CB 345.

¶25,062 Deducting Capital Expenses. The cost of capital assets generally cannot be deducted currently. However, in the year that a professional places in service tangible personal property (for example, furniture and equipment, but not land or buildings) that is used in the professional's trade or business, up to $102,000 of the cost of such property may be deducted for property placed in service in 2004 (.05). The cost of a car used for business purposes can also be expensed under this rule, but there are special rules that must be used to determine the maximum amount that may be expensed (.10).

The professional may also recover the cost of most capital assets, except land, through depreciation deductions (.15).

.05 Code Sec. 179.

.10 Code Sec. 280F(d)(1).

.15 Code Sec. 167 and Code Sec. 168.

¶25,063 Deductible or Excludable Educational Expenses. Educational expenditures are deductible if:

(1) the education maintains or improves skills required in the professional's trade or business; or

(2) the education meets the express requirements of the professional's employer (.05).

Two important limitations on the deductibility of educational expenses *as a business expense* are the "minimum educational requirement" and the "qualification for a new trade or business" restriction (.10). Accordingly, if the education sought is a minimum educational requirement for qualification in a profession or part of a program of study that will lead to qualifying an individual for a new profession, trade or business, then the expenditures are nondeductible (.15).

The minimum education necessary to qualify for a profession, trade, or business must be determined from a consideration of such factors as the requirements of the applicable law and regulations and the standards of the profession, trade, or business involved. However, once an individual has met the minimum educational requirements for qualification in his trade or business (as in effect when entering the trade or business), the individual is considered as continuing to meet those requirements even though they are changed.

Furthermore, to be considered as maintaining or improving professional skills, the taxpayer must be engaged in the profession *at the time* the educational expenses are incurred (.20). Merely being a member in good standing in a profession is not the same as carrying on a profession (.25). Thus, a licensed attorney who had never practiced law was not entitled to deduct expenses incurred in earning a Master of Law degree because these expenses were not incident to the trade or business of practicing law (.30).

See, also, ¶7225 and following for a full explanation of the deductibility of educational expenses as trade or business expenses.

An above-the-line deduction for qualified tuition and related expenses is available to individual taxpayers in tax years beginning after December 31, 2001, and before January 1, 2006 (.35). This deduction is equal to the qualified tuition and related expenses paid by the taxpayer during the tax year and is limited depending on (1) the taxpayer's adjusted gross income (AGI) and (2) the tax year in which the deduction is claimed. For the details concerning this deduction see ¶6434.

If the educational expenses of an employee are reimbursed under an employer-sponsored educational assistance program, up to $5,250 of the reimbursed expenses are excludable from gross income (.40). Employer-provided educational assistance for courses leading to advanced academic or professional degrees (graduate level courses) is excludable from the employee's income (.45).

.05 Code Sec. 162(a); Reg. §1.162-5.

.10 Reg. §1.162-5(b)(2) and Reg. §1.162-5(b)(3).

.15 *M.J. Goldberg,* 49 TCM 168, CCH Dec. 41,637(M), T.C. Memo. 1984-617.

.20 *A.M. Jungreis,* 55 TC 581, CCH Dec. 30,600.

.25 *J.C. Ford,* 56 TC 1300, CCH Dec. 30,986; *P.R. Wassenaar,* 72 TC 1195, CCH Dec. 36,359, aff'd CA-9, 73-2 USTC ¶9798.

.30 *M.S. Frankel,* 47 TCM 1208, CCH Dec. 41,032(M), TC Memo. 1984-103.

.35 Code Sec. 222.

.40 Code Sec. 127(a)(2).

.45 Code Sec. 127(c)(1).

¶25,064 Travel Expenses. A deduction is allowed for travel expenses incurred by a professional while away from home in the pursuit of a trade of business. In order to be deductible, the expenses must be ordinary and necessary. A deduction is allowed for the cost of meals and lodging as well as transportation expenses incurred by a professional in business travels (.05).

Local travel expenses incurred as part of the professional's trade or business, such as traveling between one client and another, are also deductible. However, commuting expenses between home and work are not deductible (.10).

Only travel expenses incurred by an employee under a reimbursement or other expense allowance arrangement with the employer are fully deductible in arriving at adjusted gross income. If full reimbursement is not made pursuant to an expense allowance arrangement, the unreimbursed portion of the travel expense is allowable only as a miscellaneous itemized deduction, subject to a two-percent floor.

.05 Code Sec. 162; Reg. §1.162-2.

.10 Reg. §1.162-2(e).

¶25,065 Substantiating Travel Expenses. Careful recordkeeping is required so that a professional will be able to substantiate claims for travel expense deductions with adequate records or by sufficient evidence that corroborates the taxpayer's own statement (.05). Expenditures that are lavish or extravagant are not deductible no matter how well the records are kept (.10). The professional should keep the following tax records of business travel expenses:

(1) each separate amount spent for travel away from home, such as for transportation and lodging, although individual meals and travel expenses may be added together for daily totals;

(2) the date of departure and return for each trip and the number of days spent on business on each trip;

(3) the name of the city or town visited; and

(4) the business reason for the travel or the business benefit expected to be derived.

.05 Code Sec. 274(d). **.10** Reg. §1.274-1.

¶25,066 Convention and Seminar Expenses. Usually, a professional may deduct the expenses of attending a business seminar or convention (.05). The deductibility of such expenses turns upon whether there is a sufficient relationship between the taxpayer's profession and attendance at the convention. In general, if the professional is benefiting or advancing the interest of the taxpayer's trade or business by attendance, the expenses are deductible. However, if attendance at the convention is for political, social, or other purposes unrelated to the taxpayer's trade or business, the expenses are not deductible.

When there is a sufficient relationship between the individual's business and attendance at the convention, then expenses for travel to and from the convention and expenses for meals, lodging and other incidentals are deductible. However, if, while attending a business-related convention, the individual engages in personal activities such as social entertaining or sightseeing, the expenses allocable to the personal activities are not deductible. When convention attendance is not business related, for example, when it is, in effect, a personal vacation, only the expenses that are ordinary, necessary, and directly related to the individual's business activity may be deducted.

Deductions are allowed only for expenses related to a trade or business; thus expenses for attending a convention, seminar, or similar meeting for investment purposes or financial planning are not deductible.

.05 Reg. §1.162-2.

¶25,067 Foreign Conventions. Generally, no deduction is allowed for expenses relating to attendance at conventions outside North America (.05). In addition, the profession must establish that the meeting is directly related to his profession (or to an income-producing activity), and that, after taking certain factors into account, it is as reasonable to hold the meeting outside the permitted countries or areas as within them (.10).

Conventions on cruise ships

For a professional to be able to deduct expenses for attending a convention on a cruise ship, the ship must be a vessel registered in the United States and all ports of call of the ship must be located in the United States or possessions of the United States. In addition, the professional must establish that the meeting is directly related to the active conduct of a trade or business. Also, the professional must attach two written information statements to the professional's federal income tax return. One statement must be signed by the professional and include (1) the total number of days of the trip and the number of hours each day was devoted to scheduled business activities and (2) a program of scheduled business activities and meetings. The second statement must be signed by an officer of the organization or group sponsoring the meeting and include (1) the schedule of the business activities for each day and (2) the number of hours the professional attended such scheduled business activities (.15).

.05 Rev. Rul. 87-95, 1987-2 CB 79, modified by Rev. Rul. 94-56, 1994-2 CB 37.
.10 Code Sec. 274(h).
.15 Code Sec. 274(h)(2).

¶25,068 Business Entertainment Costs. Fifty percent of sums spent by a professional for entertainment activities may be deductible if the sums are reasonable in amount and are an ordinary and necessary trade or business expense (.05). However, entertainment deductions for expenses incurred with respect to certain entertainment facilities, with some exceptions, are not allowed. The nondeductible facilities include yachts, hunting and fishing lodges, swimming pools, vacation resorts, hotel suites, and dining rooms (.10). Club dues are not deductible. See ¶25,071.

If an entertainment expense is incurred with respect to an activity rather than a facility, 50 percent of it may be deductible if the individual establishes that the expense is directly related to that trade or business. The individual also must have a reasonable expectation that the business will benefit. See also ¶25,071.

The amount of the entertainment deduction must be properly substantiated and its reasonableness determined. Deductions must be substantiated by adequate records or by sufficient evidence corroborating the taxpayer's statement. Documentary evidence of a business expense normally is required if the expense is $75 or more. If the expense is less than $75, a professional's business records may be used to substantiate the expense (.15).

Once the amount of the expense is established, the deduction may be claimed only when the taxpayer is able to show that the entertainment had a direct relationship to the conduct of his business, and that the business benefit can reasonably be expected from the expenditure. This benefit cannot consist solely of the goodwill of the person being entertained (.20). A general statement of expected referrals or new patients as a result of the entertainment is not enough. If personal reasons predominate, the expenditure may not be deducted, even though there is some possibility of a business benefit.

.05 Code Sec. 274(d).
.10 Reg. §1.274-4(e)(2).
.15 Reg. §1.274-5(c)(2)(iii)(B).
.20 Reg. §1.274-2(c)(3)(i).

¶25,069 Business Meals. As in the case of other entertainment expenses (see ¶25,068), 50 percent of the cost of business meals or food and beverages is deductible only if they are directly related to the trade or business, or, in the case of meals directly preceding or following a business discussion, if they are associated with the trade or business (.05). Further, it is important to note that meal expenses are not deductible if neither the taxpayer nor one of the taxpayer's employees is present at the meal. Likewise, no deduction is allowed for food and beverages to the extent that the amount spent is lavish or extravagant under the circumstances (.10).

"Working lunches" are not deductible where all the parties to the lunch meetings are co-workers. Thus, daily lunch meetings between law partners did not qualify for a business expense deduction. The expenses did not qualify as "necessary" (.15).

When business associates regularly lunch or dine together, no deduction for meals is allowed unless the specific meal being deducted meets the requirements set out above. Unless the deduction requirements are met, such a meal is considered a personal expense.

.05 Code Sec. 274(d) and Code Sec. 274(k).
.10 Rev. Rul. 63-144, 1963-2 CB 129.
.15 *D. Kaufman*, CA-1, 85-1 USTC ¶9278, 758 F2d 1, aff'g DC Me., 84-1 USTC ¶9500, 584 F.Supp. 872.

¶25,070 Host's Share of the Expense. The deductible amount of the total expenses incurred by professional persons for themselves while entertaining clients is generally the amount that exceeds the sum they normally would spend on themselves in such a situation (.05).

> ***Example:*** Lorna Summer, an attorney, invites a client to lunch to close a pending deal and pays a $80 check, $40 for herself and $40 for her client. If Summer can prove that she normally pays only $10 for her lunch, she is entitled to deduct $70, which is 50 percent of the entertainment expenses: $40 for the client and $30 for herself.

This rule is generally applied in abuse situations when taxpayers claim deductions for substantial amounts of personal living expenses.

However, the IRS has, with judicial approval, applied the rule at its option and will not permit taxpayers to prevent its application (.10). In clear business settings, such as a hospitality room at a convention, the full cost of the professional person's meal with a client is deductible (.15).

.05 Rev. Rul. 63-144, 1963-2 CB 129, Question 31.

.10 *J.P. Fenstermaker,* 37 TCM 898, CCH Dec. 35,200(M), TC Memo. 1978-210; Rev. Rul. 63-144, 1963-1 CB 129.

.15 Reg. §1.274-2(a)(4).

¶25,071 Entertainment Facilities, Club Dues, and Tickets. No business deduction is allowed for any expense paid or incurred with respect to an entertainment facility. Entertainment facilities include yachts, hunting lodges, fishing camps, swimming pools, tennis courts, and bowling alleys (.05). Thus, an entertainment facility is considered a non-business asset. When an individual purchases such a facility, no investment credit, depreciation deduction, or other business deductions may be claimed. (Non-business deductions such as taxes and interest may still be claimed.) If, however, the facility otherwise qualifies as a business asset, the normal business deductions may be claimed.

> ***Example 1:*** Attorney Farleigh Smith owns a fishing yacht that he uses to entertain clients. He may not claim any business deductions with respect to the yacht. If, however, the same yacht were owned by an individual who was in the business of leasing the boat for charter fishing, then the normal business deductions could be claimed.

In addition, if any entertainment facility is used to provide a deductible entertainment activity, the expense of the activity may still be deducted.

> ***Example 2:*** Assume the same facts as in Example (1). If Smith serves a qualified business meal on the yacht, the expense of the meal may be deducted even though no business expense may be claimed with respect to the yacht.

Club dues paid are not deductible (.10).

Fifty percent of the cost of tickets to a place of entertainment is a gift if the professional does not accompany the recipient unless the taxpayer elects to treat such cost as entertainment (.15). However, business gifts are limited to no more than $25 per year per person (.20).

.05 Code Sec. 274(a)(1).

.10 Code Sec. 274(a)(3).

.15 Reg. §1.274-2(b)(1)(iii)(*b*).

.20 Reg. §1.274-3.

¶25,072 Professional Office at Home. If a professional uses one structure for both a residence and a place of business, a portion of the expenses incurred in the business may be deducted (.05). Generally, the professional taxpayer must show that a portion of the building has been exclusively and regularly used as the principal place of business or as a place used by clients, customers or patients for meeting or dealing with the taxpayer (.10). However, the deduction also is available if (1) the office is used by the taxpayer to conduct administrative or management activities of his trade or business, and (2) there is no other fixed location of the trade or business where the taxpayer conducts substantial administrative or management activities of the trade or business (.15).

Those professionals satisfying the exclusive-use and regular-basis rules can deduct the expenses attributable to the business use of the home that do not exceed the amount of gross income derived from such business use after reduction by the allocable portion of the deductions allowed that have no connection with the taxpayer's trade or business (such as mortgage interest and real estate taxes).

The home office deduction is barred if an employee leases a portion of the home to the employer. Further, the home office deduction limitation is additionally reduced by trade or business deductions allocable to the home office business activity but not allocable to the use of the home (such as supplies and compensation paid); amounts disallowed because of the limitations, however, may be carried over to the next year. In addition, the home office deduction is treated as a miscellaneous expense subject to the two-percent floor.

.05 Code Sec. 280A.

.10 *E.R. Curphey*, 73 TC 766, CCH Dec. 36,753.

.15 Code Sec. 280A(c)(1).

¶25,073 Gift-Leasebacks and Sale-Leasebacks. Gifts of income-producing rental properties under a gift-leaseback or a sale-leaseback arrangement offer a professional person an opportunity for substantial tax savings over a period of years. Generally, such a transaction involves a taxpayer in a high income bracket who sets up a trust or a corporation, gives or sells property to it, and then leases the property back. The transaction gives the taxpayer a rental deduction, and income is thus transferred to the lower-bracket trust or corporation. For example, a doctor's practice was incorporated and the corporation then leased medical furnishings and equipment from a trust for the doctor's children to which the doctor had previously transferred the equipment. The Tax Court held that the rent was deductible by the corporation and was taxable to the trust (.05).

For such an arrangement to produce the desired results, it must involve a valid transfer of the property by the professional person. For a discussion of the factors that a court will examine to determine the genuineness of the transfer, see ¶25,073.

.05 *H.A. Lerner*, 71 TC 290, CCH Dec. 35,544.

RETAILERS-MANUFACTURERS-WHOLESALERS

Introduction

¶25,075 Retailers, wholesalers, distributors, jobbers, manufacturers and processors have similar tax situations. This is because they all sell merchandise and, with some variations, determine their taxable income in the same basic way (sales, less cost of goods sold, less operating expenses). The determination of a manufacturer's cost of goods sold, however, is usually more complex because the costs involved in the manufacture of the product have to be determined and used in the computation.

Since the tax treatment of retailers, manufacturers and wholesalers is very similar, the following explanations, beginning at ¶25,077, discuss all such businesses together, pointing out differences where they occur, and highlighting opportunities for tax savings.

Accounting for Income and Expense

¶25,077 Cash or Accrual Method. A taxpayer's method of accounting for income and expenses determines when such items are reported for income tax purposes (.05). If income is realized from the production, purchase or sale of merchandise, the taxpayer must keep inventories (see ¶25,088-¶25,098) and the accrual method of accounting must be used to account for those inventories.

This means that manufacturers, retailers, and wholesalers must use the accrual method of accounting to account for purchases, production costs, and sales. Ordinarily, "purchases" includes all goods (or title to goods) that have been received during the year (including goods in transit), whether paid for or not. "Sales" are transactions in which goods (or title to them) have passed into the hands of the buyer during the year, regardless of whether payment has been received (but, see ¶25,078). Manufacturing and processing costs for the year are those for which a liability has arisen during the year.

Although the accrual method must be used for inventories, generally it does not have to be used for other operating or non operating expenses, such as financial income and expenses. For these items, the cash method may be used. Since a taxpayer has more control over the timing of income and expense using the cash method, some shifting of income and expense from one tax year to another may be possible, which may result in tax savings.

> ***Example:*** Shifting income from a high income year into a lower income year will lower the taxpayer's tax liability for the high income tax year by reducing

income. Similarly, shifting expenses into a high income tax year from a low income tax year will lower the taxpayer's tax liability by reducing taxable income.

The use of the cash method of accounting is restricted for certain taxpayers. Tax shelters, C corporations and partnerships that have a C corporation as a partner may not use the cash method. However, this restriction does not apply to farming businesses, personal service corporations, and business entities with average annual gross receipts of $5 million or less (.10).

Planning Note

CCH Analysts note that the use of the cash method by a small business is not engraved in stone. In the first case, the tax court found that the IRS did not abuse discretion when it required a software developer that generated gross receipts of less than fivc million dollars to use an overall accrual accounting method to clearly reflect its income. Although corporations with gross receipts of less than $5 million are excepted from the requirement to use the accrual method by statute, the IRS retains the authority to require such a corporation to use the accrual method if necessary to clearly reflect its income. In the second case, a mom-and-pop oil company with gross receipts of less than five million dollars could not use the cash method of accounting because the purchase and resale of petroleum products was an income-producing factor in its business. Thus, the taxpayer was required to take inventories and use the accrual method of accounting to accurately reflect its business income (.15).

.05 Code Sec. 446(c), Code Sec. 448 and Code Sec. 471; Reg. §1.446-1(c) and Reg. §1.471-1.

.10 Code Sec. 448(b).

.15 *Nemetschek North America*, CCH Dec. 54,532(M), TC Memo. 2001-288; *Cross Oil Company, Inc,*, 81 TCM 1682, CCH Dec. 54,352(M).

¶25,078 Timing of Sales and Purchases. Generally, an accrual-method business must recognize income at the time of a sale, whether or not payment is received at that time (.05). Therefore, when a sale occurs is critical.

Ordinarily, a sale on credit or open account occurs when the item sold is delivered to the buyer. If title to the item does not pass to the buyer at that time, however, the sale is not complete. For instance, in a "sale on approval" the property is delivered to the buyer, but title does not pass until the buyer decides to keep the merchandise. In a "consignment sale," title passes only when the consignee sells the goods.

In contrast, "sale or return" contracts, which are prominent in the record and book retailing business, do not create a condition of acceptance or resale, and income is accrued when the goods are delivered to the buyer or title passes. The distinction between consignment and "sale or return" transactions is based on the parties' intent when executing the contract. A typical "sale or return" contract permits periodic shipments and accords the buyer the right to return any unsold individual parts of the shipment.

In the case of a conditional sale, title usually does not pass to the buyer until the buyer has paid all installments of the purchase price. When there is a lease of property with an option to purchase, the arrangement may be treated as a sale, depending upon the circumstances.

Planning Note

CCH Analysts note that when it is expected that the seller's income will be taxed at a lower rate in the next year (either because of a reduction in tax rates or because the seller will be in a lower tax bracket due to a smaller estimated income from sales), taxes can be saved by deferring year-end sales until the next year and by expediting the issuance of credit memos on sales returns and allowances at the year's end. The reverse holds true if the tax rates are expected to be higher in the next tax year.

One way to defer year-end sales to the next year is to sell goods "on approval" (if the buyers are agreeable), instead of on open account or as a "sale or return." Many such sales would probably not be approved until the next year. To accelerate next year's sales, make the sale on open account or as a "sale or return," accelerate year-end billings, and encourage customers to pay ahead of time.

Commissions on sales

Under the accrual method, commissions on sales are deductible in the year in which the income from the sales is reported. Thus, when income was reported upon shipment of goods, the commissions were fixed and definite liabilities and deductible in the same year even though they were dependent upon collection of the sales price (.10). Moreover, when income was reported upon shipment and billing, the commissions were deductible at the time the orders were shipped and billed and not in the prior year when they were accepted (.15).

.05 Code Sec. 451.

.10 *Ohmer Register Co.*, CA-6, 42-2 USTC ¶9777, 131 F2d 682.

.15 *Shelby Salesbook Co.*, DC, 52-1 USTC ¶9250, 104 FSupp 237.

¶25,079 Installment Sellers. The installment method of accounting may not be used for sales of personal property under a revolving credit plan. Consequently, all payments for such property are deemed to have been received in the year of sale (.05). A revolving credit plan includes cycle budget accounts, flexible budget accounts, continuous budget accounts and other plans under which the customer agrees to pay a part of the outstanding balance of the account periodically (.10).

.05 Code Sec. 453(k)(1).

.10 Reg. §1.453A-(2)(c).

¶25,080 Bad Debts. There are two ways to deduct a bad debt loss (.05). Under the "specific charge-off" method, the creditor deducts the debt as it becomes wholly or partially worthless. Under the "reserve" method, the creditor sets up bad debt reserves. However, only small banks can use the reserve method to deduct bad debts. Thus, nearly all taxpayers employ the specific charge-off method.

Once it has been determined that the debt is a genuine business debt that has become worthless, the next step is to determine the tax year in which the bad debt loss deduction can be claimed (.10). A bad debt generally is deductible for the tax year in which the debt became worthless. Thus, the proper timing of the deduction depends upon the proper determination of the debt's worthlessness. A debt becomes worthless or uncollectible when identifiable events occur that reasonably cause the creditor to abandon hope of ever recovering any part of the loan. If there is any possibility of recovery, the creditor cannot claim a bad debt deduction.

This rule (the date of worthlessness determines the tax year in which the bad debt deduction can be taken) also applies to partially worthless business debt.

Comment

If a creditor has deducted a partially worthless debt in one year, he cannot later amend his return to deduct the balance of the debt when it becomes worthless in the next year. However, the balance of the bad debt can be deducted in the next year, when that portion became worthless.

.05 Reg. §1.166-1(a).

.10 Code Sec. 166(a).

¶25,081 Containers. Many manufacturers, retailers, or wholesalers sell merchandise in permanent-type containers, such as bottles, barrels, wooden cases, milk cans, or reels on which to wind cable or wire etc. It title to these containers passes to the buyer of the product sold in the container, the containers are treated as part of the seller's inventory.

Example: Cola Company sells soda in plastic containers. The buyers do not pay a deposit for the container and do not return the containers to the seller. Therefore, these containers are included in Cola Company's inventory.

If a container is sold, but the seller later repurchases the container for reuse, the container is still treated as merchandise in the seller's inventory. When sold containers are repurchased, they should be valued in inventory at their repurchase price, or at the lower of the repurchase price or market value.

If the seller retains title to the containers and merely lends them to the buyer, usually in return for a deposit, or leases them to the buyer the containers are not included in the seller's inventory but are instead treated as assets used in a trade or business. Depreciation deductions have been allowed on such containers, and, in one case, the taxpayer was permitted to treat the cost of the container as an expense (.05).

Taxability of retained deposits

When a retailer retains title to the containers and merely accepts a deposit on them, the deposits must be included in income when received and may be deducted only when the empty containers are returned (.10). Deposits retained when returnable containers are kept by the buyers are also taxable.

Any gain or loss created by forfeited deposits is capital in nature but is also subject to the recapture rules of Code Sec. 1245 (.15).

.05 *Est. of H. Smith* 6 TCM 358, CCH Dec. 15,716(M).

.10 Rev. Rul. 78-273, 1978-2 CB 163.

.15 Rev. Rul. 75-34, 1975-1 CB 271; *Philadelphia Quartz Co.*, CtCls, 67-1 USTC ¶9304, 374 F2d 512.

¶25,082 Coupons and Trading Stamps. If an accrual-basis taxpayer issues coupons when it sells merchandise, or is in the business of selling coupons, and the coupons are redeemable by the taxpayer in merchandise, cash or other property, the taxpayer is allowed a reduction from gross receipts for the cost of current and future estimated redemptions (.05). However, this provision does not apply to coupons that entitle the holder to a discount from the sales price of specified products.

.05 Reg. §1.451-4.

¶25,083 Advance Payments for Goods and Services. Regardless of the taxpayer's method of accounting, prepaid income generally is includible in gross income in the year received. However, deferral privileges are available. Qualifying taxpayers generally may choose to defer advance payments for certain goods or services to the next succeeding tax year to the extent the advance payments are not recognized in financial statement revenues (or, in certain cases, are not earned) in the tax year of receipt (.20). Except for a limited exception involving short tax years, these rules do not permit deferral to a tax year later than the next succeeding tax year.

A payment received by a taxpayer is an "advance payment" if the payment is recognized by the taxpayer (in whole or in part) in revenues in its applicable financial statement for a tax year after receipt or, for taxpayers without an applicable financial statement if the payment is earned by the taxpayer (in whole or in part) in a subsequent tax year. The payment must be for services, the sale of goods, the use (including by license or lease) of intellectual property, the occupancy or use of property if the occupancy or use is ancillary to the provision of services (for example, advance payments for the use of rooms or other quarters in a hotel, booth space at a trade show, campsite space at a mobile home park, and recreational or banquet facilities, or other uses of property, so long as the use is ancillary to the provision of services to the property user), the sale, lease, or license of computer software, related guaranty or warranty contracts, certain subscriptions, certain memberships in an organization, or any combination of items.

The term advance payment generally does not include rent, insurance premiums, payments with respect to financial instruments (for example, debt instruments, deposits, letters of credit, notional principal contracts, options, forward contracts, futures contracts, foreign currency contracts, credit card agreements, financial derivatives, etc.), including purported prepayments of interest, payments with respect to certain service warranty contracts, payments with respect to warranty and guaranty contracts under which a third party is the primary obligor, or payments in property such as certain stock.

Longer deferral for goods. Taxpayers may gain a longer deferral for certain advance payments for goods (.20). Again, the payment may be deferred until no later than the time such advance payments are included in gross receipts for purposes of all of the taxpayer's reports (including consolidated financial statements) to shareholders, partners, beneficiaries, other proprietors, and for credit purposes. However, the deferral isn't limited to the tax year following the tax year of receipt as it is under the general advance payment deferral rules.

Although a longer deferral period is sometimes permitted for advance payments for goods, even the longer deferral period is limited if a taxpayer receives substantial advance payments in a tax year for the sale of goods includible in his inventory, or for an agreement (such as a gift certificate) that can be satisfied with goods or a type of goods that cannot be identified in that tax year. The deferral that would otherwise apply is limited if the taxpayer has on hand (or available to him in such year through his normal source of supply) goods of substantially similar kind and in sufficient quantity to satisfy the agreement in that year. In such a case, all advance payments received with respect to such agreement by the last day of the second tax year following the year in which the substantial advance payments are received, and not previously included in income must be included in income in the second tax year.

Deduction for future expenses

Under the "all-events test," an accrual-basis taxpayer generally is entitled to deduct an accrued expense in the tax year in which: (1) all of the events have occurred that determine the fact of liability, and (2) the amount of the liability can be determined with reasonable accuracy. Generally, the all events test is not met before economic performance occurs with respect to the particular item of expense or obligation that underlies the taxpayer's liability (.20).

Economic performance

The Code specifies when economic performance occurs for certain types of liabilities (.25). The types of liabilities specified include:

(1) *Property and services provided to taxpayer.* If the taxpayer's liability involves property or services provided to the taxpayer by another person, economic performance occurs as the property or services are provided to the taxpayer. However, economic performance occurs for such property or services, even when they have not yet been provided, if the taxpayer pays for the property or services, and the taxpayer can reasonably expect the person to provide the property or services within 3 ½ months. Alternatively, a taxpayer may treat property as being provided either when delivered to or accepted by the taxpayer or when title to the property passes. Incidental costs for services or property need not be treated separately if they are treated by the taxpayer on its books as part of a cost of other property or services and if, in the aggregate, incidental costs do not exceed 10 percent of the total contract price.If a taxpayer accounts for property or services received under a long-term contract using the percent-

age-of-completion method, the economic performance standard may be met as the service or property is provided, or, if earlier, as payments are made prior to the receipt of the property or service (.30). If a liability arises from the taxpayer's use of property, economic performance occurs ratably over the period of time that the taxpayer is entitled to use the property (.35)

(2) *Property and services provided by taxpayer.* If the taxpayer's liability requires it to provide services or property, then economic performance occurs as the taxpayer incurs costs in connection with its obligation. In a "barter transaction" where the taxpayer both receives and provides property and/or services, economic performance occurs for the taxpayer's provision of property or services to the extent of the lesser of (1) the taxpayer's costs or (2) the property or services provided to the taxpayer (.40).

(3) *Workers' compensation and tort liabilities.* In the case of a taxpayer's liability to another person that arises under workers' compensation laws or out of any tort, economic performance occurs when payments to that person are made. In addition, economic performance does not occur until payments are made to a claimant for a liability arising from a breach of contract (if the payments are in the nature of incidental, consequential, or liquidated damages) or from a violation of law (.45). The effect of the establishment of a settlement fund on the deduction of such liabilities is explained at ¶15,535.

(4) *Exception for certain recurring items.* Certain recurring items are treated as incurred in advance of economic performance, provided that the all-events test is otherwise satisfied. This exception is intended to prevent the disruption of normal business and accounting practices and to avoid the imposition of unnecessary burdens on taxpayers. Under the exception, an item is treated as incurred during a tax year if:

(a) as of the end of such tax year, all events have occurred that establish the fact of the liability and the amount of the liability can be determined with reasonable accuracy;

(b) the economic performance test is met within the shorter of 8 ½ months or by the return due date (including extensions) for such tax year;

(c) the item is recurring in nature; and

(d) either the item is not material, or accrual of the item in the year in which the all-events test is met results in a better matching against the income to which it relates than accrual of the item in the tax year of economic performance.

An item that is generally expected to be incurred from one tax year to the next is recurring; even if an item is not incurred in each tax year, it may be treated as a recurring item. In determining whether an item is material, or whether a more proper matching against income results from deduction of an expense prior to economic performance for purposes of (d), above, the treatment of the expense on financial statements is taken into account. The recurring expense exception does not apply to workers' compensation liabilities or tort liabilities requiring payment by the taxpayer to another person (.50). Adopting the recurring item exception for any liability (i.e., item) of the taxpayer is generally a change of accounting method requiring IRS consent (.55).

Reserves. The economic performance rule does not apply to any deductions for additions to reserves for estimated expenses that are specifically allowed by the tax law (.60).

Rebates and refunds

With respect to a taxpayer's liability for a rebate or refund to another person, economic performance occurs as payments are made. Thus, unless the recurring item exception applies, deductions may not be claimed by an accrual-method taxpayer prior to payment. This rule applies whether rebates or refunds are made by actual payment in money or property or are reflected by a reduction in the cost of goods or services to be provided in the future by the taxpayer(.65).

.20 Rev. Proc. 2004-34, I.R.B. 2004-22, 991.
.20 Reg. §1.451-5.
.20 Code Sec. 461(h).
.25 Code Sec. 461(h).
.30 Reg. § §1.461-4(d)(2) and 1.461-4(d)(6).
.35 Reg. §1.461-4(d)(3).
.40 Reg. §1.461-4(d)(4).
.45 Reg. §1.461-4(g)(2).
.50 Reg. §1.461-5.
.55 Reg. §§1.461-5(d) and 1.461-5(b)(2).
.60 Code Sec. 461(h)(5).
.65 Reg. §1.461-4(g)(3).

¶25,084 Research and Experimentation Expenditures. A taxpayer may elect to treat research and experimental expenditures in one of four ways, that is, they may be: (1) currently deducted, (2) capitalized and amortized over a 10-year period beginning with the year incurred, (3) capitalized and amortized over a period of at least 60 months, beginning with the month that the project first generates economic benefits or (4) charged to a capital account (.05). If option (2) is elected, the costs subject to the election will not generate a tax preference adjustment for alternative minimum tax purposes. Costs charged to a capital account are included in the basis of the property resulting from the project and may be taken as a loss if the project is a failure.

Research and experimental expenditures include all expenditures paid or incurred during the tax year on a research project, whether the expenditures are made by the taxpayer or by another person or organization on behalf of the taxpayer.

Comment

Whether an election should be made to expense rather than amortize research and experimental expenditures depends on several factors. Expensing the costs is the easiest option: the election is made simply by taking the deduction on the return. This method avoids postponing deductions for current cash outlays and also avoids the detailed bookkeeping that may be required when costs are amortized. In addition, recapture is not required when the technology or assets resulting from the research and experimental expenditures are later sold.

However, currently expensing may not be the best choice in all situations. The taxpayer's current and future income should be considered in determining whether to expense or amortize research and experimental expenditures. If a taxpayer has current income to offset, the choice of ten-year amortization may also be attractive. This option can be preferable to the minimum 60-month amortization option because it allows the taxpayer a current deduction rather than requiring that any deduction be postponed until benefits from the research and experimental expenditures are realized, yet it reserves a portion of the deduction for future years when increased income from the expenditures can be expected. This can be an advantage over currently deducting all expenditures when income may be lower. The disadvantage, of course, is that the ten-year amortization period is twice as long as the 60-month amortization period otherwise available and detailed records must be maintained.

Research and experimentation credit

A nonrefundable tax credit for incremental research and experimentation expenditures may be available (.10).

Trade names, trademarks

Under some circumstances, a trade name or trademark may be amortized over 15 years.

Clinical testing

A credit may be available for qualified clinical testing expenses paid or incurred for the clinical testing of a drug developed for a rare disease or condition (.15).

.05 Code Sec. 41, Code Sec. 174 and Code Sec. 197; Reg. §§1.174-1—1.174-4.

.10 Code Sec. 41 and Code Sec. 280C.

.15 Code Sec. 45C.

¶25,085 Computer Software Costs. The cost of *developing* computer software may be currently deducted under Code Sec. 174(a). Development costs that are not treated as current expenses may be amortized over 60 months from the date of completion of the development or 36 months from the date the software is placed in service (.05). The taxpayer's treatment of these costs must be consistent. The cost of research for computer software that is developed by a taxpayer primarily for its own internal use may be eligible for the research and experimentation credit (see ¶2453).

Tax treatment of the costs of purchased computer software depends on whether such costs are separately stated. If the software costs are included in the cost of hardware without being separately stated, the costs are treated as part of the cost of the computer hardware and are depreciated over the useful life of the computer hardware. Regulations provide that the capitalized cost of separately acquired computer software is depreciated on a straight-line basis over a 36-month useful life if the costs are separately stated from the hardware (.10).

If the costs of the computer software are separately stated, the costs are amortized ratably over a five-year period or any shorter period that the taxpayer can establish as its useful life. Computer software is considered purchased if the software is custom made for a taxpayer and the developing party is responsible for its operability. However, computer software is considered to be self-developed if the taxpayer bears the risk of the functional utility of the software

.05 Rev. Proc. 2000-50, 2000-2 CB 601.

.10 Reg. §1.167(a)-14.

¶25,086 Advertising and Sales Promotion Expenses. Advertising and other ordinary and necessary selling expenses that bear reasonable relation to taxpayer's trade or business are deductible unless advertising expenses constitute capital expenditures (.05). Deductible advertising expenses include expenditures for advertisements to reach ultimate consumers, amounts paid to association of merchants that uses payment for advertising purposes, and costs to solicit merchants to become franchise outlets. Advertising expenses that will have benefits for more than one year must be capitalized unless benefit period of advertising campaign cannot be ascertained (.10).

.05 Reg. §§1.162-1.

.10 Rev. Rul. 69-331, 1969-1 CB 87.

Inventories

¶25,088 Overview. Inventories are an essential element in determining the cost of goods sold during the tax year. Inventories are required to be used in every case in which the production, purchase, or sale of merchandise is an income-producing factor (.05). The IRS may also require the use of inventories if needed to clearly reflect income.

Gross profit from business operations are computed by deducting the cost of goods sold from gross receipts. The cost of goods sold is determined either (1) by aggregating the cost of each specific item sold or (2) by adding the inventory at the beginning of the year to the cost of goods purchased or produced during the year and deducting the inventory at the end of the year. When a taxpayer withdraws merchandise or stock in trade from inventory for personal use, the cost of goods sold must be reduced by the cost of such goods. When method (2) is used, this is done by subtracting the cost of such goods from purchases.

By using the accrual method and inventories, gross income of an accounting period is more clearly reflected because the proceeds from the sale of goods is matched with their cost.

Inventory items

An inventory is an itemized list, with valuations, of goods held for sale or consumption in a manufacturing or merchandising business. The quantities shown on the list should be verified by physical inventories at reasonable intervals and should be adjusted to conform with this physical count.

Inventories should include all finished or partly finished goods. Also included in inventory are:

(1) raw materials and supplies, or materials that are to become a part of goods for sale;

(2) containers on hand, if title passes to the customer;

(3) items shipped on consignment, if not sold by the consignee;

(4) items sold for future delivery, if the taxpayer is still subject to risk of loss; and

(5) items in transit to customers, such as C.O.D. parcel post.

In addition, under the uniform capitalization rules, certain taxpayers are required to include direct costs and the allocable portion of indirect costs in the cost of inventory (see, "Uniform Capitalization Rules," below.)

Merchandise should be included in inventory only if the taxpayer is the legal owner (has title) of the goods (.10). A seller should include in the inventory goods under contract for sale but not yet segregated and applied to the contract, and goods out on consignment. The seller should not include goods sold when title has passed to the buyer.

A buyer should include in inventory merchandise purchased (including containers) where title has passed to the buyer, even where the merchandise is in transit or has not been reduced to physical possession, but should not include goods ordered for future delivery, transfer of title to which has not yet been effected.

Unless each item in inventory is specifically identified as to its cost, the taxpayer must choose to use either the first-in, first-out (FIFO) (¶25,092) or the last-in, first-out (LIFO) (¶25,093) identification method.

Inventory valuations

An inventory method must (1) conform as nearly as possible to the best accounting practice in the trade or business, and (2) clearly reflect income(.15).

For purposes of the first test, the term "best accounting practice" is somewhat synonymous with "generally accepted accounting principles." However, no method of accounting is acceptable unless, in the IRS's opinion, it clearly reflects income. The fact that a taxpayer's approach may conform to generally accepted accounting practices (designed mainly to provide useful data to management and shareholders) is no guarantee that it is acceptable for tax purposes. The primary goal of the income tax system is to ensure the collection of revenue in a manner that is equitable and that protects the public interest. Although in many instances a generally accepted practice may suffice for tax purposes, this does not create a presumption that such practice clearly reflects income and does not shift the burden to the IRS to show that such a method distorts income (.20).

There are two basic methods of valuing inventory. These methods are:

(1) cost, and

(2) lower of cost or market.

Retail merchants may use the retail method (¶25,091) to approximate the lower-of-cost-or-market method.

Opening and closing inventory must be valued by the same method. Where the inventory is valued by using the lower-of-cost-or-market method, the market value of *each* article on hand at the inventory date must be compared with the cost of the article, and the lower of such values must be taken as the inventory value of the article. A taxpayer is not permitted to inventory the *entire* stock at cost and also at market and use the lower of the two totals in order to arrive at the lowest possible profit.

A business is generally permitted to determine its year-end closing inventory by taking a reasonable deduction for shrinkage (e.g., inventory loss due to undetected theft, breakage and bookkeeping errors). A business is not required to actually take a year-end inventory in order to determine if any inventory shrinkage has occurred. However, the deduction for the estimated shrinkage may only be claimed if the business: (1) normally takes a physical count of its inventories at each business location on a regular and consistent basis; and (2) makes proper adjustments to its inventories and to its estimating methods to the extent its estimates are more or less than the actual shrinkage (.25). The IRS has issued a retail safe harbor method that may be used by retailers to estimate inventory shrinkage as well as guidance for any other taxpayers who want to change to a method of accounting for estimating inventory shrinkage (.30).

Uniform capitalization rules

Generally, taxpayers who *produce* real and tangible personal property or who *acquire* such property for resale are subject to uniform capitalization rules. The rules apply to all property produced by a taxpayer. However, in the case of personal property acquired by the taxpayer for resale, the rules apply only if the average of annual gross receipts of the taxpayer for the past three years exceeds $10 million (.35).

Basically, the uniform capitalization (UNICAP) rules require that costs attributable to inventory be added to the cost of producing or acquiring the inventory and that costs attributable to producing or acquiring other property be capitalized. The rules apply to the direct costs of producing or acquiring property and to an allocable portion of those indirect costs that benefit the assets being produced or acquired for resale. The obvious effect of these rules is that taxpayers are not able to claim current deductions for those costs that have to be included in inventory or capitalized.

For example, under these standards retailers and wholesalers are required to treat the following as inventory costs: (1) wages and salaries of employees responsible for purchasing the inventory, (2) repacking, assembly, and other costs incurred in processing the goods while in the taxpayer's possession, (3) storage, and (4) the portion of general and administrative costs that is allocable to these functions. Certain costs, such as selling, marketing, advertising and distribution, are not required to be included in inventory under the UNICAP rules. (.40)

.05 Code Sec. 471; Reg. §§1.471-1—1.471-4.

.10 Rev. Rul. 81-272, 1981-1 CB 116.

.15 Code Sec. 471.

.20 *Thor Power Tool Company*, SCt, 79-1 USTC ¶9139, 99 SCt 773.

.25 Code Sec. 471(b), as amended by P.L. 105-34.

.30 Rev. Proc. 98-29, I.R.B. 1998-15.

.35 Code Sec. 263A.

.40 Code Sec. 263A.

¶25,089 Inventories at Cost. When a retailer or wholesaler values inventories at cost, goods are included in inventory at the purchase price including freight-in, commissions to buyers, interest expense on long-term purchase contracts, and manufacturers' excise taxes, less cash and trade discounts and freight-out on purchase returns (.05). For example, car dealers must reduce the cost of new cars in inventory by the amount of the manufacturer's rebate even though such rebates are received in the year following the year of purchase (.10). According to the IRS, such rebates are trade discounts that are allowed irrespective of the time of payments.

A manufacturer, however, takes finished goods into inventory at the cost of their manufacture (cost of raw materials, direct labor and factory overhead). Further, the manufacturer must take both direct and indirect production costs into account in the computation of inventoriable costs in accordance with the "full absorption" method of inventory costing.

Production costs include costs that are incurred as a result of processes intended to add utility to a product or to transform an already manufactured material. Production costs are not necessarily manufacturing costs, but can include such processes as assembly and printing. Production processes do not have to be performed by the taxpayer so long as the taxpayer pays for the costs of the processes.

Inventory costs incurred are subject to the Uniform Capitalization Rules (.15). (see ¶25,088.)

.05 Reg. §1.471-3, Reg. § 1.471-11.
.10 Rev. Rul. 84-41, 1984-1 CB 130.
.15 Code Sec. 263A.

¶25,090 Inventories at Lower of Cost or Market. Under the lower-of-cost-or-market method of valuing inventories, market losses are realized by valuing inventory at the market price when it drops below cost (the loss is realized by the increased deduction for cost of goods sold which results because the ending inventory is smaller) (.05). Each item must be valued first at cost and then at market, and the smaller amount included in inventory. The lower of cost or market of the *total* inventory (rather than of specific items) may not be used.

Market value for a wholesaler or retailer is the replacement cost at the inventory date. For a manufacturer, market value is reproduction cost at the inventory date, taking into consideration the prices of raw materials and direct labor and the rates of factory overhead then effective.

Uniform capitalization rules apply to inventories valued at cost by a taxpayer using the lower-of-cost-or-market method (.10). (see ¶25,088 "Uniform Capitalization Rules")

Writedowns

Inventory writedowns must be based on closed transactions or identifiable events and on objective evidence (.15). For example, a manufacturer could not reduce its ending inventory because of purported sales of "excess" inventory at scrap value when, under the sales arrangement, the manufacturer continued to possess the benefits and burdens of ownership with respect to the "excess" inventory (.20) or when the seller had the exclusive right to repurchase parts purportedly "sold" (.25). Such transactions did not constitute a bona fide sale.

.05 Reg. §1.471-4.
.10 Code Sec. 263A.
.15 *Rockwell International Corp.*, CA-3, 82-2 USTC ¶9698, 694 F2d 60, aff'g TC, 77 TC 780, CCH Dec. 38,337.
.20 Rev. Rul. 83-59, 1983-1 CB 103.
.25 *Paccar, Inc.*, CA-9, 88-1 USTC ¶9380, 849 F2d 393, aff'g 85 TC 754, CCH Dec. 42,476.

¶25,091 Retail Method. Retail merchants may use the retail method to estimate cost or the lower of cost or market in pricing their inventories (.05). Under this method, the retailer inventories goods at the retail selling price by departments or classes of goods and then converts the inventory at retail to either cost or the lower of cost or market by reducing it by the mark-on percentage (percentage of expected gross margin to retail value). When converting to cost, the mark-on percentage is computed after adjusting the retail value of the goods available for sale for both net mark-ups and mark-downs; when converting to lower of cost or market, it is computed after adjusting such retail value for mark-ups only (excluding mark-ups made to cancel or correct mark-downs and reduced by mark-downs made to cancel or correct mark-ups).

> ***Example 1:*** The shoe department of a retail store has an ending inventory at retail value of $26,000. From the store's records pertaining to the department's beginning inventory, purchases, mark-ups and mark-downs, the department's inventory is converted to either cost or the lower of cost and market, as follows:

	Cost	*Mark-On*	*Retail Value*	*Mark-On %*
Beginning inventory	$14,000	$6,000	$20,000	
Purchases	48,000	30,000	78,000	
Total	$62,000	$36,000	$98,000	
Add: Net mark-ups		2,000	2,000	
After mark-ups		$38,000	$100,000	38%
Less: Net mark-downs		4,000	4,000	
After mark-ups and mark-downs		$34,000	$96,000	35%

> The ending inventory at either cost or the lower of cost or market is equal to—

	At Cost	*At Cost or Market*
Retail value	$ 26,000	$ 26,000
Less: Mark–on %:		
(35% X $26,000)	9,100	
(38% X $26,000)		9,880
	$ 16,900	$ 16,120

Net mark-ups are mark-ups (above the original retail price) less mark-up cancellations. Net mark-downs are mark-downs (below original retail price) less mark-down cancellations. Where the price is marked up and then marked down below the original retail price, the mark-down is partly a mark-up cancellation and partly a mark-down.

> ***Example 2:*** The selling price of an item is marked up from an original retail price of $10 to $12 and then marked down to $8. The mark-down from $12 to $8 was a $2 mark-up cancellation and a $2 mark-down.

Similarly, a mark-down cancellation that brings the selling price above the original retail price is partly a mark-down cancellation and partly a mark-up.

The retail method may be used only if the retailer keeps accurate accounts and records to provide the necessary information for computing the mark-on percentage. The records must show the original retail value, the cost, and the net mark-ups and mark-downs.

Planning Note

CCH Analysts note that under the retail method, the retail inventory value can be conveniently estimated at any time from the books without taking a physical count. Simply subtract sales from the retail value of the beginning inventory plus purchases after adjusting for mark-ups and mark-downs. Thus, sales for the department in Example (1), above, would have been approximately $70,000 ($96,000 (beginning inventory plus purchases after mark-ups and mark-downs) minus $26,000 (ending inventory)).

The cost of the inventory must be computed under the uniform capitalization rules (see ¶25,088).

.05 Reg. §1.471-8.

¶25,092 First-In, First-Out Identification. When each item in a wholesaler, retailer, or manufacturer's inventory is not specifically identified as to its cost, it is assumed that the first (or earliest) items purchased or produced are the first ones sold (FIFO method) -unless the taxpayer elects the last-in, first-out (LIFO) method (.05). (See, ¶25,093.) Then, the ending inventory will be composed of the latest goods purchased or produced.

> ***Example:*** A wholesaler has 20 radios of a particular type on hand at the end of the year. The wholesaler's records show no beginning inventory and purchases of the radios during the year as follows:

Date	*Units*	*Price*	*Total Price*
December 6	8	$ 20	$ 160
November 5	8	19	152
October 12	10	18	180

> If the wholesaler values the inventory at cost and identifies items in it by the first-in, first-out (FIFO) method, the ending inventory value for the 20 radios would be $372: $40 (2 radios at $20 each) + $152 (8 radios at $19) + $180 (10 radios at $18).

The cost of the inventory may be required to be computed under the uniform capitalization rules (see ¶25,088).

.05 Reg. §1.471-2.

¶25,093 Last-In, First-Out Identification. Rather than use the first-in, first-out (FIFO) method of identification, a retailer, wholesaler or manufacturer may elect to use the last-in, first-out (LIFO) method (.05). This method assumes that the last items purchased or produced are the first ones sold. Thus, the ending inventory is composed of the opening inventory plus the earliest purchases of the year.

> ***Example 1:*** A manufacturer's opening inventory includes 20 vases at a total cost of $240 ($12 each). The manufacturer produced 80 vases during the year. The first 20 vases produced during the year had a cost of $13 per vase, the last 60 had a cost of $15. There are 40 vases in the ending inventory. The ending inventory value of the 40 vases is $500 ($240 (opening inventory) + $260 (20 × $13)).

When using LIFO, there are two other ways of pricing the increase in inventory during the year (the increase in Example (1) was based on the cost of the earliest-produced items). The increase may be priced by using (1) the *average cost* or (2) the *latest cost* of goods purchased or produced. In no event may the market value be used.

> ***Example 2:*** If the *average cost* of producing vases for the year in Example (1) was $14.50, the LIFO value of the inventory (with the increase at average cost) would be $530 ($240 (opening inventory) + $290 (20 vases at $14.50)). If the last 20 vases produced during the year were at a cost of $15 each, the ending inventory is $540 ($240 + $300 (20 vases at $15 each)).

In a period of rising costs, the LIFO method reduces taxes. This is because the cost of sales, which is matched against income, is calculated at the later, higher prices (inventory being valued at the lower, earlier prices). Under FIFO, the cost of sales is calculated at the older, lower prices. Of course, in a period of falling costs the reverse is true—income and taxes are increased under LIFO.

> ***Example 3:*** Assume that the manufacturer in Examples (1) and (2), during the year, has vase sales of $2,500 and its cost of manufacturing the vases is $1160.

Assuming the last 40 vases were produced at a cost of $15 each, the manufacturer's gross profit under FIFO and LIFO is computed as follows:

	FIFO		*LIFO*	
Sales		$ 2,500		$ 2,500
Cost of Sales:				
Inventory, January 1	$ 240		$ 240	
Manufactured goods	$1160		$1160	
Total	$ 1,400		$ 1,400	
Inventory, December 31	600[1]	800	500[2]	900
Gross Profit		$ 1,700		$ 1,600

[1]40 vases at $15 each.
[2]See Example (1).

In order to use the LIFO inventory method, retailers, wholesalers, and manufacturers must file Form 970 (Application to Use LIFO Inventory Method) or a similar statement with their timely filed tax return for the year in which LIFO is first used (.10). Additionally, a taxpayer must use the LIFO method to determine profit or loss for credit purposes or for reports to shareholders, partners or proprietors if the method is used for tax purposes. Furthermore, the LIFO method cannot be used in conjunction with the lower-of-cost-or- market method (¶25,090) of valuing inventories.

A manufacturer may elect to use the LIFO method with respect to raw materials only (including those in finished goods and work in process) (.15).

The cost of the inventory may be required to be computed under the uniform capitalization rules.

Related corporations

Members of the same group of financially related corporations are treated as a single taxpayer for purposes of LIFO. The term "group of financially related corporations" means (1) any affiliated group after applying the 50-percent stock ownership test or (2) any other group of corporations that generally issues consolidated financial statements or reports to shareholders and others (.20).

.05 Code Sec. 472; Reg. §1.472-1, Reg. §1.472-2.

.10 Reg. §1.472-1(c).

.15 Reg. §1.472-1(c).

.20 Code Sec. 472(g).

¶25,094 Dollar-Value LIFO. The computation of the LIFO value of an inventory with a large number of items is complex because of the number of mechanical steps involved (.05). The increase in quantity for each item in the inventory must be determined by comparing quantities in the opening and closing inventories and the price of the increase or decrease for each item must be determined.

The dollar-value LIFO method is designed to overcome the problem of determining the quantity increase or decrease for each item. Under this method, the quantity increase or decrease is measured by comparing the *total* dollar value of the beginning and ending inventories. The assumption is that all items in the inventory are homogeneous or similar. But because prices change over the years, the quantity measurement must be in constant dollars or prices.

> ***Example 1:*** An item in inventory costs $1. Total dollar value of the beginning inventory consisting of six items is $6. At the end of the year, the item costs $1.50. The dollar value of the ending inventory is $12.00, and there are 8 items in it. The increase in dollar value indicates a quantity increase from 6 to 12, although the actual quantity increased only from 6 to 8 ($12 ÷ $1.50), an increase of 2. But if the

ending inventory is valued at beginning-of-the-year prices (8 × $1 = $8), the true quantity increase is shown.

Thus, the beginning and ending inventories are both valued at the prices in effect at the beginning of the first LIFO year (called "base year"). The conversion is made by use of price indexes (¶25,096).

Example 2: Assume that the year in Example (1) was the first LIFO year. The price index was 100% at the beginning and 150% at the end of the year (price went from $1 to $1.50). The year-end inventory is converted to beginning-of-the-year prices by dividing by the price index ($12 ÷ 150% = $8).

Once a quantity increase (excess of closing over opening inventory, both at base-year prices) is determined, it must be valued at the price at which it was produced or acquired. To do this, the quantity increase (in base-year dollars) is reconverted to current-year prices by means of a price index for either the earliest, average or latest prices in the year acquired.

Example 3: In Examples (1) and (2), assuming that the earliest acquisitions were made at the same price as items in the beginning inventory, the LIFO value of the ending inventory is $8, computing the increase at earliest prices ($6 (opening inventory) + $2 ($2 quantity increase × 100%)).

The cost of the inventory may be required to be computed under the uniform capitalization rules.

Indexes

The indexes that can be used for converting to base-year prices and back again are:

(1) retail price indexes prepared by the U.S. Bureau of Labor Statistics for certain retailers using Retail LIFO (see ¶25,097);

(2) indexes computed under the "double-extension" method (.10); and, where this method is impractical because of technological changes or the extensive variety or extreme fluctuation of items in the inventory, either

(3) an IRS approved custom index, computed by other sound and consistent statistical methods, presumably using industry and government data; or, if it can be shown that neither index (2) nor (3) is practical,

(4) indexes computed by the "link-chain" method, under which an annual index (1) is computed each year (ending inventory at year-end prices divided by its value at beginning-of-the-year prices) and (2) is made cumulative by multiplying the second year's annual index times the first year's, and, for every year thereafter, by multiplying the annual index times the preceding year's cumulative index.

(5) consumer or producer price indexes prepared by the U.S. Bureau of Labor Statistics (see ¶25,096). Such indexes may not be used, however, by taxpayers using the retail LIFO method who are eligible to use retail price indexes prepared by the U.S. Bureau of Labor Statistics (.15).

Dual indexes

Dual indexes may be used to compute the LIFO value of a dollar value pool, but only if the use clearly reflects the value of the LIFO inventory.

See ¶25,096 for further details regarding price indexes.

.05 Reg. §1.472-8.
.10 Reg. §1.472-8(e)(2).
.15 Reg. §1.472-8(e)(3).

¶25,095 Pooling Under Dollar-Value LIFO. The dollar-value LIFO method assumes that the items in the inventory are homogeneous (.05). See, ¶25,094. Generally, it is required that the inventory be grouped into homogeneous pools based upon the kinds of goods or products in the inventories. (But see, "Simplified dollar-value LIFO method for small businesses," in this paragraph.) Inventory pools that comprise less than five percent of total inventory value may be combined to form a single miscellaneous inventory pool. If such a pool comprises less than five percent of inventory value, that pool may only be combined with the largest inventory pool.

Natural units

For manufacturers and processors, inventory pools must consist of all inventory items in a natural business unit (NBU). Usually, a natural business unit consists of the entire productive activity of the manufacturer within one or more related product lines. Raw materials, goods-in-process and finished goods are all included in the inventory pool for each business unit. How many natural business units a manufacturer or processor may pool depends on (1) how the business is divided for internal management, (2) whether there are separate and distinct production facilities, and (3) whether separate profit and loss records are kept (.10).

Multiple pools in a natural unit

A manufacturer may elect to break down the pool for a natural business unit into a number of smaller pools. Under this election, raw materials that are substantially similar have to be pooled together, and goods-in-process and finished goods would have to be placed into pools classified by major types or classes of goods. Or dollar-value LIFO may be applied to only the raw materials (including those in goods-in-process and finished goods). If they are so applied, those raw materials that are substantially similar have to be pooled together.

Guides

Wholesalers, retailers, jobbers and distributors must pool their goods by major lines, types or classes. The customary business classifications of the taxpayer's trade or industry are considered important pooling guides. An example of a customary business classification is the department in the department store. In such cases, practices are relatively uniform throughout the trade, and departmental grouping is adapted to the customs and needs of the business. Wholesalers, retailers, distributors, and jobbers may elect, where appropriate, to pool by natural business units, as is prescribed for manufacturers.

A manufacturer who is also a wholesaler or retailer, etc., must pool manufacturing inventories according to the rules for manufacturers, and wholesale or retail inventories must be pooled separately, even if an election is made to pool them under manufacturers' rules. For example, a domestic manufacturer of leather goods was required to keep two separate inventory pools for valuation purposes—one pool for finished goods it manufactured and one pool for goods it purchased for resale from its subsidiary (.15). On the other hand, a newly formed manufacturing corporation that acquired its predecessor's raw materials, work in process and finished inventory did not become a retailer with respect to the inventory of finished goods. Thus, the acquired finished goods inventory was correctly included in a single LIFO pool with the firm's subsequently produced inventory (.20).

Careful records must be kept separately for each inventory pool. The base-year inventory, the base-year and current-year cost of each succeeding inventory, each quantity increase and the index percentage by which it is converted to current-year prices, quantity decreases, and the methods of computing indexes must all be accounted for.

The rules for electing the dollar-value LIFO method, for changing to it from another LIFO method, or for changing the method of pooling are detailed in the regulations.

Simplified dollar-value LIFO method for small businesses

Businesses with average annual gross receipts of $5 million or less for the three preceding years may elect to use a simplified dollar-value LIFO method to account for their inventories (.25). Some taxpayers who have elected to use the single-pool method (for tax years prior to 1987) may continue to do so as long as they are eligible.

.05 Reg. §1.472-8; T.D. 8976, I.R.B. 2002-5.
.10 Reg. §§1.472-8.
.15 *Amity Leather Products Co.*, 82 TC 726, CCH Dec. 41,221.
.20 *UFE, Inc.*, 92 TC 1314, CCH Dec. 45,793.
.25 Code Sec. 474(b).

¶25,096 Use of Price Indexes to Compute Dollar-Value LIFO Inventories. Taxpayers may use an inventory price index based on selected consumer or producer price indexes prepared by the U.S. Bureau of Labor Statistics (BLS) (.05). Indexes must be selected from the Consumers Price Index Detailed Report (CPI) or Producer Prices and Price Indexes (PPI).

Eligible small businesses (see ¶25,095), defined as those whose average annual gross receipts do not exceed $5 million for the three-tax-year period ending with the tax year in which they elect to use published price indexes to adjust the value of their inventory, are entitled to use an inventory price index of 100 percent of the percent change in the applicable price indexes. For tax years ending on or after December 31, 2001, all taxpayers electing to use the IPI method may use 100 percent of the percent change in the applicable price indexes.

> ***Example 1:*** Assume that a taxpayer began a retail business with newly acquired inventory on December 31, 2002. Also assume that the applicable index increased 10 percent per year for the period December 2002 to December 2004. Further assume that the original index was at 100 in December 2002.

Original Value	100
Year 1 increase (10% of 100)	10
Value at beginning of year 2	110
Year 2 increase (10% of 110)	11
Value at end of year 2	121
Cumulative increase (121 ÷ 100 = 1.21 or a 21 percent increase)	.21
Cumulative increase times 80% limitation if applicable (.21 X .8)	.168

The inventory price index computation method may not be used by a taxpayer eligible to use inventory price indexes prepared by the BLS for a specific industry. Therefore, a taxpayer eligible to use the Department Store Inventory Price Indexes prepared by the BLS in connection with the retail LIFO method may not use the inventory price index method of computing its inventory (.10).

Selection of index

The taxpayer must follow a two-step process for determining the appropriate consumer or producer price index. First, the inventory items in each pool should be classified according to the detailed listings in the appropriate tables of the CPI or PPI. Second, an appropriate consumer or producer price index must be determined for each index category to which inventory items have been assigned.

Index categories are assigned by process of elimination according to the following steps:

(1) Whenever a specific item in the taxpayer's inventory comprises 10 percent or more of the total inventory value, such an item must be placed in its own inventory category. The index category must be the most detailed index category that includes the inventory item.

(2) If there are inventory items remaining in the pool that have not been included in an index category, the taxpayer must select the most detailed index category that in the aggregate comprises 10 percent or more of the total inventory value.

(3) If there are inventory items still remaining in the pool that comprise less than 10 percent of the total inventory value, the index category to be selected for these items must be the most detailed index category that includes such items. In no event may an index category be selected, however, that is less detailed than either the 11 general categories of the CPI or the 15 general categories of the PPI.

In the first year the index method is used, small businesses must report the inventory pools used, the types of goods included in each pool and the consumer or producer price indexes selected for each pool. The taxpayer therefore must maintain adequate books and records to substantiate the selection of pools and indexes and the computation of changes in inventory price indexes.

Manufacturers, processors, wholesalers, jobbers and distributors may select indexes only from the PPI. Retailers may select indexes from either the CPI or the PPI. If indexes could be selected from either publication, a retailer using the retail inventory method must select the index from the CPI Detailed Report and a retailer not using the retail method must select the index from the PPI. If a retailer using the retail inventory method selects a price index from the PPI, the index must be converted into a retail price index.

In the case of taxpayers using the CPI Detailed Report, indexes may be selected only from Table 3 (Consumer Price Index for All Urban Consumers: Food Expenditure Categories, U.S. City Average) of the report. In the case of the PPI, indexes may be selected only from Table 6 (Producer Prices and Price Indexes for Commodity Groupings and Individual Items), unless the taxpayer can demonstrate that the selection of an index from another PPI table would be more appropriate.

A taxpayer using the retail inventory method must select the index of the last month of its tax year. Taxpayers who do not use the retail method must use indexes as of the month or months most appropriate to the taxpayer's method of determining the current year cost of items making up their inventory pools. Otherwise, taxpayers must make a one-time binding election of an appropriate month for determining the current year cost of inventory. The election should be made on Form 970 (Application to Adopt LIFO Method of Inventory Valuation).

Inventory pools

A retailer, wholesaler, jobber, or distributor computing an inventory price index may establish an inventory pool for any group of goods included within one of 11 general categories of consumer goods described in the CPI Detailed Report. Inventory pools that comprise less than five percent of inventory value may be combined into a single miscellaneous inventory pool. If the resulting pool itself comprises less than five percent of inventory value, it may be combined only with the largest inventory pool. A small business that elects to use published price indexes to adjust the value of its inventory may use a single LIFO pool (see ¶25,095).

Computation of dollar-value LIFO inventories

The amount of dollar-value LIFO inventories may be computed by first dividing the dollar amount of the taxpayer's ending inventory by the end-of-the-year price index for the goods comprising the inventory pool. The beginning inventory at the base-year price is then subtracted. This figure is the previous year's inventory at the base year's price and is computed by dividing the previous year's ending inventory by the price index at the time the inventory is taken. The difference between the beginning inventory and the ending inventory at the base year's prices is converted to the current year's prices by multiplying it by the end-of-the-year price index. This product is then added to or subtracted from the LIFO value of the beginning inventory to yield the LIFO value of the ending inventory.

Example 2: The taxpayer is an eligible small business and, therefore, uses 100 percent of the percent change in the applicable CPI.

Year 1 The taxpayer elects to use the dollar value method of inventory valuation and further elects to use the consumer price index to adjust the value of its inventory. Year 1 opening inventory is $25,000, and the ending inventory is $36,000. The price index for the goods making up the inventory pool is 100 at the beginning of the year and 104.4 at the end of the year.

Ending inventory at base year price ($36,000 ÷ 1.044)	$ 34,483
Beginning inventory at base year price ($25,000 X 1.00)	25,000
Dollar value quantity increase	$ 9,483
Increase converted to current prices ($9,483 X 1.044)	$ 9,900
LIFO value of beginning inventory	25,000
LIFO value of ending inventory	$ 34,900

Year 2 The price index has risen from 104.4 to 107.2 and the dollar value of the ending inventory is $43,000.

Ending inventory at base year price ($43,000 ÷ 1.072)	$ 40,112
Beginning inventory at base year price (Year 1 ending inventory, $36,000 ÷ 1.044)	34,483
Dollar value quantity increase	$ 5,629
Increase converted to current year's price ($5,629 X 1.072)	$ 6,034
LIFO value of beginning inventory (Last year's LIFO value of ending inventory)	34,900
LIFO value of ending inventory	$ 40,934

Year 3 The price index has risen to 110, but the dollar value of the ending inventory is $34,000. There has been a net liquidation of inventory.

Ending inventory at base year price ($34,000 ÷ 1.10)	$ 30,909
Beginning inventory at base year price (year 2 ending inventory, ($43,000 ÷ 1.072)	40,112
Decrease	($ 9,203)
Decrease converted to current year's prices ($9,203 X 1.10)	($ 10,123)
LIFO value of beginning inventory (LIFO value of last year's ending inventory)	$ 40,934
LIFO value of ending inventory ($40,934 - $10,123)	$ 30,811

Year 4 The price index has fallen from 110 to 107.5, but ending inventory has increased to $45,000.

Ending inventory at base year price ($45,000 ÷ 1.075)	$ 41,860
Beginning inventory at base year price (Year 3 ending inventory, $34,000 ÷ 1.10)	30,909
Dollar value quantity increase	$ 10,951
Increase converted to current year's price ($10,951 X 1.075)	$ 11,772
LIFO value of beginning inventory (last year's LIFO value of ending inventory)	30,811
LIFO value of ending inventory ($11,772 + $30,811)	$ 42,583

As this example illustrates, in a period of generally rising costs, the dollar value LIFO amount of the ending inventory is lower than the dollar value amount. Because ending inventory is lower, the cost of goods sold is greater and net income is less, and this method of inventory valuation has the effect of reducing taxes.

.05 Reg. §1.472-8(e)(3); T.D. 8976, I.R.B. 2002-5.

.10 Rev. Proc. 86-46, 1986-2 CB 739.

¶25,097 Retail LIFO. The retail method of last-in, first-out (LIFO) is a combination of the retail inventory method (see ¶25,091) and dollar-value LIFO (see ¶25,094) (.05). At the beginning of the first LIFO year (base year), the retail inventory is converted to cost (not lower of cost or market) by the retail method described at ¶25,091. The next retail inventory and succeeding ones are converted to base-year retail prices by means of price indexes. Each increase of the closing over the opening inventory at base-year retail prices (retail dollar-value quantity increase) has to be converted to the current-year retail prices by using the indexes and thereafter adjusted to its cost by reducing it by the mark-on percentage for purchases of the current year.

The mark-on percentage for the year's purchases must be figured after adjusting for both markups and markdowns in order to approximate cost.

> ***Example:*** At the beginning of the first LIFO year, the notions department of a retail store has an inventory at retail of $10,000. The mark-on percentage is 30%. The LIFO value of the opening inventory is thus $7,000 ($10,000 – $3,000 (30% × $10,000)). The ending inventory at retail for that year is $13,200; the price index at the end of the year is 110% (assuming it was 100% at the beginning); and the mark-on percentage for purchases during the year was 32%. The LIFO value of the ending inventory is computed as follows:

Ending inventory at base-year retail ($13,200 ÷ 110%)	$ 12,000
Beginning inventory at base-year retail	10,000
Retail dollar-value quantity increase	$ 2,000
Increase converted to current (latest) prices ($2,000 X 110%)	$ 2,200
Less purchases' mark-on percentage ($2,200 X 32%)	704
LIFO value of 1st year's increase	$ 1,496
LIFO value of beginning inventory	7,000
LIFO value of ending inventory	$ 8,496

All department stores and retail "specialty" stores may use the monthly price indexes published by the U. S. Bureau of Labor Statistics for converting from current-year to base-year prices and back again (.15). Also, a retail store may use such indexes for one or more of its departments if it can show that the inventories in them are reasonably representative of the goods in the same departments of a department store (.20). Because the IRS has discovered misuse of the price indexes prepared by the U. S. Bureau of Labor Statistics (BLS), these indexes will not be accepted in connection with the use of the LIFO method unless the taxpayer can demonstrate the accuracy, reliability and suitability of the use of such indexes to the satisfaction of the IRS (.25). (Department stores are excepted from this prohibition.)

If a retail department store does not use BLS indexes for retail stores, it may be able to use consumer or producer price indexes in conjunction with the dollar-value LIFO method (see ¶25,096). It may also use its own indexes computed on sound statistical principles if such indexes are acceptable to the IRS.

.05 Reg. §1.472-8.

.15 Rev. Proc. 86-46, 1986-2 CB 739.

.20 Rev. Rul. 23, 1953-1 CB 34.

.25 Rev. Rul. 75-181, 1975-1 CB 150; T.I.R. 1342, January 27, 1975; IRS Letter Ruling 8503003, 9-28-84, CCH IRS Letter Rulings Reports.

¶25,098 Donations of Inventory to Charity. A C corporation may deduct the basis of and one-half of the appreciation on inventory or stock in trade contributed to a public charity or a private operating foundation (.05). However, the total amount of the deduction is limited to twice the property's basis. Regardless of the amount of the deduction allowed, the reduction of cost of goods sold for such contributed property must be made for the lesser of the property's basis or its fair market value (.10).

The deduction does not apply to property that does not satisfy the relevant requirements of the Federal Food, Drug, and Cosmetic Act, or to unrealized appreciation that would have been ordinary income (if the property had been sold) because of the recapture rules (see ¶25,103.

A charitable deduction may also be claimed for certain manufactured property that will be used for research purposes by colleges, universities and certain exempt scientific organizations (.15).

A C corporation may deduct charitable contributions of computer technology and equipment to qualifying educational institutions through the end of 2005. Beginning in 2001, public libraries are included as qualified recipients. The amount of the deduction is equal to the donor's basis in the donated property plus one-half of the amount of ordinary income that would have been realized if the property had been sold (.20).

.05 Code Sec. 170(e)(3), (4); Reg. §1.170A-4A(c).

.10 Reg. §1.170A-4A(c)(3).

.15 Code Sec. 170(e)(4).

.20 Code Sec. 170(e)(6), as amended by the Working Families Tax Relief Act of 2004 (P.L. 108-311).

Depreciation and Cost Recovery

¶25,100 Depreciable Property. A percentage of the cost or other basis of depreciable property is deductible from income over a number of tax years (.05). In order for a wholesaler, retailer, or manufacturer to claim depreciation, such taxpayer must have an ownership interest in the property. Additionally, the depreciable property must be used in a trade or business or held for the production of income.

Generally, depreciable assets of manufacturers, wholesalers, and retailers include:

(1) Buildings and permanent improvements

(2) Building equipment (such as furnaces, air conditioning, etc.)

(3) Plant machinery and equipment

(4) Office equipment

(5) Furniture and fixtures

(6) Transportation equipment

(7) Returnable containers (see ¶25,081)

(8) Cost of railroad siding or spur (if owned by taxpayer)

(9) Private roadways, tunnels, parking lots used for business

Uniform capitalization rules

Uniform capitalization rules may be applicable in determining what costs and expenditures must be capitalized by a taxpayer.

Items temporarily not in use

Depreciation may be claimed for tangible assets even though they are temporarily not in use, such as in an idle plant situation (.10). Although they are not actually being used, they are still considered as being used in the business. If depreciation is not taken in the year in which it is supposed to be claimed it will be lost, because the taxpayer's basis in the property will be reduced by the amount of the allowable deduction.

Intangible assets

Traditionally, in order to be depreciable, an intangible asset must have an ascertainable limited useful life. However, certain intangible property (e.g., goodwill) acquired after August 10, 1993, may be amortized over 15 years (.15). An election may be made to use the amortization period for intangible assets acquired after July 25, 1991.

Luxury cars, "listed" property not predominantly used in business

The depreciation deduction for cars that are used for business reasons is subject to strict limits. For cars (other than electric cars) first placed in service in 2004, the maximum allowable depreciation deduction for the first year is limited to $2,960 ($10,610 if 50% bonus depreciation is claimed). The maximum allowable deduction for the second year is $4,800; for the third year, $2,850; and for each succeeding year in the recovery period, $1,675. For electric cars first placed in service in 2004, the maximum allowable depreciation deduction for the first year is limited to $8,880 ($31,830 if 50 percent bonus depreciation is claimed.) The maximum allowable deduction for the second year is $14,300; for the third year, $8,550; and for each succeeding year in the recovery period, $5,125 (.20).

The cost of "listed" property that is not predominantly used in business (business use percentage must exceed 50 percent for predominant use) is recovered under the straight-line method over the alternative MACRS recovery period. Listed property includes passenger cars, computers, and other types of property (.25).

.05 Code Sec. 167 and Code Sec. 168.

.10 *B.R. Kittredge*, CA-2, 37-1 USTC ¶9165, 88 F2d 632.

.15 Code Sec. 197.

.20 Rev. Proc. 2004-20, I.R.B. 2004-13, 642.

.25 Code Sec. 280F.

¶25,101 Available Methods. Retailers, manufacturers, and wholesalers are entitled to a depreciation deduction for property used in a trade or business (.05). The method used in computing depreciation depends on when the property is placed in service. Once the method to be used is determined, it must be used for the prescribed life of the asset.

Assets placed in service after 1986

Generally, for property placed in service after December 31, 1986, depreciation on tangible assets must be computed under the Modified Accelerated Cost Recovery System (MACRS). With respect to certain types of property placed in service after 1986, however, the alternative MACRS method must be used.

Under MACRS, each item of property is assigned to one of eight classes of property. The class of the recovery property determines its recovery period, the applicable depreciation method, and the appropriate averaging convention.

See ¶9100 and following for a discussion of the MACRS rules.

Assets placed in service after 1980 and before 1987

For most tangible assets placed in service after 1980 and before 1987, depreciation must be computed under the Accelerated Cost Recovery System (ACRS).

The ACRS allowance is determined by applying the statutory percentage for the respective class of property to the unadjusted basis of the recovery property. Salvage value is disregarded in computing ACRS deductions.

See ¶9200-¶9250 for a discussion of the ACRS rules.

Assets placed in service before 1981

The methods for figuring depreciation with respect to property that was placed in service before 1981 or is otherwise ineligible for recovery under ACRS include the straight-line method and the sum of the years-digits method.

Section 179 expense

An expense deduction is available for taxpayers who elect to treat the cost of qualifying property as an expense, rather than as a capital expenditure (.10).

For 2004, the expense deduction may not exceed $102,000. The maximum deduction will increase to $105,000 in 2005. It will be further adjusted for inflation for 2006 and 2007. Barring legislative action, it is scheduled to be reduced to $25,000 in 2008. In addition, when the cost of qualified property placed into service during the year exceeds $410,000 in 2004, $420,000 in 2005 or such other inflation adjusted amount for 2006 and 2007 (this dollar threshhold is scheduled to drop down to $200,000 in 2008) the maximum dollar amount is reduced by the amount of the excess. For example, if more than $5120,000 of qualified property is place in service in 2004, no expense deduction is allowed ($102,000 maximum 2004 deduction - ($512,000-410,000 2004 phase-out threshhold))

Planning Note

CCH Analysts note that certain qualified businesses that are operated within specified "enterprise zones" may be entitled to an increased Code Sec. 179expense allowance. For such qualified businesses, the deduction cap is $135,000 in 2004 (.15). While some types of businesses may not claim the increased Code Sec. 179 expense deduction even if they operate within an enterprise zone, most retailers, manufactures and wholesalers should qualify.

.05 Code Sec. 167 and Code Sec. 168.

.10 Code Sec. 179.

.15 Code Sec. 1397A.

¶25,102 Options Under MACRS and ACRS. Both the Accelerated Cost Recovery System (ACRS) and the Modified Accelerated Cost Recovery System (MACRS) are designed to simplify the recovery of capital costs incurred with respect to depreciable property (.05). Under these systems, the useful life of an asset is irrelevant; rather, the depreciation deduction is tied to a cost recovery period for the particular class of depreciable property.

Under either system, the taxpayer may elect to apply special straight-line methods to determine depreciation, rather than the regular accelerated methods provided by the respective systems. Although the depreciation deductions provided under the special straight-line methods will be smaller than those provided under the respective systems, some taxpayers prefer to use the straight-line methods due to the favorable alternative minimum tax treatment that arises from electing to use the straight-line methods.

MACRS straight-line methods

In lieu of applying the MACRS method, taxpayers may elect to apply the alternative MACRS method that is mandatory for certain property or the straight-line MACRS method with respect to any class of property in calculating depreciation. Although similar to the alternative MACRS system, the straight-line MACRS system is applied over the regular MACRS recovery periods. Therefore, the straight-line MACRS method is applied over shorter recovery periods and will produce a larger depreciation deduction than that produced under the alternative MACRS method.

Planning Note

A special first year depreciation allowance may be claimed for certain on new MACRS property for which the recovery period is 20 years or less. Generally, Code Sec. 168(k)(1) allows a 30-percent additional first-year depreciation deduction for qualified property acquired after September 10, 2001, and placed in service before January 1, 2005. Code Sec. 168(k)(4) allows a 50-percent additional first-year depreciation deduction for "50-percent bonus depreciation property" acquired after May 5, 2003, and, generally, placed in service before January 1, 2005.

Additionally, Code Sec. 1400L(b) allows a 30-percent additional first-year depreciation deduction for qualified New York Liberty Zone property acquired after September 10, 2001, and placed in service before January 1, 2007 (January 1, 2010, in the case of qualifying nonresidential real property and residential rental property) (.10).

See ¶9131 for a discussion of the MACRS Bonus Depreciation Allowance.

ACRS straight-line method

Instead of the regular ACRS deduction, wholesalers, retailers, and manufacturers could have elected to claim straight-line ACRS deductions over the regular recovery period or over optional, longer recovery periods. However, the rules varied depending on whether the property was personal property, real property, or property used predominantly outside the United States.

.05 Code Sec. 168. **.10** 1400L(b).

¶25,103 Recapture of Cost Recovery. Gain or loss is generally recognized on the disposition (including retirement) of depreciable assets, whether real or personal (.05). Generally, any gain realized on the disposition of personal recovery property (Code Sec. 1245 property) is treated as ordinary income to the extent of prior depreciation deductions.

Gain on the sale or other disposition of real recovery property (Code Sec. 1250 property) is treated as ordinary income to the extent of excess cost recovery claimed over straight-line depreciation. Any remaining gain is treated as long-term capital gain.

.05 Code Sec. 1245 and Code Sec. 1250.

General Business Tax Credit

¶25,105 General Business Credit. Manufacturers, retailers, and wholesalers, like others in business, are eligible for the general business credit (.05). For purposes of the general business credit, certain tax credits (e.g., the research and development credit, the work opportunity tax credit, and the alcohol fuels credit) are combined to provide a uniform limitation on the credit that may be claimed.

In determining the general business credit, each of the integral credits is computed separately. Then, the total of these credits becomes the general business credit for purposes of applying the maximum tax liability rules and the carryback and carryforward rules.

Planning Note

CCH Analysts note that eligible businesses that operate within an "empowerment zone" may be entitled to a 20 percent credit for the first $15,000 of qualified wages paid to full-or part-time employees who live within the designated zone and who perform substantially all of their work within that zone (.10). The maximum credit per employee is $3,000 per year. This credit must be included as part of the taxpayer's general business tax credit.

.05 Code Sec. 38.

.10 Code Sec. 1396.

Other Important Taxes

¶25,106 Accumulated Earnings. In addition to regular income taxes, a corporation may be liable for a tax on its accumulated earnings (.05). The tax applies if the corporation is used or formed for the purpose of tax avoidance by means of the expedient of permitting earnings and profits to accumulate instead of being divided or distributed. Generally, it is imposed on closely held corporations, although public corporations may also be liable. In order to justify an accumulation of income, a corporation must show a reasonable business need for such accumulation and a definite plan for its use. Otherwise, the accumulations may be taxed.

For tax years commencing after December 31, 2002, and before January 1, 2009, accumulated taxable income is taxed at the rate of 15 percent (.10).

Corporations may also be liable for an alternative minimum tax. The alternative minimum tax (AMT) is imposed to the extent that a corporation's tentative minimum tax exceeds its regular tax liability.

Wholesalers and retailers also may be subject to a multitude of excise taxes.

.05 Code Sec. 55 and Code Sec. 531- Code Sec. 537.

.10 Code Sec. 531.

DEVELOPERS-CONTRACTORS

Introduction

¶25,108 The special income tax provisions relating to the real estate development and construction industry, along with the tax application and effects of these rules, are discussed in the following paragraphs.

One of the major tax issues for businesses in the construction/development industries is when to include income from a project in taxable income. The problem is that many construction/development projects are not completed in the year in which a contract to undertake a project has been agreed to. In fact, several years may pass before the contract is fulfilled, giving rise to questions whether income from a project should be reported in the year in which a contract is agreed to, in the year in which it is fulfilled, or year-by-year over the course of contract.

Other tax issues that tend to have greater importance in the construction/development industries than in other businesses are the passive activity loss rules and the at-risk rules.

Under the at-risk rules, which must be applied before the passive loss rules, a taxpayer cannot claim business deductions, such as deductions that grow out of a taxpayer's real estate ventures, that exceed the amount the taxpayer has "at risk" in the business (¶25,132). A person is at risk for an activity if he has contributed money or property to the business or if he is personally liable on indebtedness used to finance the business. These rules are designed to discourage investors from using nonrecourse loans (loans for which they are not personally liable) to invest in a business that produces losses that are greater than the amount they have invested. However, real estate investors are treated as being at risk for certain types of nonrecourse financing (¶25,132). As with the passive loss rules, the at-risk rules are a means of preventing the sheltering of taxable income from an at-risk source with losses from activities in which little investment is at risk.

Under the passive activity loss rules, investors who do not materially participate in a business in which they have invested may claim tax deductions (passive losses) arising out of their investments in an amount that is no larger than the income (passive income) they have earned from these or similar passive activity investments. This means that passive losses may not offset nonpassive income from other sources such as salaries, professional fees, and portfolio income (such as interest and dividend income) (¶25,133). Furthermore, tax credits generated by passive investments may offset only tax liability for passive income. These rules are designed to prevent investors from making passive investments solely to take advantage of inflated loss deductions as a means of offsetting their nonpassive income.

Also covered are business expense deductions and depreciation deductions as they apply to the real estate industry.

Accounting Methods and Problems

¶25,110 Choice of Accounting Methods. A developer or contractor generally may use any method of accounting that clearly reflects income, including the cash or accrual method (.05). However, where maintenance of inventories is necessary, developers and contractors are required to use the accrual method to account for their purchases, sales and other items that affect income (.10). Furthermore, the accrual method of accounting must be used by:

(1) C corporations,

(2) partnerships that have one or more C corporations as partners, and

(3) tax shelters

(.15)

Long-term contract methods

Since many contracts for construction projects run for long periods of time and have special accounting needs, alternative accounting methods have been provided for long-term contracts. A long-term contract is a building, installation, or construction contract that is not completed within the tax year in which it is entered into (.20). The special rules that apply to the manufacture of personal property do not apply to contracts for the building, installation, construction of real property or improvements to real property. Thus, contracts for construction of, or improvements to, real property that are not completed in the tax year in which they are entered into are treated as long-term contracts even where the property is not unique and does not normally require more than 12 months to complete.

Long-term contracts generally must be accounted for under the percentage-of-completion method (.25). However, three types of long-term real estate construction contracts—small real estate construction contracts, home construction contracts and residential construction contracts—are subject to special accounting rules. See ¶25,115.

If a contractor incurs additional expenses because of owner-related causes (changes in plans, "extras" and the like) income must include "claim revenue" if under the circumstances it would be reasonable to conclude that the contractor will be paid for the additional work (.30).

.05 Code Sec. 451; Reg. §1.451-3; Rev. Rul. 78-180, 1978-1 CB 136.

.10 Code Sec. 471 and Code Sec. 472.

.15 Code Sec. 451; Code Sec. 461(i)(3), and Code Sec. 6662(d)(2)(C)(ii).

.20 Code Sec. 460(f).

.25 Code Sec. 460(a).

.30 IRS Industry Specialization Program (ISP) Claim Revenue Under a Long-Term Contract, October 19, 1996.

¶25,111 Percentage-of-Completion Method. Under the percentage-of-completion method of accounting for long-term contracts, the contractor reports part of the contract profit as income for the year based on costs incurred under the contract in each particular tax year. Thus, the contractor can spread the income and the taxes over the term of the contract (.05).

Using this method, the portion of the gross contract price that corresponds to the percentage of the entire contract completed during the tax year is included in gross income for that tax year. This percentage-of-completion ratio is based on a comparison of the total costs incurred during each tax year with the total estimated costs for the contract. For small real estate construction contracts, the percentage-of-completion ratio is based either on a comparison of the work performed during the tax year with estimated total work to be performed under the contract or on a comparison of contract costs.

The contract costs taken into account in determining the percentage of completion include those costs that are required to be allocated to the contract and capitalized). Costs incurred with respect to the long-term contract that are not capitalized are deductible in the year incurred, subject to general accounting principles.

Example: Midwest Construction, Inc. entered into a contract on March 7, 2003 to build an office building for a total contract price of $7,500,000. Construction began on September 28, 2003 and the building will be completed in April 2005. The company is a calendar-year taxpayer and accounts for its long-term contracts under the percentage-of-completion method.

The total estimated contract costs are $6,000,000. The total cumulative costs incurred before the close of 2003 and 2004 are $1,200,000 and $4,500,000, respectively. Midwest would compute its gross income for 2003 and 2004 under the percentage-of-completion method as follows:

	2003	*2004*
Total cumulative costs incurred before end of year	$ 1,200,000	$ 4,500,000
Total estimated costs	6,000,000	6,000,000
Percentage-of-completion (Total cumulative costs ÷ Total estimated costs)	20%	75%
Contract price	7,500,000	7,500,000
Cumulative income (Percentage-of-completion X Contract price)	$ 1,500,000	$ 5,625,000
Income recognized in prior years	0	1,500,000
Gross income for each year	$ 1,500,000	$ 4,125,000

Modified percentage-of-completion method

Taxpayers using the percentage-of-completion method to account for long-term contracts may elect to defer recognition of income and cost accounting until the first tax year in which a 10-percent threshold of estimated costs is reached (.10). Once made, an election to use the 10-percent method applies to all of the taxpayer's long-term contracts that are entered into during the tax year in which the election is made or during any subsequent years (.15). This election is not available to taxpayers who use a simplified method of allocating costs (.20).

Abuse of percentage-of-completion method

According to the IRS, many contractors attempt to use the percentage-of-completion method to improperly delay recognition of income (.25). The Code requires that income from the contract be reported over the life of the contract and requires that contract expenses be deducted in the year they are incurred. Under the percentage-of-completion method, contract income is computed by multiplying the contract price by the ratio of first-year contract costs to estimated total contract costs. Because the recognition of income under the percentage-of-completion method is based on the amount of costs incurred to date, deferring costs also delay the recognition of income. Given this potential benefit, according to the IRS, many contractors have been attempting to postpone the time that certain costs are deemed to have been incurred under the economic performance rules.

The contractors' position is that the cost of paying their subcontractors should not be deemed incurred until actual payment. They argue that the subcontracts represent contracts for the provision of property and that the property should not be deemed provided until the property is finally accepted by the land owner. It is industry practice that the landowner does not accept the subcontractor's work until the time when the subcontractor's work is substantially complete.

To this, the IRS replies that a subcontractor furnishes services as well as materials. Therefore, economic performance is not governed solely by acceptance. Economic performance with respect to construction services occurs as the construction services are rendered.

Next, with respect to liabilities for property (the raw materials) acceptance by the owner may be irrelevant. The subcontractor really is working for the contractor, and, if this is the case, acceptance by the contract would trigger economic performance with respect to this portion of the liability.

This acceptance of property generally is governed by contract. It may occur, for example, as the raw materials are (1) delivered to the job, (2) billed, and (3) the bill is accepted as correct by the contractor. There may be a reasonable time for inspection provided in the contract. Further, acceptance usually occurs in stages, as periodic subcontractor bills are accepted by the contractor. It is not dependent on the subcontractor's substantial completion of the project, which could take years. Treasury regulations state that, with respect to long-term contracts expenses, economic performance occurs as the services or property is provided or, if earlier, as the taxpayer makes payment.

"Look-back" rule

In the tax year in which the contract is completed, a determination will be made as to whether the taxes paid with respect to the contract in each year of the contract were more or less than the amount that would have been paid if the actual gross contract price and the actual total contract costs (rather than the anticipated contract price and costs) had been used to compute gross income. Under this "look-back" procedure, interest must be paid by the contractor if there is an underpayment with respect to a tax year (.30). Similarly, interest will be paid to the contractor if there is an overpayment. The amount of interest due or to be refunded is reported on Form 8697, "Interest Computation Under the Look-Back Method for Completed Long-Term Contracts." For purposes of the look-back rule, the contract price reflects all amounts received under the contract, including amounts received after the contract completion date as a result of disputes, litigation, or settlements relating to the contract (.35).

.05 Code Sec. 451, Code Sec. 460; Reg. §1.451-3(c).

.10 Code Sec. 460(b)(5).

.15 Code Sec. 460(b)(5)(C).

.20 Code Sec. 460(b)(5)(D)(i).

.25 IRS Industry Specialization Program (ISP) Percentage-of-Completion Method—Timing of Cost Recognition, March 21, 1997.

.30 Code Sec. 460(b)(2); Reg. §1.460-6.

.35 Code Sec. 460.

¶25,112 Completed-Contract Method. Most long-term contracts must be accounted for under the percentage-of-completion method of accounting. The completed-contract method under which income and deductions from the contract were not reported until the work under the contract was completed, may be used only for "small" construction contracts and in very limited circumstances (see ¶25,115). Although the percentage of completion method generally requires taxpayers to recognize income and costs from a long-term contract as the contract is being completed, taxpayers may elect to postpone such recognition until the first tax year in which at least 10 percent of the contract costs have been incurred as of the end of that year.

Generally, a long-term contract is any contract for the building, installation, or construction of property where the contract is not completed within the tax year in which it is entered into (.05). Contracts for the production or installation of real property or improvements to real property are considered to be long-term contracts if they are not completed within the tax year in which they are entered into.

In determining if a contract is completed within the tax year in which it is entered into, all contract costs incurred and activities performed by the taxpayer, by any parties related to the taxpayer, and by the customer must be taken into account (.10).

Contracts characterized as for the sale of property may still qualify as long-term contracts, if manufacture, building, installation or construction of the property was necessary in order for the taxpayer's contractual obligations to be fulfilled and if such manufacture, building, installation or construction was not completed at the time that the contract was entered into (.15).

Modified percentage of completion method

Taxpayers may elect not to recognize income and not to take into account any costs from long-term contracts accounted for under the percentage-of-completion method until the first tax year in which a 10-percent threshold of estimated costs is reached. Thus, an electing taxpayer can postpone recognition of income and accounting for costs until the first tax year in which at least 10 percent of the estimated total contract costs have been incurred as of the end of that year (.20).

The exempt-contract percentage of completion method (EPCM) is a permissible method of accounting for the exempt construction contracts discussed at ¶25,115. A taxpayer using the EPCM generally must include in income the portion of the total contract price that corresponds to the percentage of the entire contract that has been completed during the tax year. The percentage of completion may be determined as of the end of the tax year by using any method of cost comparison (such as comparing direct labor costs incurred to date to estimated total direct labor costs) or by comparing the work performed on the contract with the estimated total work to be performed. The method of comparison must be used consistently and clearly reflect income. The 10-percent method cannot be used with the EPCM (.25).

In applying the percentage-of-completion method to long-term contracts, incorrect cost or income estimates generally give rise to interest liability or income upon completion of the contract under the look-back method.

Look-back method

Generally, the look-back method applies to any income from a long-term contract entered into after February 28, 1986, that is reported under the percentage of completion method.

Under the percentage of completion method, a taxpayer is required to estimate the contract costs and price in order to report income from a long-term contract that is in progress. Upon completion of the contract, it may be determined that the estimates were incorrect. Consequently, the income tax liability that would have been reported if actual contract costs and price were used in lieu of estimates may have been accelerated or deferred depending on whether the contract costs and price were overestimated or underestimated.

The look-back method compensates for timing differences that result from erroneous estimates of contract price or costs by requiring the taxpayer to either pay or receive interest upon completion of the contract (.30). This interest is computed on hypothetical underpayments or overpayments of tax that are assumed to have occurred while the contract was in progress. The application of the look-back method does not result in an adjustment to the taxpayer's tax liability as originally reported, as reported on an amended return, or as adjusted upon IRS examination (.35) Thus, the look-back method does not correct for differences in tax liability that result from permanent tax differences, such as changes in tax rates during the term of the contract.

The look-back method does not apply to computing taxable income from a long-term construction contract that: (1) is a home construction contract or (2) is estimated to be completed within a two-year period by a taxpayer whose average annual gross receipts for the three tax years preceding the tax year in which the contract was entered into do not exceed $10 million (.40).

☐ For further discussion of issues relating to the look-back method, see ¶15,465.

☐ For a discussion of the allocation of costs to contracts accounted for under the completed-contract method, see ¶25,114.

.05 Code Sec. 460(f); Reg. §1.460-1(b)(1).
.10 Reg. §1.460-1(c)(1).
.15 Reg. §1.460-1(b)((2)(i).
.20 Code Sec. 460(b)(5), Reg. §1.460-4(B)(6).
.25 Reg. §1.460-4(c)(2).
.30 Code Sec. 460(b)(1)(B).
.35 Reg. §1.460-6(a)(1).
.40 Code Sec. 460(e)(1); Reg. §1.460-6(b)(2).

¶25,114 Allocation of Costs to Long-Term Contracts In general, all costs that directly benefit or are incurred by reason of the long-term contract activities of the taxpayer, other than small construction or home construction contract activities, must be allocated to those contract (.05). In the case of small construction or home construction contracts, production period interest is the only interest allocated to the contract.

Costs that must be allocated to long-term contracts also include all storage, handling and processing costs incurred with respect to the long-term contract activities of the taxpayer. In addition, an allocable share of all otherwise allowable contributions to a pension or annuity plan representing current or past service costs must be included in the basis of property produced under a long-term contract, and such contributions are no longer currently deductible. For contracts with the federal government or cost-plus long-term contracts, any costs identified by the contractor or by federal, state or local law as being attributable to the contract are capitalized.

Production period interest incurred in connection with a long-term contract must be capitalized in most cases. The production period begins on either (1) the date on which the contractor incurs any costs under the contract, or (2) for accrual-method taxpayers, the later of the date in (1) or the date on which at least five percent of the total estimated costs under the contract have been incurred. The production period ends on the date the contract is completed. Under a special exception for certain accrual-method taxpayers, production period interest does not have to be capitalized for property that will take less than one year to complete and that will cost $1 million or less.

Independent research and development expenses, expenses for unsuccessful bids and proposals, and marketing, selling and advertising expenses are not subject to capitalization.

.05 Code Sec. 460(c).

¶25,115 Real Estate Construction Contracts. For certain real estate construction contracts, the long-term accounting methods (described at ¶25,110) and the cost allocation rules (¶25,114), other than the production period interest allocation rules, do not apply. These types of special construction contracts include small real estate construction contracts, home construction contracts and residential construction contracts (.05).

Small real estate construction contracts

The use of the percentage-of-completion method is not required for certain small real estate construction contracts. Contracts within this exception are those contracts for the construction or improvement of real property that are:

(1) expected to be completed within the two-year period beginning on the commencement date of the contract and

(2) performed by a contractor whose average annual gross receipts for the three tax years preceding the tax year in which the contract is entered into do not exceed $10 million.

In determining the $10 million limit, the gross receipts of parent-subsidiary and brother-sister corporations are combined or any other group under common control are combined.(.10)

The uniform capitalization rules of Code Sec. 263A apply to home construction contracts other than home construction contracts of small contractors as described above (see ¶15,800and following). In addition, home construction contracts of small contractors will not be considered long-term contracts for purposes of the adjustments in computing alternative minimum taxable income (AMTI) of Code Sec. 56 (.15). If a contract involves construction of a mixed-use building with both commercial units and dwelling units, the taxpayer must allocate the costs among the commercial and dwelling units using a reasonable method or a combination of reasonable methods, such as specific identification, square footage, or fair market value (.20)

Home construction contracts

The long-term contract rules—including the generally required use of the percentage of completion method and the percentage of completion-capitalized cost method—and the cost allocation rules, except for the allocation of production period interest, do not apply to home construction contracts.

A home construction contract is one where 80 percent or more of the estimated total contract costs, as of the close of the tax year in which the contract was entered into, are reasonably expected to be attributable to the building, construction, reconstruction or rehabilitation of (1) dwelling units contained in buildings containing four or fewer dwelling units (with each townhouse or rowhouse treated as a separate building), and (2) improvements to real property directly related to such dwelling units and located on the site of such dwelling units (.25) .

Residential construction contracts

Special rules apply to residential construction contracts for buildings containing more than four dwelling units. Residential construction contracts are contracts other than home construction contracts for which 80 percent or more of the total estimated costs under the contract are reasonably expected to be attributed to the building, construction, reconstruction, or rehabilitation of, or improvements to real estate directly related to and located on the site of dwelling units (.30). A dwelling unit, only for purposes of this exception, is a house or apartment used to provide living accommodations in a building or structure, but does not include a unit in a hotel, motel, inn, or other establishment more than one-half of the units in which are used on a transient basis (.35)

Taxpayers who enter into residential construction contracts that are not also home construction contracts may use the percentage of completion method or the percentage of completion-capitalized cost method (.40) . Under this special rule, the percentage of completion-capitalized cost method of accounting is applied with 70 percent of the items under the contract taken into account under the percentage of completion method and the remaining 30 percent taken into account under the taxpayer's normal method of accounting (.45).

.05 Code Sec. 460(e).

.10 Conference Committee Report to the Technical and Miscellaneous Revenue Act of 1988, P. L. 100-647.

.15 Conference Committee Report to the Technical and Miscellaneous Revenue Act of 1988, P.L. 100-647.

.20 Reg. §1.460-3(b)(2)(iv).

.25 Code Sec. 460(e)(6); Reg. §1.460-3(b)(2).

.30 Code Sec. 168(e)(2)(A)(ii), Code Sec. 460(e)(5), Code Sec. 460(e)(6)(B); Reg. §1.460-3(c).

.35 Code Sec. 168(e)(2)(a)(ii).

.40 Reg. §1.460-3(c).

.45 Code Sec. 460(e)(5); Reg. §1.460-4(e).

¶25,116 How to Elect. A taxpayer may use a long-term contract method of accounting without obtaining the IRS's consent in the year he first enters into a long-term contract. Alternatively, he may use any other permissible method, such as the cash or accrual method. But he may not change thereafter from the long-term method to any other method, or *vice* *versa,* without first obtaining the IRS's permission. An application for such permission must be made on Form 3115 within 180 days after the beginning of the tax year to be covered by the return (.05).

.05 Code Sec. 446(e); Reg. §1.446-1 and Reg. §451-3(f).

¶25,117 Reporting Other Expense and Income. Generally, the long-term contract methods of accounting apply only to expenses and income attributable to long-term contracts. All other items of income or expense not attributable to long-term contracts must be accounted for under a method of accounting that clearly reflects income (.05). For instance, the salaries of officers or employees not attributable to a long-term contract generally can be deducted when paid.

Home builders

A contractor engaged in the business of developing real estate may not use the last-in, first-out (LIFO) method or other inventory identification methods to account for the total cost of completed homes and homes under construction because the costs of such construction must be capitalized and are not currently deductible. Such costs are recovered when the specific property is sold. The use of inventories is usually unnecessary for the determination of a developer's income and is generally impractical as a method of valuing real estate (but see ¶25,112). Although the job order cost method used to accumulate the costs of completed homes and construction in progress is a capitalization method and not an inventory method, when used in conjunction with a LIFO inventory method, distortion of income results (.10).

.05 Code Sec. 446(c), Code Sec. 451; Reg. §1.446-1(c) and Reg. §1.451-3(a).

.10 Rev. Rul. 86-149, 1986-2 CB 67, amplifying Rev. Rul. 69-536, 1969-2 CB 109.

¶25,118 Contracts with Maintenance Provisions. Construction contracts that provide that the contractor maintain the completed construction work for an extended time have generally been held to be completed (and the total income recognizable) when the construction work is finished, rather than when the maintenance period expires (.05). The maintenance expenses are not deductible until they have been incurred upon the performance of services (.10).

The existence of maintenance provisions ordinarily will not delay completion of a contract under the completed-contract method of accounting for federal income tax purposes (.15).

.05 *E.J. Harrison, Receivers,* DC PA., 1 USTC ¶332, 28 F2d 985.

.10 *W.J. Strickland Co.,* 33 TCM 484, CCH Dec. 32,552(M), TC Memo. 1974-98; Code Sec. 461(h)(2)(B).

.15 *E.J. Harrison, Receivers,* see .05, above; *Chaplin Construction Co.,* 3 BTA 1377, CCH Dec. 1019; *Scholl Co.,* 30 BTA 993, CCH Dec. 8608.

¶25,119 Damages Received for Breach of Contract. Developers and contractors must treat income received by way of damages for a breach of contract under the same general rules as other taxpayers. Thus, a cash-method taxpayer must report damages when received; an accrual-method taxpayer must report them when the right to receive damages and the amount of the damages are fixed and determinate.

Where the contractor is using a completed-contract method and damages are received for a breach of part of a contract, income can be deferred until the contract is completed (.05). However, a subway contractor using the completed-contract method who completed a city contract at a loss was required to report as income in the year received a sum received 15 years later from the city as compensation for the loss. The contractor was not permitted to amend the income tax return for the year in which the loss from the contract was originally reported (.10).

.05 *Fort Pitt Bridge Works*, CA-3, 37-2 USTC ¶9490, 92 F2d 825, SCt, cert. denied, 303 U.S. 659.

.10 *Newman & Carey Subway Const. Co.*, 37 BTA 1163, CCH Dec. 10,072 (Acq.).

¶25,120 Mortgage-Financing Reserves. Frequently, developers engaged in the construction and sale of homes sell them under a financing arrangement with a financing institution that requires the developer to deposit, in a savings account with the institution, a percentage of the proceeds of first mortgage loans made by the institution to the purchaser of the home. An accrual-method developer who guarantees a home buyer's loan must accrue as income the amounts deposited in the year of deposit, even though the account is to be released only when the purchaser reduces the mortgage to a specified sum (.05).

As to a cash-method taxpayer, however, the pledged amounts have been held taxable only as they became available for withdrawal where the pledged amount was in a restricted savings account and could be withdrawn in specified amounts only as the buyer reduced the loan principal by certain amounts (.10).

.05 *G. L. Bolling*, CA-8, 66-1 USTC ¶9264, 357 F2d 3; *Key Homes, Inc.*, CA-6, 59-2 USTC ¶9732, 271 F2d 280; *Western Oaks Bldg. Corp.*, 49 TC 365, CCH Dec. 28,819; *I. J. Hayutin*, CA-10, 75-1 USTC ¶9108, 508 F2d 462.

.10 *Western Oaks Bldg. Corp.*, 49 TC 365, CCH Dec. 28,819.

¶25,121 Advance Payments for Services. Builders, construction managers and architects often receive advance payments for services which are to be provided in later tax years. The prepayments initially are recorded as deferred income. The IRS has taken the position (.05) that such fees are taxable in the year received. The IRS's general policy applies to contract to furnish services and to other types of prepaid income, regardless of whether the period of proration is definite or indefinite, unless a different treatment is specifically provided in the Code or regulations (.10).

However, there is an exception for certain limited circumstances which allows accrual method taxpayers to defer the inclusion of advance payments where all of the services are to be performed before the end of the next succeeding tax year (.15). Other than for this exception, the IRS's position normally is that any accounting method which delays the reporting the advance payment for services does not clearly reflect income (.20).

Mixed contracts

In many cases, contracts call for both physical construction of a building and also construction management services. For example, a builder may enter into a contract to design and construct a building. The IRS's general rule is that income and expenses attributable to engineering or other similar services must be accounted for as part of a long-term contract (.25). This is because the service are functionally related to, directly benefit and are performed by reason of the taxpayer's building installation, or construction obligation under the same contract. Thus, if the taxpayer contract to design and build a building, the design services are directly related to the subject matter of the taxpayer's construction activity. The income and expenses attributable to the design services must be accounted for under along with the income and expenses attributable to the construction activity.

However, the IRS's position is that a contract that provides for the performances of services, but does not provide for a qualifying long-term contract activity, may not be bootstrapped into Code Sec. 460 simply by adding a construction obligation to which the service obligations to not relate (.30).

Construction services contracts

Contractors may enter into contracts to perform construction services (design, engineering and construction management) only. For tax purposes, a contractor generally must use the accrual method for reporting income from construction services contracts. On the other hand, a construction contractor that enters into a construction contract that will not be completed before the end of the tax year in which it is entered, and whose average annual gross receipts for the three tax years preceding the year in which the contract is entered into exceed $10 million, generally must report gross income from the contract under the percentage-of-completion method (see ¶25,115).

> ***Example:*** Tom Moses, an accrual-method contractor is enters into construction services contracts. Under these contracts, Moses is paid for certain defined costs incurred in performing the services (primarily labor and salaries), and a few for the services, based on either a percentage of the costs or a set amount. The contracts require Moses's client to advance funds to him based on his costs he estimates he will incur in the next month. The contracts also provide that advanced funds must be applied to the taxpayer's costs incurred on the contract, and that any excess determined at the time the contract is either completed or terminated must be returned to the client. Likewise, excess fee payments, if any, must be returned to the client.
>
> With respect to the cost-plus contracts, Moses determines the gross income both for financial and for tax purposes by taking into account an amount equal to the costs incurred during the year plus the stated percentage of the costs. For the fixed-fee contracts, he determines gross income gross income for financial and for tax purposes by taking into account an amount equal to the costs and the appropriate portion of the fixed fee.
>
> According to the IRS, both these percentage-of-completion methods are permissible under generally accepted accounting principles for determining gross income from a construction service contracts for financial accounting purposes. *However, they are not permissible methods for federal income tax purposes.* Accrual-method taxpayers must report gross income in the tax year when (1) the required performance takes place, (2) payment is due, or (3) payment is made, whichever happens first. Thus, this principle requires an accrual-method taxpayer to include advance payments received from construction service contracts in gross income in the tax year in which they are actually or constructively received, rather than when earned at a later time under general accrual accounting principles (.35).

.05 IRS Industry Specialization Program (ISP) Advance Payments for Personal Services.

.10 Rev. Rul. 60-85, 1960-1 CB 181.

.15 Rev. Proc. 71-21, 1971-2 CB 549.

.20 Code Sec. 446.

.25 Code Sec. 460.

.30 IRS Industry Specialization Program (ISP) Construction Management Contracts, April 17, 1995.

.35 IRS Industry Specialization Program (ISP) Advance Payments from Construction Services Contracts, October 19, 1996.

Business Expense Deductions

¶25,122 In General. Developers and contractors, like those engaged in any other business, trade, or profession, may deduct all ordinary and necessary business expenses paid or incurred during the tax year (.05). Such expenses include management expenses, commissions, labor, supplies, incidental repairs, operating expenses of automobiles used in the trade or business, travel expenses while away from home solely in the pursuit of a trade or business, advertising and selling expenses, together with insurance premiums against fire, storm, theft, accident, or other similar losses in the case of a business, and rental of business property. However, the amount allowable as a deduction for business meal and entertainment expenses is limited to 50 percent of such expenses, subject to certain exceptions (.10). Moreover, an expenditure is not currently deductible as a business expense if it is in the nature of a capital expenditure (.15).

.05 Code Sec. 162; Reg. §1.162-1.
.10 Code Sec. 274(n).
.15 Code Sec. 263(a) and Code Sec. 263A.

¶25,123 Equipment Costs. The cost of equipment such as tractors, bulldozers, concrete mixers, etc., is normally a capital expenditure (.05). Such cost is usually recoverable through depreciation, rather than as a deductible business expense. This also applies to the cost of reconditioned equipment (.10).

☐For further discussion of depreciation, see ¶25,130 and ¶25,131. See, also, ¶9001 and following.

The costs of small tools with comparatively short lives can be deducted in the year of purchase. But if the lives of tools extend substantially beyond the end of the tax year, the costs of such tools must be capitalized and recovered through depreciation.

Depreciation related to construction equipment owned by a general contractor where such equipment was used in the erection of capital improvements for the contractor's own use was not an allowable deduction, but was to be added to the contractor's basis in the improvement. That part applicable to the cost of depreciable capital improvements was recoverable through depreciation deductions over the useful life of the improvements (.15).

Rentals

If costs paid for use of equipment are attributable to lease of the equipment rather than for purchase of the equipment, a tax advantage can be obtained, since rental costs are immediately deductible as a business expense, while capital costs are recoverable only through depreciation deductions over the equipment's recovery period.

If the lease agreement does not include an option to purchase, the lessee-contractor is usually permitted to deduct the rents paid as business expenses. This was so where a road contractor regularly purchased all of its leased heavy equipment at the expiration of the lease at fair market value without the benefit of options to purchase (.20). Where the lease payments were applied or credited to the purchase price of the leased equipment, however, the payments were not deductible (.25).

If the lease agreement includes an option to purchase that is clearly exercisable before the end of the property's useful life and the rental payments cover a substantial part of what would be the purchase price of the property, the Tax Court would probably hold that a sale and purchase are intended ("economic reality" or "intent to purchase" test) (.30). The U.S. Court of Appeals for the Seventh Circuit has held, however, that a lease agreement was not a sale and purchase where, on the facts, the exercise of the option did not indicate that the parties intended to have rental payments apply toward the purchase price of, or build up an equity in, the leased property (.35).

.05 Code Sec. 162.

.10 *C. F. Lytle,* 21 BTA 1423, CCH Dec. 6673 (Acq.).

.15 Rev. Rul. 59-380, 1959-2 CB 87, clarified by Rev. Rul. 77-325, 1977-2 CB 67.

.20 *Western Contracting Corp.,* CA-8, 59-2 USTC ¶9751, 271 F2d 694.

.25 *E. J. Abramson,* DC IA., 55-2 USTC ¶9563, 133 FSupp 677.

.30 *N.P. Van Valkenburgh,* 26 TCM 753, CCH Dec. 28,562(M), TC Memo. 1967-162.

.35 *Breece Veneer and Panel Co.,* CA-7, 56-1 USTC ¶9485, 232 F2d 319.

¶25,124 Salaries and Compensation. Developers and contractors may deduct reasonable amounts paid for salaries and other compensation. What is reasonable depends upon the facts in each case and no hard and fast rules can be laid down to control in all situations. Where the IRS has made a determination that the compensation or salary deducted or claimed was unreasonable or excessive in amount, the contractor or developer—just like any other taxpayer—has the burden of proving the reasonableness of the amount. Amounts in excess of reasonable compensation may not be disguised and deducted as some other business expense. For example, excessive amounts of salary paid to the president of a construction company could not be deducted as "additional rent" for premises leased from the president (.05).

In considering the facts, courts have generally attached considerable weight to the testimony of disinterested witnesses regarding average or comparable salary and wage payments in the industry to similar officers and employees. They have also weighed the qualifications, duties, responsibilities, and importance of the particular officer or employee involved as well as any other pertinent or relevant facts.

Withholding responsibilities

Developers and contractors may be required to withhold taxes on wages and benefits paid to employees. Moreover, they can be held liable for such taxes if they fail to withhold them. For instance, a general contractor was held liable for unpaid withholding taxes on salary payments made to employees of a subcontractor, where the general contractor had control over the payroll accounts (.10).

.05 *Roehl Construction Co., Inc.*, 17 TC 1037, CCH Dec. 18,679.

.10 *Towne Realty, Inc.*, DC Wis., 83-2 USTC ¶9671, 575 FSupp 77.

¶25,125 Payment of Bribes and Kickbacks. Although payments to third persons for personal services are generally deductible if such payments are ordinary and necessary business expenses, the IRS and the courts give special scrutiny to payments in the nature of graft (.05).

Any bribe or illegal kickback paid to a public official or government employee, including payments to officials or employees of a foreign government that are illegal under the Foreign Corrupt Practices Act of 1977, is nondeductible. The burden, as in fraud cases, of proving that the payment was a bribe or kickback rests with the IRS.

Domestically, a payment to any person is not deductible if it is an illegal payment under a federal or a state law (but only if such state law is generally enforced) that subjects the payor to a criminal penalty or the loss of his license to engage in business. In addition, graft payments cannot be deductible as business expenses unless they constitute normal or customary industry practice in the locale of the taxpayer's activities. For example, an excavation subcontractor had to make kickback payments to the general contractor's supervisor if it wished to keep working on a large shopping mall job. Since the payments were conceded to be necessary to obtain contracts and no laws were violated, the kickback payments were allowed as business expenses (.10).

However, payments made by a subcontractor for work done on a supervisor's home were not deductible business expenses, even though such payments were not illegal. The payments were found to be neither appropriate nor helpful to the subcontractor's business and, thus, not ordinary or necessary to obtain construction contracts. This conclusion was reached despite the fact that the subcontractor might have lost up to $1 million in construction work without the kickback payments (.15).

.05 Code Sec. 162(c); Reg. §1.162-1.

.10 *Raymond Bertolini Trucking Co.*, CA-6, 84-2 USTC ¶9591, 736 F2d 1120.

.15 *Car-Ron Asphalt Paving Co.*, CA-6, 85-1 USTC ¶9298, 758 F2d 1132.

¶25,126 Bond Expenses and Losses. The expenses of securing surety bonds, such as bid and performance bonds, are deductible like any other business expense. Such bonds are normally procured from a bonding company that acts as surety for the satisfactory completion of the contractor's or subcontractor's work. In one case, a construction corporation that paid 50 percent of the net profits from contracts to two of its shareholders, who signed performance bonds as indemnitors, was allowed to deduct such payments as business expenses. In that case, the surety companies would not have issued bonds for the corporation without indemnitors, and the practice of paying part of contract profits to indemnitors was not unusual in the construction industry (.05).

Where a corporation bought and posted U.S. Government bonds as required to guarantee the performance of a contract and, upon completion of the contract, sold the bonds at a loss, the corporation was allowed to deduct the loss as a business expense (.10). However, a contrary result was reached where bonds deposited as a substitute for retained percentages were intended to be held as an investment (.15).

.05 *A.A. Jones Co.*, 19 TCM 1561, CCH Dec. 24,593(M), TC Memo. 1960-284.

.10 *Bagley and Sewall Co.*, CA-2, 55-1 USTC ¶9381, 221 F2d 944.

.15 *Wilaka Builders, Inc.*, DC NY, 64-2 USTC ¶9519.

¶25,127 Fines and Penalties. Fines and penalties paid by a taxpayer to a government or public official for the violation of any law are nondeductible, even though the commission of the offense was in connection with the carrying on of a trade or business (.05). For example, payments of damages for child labor violations under a federal law are not deductible (.10). Further, fines for overloading vehicles, whether such overloading was intentional or not, are not deductible as ordinary and necessary business expenses (.15), but liquidated damages paid separately and in addition to such fines are compensatory in nature and therefore deductible (.20). A deduction for an otherwise allowable business expense will not be denied on the ground that allowance of such deduction would frustrate a sharply defined public policy (.25).

A building material supplier could not deduct fines imposed for violation of a state antitrust act as business expenses (.30). However, attorney fees and legal expenses incident to a suit for alleged violation of state antitrust laws were deductible (.35).

The payment of a penalty assessed against the responsible officer of a corporation for the corporation's failure to pay over withholding and FICA (social security) taxes was not deductible as a business expense (.40). Additionally, amounts paid by a corporate officer under a court-approved settlement to reimburse his corporation for an illegal political contribution approved by the officer, and to pay the resulting fine, were not deductible by the officer as a business expense (.45).

.05 Code Sec. 162(f).

.10 *Davenshire, Inc.*, 12 TC 958, CCH Dec. 17,019.

.15 *Hoover Motor Express Co., Inc.*, SCt, 58-1 USTC ¶9367, 356 U.S. 38.

.20 *Mason and Dixon Lines, Inc.*, CA-6, 83-1 USTC ¶9385, 708 F2d 1043.

.25 Reg. §1.162-1.

.30 *Burroughs Bldg. Material Co.*, CA-2, 2 USTC ¶641, 47 F2d 178.

.35 *Longhorn Portland Cement Co.*, CA-5, 45-1 USTC ¶9242, 148 F2d 276, SCt, cert. denied, 326 U.S. 728.

.40 *J. W. Patton*, 71 TC 389, CCH Dec. 35,589.

.45 Rev. Rul. 81-151, 1981-1 CB 74.

¶25,128 Interest. Under general accounting rules, cash-method taxpayers must deduct interest expense in the year paid. Also some developers and contractors using an accrual method will deduct interest when it is payable, even though it has not yet been paid. Further, both cash-and accrual-method taxpayers sometimes deduct prepaid interest over the period to which it relates (.05). However, most developers and contractors capitalize production period interest (see ¶25,114).

Although a cash-method taxpayer is not considered to have paid interest when the lender withholds the amount of interest from the principal amount of the loan, an interest expense deduction was allowed to a shopping center developer who borrowed cash from its original lender to repay interest on a construction loan owed to the same lender (.10). The developer had unrestricted control over the borrowed funds.

Where a taxpayer in the trade or business of building and selling single-family residences entered into an agreement with a financial institution whereby the financial institution made mortgage loans below market rates to the home buyers and the taxpayer then bought the loans at a premium, the difference between the fair market value of the loans and the amount paid by the taxpayer was deductible as an ordinary and necessary business expense. The premium was a cost incurred in the taxpayer's trade or business that enabled it to sell its product (.15).

.05 Code Sec. 461(g).

.10 *J.B. Noble, Jr.*, 79 TC 751, CCH Dec. 39,470.

.15 IRS Letter Ruling 8229120, 4-23-82.

Depreciation

¶25,130 MACRS and ACRS. The recovery of the costs of equipment, tools and other property through cost recovery or depreciation deductions is extremely important to builders and contractors. The relatively short useful lives of expensive construction equipment as a whole, coupled with continuous production of improved and more efficient equipment, frequently require the quickest possible recovery of the costs of such assets.

For most tangible assets placed in service after 1986, depreciation must be computed under the Modified Accelerated Cost Recovery System (MACRS) (.05). Depreciation taken after 1987 for most assets placed in service after 1980 and before 1987 must be computed under the Accelerated Cost Recovery System (ACRS). Depreciation taken after 1980 for assets placed in service in 1980 or earlier must be computed under the method elected by the taxpayer when the property was placed in service.

MACRS

MACRS applies to assets placed in service after 1986. Under MACRS, the cost of eligible property is recovered over a three-year, five-year, seven-year, 10-year, 15-year, 20-year, 25-year (water utility property), 27.5-year, or 39-year period using different accelerated methods, except for real property which utilizes the straight-line method. Real property is generally classified as 27.5-year property for residential real property and 39-year property for nonresidential real property (31.5-year property, for nonresidential real property placed in service before May 13, 1993). Additionally, the MACRS rules provide that an alternative MACRS method, which uses the straight-line method and longer recovery periods, must be used for: (1) tax-exempt bond-financed property, (2) tax-exempt use property, (3) property imported from a foreign country for which an executive order is in effect because the country maintains trade restrictions or engages in other discriminatory acts, (4) tangible property used predominantly outside of the U.S., and (5) property for which an alternative MACRS election has been made.

ACRS

For most tangible depreciable property placed in service after 1980 and before 1987, capital costs are recovered under ACRS by using accelerated methods over statutory recovery periods. The cost of eligible property is recovered over a three-year, five-year, 10-year, 15-year, 18-year, or 19-year period, depending upon the type of property and when it was placed in service. Real property is generally classed as 15-year property if it was placed in service on March 15, 1984 or earlier, as 18-year property if it was placed in service after March 15, 1984 and before May 9, 1985, and as 19-year property if it was placed in service after May 8, 1985. Low-income housing is classified as 15-year property.

Eligible property includes depreciable property other than (1) most property for which an election was made to use a depreciation method not expressed in terms of years (for example, units-of-production or income forecast methods), (2) intangible property, and (3) public utility property for which the normalization method of accounting is not used (.10).

Expense deduction

In general, developers and contractors can elect to treat a portion of the cost of qualifying Code Sec. 179 property as an expense rather than as a capital expenditure (.15). Section 179 property is recovery property purchased for use *in the active conduct* of a trade or business.

For tax years beginning in 2003, 2004, 2005, 2006 and 2007, the maximum amount of the deduction (the dollar limitation) is $100,000 and the investment limitation is $400,000. Under the investment limitation, the applicable dollar limit for the tax year is reduced by the amount by which the applicable investment limitation. The threshold is indexed for inflation beginning in 2004. Thus, for 2004, the dollar limitation is $102,000 and the investment limitation is $410,000 (.20).

In addition to the annual limitation, the total cost of section 179 property that may be expensed for any year cannot exceed the total amount of taxable income that is derived from the active conduct of any trade or business during the tax year. For this purpose, taxable income from the active conduct of a trade or business is computed without regard to the deduction allowed under Sec. 179 for the cost of the qualifying property.

.05 Code Sec. 168.

.10 Code Sec. 168(e).

.15 Code Sec. 179.

.20 Code Sec. 179(b)(5), as amended by the American Jobs Creation Act of 2004 (P.L. 108-357).

¶25,131 Recapture of Depreciation. Gain on the disposition of certain depreciable property (¶5802) that would otherwise be capital in nature must be recaptured as ordinary income to the extent of the cost recovery or depreciation previously taken with respect to such property (.05).

Different rules apply with regard to the recapture of depreciation on real and personal property placed in service before 1987 and with regard to property placed in service after December 31, 1986.

Real property

Depreciable real property (Code Sec. 1250 property) includes all intangible real property (such as leases of land) and all tangible real property except property that is used as an integral part of manufacturing, production, or extraction, or of furnishing transportation, communications, electrical energy, gas, water or sewage disposal services or research or storage facilities used in connection with these activities.

If this recapture amount is equal to or more than the gain on the sale, all gain is treated as ordinary income. If the recapture is less than the gain, then the "additional depreciation" may be partially or fully recaptured. "Additional depreciation" is that amount of depreciation deductions taken that is in excess of the depreciation deductions that would have been allowed if the property had been depreciated using straight-line depreciation. There are special recapture rules for rental and low-income housing and for pre-1970 dispositions of Code Sec. 1250 property.

If Code Sec. 1250 property (depreciable real property) is sold, exchanged, or otherwise disposed of, part or all of the gain must be recaptured as ordinary income under the following rules:

(1) If the depreciable realty was held for 12 months or less, all depreciation—not just the excess over straight-line—must be recaptured to the extent of the gain on the disposition.

(2) If the realty was held for more than 12 months, "additional depreciation"—the excess of depreciation deductions taken over straight-line depreciation—must be recaptured to the extent of the gain.

Post-1986 real property. For real property placed in service after December 31, 1986, recapture is not necessary since the straight-line method of depreciation is required for such property (.10). Additionally, a deduction is generally available in the year of disposition and in the year the property is placed in service under the mid-month convention applicable to such property (.15).

Personal property

As with real estate, depreciation is recaptured on the disposition of personal property (Code Sec. 1245 property), but with some differences.

For personal property placed in service after December 31, 1986, *all* of the depreciation deductions taken by the taxpayer are recaptured as ordinary income when the property is disposed of, up to the amount of the realized gain. Unlike previous provisions, depreciation is generally allowed in the year of disposition and in the year that the property is placed in service under a half-year convention (.20). However, if more than 40 percent of the aggregate bases of property placed in service during the tax year are placed in service during the last quarter of the tax year, a mid-quarter convention applies (.25).

Expense deduction

Generally, in determining the amount of gain that is recaptured as ordinary income on a sale or disposition of either personal property or real estate, the amount of the investment credit basis adjustment is treated as a deduction allowed for depreciation (.30). Accordingly, the amount of such basis adjustment is treated as depreciation subject to ordinary income recapture. Also recaptured is any deduction taken for a Code Sec. 179 election to expense certain depreciable business assets.

.05 Code Sec. 1245 and Code Sec. 1250.
.10 Code Sec. 168(b)(3) and Code Sec. 1250.
.15 Code Sec. 168(d)(2).
.20 Code Sec. 168(d)(1).
.25 Code Sec. 168(d)(3).
.30 Code Sec. 50(c)(4).

At-Risk and Passive Loss Rules

¶25,132 At-risk rules. The at-risk rules apply to real estate only in a nominal fashion. Although Code Sec. 165 no longer has the special stated exception exempting real estate from the at-risk rules, the rules have not really changed.

The at-risk rules were enacted to prevent investors from deducting losses in excess of what was their actual investment in a property, but there are exceptions to this rule. One of these exceptions is for "qualified nonrecourse financing" (.05). Qualified nonrecourse financing in any financing relating to real property from a "qualified person." A qualified person is "any person which is actively and regularly engaged in the business of lending money and which is not: (1) a related person with respect to the taxpayer, (2) a person from which the taxpayer acquired the property (or a related person to such person, or (3) a person who receives a fee with respect to the taxpayer's investment in the property (or a related person to such person)" (.10). For this purpose, a "person" is an individual or a non-human entity.

The result is that any real estate financing procured through the normal means of borrowing from a bank, an insurance company, a savings and loan, a credit union, or any other entity that is not a "relation" of the taxpayer is exempt from the at-risk rules. This covers virtually all home, apartment, condominium, shopping center, office building and any other kind of real estate lending.

Furthermore, even if the lender and borrower are related, the financing is not subject to the at-risk rules if the loan is "commercially reasonable and on substantially the same terms as loans involving unrelated persons" (.15).

.05 Code Sec. 465(b)(6).

.10 Code Sec. 49(a)(1)(D)(iv) and Code Sec. 465(b)(6)(D)(1).

.15 Code Sec. 465(b)(6)(D)(ii).

¶25,133 Passive Losses Limited to Passive Income. Out of a fear that many investments might be made primarily to get a share of tax losses that far exceed amounts invested in a venture, the passive loss rules have been created (.05). The goal: to stop the use of these losses as a means of offsetting highly taxed income from other sources. For example, an investor who does little more than contribute $8,000 to a venture operated by others while he actively pursues his own business interests may, without the proscriptions of the passive loss rules, find that his assumed $60,000 share of losses in the venture can be deducted from his assumed $150,000 income from his salary. The passive activity loss rules were designed to prevent the expansion of tax shelters in order to restore equity to the tax system. These goals were accomplished by preventing an investor in an activity in which he did not materially participate from using losses generated by that activity to shelter income unrelated to that activity.

The activities in which a taxpayer does not materially participate are considered passive activities. However, rental activities (other than certain real estate rental activities in post-1993 tax years) are considered passive activities even if there is material participation. Under the passive loss rules, losses from such passive activities may be deducted only against passive income and may not offset salaries, professional fees, or income from businesses in which the taxpayer materially participates or "portfolio" income, income such as dividends, and interest income. In addition, tax credits that arise out of passive investments may reduce only the tax bill for passive income. Passive losses and credits that may not be used in one tax year may be carried over to future tax years and applied against passive income and passive tax liabilities for those years. Passive loss rules are different from at-risk rules (see ¶25,132) in that they apply to a wider range of persons and to persons who do not actively participate in a trade or business even where their investment in the passive activity is at risk.

Although the form of ownership is not normally controlling, all limited partnership interests are generally considered passive activity interests unless (1) the limited partner is also a general partner in the partnership at all times during the partnership's tax year ending with or within the limited partner's tax year, (2) the limited partner participates in the activity for more than 500 hours during the tax year, (3) the limited partner materially participated in the activity for any five tax years during the 10 tax years immediately preceding the tax year in question, or (4) the activity is a personal service activity and the limited partner materially participated in the activity for any three tax years preceding the tax year in question (.10).

.05 Code Sec. 469.

.10 Temp. Reg. § 1.469-5T(e).

¶25,134 Rental Real Estate Activities. Normally, rental activities are automatically considered passive activities, regardless of the taxpayer's participation in the activity. Thus, contrary to what most taxpayers would prefer, losses from the activity can only be deducted from other passive income. On the other hand, operating income and other income from the sale of property used in such activities is normally considered passive income that can be used to offset losses from other passive activities, a result that many investors prefer.

Certain special rules may apply to treat certain losses and certain income from real estate activities that involve the rental of property as being derived from nonpassive activities.

Real estate rental activities of the taxpayer are not considered passive activities if more than half of the personal services performed by the taxpayer during the tax year are performed in a broad variety of real property trades or businesses in which the taxpayer materially participates, and the taxpayer performs more than 750 hours of services during the tax year in those real property trades or businesses (.05). In the case of losses claimed on a joint tax return, these requirements are met only if either spouse separately satisfied the requirements. In such cases, the deduction of losses from the activity is not barred by the passive activity loss rules, but any income from the activity will also be considered nonpassive.

For taxpayers whose participation in a real estate rental activity does not rise to the level of material participation, but does meet the less-demanding active participation standard, up to $25,000 of losses from such passive activities may be used to offset nonpassive income (.10).

Another special rule has the undesirable consequences of treating only the gain realized upon the sale of a real estate development as nonpassive income to the extent of net rental income from the property (.15). This rule applies where the real estate developer has materially or significantly participated in "value-enhancing" services for the property and has used the property in a rental activity less than 12 months before the date of the property's disposition. In addition to development and renovation activities, a taxpayer who participates in soliciting tenants for the property will normally be treated as materially participating in a "value-enhancing" service where his interest was acquired before more than 50% of the property was leased. The net rental income is loosely defined as the gross income from the rental or disposition of the property less any passive activity deductions and suspended losses allocable to the property.

☐ For a full discussion of the passive activity loss rules, see ¶10,500 and following.

.05 Code Sec. 469(c)(7).

.10 Reg. §1.469-2(f)(5) and Temp. Reg. § 1.469-2T(f)(5).

.15 Code Sec. 469(i).

Form of Doing Business

¶25,135 Choice of Form. As with other business persons, developers may choose any legal form for doing business. The most common forms for owning and developing real estate (other than sole proprietorship) are the corporation, the partnership, and the limited liability company (LLC). Generally, however, corporations are not well suited to the ownership of improved real estate for investment because of the double taxation of income and the corporation's inability to pass corporate depreciation deductions through to the shareholder. However, an S corporation (see ¶25,136) may be suitable for holding real estate under certain circumstances. Still, the partnership, either general or limited, remains the most popular form for the multiple ownership of real estate.

¶25,136 S Corporations. S corporations are not taxed at the corporate level like other corporations, but instead are treated for federal income tax purposes like partnerships, with all the business's income and deductions passed on to the shareholders and then taxed as part of their respective incomes (.05). (However, the aggregate amount of a taxpayer's deductions cannot exceed his basis in his stock plus the basis of any indebtedness owed by the corporation to the taxpayer (.10).) Thus, taxpayers are offered the legal advantages of the corporate form without taxation at both the corporate and the shareholder levels.

To qualify for tax treatment under subchapter S, a corporation must *not* have:

(1) more than one class of stock,

(2) more than 100 shareholders, or

(3) a nonresident alien or an entity, other than an estate or certain trusts, as a shareholder.

An S corporation must also be a domestic corporation (that is to say, a corporation organized or created under the laws of the United States or a state or territory) (.15).

An S corporation election terminates if the S corporation has both passive investment income in excess of 25 percent of total gross receipts and Subchapter C earnings and profits at the close of each of three consecutive tax years during which it has been an S corporation (.20). The accumulated earnings and profits of an S corporation during its first tax year beginning after that date are reduced by the earnings and profits accumulated in any tax year beginning before January 1, 1983, for which the corporation was an S corporation (.25). This reduction ensures that an S corporation's accumulated earnings and profits are solely attributable to tax years for which its S election was not in effect and eliminates unnecessarily complicated corporate recordkeeping.

Passive investment income includes gross receipts derived from royalties, rents, dividends, interest, annuities, and gains from sales or exchanges of stock or securities. Royalties derived in the ordinary course of a trade or business and rents derived in the active trade or business of renting property are not included in passive investment income (.30). Income derived from leasing self-produced tangible property is also excluded from the definition of rents.

If an S corporation holds stock in a C corporation meeting the requirements of Code Sec. 1504(a)(2) (relating to the 80-percent voting and value test for affiliated groups), the term "passive investment income" does not include dividends from the C corporation to the extent that the dividends are attributable to the earnings and profits of the C corporation derived from the active conduct of a trade or business (.35).

Passive investment income also includes rental income where no significant services are rendered as part of the rental agreement (.40). The rental of hotel rooms, for example, includes the sale of significant services. However, the normal maintenance and cleaning services involved in the renting of office space (.45), the maintenance and repair required of a landlord of a shopping mall (.50) and the cleaning and decorating for new tenants in a residential property (.55) all failed to qualify as significant services; thus, income derived from these properties constituted rent and was classified as passive investment income.

Contrast with partnerships

Partnerships allow investors current utilization of losses from the investment activity that are made available to offset other sources of income. However, losses from limited partnerships are treated as losses from passive activities in most cases and cannot be used to offset nonpassive income (.60). The losses immediately recognizable by an S corporation shareholder are limited to his basis in the S corporation stock and in loans made to the corporation. In addition, partnerships can allocate specific items of gain and loss among the partners provided there is substantial economic effect to the allocation. For a partnership that uses the cash basis of accounting for certain items, these items must be allocated among the partners on a daily basis in proportion to their interests in the partnership. No special allocation is allowed among S corporation shareholders.

.05 Code Sec. 1361, Code Sec. 1363(a) and Code Sec. 1366.

.10 Code Sec. 1366(d).

.15 Code Sec. 1361(b) as amended by the American Jobs Creation Act of 2004 (P.L. 108-357).

.20 Code Sec. 1362(d)(3)(A); Reg. §1.1362-2(c)(1).

.25 Act Sec. 1311(a), Small Business Job Protection Act of 1996 (P.L. 104-188)

.30 Reg. §1.1362-2(c)(5)(i) and Reg. §1.1362-2(c)(5)(ii)(B)(2).

.35 Code Sec. 1362(d)(3)(E).

.40 Code Sec. 1362(d)(3)(D)(i).

.45 *Bramlette Building Corporation, Inc.*, CA-5, 70-1 USTC ¶9361, 424 F2d 751.

.50 *J.J. McIlhinney*, 39 TCM 554, CCH Dec. 36,463(M), TC Memo. 1979-473, aff'd by CA-3, in an opinion unpublished under court rules, 1-19-81.

.55 *H.E. Lillis*, 45 TCM 1000, CCH Dec. 39,967(M), TC Memo. 1983-142, aff'd by CA-9, in an opinion unpublished under court rules.

.60 Code Sec. 469.

¶25,137 Partnership/Joint Venture. Partnerships and joint ventures are subject to similar treatment for federal income tax purposes. It has been said that the difference between a partnership and a joint venture is that the joint venture relates to the conduct of a specific project (such as the development of a specific piece of real estate) while a partnership involves a continuing business of some kind (.05).

The income of a partnership is attributable directly to the partners and not to the partnership itself. This income is taxed to the partners whether or not it has actually been distributed to them (.10).

Since an interest in a partnership or a joint venture is considered to be a capital asset, the sale or exchange of such an interest results in any gain or loss being treated as a capital gain or loss. In one case, the taking over of the assets and business of a joint venture by a second joint venture composed of some of the members of the first joint venture was an additional capital investment on the part of the second joint venturers. There was no sale giving rise to deductible losses (.15).

Limited partnerships

A limited partnership is a partnership that has one or more general partners who are personally liable for the obligations of the partnership and one or more limited partners whose potential personal liability for partnership debts is limited to the amount of money or other property that the partner contributed or is required to contribute to the partnership (.20). As with other partnerships, the income of a limited partnership is not taxed to the partnership, but is taxable to the partners themselves. However, larger limited partnerships, known as master limited partnerships, may be taxed like corporations.

Most importantly, in most cases, limited partnership interests are treated as being passive activity interests for purposes of the passive loss rules. Thus, a developer must assess the market for limited partnership interests in general before determining to use this form of doing business.

Limited liability companies

The tax and business benefits available to a state-registered limited liability company (LLC) are making this an ever-more attractive vehicle for conducting various types of business and investment activities. A properly structured LLC is normally taxed as a partnership for federal tax purposes, but its members, like corporate shareholders, are not personally liable for its debts and liabilities.

One major advantage that partnerships and LLCs have over S corporations regarding the ownership of real estate is that nonrecourse financing relating to property held by a partnership or LLC can increase the basis of the partners in their partnership interests. This, in turn, allows the deduction of losses arising from the operation of the real estate activity to be deducted in excess of a partner's actual investment in the property. With S corporations, a shareholder's basis in his stock is basically limited to what was paid for it. An S corporation's nonrecourse mortgage would have no effect on the shareholder's bases in their shares.

.05 *H. Bartholemew*, CA-8, 51-1 USTC ¶9150, 186 F2d 315.

.10 Code Sec. 761, Code Sec. 7701(a)(2); Reg. §301.7701-3.

.15 *A.E. Bell Corp.*, CA-9, 44-2 USTC ¶9476, 145 F2d 157.

.20 Form 1065, CCH FEDERAL TAX FORMS, Reg. §301.7701-2, and *P.G. Larson*, 66 TC 159, CCH Dec. 33,793 (1976), Acq. on another issue.

Liens

¶25,138 Liens for Taxes. The United States has a lien against the property of any person who neglects or refuses to pay taxes after demand. Such a lien attaches at the time the assessment for a delinquency is made (.05). A federal tax lien is invalid as against any purchaser, judgment lien creditor, mechanic's lienor, or holder of security interests until notice of the tax lien has been filed in the appropriate state office or in the office of the clerk of the U.S. District Court if no such state office has been designated for the filing.

Liens that affect real property must be filed with the appropriate state or local office for filing such tax liens. This requirement applies, however, only if (1) applicable state law requires public indexing of a deed before it will be valid against a purchaser of the property who does not have actual notice or knowledge and (2) the state or local office where notices of tax liens are filed has an adequate system for the indexing of federal tax liens. If these two conditions are not satisfied, indexing apparently is not required in order to give the lien priority over purchasers and other creditors.

Any person who has had a notice of federal tax lien filed on his property or rights to property may appeal to the IRS for a release of the lien (.10). Such an administrative appeal may be used only for the purpose of correcting the erroneous filing of a notice of lien and not for challenging the underlying deficiency that led to the imposition of the lien.

Certain mechanic's liens are protected against federal tax liens, even though notice of the tax lien has been filed (.15). Thus, a federal tax lien is not valid with respect to real property subject to a mechanic's lien for repair or improvement of a personal residence occupied by the owner where the contract price for the work is not more than $5,660 for 2002 (.20).

Even if a mechanic's lien is junior to a federal tax lien, the lien creditor has several rights which may aid him in satisfying his lien. For instance, if the government realizes surplus funds on the sale of property following a levy, the mechanic has the right to reach the surplus funds by bringing a civil action against the United States in a district court. Also, if a dispute exists among competing lienors, including the United States, concerning their rights to specific property, the IRS may issue a certificate of discharge where property subject to a tax lien is sold and, under an agreement with the IRS, the proceeds from the sale are to be held as a fund subject to the liens and claims of the United States in the same manner and with the same priority as the liens and claims on the discharged property. In such case, any person who claims to be legally entitled to the proceeds of the sale may bring a civil action against the United States in a U.S. District Court (.25).

.05 Code Sec. 6321, Code Sec. 6322 and Code Sec. 6323.

.10 Code Sec. 6326; Reg. §301.6326-1.

.15 Code Sec. 6323(b)(7).

.20 Rev. Proc. 2002-66,.

.25 Code Sec. 7426.

FIDUCIARIES AND BENEFICIARIES OF ESTATES AND TRUSTS

Introduction

¶25,140 Persons who act as fiduciaries, such as trustees, executors, and administrators, are faced with tax problems that are peculiar to their positions. For federal income tax purposes, a "fiduciary" is a person who is in a position of confidence or trust as to others, which creates income tax responsibilities (¶25,142). Thus, the fiduciary is a person who holds legal title to property in which another has the beneficial title or interest or, in the case of a receiver, who receives and controls the income of another. A committee or guardian of the property of an incompetent person is also considered a fiduciary. The party holding the beneficial interest is known as the beneficiary, who must also face some unique tax planning considerations.

Although there may be a fiduciary relationship between an agent and a principal, an "agent" is not necessarily a fiduciary. For example, an agent is not a fiduciary within the meaning of the Internal Revenue Code if a power of attorney confers upon him the entire charge of property, including the authority to enter into leases with tenants on his own responsibility, and merely requires him to turn over the net profits from the property to his principal periodically (Reg. §301.7701-7).

Responsibilities of Fiduciaries

¶25,142 "Fiduciary" Defined. A "fiduciary" is a person who occupies a position of special confidence towards others under the law, such as a trustee, executor, administrator, receiver, conservator, or guardian of an incompetent (.05), and is generally held responsible for the federal income tax rights and duties of the taxpayer he represents (see ¶19,260 and ¶25,148).

Where a person acting as a mere agent, debtor, intermediary or conduit receives income that is paid over to another, no fiduciary return for income tax purposes is required, because the income is taxable to the principal (.10). For instance, a manager for others of a joint venture, one member of a family managing properties for others, or a broker receiving dividends on stock that is in his possession, but legal title to which is in another's, is not treated as a fiduciary for income tax purposes. Likewise, it seems that a bailee who takes title to property that he sells for another, or the pledgee or assignee of property held to secure a debt, would not be acting in a fiduciary capacity for tax purposes.

However, a trustee for a life tenant or a remainderman appointed by the court as the result of a judicial sale of certain property is required to file a return as fiduciary and to pay the tax thereon (.15). Also, a trustee in a Chapter 7 (liquidation) or Chapter 11 (reorganization) bankruptcy for an individual is considered a fiduciary and is required to file a fiduciary income tax return for the bankruptcy estate. A separate taxable entity is not created when an individual undertakes a Chapter 13 reorganization (.20). See ¶25,657–¶25,682.

The commencement of a bankruptcy proceeding for a partnership or a corporation does not create a taxable entity separate and apart from the debtor and, hence, no fiduciary return is required (.25). However, a court-appointed custodian of property, pending final determination of the rightful owner, is a fiduciary if the custodian is vested with broad discretionary powers of administration and management and, as such, is required to file a fiduciary's income tax return reporting income from the property (.30).

.05 Code Sec. 7701(a)(6).
.10 Reg. §§301.7701-6 and 301.7701-7.
.15 *Nat'l City Bank of N.Y.*, DC NY, 37-2 USTC ¶9423, 9562, 9596, 21 FSupp 791.
.20 Code Sec. 1398; Rev. Rul. 68-48, 1968-1 CB 301; Rev. Rul. 73-94, 1973-1 CB 322.
.25 Code Sec. 1399.
.30 Rev. Rul. 69-300, 1969-1 CB 167.

¶25,143 Compensation for Services. The rule that all compensation for personal services, regardless of the form of payment (whether cash, notes, stock, commissions, fringe benefits or other property), is taxable applies to commissions paid to a fiduciary for his services (.05). Of course, a fiduciary, such as an executor, may waive his right to commissions allowed under state law. The crucial test of whether a fiduciary may waive his right to receive statutory commissions without incurring any income or gift tax liability is whether the waiver involved gives evidence of a primary intent to render a gratuitous service.

Intent to serve on gratuitous basis

The requisite intention to serve on a gratuitous basis will ordinarily be deemed to have been adequately manifested if the fiduciary supplies one or more of the principal beneficiaries, within six months after his initial appointment as fiduciary, with a formal waiver of any right to compensation for his services. The intention to serve gratuitously may also be adequately shown through an implied waiver, if the fiduciary fails to claim fees or commissions at the time of filing the usual accountings and if all the other attendant facts and circumstances are consistent with a fixed, continuing intention to serve gratuitously. Thus, for example, if an executor or administrator claims his statutory fees or commissions as a deduction on one or more of the estate, inheritance, or income tax returns that are filed on behalf of an estate, such action will ordinarily be considered inconsistent with any fixed or definite intention to serve on a gratuitous basis (.10). An assignment of fees to a third party will not prevent taxation to the executor, even if the assignment is to compensate the third party for work performed for the estate (.15).

.05 Code Sec. 61; Reg. §1.61-2.
.10 Rev. Rul. 66-167, 1966-1 CB 20, clarifying Rev. Rul. 56-472, 1956-2 CB 21, and distinguishing Rev. Rul. 64-225, 1964-2 CB 15.
.15 *J. O'Connell*, 41 TCM 62, CCH Dec. 37,302(M), TC Memo. 1980-432, aff'd by CA-2 in an unpublished opinion.

¶25,144 Fiduciaries as Beneficiaries. There is nothing unusual about naming a beneficiary of an estate or trust as its executor or trustee (.05). The fiduciary and the estate or trust for which he acts are separate taxable entities, even though the fiduciary may be the sole beneficiary. Thus, a trustee who is also the beneficiary of the trust should file a return for the trust, and he should report this income on his individual return.

.05 Code Sec. 6012; Reg. §1.6012-3.

¶25,145 Bequest in Lieu of Commissions. Although an executor's fees or commissions for services performed for the estate are taxable as compensation, the executor is not subject to income tax on a bequest from the estate, because bequests are tax-free gifts for income tax purposes (.05). This rule applies as long as a bequest to an executor, in lieu of a commission, is a recognized device for saving taxes for the executor (.10). To provide this benefit, the testator should make a bequest to the executor named in the will, state specifically that it is "in lieu of all compensation or commissions," and specify that the bequest is to be unconditionally payable whether or not the individual named as executor acts in this capacity.

.05 Code Sec. 102; Reg. §1.102-1.

.10 *F. L. Merriam*, SCt, 1 USTC ¶84, 263 U.S. 179; Rev. Rul. 57-398, 1957-2 CB 93, distinguished by Rev. Rul. 67-375, 1967-2 CB 60. See, also, *R. C. Ream v. Bowers*, CA-2, 1 USTC ¶257, 22 F2d 465.

¶25,146 Commissions as Self-Employment Income. Fees received by professional fiduciaries (.05) are always treated as earnings from self-employment, regardless of the assets contained in the estate (.10).

Generally, fees received by nonprofessional fiduciaries (for example, persons who serve as executors or administrators in isolated instances, usually as personal representatives for the estate of a deceased friend or relative) are not treated as self-employment income unless all of the following conditions are met:

(1) one of the assets of the estate is a trade or business;

(2) the executor actively participates in the operation of this trade or business; and

(3) the fees of the executor are related to the operation of the trade or business.

Only that part of a nonprofessional fiduciary's fees that is received from the trade or business is subject to the self-employment tax.

In some cases, the activities of the executor of a single estate may amount to the conduct of a trade or business even though the assets of the estate do not include a trade or business as such. If, for example, an executor manages an estate that requires extensive management activities on the executor's part over a long period of time, such activities may be of sufficient scope and duration to amount to the carrying on of a trade or business.

.05 Code Sec. 1402; Reg. §1.1402(c)-1.

.10 Rev. Rul. 58-5, 1958-1 CB 322, as distinguished by Rev. Rul. 72-86, 1972-1 CB 273.

¶25,147 Employer or Employee—Income Tax Withholding. Generally, a fiduciary, whether a receiver, trustee in bankruptcy, or representative of an estate or liquidator of a bank, is not an employee with respect to the services performed in a fiduciary capacity (.05). It is only under unusual circumstances that a fiduciary becomes the employee of an estate or trust. This may occur, however, where two or more fiduciaries engage one of their number to perform certain services for the estate that are specifically recognized as being outside the scope of the fiduciary's official duties and that fiduciary is subject to the supervision and control of the others and is paid extra compensation for such services (.10). In those cases, income tax withholding applies to the remuneration for those special services only.

On the other hand, persons performing services for a trust or estate administered by a fiduciary are generally employees of the trust or estate (.15), and the withholding and related returns are required to be handled by the fiduciary on behalf of the trust or estate (.20). This rule applies not only to trusts, but also to corporations and estates whose affairs are being administered or liquidated by trustees in bankruptcy or by state or federal receivers, including bank liquidators (.25). For this reason, a trustee in bankruptcy with authority to pay the wage claims of former employees of a bankrupt was held to be responsible for the withholding taxes on behalf of the bankrupt employer (.30).

.05 Code Sec. 3401; Reg. §§31.3401(c)-1 and 31.3401(d)-1.

.10 Rev. Rul. 69-656, 1969-2 CB 188.

.15 Code Sec. 3401.

.20 Code Sec. 3504; Reg. §31.3504-1.

.25 Rev. Rul. 69-657, 1969-2 CB 189.

.30 *E.L. Fogarty*, CA-8, 47-2 USTC ¶9383, 164 F2d 26.

¶25,148 Notice of Fiduciary Relationship. Every person acting for a taxpayer in a fiduciary capacity is required to give notice in writing of that capacity to the IRS (.05). The IRS has provided Form 56 (Notice Concerning Fiduciary Relationship) for this purpose. As soon as the notice is filed, the fiduciary assumes the powers, rights, duties, and privileges of the taxpayer whom the fiduciary represents, or, if an estate is the taxpayer, of the estate for which the fiduciary is responsible. The same applies if the fiduciary acts for the transferee of a taxpayer.

The function of the notice of fiduciary relationship is to assure receipt by the fiduciary of the statutory notice of deficiency determined against an estate, trust, transferee, or other person for whom he is acting, and thus to afford him an opportunity of contesting the deficiency. A failure to file the fiduciary notice may otherwise prejudice the interests of the person the fiduciary is representing. For example, in the absence of such a notice, the sending of the deficiency notice to the last known address of the taxpayer, transferee, or other person will be sufficient compliance with the deficiency notice rules (.10) even though the taxpayer, transferee, or other person may be deceased, or, in the case of a corporation, may have terminated its existence.

The notice of fiduciary relationship must be in writing, signed by the fiduciary, and filed with the IRS office where the person for whom the fiduciary is acting is required to file a return. It must state the name and address of the person for whom the fiduciary is acting and the nature of the liability of such person; that is, whether it is a liability for tax, and, if so, the year or years involved, or a liability at law or in equity of the transferee of property of a taxpayer, or a liability of a fiduciary. Unless satisfactory evidence of authority of the fiduciary to act for such person in a fiduciary capacity is already on file with the IRS, this evidence must be filed with and made a part of the notice. If the fiduciary capacity exists by order of a court, a certified copy of the order may be regarded as satisfactory evidence.

Trustees in bankruptcy, executors, receivers, a debtor in possession of property, assignees for the benefit of creditors, and other fiduciaries in control of the assets of a debtor are also required to notify the IRS of the appointment or authorization to act as a receiver or like fiduciary. The notice must be given in writing within 10 days after the appointment or authorization. However, if written notice has been given to the Secretary or other appropriate officer of the Treasury as required by Title 11 of the Bankruptcy Act, then separate notice to the IRS is not necessary. Executors and administrators who are also required to give notice of fiduciary relationship (above) will be treated as having complied with this requirement if they give the notice of qualification as executors or receivers.

Termination of fiduciary capacity

When the fiduciary capacity has terminated, the fiduciary, in order to be relieved of any further duty or liability as such, should file with the IRS written notice that the fiduciary capacity has terminated. This notice must be accompanied by satisfactory evidence of the termination of the fiduciary capacity. Form 56 may also be used to notify the IRS of the termination of the fiduciary relationship. The notice of termination should state the name and address of the person, if any, who has been substituted as fiduciary.

The IRS is not authorized to waive notice that a fiduciary has been discharged. Consequently, even though the IRS's answer to a petition filed in the Tax Court concedes that a fiduciary had been discharged, such admission is not an admission that the statutory responsibility of a fiduciary for a tax was terminated (.15).

The termination notice cannot, of course, affect any liability for taxes already incurred by the fiduciary.

.05 Code Sec. 6036 and Code Sec. 6903; Reg. §§301.6036-1 and 301.6903-1.

.10 Code Sec. 6212.

.15 M.M. *Sanborn*, CA-8, 40-1 USTC ¶9173, 108 F2d 311; *C. Coates Est.*, 52 TCM 1122, CCH Dec. 43,523(M), TC Memo. 1987-383.

¶25,149 Personal Liability for Payment of Tax. An executor or administrator of an estate or the trustee of a trust must make and file a Form 1041 (U.S. Fiduciary Income Tax Return) and pay the tax on the taxable income of the estate or trust (.05). The tax is ordinarily collectible from the estate or trust, or from the estate of a transferee or other persons subject to liability for taxes of another as the transferee of property.

In effect, every executor, administrator, or assignee or other person who pays, in whole or in part, any debt due by the person or estate for whom or for which he acts, without first satisfying and paying debts due the United States, is personally liable to the extent of such payments (.10).

The debts due the United States must have been determined or determinable at the time the other debts were paid. The fiduciary must also have been "chargeable" with knowledge of the debts due the United States (.15). Generally, this means that the fiduciary must either have personal knowledge of the debt or have such knowledge as would put a reasonably prudent person on inquiry (.20). The burden of proving lack of knowledge of the debt shifts to the fiduciary once the government makes a prima facie case (.25). Despite receiving notice of an estate's potential income tax liability, an executor's good faith reliance on the advice of counsel that no tax was owed the government can suffice to show lack of knowledge, (.30) but not if the executor had actual knowledge of the estate's liability and litigation over the extent of that liability. (.35)

According to the Tax Court (.40), before liability can attach to the fiduciary, the fiduciary must have had a choice between payment of the tax due and payment of a debt owed by the estate. However, a fiduciary may not take advantage of this rule by hastening payment of debts and distribution of an estate before federal taxes are finally determined in order to avoid personal responsibility for the taxes (.45). Thus, a fiduciary should not make distributions before the IRS's examination of the final return is completed, particularly if there is a difference of opinion (or possibility thereof) as to treatment of an item.

There is no personal liability on the part of a fiduciary for amounts paid on debts that have priority over federal taxes. Such debts include probate costs of administration, expenses for the decedent's funeral and headstone (.50), and the statutory allowance to a surviving spouse required by local law where the assets used in payment of the allowance are assets of the estate (.55). A distinction was made where the assets used to pay the allowance were assets to which the estate was not entitled but which it, as transferee, held subject to liabilities of the insolvent transferor (.60).

To facilitate closing the estate and to avoid personal liability, after the tax return has been filed, an executor, administrator or other fiduciary of a decedent's estate may file a written request for prompt assessment of taxes with the IRS office where the return was filed. See ¶25,155 (.65). In order to indemnify himself against personal liability for taxes later found due, a fiduciary who distributes property may safeguard his interests in doubtful cases by exacting a bond from the distributees.

See ¶25,151 as to transferee liability of the executor or administrator.

Discharge of fiduciary by state court

Discharge of the administrator or executor by the state probate court does not terminate his liability where he paid the other debts of the estate without satisfying a prior claim for federal taxes (.70).

Release from personal liability

An executor of an estate may also request a release from personal liability for the decedent's income and gift taxes (.75). The request must be made after the income or gift tax return is filed. In such situations, the IRS may notify the executor of the amount of such taxes. Upon payment of the amount of which the executor is notified, or nine months after the receipt of the application for discharge if the executor is not notified of any payments due, the executor is discharged from personal liability for any income or gift taxes thereafter found to be due by reason of the tax liability of the decedent.

.05 Code Sec. 641, 6012, 6036, 6905; 31 USC §3713; Reg. §§1.641(b)-2, 1.6012-3, and 301.6036-1.

.10 Code Sec. 6901; *L.L. Morris*, 36 BTA 516, CCH Dec. 9750; Reg. §1.641(b)-2.

.15 *Irving Trust Co.*, 36 BTA 146, CCH Dec. 9684 (Acq.).

.20 Rev. Rul. 66-43, 1966-1 CB 291.

.25 *L.T. McCourt*, 15 TC 734, CCH Dec. 17,951.

.30 *W.D. Little*, 113 TC 474, Dec. 53,676.

.35 *E. Bartlett*, DC Ill., 2002-1 USTC ¶60,429.

.40 *G.P. Fitzgerald*, 4 TC 494, CCH Dec. 14,291.

.45 *J.T. Hurst*, DC Wyo., 1925 CCH ¶7017, 2 F2d 73; *Pennsylvania Cement Co. v. Bradley Contracting Co.*, DC N.Y., 274 Fed. 1003.

.50 *K. Weisburn*, DC Pa., 43-1 USTC ¶9247, 48 FSupp 393.

.55 *J. Smith*, 24 BTA 807, CCH Dec. 7275.

.60 *L.T. McCourt*, 15 TC 734, CCH Dec. 17,951.

.65 Code Sec. 6501(d).

.70 *M. Viles*, CA-6, 56-1 USTC ¶9539, 233 F2d 376.

.75 Code Sec. 6905.

¶25,150 Enforcing the Fiduciary's Personal Liability. Generally, the personal liability of a fiduciary is assessed, collected, and paid in the same way as a deficiency in tax.

Criminal penalties, however, may be imposed when the fiduciary willfully fails to make a return when required by law or regulations to do so or when the fiduciary willfully attempts in any manner to evade or defeat the tax. These penalties are in addition to the civil penalties applicable to the tax due by the estate or trust.

The estate of a decedent is liable for civil penalties incurred by the decedent during his lifetime (.05). These civil penalties are remedial compensation for loss to the federal government, and not personal punishment (.10). Thus, they survive the death of the taxpayer.

Estates of mentally disabled, deceased, or insolvent persons are not exempt from penalties for delinquencies or violations, because the administrators, executors, etc., are personally liable in such cases.

.05 *F.P. Kirk (Briden Est.)*, CA-1, 50-1 USTC ¶9169, 179 F2d 619; *M. J. Reimer Est.*, 12 TC 913, CCH Dec. 16,997, aff'd *per curiam* by CA-6, 50-1 USTC ¶9189, 180 F2d 159; Rev. Rul. 73-293, 1973-2 CB 413.

.10 *C.E. Mitchell*, SCt, 38-1 USTC ¶9152, 303 U.S. 391; Rev. Rul. 73-293, 1973-2 CB 413.

¶25,151 Transferee Liability of Executor or Administrator. Generally, a transferee is liable for the taxes already accrued (.05) against the transferor before the transfer (.10) to the extent of the value of the property transferred (.15), if the transferor was insolvent at the time of the transfer or was made insolvent by the transfer (.20). This rule holds even if the property was previously gifted to the transferee with gift taxes paid in full and included in the estate only because it was transferred within three years of the decedent's death (.25). If a transferee received the property from a preceding transferee, then the liability is the same as that of the preceding transferee. Where there are several transferees, the IRS may proceed against any one of them to collect the entire tax, to the extent of the property received by him. That transferee will then have a right of contribution from the other transferees (.30).

Taxes are assessed and collected from the transferee of property of a taxpayer in the same way as any other deficiency imposed by the IRS. When a deficiency is determined against an estate, the executor, as transferee, is liable for the unpaid taxes as a representative of the decedent's estate, not as a fiduciary (.35). This is an important distinction, because it means that the government has recourse against the estate, heirs, legatees, devisees, or transferees of the property of the estate, but not against the executor personally (see ¶25,149).

If the insolvency of the estate results from the failure of the personal representative to observe priority of payment of debts and legacies, it seems that the IRS may elect to proceed against the fiduciary to enforce his personal liability, against the estate, against the fiduciary as representative of the estate, or against the beneficiary, or it may invoke several remedies to the extent necessary for the collection of the tax.

See ¶25,150 as to personal liability of the executor or administrator.

.05 Code Sec. 6901; Reg. §§301.6901-1 and 301.6902-1.

.10 *Western Union Telegraph Co.*, CA-2, 3 USTC ¶1200, 68 F2d 16, cert. den., 292 U.S. 636; *Est. of V. DeNiro*, 38 TCM 721, CCH Dec. 36,042(M), TC Memo. 1979-168.

.15 *R.T. Buzard*, CA-DC, 35-1 USTC ¶9288, 77 F2d 391.

.20 *S. Keller*, CA-7, 3 USTC ¶964, 59 F2d 499; *R.L. Ewart*, 85 TC 544, CCH Dec. 42,432.

.25 *Armstrong, III v Commr*, 114 TC 94, Dec 53,765 (2000).

.30 *A.G. Phillips*, SCt, 2 USTC ¶743, 283 U.S. 589.

.35 *Est. of L.E. McKnight*, 8 TC 871, CCH Dec. 15,736.

¶25,152 Insurance Proceeds Received by Fiduciary. When an executor, administrator or trustee receives life insurance proceeds for a beneficiary of the estate or trust for which he acts, his liability with respect to such assets is probably no different from what it would be for other assets. Without some special provision in federal or state law, the life insurance proceeds received by an estate or trust might not seem to have special status freeing it as a source for the collection of unpaid income taxes. However, it is possible that, because the beneficiary of the estate or trust is an individual within a special state law category, the life insurance proceeds received by the estate or trust would be entitled to the same protection. Therefore, the U.S. Supreme Court's decisions in *J.F. Stern* (.05) and *M.G. Bess* (.10) may affect the fiduciary's duty in this area. In these cases, the U.S. Supreme Court stated that recovery of unpaid federal income taxes from a beneficiary of life insurance, in the absence of a lien, may be sustained only to the extent that state law imposes liability on the beneficiary in favor of other creditors of the insured. Although the cases dealt specifically with life insurance, they affect the entire field of transferee liability, because the Court:

(1) clearly stated that the existence and extent of transferee liability are to be determined under state law;

(2) apparently recognized the need for formal notice and demand by the government in order to establish a lien, and may have broadened the area in which a recipient or adverse claimant to a tax debtor's property could argue that no lien came into existence because the taxpayer had not refused or neglected to pay the tax even after notice and demand; and

(3) may have modified the extent to which a transferee of an insolvent taxpayer is liable for the debtor's taxes. (It is the prevailing view that the transferee is liable to the full extent of the property received.)

What the Court specifically decided in *Stern* was that, under Kentucky law, a beneficiary of life insurance proceeds was not liable as a transferee for any part of the decedent's unpaid taxes. In *Bess*, the Court reached the same conclusion under New Jersey law, except that, in this instance, the IRS had made notice and demand for taxes during the decedent's lifetime and, because he had "refused" to make payment, a lien against the cash surrender values of his policies came into existence, survived his death, and could be enforced against the amounts received by the beneficiary.

.05 *J.F. Stern*, SCt, 58-2 USTC ¶9594, 357 U.S. 39.

.10 *M.G. Bess*, SCt, 58-2 USTC ¶9595, 357 U.S. 51.

¶25,153 Filing the Claim for Credit or Refund. A fiduciary is the proper person to file a claim for credit or refund of overpayments made by an estate or trust (.05). This fiduciary duty may be overlooked with respect to an estate because of the estate's short duration and the desire of the heirs or legatees to curtail administrative expenses.

The administrators or executors of a deceased taxpayer may file claims for refund if they are acting as such at the time. Upon their discharge, the right passes to the beneficiaries entitled to the estate. A beneficiary could be a trustee if the decedent created a testamentary trust. Signature of only one coexecutor is required on the claim (.10).

Claims for refund of income tax generally are made using the type of income tax form previously filed. Thus, a claim for a refund for taxes reported on Form 1041 is made by filing an amended Form 1041. However, a claim for a refund of taxes reported and paid on Form 1040, 1040A or 1040-EZ (U.S. Individual Income Tax Return) is to be made using Form 1040X (Amended U.S. Individual Income Tax Return). Claims for refunds of taxes other than income taxes, such as an overpayment of estate tax, should be made on Form 843 (Claim for Refund and Request for Abatement).

If a refund claim is filed with respect to a return that had been filed by the individual prior to death, the fiduciary must attach certified copies of the letters testamentary, letters of administration or similar evidence to establish authority to file the claim. Further, if the person filing the claim is not the surviving spouse or a court-appointed representative, a completed Form 1310 (Statement of Person Claiming Refund Due a Deceased Taxpayer) must be attached to the appropriate claim form.

.05 Code Sec. 6402; Reg. § §301.6402-2 and 301.6402-3.

.10 Rev. Rul. 54-468, 1954-2 CB 248.

¶25,154 Joint Return by the Surviving Spouse. A surviving spouse may file a joint return on Form 1040 or 1040A for the tax year in which the other spouse died if no return for the tax year has been made by the decedent and if no personal representative has been appointed (.05). If an executor or administrator is appointed on or before the last day for filing the return of the surviving spouse, the surviving spouse may not independently elect to make a joint return, regardless of whether a separate return for the deceased spouse is made by the executor or administrator. However, the surviving spouse and the deceased's legal representative may join together to file a joint return on behalf of the deceased and the surviving spouse. The surviving spouse loses the right to file a joint return with the deceased if the survivor remarries before the close of the tax year in which the decedent's death occurs.

The executor or administrator thereafter appointed may disaffirm the surviving spouse's election to file a joint return by filing a separate return for the tax year of the decedent with respect to which the joint return was made. In order for this disaffirmance to be effective, it must be made within one year after the last day for filing the surviving spouse's return (including any extension of time). Thus, if a joint return is going to be made, it should be made by both the executor or administrator and the surviving spouse.

If the return is filed by the executor or administrator, it must be signed by the executor or administrator on the line indicated for the taxpayer. For example, an executor would sign "John Smith, Executor of the Last Will and Testament of John Brown, Deceased." If the legal representative is the administrator of an intestate estate, then that representative would sign as follows: "John Smith, Administrator of the Estate of John Brown, Deceased." A certified copy of Letters Testamentary or Letters of Administration, as appropriate, should accompany the return.

Where a refund is due, Form 1310 must also be filed, unless the return is being made by the surviving spouse and/or a court-appointed representative.

.05 Code Sec. 6013(a)(3); Reg. §1.6013-1.

¶25,155 Request for Prompt Assessment. A fiduciary may shorten the regular three-year period (after the return is filed) for the assessment and collection of any tax other than estate tax due from a decedent's estate (.05). The prompt assessment request privilege does not apply to trusts. Special rules apply to corporations. See ¶22,445.

The effect of such a request is to limit the time in which an assessment of tax may be made, or the time that a proceeding in court without assessment for collection of tax may be begun, to a period of 18 months from the date the request is received by the proper District Director. The request will not extend the time within which an assessment may be made, or the time that a proceeding in court without assessment may be begun, beyond three years from the date the return was filed. This special period of limitations will not apply to any return filed after a request for prompt assessment has been made, unless an additional request is filed. Nor does the privilege apply if the income tax returns filed by the decedent or estate were fraudulent.

To shorten the assessment and collection period, the fiduciary must file a written request for prompt assessment with the IRS office where the regular return was filed. (This office will usually be an IRS Service Center.) The request, in order to be effective, must set forth the classes of tax and the period for which the prompt assessment is requested, and must clearly indicate that it is a request for prompt assessment. The request must also be filed after the return in question has been filed and must be transmitted to the IRS in an envelope separate from any other document. Form 4810 (Request for Prompt Assessment Under Internal Revenue Code Sec. 6501(d)) may be used for this purpose.

.05 Code Sec. 6501(d); Reg. §301.6501(d)-1.

Tax Characteristics of Estate and Trusts

¶25,157 Fiduciary's Involvement for Income Tax Purposes. In whatever capacity a fiduciary may act, whether as the guardian of a minor, the guardian of an incompetent, an executor or administrator, receiver, trustee, conservator, or in any other fiduciary capacity, he is almost certain to become involved with some phase of income taxation. In this connection, the taxation of estates and trusts is one of the major areas of involvement for the fiduciary. This being so, the following material focuses on such tax entities primarily as a means of demonstrating to the executor, administrator, or trustee the federal income tax problems that may be encountered.

¶25,158 Estates and Trusts as Tax Entities. Trusts and estates of deceased persons are separate and distinct tax entities for federal income tax purposes (.05). They are subject to the same income taxes (but not the self-employment tax) as individuals, with certain differences in the computation of credits and deductions. Furthermore, the gross income of an estate or trust is generally determined in the same way as that of an individual. An estate or trust files an income tax return and pays its tax, if any, through a fiduciary, without regard to the tax year or accounting method of the decedent, grantor, or "predecessor estate" (in the case of a testamentary trust) from whom assets were received.

Estates

The estate of a minor, incompetent, or other person under a disability, or of an individual or corporation in receivership or bankruptcy is not a taxable entity separate from the person for whom the fiduciary is acting. Thus, the tax treatment differs in that respect from the estate of a deceased person or a trust. For tax treatment of bankruptcy estates, see ¶25,657 and following.

When a taxpayer dies, the late taxpayer's tax role is taken on by a new taxable entity, the taxpayer's estate. The estate must go through a process of administration under the supervision of a court. This process is necessary to ensure that the wishes of the deceased are carried out in orderly fashion. Even if these wishes were not expressed (i.e., if no will was executed), it is still necessary that the estate be distributed according to the laws of the state. Before administration may begin, the court must authorize the personal representative (termed the "executor" if the decedent left a will in which a representative was nominated, or the "administrator" if there was no will or if a will did not name a representative to proceed with settlement of the estate).

Trusts

In general, the trusts considered here are created either by a will or by an *inter vivos* (lifetime) declaration whereby trustees take title to property for the purpose of protecting or conserving it for the beneficiaries under the ordinary rules applied in chancery or probate courts. Usually, the beneficiaries of such a trust do no more than accept its benefits and are not the voluntary planners or creators of the trust arrangement. However, the beneficiaries of such a trust may be the persons who create it, and it will be recognized as a trust for federal income tax purposes if it has been created for the purpose of protecting or conserving the trust property for beneficiaries who stand in the same relation to the trust as they would if the trust had been created by others for them.

Generally, an arrangement will be treated as a trust for federal income tax purposes if it can be shown that the purpose of the arrangement is to vest in trustees responsibility for the protection and conservation of property for beneficiaries who cannot share in the discharge of this responsibility and who, therefore, are not associates in a joint enterprise for the conduct of business for profit. However, an attempt to create a trust will be unsuccessful and the trust will be disregarded if the grantor retains certain prohibited rights and powers. In this case, the income is taxed to the grantor as if no trust existed.

There are other arrangements that are known as trusts because the legal title to property is conveyed to trustees for the benefit of beneficiaries, but that are not classified as trusts for federal income tax purposes because they are not simply arrangements to protect or conserve the property for the beneficiaries. These trusts, often known as business or commercial trusts, generally are created by the beneficiaries as a device to carry on a profit-making business that normally would be carried on through business organizations classified as corporations or partnerships for tax purposes.

☐ See, also, "Grantor trusts" at ¶25,175.

However, the fact that the corpus of the trust is not supplied by the beneficiaries is not sufficient reason in itself for classifying the arrangement as an ordinary trust rather than as an association or partnership. The fact that any organization is technically cast in the trust form, by conveying title to property to trustees for the benefit of persons designated as beneficiaries, does not change the real character of the organization if the organization more nearly resembles an association or a partnership than a trust. For example, where, under the terms of a trust agreement, the beneficiaries have the sole right to operate the trust property, such operation results in the creation of a partnership or joint venture for federal income and self-employment tax purposes (.10). On the other hand, a trust established by a decedent to run his family business was not classified as an association because it did not include any parties who had freely associated together to form a business enterprise (.15).

.05 Code Sec. 641 and 7701; Reg. §§1.641(b)-2 and 301.7701-4.

.10 Rev. Rul. 64-220, 1964-2 CB 335.

.15 *H.M. Bedell, Jr.*, 86 TC 1207, CCH Dec. 43,116 (Acq.).

¶25,159 Principle for Taxing Estates and Trusts. The underlying principle in the taxation of estates and trusts is that all income of whatever kind and from whatever source derived (other than exempt income, such as tax-free interest on municipal obligations, etc.) is taxable to someone (.05): to the trust or estate, to the beneficiary, or, less frequently, to the grantor (.10). (See, also, ¶25,216.) Regardless of who is taxed, the income retains the same character, and the taxpayer is allowed the credits, exclusions, capital gain benefits (see ¶25,181), or other privileges attaching to the income on which the tax is imposed. This is the "conduit" rule for taxing estates and trusts. (See, also, ¶25,197.)

.05 Code Sec. 641; Reg. §1.641(a)-0.

.10 Code Sec. 673-677.

¶25,160 Period of Estate's Existence. The estate of a deceased person exists as long as is necessary for the executor or administrator to perform the ordinary duties of administration, such as the collection of assets and the payment of debts, taxes, legacies and bequests (.05). This is so regardless of whether the period is longer or shorter than the period specified under local law for the settlement of estates, although the IRS has ruled that local law may be considered in reaching a decision as to when the estate has ceased to exist (.10).

> ***Example:*** An executor, who is also named as trustee under a will, fails to obtain his discharge as executor. The period of estate administration continues only until his duties of administering the estate as executor are complete and he actually assumes his duties as trustee, whether or not pursuant to a court order.

Undue delay

As a general rule, where the executor or administrator is not the sole beneficiary, final distribution of the assets to the beneficiaries determines the closing of administration of the estate. The period of administration of an estate may not be unduly prolonged, however. If the administration of an estate is unreasonably prolonged, the estate is considered terminated for federal income tax purposes after the expiration of a reasonable period for the performance by the executor of all the duties of administration.

Further, an estate will be considered terminated when all assets have been distributed except for a reasonable amount that is set aside in good faith for the payment of unascertained or contingent liabilities and expenses (not including a claim by a beneficiary in the capacity of beneficiary). Administration of an estate may, thus, be considered complete even in the face of an unsettled federal tax liability (.15).

Whether there is undue delay in winding up an estate is a question of fact to be determined in every case. Continuance of the estate has been upheld where litigation was pending (.20) and where the principal creditor was still unpaid (.25). But where debts had been paid, administration was effectively ended notwithstanding provision for the decedent's personal representative to take his place as a partner for five years (.30), to hold property subject to partnership and annuity claims (.35), to continue collections on a debt owed the estate, or to continue operation of the decedent's business because of its extensive holdings, or to build up its credit rating (.40). If an estate is considered terminated for federal income tax purposes, then the gross income, deductions and credits of the estate are, subsequent to the termination, considered the gross income, deductions and credits of the person (or persons) succeeding to the estate's property (.45).

.05 Code Sec. 641; Reg. §1.641(b)-3.

.10 Rev. Rul. 73-397, 1973-2 CB 211.

.15 *L.V. Kohn*, 16 BTA 662, CCH Dec. 5196 (Nonacq.).

.20 *E.W. Brown, Jr.*, CA-5, 54-2 USTC ¶9591, 215 F2d 679; *I. Stephenson*, 33 BTA 252, CCH Dec. 9105 (Acq.).

.25 *H.R. King*, 3 TCM 11, CCH Dec. 13,678(M).

.30 *J. Stewart*, CA-5, 52-1 USTC ¶9315, 196 F2d 397.

.35 *S.N. LeFiell*, 19 TC 1162, CCH Dec. 19,542.

.40 *W.G. Farrier Est.*, 15 TC 277, CCH Dec. 17,846 (Acq.).

.45 Reg. §1.641(b)-3(d); *A.T. Miller*, CA-8, 64-2 USTC ¶9579, 333 F2d 400.

¶25,161 Estate Representative's Title to Personal Property. The passing of title to an executor or administrator on the death of the decedent is not a realization of income by the estate, even though the property may have appreciated in value after its acquisition by the decedent (.05). Upon acceptance of the appointment, title to all personal property belonging to the estate vests in the administrator or executor as of the date of the decedent's death. This vesting of title is deemed necessary for the proper administration of the estate and for its distribution.

Upon distribution, the title to personal property is regarded, for tax purposes, as having passed to the legatees on the date of the decedent's death (.10). The interim title vests in the executor or administrator as a matter of convenience and necessity only, but income from personal property nevertheless is taxable to the legatee then holding title.

.05 Code Sec. 641.

.10 *E.F. Brewster*, SCt, 2 USTC ¶451, 280 U.S. 327.

¶25,162 Period of Existence of a Trust. The trust entity begins when legal title to property is transferred to a trustee who undertakes to hold and manage the property for the benefit of designated beneficiaries (.05). It may be created by a will (testamentary) or during a person's lifetime (*inter vivos* trust). Generally, a testamentary trust may begin only when the estate terminates, and it is not permissible for a testamentary trust and an estate to be in existence simultaneously to secure tax advantages (.10). Administration of an estate may be considered completed even though the estate has not yet been officially terminated (see ¶25,160).

Whether a trust has terminated depends upon whether the property held in trust has been distributed to the persons entitled to succeed to the property upon termination of the trust, rather than upon the technicality of whether or not the trustee has rendered his final accounting. A trust does not automatically terminate upon the happening of the event by which the duration of the trust may be measured. A reasonable time is permitted after such event for the trustee to perform the duties necessary to complete the administration of the trust.

Undue delay in winding up trust

The winding up of a trust, however, may not be unduly postponed. If distribution of the trust corpus is unreasonably delayed, the trust is considered terminated for federal income tax purposes after the expiration of a reasonable period for the trustee to complete the administration of the trust. In addition, a trust will be considered terminated when all the assets have been distributed except for a reasonable amount which has been set aside in good faith for the payment of unascertained or contingent liabilities and expenses (not including a claim by a beneficiary in the capacity of beneficiary).

.05 Code Sec. 641; Reg. §1.641(b)-3(b).

.10 *E.F. Britten, Jr.*, CA-3, 47-1 USTC ¶9273, 161 F2d 921.

¶25,163 Trustees as Partners. Regardless of state law, trusts may be recognized as general or limited partners for federal tax purposes (.05). A trustee who is unrelated to and independent of the grantor, and who participates as a partner and receives distribution of the income distributable to the trust, is recognized as a partner unless the grantor retains controls inconsistent with such ownership.

If the grantor is the trustee, or if the trustee is subservient to the grantor's will, then the provisions of the trust instrument (particularly as to whether the trustee is subject to the responsibilities of a fiduciary), the partnership agreement provisions, and the conduct of the parties are all considered in determining whether the trustee really owns the partnership interest. In such a case, the trust will be recognized as a partner only if the trustee actively represents and protects the interests of the beneficiaries and not those of the grantor (.10).

.05 Reg. §1.704-1(e)(2)(vii).

.10 *M. Kuney, Jr.*, CA-9, 62-2 USTC ¶9769, 308 F2d 719; *M.J. Kuney, Jr.*, CA-9, 71-2 USTC ¶9646, 448 F2d 22 and 75-2 USTC ¶9767, 524 F2d 795.

Return and Tax Payment Requirements for Estates and Trusts

¶25,165 When an Income Tax Return Must Be Filed. A fiduciary, the executor or administrator of an estate of a deceased person, or the trustee of a trust, must file a return on Form 1041 (U.S. Fiduciary Income Tax Return) for the estate or trust for which he acts (.05):

(1) when the gross income of the estate for the tax year is $600 or over, before making deductions allowed for amounts paid or credited to beneficiaries or amounts required to be currently distributed;

(2) when a trust (other than a tax-exempt Code Sec. 501(a) trust) has any taxable income for the tax year, or has gross income of $600 or over, regardless of the amount of taxable income; or

(3) when any beneficiary of the estate or trust is a nonresident alien, regardless of the amount of gross income.

In connection with item (2), above, a "complex" trust is entitled to a deduction for a personal exemption of $100. A "simple" trust (one that must, under its governing instrument, distribute all of its income currently and that makes no charitable gifts) is entitled to a $300 exemption.(.10) Thus, if a trust has less than $600 of gross income but has any taxable income left after deducting the $100 or $300 exemption, as the case may be, it may still have to file a return.

The filing requirements for trusts with charitable interests vary, depending on whether the trust is treated as a private foundation and on the type of charitable interest involved.

☐ As to joint fiduciaries, see ¶25,166.

Grantor trusts file Form 1040

There are two circumstances under which a Form 1041 should not be filed for a grantor trust:

(1) when the same person is both grantor and trustee (or co-trustee), and he is treated, by operation of law, as the owner of all trust assets for the year, all items of income, credit and deduction from the trust being reported on his individual Form 1040, and

(2) when a jointly filing husband and wife are the sole grantors, at least one is a trustee (or co-trustee) and one or both are treated, by operation of law, as the owner of

all trust assets for the year. The appropriate reporting should be made on their Form 1040.

Multiple trusts

A trustee for two or more trusts must make a separate return for each trust. Generally, as explained at ¶25,180 multiple trusts will be treated as a single trust.

Domiciliary and ancillary representatives

If an estate has both domiciliary and ancillary representatives, each must file a return (see ¶25,173).

Other documents

Upon a request by the IRS, the fiduciary must file with the return a copy of the will or trust instrument, accompanied by a written declaration of the fiduciary under penalty of perjury that it is a true and complete copy, and a statement indicating the provisions that determine the extent to which the income of the estate or trust is taxable to the estate, the trust, the beneficiaries, or the grantor.

.05 Code Sec. 6012; Reg. §1.6012-3(a). **.10** Code Sec. 642(b)(2).

¶25,166 Joint Fiduciaries. In case of an estate or trust having joint fiduciaries, the return may be made by only one of them (.05). The return must contain a statement that the fiduciary has sufficient knowledge of the affairs of the estate or trust for which the return is made to enable him to make the return, and that the return is, to the best of his knowledge and belief, true and correct.

.05 Code Sec. 6012(b)(5); Reg. §1.6012-3(c).

¶25,167 Accounting Period of Estate or Trust. In filing its first return, an estate may choose the same accounting period as the decedent (i.e., a calendar year or fiscal year), or it may choose a different accounting period (.05). Thus, if an estate came into existence on March 15, the estate could choose as its tax year the period ending on March 31 or February 28 of the next year, or the last day of any intervening month. If it chooses the same accounting period used by the decedent, its first return is for a short period to fill out the unexpired full year of the decedent. The first tax year of an estate begins the day after a decedent's death. There is no double taxation of decedent and estate, and no omission of income earned on the day of the decedent's death. The personal exemption of the estate need not be prorated.

The choice of a tax year is not a matter to be approached casually. It offers opportunities for important income tax savings. In making the choice, the executor needs information (or estimates) concerning probable duration of administration, probable estate income and the timing of its receipt, probable deductions of the estate and their timing, and the tax years and probable income and deductions of beneficiaries.

Because an estate is entitled to one $600 exemption each time it files a return, maximizing the number of tax periods can save taxes.

> ***Example:*** An estate comes into being on May 1 and it is expected that administration will take 10 months. The executor might simply proceed to wind up the estate and file a single return for the 10-month period May 1 through February 28. But, because an estate has no income in the year of final distribution, the $600 exemption will be wasted.
>
> On the other hand, suppose the executor chooses a fiscal year ending January 31. Here, he has a $600 exemption to offset against nine months of estate income. He may then proceed to close the estate and file another return for the final month of the estate's duration. By providing two tax periods where only one was required, the executor utilizes a $600 deduction that otherwise would have been wasted.

Trusts

Most trusts do not have the option of selecting fiscal tax years that estates are granted. Instead, trusts (other than tax-exempt and wholly charitable trusts) must use a calendar tax year (.10).

.05 Code Sec. 441, 443, 444 and 645; Reg. §§1.441-1(c) and 1.443-1(a)(2).

.10 Code Sec. 645.

¶25,168 Time to File Returns. Estates and trusts must file their returns on or before the 15th day of the 4th month following the close of the entity's tax year (.05).

If an executor is filing a decedent's final return (on Form 1040EZ, 1040A or 1040) for a short tax year, the due date is the same as if the decedent had lived to the end of his last tax year. Thus, if he had been on a calendar-year basis, the return would be due on or before April 15 following the close of the calendar year in which he died. If the decedent had been on a fiscal-year basis, the return would be due on or before the 15th day of the 4th month following the close of the fiscal year in which he died.

.05 Code Sec. 6012 and 6072; Reg. §§1.6013-3 and 1.6072-1.

¶25,169 Extension of Time to File Returns. The fiduciary of an estate may request an extension of time for filing Form 1041 (.05). This extension of time is not automatic, so it should be requested early enough to enable the IRS to act upon the request before the due date for filing the return. The request may be made on Form 2758 (Application for Extension of Time to File Certain Excise, Income, Information, and Other Returns). A tentative return on Form 1041 does not have to be filed with the request for an extension of time on Form 2758. The taxpayer must fill in the data on Form 2758, clearly describing the reasons that will cause the delay, and pay the estimated tax as computed on the form.

When an extension of time to file is denied, the return must be filed by the regular due date or 10 days from the date of denial, whichever is later. Elections required to be made within the time prescribed by law (including any extension thereof) for filing the return are timely made if the return is filed within the 10-day period, if granted (.10).

An automatic three-month filing extension is available to trusts upon filing Form 8736 (Application for Automatic Extension of Time to File Return for a U.S. Partnership, REMIC, or for Certain Trusts) with the IRS Service Center where the trust's return will be filed. The request must be filed on or before the due date of the return and the full amount of the trust's unpaid estimated tax liability must be remitted (.15).

Interest is charged at the current annual rate on the difference between the amount of tax shown on the request for the extension of time and the final return. It is computed for the period beginning on the date the tax is due and continues through the date of payment.

.05 Code Sec. 6081; Reg. §1.6081-1.

.10 Rev. Rul. 64-214, 1964-2 CB 472.

.15 Reg. §1.6081-6.

¶25,170 Estimated Tax Payments. Trusts and estates must make quarterly estimated tax payments in the same manner as individuals, except that an estate does not have to make such payments during its first two tax years (.05). Accordingly, the penalties for underpayment of income tax are applicable to trusts and estates as well as to individuals. The due dates of the estimated tax installments for a calendar year are April 15, June 15, September 15, and January 15 of the following year.

The balance of any tax required to be reported on Form 1041 (or, in a case where an executor or administrator is filing the final return of a decedent on Form 1040EZ, 1040A or 1040) is due and payable at the same time that the return is due. The return has to be filed with, and payment made to, the IRS Service Center specified in the instructions.

Crediting excess estimated tax payments to beneficiary

In the case of trusts making quarterly estimated payments, the trustee may elect to treat any amount of an excess estimated payment for any tax year of the trust as a payment made by a beneficiary or beneficiaries. Estates that make estimated tax payments in their final tax year may also take advantage of this election. The election must be made using Form 1041-T, "Allocation of Estimated Tax Payments to Beneficiaries," within 65 days after the end of the tax year for which the election is being made (March 6 for calendar tax years other than a leap year). The beneficiary who is treated as making the payment is deemed to receive a distribution on the last day of the trust's tax year for federal income tax purposes and is deemed to make a payment of estimated tax on January 15 following the tax year. These provisions apply only to the extent the payments of estimated tax made by the trust for the tax year exceed the tax shown as due on its return for the same tax year.

.05 Code Sec. 643(g), 6091, 6151 and 6654(l); Reg. §§1.6091-2 and 1.6151-1.

¶25,171 Extension of Time to Pay the Tax. An extension of time for filing a return does not generally extend the time for payment (.05). An extension of time to pay will be granted only if payment on the due date will result in "undue hardship." This means that the taxpayer will sustain substantial financial loss, not just financial inconvenience, if prompt payment is required. For example, having to liquidate assets below market value could constitute cause for an extension of time to pay. Even if the time for payment is postponed, interest is due from the statutory due date (see ¶22,257 and ¶22,239).

Payment of income tax. An application for extension of time to pay the tax shown on Form 1041 (or on Form 1040EZ, 1040A or 1040, if the administrator or executor is filing a final return for the decedent) is made on Form 1127 (Application for Extension of Time for Payment of Tax). The application must also be accompanied by a statement showing the financial condition of the estate or trust. Form 1127 must be filed with the IRS office where the tax is required to be paid on or before the date for payment of the tax. If an extension is justified, it will be granted for a period not exceeding six months (longer for taxpayers living abroad) from the date fixed for payment of the tax or an installment thereof. Ordinarily, security for the payment of the tax will have to be furnished. If a bond is furnished, the IRS may require an amount not greater than twice the amount of the tax.

Payment of estate and generation-skipping tax. An extension of time to pay estate and generation-skipping taxes may be granted upon application to the IRS. Form 4768 (Application for Extension of Time to File a Return and/or Pay U.S. Estate (and Generation-Skipping Transfer) Taxes) is used to request an extension to pay estate taxes, as well as to request an extension of time to file the estate tax returns. The extension is generally for 12 months, but may be for up to 10 years. As with a request for an extension of time to pay other taxes, the request must demonstrate why it is impractical or impossible to timely pay the tax. For example, the bulk of the estate assets are rights to receive payments in the future, and, thus, there is insufficient cash available for the payment of taxes.

Extension of time to pay deficiencies. Upon demonstration of reasonable cause and by use of the above-described procedures for application of an extension of time, the time for the payment of any deficiency of estate taxes may be extended for a reasonable period not to exceed four years from the date otherwise fixed for the payment of the deficiency (.10). If an estate elects to postpone payment of that part of the estate tax attributable to a reversionary or remainder interest, a portion of the outstanding liability may be prepaid without payment of accrued interest or acceleration of the remaining tax (.15).

.05 Code Sec. 6161.
.10 Code Sec. 6161(b)(2).
.15 Rev. Rul. 83-103, 1983-2 CB 238.

¶25,172 Resident Fiduciary for Nonresident Alien Beneficiary. A resident fiduciary for an estate or trust, any beneficiary of which is a nonresident alien, is required to file Form 1041, and also a return for the beneficiary (Form 1040NR (U.S. Nonresident Alien Income Tax Return)), in all cases in which such a return is required of the nonresident alien (.05). He is relieved of the duty of filing Form 1040NR for the nonresident alien beneficiary if the latter has appointed a person in the United States to act as his agent for the purpose of filing income tax returns. In such a case, the fiduciary has to make a return on Form 1041 and attach thereto a copy of the notice of appointment of such agent.

The fiduciary must also withhold income taxes from distributions to foreign beneficiaries. See ¶18,605.

.05 Code Sec. 6012; Reg. §1.6012-3.

¶25,173 "Ancillary" Fiduciaries. The domiciliary representative (the executor or administrator who is appointed to act for an estate in the state of domicile of the decedent) is required to include the entire income of the estate on Form 1041 (.05). It is not unusual for a decedent to have owned property in a state other than the state of his domicile. In such a case, administration may be granted in the foreign state to collect the assets and pay the debts there, bringing what remains into the general administration of the estate. This is referred to as "ancillary" administration by an "ancillary" representative.

An ancillary representative who collects income of a decedent from property located outside the state of the domicile of the decedent is required to file an information return on Form 1041, showing the gross income received by him and the deductions to be claimed against that income, including any amount of income properly paid or credited by the ancillary representative to a legatee, heir, or beneficiary.

As pointed out above, the domiciliary representative must file a return showing all the income and deductions of the estate, including that reported by the ancillary representative, and pay the entire tax due. Where the domiciliary representative is a nonresident alien and the ancillary representative is a resident or citizen, the ancillary representative must file the return otherwise required of the domiciliary representative and, therefore, would probably be allowed the estate's $600 exemption.

The information return of the ancillary representative of the estate is required to be filed with the District Director for the district in which the ancillary representative is located, or with an IRS Service Center as specified in the Form 1041 instructions.

.05 Code Sec. 6012; Reg. §1.6012-3(a) (3).

Income Taxable to the Estate or Trust

¶25,175 Determining Gross Income. Generally, the gross income of an estate or trust is determined in the same manner as that of an individual (.05). For instance, interest and rents earned and accrued after a decedent's death are includible in the gross income of an estate or trust to the same extent that they would be includible if received by an individual. A more definitive discussion of this area appears at ¶19,065.

The explanations that follow are keyed to a few of the collateral aspects of income realization. These involve the answers to questions concerning gain or loss on the passage of property to the fiduciary (¶25,177), sale of real estate for payment of legacies (¶25,178), transfer of personal property to a trust (¶25,179), the treatment of capital gains and losses (¶25,181) and the special relief provision applicable in the case of stock redemptions to pay death taxes (¶25,182).

Grantor trusts

It is important to remember that the grantor of a trust may be treated as owning income from the trust corpus, and such income is taxed to the grantor without regard to the existence of a trust, if:

(1) for transfers in trust generally after March 1, 1986, the trust corpus or income will revert to either the grantor or the grantor's spouse and the value of the reversionary interest, measured as of the inception of that portion of the trust, exceeds five percent of the value of that portion of the trust, unless the grantor or the grantor's spouse retains a reversionary interest that takes effect only upon the death of a minor lineal descendant (under age 21) (.10);

(2) for transfers in trust before March 2, 1986, the trust corpus or income will, or reasonably may be expected to, revert to him within 10 years after the transfer in trust (.15);

(3) the trust grantor or a nonadverse party, or both, may exercise a power of disposition over the beneficial enjoyment of the trust income or corpus (.20);

(4) administrative control of the trust is exercisable primarily for the grantor's benefit (.25);

(5) a grantor creates a trust and reserves a right to revoke it and the power to revoke amounts to a reversionary interest (.30); or

(6) trust income is, or in the discretion of the grantor or a nonadverse party may be, distributed to the grantor, held or accumulated for future distribution to the grantor, or applied to payment of premiums on life insurance covering the grantor, except policies irrevocably payable to charities (.35) (see also, ¶25,216).

.05 Code Sec. 641; Reg. §1.641(a)-2.
.10 Code Sec. 672 and 673.
.15 Code Sec. 673, prior to amendment by P.L. 99-514.
.20 Code Sec. 674.
.25 Code Sec. 675.
.30 Code Sec. 676.
.35 Code Sec. 677.

¶25,176 Alternative Minimum Tax. As in the case of other taxpayers, trusts and estates are subject to the alternative minimum tax (.05).

The alternative minimum tax on an estate or trust is the excess of the tentative minimum tax over the amount of the estate's or trust's regular tax.

☐ See ¶19,005 for the rules for calculating the alternative minimum tax for an estate or trust.

.05 Code Secs. 55-59.

¶25,177 Is Gain or Loss Realized on Passage of Property to the Fiduciary? With respect to property acquired from a decedent, no gain or loss from the passage of property to the executor or administrator from the decedent need be recognized (.05). For details, see ¶5180.

.05 Code Sec. 1014.

¶25,178 Income from Real Estate. State law determines whether income from real estate during the period of administration is taxable to the decedent's estate or to the heirs or devisees. Where state law provides that real property is subject to probate administration (whether through an administrator or executor), income derived from the property is taxable to the estate, even though legal title may pass directly to the heirs or devisees. However, if the administrator or executor is not entitled to possession or control of real property, income from the property is taxable to the heirs or devisees, and not to the estate. Even if the property is not subject to the personal representative's control, all or a part of a gain from a sale of real property is taxable to the estate to the extent that the property was sold, under state law, to raise funds for the administration of the estate (.05).

If a conversion by the terms of the will or the local law changes the realty into personalty, a sale of the real estate by the executor or administrator for any purpose changes the character thereof to the extent of making gain or loss attributable to the estate, and absolves from tax liability the heir or devisee who would otherwise possess and control the property.

The decedent's will may authorize the sale of real property, not only for the purpose of the payment of debts or legacies, but also because it is the express intention of the testator that the executor should conduct such a sale for the purpose of forestalling vexatious and expensive partition proceedings that could ensue with respect to an undivided ownership otherwise vesting in the devisees upon death. The sale for the purpose of payment of debts and legacies only would be clearly incidental in the ordinary administration of an estate.

It may seem that a distribution by an executor of real property to devisees by means of a sale (if it is determined the property is not susceptible of voluntary division by metes and bounds) is no different in principle from a sale for payment of general legacies. However, the extent of the power of an executor to carry out a division and distribution of real property in this manner, and the ensuing question of whether the direction in the will itself effected a conversion of the realty into personalty, depends wholly upon the express provisions of the will and the local law. It may develop, for instance, that the executor in such a case has, in the beginning, no title to the property, but only a power in trust to sell if the devisees cannot agree to a voluntary division of the real estate.

As stated in one case, a "mere donee of a power is not the owner of an estate, nor to be classed as a juristic entity to which a loss can be attributed" (.10). If the converse were true, gain or loss on a sale would be attributable to the devisees and not to the estate. On the other hand, a view might be taken under local law that, in directing a partition of the property, the executors were charged with active duties not susceptible of fulfillment without possession and dominion of title from the inception of the estate. Inquiry may also be directed to the question of whether such a provision in the will created a discretionary or a mandatory power in the executor.

.05 Rev. Rul. 57-133, 1957-1 CB 200; Rev. Rul. 59-375, 1959-2 CB 161; Rev. Rul. 75-61, 1975-1 CB 180.

.10 *M.S. Wilson,* SCt, 3 USTC ¶1066, 289 U.S. 20.

¶25,179 Transfer of Personal Property to a Trust. It is the general rule that income from personal property is always taxable to the estate because title to personal property vests in the administrator or executor immediately upon his appointment and does not pass to the legatees until it is distributed by court order (.05). Where a decedent's will calls for the transfer of personal property to a trust, the income from the personal property before the transfer is taxable to the estate, because the trust cannot come into existence as to specific property until after probate administration. Thereafter, the trust will have to report the income. In this connection, income from personal property in the hands of an *inter vivos* trust is taxable to the trust except where it is considered to belong to the grantor because of his power to control the beneficial enjoyment of the trust income or corpus.

.05 Code Sec. 641; Reg. §1.641(a)-2.

¶25,180 Multiple Trusts. A grantor or a testator may create several trusts for several beneficiaries by means of one instrument (.05). Two or more trusts will be treated as one trust if:

(1) the trusts have substantially the same grantor or grantors and substantially the same primary beneficiary or beneficiaries; and

(2) a principal purpose of the trusts is tax avoidance.

For these purposes, a husband and wife are treated as one person.

Tax avoidance need not be the only principal purpose of the trusts, so long as it is a principal purpose, for multiple trusts to be aggregated. In addition, it does not matter whether or not the trusts have substantially independent purposes (.10).

These limitations do not apply to any trust that was irrevocable as of March 1, 1984, except to the extent that corpus is contributed to the trust after that date.

.05 Code Sec. 643(f). **.10** Reg. §1.641(a)-0(c).

¶25,181 Capital Gains and Losses. For purposes of determining taxable income, trusts and estates ordinarily account for capital gains and losses in the same manner as does an individual (.05). Generally, capital gains are taxed in the same manner as ordinary income. However, 50% of the gain resulting from the sale of stock in a qualified small business corporation that is acquired on or after January 1, 1994, and held for more than five years may be excluded. Such excluded gain can not also be taken as a charitable deduction (.10). In computing capital gains and losses, no distinction is made between those allocable to income and those allocable to corpus.

The gain realized by an estate or trust upon the sale of its capital assets is taxable even though the sale is for the purpose of liquidation to pay creditors or to make distribution of shares to heirs or beneficiaries, regardless of the fact that the tax will diminish the amount the heirs or beneficiaries receive. Where a specific dollar amount bequest is satisfied in property that has increased in value since its acquisition by the estate or trust that distributed it, taxable income is realized in the amount of such increase (.15). A distribution of cost recovery or depreciable tangible personal property by an executor in satisfaction of a specific dollar bequest is subject to the recapture provisions (.20), and distributions of realty are subject to "cost recovery or depreciation recapture" (.25).

Whether gain or loss is ordinary or capital in nature depends on the character of the property in the hands of the estate or trust—that is, whether the property was held for investment purposes, for sale to customers, or for use in a trade or business. It is possible for the character of income to change in the hands of the executor of an estate. Thus, subdivision lots held by a real estate dealer became capital assets in the hands of the executor who held them only for liquidation and not for sale to customers in the ordinary course of business (.30).

In reporting the income from sale of capital assets, estates and trusts may, like an individual, avail themselves of the net capital gain provisions of the Code. Estates and trusts are also entitled to capital gain and loss treatment with respect to trade or business property and involuntary conversions (.35). As noted above, they are also subject to the "cost recovery and depreciation recapture" provisions (.40). See ¶5702, ¶5800 and ¶5810 for a discussion of the above capital gains and recapture rules.

If a part of the corpus is sold at a loss, the beneficiary may conceivably suffer because there will be fewer sources of income from the trust or estate. The trust or estate, as legal owner of the assets, may avail itself of the losses resulting from such sales, but the beneficiary, even though he is a remainderman, may not deduct the losses (.45) (except as a capital loss carryover) upon termination of the trust or estate.

Holding period

For capital gain and loss purposes, the holding period of property acquired by the estate from a decedent generally begins on the date of the decedent's death.

If the recipient of property acquired from a decedent sells or disposes of the property within one year, the recipient will still be considered to have held the property for more than one year, provided:

(1) the basis of the property in the hands of the recipient was determined under the ordinary basis rules (.50) by reference to its value at the time of the decedent's death (or alternate valuation date); and

(2) the property was sold within one year of the decedent's death.

□ See ¶5180 and ¶5672 for a discussion of the above holding period and basis rules.

.05 Code Sec. 642; Reg. §1.642(h)-1.

.10 Code Sec. 642(c)(4).

.15 Reg. §1.661(a).

.20 Code Sec. 1245.

.25 Code Sec. 1250.

.30 *W.D. Haden Est.*, 12 TCM 825, CCH Dec. 19,813(M); petition for review dismissed by CA-5, 55-2 USTC ¶9639.

.35 Code Sec. 1231.

.40 Code Sec. 1245 and Code Sec. 1250.

.45 *W.W. Abell*, CA-4, 1 USTC ¶355, 30 F2d 54, cert. denied, 279 U.S. 849.

.50 Code Sec. 1014(b).

¶25,182 Redemption of Stock to Pay Death Taxes. A closely held corporation may redeem its stock from the estate of a stockholder without taxation of the redemption as a dividend (.05). However, the stock redemption proceeds may not exceed the sum of death taxes (including interest) imposed because of the decedent's death plus funeral and administration expenses allowable as deductions from the gross estate. The IRS will not apply the step transaction doctrine (i.e., the breaking down of a transaction into its component parts) to a stock redemption to pay death taxes (.10) that would thereby deny the favorable tax consequences of such redemptions.

The redemption must also be made within the three-year period of the statute of limitations for the assessment of the estate taxes due or within 90 days after the expiration of that period, or, if a timely petition for redetermination of the estate tax has been filed with the Tax Court, at any time before the expiration of 60 days after the court's decision becomes final.

In order for an estate to be eligible for this type of redemption, the stock must amount to more than 35 percent of the excess of the gross estate over the sum of the expenses, debts, taxes and loss deductions allowable for estate tax purposes (.15). See ¶20,360. For the purpose of the 35-percent requirement, stock of two or more corporations (with respect to each of which there is included in determining the value of the decedent's gross estate more than 20 percent in value of the outstanding stock) is treated as the stock of a single corporation.

> ***Example:*** The value of Thomas Price's gross estate at death is $1,000,000, the taxable estate is $700,000, and the sum of the death taxes and funeral and administration expenses is $275,000. Included in the gross estate are stocks in three corporations, valued as follows:

Corp. A	$ 200,000
Corp. B	400,000
Corp. C	200,000

The stock of Corp. A and Corp. B included in the estate is all of the outstanding stock of these two corporations. The total of deductions allowable to the estate for expenses and taxes is $275,000. The stock of Corp. A and Corp. B has a combined value in excess of $253,750 (35% of $725,000, the difference between the gross estate of $1,000,000 and the allowable deduction total of $275,000). Therefore, the distribution by one or more of the three corporations of amounts not exceeding, in the aggregate, $275,000 in redemption of any of the stock of the corporations will be treated as a full payment in exchange for the stock so redeemed.

A corporation may accumulate earnings in order to fund such a redemption without risking the imposition of accumulated earnings tax. See ¶12,415.

Tax advantages of redemption treatment

Although capital gains are generally taxed as ordinary income, the use of Code Sec. 303 to treat stock redemptions as sales, rather than as dividend distributions, can save large amounts of income taxes. This is so because, if Code Sec. 303 is complied with, the stock will have a stepped-up basis in the hands of the estate, and little or no gain will be realized on the sale. However, if Code Sec. 303 is not utilized, dividend treatment will apply to the extent of the corporation's earnings and profits.

If the amount realized exceeds the amounts of estate and death taxes and funeral and administrative expenses, the excess may be taxed as a dividend, unless the redemption qualifies as a sale under Code Sec. 302 (see ¶25,184).

.05 Code Sec. 303; Reg. §1.303-2.

.10 General Counsel Memorandum 39027, 2-10-83.

.15 Code Sec. 2053 and 2054.

¶25,183 Timing the Redemption. Timing of redemptions may avoid loss of capital gain benefits where both the estate and beneficiary own stock in the corporation and one of them intends to redeem all the stock (.05). For example, if an estate holds stock intended to be redeemed in order to pay death taxes and the surviving spouse also holds stock in the same corporation that he or she intends to redeem in any event, it would be best for the estate to redeem stock first and use the proceeds to pay death taxes. Then the surviving spouse, by completely terminating his or her interest in the corporation, would get the benefit of the capital gains provisions, leaving the estate's entire holdings to be applied for payment of death taxes, with only the remainder of its holdings being vulnerable to ordinary dividend treatment.

.05 Code Sec. 303.

¶25,184 Distributions in Redemption of Stock. An estate may liquidate (.05) all its shareholdings in a corporation so as to treat the redemption as a sale (.10) and avoid having redemption amounts treated as a dividend. Generally, a redemption will qualify as a sale or exchange if the redemption:

(1) is substantially disproportionate with respect to the shareholder;

(2) terminates the shareholder's entire interest in the corporation;

(3) is not substantially equivalent to a dividend; or

(4) is of stock held by a noncorporate shareholder and is in partial liquidation of the distributing corporation. See ¶12,150 and following.

One of the easiest ways to obtain capital gain treatment for amounts received in a redemption is to redeem all the stock owned by the estate, thus terminating its interest in the corporation (.15). Often, especially with closely held or family corporations, funds for the redemption come from an insurance policy taken out on the decedent's behalf by the corporation. This planning technique can be a great advantage to both the estate and the corporation. The estate receives a liquid asset (cash) that better enables it to pay creditors, and the corporation may easily redeem the stock without depleting its assets.

One problem that may be faced by estates using this planning technique is the application of the constructive ownership rules, also known as the attribution of ownership rules. With respect to an estate, these rules would attribute to the estate corporate stock owned by the estate's beneficiaries (.20). If this occurs, the estate's interest in the corporation will not be terminated and the redemption amounts will receive dividend treatment.

Waiver of attribution rules

Trusts as well as estates may waive the rules that attribute to a family member stock owned by another. However, like estates, trusts may not waive the provisions that attribute stock owned by its beneficiary to the trust (.25).

.05 Reg. §§1.302-1—1.302-4.
.10 Code Sec. 302.
.15 Code Sec. 302(b)(3).
.20 Code Sec. 318(a)(2).
.25 Code Sec. 302(c).

Ordinary Deductions of the Estate or Trust

¶25,186 Deductions in General. In general, an estate or trust is allowed the same deductions for expenses incurred in carrying on a trade or business or in the production of income as is an individual (.05). In addition, estates and trusts, like individuals, are not permitted to deduct such expenses to the extent they are allocable to the production or collection of tax-exempt income. See ¶8435.

Estates and trusts are entitled to deduct reasonable amounts paid or incurred by fiduciaries on account of administration and business expenses, including fiduciaries' fees and expenses of litigation. It is immaterial whether the administration or business expenses, if deductible, are paid from the corpus or from the income of the estate or trust. They derive their deductible character not from the fund from which they are paid, but from the purpose for which they were incurred. However, such expenses are deductible only if they have not been claimed as deductions for estate tax purposes (see ¶25,225). The rule against double deductions does not apply to deductions for taxes, interest, business expenses, and other items accrued at the date of the decedent's death, so that they are allowable as deductions for estate tax purposes as claims against the estate and are also allowable to the estate as deductions in respect of a decedent for income tax purposes (.10).

Deductions for losses are allowed to an estate or trust to the same extent as in the case of an individual—that is, the losses sustained during the tax year, not compensated for by insurance or otherwise, from a trade or business, from a transaction entered into for profit, or from a casualty or theft are deductible. However, an estate cannot deduct capital and net operating losses sustained by a decedent during the period ending with the date of death (.15). This rule also applies to the carryovers of such losses that the decedent had at the date of death.

Special rules govern certain deductions, such as those for cost recovery, or depreciation and depletion. Therefore, special mention is made concerning these deductions at ¶25,193.

In addition to the usual deductions, estates and trusts are allowed deductions for income distributed or distributable to beneficiaries. See ¶25,198, ¶25,200 – ¶25,203 and following.

Two-percent floor on miscellaneous deductions

Certain miscellaneous itemized deductions are deductible by estates and trusts (as well as individuals) only if the aggregate amount of the deductions exceeds two percent of the estate or trust's adjusted gross income (.20). Miscellaneous itemized deductions are all itemized deductions except those specifically excepted by statute. For this purpose, the adjusted gross income of an estate or trust is computed in the same manner as the adjusted gross income of an individual. However, deductions for expenses incurred in connection with the administration of a trust or estate that would not have been incurred if the property were not held in a trust or estate are treated as allowable in arriving at adjusted gross income and, thus, are not subject to the two-percent floor. The Code Sec. 642(c) deduction, relating to amounts paid or permanently set aside for charitable purposes, and the distribution deductions allowed under Code Sec. 651 and 661 are subtracted from the estate's or trust's gross income in arriving at adjusted gross income. Accordingly, these deductions are not subject to the two-percent floor.

Although there is some authority supporting the view that the cost of investment advice is a deduction not subject to the two-percent floor, the IRS takes the position that investment advice would be necessary whether the property were held in trust or not and therefore it is subject to the two-percent floor.

The two-percent floor does not apply to the deduction for estate tax paid in the case of income in respect of a decedent (.25). The two-percent floor does apply with respect to indirect deductions through grantor trusts by virtue of the grantor trust rules (.30)The pass-through entity provision does not, however, apply to estates or nongrantor trusts.

In addition, under an exception to the full deduction of trusts' and estates' administrative expenses, the carryover deduction allowed beneficiaries of an estate or trust that terminates with unused excess deductions for administrative expenses may be taken only if such excess deductions exceed two percent of a beneficiary's adjusted gross income (.35).

.05 Code Sec. 641 and 642; Reg. §§1.641(b)-1 and 1.642(a)(1)-1—1.642(h)-5.

.10 Reg. §1.642(g)-2.

.15 Rev. Rul. 74-175, 1974-1 CB 52.

.20 Code Sec. 67.

.25 Code Sec. 691(c).

.30 Reg. §1.67-2T(b).

.35 Code Sec. 642(h).

¶25,187 Charitable Deduction. Charitable contributions actually paid out of income by a complex trust or estate during the tax year to recognized charities qualify for an unlimited deduction (.05).

The income tax charitable deduction is allowable only for taxable income that is paid (or set aside in the case of some estates and pooled income funds) to recognized charities by the specific terms of the governing instrument. No deduction may be claimed for charitable contributions that are payable from corpus or principal by the terms of the governing instrument. If the governing instrument is silent as to whether contributions are to be made from income or principal, a deduction will be allowed, in the case of a complex trust, to the extent of the amount of the trust income if state law provides that contributions are considered to be paid first from income and then from principal (.10). Note that gain excluded under Code Sec. 1202 may not be taken as a charitable deduction (.15) (see ¶25,181).

See ¶19,160 for deduction of amounts permanently set aside for charitable purposes.

The law prohibits a double deduction from income taxes by providing that charitable contributions that qualify for the deduction for contributions distributed from income are not deductible as distributions to beneficiaries (.20). The regulations go a step further and provide that charitable contributions by estates from income are deductible only if qualified as contributions distributed from income (.25).

Under the choice-of-tax-year rules (.30), a fiduciary of an estate may make an election that may save taxes by choosing either a fiscal or a calendar tax year, depending upon which period best uses the annual deduction and other allowable deductions.

.05 Code Sec. 642(c); Reg. §1.642(c)-1.
.10 Rev. Rul. 71-285, 1971-2 CB 248.
.15 Code Sec. 642(c)(4).
.20 Code Sec. 661.
.25 Reg. §1.663(a)-2.
.30 Code Sec. 441.

¶25,188 Charitable Deduction for Remainder Interests. Income, estate, and gift tax charitable deductions for contributions of remainder interests are strictly limited and must pass to the charity by means of a pooled income fund, charitable remainder annuity trust (CRAT), or a charitable remainder unitrust (.05). A pooled income fund is a trust set up by a public charity to which an individual transfers property and retains an income interest in such property for the life of one or more beneficiaries living at the time of the transfer. Thus, the public charity has a remainder interest in the property transferred to it. A CRAT is a private trust that pays an fixed sum annuity to one or more noncharitable beneficiaries prior to the remainder interest passing to the charity. A unitrust is a private trust that pays a percentage of trust assets or trust income to one or more noncharitable beneficiaries prior to the remainder interest passing to the charity.

Pooled Income Fund

A pooled income fund must meet the following requirements:

(1) The fund must commingle all property transferred to it by all persons making property contributions to it.

(2) The fund may not invest in securities whose income is tax-exempt.

(3) The fund must be maintained by the recipient charity, and no donor or income beneficiary may be a trustee of the trust. However, the charity does not have to act as trustee of the fund.

(4) The fund may not include any contributions of property from other sources.

(5) The fund may not accumulate income for any beneficiary. Each person who has an income interest resulting from a transfer of property to the fund must be paid an annual amount of income based on the fund's rate of return (.10).

The IRS has provided examples of arrangements that meet the foregoing requirements (.15). A pooled income fund that meets those requirements will be taxed as a trust.

No gain or loss will be recognized by a donor on the transfer of property to a pooled income fund, except where he receives property other than an income interest or where the fund assumes an indebtedness on the property. The present value of the charitable remainder interest in the property transferred to the fund is allowed as a charitable deduction. Where there is only one income beneficiary, tables (.20) are used to compute the value of the remainder interest.

Alternative Charitable Remaindermen. See ¶19,035 for a discussion of the options available to the trustee in the event that the public charity designated as the remainderman of a pooled income fund goes out of business or loses its qualification.

Charitable Remainder Annuity Trust (CRAT)

A CRAT is a trust that pays a fixed amount not less than 5 percent of the initial net fair market value of all property placed in the trust at least once a year to one or more persons (at least one of whom is not a charitable organization and, in the case of individuals, only to an individual who is living at the time of the creation of the trust) for a term of years (not in excess of 20) or for the life or lives of such individual or individuals. No amount other than these payments may be paid to or for the use of any person other than a charitable organization. Following the termination of these payments, the remainder interest in the trust is to be transferred to, or for the use of, a charitable organization or is to be retained by the trust for such a use. However, a CRAT may pay the remainder to a qualified employee stock ownership plan. (.30). These requirements are applied strictly. For example, failure on the part of a trustee of a CRAT to make annual payments to non-charitable beneficiaries caused the estate to lose the charitable deduction for the entire charitable remainder (.35).

Charitable Remainder Unitrust (CRUT)

A charitable remainder unitrust is a trust that from its inception must pay a fixed percentage of not less than 5 percent of the annual net fair market value of its assets, the unitrust amount, to one or more persons, at least one of which is not a qualifying charitable organization. In addition, the unitrust amount paid cannot exceed 50 percent of the fair market value of the trust's assets. Alternatively, a unitrust can base distributions on income. If all or part of the unitrust amount is payable to an individual, that individual must be living when the trust is created. The unitrust amount must be payable at least annually for a term of years not exceeding 20 years, or for the life or lives of the individual or individuals to whom the unitrust amount is payable. No amount other than the unitrust amount can be paid by the trust to, or for the use of, any person other than a qualifying charitable organization. When the unitrust payment period terminates, the remainder interest in the trust must be paid to, or for the use of, a qualifying charitable organization or be retained by the trust for that use. However, like an annuity trust, a charitable remainder unitrust may pay the remainder to a qualified employee stock ownership plan (.40)

.05 Code Sec. 2055(e)(2)(A).

.10 Code Sec. 642(c)(3)–(5); Reg. §§1.642(c)-5–1.642(c)-7.

.15 Rev. Proc. 2003-53, 2003-31 I.R.B. 230; Rev. Proc. 2003-54, 2003-31 I.R.B. 236; Rev. Proc. 2003-55, 2003-31 I.R.B. 242; Rev. Proc. 2003-56, 2003-31 I.R.B. 249; Rev. Proc. 2003-57, 2003-31 I.R.B. 257; Rev. Proc. 2003-58, 2003-31 I.R.B. 262; Rev. Proc. 2003-59, 2003-31 I.R.B. 268; Rev. Proc. 2003-60, 2003-31 I.R.B. 274.

.20 Reg. §1.642(c)-6(d) and (e); Prop. Reg. §§ 1.642(c)-6A and 20.7520-1.

.30 Code Sec. 664(d)(1).

.35 *Est. of M.B. Atkinson*, CA-11, 2002-2 USTC ¶ 60,449.

.40 Code Sec. 664(d)(2).

¶25,189 Decedent's Medical Expenses. No medical deduction is available to an estate or trust because it may not incur the expenses on its own behalf and it has no dependents, as that term is defined in the law (.05). However, medical expenses incurred for the care of a decedent during his last illness and paid by an estate within one year after the decedent's death are treated as having been paid by the decedent when incurred, and, accordingly, may be deducted on the decedent's return for the year incurred (usually his final return). The deductions, however, are subject to the percentage-of-income limitations (.10) See ¶6503. A statement must be filed showing that the amounts claimed as income tax deductions have not been "allowed" and are waived as deductions for federal estate tax purposes (see ¶25,225).

Medical expenses that are not paid within one year of a decedent's death may be deducted only on the estate tax return and may not be claimed as income tax deductions on the decedent's final income tax return (.15). The medical expenses that are not deductible for income tax purposes because of the 7.5-percent income limitation are also not deductible for estate tax purposes (.20).

Medical expenses can create problems when an estate receives insurance reimbursements for such expenses paid on behalf of the decedent. When an estate administrator or executor claims deductions for medical expenses on the decedent's final return and, in the following tax year, receives reimbursement for the expenses, such reimbursement generates additional income tax liability as income received in respect of a decedent and additional estate tax liability as an amount includible in the gross estate (.25). If no deduction had been claimed, the reimbursement would not have been income in respect of the decedent and, therefore, would only have been includible in the gross estate (.30).

The choice of whether to deduct the medical expenses on the decedent's final return depends upon the circumstances of each situation. Executors or administrators should compute the total income and estate liability under both alternatives (i.e., claiming or not claiming the medical expenses as an itemized deduction on the decedent's last return) in order to determine the method that will save the most tax.

Keep in mind that funeral expenses are deductible for estate tax purposes, but not for income tax purposes. The election that may be made to treat administrative expenses as deductions from the estate tax or the income tax does not apply to funeral expenses (.35). Therefore, if funeral expenses are not taken as a deduction from the estate tax, their use as a deduction is lost.

.05 Code Sec. 642(g); Reg. §1.642(g)-2.
.10 Code Sec. 213(c).
.15 Code Sec. 213(a) -(d); Reg. §1.213-1(d).
.20 Rev. Rul. 77-357, 1977-2 CB 328.
.25 Rev. Rul. 78-292, 1978-2 CB 233.
.30 Code Sec. 105 and 691(a).
.35 Reg. §1.642(g)-1; Code Sec. 2053(a).

¶25,190 Alimony and Separate Maintenance. In computing its net income, a trust or estate is entitled to a deduction for amounts in the nature of alimony and separate maintenance payments (including amounts paid under a private separation agreement) that are required to be included in the income of the spouse receiving the payments (.05). This deduction is limited to the extent that such amounts are paid, credited or required to be distributed out of income of the estate or trust for its tax year. However, generally, the spouse receiving the payments is taxed on such payments whether made out of income or corpus. See ¶19,050.

Where an "alimony trust" is created in contemplation of divorce, the trust income that may be used for the benefit of the grantor's spouse is taxed to the grantor. However, this rule is not applicable to an alimony trust created prior to divorce or separation. The income from such trusts is taxed under the usual trust rules.

.05 Code Sec. 62, 71, and 682; Reg. §1.682(b)-1.

¶25,191 Losses on the Sale of Corpus. Capital losses from the sale of trust or estate corpus, title to which is in the trust or estate, are deductible only by the estate or trust, not by the beneficiaries (.05). Therefore, if a trust or estate sells part of its corpus at a loss, even though the beneficiary may conceivably suffer to the extent that the amount of trust or estate sources of future income will be less than formerly, only the trust or estate, as legal owner of the capital assets, may avail itself of the losses resulting from such sales (.10). However, if, under local law, legal title to real estate is considered to be in the residuary legatee from the moment of the decedent's death, a loss on the sale of the property may be deductible by the residuary legatee. In this case, the sale is considered as having been made by the estate or trust as an agent (.15).

.05 Code Sec. 641; Reg. §1.641(b)-1.

.10 *W.W. Abell*, CA-4, 1 USTC ¶355, 30 F2d 54, cert. denied, 279 U.S. 849, 49 SCt 346; *T.R. Beatty*, 28 BTA 1286, CCH Dec. 8221; *M.S. Wilson*, SCt, 3 USTC ¶1066, 289 U.S. 20.

.15 *L.R. Arrott*, CA-3, 37-2 USTC ¶9491, 92 F2d 773.

¶25,192 Apportionment of Casualty Losses. Casualty and theft losses are deductible on an estate's income tax return only if, at the time of the filing of the return, the loss has not been claimed as a deduction from the gross estate of the decedent on a federal estate tax return (see ¶25,225) (.05). An individual who has a legal life estate in property is entitled to any casualty loss deduction (.10). Because the damage sustained by the property constitutes an injury to both the life estate and the remainder interest, it may be necessary to apportion the loss between the two interests. However, if, as a practical matter, the entire burden falls on the life tenant, he or she alone will be entitled to the casualty loss deduction. If an apportionment is warranted by the facts, however, both the life tenant and the remainderman would be entitled to deduct their proportionate shares, subject to the usual limitation that the deductible loss may not exceed the taxpayer's adjusted basis.

.05 Code Sec. 165(c)(3); Reg. §1.165-7(c).

.10 *K.B. Bliss*, CA-2, 58-2 USTC ¶9618, 256 F2d 533.

¶25,193 Apportionment of Cost Recovery or Depreciation and Depletion. An estate or trust is allowed the deductions for cost recovery or depreciation and depletion only to the extent that these deductions are not allocable to beneficiaries (.05).

In the case of a trust, the allowable deduction is apportioned between the income beneficiaries and the trust or estate on the basis of the trust income allocable to each, unless the governing instrument (or local law) requires or permits the trustee to maintain a reserve in any amount. If this is the case, the deduction amount is first allocated to the trustee to the extent that income is set aside for a reserve, and any part of the deduction amount in excess of the income set aside for the reserve is apportioned between the income beneficiaries and the trustee on the basis of the trust income (in excess of the income set aside for the reserve) allocable to each.

In the case of an estate, the allowable deductions for cost recovery or depreciation and depletion are apportioned between the estate and the heirs, legatees, or devisees on the basis of the income of the estate allocable to each. See ¶19,140.

.05 Code Sec. 642; Reg. §1.642(e)-1.

¶25,194 Cemetery Perpetual Care Funds. Perpetual care fund trusts may deduct amounts that are distributed to cemeteries for the care and maintenance of gravesites (.05). The deduction is limited each year to $5 times the number of gravesites that have been sold before the beginning of the tax year. The deduction is available only for a fund that is taxable as a trust, and then only if it was created pursuant to a local law by a taxable cemetery corporation for the care and maintenance of cemetery property.

The distributions for the care and maintenance of gravesites must be for those gravesites that the fund actually has an obligation to maintain. The deduction is allowed to the extent that the cemetery company actually expends the funds for the care and maintenance of gravesites. Thus, a perpetual fund is not entitled to deductions for care and maintenance payments that are used to pay other types of expenses, such as officers' salaries.

Such payments are treated as distributions (.10) that limit deductions for trust distributions to distributable net income. Gravesite owners, heirs and the general public are not treated as trust beneficiaries required to include such distributions in income. The amounts distributed are taxable to the cemetery company as ordinary income (.15) and are not treated as a trust distribution in its hands (.20).

.05 Code Sec. 642(i).

.10 Code Sec. 651 and 661.

.15 Code Sec. 61.

.20 Code Sec. 652 and 662.

Taxing Estates and Trusts and Their Beneficiaries

¶25,196 Rates and Basis of Taxation. The tax rate schedule ordinarily used by estates and trusts is reproduced at ¶167 (.05). These rates apply to estates and nongrantor trusts only—income from a grantor trust is taxed directly to the grantor. Income tax liability is computed generally in the same manner and on the same basis as for an individual taxpayer, with some differences. For instance, an estate is allowed one exemption of $600, a simple trust is allowed an exemption of $300, and a complex trust is allowed an exemption of only $100.

Estates and trusts may claim the foreign tax credit and any other applicable tax credit in computing their income tax liabilities. All of these credits, however, are allocable between the fiduciary and the beneficiaries.

There is no statutory authority that permits the beneficiaries of an estate or trust to claim any unused tax credits upon the termination of the estate or trust. Thus, a real tax loss may result to the extent of the estate or trust's unused tax credit. The loss may be eliminated or reduced by making additional discretionary distributions to beneficiaries prior to termination, if this is permissible. Alternatively, fiduciaries should refrain from making qualifying investment credit expenditures shortly before termination if the fiduciaries are unable to utilize the full amount of the credit to which they are entitled.

It is also necessary to remember that this discussion is concerned with the ordinary *inter vivos* (during lifetime) or testamentary trust in which particular property is conveyed to a trustee or trustees for the benefit of designated beneficiaries, with the trustees conserving the property and collecting the income for such persons. Coverage here does not include trusts that are treated as associations and taxed as corporations.

.05 Code Sec. 641 and 642; Reg. §§1.641(a)-1—1.641(b)-1, Reg. §1.642(b)-1.

¶25,197 Conduit Principle. Estates and trusts are separate taxable entities, but they also are the channels or "conduits" through which income flows to the beneficiaries, although the flow may stop temporarily when it is required to be accumulated for future distribution (.05). Generally, the income that flows to the beneficiary has the same character that it had in the hands of the estate or trust. In connection with the passage of income to the beneficiary, questions concerning the taxation and deduction of income necessarily follow. The measure for determining the taxability of beneficiaries and the deductibility of distributions by an estate or trust is "distributable net income." In addition, amounts required to be distributed currently or properly paid or credited to the beneficiaries are deductible by the estate or trust to the extent of "distributable net income," regardless of the source of the distribution.

☐ See, further, ¶25,203.

.05 Code Sec. 651, 652, 661 and 662; Reg. §§1.651(b)-1, 1.652(a)-1, 1.661(a)-2 and 1.662(a)-1.

¶25,198 Simple Trusts. A deduction is available to a trust for the amount of the income for the tax year that is required to be distributed currently if the trust (.05)

(1) only distributes current income,

(2) is required, under the terms of its governing instrument, to distribute all of its income currently whether or not the trustee actually does so, and

(3) is not to pay, permanently set aside, or use any amounts for charitable purposes.

Such a trust is a "simple" trust (as distinguished from a "complex trust," as explained at ¶25,201) and, as pointed out above, its deduction for amounts required to be distributed currently is limited only by the distributable net income for the tax year, whether or not such distributions of current income are in fact made, and even if the trustee makes the actual distribution after the close of that year.

Decedents' estates are not governed by the rules applicable to simple trusts but are subject to the provisions of estates and complex trusts (.10) (see ¶25,201).

.05 Code Sec. 651; Reg. §§1.651(a)-1 and 1.651(a)-5.

.10 Code Sec. 661.

¶25,199 Capital Gains of a Simple Trust. Allocation of capital gains to corpus will not prevent a trust from qualifying as a simple trust (.05). The determination of what is "income" depends upon the terms of the governing instrument and upon applicable local law. Consequently, capital gains are not "income" if they are properly allocable to corpus, even though they are includible in gross income of the trust for income tax purposes. However, capital gains are "income" if the trust instrument specifically provides that all capital gains are currently distributable to beneficiaries.

.05 Code Sec. 643(a)(3); Reg. §1.643(b)-1.

¶25,200 Distribution of Other Amounts by Simple Trusts. If a trust distributes amounts other than income (e.g., payments out of the trust corpus), the trust will be governed by the complex trust rules for the tax year in which such other amounts are distributed, including the allowable exemption amount (.05). The trust may, however, again qualify under the simple trust provisions for other years. The fact that a trust that is required to distribute all of its income currently also makes a distribution of corpus that disqualifies it in that year from treatment as a simple trust does not disqualify it from taking a $300 exemption in subsequent years.

.05 Code Sec. 651; Reg. §1.651(a)-3.

¶25,201 Estates and Complex Trusts. Trusts that accumulate income, distribute corpus or pay, permanently set aside, or use any amounts for charitable purposes are called "complex" trusts (.05). Included in this category are all trusts in the final year of administration. Such trusts are subject to special provisions that also apply to decedents' estates.

Estates and complex trusts are allowed to deduct the amount of income for the tax year that is required to be distributed currently and any "other" amounts properly paid or credited or required to be distributed for the tax year. The deduction, however, is limited to distributable net income. Income that is required to be distributed currently includes any amount required to be distributed that may be paid out of income or corpus, such as an annuity, to the extent that it is paid out of income for the tax year.

Other amounts for which a deduction is allowed include all amounts properly paid, credited or required to be distributed during the tax year other than income required to be distributed currently. The term "other amounts" includes

(1) an amount distributed in the discretion of the fiduciary,

(2) payment of an annuity to the extent that it is not paid out of income for the taxable year,

(3) a distribution of property in kind,

(4) an amount applied or distributed out of corpus or out of other than income for the tax year in discharge of obligations of support, and

(5) any amount used to discharge or satisfy any person's legal obligation.

Estates may claim deductions for statutory widows' and dependents' allowances that are paid from either income or principal to the extent of the estate's distributable net income for the year. In addition, surviving spouses and family members receiving such payments will have to include these amounts in their gross incomes to the extent of the estate's distributable net income (.10).

.05 Code Sec. 661; Reg. § §1.661(a)-1 and 1.661(a)-2.

.10 Rev. Proc. 73-4, 1973-1 CB 751.

¶25,202 Limitations. If the amount of income that is required to be distributed currently plus any other amounts properly paid, credited or required to be distributed by an estate or a complex trust exceed its distributable net income, the deduction allowed to the estate or trust is limited to its distributable net income (see ¶25,203) (.05). For this purpose, however, distributable net income must be decreased for any item of distributable net income, such as tax-exempt interest, that is not included in the gross income of the estate or trust for the purpose of computing its taxable income (see ¶25,175). In addition, capital gains from the sale of qualified small business stock that are excludable under Code Sec. 1202 will not be taken into account in computing the exclusion of capital gains in determining distributable net income (.10).

.05 Code Sec. 651 and 661; Reg. §§1.651(a)-3(a), 1.661(a)-2 and 1.661(c)-1.

.10 Code Sec. 643(c).

¶25,203 Distributable Net Income. As noted previously, "distributable net income" is the yardstick that is used to measure the amount deductible by an estate or trust, amounts paid, credited or required to be distributed to beneficiaries, and the amount taxable to the beneficiaries. It also includes the taxable income of the estate or trust, with some modifications (see ¶19,200) (.05). Because the distributable net income concept is used to determine the character of amounts distributed to the beneficiaries, it is necessary to adjust taxable income by adding to it items that are not includible in the gross income of the estate or trust but that may nevertheless be available for distribution to the beneficiaries, such as tax-exempt interest (.10). The deductions for personal exemptions, capital losses not offset against distributable gains, and for amounts paid, credited or required to be distributed to the beneficiaries are disallowed, thus restricting the benefit of these deductions to the estate or trust.

Because a trust's taxable income does not include the amount of any "includible gain" from certain sales or exchanges of property transferred to the trust at less than fair market value reduced by related deductions (¶25,211), such gain is excluded from distributable net income (.15).

.05 Code Sec. 643; Reg. §1.643(a)-0.

.10 Code Sec. 666(c).

.15 Code Sec. 641(c).

¶25,204 Deductions Against Corpus. All deductible charges against an estate or trust, whether paid from income or from principal (corpus), are allowed as deductions in computing distributable net income (.05). Thus, the primary benefit of the deductions goes to the income beneficiaries. It is only when such deductions exceed distributable net income (see ¶25,203) that they are allowed to offset income allocated to corpus and taxable to the trust. The effect is that, even where the deductions are properly chargeable against corpus and borne by the remaindermen, they are allowed to benefit first the income beneficiaries. Therefore, in many instances, the remaindermen are deprived of tax deductions.

.05 Code Sec. 661; Reg. §1.661(a)-2.

¶25,205 Taxing Beneficiaries of a Simple Trust. Income (in the accounting sense) that is required to be distributed to beneficiaries is taxable to them, whether or not it is actually distributed to them during the tax year, up to the amount of distributable net income (.05). If the income required to be distributed exceeds distributable net income, only a proportionate part of each item is includible in the beneficiaries' income. In making this apportionment, each item retains the same character (such as rents, dividends, etc.) it had in the hands of the trust, unless the trust instrument specifically allocates a particular type of income to a particular beneficiary.

Under a special provision, applicable only to simple trusts, any "extraordinary" or taxable stock dividends that the fiduciary determines in good faith must be allocated to corpus under local law are not included in the trust's distributable net income and so will not be included in the taxable income of a beneficiary. These dividends are intended to be taxed only to the trust.

Where a taxpayer is the beneficiary of a trust receiving all its income from foreign sources, the beneficiary is taxable on the net income realized by the trust in that part of the year during which he is a U.S. citizen, even though he has not received the full amount of that income (.10).

.05 Code Sec. 652; Reg. § §1.652(a)-1—1.652(c)-4.

.10 *E.N. Petschek Estate*, CA-2, 84-2 USTC ¶9598, 738 F2d 67.

¶25,206 "Tier" System for Taxing Beneficiaries of Estates and Complex Trusts. Where there is more than one beneficiary receiving distributions, it is necessary to determine the order of priority in which distributions to beneficiaries are to be treated as consisting of income distributed by the estate or complex trust (.05). This is accomplished by a mechanical device known as the "two-tier" system. In accordance with this system, the "distributable net income" (see ¶25,203) is first treated as paid to those beneficiaries receiving income required to be distributed currently (the first tier), and then, as to any remaining distributable net income, to all other beneficiaries (the second tier).

For purposes of allocating estate or trust income, beneficiaries receiving discretionary distributions of income are placed in the same class or tier with those beneficiaries receiving distributions from corpus. Then, if distributions to "tier one," that is, required income beneficiaries, do not use up the full amount of distributable net income, a beneficiary who may receive distributions only out of corpus ("tier two") is taxed on a pro rata share of the remaining distributable net income along with a beneficiary receiving discretionary payments out of income (also a "tier two" beneficiary), even if the distributable net income was in fact only sufficient to satisfy the distributions to the income beneficiaries.

Any distributable net income remaining after an allocation is made to the first tier beneficiaries is allocated to the charitable deduction before being allocated to beneficiaries coming within the second tier. Thus, in the case of a trust that requires the current income to be paid to charity, and an equal amount of corpus to be paid to a noncharitable beneficiary, the latter is not taxed on the amount he receives.

.05 Code Sec. 662; Reg. §§1.662(a)-2 and 1.662(a)-3.

¶25,207 The 65-Day Distribution Rule. The fiduciary of a complex trust may elect to treat any distribution or any portion of any distribution to a beneficiary within the first 65 days following the end of a tax year as an amount that was paid or credited on the last day of such tax year (.05). This election is also available to executors of estates of decedents dying after August 5, 1997 (.10).

If the election is made, the fiduciary must deduct the amounts covered in the election in the tax year of the election, and the beneficiary must include the amounts covered by the election in his income for the tax year covered by the election. Moreover, although the taxpayer-beneficiary who receives income distributions from the trust after the close of the previous tax year must include the payments as part of his income for the previous tax year, he need not include them in the previous year's income for purposes of determining liability for the penalty for underpayment of estimated taxes (.15).

.05 Code Sec. 663.
.10 Code Sec. 663(b).
.15 Rev. Rul. 78-158, 1978-1 CB 437.

¶25,208 Accumulation Trusts. The tax savings to beneficiaries are reduced by application of the "throwback" rules that are applicable in taxing accumulation distributions made to trust beneficiaries (.05). These rules have the effect of taxing accumulation distributions to the beneficiaries as if the distributions were distributed to them by the trust in the year or years when the income was accumulated. These throwback rules do not apply to beneficiaries of *estates*. Further, the throwback rules have been repealed, effective with respect to distributions made from domestic trusts in tax years beginning after August 5, 1997 (.10).

Usually, a beneficiary receiving an accumulation distribution treats it as if it had been received in the year or years such income was earned by the trust. However, in the case of a trust accumulation, additional tax that the beneficiary would have paid in the year or years when the trust earned the income is added to his tax in the year of the accumulation distribution. This partial tax on an accumulation distribution is computed on the basis of taxable income received during three of the beneficiary's five tax years preceding the year of distribution. (The two years with the highest and lowest taxable income are disregarded.)

An accumulation distribution is not deemed made in a given year if the amounts properly paid, credited, or required to be distributed by the trust for the year do not exceed the income of the trust for that year. This is intended to prevent distributions of a current year's trust income to a beneficiary from being treated as an accumulation distribution where the trust's accounting income is greater than its distributable net income.

Distributions of income accumulated by a domestic trust prior to a beneficiary's attaining majority are not considered to be accumulation distributions, and so are not subject to the throwback rules.

☐ For details, see ¶19,345 et. seq.

.05 Code Sec. 665-667.
.10 Code Sec. 665(b) and 665(c).

¶25,209 Termination Without Taxation. A stumbling block to passing the residue of an estate or trust to a residuary legatee or remainderman free of tax is the well-established rule that, on termination of an estate or trust, the income for the year of termination becomes "currently distributable" (.05). This means that, to the extent of distributable net income, the income is deductible by the estate and taxable to the beneficiary.

Ordinarily, gains from the sale or exchange of capital assets that are allocated to corpus under the terms of the governing instrument or under local law are excluded from distributable net income. However, this will only be true, and the gains will not be considered as paid, credited, or required to be distributed to any beneficiary, if the gains are not actually distributed to the beneficiaries during the tax year (.10).

Example 1: The trustee of a trust containing Blackacre and other property is directed to hold Blackacre for 10 years, and then sell it and distribute its proceeds to A. Any capital gain realized from the sale will be included in distributable net income.

Example 2: The executor of an estate is directed by the will to sell Whiteacre when the price is right, but in no event later than three years after the testator's death. He is then to distribute the proceeds to A and B in equal shares. Whiteacre is sold at a gain within three years of the testator's death and the proceeds are distributed to A and B in the year of sale. The capital gain was included in distributable net income.

It makes no difference whether capital gains are allocated to, and become part of, principal under state law (.15). On termination of an estate, the income for the year of termination becomes "currently distributable" to the residuary legatee regardless of the fact that, under state law, such income is considered principal to the legatee, except where the distribution is made in satisfaction of a pecuniary legacy.

Thus, getting the residuary estate to the residuary legatee tax-free calls for astute planning. Essentially, the fiduciary should consider deferring the termination of the estate (or trust) to a year when it is reasonable to expect that the estate will have little or no distributable net income. This situation may be created by arranging to distribute all income that is in the category of "currently distributable income" (including accumulated income) in advance of the termination year, or to distribute it to a beneficiary other than the residuary legatee in such a way that the latter is a "tier two" beneficiary subject to tax on excess currently distributable income.

Example 3: A decedent's will requires payments of $10,000 annually to A payable only out of net income and $5,000 per year to B, the residuary legatee, payable out of income or corpus. In the year of termination, the estate has $10,000 of net income all of which is distributed to A. It also has $10,000 of distributable net income in the year of termination. A is taxable on the full amount of the distribution. There is no tax on the distribution to B because the distributable net income after reduction by the amount required to be distributed currently is zero.

The above is a result of the application of the "tier system" rule (see ¶25,206). To restate that rule: if the income required to be distributed currently (tier 1) plus the tier 2 "other" amounts which are properly paid, credited or required to be distributed to a beneficiary for the tax year exceed the distributable net income, then the beneficiary's share of such "other" amounts is a proportionate part of the distributable net income (after subtracting the amounts required to be distributed) equal to the proportion that the beneficiary's share of "other" amounts is of the total "other" amounts for all beneficiaries.

To accomplish the above result, the fiduciary will have to be especially concerned with avoiding the possibility that the trust or the estate is not treated as terminated in advance (for example, because administration has been unduly prolonged). Should that happen, all the careful planning will have been wasted because, if an estate is held to have been terminated for federal income tax purposes, the residuary legatee could be taxed with the income regarded as currently distributable in the year of forced termination.

.05 Code Sec. 641, 643, 661 and 662; Reg. §§1.641(b)-3(c), 1.643(a)-3, 1.661(a)-2 and 1.662(a)-2.

.10 Reg. §1.643(a)-3(a)(2).

.15 *H.K. Carlisle*, CA-6, 48-1 USTC ¶9171, 165 F2d 645.

¶25,210 Distributions by Foreign Trusts. In addition to the partial tax imposed on accumulation distributions (¶25,208), a nondeductible annual "interest charge" is imposed on U. S. beneficiaries receiving taxable accumulation distributions from foreign trusts (.05). This charge is applicable whenever foreign trust income is not taxable to the grantor under the grantor trust rules (.10) (¶19,475). For distributions after August 20, 1996, the interest charge is equal to the rate charged on underpayments of tax under Code Sec. 6621(a)(2), with compounding; however, simple interest continues to accrue through 1995 (.15). For distributions prior to August 21, 1996, the charge is six percent of the partial tax imposed on beneficiaries (.20) after reduction for foreign tax credits attributable to the distribution and the U.S. taxes paid by the trust.

□ See ¶19,375–¶19,380 for a detailed discussion of the throwback rules as they apply to foreign trusts and accumulation distributions to foreigners.

.05 Code Sec. 665, 668 and 669.
.10 Code Sec. 679.
.15 Code Sec. 668(a).
.20 Code Sec. 667(b).

¶25,211 Tax on Trusts Selling Appreciated Property. A special tax is imposed on a trust that sells property within two years after the property has been transferred to it in order to shift the tax liability to the trust, so that income on the sale may be taxed at the trust's lower progressive rates (.05). The tax has been repealed, however, with respect to sales or exchanges occurring after August 5, 1997. For pre-August 6, 1997 sales or exchanges, this special tax is imposed only if:

(1) the fair market value of the property exceeds the price paid (if any) for the property by the trust, and

(2) the trust sells the property at a gain (called "includible gain"; see ¶25,213) within two years from the date of the transfer.

If both of these conditions are met, the trust's special tax is the amount of the additional tax that the transferor would have to pay (including any alternative minimum tax) if he had disposed of the property in the same tax year as the trust. This special tax does not apply with respect to property acquired under the following circumstances:

(1) by a trust from a decedent or which has passed to a trust from a decedent (.10);

(2) by a pooled income fund;

(3) by a charitable remainder annuity trust or a charitable remainder unitrust; or

(4) by a sale or exchange of property that occurs after the death of the transferor, even if such disposition is within two years of the initial transfer to the trust.

The property in question can be acquired by the disposing trust by means of:

(1) an outright gift in trust from the transferor,

(2) a bargain sale of the property by the transferor, or

(3) a transfer of property from one trust to another.

However, where the property has been transferred from one trust to another, the two-year holding period begins running on the date of the initial transfer of the property in trust by the transferor.

In order to prevent the circumvention of the two-year period through a short sale during such period, a special rule extends the two-year period to the closing of the short sale. Special rules also apply if the trust elects to use the installment method of reporting gain. See ¶25,214.

.05 Code Sec. 644, prior to repeal by P.L. 105-34.
.10 Code Sec. 1014.

¶25,212 Computation of Tax on Sales of Appreciated Trust Property. If a trust sells appreciated property both at a gain and within the two-year period, the special tax imposed on the trust is based on what is called the "amount of the includible gain" realized by the trust (.05). The amount of the "includible gain" is the lesser of:

(1) the amount of the gain realized by the trust on the sale or exchange of the property, or

(2) the excess of the fair market value of the property at the time of the initial transfer in trust by the transferor over the trust's basis in such property immediately after such transfer.

The special tax must be paid by the trust in the year it disposes of the property and is the difference between:

(1) the amount of income tax (including the alternative minimum tax) that the transferor would have to pay on the "includible gain" (and related deductions incurred by the trust) if this gain had been included in his taxable income in the year in which the trust disposed of the property, and

(2) the tax (including the minimum tax) actually imposed on the transferor for such year (.10).

.05 Code Sec. 644(b).

.10 Code Sec. 644(a)(2).

¶25,213 Includible Gain to Which Special Tax Applies. The character of the includible gain to which the special tax applies (on sales of property within two years; see ¶25,211) is determined as if the property had actually been sold or exchanged by the transferor, and any activities of the trust regarding the sale of the property are deemed to be the activities of the transferor (.05). In essence, the above rule provides that, for purposes of determining whether the property is a capital asset and subject to capital gain treatment, the character of the property is determined by reference to its character in the hands of the transferor. Consequently, capital gain treatment will not be available if the property was not a capital asset in the hands of the transferor, even though the property is a capital asset in the hands of the trust. For 2004, the maximum long-term capital gain rate for individuals is 15percent (5 percent for taxpayers in the 10- or 15-percent brackets). However, the capital gains tax rate on certain types of collectibles is 28 percent. Because the highest tax rate that may be imposed on net long-term capital gains is limited to 28 percent, the status of property as a capital asset can be significant since the maximum income tax rate is 35 percent.

Also, the portion of the includible gain subject to the cost recovery or depreciation recapture provisions (.10) is determined in accordance with regulations to be prescribed by the IRS. Because most transfers of property to trusts involve outright gift situations, the amount of cost recovery or depreciation that is subject to recapture by the transferor will also have to be taken into account in determining the ordinary income portion of the gain for purposes of determining the special tax.

The special tax on sale of appreciated property discussed at ¶25,211 is reported by the trust for the tax year of the trust that begins with or within the tax year of the transferor in which the sale or exchange occurs. In order to prevent double taxation of the includible gain, the law specifically excludes the includible gain, minus any deductions, from the trust's taxable income for the year. This exclusion achieves two results:

(1) It means that the special tax on the includible gain is computed separately from the trust's tax liability for its income from other sources. Thus, a trust's tax liability in the year it disposes of property is the sum of (a) the special tax computed on the property, and (b) its tax liability on its other sources of income, which is to be determined by deducting the gain and any related deductions from the trust's taxable income.

(2) Because the includible gain is excluded from the trust's taxable income, the gain is not included in the trust's distributable net income and, consequently, the includible gain may not be taxed to a beneficiary if the gain is currently distributed to him. Furthermore, since the includible gain is excluded from the trust's distributable net income, the gain will also not be subject to the accumulation distribution rules.

Note, however, that capital gains from the sale of qualified small business stock that are excludable under Code Sec. 1202 will not be taken into account in computing the exclusion of capital gains in determining distributable net income (.15).

.05 Code Sec. 641(c) and 644(c).

.10 Code Sec. 1245 and 1250.

.15 Code Sec. 643(c).

¶25,214 Additional Tax on Fiscal-Year Deferments. Another special rule allows a trust using a tax year that differs from that of the transferor to defer reporting a gain from a sale of property within two years of receipt, with the result that the trustee may not ascertain the amount of tax that the transferor would have to pay on the "includible gain" because the sale occurs within a tax year of the transferor that ends after the end of the tax year of the trust in which the sale occurs (.05).

For example, assume that a trust uses a calendar year and the transferor uses a fiscal year ending on June 30, that the transferor transfers the appreciated property to the trust during calendar year 2003, and that the trustee sells the property during the last six months of calendar year 2004. In such a case, the trust will report the gain and pay the special tax with its return that is to be filed for the calendar year 2005, and not its return for the calendar year 2004. It is deferred because it is impossible to determine the amount of tax that the transferor would have paid for the fiscal year ending on June 30, 2005, until the trust's 2004 calendar year has ended.

However, a trust must pay an additional tax in those cases where gain on a sale is deferred in accordance with the above rule. This additional tax is computed by multiplying the amount of the special tax on the amount of deferred gain by the annual rate of interest (.10). This rule also applies to installment payments that are deferred.

If a trust elects to report gain realized on the sale of property acquired from a transferor under the installment method (see ¶15,355 and following paragraphs), the trust is allowed to report the special tax on includible gain under the installment method as well.

Where the trust and transferor have the same tax years, the additional tax is the amount of tax that the transferor would have paid on the installments received by the trust, less any amount of the tax actually paid by the transferor. However, where the trust and beneficiary have different tax years, the trust has to pay only the additional tax on those installments that it receives within the period of its tax year that ends with the end of the transferor's tax year, and, moreover, the deferment rule applies for any later installments. Thus, the additional tax must be paid on these deferred installments.

It is important to note that, if an installment sale occurs within two years after the transfer to the trust, each installment (including installments received more than two years after the initial transfer) is taxed at the transferor's tax rate. In other words, the special tax applies where a trust reports income under the installment sale method as if each installment were a separate sale or exchange of property, without regard to the two-year rule.

The installment payment rules apply only for the period the transferor is alive. After the transferor's death, the tax on the "includible gain" is based on the trust tax rates.

.05 Code Sec. 644(f).

.10 Code Sec. 6621.

Grantor Trusts

¶25,216 Statutory Compliance. Income earned from a "grantor trust," a trust where the grantor is treated as the owner of the trust income, is taxed to the grantor at his tax rate (.05). The Code (.10) prescribes rules for determining when trust income is taxed to the grantor because of:

(1) the reversion of the trust property to the grantor after creation of the trust,

(2) the reservation of the power to determine who should enjoy the corpus or income, and

(3) the reservation of important administrative controls in a nonfiduciary capacity.

For transfers in trust made after March 1, 1986, except for transfers in trust made after that date pursuant to a binding property settlement agreement entered into on or before that date, the grantor trust rules have been expanded so that the income of a trust also is generally taxed to its grantor if the trust corpus will revert to either the grantor or the grantor's spouse (.15). The use of short-term (*Clifford*) trusts—trusts where the application of the grantor trust provisions could be avoided when certain retained powers and interests did not become effective in the grantor until after a period of 10 years—has been repealed.

A grantor is now considered to be the owner of any portion of a trust in which he has a reversionary interest in either the trust corpus or the income if the value of the reversionary interest exceeds five percent of the value of that portion of the trust. The value of the reversionary interest is measured as of the inception of the portion of the trust in which the grantor holds an interest.

However, a grantor is exempt from the above-mentioned rule if he retains a reversionary interest that takes effect only upon the death of a minor (under age 21) lineal descendant. In order for this exception to be applicable, the beneficiary must have the entire present interest in the trust or a trust portion.

It should be noted that intra-family transfers of income-producing property to a child under age 14 may no longer be used to reduce income tax liability by shifting income from the parents' high marginal tax rate to the child's generally lower tax bracket (.20). Instead, for 2004, a child's net unearned income in excess of $800, reduced by the child's standard or itemized deductions allocated to such income, is subject to tax at his parents' top marginal rate. Because the applicable standard deduction for dependents is generally limited to $800, unearned income of a minor child in excess of $1,600 for 2004 will be taxed at the parents' rate. See, also, ¶1070.

.05 Code Sec. 671.
.10 Code Sec. 673-677.
.15 Code Sec. 672.
.20 Code Sec. 1(g).

¶25,217 Short-Term (*Clifford*) Trusts. The favorable tax treatment available for short-term (*Clifford*) trusts has been eliminated for transfers in trust made after March 1, 1986, except for transfers in trust made after that date pursuant to a binding property settlement agreement entered into on or before that date (.05). See ¶19,405.

.05 Code Sec. 671.

¶25,218 Family Estate Trusts. Despite the fact that the right of parents to transfer a part of their property to a trust for the benefit of a member of their family, (thereby relieving themselves of federal tax liability) has been well established, the tax benefits often associated with what are known as family estate trusts may be illusory (.05). By transferring their property and lifetime services to a trust and having the trust pay their personal expenses, such taxpayers have attempted to avoid personal income tax liability. However, the tax benefits claimed for these devices in so-called tax kits by their promoters have been successfully attacked by the IRS in the courts. The IRS has used two general approaches in its successful attempts to tax trust income to the grantors: the first is to consistently rule that such trusts are nullities for tax purposes, and the second is to combine the assignment of income and grantor trust rules (.10).

Another, and potentially more serious, problem with family estate trusts is that improper use of them may render a taxpayer liable for civil penalties (.15).

.05 Code Sec. 671; Reg. §1.671-1.

.10 *L. Markosian*, 73 TC 98, CCH Dec. 36,858; *W.M. Raemer*, 41 TCM 1149, TC Memo. 1981-138, CCH Dec. 37,776(M); *L.R. Liljequist Est.*, 41 TCM 1103, TC Memo. 1981-121, CCH Dec. 37,757(M); *A. Lundgren*, 41 TCM 1139, TC Memo. 1981-136, CCH Dec. 37,774(M); *J.L. Landphier*, 41 TCM 1172, TC Memo. 1981-145, CCH Dec. 37,786(M).

.15 *E.G. Bass, Jr.*, 41 TCM 1176, TC Memo. 1981-146, CCH Dec. 37,789(M).

Elections by the Estate

¶25,220 Tax-Saving Elections Available. The executor or administrator of an estate may make several important elections that affect the estate's or the beneficiary's total tax costs. The elections that affect estate tax liability are discussed below.

¶25,221 Alternate Valuation Date. Under certain circumstances, the valuation of an estate for tax purposes may be made as of the date six months after the date of the decedent's death, or if an asset is sold within the six-month period, as of the sale date (the alternate valuation date (.05)). The election to value the estate as of the alternate valuation date may be made only where the election will reduce both the value of the decedent's gross estate and the sum of the federal estate tax and generation-skipping transfer tax liabilities. For details, see ¶20,340.

Consequently, executors of decedents' estates having no estate tax or generation-skipping transfer tax liability may not elect to value estate assets on the alternate valuation date if doing so would result in a higher valuation. Such a higher valuation may not be used to reduce the beneficiary's income tax liability upon a later sale of the assets, because property acquired from a decedent receives a stepped-up basis as of the date of valuation.

.05 Code Sec. 2032(c).

¶25,222 Special Use Valuation. If certain conditions are met, the fiduciary of an estate may elect to value certain real property that is used for the family farm or closely held business at its actual value rather than at its highest and best use value (.05). (See ¶20,350) This election may be made in conjunction with the alternate valuation date election discussed at ¶25,221. The election is made by checking the appropriate box on Form 706 (United States Estate (and Generation-Skipping Transfer) Tax Return). It may be made on a late return, provided that it is made on the first return filed. The special use valuation election is irrevocable.

However, a fiduciary may preserve the estate's options in situations where it is unclear that the property will qualify as special use property by making a protective election. Thus, the fiduciary can value the real property at its fair market value, not the special use value, and make a protective election to specially value qualified real property by checking the appropriate box on Form 706 and completing Schedule A-1 (Section 2032A Valuation) (see ¶20,350).

.05 Code Sec. 2032A.

¶25,223 Postponement of Tax Attributable to Reversionary or Remainder Interests. The fiduciary of an estate may elect to postpone the payment of tax attributable to a reversionary or remainder interest until six months after the termination of the preceding property interests (.05). The election to postpone payment of tax is made on Form 706 at part 3.

.05 Code Sec. 6163; Reg. §20.6163-1.

¶25,224 Payment of Estate Tax in Installments. Estate tax of an estate containing an interest in a closely held business can be paid in installments if the fiduciary so elects by checking the appropriate election box on Form 706 at part 3 (.05). See ¶20,385. In addition, the fiduciary who elects to defer payment of tax can also select a special lien procedure in order to be discharged from personal liability. (See ¶20,385.)

.05 Code Sec. 6166 and 6324A.

¶25,225 Treatment of Expenses. One important election available to the executor involves the treatment of administration expenses, casualty losses, and other expenses (.05). The executor has the choice of claiming these as deductions on either (but not both) the estate tax return or the fiduciary income tax return. The starting point for planning, of course, is a comparison of rates. If the estate's income tax bracket is higher than its estate tax bracket, greater overall savings will result from utilizing the deductions on the income tax return.

It is not necessary that all administration expenses be claimed on one return or the other. The decision may be made on an item-by-item basis. Nor is it required that the total deductions, or the total amount of any deduction, be treated in the same way. One deduction or a portion of a deduction may be allowed for income tax purposes if the appropriate statement is filed, while another deduction or portion may be allowed for estate tax purposes. A particular item may be deductible on one return but not on the other. For example, expenses incurred in earning tax-exempt income are not deductible for income tax purposes, but may be deductible for estate tax purposes.

Expenses incurred by an estate in selling property to raise funds to pay administration expenses and taxes are also subject to this double-deduction prohibition. Such expenses can be claimed only as an administration expense deduction on a decedent's estate tax return or claimed as an offset against the sale price for computing the capital gain on the fiduciary's income tax return.

The rule against double deductions also does not apply to deductions for taxes, interest, business expenses, and other items that are accrued at the date of a decedent's death and that, therefore, are claims against his or her estate. These expenses can be claimed as an estate tax deduction and as a deduction in respect of a decedent for income tax purposes (.10).

Possible conflicts

In making an election concerning administration expenses, there are possible conflicts that may result between beneficiaries because of the shifting of burdens and benefits that may be brought about. If the executor takes the administration expenses as deductions on the estate's income tax return, a life beneficiary will be enriched at the expense of a remainderman. This is the case because administration expenses allowable as income tax deductions are usually paid from principal rather than income. Thus, the income beneficiary receives increased after-tax income by virtue of the reduction in federal income taxes but does not share any of the burden of the payment of administration expenses that produced the tax savings. The remainderman may complain that reimbursement of the additional estate tax should be made to principal since it will be reduced by:

(1) the amount of administration expenses chargeable to principal, and

(2) the additional estate tax caused by the executor's election to take administration expenses on the estate's income tax return instead of the estate tax return.

Furthermore, the executor may be confronted under local law with the duty to make an adjustment against the surviving spouse in favor of the residuary beneficiaries unless the decedent's will relieves the executor from any such duty. This could affect the marital deduction, as it reduces the income of the surviving spouse. In addition, an election to deduct administration expenses on the income tax return rather than on the estate tax return will increase the taxable estate and, thus, increase the amount of federal estate taxes.

Redemption of stock to pay tax

Many estates take advantage of the election to redeem stock to pay death taxes (.15). This election permits a specified amount of stock to be redeemed by a corporation without dividend implications. That specified amount is the sum of death taxes (including interest), plus funeral and administration expenses allowed as deductions from the gross estate. Through careful handling of administration expenses, it may be possible for the executor to qualify a stock redemption for this treatment that might otherwise not qualify because the redeemed shares fail to meet the percentage requirements.

☐ See ¶25,182.

.05 Code Sec. 642, 2053 and 2054.
.10 Code Sec. 691.
.15 Code Sec. 303.

¶25,226 Consideration of Tax Brackets. For the most part, estates and trusts have the same tax rates as individuals. In 2004, the estate and trust rates are 15, 25, 28, 33, and 35 percent. These rates are the same as the individual rates except that individuals benefit from an initial 10 percent rate. Although the rates are very similar for individuals on the one hand, and estates and trusts on the other, the schedules nevertheless differ substantially because the estates and trust brackets are compressed. For example, for 2004, the 25 percent bracket begins at income amounts over $1,900 for estates and trusts compared to $29,050 for an unmarried taxpayer. Thus, it may be better to shift income from the estate or trust to the beneficiary rather than retain it.

¶25,227 U.S. Savings Bonds. If a cash-basis decedent did not elect to report the increment in value of Series E savings bonds as income, the increment in value up to the date of his death becomes income in respect of a decedent (.05). This rule applies to the following types of bonds (.10):

(1) bonds that were purchased by the decedent and registered solely in his name;

(2) bonds that were registered in the names of the decedent and another person, as co-owners, and that were purchased by the decedent solely with his own funds; and

(3) bonds that were acquired by the decedent, as the surviving co-owner, and that were purchased by the other co-owner, where neither reported the increment as income.

There are a number of optional tax-saving ways to report the increment on the above types of bonds as income:

(1) An executor, administrator, or any other person charged with the property of a decedent may elect to report the increment in value up to the date of the decedent's death on the decedent's final income tax return (.15).

(2) A cash-basis estate may elect to report all the unreported interest on all of the decedent's bonds, from the dates of their purchase to the year of the election, on its income tax return. An election by the estate will not preclude the person who ultimately receives the bonds from electing to report the discount as income when the bonds are redeemed or finally mature. (The IRS has ruled that a testamentary trust which acquired a decedent's savings bonds was not bound by the executor's election and could report any remaining accrued increment upon the bonds' maturity or redemption, even though the executor was also the trustee (.20).)

(3) A cash-basis beneficiary who acquires the savings bonds also has the option of reporting the increment when he acquires the bonds or of holding the bonds until maturity or redemption and then reporting the unreported increment as income. However, the IRS has ruled that, if a "recipient" acquiring savings bonds from a decedent makes the election to report the increment, he must include in gross income all of the unreported increment in value of all Series E bonds held by him and not just the increment attributable to the decedent's bonds. Thereafter, he should report in each tax year the increment in value actually accruing within such tax year.

.05 Code Sec. 691; Rev. Rul. 64-104, 1964-1 (Part 1) CB 223.

.10 Rev. Rul. 58-435, 1958-2 CB 370.

.15 Rev. Rul. 68-145, 1968-1 CB 203.

.20 Rev. Rul. 58-435, 1958-2 CB 370.

¶25,228 65-Day Distribution Rule. For tax years beginning after August 5, 1997, a decedent's estate may elect to treat distributions made to beneficiaries within 65 days after the close of its tax year as if they were made of the last day of the tax year (.05). Previously, this election was available only to trusts, not estates.

.05 Code Sec. 663(b).

¶25,228A Pre-Need Funeral Trusts. A funeral trust is an arrangement whereby an individual purchases funeral services or merchandise from a funeral home prior to his or her death. The payment amount is held in trust and paid to the seller upon the individual's death. Under prior law, a pre-need funeral trust was generally treated as a grantor trust, and the annual income earned by the trust was taxed to the purchaser/grantor. If a trustee elects special tax treatment, a "pre-need qualified funeral trust" is not treated as a grantor trust, and the tax on the annual earnings of the trust is payable by the trustee (.05). Previously, this election was available only to trusts, not estates.

If the election is made, the Code Sec. 1(e) income tax rate schedule generally applicable to estates and trusts is applied to the trust by treating each beneficiary's interest as a separate trust. However, the trust is not entitled to a Code Sec. 642(b) personal exemption in calculating the tax. The trustee's election must be made separately for each purchaser's trust. No gain or loss is recognized to a purchaser of a pre-need funeral trust contract as a result of any payment from the trust to the purchaser due to the cancellation of the contract.

.05 Code Sec. 685.

¶25,228B Election to Include Revocable Trust in Estate. If elected, a qualified revocable trust (QRT) may be treated as part of a decedent's estate for federal income tax purposes and not as a separate trust. A QRT trust is a trust or portion of a trust that is treated as owned by the decedent as a result of a power the decedent held as grantor. A decedent for these purposes is the individual treated as the owner of the QRT on the date of that individual's death (.05).

The election is made by filing Form 8855, Election to Treat a Qualified Revocable Trust as Part of an Estate.

.05 Code Sec. 645.

INVESTORS

Introduction

¶25,229 Tax legislation during 2003, brought about dramatic reductions in the taxation of capital gains and dividends. These reductions should cause a fundamental shift in the way individuals think about their long-range investment planning and how they structure their investment portfolios. Generally, starting in 2003, qualified dividend income is taxed at a maximum rate of 15% (a 5% rate for those in the 10% or 15% tax brackets). Long-term capital gain recognized after May 5, 2003 is taxed at a maximum rate of 15% (a 5% rate for those in the 10% or 15% tax brackets.) Long-term capital gain recognized before May 6, 2003 was taxed at a maximum rate of 20% (10% for taxpayers in a 10% or 15% tax bracket). For 2004, the highest regular income tax rate applicable to individuals is 35%. Because of the spread between the rates imposed on ordinary income (i.e., maximum of 35%) and the rates imposed on long-term capital gains and dividend income (i.e., maximums of 5% or 15%), individuals should place more emphasis on the receipt of long-term capital gain and/or dividend income as opposed to ordinary income (e.g., interest income).

The following are some of the steps that individual investors should consider in order to minimize their federal income tax liabilities:

(1) Consider holding your investments that generate interest income in tax-sheltered accounts (e.g., retirement plans, such as traditional IRAs, 401(k) plans, SEPs) and holding investments that generate qualified dividend income and/or long-term capital gains in taxable accounts. (The exception to this general rule is a Roth IRA, that provides the opportunity of tax-free distributions no matter the source of the income.) This practice may prove an effective tax reduction strategy due to the fact that distributions from tax-sheltered accounts are generally taxed as ordinary income. Thus, when dividend and capital gains are eventually distributed from your retirement plan, they will not eligible for the lower tax rates that generally apply to investment income. On the other hand, interest income is taxed as ordinary income no matter whether it is distributed from a retirement plan or regular account.

(2) Make investments in order to maximize rate of return and appreciation in the property, and not merely to reduce taxes. The saving of taxes is an important goal, but it should not override these considerations. Investors

who are in the higher tax brackets, should consider investing in tax-exempt bonds when the rate of return on these bonds is greater than the after tax return on taxable bonds. However, the risk inherent in any investment must be evaluated.

(3) Earn tax-exempt income. Investments in tax-exempt bonds and Roth IRAs are key examples of such opportunities.

(4) Defer the recognition of gain and/or income (for example, see, ¶25,256). Delaying the recognition of gain is especially important given the low tax rates that now apply to long-term capital gains (see ¶25,232).

(5) Maintain adequate records. In order to achieve the maximum tax benefit available, investors must be able to identify the assets that are being sold (see ¶25,234), the dates of purchase and sale (see ¶25,243), cost or other basis (see ¶25,271).

(6) Offset taxable income with more deductions. However, do not overlook a potential tax liability under the alternative minimum tax.

(7) Minimize expenditures that are made for nondeductible items. There is, for example, a cap on deductions for investment interest.

(8) Minimize activities that may produce losses that will be nondeductible in the current year. Investors, for example, should give some consideration to the limits that are applicable to passive losses. Investors must also avoid transactions that will result in wash sales (see ¶25,243).

(9) Comply with the law in order to avoid penalties. For example, pay estimated taxes when they are due (see ¶25,231) and do not invest in or claim losses from abusive tax shelters.

The material at ¶25,231 outlines these rules as they apply to the following typical investments:

(1) stocks (see ¶25,239 and following);

(2) bonds (see ¶25,249 and following);

(3) commodity futures, including straddles (see ¶25,258 and following);

(4) options: puts and calls, including straddles (see ¶25,262 and following);

(5) mutual funds (see ¶25,269 and following);

(6) real estate (see ¶25,274 and following);

(7) real estate investment trusts (REITs) (see ¶25,277 and following); and

(8) real estate mortgage investment conduits (REMICs) (see ¶25,280 and following).

This division concludes with discussions of investments held in life insurance and annuity contracts (see ¶25,283 and following) and in retirement savings (see ¶25,287 and following), and of the pros and cons of holding investments in corporations, personal holding companies and S corporations (see ¶25,291 and following). The introductory material (¶25,231-¶25,236) contains general rules applicable to most investments.

Overview

¶25,231 Taxation of Investors. Investors receive a number of specialized types of income from their investments, each governed by its own unique rules. Investors who have a capital gain or loss for the year must generally attach Schedule D (Capital Gains and Losses) to their Form 1040. Dividends (see ¶25,244) and interest (see ¶25,250), two other important sources of investment income, are usually required to be reported on Schedule B (Interest and Dividend Income). Rents from rental real estate, royalties, and income from partnerships are reported on Schedule E (Supplemental Income Schedule).

The rules regarding expenses of producing income are discussed at ¶25,236. Limitations on the deductibility of interest paid on loans used to purchase or carry investments are discussed at ¶25,235. Depreciation deductions that are available to investors in real estate are discussed at ¶25,274. Investment clubs, formed by groups of individuals who pool their money to invest in stocks or other securities, are discussed at ¶25,237.

Estimated tax

All investors should consider whether they have an obligation to pay estimated tax. If necessary, investors should consider having additional amounts withheld from wages. Failure to have the required tax paid through estimated taxes and/or withholding may result in penalties being assessed.

¶25,232 Capital Gains and Losses. In most situations, a taxpayer generally receives two types of income from investments:

(1) income from ownership of the investment (e.g., dividends from stocks, interest from bonds, and rents from real estate); and

(2) gain or loss from disposing of the property.

Income derived from holding an investment is generally taxed as ordinary income unless the taxpayer satisfies a *more than 12 months* holding period. Special rules may apply to exclude all or part of such income, as is the case with dividends when there is a return of capital (see ¶25,244).

Amount of gain or loss—Basis

The first step in determining the tax effect of a sale or other disposition of investment property is calculating gain or loss on the transaction. *Gain* is equal to the excess of the selling price (i.e., cash or fair market value of other property received reduced by commissions paid on the sale), over the property's adjusted basis. *Loss* is equal to the excess of the property's adjusted basis over the selling price (.05).

An investor's *basis* in a particular piece of investment property depends on how the property was acquired.

(1) *Purchase.* If an investor acquired investment property by purchase, basis in the property is generally its cost (.10). *Cost* is the amount of cash, if any, plus the fair market value of other property, if any, paid for the investment. Cost also includes commissions paid in acquiring the property. An exception to the cost rule for computing

basis exists in the case of certain tax-free exchanges, which are discussed as item (4), below.

(2) *Gift.* If the fair market value (FMV) of the property at the time of the gift is less than the donor's adjusted basis, the investor's basis depends on whether he has a gain or a loss when he disposes of the property. The basis for figuring *gain* is the same as the donor's adjusted basis plus or minus any required adjustment to basis while the investor held the property. The basis for figuring *loss* is its FMV when the investor received the gift plus or minus any required adjustment to basis while he held the property. If the investor uses the donor's adjusted basis for figuring a gain and gets a loss, and then uses the FMV for figuring a loss and has a gain, he has neither gain nor loss on the sale or disposition of the property. If the FMV of the property is equal to or greater than the donor's adjusted basis, the investor's basis is the donor's adjusted basis at the time the investor received the gift.(.15).

> ***Example:*** Bob Green received an acre of land as a gift. At the time of the gift, the land had an FMV of $8,000. The donor's adjusted basis was $10,000. After he received the land, no events occurred to increase or decrease his basis. If Bob sold the land for $12,000, he will have a $2,000 gain because he must use the donor's adjusted basis ($10,000) at the time of the gift as his basis to figure gain. If he sells the land for $7,000, he will have a $1,000 loss because he must use the FMV ($8,000) at the time of the gift as his basis to figure a loss. If the sales price is between $8,000 and $10,000, Bob would have neither gain nor loss. For instance, if the sales price was $9,000 and he tried to figure a gain using the donor's adjusted basis ($10,000), Bob would get a $1,000 loss. If he then tried to figure a loss using the FMV ($8,000), he would get a $1,000 gain.

(3) *Inheritance.* Investment property acquired by inheritance has a basis equal to the fair market value of the property at the date of death (or, if alternate valuation is elected, the fair market value six months after death or at the time of earlier disposition) (.20).

(4) *Tax-free exchanges.* Investment property acquired in a tax-free exchange of like-kind property (.25) or exchanges of stock made in connection with tax-free reorganizations (.30) generally have a basis equal to the basis of the property given up in the transaction plus any additional cash paid minus the amount, if any, of gain recognized on the transaction.

(5) *Distributions from employee retirement plans.* Securities distributed by a qualified employee plan (i.e., pension plans, thrift plans, and employee stock ownership plans (ESOPs)) generally have a basis equal to the total amount of employee contributions to the plan plus any gain realized on the distribution minus the amount of cash received on the distribution (.35).

(6) *Stock dividends.* Special rules for computing basis in the case of stock dividends are discussed at ¶25,245.

(7) *Stripped bonds.* Special rules for computing basis in the case of stripped bonds or coupons are discussed at ¶25,254.

During the life of an investment, additions to and subtractions from basis may have to be made. An increase in basis reduces the amount of gain that will be taxed when the property is eventually disposed of, and a decrease in basis increases such gain. The following are some adjustments to basis that a typical investor is likely to encounter:

(1) *Capital expenditures.* The basis of real property and other capital assets is increased when a taxpayer makes capital additions or improvements to it (e.g., by adding a wing to a building) (.40).

(2) *Depreciation.* The basis of real estate is decreased for allowable depreciation deductions (.45).

(3) *Tax-free dividends.* The basis of stock is increased to the extent that a dividend received is in excess of the corporation's earnings and profits (.50). (See ¶25,244.)

(4) *Bond premiums.* The basis of bonds is decreased when deductions are taken to amortize bond premiums (.55). (See ¶25,252.)

(5) *Bond discounts.* The basis of bonds is increased when original issue discount income (.60) or market discount income (.65) is reported. (See ¶25,253.)

Recaptured depreciation

Also, investors who sell or otherwise dispose of real estate for which depreciation has been taken may be required to report all or part of the previously claimed depreciation as ordinary income when the recapture rules are applicable. For a discussion of recapture, see ¶25,274.

Taxation of capital gains and losses

In order to calculate the capital gains tax, taxpayers must aggregate capital gains and losses. For 2003, net capital gain income (excess of net long-term capital gain over net short-term capital loss) is taxed at rates ranging from 5% to 28% depending on the timing of the sale, the individual's tax bracket, and the holding period of the asset.

General rules. For 2004, if a capital asset has been held more than 12 months it will generally be taxed at a 15% maximum capital gains rate (.75). However, for individuals in the 10% or 15% brackets the gain will generally be taxed at a 5% rate.

Collectibles. Collectibles (as defined under Code Sec. 408(m) (e.g., works of art, rugs or antiques, metals or gem, and stamps or coins) are taxed at a maximum capital gains rate of 28% even for a holding period of more than 12 months.

Real estate depreciation recapture. "Unrecaptured Section 1250 gain" is subject to a maximum capital gains tax rate of 25% (.80). Generally, "unrecaptured Section 1250 gain" is the amount of depreciation claimed on Section 1250 property (i.e., real property) which is not recaptured as ordinary income under the Code Sec. 1250 recapture rules. Unrecaptured depreciation taken into account in computing unrecaptured Section 1250 gain cannot exceed the amount of gain recognized on the property after the gain is reduced by any ordinary income depreciation recapture. Gain on an item of Section 1250 property which is in excess of any ordinary income depreciation recapture and unrecaptured Section 1250 gain is eligible for the 15% capital gains rate.

Specifically unrecaptured Section 1250 gain is the *excees* of:

(1) the amount of long-term capital gain (not otherwise treated as ordinary income) that would be treated as ordinary income if (a) Code Sec. 1250(b)(1) included all depreciation and the applicable percentage that applied under Code Sec. 1250(a) were 100%, and (b) only gain from property held for more than 12 months were taken into account, over

(2) the excess of 28% rate loss over 28% rate gain.

The upshot of this computational process is that any net 28% rate loss acts first to offset unrecaptured Section 1250 gain, and the excess of such loss, if any, is then applied to offset capital gains that are taxed at the maximum 20% (or 15%) rate.

Under the capital gains rules, Code Sec. 1250 will continue to treat some prior claimed depreciation (i.e., usually the amount claimed in excess of the amount allowable under the straight-line method) as ordinary income. This fact is illustrated in the following example.

Example 1: On December 8, 2004, William Drake sold a building for $1,000,000. The building had originally cost $500,000 and, over the years, Drake had claimed $400,000 in depreciation. Drake recognized a $900,000 gain. Of the $400,000 in depreciation, $100,000 was in excess of that allowed under the straight line method and recaptured as ordinary income. Under the capital gains rules, $300,000 of the depreciation is classified as unrecaptured Section 1250 gain and subject to a 25% tax rate. The remaining $500,000 of gain is subject to a maximum 15% rate.

Under MACRS, all depreciation on real property must be computed using the straight-line method. As a result, any gain on the sale of MACRS real property that is due to claimed depreciation will be classified as "unrecaptured Section 1250 gain" and thus subject to a maximum capital gains rate of 25%. Of course, the property will have to be held more than 12 months for this rule to apply.

Example 2: On December 30, 2004, Nat Spar sold a building for $100,000. He had owned the property for more than 12 months. Spar had purchased the building for $50,000 and under MACRS had claimed $20,000 in straight-line depreciation. His basis in the building at the time of sale was $30,000. As a result, his long-term capital gain was $70,000. However, in determining Spar's "adjusted net capital gain", he must subtract his $20,000 of unrecaptured Section 1250 gain. The $20,000 will be taxed at a maximum rate of 25% and his remaining $50,000 in adjusted net capital gain will be taxed as a maximum rate of 15%.

A net capital loss for the year is deductible from ordinary income up to a maximum of $3,000 annually.

Tax-free exchanges

An investor may escape tax on a disposition of investment property under certain circumstances. The two most common tax-free dispositions are (1) like-kind exchanges, which are of particular interest to investors in real estate, and (2) exchanges of stock made in connection with a tax-free corporate reorganization.

.05 Code Sec. 1001.
.10 Code Sec. 1012.
.15 Code Sec. 1015.
.20 Code Sec. 1014.
.25 Code Sec. 1031.
.30 Code Sec. 1036.
.35 Reg. §1.402(a)-1(b).
.40 Code Sec. 1016.
.45 Code Sec. 1016.
.50 Code Sec. 301.
.55 Code Sec. 171.
.60 Code Sec. 1272.
.65 Code Sec. 1276.
.75 Code Sec. 1(h)
.80 Code Sec. 1(h)(7).

¶25,233 Installment Sales. The installment method of accounting may not be used to report gain on sales of stock or securities (.05). Thus, an investor who is a cash-method taxpayer and who sells stock on a stock exchange at a gain near the end of the year does not have the option of either postponing the reporting of such gain until the following year or reporting it in the year of sale. Instead, both cash- and accrual-basis taxpayers must report the gain in the year the transaction is executed.

.05 Code Sec. 453.

¶25,234 Identification of Securities. An investor who owns several certificates of the same security should be careful to identify the shares intended to be sold, particularly if the securities were acquired at different times and for different prices. If adequate identification is made at the time of the sale, the amount of gain and the holding period of the securities sold is determined by using the basis and acquisition date of the identified securities (.05). If an identification is not made, the first-in, first-out (FIFO) rule is applied: the earliest acquired securities are deemed to be sold first.

Adequate identification

Adequate identification may be made in the following manner:

(1) If the securities are held by the investor, adequate identification is made when the certificates representing the securities to be sold are delivered to the investor's broker.

(2) If the securities are held by the investor's broker or bank (for convenience or as margin or collateral for other loans), adequate identification is made where the investor notifies the broker as to the specific securities (by acquisition date and price) to be sold. The broker must then confirm the identification in writing. Adequate identification is not made if the investor merely makes note of the transaction in personal records.

The FIFO rule does not apply to stock received in a reorganization exchange when the basis for the new shares is the average of the basis of the old shares given up in the exchange. When there is a stock split, however, the FIFO rule applies. The identification is made by assigning the lowest numbered certificates to the earliest purchases of the original stock. The transfer agent's statement as to which new certificate was issued for each old share is the identification record.

When shares in a mutual fund are sold, the general rules concerning the determination of basis are the same as those applied to shares of stock in a corporation. If certain requirements are met, however, mutual fund shareholders may elect to determine the basis of mutual fund shares using an "average basis" method for the shares sold. (See ¶25,271.)

.05 Reg. §1.1012-1(c).

¶25,235 Investment Interest Expense. For many investors, interest is a major expense associated with the acquisition and carrying of investment property. Investors who itemize their deductions may generally deduct their interest expense. The deduction for this type of interest is limited to the amount of net investment income (.05).

Definitions

For purposes of the limitation on the deductibility of investment interest:

Investment interest means interest paid or accrued on debt incurred or continued to buy or carry property held for investment. For short sales, the term also includes any amount allowable as a deduction in connection with property used in the short sale. Interest on home mortgages, car loans, or loans taken in connection with the taxpayer's trade or business, however, are not subject to the investment interest limitation. Investment interest also does not include interest that is taken into account under Code Sec. 469 in computing income or loss from a passive activity or interest allocable to a rental real estate activity in which the taxpayer actively participates, within the meaning of the passive loss rules.

Net investment income is the excess of a taxpayer's investment income over investment expenses.

Investment income includes interest, dividends, rents from net lease property, and royalties, plus any net gain attributable to the disposition of property held for investment. Investors may elect to classify all or part of their capital gains that are subject to the maximum tax rate of 28 percent as investment income in order to offset additional investment interest. However, they must also subject the amount of their capital gains that was classified as investment income to their ordinary income tax rates.

Investment expenses include any expenses other than interest that are directly connected with the production of investment income, such as office rent, investment counsel fees, accounting expenses, storage fees, insurance, or legal expenses.

Disallowed investment interest

If the full amount of the investment interest is not deductible because of the investment interest limitation, the excess amount may generally be carried over to later years to the extent of net investment income in such years (.10).

Interest on margin accounts

An investor who establishes a margin account with a broker may purchase securities by depositing with the broker only a portion of the purchase price. The balance represents a loan from the broker to the investor, for which interest is charged. Such interest is deductible investment interest, but, for an investor using the cash method of accounting, it is not deductible until it is actually or constructively paid to the broker. Such payments may consist of amounts received by the broker from:

(1) the collection of dividends or interest for the investor's account;

(2) the sale of the investor's securities that are held by the broker; or

(3) the deposit of cash by the investor, voluntarily or in answer to a call from the broker for additional margin (.15).

Interest to carry tax-exempt securities

No deduction is allowed for interest on indebtedness of an investor or related person incurred or continued to purchase or carry tax-exempt securities (.20).

Market discount bonds and short-term obligations

Interest to purchase or carry market discount bonds acquired after July 18, 1984, may be disallowed to the extent of accrued market discount for the year. A similar limitation applies to interest incurred to purchase or carry short-term obligations such as Treasury bills.

.05 Code Sec. 163(d).

.10 Code Sec. 163(d)(2); *A. Beyer*, CA-4, 90-2 USTC ¶ 50,536.

.15 Rev. Rul. 70-221, 1970-1 CB 33.

.20 Code Sec. 265.

¶25,236 Expenses of Producing Income. An individual's investment expenses are deductible only as expenses of producing income, not as business expenses (.05). This means that they must be itemized on Schedule A of Form 1040 and may not be taken if the taxpayer does not itemize deductions. The aggregate of most investment expenses and other miscellaneous deductions must exceed 2% of adjusted gross income in order to be deductible.

"Investment," as used here, means buying and selling stocks, bonds, certificates of interest in mortgages, notes, etc., for one's own account. The term does not refer to the handling of rents and royalties, even though such activities may, for income tax purposes, be an investment rather than a business. Expenses incurred in connection with rental real estate and royalties are usually deductible on Schedule E of Form 1040.

Deductible expenses

An investor's nonbusiness expenses may include the following: office rent, investment counsel fees, legal and accounting expenses, secretary's salary, safe deposit rent, stamp taxes, and statistical services. Expenses incurred in making trips to look after one's investments are deductible (.10). Travel expenses incurred to attend investment seminars or conventions are deductible only if they are connected with a trade or business. These expenses are not deductible as expenses incurred for the production of income (.15).

☐ For a discussion of the deductibility of investment interest, see ¶ 25,235.

Commissions

Commissions paid on the purchase of stock, bonds, and other investment property must be included in the basis of the acquired property. Commissions paid on the sale of such property is applied as an offset against the selling price. (See ¶25,232.)

Legal expenses

Legal expenses that are reasonable in amount and bear a proximate relation to an individual's investments or to the maintenance of property held for the production of income are deductible. However, nonbusiness legal expenses connected with the purchase of property are part of the cost of the property and must be capitalized (.20).

Expenses allocable to tax-exempt income

No deduction is allowed for expenses to the extent that they are allocable to tax-exempt income (.25). When an investor incurs expenses that are not clearly allocable to either taxable or tax-exempt income, the expenses must be apportioned on the basis of their proportionate contributions to gross income (.30).

Short-sale expenses

No deduction is allowed to a short seller for payments made in lieu of dividends on stock sold short (see ¶25,242) if the short sale is closed on or before the 45th day after the date of the short sale (.35). The 45-day period is extended to one year in the case of payments made in lieu of extraordinary dividends. Extraordinary dividends are dividends in excess of five percent of the amount the investor realized on the short sale in the case of preferred stock and 10 percent in the case of any other stock. Aggregate dividends within a 365-day period in excess of 20 percent of the amount the investor realized on the short sale are also considered extraordinary dividends (.40).

When the deduction is disallowed, such payments are added to the basis of the stock used to close the short sale. If the deduction is allowed, i.e., when the payments are made after the required holding period, the deduction is not considered an "expense of producing income." Instead, such payments are considered investment interest and are subject to the deduction limits applicable to investment interest (see ¶25,235).

In determining how long a short sale is kept open, any period during which the investor holds, has an option to buy, or is under a contractual obligation to buy, substantially identical stock or securities or is otherwise substantially protected from the risk of loss on the short sale by holding related positions is not counted.

Straddle expenses

Investors are required to capitalize certain otherwise deductible expenditures for actively traded personal property if the property is held as part of an offsetting position that substantially diminishes the taxpayer's risk of loss by means of buy-and-sell orders in the same property, i.e., a straddle (.45). Such expenditures must be charged to the capital account of the property for which the expenditures are made. Thus, these expenditures will reduce the gain or increase the loss recognized upon the disposition of the property.

Expenditures subject to this capitalization requirement are interest on indebtedness incurred or continued in order to purchase or carry the property, as well as amounts paid or incurred for insuring, storing or transporting the property. The amount of expenditures to be capitalized (called carrying charges) is reduced by: (1) any interest income from the property (including original issue discount) that is includible in gross income for the tax year, (2) dividends on stock included in a straddle, but only to the extent that they are included in income after allowance of the dividends-received deduction, (3) any amount of ordinary income acquisition discount includible in gross income for the tax year, and (4) any compensating payments made to the lender of securities used in a short sale.

The capitalization requirements do not apply to any identified hedging transactions or to any position that is not part of a straddle. Thus, for example, a farmer may deduct currently the costs of financing crops. Similarly, securities dealers' expenses for financing their inventory and trading accounts that generate ordinary income or loss are deductible.

.05 Code Sec. 212; Reg. §1.212-1.
.10 *P.J. Preseault,* 34 TCM 685, CCH Dec. 33,203(M), TC Memo. 1975-146; *E. McBee,* 25 TCM 931, CCH Dec. 28,062(M), TC Memo. 1966-180.
.15 Code Sec. 274(h)(7).
.20 Reg. §1.212-1(k).
.25 Code Sec. 265.
.30 Rev. Rul. 73-565, 1973-2 CB 90.
.35 Code Sec. 263(h)(1).
.40 Code Sec. 263(h)(3) and 1059(c).
.45 Code Sec. 263(g).

¶25,237 Investment Clubs. A common form of buying and selling stocks and other securities among small investors is through an investment club. Individuals may combine their resources and take advantage of the club's ability to create a diversified investment portfolio.

Choice of entity plays an important role because, depending on its organization, an investment club may be an entity treated as a partnership, a C corporation, or an S corporation (.05). If the investment club is treated as a partnership, it must file an information partnership return on Form 1065, but does not pay tax. Instead, the investor/ partners report their share of the partnership items separately on their own returns, whether or not the club makes any distributions, according to the amounts reported on a Schedule K-1 (Partner's Share of Income, Credit Deductions, Etc.). The investment club cannot net its investment expenses against its income as business expenses but must separately report to each partner his or her share of such expenses because this type of investment activity does not constitute a trade or business for an individual (.10). The expenses passed through to partners are subject to the 2% of AGI floor on miscellaneous itemized deductions.

An investment club formed after 1996 is taxed as a corporation if it: (1) is formed under a federal or state law that refers to it as incorporated or as a corporation, body corporate, or body politic, (2) is formed under a state law that refers to it as a joint-stock company or joint-stock association, or (3) chooses to be taxed as a corporation (.15).

An investment club that is a corporation for tax purposes will file a corporate tax return on Form 1120, or 1120-A, if appropriate, and pay tax on the income earned by the club. Later, when the income is distributed to the investor shareholders, it will again be taxed to them individually. This double taxation may be avoided by electing subchapter S status if the incorporated club has 75 or fewer individual investors, none of whom are nonresident aliens. S corporation income, losses and credits are passed through and reported on their investor shareholder's tax returns, in proportion to their ownership interests.

.05 Rev. Rul. 75-523, 1975-2 CB 257.
.10 Rev. Rul. 75-525, 1975-2 CB 350.
.15 IRS Publication 550, "Investment Income and Expenses," (for 2001 returns).

Stocks

¶25,239 Investment in Stocks. Stocks offer investors two basic types of income: income from appreciation of the stock that may be realized upon sale of the stock and distributions of profits earned by the corporation that issued the stock. Special rules for the taxation of these types of income can be found in the following paragraphs:

(1) The rules regarding the taxation of appreciation in the value of stock and capital gains are discussed at ¶25,240 -¶25,243.

(2) The rules regarding the taxation of corporate distributions are discussed at ¶25,244-¶25,247.

¶25,240 Sale of Stocks. Gains or losses on the sale of stock by an investor are treated as capital gains or losses.

Both net long-term capital losses and net short-term capital losses may be offset dollar for dollar against ordinary income with an annual $3,000 limit for such offsets.

¶25,241 Small Business Corporation Stock. Individuals and partnerships owning qualifying stock issued by a qualifying small business corporation may treat losses sustained from the sale of such stock as ordinary losses (.05). A small business corporation should not be confused with an S corporation. The maximum ordinary loss that may be claimed from a sale of qualifying stock is $50,000, or $100,000 on a joint return.

A corporation is considered "a small business corporation" if the sum of all money and all property received for stock as a contribution to capital and as paid-in surplus does not exceed $1,000,000.

Stock issued by a small business corporation is considered Sec. 1244 stock if:

(1) the stock was issued in exchange for money or property (but not stock or securities); and

(2) during the corporation's five most recent tax years ending on the date on which the stock is sold by the taxpayer, more than 50 percent of the corporation's gross income was derived from sources other than royalties, rents, dividends, interest, annuities, or gains from the sale of securities. This requirement does not apply if the corporation's deductions (other than those for dividends and net operating losses) exceed its gross income.

Investors in small business stock may exclude 50 percent of the gain realized on the sale of such stock. The exclusion applies to stock issued by qualifying corporations after August 10, 1993, which must be held for more than five years.

Small business investment company

Investors in stock in a small business investment company operating under the Small Business Investment Company Act of 1958 are also allowed an ordinary loss deduction for loss on the sale or exchange of, or worthlessness of, their stock (.05).

Individual and corporate investors may defer taxation on gains from the sale of publicly held securities if the proceeds are used to buy an interest in a specialized SBIC within 60 days of the sale.

.05 Code Sec. 1244.

.05 Code Sec. 1242 and 1243.

¶25,242 Short Sales. A short sale is a sale of stock in which the seller borrows the stock that is delivered to the buyer. At a later date, the seller "closes" the short sale by covering the loan either with stock purchased for that purpose or with stock the investor held at the time of the short sale but did not wish to transfer at the earlier date. An investor who enters into a short sale realizes profits when the price of the stock declines.

Because a short sale promises profits from the decline in the value of stock, an investor may use short sales to protect unrealized profits in long positions (ownership of the stock he sold short) that are held. By holding simultaneous long and short positions, a loss on one position will be exactly offset by a gain on the other.

Capital gains and losses on short sales

The taxable event in a short sale is the closing of the transaction. Any gain or loss realized upon closing a short sale is treated as a capital gain or loss, provided that the stock used to close the short sale is a capital asset in the investor's hands (.10).

An investor who enters into a short sale and, at the time of the short sale, does *not* hold substantially identical property will recognize capital gains or losses of the following types when the sale is closed:

(1) *all gains* are short-term capital gains (.10);

(2) losses are long- or short-term depending on the holding period of the stock used to close the short sale.

Simultaneous long and short positions

If, at the time of a short sale, an investor holds a long position in substantially identical property, the following rules apply:

(1) *Short-term property.* If property that is substantially identical to the property that has been sold short was held for one year or less at the time of the short sale, its holding period is considered to begin on the date that the short sale is closed or on the date of a sale, gift, or other disposition of such property, whichever occurs the earliest (.20). This rule does not apply to so much of the substantially identical property as exceeds the property sold short, nor does it apply to securities involved in bona fide arbitrage transactions.

(2) *Long-term property.* If property substantially identical to that sold short has been held for more than one year on the date of the short sale, loss on closing the short sale is long-term capital loss, regardless of how long any property used to close the short sale has been held. The rule does not apply to so much of the property sold short as exceeds in quantity the substantially identical property held for more than one year.

(3) *Long- and short-term property.* If substantially identical property has been held by an investor on the date of the short sale for not more than one year, or is acquired by him after the short sale and on or before the date of closing, gain on the closing of the short sale is short-term capital gain (.30). This rule applies to stocks and securities (including stocks and securities dealt with on a "when issued" basis that are capital assets in the hands of the taxpayer. It does not apply to the portion of property sold short that exceeds the quantity of substantially identical property held for one year or less.

These above rules only apply to the extent that the number of shares sold short equals the number of shares held long. If more shares are sold short than are held long, gains or losses on the excess are treated under the regular short sale rules discussed at "Capital gains and losses on short sales," above.

"Short against the box"

In the past, one way to defer recognition of gain or loss on a stock was to sell the stock "short against the box." This occurred when an investor who held a long position in a particular stock sold the stock short before year's end and closed the short sale by delivering the previously held stock in the new year. This strategy was generally eliminated under the Taxpayer Relief Act of 1997 (.30).

Effect on owners of the borrowed stock

A margin buyer or other investor who allows his broker to lend his stock to be sold short receives a credit to his account (called a "short dividend") in the amount of the forgone dividend. The borrower is not considered to be the owner of the stock sold short; the purchaser in the short sale is the owner. The margin buyer is, therefore, taxed on the short dividend.

☐ Short sales are covered by the wash sale rules (see ¶25,243). For a discussion of the deductibility of payments made by the short seller in lieu of dividends, see ¶25,236.

.10 Code Sec. 1233(a).
.10 Code Sec. 1233(b)(1); Reg. §1.1233-1(c)(2).
.20 Code Sec. 1233(b)(2); Reg. §1.1233-1.
.30 Code Sec. 1233(b); Reg. §1.1233-1.
.30 Code Sec. 1259.

¶25,243 Wash Sales. Losses on the sale or other disposition of stock (including margin transactions) may not be deducted if, within a 61-day period beginning 30 days before the date of sale and ending 30 days after the sale, the investor acquires (by purchase or taxable exchange) substantially identical stock or securities—a wash sale (.05). The wash sale rules also apply to disallow losses when, within the 61-day period, the investor acquires a contract or option to acquire substantially identical stock or securities.

Basis and holding periods

If a loss deduction is denied because of the wash sale rules, the cost basis (see ¶25,232) of the acquired stock is increased by the amount of loss that was disallowed on the sale of the old stock.

Application to short sales

Losses realized on the closing of a short sale are disallowed if, within 30 days before or after the closing:

(1) the investor sells substantially identical stock or securities; or

(2) the investor enters into another short sale of substantially identical stock or securities (.10).

> ***Example:*** Jean Smith sold short 100 shares of Tech Corp. common stock at 35⅞ early in 2003. On December 20, 2003, she closed the short sale at 43¼ , realizing a loss of $737.50 (ignoring commissions). On January 14, 2004, Jean again sold 100 shares of Tech Corp. common stock short. Her 2000 realized loss of $737.50, therefore, is disallowed. When the second short sale is closed, however, any gain will be decreased by $737.50 and any loss will be increased by the same amount.

Avoiding the wash sale rules

An investor who desires to recognize a loss on stock or securities in a particular year but does not want to abandon the investment may employ the following techniques to avoid application of the wash sale rules:

(1) The simplest method of avoiding the wash sale rules is to sell the loss securities and wait at least 31 days before repurchasing, or entering into a contract or option to repurchase, them. The risk of this technique is that the investor might miss out on any gain on the stock that occurs during the waiting period.

(2) Another method, known as "doubling up," is to buy a second lot that is equal to the original holding, to wait at least 31 days, and then to sell the original lot, thereby recognizing the loss. Under this method, the investor maintains a continuing interest in the stock, but additional funds must be tied up for at least 31 days in order to complete the transaction.

(3) Some investors avoid the wash sale rules by selling the loss stock and reinvesting the proceeds in stock of another company, preferably in the same industry, that has historically performed the same way the loss stock has. After at least 31 days,

the investor can reverse the process to restore the original holding. This method minimizes the investor's risk during the waiting period.

Taking advantage of the wash sale rules

Occasionally, the wash sale rules may prove to be a help for investors who have sold stock at a loss and later realize that they do not want to recognize the loss at that time (see ¶25,240). If an investor learns of the bad timing within 30 days of the sale, a repurchase of the stock can be made to avoid the loss. The disallowed loss is added to the basis of the replacement stock, and the holding period of the old stock is added to the holding period of the new stock. The investor is thereby effectively restored to the original position without any tax consequences from the poorly timed sale.

.05 Code Sec. 1091; Rev. Rul. 71-316, 1971-2 CB 311.

.10 Code Sec. 1091(e).

¶25,244 Dividends—Taxable and Nontaxable. Corporations make various kinds of distributions to their shareholders to which special tax rules apply. The most common type of distribution is cash dividends, which are discussed below. Stock dividends are discussed at ¶25,245 and stock rights are discussed at ¶25,246. Distributions made in connection with corporate reorganizations and liquidations are discussed at ¶25,247.

Taxable dividends

Dividends of cash (or property other than stock in the distributing corporation) are taxable to the extent that they are paid out of the corporation's earnings and profits (.05).

Tax rate on taxable dividends

Qualified dividends are taxed at a maximum rate of 15%. Investors in a 10% or 15% bracket will be taxed at a maximum rate of 5% (.10).

Nontaxable dividends

Dividends are not taxable to the extent that they are a return of capital and are *not* paid out of the corporation's earnings and profits. Instead, an investor must reduce the basis of the stock by the amount of the dividend.

Determining tax status of dividends

The tax status of dividends paid by publicly held corporations may be found by consulting published dividend records. Information concerning dividends, stock dividends, stock rights, splits, reverse splits, stock issuance, redemptions, and other capital changes together with the tax status of such transactions may be found in the CCH CAPITAL CHANGES REPORTER.

.05 Code Sec. 316.

.10 Code Sec. 1(h)(11).

¶25,245 Stock Dividends and Stock Splits. Most stock dividends are tax free. They are taxed only if the shareholder has an option to receive the distribution in money or property other than the stock or if the distribution is in discharge of preference dividends for the year of distribution or an earlier year. Stock dividends may also be taxed if they are disproportionate, if preferred shareholders receive common stock, or if common shareholders receive convertible preferred stock (.05).

Fractional shares

Frequently, the formula for computing a stock dividend results in the necessity of distributing fractional shares to some shareholders. For example, if a corporation declares a stock dividend of one share for every 30 shares a shareholder owns, a shareholder owning 100 shares would be entitled to three-and-one-third new shares.

If, in place of distributing fractional shares, the corporation distributes cash, the cash is taxed at ordinary income rates.

Basis and holding period

An investor who receives a nontaxable stock dividend is required to allocate part of his basis in the old stock to the new shares received. This allocation must be made in proportion to the respective fair market values of the new and old stock (.10). If the stock dividend was taxable, however, the basis of the new stock is equal to the amount of dividend income that was recognized on the distribution (usually the fair market value of the stock distributed at the time of the distribution). The holding period of stock received in a nontaxable distribution is the same as the holding period of the old stock.

For easy determination of the proper treatment of stock dividends, see the CCH CAPITAL CHANGES REPORTER.

Stock split

A stock split, as distinguished from a stock dividend, never results in the recognition of income by the shareholder. A stock split is a division of outstanding shares into a greater number of share units that merely reduces the per-share value of the outstanding stock. Although the reduction is proportionate to the split on the corporate books, the market value may tend to be greater than would be expected based solely on the split ratio. A stock dividend, on the other hand, entails a transfer from a surplus account of the corporation to the capital account for the outstanding stock.

The basis of an investor's old shares is allocated to the new split shares in proportion to their fair market values. The holding period of the new shares includes the holding period of the old.

.05 Code Sec. 305. **.10** Code Sec. 307.

¶25,246 Stock Rights. A corporation may issue stock rights to shareholders that entitle them to purchase new shares of stock in the corporation for a stated price that is often substantially less than the fair market value of the stock. These rights may be exercised by paying the stated price, may be sold, or may be allowed to expire or lapse.

Distribution of stock rights

An investor is generally not taxed on the receipt of stock rights in the issuing corporation. An exception to this applies if the investor is given the option to receive cash or other property instead of the stock rights (.05).

Basis and holding period of stock rights

The basis of stock with respect to which nontaxable stock rights are distributed is allocated between the stock and the stock rights in proportion to the fair market values of each on the date of distribution (.10). If the fair market value of the stock rights is less than 15 percent of the fair market value of the stock, no allocation needs to be made and the basis of the stock rights is zero, unless the investor elects to make the allocation (.15). The basis of stock received in a taxable distribution is equal to the amount of income recognized (generally, the fair market value of the rights at that time).

The holding period of unexercised rights that are nontaxable includes the holding period of the old stock on which the rights were issued. In the case of taxable rights, the holding period dates only from the time of acquisition of the rights.

If an investor sells stock rights, any gain or loss is a capital gain or loss.

Exercise of stock rights—basis and holding period of acquired stock

The exercise of stock rights is not a taxable event. The basis of stock acquired by the exercise of rights is equal to the investor's basis in the rights plus the exercise price (purchase price) of the stock. The holding period of stock acquired by the exercise of stock rights begins on the date the rights are exercised (.20). However, in the case of stock or other property acquired by exercise of a purchase option, the holding period begins on the day after its exercise (.25).

Lapse of stock rights

An investor who allows a stock right to lapse is not taxed on the lapse. The rule requiring the allocation of basis between stock and stock rights (see "Basis and holding period of stock rights," above) applies only if the stock rights are exercised or sold (.30). Therefore, no adjustment is made to the basis of the stock with respect to which the rights were distributed.

.05 Code Sec. 305.
.10 Code Sec. 307(a).
.15 Reg. §1.307-2.
.20 Rev. Rul. 56-572, 1956-2 CB 182.
.25 *E.T. Weir*, CA-3, 49-1 USTC ¶9190, 173 F2d 222.
.30 Reg. §1.307-1.

¶25,247 Corporate Reorganizations and Liquidations. Corporate reorganizations and liquidations may result in stock exchanges or distributions with respect to stock that have significant tax consequences for the investor.

Reorganizations

An investor recognizes no gain or loss if the stock held in a corporation that is a party to a reorganization is, pursuant to the plan of reorganization, exchanged solely for new stock in the same corporation or in another corporation (.05). The types of reorganizations covered by this rule include (.10):

(1) a statutory merger or consolidation;

(2) the acquisition by one corporation of a controlling interest in the stock of another solely in exchange for voting stock in the acquiring corporation or in the parent of the acquiring corporation;

(3) the acquisition by one corporation of substantially all the assets of another corporation solely in exchange for voting stock in the acquiring corporation or in the parent of the acquiring corporation;

(4) corporate "spin-offs," "split-offs," or "split-ups" (.15);

(5) a recapitalization;

(6) certain reorganizations in bankruptcy; and

(7) minor changes in corporate form.

If property or money ("boot") is received in one of these exchanges, the gain on the transaction is taxed, but only up to the amount of the money and property received (.20).

.05 Code Sec. 354.
.10 Code Sec. 368.
.15 Code Sec. 355.
.20 Code Sec. 356.

Bonds

¶25,249 Gains and Losses on Bonds. Gains or losses on the sale or other disposition of bonds, like stocks, are generally capital gains or losses (see ¶25,232). Short sale (see ¶25,242) and wash sale (see ¶25,243) rules that apply to stocks are also generally applicable to bonds.

The distinguishing features of bonds are that they are a fixed obligation of the issuer, they generally pay interest (rather than dividends), and they generally have a principal amount that is paid when the bond matures. This division discusses:

(1) how interest is taxed (see ¶25,250);

(2) how income and the basis of bonds are affected if bonds are purchased at a premium (see ¶25,252) or at a discount (see ¶25,253); and

(3) tax-free bonds (see ¶25,255).

¶25,250 Interest Income. Interest received on bonds, debentures, or notes is generally includible in an investor's gross income and is fully taxable at ordinary income rates (.05). Such interest is usually taxed when received, but in some circumstances when bonds are purchased at a discount, interest may be taxed proportionally over the life of the bond (see ¶25,253).

Interest on obligations of the United States and its agencies is subject to tax to the same extent as private obligations. Interest on state, local, and municipal obligations, however, may be exempt (see ¶25,255).

☐ See ¶25,251 for a discussion of the treatment of interest when bonds are sold between interest dates.

.05 Reg. §1.61-7.

¶25,251 Bonds Sold with Accrued Interest. When a bond is sold between interest dates, an amount for interest accrued to the date of the sale is added to the selling price of the bond and the seller must report this amount as interest income (.05). When the buyer receives payment of the interest, he reports as income only the excess over what he paid the seller for the interest. Since the buyer purchased the interest accrued up to the date of the purchase, it is a return of capital when it is paid to him. This interest income adjustment has no effect on the cost basis of the bond because the amount paid for the interest was not included in the basis of the bond. Additional interest earned on the bond after the date of purchase is taxable interest income to the buyer.

Bonds purchased "flat"

Bonds that are in default as to principal or interest, or as to which the payment of interest is contingent on earnings or other future conditions, are ordinarily quoted "flat"—that is, the price of the bond covers not only the unpaid principal but also the right to receive interest accrued and unpaid. Generally, when the buyer later collects the interest that accrued *before* the purchase, he realizes no income. Until an amount equal to the prepurchase interest is received, all payments, whether they are described as principal or interest, are first treated as a return of capital and reduce the basis of the bond. Recoveries in excess of basis are treated as amounts received on retirement of the bond and, therefore, are usually taxable as capital gain. Payments of interest accrued *after* the purchase are taxable as interest income (.10).

.05 Reg. §1.61-7(d).

.10 Reg. §1.61-7(c).

¶25,252 Bonds Purchased at a Premium. If a taxable bond is purchased for more than its face value, the investor may elect to amortize the premium—that is, deduct a portion of the excess each year over the life of the bond. The basis of the bond is correspondingly reduced by the deductible amounts. If the bond is held until it is redeemed, its basis will equal its face value and no loss will be realized on its redemption (.05).

A premium on a taxable, callable bond is amortizable to maturity or an earlier call date. The earlier call date may be substituted for the maturity date, however, only if a smaller deduction results from amortizing the premium to the earlier call date. Amortization is not allowed for that portion of the premium on a convertible bond that is attributable to the conversion features of the bond.

An investor is not required to amortize the premium. If he elects not to, the amount of the premium will be a capital loss on the redemption of the bond. Amortization is generally advantageous as it allows the investor to take the loss in earlier years and possibly offset the income from the bond. An election, once made, is irrevocable, and the basis of the bond must be reduced each year regardless of whether the deduction is of any use to the investor. Therefore, an investor who expects little or no taxable income during the amortization years might be better off not making the election.

Tax-exempt bonds

No amortization deduction is allowed for tax-exempt bonds (see ¶25,255). To allow a deduction would permit a reduction of income by what is really an expense attributable to the earning of tax-exempt income (see ¶25,236). Reduction of the basis of the bond by the amount of the amortizable bond premium is nevertheless required. This prevents the investor from deducting the premium as a loss on sale or maturity.

.05 Code Sec. 171; Reg. § §1.171-1—1.171-4.

¶25,253 Bonds Issued at a Discount. When bonds are issued at a discount, their eventual redemption consists of a payment in return of capital (the portion equal to the original investment) and a payment in lieu of interest (the portion equal to the discount). To prevent the interest portion of the redemption from being deferred, the tax law generally requires that imputed interest be accrued and recognized as interest income over the life of the bond. The amount of original issue discount (OID) that must be accrued each year depends on when the bond was issued.

Bonds issued before July 2, 1982

The holder of a corporate bond or other evidence of indebtedness issued before July 2, 1982, and after May 27, 1969, must include equal monthly portions of the original issue discount in income as interest income. The investor's basis in the bond is increased by the portion of the OID included in income. Any gain or loss on the sale or redemption of the bond, computed after this adjustment is made, is treated as a capital gain or loss.

If noninterest-bearing bonds were issued at a discount before July 2, 1982, and are redeemable for fixed amounts increasing at stated intervals, a cash-method taxpayer may report the increases as income for each of the stated intervals. A cash-method taxpayer who makes the election must treat all such bonds similarly. In the year the election is made, the accrued increase in redemption value from the time of acquisition of the obligations to the beginning of the tax year must be reported in that year. The election cannot be changed without IRS consent. Accrual-method taxpayers must accrue the increases as income as they occur (.05).

Bonds issued after July 1, 1982

The method used to compute imputed interest on bonds issued before July 2, 1982, resulted in equal annual deductions for the issuers and equal annual inclusions for the holders of bonds. Beginning with bonds issued after July 1, 1982, however, a different method for computing imputed interest is required that results in smaller amounts of imputed interest in early years and greater amounts in later years, corresponding more closely to the actual accrual of interest (.10).

The first step in computing imputed interest for bonds issued after July 1, 1982, is to determine the bond's yield to maturity, which is the assumed interest (or discount) rate that, if applied to the bond's issue price and compounded semiannually, would produce both the increase in value from the issue price to the maturity price and also all the interest payments called for during the life of the bond. This discount rate is then applied to the bond's issue price to determine the first year's imputed interest. The portion of imputed interest that is not actually paid out as interest is added back to the bond's issue price (i.e., the principal amount). On the anniversary of the bond's issue date, the discount rate is applied to the new principal amount of the obligation to determine the next year's imputed interest. Again, the portion of the imputed interest that is not actually paid out is added back to the principal. This procedure is repeated each year until the bond is redeemed.

The following examples illustrate the difference in tax treatment between a discounted bond issued before July 2, 1982, and a similar bond issued after July 1, 1982.

Example 1: A 30-year zero-coupon bond with a face value of $10,000,000 is issued by a corporation on January 1, 1982, for $990,000. The purchaser must report annual interest income of $300,333, an amount equal to the total discount of $9,010,000 ($10,000,000 – $990,000) divided by 30, the number of years to maturity.

Example 2: Assume the above facts, except that the bond is issued and purchased on July 1, 2002, and the yield to maturity of the obligation based on annual compounding is 8%. The interest amount for the first accrual period is $79,200, which is the value of the obligation at the date of issue ($990,000) multiplied by 8%. Thus, the purchaser must include $39,492 (182/365 × $79,200) in income for 2002.

As gain is recognized for the ratable portion of OID (under either rule), the holder's basis in the bond is increased by the amount of OID included in income. This prevents such amounts from being taxed a second time when the bond is sold or exchanged.

A subsequent purchaser of an OID bond is required to continue to report income based on the discount remaining when the bond is purchased, less any amount paid for the bond over the adjusted issue price (issue price of the bond plus the amount of OID amortized up to that date).

Government bonds issued at discount

This method also applies to bonds issued by any government or political subdivision. However, this does not include tax-exempt bonds bought before May 1, 1993 (other than certain industrial development bonds that generate interest deductions to a taxable issuer), short-term government bonds, or U.S. savings bonds (.15).

Any gain realized on the sale or exchange of a short-term governmental obligation is treated as ordinary income up to the amount of what is called the ratable share of the acquisition discount (.20). "Acquisition discount" is the excess of the stated redemption price at maturity over the taxpayer's basis for the obligation. The ratable share is the portion equal to the ratio of the number of days the bond is held by the taxpayer to the number of days between the date of acquisition by the taxpayer and the date of maturity.

.05 Code Sec. 454.
.10 Code Sec. 1271 and 1272.
.15 Code Sec. 1272(a)(2).
.20 Code Sec. 1271(a)(3).

¶25,254 Stripped Bonds. When a stripped bond or detached, unmatured coupons are purchased, the purchaser is treated as having acquired an original issue discount bond with a discount equal to the excess of the redemption price of the bond (or amount payable on the coupon) over the purchase price of the stripped bond (or detached coupon) (.05). Thus, discount income is attributed to the stripped bond or detached coupon and is taxed to the purchaser between the purchase date and the date of maturity (or due date of the coupon) under the inclusion rule for original issue discount income (see ¶25,253).

Tax-exempt bonds

The rule requiring a seller of a stripped bond or the detached coupons to allocate the basis of the bond with coupons attached between the items retained and those disposed of applies to a tax-exempt bond. Thus, as in the case of taxable obligations, the seller of a stripped tax-exempt obligation is unable to create an artificial loss because basis is allocated to retained coupons under the rule. Also, if tax-exempt coupons are sold separately, there may be taxable gain on the sale or redemption of the retained stripped bond attributable to allocation of a portion of the seller's basis to the detached coupons.

U.S. securities

The Department of the Treasury maintains a system, known as STRIPS (Separate Trading of Registered Interest and Principal of Securities), that puts selected treasury securities in the book-entry system of the Federal Reserve Banks in a manner that permits separate trading and ownership of interest and principal payments. Purchasers of such instruments are subject to the same tax consequences that apply to purchasers of nongovernmental stripped bonds and zero coupons.

.05 Code Sec. 1286.

¶25,255 Tax-Free Bonds. Some investors may profit from investing in state and municipal bonds. Although interest on obligations of the United States, its agencies and instrumentalities is generally subject to federal income taxes to the same extent as interest on private obligations, interest on state and local obligations may be tax exempt (.05).

The term "tax-exempt bonds" includes bonds issued by states, cities, and their political subdivisions. Certain obligations of state and local governments must be in registered form in order for the interest to be tax exempt (.10). In addition, interest on certain types of state or local bonds may not be tax exempt unless certain requirements are met. These bonds include arbitrage bonds, exempt facility bonds and mortgage bonds.

□ For a discussion of tax-exempt bonds purchased at a premium, see ¶25,252. For a discussion of stripped tax-exempt bonds, see ¶25,254. For a discussion of interest expenses on loans used to purchase tax-exempt bonds, see ¶25,235. For a discussion of other expenses associated with tax-exempt bonds, see ¶25,236.

.05 Code Sec. 103, 141-150.

.10 Code Sec. 149.

¶25,256 U.S. Savings Bonds. Generally, interest on U.S. savings bonds is earned in one of two ways. It is either paid out at stated intervals (Series H or HH) or the bond is issued at a discount, then redeemed for face value at maturity (Series E or EE) (.05).

Cash basis taxpayers who purchase Series EE have a choice in reporting the interest. Reporting may be postponed until the earlier of the year the bonds are cashed in or the year they mature. Investors may also report the interest each year as it is earned.

Interest earned on Series EE bonds issued after December 31, 1989, may be excluded from interest if the bond proceeds are used for qualified higher educational expenses (see ¶3725).

Patriot Bonds. Patriot Bonds are Series EE savings bonds. The "Patriot Bond" legend has been inscribed on Series EE bonds since December 11, 2001 and will continue indefinitely.

Inflation-Indexed Bonds (I Bonds). I Bonds are designed for investors seeking to protect the purchasing power of their investment and earn a guaranteed real rate of return. I Bonds are an accrual-type security (i.e., interest is added to the bond monthly and paid when the bond is cashed). Earnings are exempt from state and local income taxes. Federal income taxes can be deferred for up to thirty years, or until redemption or other taxable disposition, whichever comes first. In addition, if the taxpayer qualifies, all or part of the interest on I Bonds (and on eligible EE bonds) can be excluded from income as long as the proceeds are used to pay for tuition and fees at eligible post-secondary educational institutions (see ¶3725).

Treasury Inflation-Indexed Securities (TIPS). Treasury Inflation-Indexed Securities, often called Treasury Inflation-Protected Securities or TIPS, are a special type of Treasury notes and bonds. As with other notes and bonds, when a taxpayer buys an Inflation-Indexed note or bond, the taxpayer receives interest payments every six months and a payment of principal when the security matures. The difference is this: Unlike the situation with other notes and bonds, the interest and redemption payments for Treasury Inflation-Indexed Securities are tied to inflation. (It should be noted that the Treasury Department has not offered a Treasury bond since its decision in October 2001 to suspend issuance of the 30-year bond.) Generally, the interest payments are taxable when received, which is consistent with the tax treatment of other Treasury securities. The inflation adjustments to the principal are taxable in the year in which such adjustments occur even though the inflation adjustments will not be paid until maturity.

.05 Code Sec. 135

Commodities Futures

¶25,258 Futures Transactions. A commodity future is a contract to buy or sell a specified amount of a commodity (such as wheat, soybeans, gold, or silver) at a future date for a fixed price. There are generally two types of futures contracts:

(1) regulated futures contracts, which are regulated by a qualified board of trade or exchange; and

(2) forward contracts, which are not regulated by a qualified board of trade or exchange.

Transactions in regulated futures contracts are taxed under special "marked-to-market" rules (see ¶25,259) unless they are "hedging transactions" (see below) or part of a "mixed straddle" (see ¶25,260). Transactions in forward contracts are taxed under the regular capital gains rules (see ¶25,232), again, unless they are hedging transactions or part of a mixed straddle.

Futures contracts have a number of different uses and each type of use carries with it its own tax consequences:

(1) The purchase or sale of futures contracts in a commodity directly related to the taxpayer's trade or business, e.g., a corn farmer trading in corn futures, is generally considered to be a "hedging transaction" if the transaction is entered into in the normal course of business to reduce the taxpayer's risk of price fluctuations with respect to the property held in the business or to reduce the risk of interest rate fluctuation with respect to borrowings of the taxpayer. the end-of-the-year marked-to-market recognition rule does not apply to such hedging transactions. The commodity involved is not considered to be a capital asset, and, thus, the transaction gives rise to ordinary gain or loss regardless of how long the contracts have been held.

(2) Futures contracts are bought and sold by investors for investment or speculation purposes. Gains and losses from such transactions are generally capital gains and

losses. Rules regarding the amount, timing, and character of such gains and losses are discussed at ¶25,259 and ¶25,260.

(3) A specialized type of investment strategy involves the purchase and sale of futures contracts for the same commodity, usually calling for delivery in different months. An individual who invests in such offsetting positions, known as "straddles," expects to realize gain through variation in prices between the two positions. As with other commodities transactions (other than hedging transactions), gains or losses on straddles are generally capital gains or losses. Special rules are provided, however, to prevent the investor from taking a loss on one "leg" of a straddle in the current year and the offsetting gain from the other leg in the next year (see ¶25,267).

¶25,259 Marked-to-Market Rules. The U.S. commodity futures exchanges employ a unique system of accounting for every contract's gain or loss in cash on a daily basis. Even though a futures trader does not close out a position but continues to hold it, the trader receives any gain on the position in cash as a matter of right for each trading day.

If a trader's position has increased in value during the day, the net increase in the position is transferred to the trader's account before the beginning of the next day's trading. The trader has the right to withdraw the full amount of such gains immediately for each trading day. However, if a trader's position decreases in value, the trader will have to meet a margin call—that is, he will have to deposit additional funds before the next business day. Money paid on position losses is paid into the exchange clearing association, which transfers such amounts to accounts that gained during the trading day. This daily accounting, which includes the determination of contract settlement prices and margin adjustments to reflect gains and losses, is called marking to market.

Taxation under marked-to-market rules

Gains and losses from "section 1256 contracts" (see "Section 1256 contracts," below) must be reported on an annual basis under a marked-to-market rule that corresponds to the daily cash settlement, marked-to-market system employed by commodity futures exchanges in the United States. When section 1256 contracts are taxed under this system, the loss deferral rule, the wash and short sale rules applicable to straddles, and the capitalization rules for interest and carrying charges are all inapplicable.

Under this system of taxation, all section 1256 contracts must be marked to market at the end of each year. Each section 1256 contract held by a taxpayer is treated as if it were sold for fair market value on the last business day of the year. Ordinarily, a contract's fair market value is the settlement price determined by the exchange for the section 1256 contract as of the last business day of the year. Any gain or loss on the contract is taken into account for the tax year, together with the gain or loss on other contracts that were held during the year but closed out before the last business day. As a result, taxpayers' net gains or losses are approximately equal to the aggregate net amounts that are credited to their margin accounts, or that they have had to pay into their accounts during the tax year. If a taxpayer holds section 1256 contracts at the beginning of a taxable year, any gain or loss subsequently realized on these contracts must be adjusted to reflect any gain or loss taken into account with respect to these contracts in a prior year.

Any capital gain or loss on a section 1256 contract under the marked-to-market tax system is treated as if: (1) 40 percent of the gain or loss is short-term capital gain or loss, and (2) 60 percent of the gain or loss is long-term capital gain or loss. Ordinary income or loss items are excluded from this rule.

Section 1256 contract transactions taxed under the marked-to-market system are initially reported on Form 6781, Gains and Losses from Section 1256 Contracts and Straddles, in Part I.

The net gain or loss from such transactions is computed in Part I, is treated as 40-percent short-term and 60-percent long-term, and is then carried over and reported on the applicable Schedule D.

The marked-to-market tax rules, including the 60-40 long-term and short-term allocation, apply to terminations (or transfers) of section 1256 contracts by taxpayers. Terminations can occur by offsetting section 1256 contracts, by taking or making delivery, by exercise or being exercised, by assignment or being assigned, or by lapse. Gain or loss is determined on the basis of the contract's fair market value at the time of termination (or transfer). In most cases, this is the actual price received or paid.

If a straddle (see ¶25,260) includes two or more section 1256 contracts, all contracts in the straddle are deemed terminated as of the date of delivery under any one of the contracts where the taxpayer takes delivery or exercises part of the straddle.

Section 1256 contracts

A "section 1256 contract" is a contract that meets both of the following conditions:

(1) is marked to market under a daily cash flow system of the type used by United States futures exchanges to determine the amount that must be deposited, in the case of losses, or the amount that may be withdrawn, in the case of gains, as a result of price changes on the contract during the business day; and

(2) is traded on or subject to the rules of a domestic board of trade that is designated as a contract market by the Commodity Futures Trading Commission, or any other board of trade or exchange that the Internal Revenue Service determines is operating under a marked-to-market system.

This type of contract is known as a "regulated futures contract." The term "section 1256 contract" also includes any foreign currency contract.

The marked-to-market rules also apply to nonequity options and dealer equity options. Generally, a nonequity option is any option (other than a right to acquire stock from the issuer) that is traded on, or subject to the rules of, a qualified board or exchange (referred to as a "listed option") *other than* an option to buy or sell stock or an option the value of which is determined directly or indirectly by reference to any stock or group of stocks or stock index. Also included is an option with respect to any group of stocks or stock index if there is in effect a designation by the Commodity Futures Trading Commission of a contract market based on the group of stocks or stock index.

A dealer equity option, with respect to an option dealer, is a listed option that: (1) settles in stock or the value of which is determined by reference to any stock or stock index, (2) is purchased or granted by an option dealer in the normal course of dealing in options, and (3) is listed on a qualified board or exchange with which the dealer is registered.

Loss carrybacks

Investors having a net loss from section 1256 contracts in a given tax year may carry back the loss to the three previous tax years. To the extent that such carryback is allowed, 40 percent of the amount so allowed is treated as a short-term capital loss from section 1256 contracts, and 60 percent is treated as a long-term capital loss from section 1256 contracts.

¶25,260 Straddles. A "straddle" is a combination of offsetting positions in futures, options, or other actively traded personal property that substantially diminishes the investor's risk of loss on either of the positions in the straddle. For example, a long and a short position in the same commodity is a straddle because losses on one position of the straddle will be offset by gains on the other. Because straddles offer the potential of taking early losses and deferring gains until later tax years under circumstances where there is little economic risk, the law places restrictions on the current deduction of *unrecognized* losses (see ¶25,267). When section 1256 contracts make up all or part of a straddle, however, all gains and losses are recognized at year's end under the marked-to-market rules (see ¶25,259). This paragraph deals with the elections that are available to investors in straddles that are made up entirely or partially of section 1256 contracts. The actual loss deferral rules applicable to these types of straddles are discussed at ¶25,267.

Section 1256 contracts only

When all of the positions in a straddle are section 1256 contracts (regulated futures contracts, foreign currency contracts, nonequity options, and dealer equity options), there is no potential for accelerating losses and deferring gains, as is the case with other straddles, because the marked-to-market rules require any gains or losses in such contracts to be recognized at year's end as if they were sold on that date. Straddles that are made up entirely of section 1256 contracts are therefore exempt from the straddle rules (.05). No election need be made and all gains and losses are 60-percent long-term gains or losses and 40-percent short-term gains or losses under the marked-to-market rules.

Mixed straddles

When some but not all the positions in a straddle are section 1256 contracts, an investor may elect not to apply the regular marked-to-market rules. Two elections are available:

(1) straddle-by-straddle identification; and

(2) mixed straddle accounts.

If no election is made, the marked-to-market rules are applied to each section 1256 contract the investor holds. Any losses recognized under the marked-to-market rules are deferred to the extent that there are unrecognized gains in offsetting positions that are nonsection 1256 positions under the loss deferral rules applicable to regular straddles (see "Loss deferral rules" at ¶25,267).

Straddle-by-straddle identification

If an investor elects straddle-by-straddle identification, the marked-to-market rules are dispensed with (at least to the extent that section 1256 gains or losses are offset by nonsection 1256 gains or losses). Instead, special rules for netting gains and losses are employed (see "Straddle-by-straddle identification" at ¶25,267).

To elect this method of reporting gains and losses, an investor must clearly identify each position that is part of the identified mixed straddle before the end of the day on which the straddle is established on a reasonable and consistently applied economic basis. An investor is presumed to have made an identification if he receives independent verification of the identification (.10). The independent verification requirement is met, for example:

(1) if an investor places one or more positions in a separate account designated as a "section 1092(b)(2) identified mixed straddle account" that is maintained by a broker, futures commission merchant, or similar person and notations are made by such person identifying all positions of the identified mixed straddle and specifying the date the straddle was established; or

(2) if an investor receives written confirmation from a broker, futures commission merchant, or similar person, or from the person from whom the position was acquired stating the date the straddle was established and identifying the other positions of the straddle.

Mixed straddle accounts

A mixed straddle account is an account for determining gains and losses from all positions held as capital assets in a designated class of activities. A separate account must be established for each class of activities. A class of activities may be designated as such if a reasonable person would expect the types of positions in the class to be offsetting positions. Gains and losses are determined on an account basis.

An election is made by attaching a statement to the investor's tax return for the tax year in which the mixed straddle account is established. In addition, a statement must be attached designating with specificity the class of activities for which the mixed straddle account is established. If an investor establishes more than one mixed straddle account, sufficient information must be given to allow the IRS to determine whether specific positions are placed in the appropriate accounts. The election applies to all positions in the designated class of activities held by the investor during the tax year (.15).

An election to establish a mixed straddle account is effective for the *entire* tax year for which the election is made and for all later years. Such an election may not be revoked without the consent of the IRS, but may be amended to expand a designated class of activities.

.05 Temp. Reg. § 1.1092(b)-1T(d).

.10 Temp. Reg. § 1.1092(b)-3T(d).

.15 Temp. Reg. § 1.1092(b)-4T(f).

Options and Straddles

¶25,262 Puts and Calls. Traded options come in two basic varieties: puts and calls. A "put" is an option to *sell* a specified number of shares of a particular stock at a fixed price (the "striking price" or "exercise price") within a specific period of time. A "call" is an option to *buy* a specified number of shares of a particular stock at a fixed price within a specified period of time. In addition to options on stock, an investor may trade options on other property such as commodity futures.

Listed and unlisted options

Options that are traded on an exchange, e.g., the Chicago Board of Options Exchange, the American Exchange, and various regional exchanges, are referred to as "listed" options. Listed options are standardized as to the size of a lot (100 shares), striking prices (in $5 or other increments), and expiration dates. Options that are traded off the exchanges are "unlisted" options. The tax rules are generally the same for listed and unlisted options. Differences are noted where appropriate.

"In-the-money" options

A call is referred to as an "in-the-money" call if its striking price is *less* than the current market price of the underlying stock. A put is referred to as an "in-the-money" put if its striking price is *more* than the current market price of the underlying stock. The purchase price of an option that is "in-the-money" is more likely to parallel the price of the underlying stock than an option that is "out-of-the-money." The purchase price of an "out-of-the-money" option is more likely to be influenced by factors such as the time remaining before the option lapses.

¶25,263 Taxation of Option Purchasers. The way an option purchaser is taxed depends on whether the option is sold, exercised or lapses.

Sale of an option

Options are normally capital assets in the hands of an investor. If the investor sells an option, he is taxed, with the sale of other capital assets (see ¶25,232), on the difference between what he paid for the option and the proceeds of the sale.

Exercise of an option

An investor who exercises a put is not taxed on the exercise. Rather, any gain or loss on the sale of the underlying stock is adjusted by decreasing the sale price of the stock by the amount paid for the put.

An investor who exercises a call is similarly not taxed on the exercise. The amount paid for the call is added to the basis of the stock. As a result, any gain on the eventual sale of the stock will be decreased and any loss will be increased. The holding period of the stock, however, does not begin until the day after the call is exercised.

Lapse of an option

An option that is allowed to expire is generally treated as if it were sold on the expiration date, thereby giving the investor a capital loss. However, if a put expires that was purchased on the same day as the stock that was to be used if the put were exercised, no loss is allowed. Instead, the cost of the put must be added to the basis of the identified stock.

¶25,264 Taxation of Option Grantors. the way a "writer" of an option is taxed depends on whether the option is exercised, terminated, or expires.

Exercise of an option

An investor who purchases stock upon the exercise of a put he wrote takes a basis in the stock equal to the exercise price he paid, less the premium he received when he wrote the put.

An investor who sells stock upon the exercise of a call must include the call premium in the proceeds from the sale of the stock. In other words, the proceeds from the sale of the stock are deemed to be the total of the exercise price and the premium.

Termination of an option

The grantor of a listed call may terminate it by repurchasing an identical call in a closing transaction. Any gain or loss realized on such a transaction is a short-term capital gain or loss.

Lapse of an option

A writer of an option recognizes income if the option expires without being exercised.

¶25,265 Dividends Paid During Option Period. In some circumstances, dividends or other distributions may be made with respect to stock during a period when it is subject to an option. Unlisted options normally provide that the exercise price is reduced by the value of any distributions. This is not the case for listed options (at least for ordinary dividends).

All dividends received during the option period are taxable dividends to the owner of the stock at the time of the dividend. The reduction in the exercise price only affects the basis of the stock acquired if the option is exercised (.05).

.05 Rev. Rul. 58-234, 1958-1 CB 279.

¶25,266 Wash Sales. If an investor sells stock or securities at a loss and within the 61-day wash-sale period (30 days before and after the day of the sale—see ¶25,243) buys a call with respect to the stock or securities sold, the loss is disallowed (.05). The same is true if, within the wash-sale period, an investor who has sold stock at a loss sells an "in-the- money" put for the same stock under circumstances that make it unlikely that the put will *not* be exercised (.10). The sales of stock options are also covered by the wash sale rules.

.05 Code Sec. 1091(a).

.10 Rev. Rul. 85-87, 1985-1 CB 268.

¶25,267 Straddles. A "straddle" is a combination of offsetting positions in futures, options, or other actively traded personal property that substantially diminishes the investor's risk of loss on either of the positions in the straddle (.05). These conditions are met, for example, by long and short positions in the same commodity, because losses on one position, or "leg," of the straddle are completely or partially offset by gains on the other leg. Straddles may be made up of two or more futures contracts, a physical commodity and an option or futures contract, a stock and a listed or unlisted option, a treasury bill and an option or futures contract, or many other combinations. The deduction of losses will be denied if the straddle lacks economic substance and was entered into solely for tax avoidance purposes (.10).

Loss deferral rules

Straddles offer the potential of taking early losses and deferring gains until later tax years under circumstances where there is little economic risk; thus, the law places restrictions on the current deduction of losses. Generally, a loss on one or more positions in a straddle may be taken into account for a tax year only to the extent that it exceeds the unrecognized gain in the positions that offset the loss position (.15). An unrecognized gain is the gain that would be taken into account if a position were disposed of at fair market value at the end of the last business day of the tax year. Any loss that is disallowed may be carried over to the next year, when it will again be subject to the loss deferral rules.

> ***Example 1:*** On December 1, 2003, Judy West entered into offsetting long and short positions. On December 10, 2003, she disposed of the short position at an $11 loss, at which time there was $5 of unrealized gain in the offsetting long position. At year's end there was $7 of unrecognized gain in the offsetting long position. West may deduct $4 of the loss in 2003. The remaining $7 is disallowed as a deduction for 2003 but may be carried over to 2004. If West continues to hold the long position through 2004, the deductibility of the $7 carryover will depend on how much unrecognized gain there is in the long position at the end of 2004.

Successor positions

The deductibility of a loss in a straddle is not limited only by unrecognized gains in the original straddle positions. An investor may also have to take into account unrecognized gains in "successor positions." If an investor disposes of one position in a straddle, he may have a successor position in the straddle if (.20):

(1) he enters into a new offsetting position (the successor position);

(2) the successor position is entered into during the 61-day wash-sale period (see ¶25,243); and

(3) the successor position is entered into no later than 30 days after the loss position is no longer included in a straddle, i.e., no later than 30 days after the straddle is terminated for reasons *other* than disposition of the loss position.

If an investor disposes of fewer than all of the positions of a straddle, any loss sustained may be recognized only to the extent that it exceeds the unrecognized gain in (.25):

(1) any position offsetting the loss position;

(2) any positions that are successor positions; and

(3) any positions that offset any successor positions.

> ***Example 2:*** Vic Smith entered into the following long (L) and short (S) positions in 2003:

DATE	TRANSACTION	GAIN OR LOSS
1-1	Enters L1 and S1, offsetting long and short positions	—
3-1	Disposes of L1	$10 gain
3-10	Disposes of S1	$10 loss
3-15	Enters S2, a short position that would have been offsetting to L1	—
4-10	Enters L2, a long position offsetting S2	—
12-31	Holds S2 and L2 at year's end	$5 unrecognized gain in S2 $4 unrecognized gain in L2

Although both positions of the original straddle are disposed of when L1 is disposed of on March 10, 2004, S2 is deemed a successor position because it is acquired within 30 days after the disposition of the loss position (S1). L2 is a position that is offsetting to the successor position (S2). Therefore, the unrecognized gain in L2 and S2 must be taken into account in deciding whether the loss on the disposition of S1 will be allowed. Because the total unrecognized gain on the successor position (S2) and the offset to the successor position (L2) is $9 ($5 + $4), only $1 of the loss on S1 will be allowed in 2004 (excess of the loss over the unrecognized gains).

If S2 had been acquired on April 2, 2004, instead of March 15, the entire loss on the disposition of S1 would have been allowed because S2 would not be deemed a successor position because it was entered into more than 30 days after the disposition of the loss position (S1). Lacking a successor position (or offsetting position), there would be no limit on the recognition of the loss on S1.

Mixed straddles

Mixed straddles are made up of both section 1256 contracts (regulated futures contracts, foreign currency contracts, nonequity options, and dealer equity options—see ¶25,259) and non-section 1256 contracts. Gain or loss on section 1256 contracts is recognized at year's end under the marked-to-market rules discussed at ¶25,259, regardless of whether the contract is disposed of at that time or not. Special rules have, therefore, been adopted to govern the reporting of gains and losses where some, but not all, of the positions in a straddle are subject to the marked-to-market rules. The two methods that may be elected are straddle-by-straddle identification (.30) and mixed straddle accounts (.35). (See ¶25,260 for a discussion of how to make these elections.)

Straddle-by-straddle identification

The treatment of gains and losses from positions that are part of identified mixed straddles depends on when the positions are disposed of in relation to their offsetting positions (.40):

(1) If *all positions* of an identified mixed straddle are disposed of on the same day, gains and losses from section 1256 contracts in the straddle and from nonsection 1256 positions in the straddle are separately netted. Net gain or loss from the section 1256 contracts is then offset against the net gain or loss from the nonsection 1256 positions to arrive at the net gain or loss from the straddle. If the net gain or loss from the straddle is "attributable" to the section 1256 contracts (i.e., the magnitude of the gain or loss from the section 1256 contracts is greater than the magnitude of the offsetting gain or loss from the nonsection 1256 positions), such gain or loss is treated as 60-percent long-term and 40-percent short-term gain or loss. If the net gain or loss from the straddle is attributable to the nonsection 1256 positions, such gain or loss is treated as short-term capital gain or loss.

Example 3: On May 1, 2004, Fred Smith enters into a straddle consisting of two nonsection 1256 positions and two section 1256 contracts and makes a valid election to treat the straddle as an identified mixed straddle. On May 10, 2004, Smith disposes of the positions in the straddle as follows:

Position Disposed of	*Gain or Loss*
§1256 contract	$ 700 loss
§1256 contract	$ 500 gain
Nonsection 1256 position	$ 400 gain
Nonsection 1256 position	$ 300 loss

The gains and losses of the two types of positions are separately netted, yielding a net loss on the section 1256 contracts of $200 ($700 – $500) and a net gain on the nonsection 1256 positions of $100 ($400 – $300). The net loss from the section 1256 contracts of $200 is then netted against the $100 net gain on the nonsection 1256 positions, giving a net loss for the straddle of $100. This loss is treated as being "attributable" to the section 1256 contracts.

(1) If *all nonsection 1256 positions* of an identified mixed straddle are disposed of on the same day, the net gain or loss from the straddle is computed as in the previous section, taking into account both realized *and unrealized* gains or losses on that day from the section 1256 contracts in the straddle. Net gain or loss from the straddle that is attributable to the nonsection 1256 positions is treated as short-term capital gain or loss on that day. Net gain or loss from the straddle that is attributable to *realized* gain or loss on section 1256 contracts is recognized and treated as 60-percent long-term and 40-percent short-term capital gain or loss. Any gain or loss subsequently realized on the section 1256 contracts is adjusted to take into account the extent to which gain or loss on the nonsection 1256 positions was offset by unrealized gain or loss on the section 1256 contracts.

(2) If *all section 1256 contracts* of an identified mixed straddle are disposed of on the same day, the net gain or loss from the straddle is similarly computed, taking into account both realized and unrealized gains or losses on that day from the nonsection 1256 positions.

(3) If *one or more, but not all, positions* of an identified mixed straddle are disposed of in one day, one of the previous two paragraphs will apply. Which of the two applies depends on the net gain or loss from the positions actually disposed of that day. If such net gain or loss is attributable to nonsection 1256 positions, paragraph (2) applies. If such net gain or loss is attributable to the section 1256 contracts, paragraph (3) applies. Special rules are provided if both types of positions yield net gains or net losses, and provision is made for determining the treatment of gain or loss subsequently realized on a position in the straddle.

(4) If *one or more positions* of an identified mixed straddle were held before the day the straddle was established, they are deemed to have been sold on the preceding business day at fair market value. If an investor holds nonsection 1256 positions that are part of an identified mixed straddle after all section 1256 contracts are disposed of, they are treated as short-term capital gain or loss to the extent they are attributable to the period when the positions were part of the straddle.

Mixed straddle accounts

A mixed straddle account is used for determining gains and losses from all positions held as capital assets in a designated class of activities. A separate account must be established for each class of activities that may be designated if a reasonable person would expect that the types of positions in the class would be offsetting positions (.45).

Gains and losses in a mixed straddle account are determined daily as if all positions in the account had been sold for their fair market value at the close of each business day. Gains and losses from all the positions (both realized and unrealized) are treated in a manner similar to that set out in method (1) above for computing gain or loss on identified mixed straddles, except that special rules are provided if both section 1256 contracts and nonsection 1256 positions yield net gains or net losses.

Interest and carrying charges

The deduction of interest and carrying charges incurred with respect to a straddle position is not permitted, except to the extent that such interest and carrying charges are offset by current income generated by the position. The excess must be capitalized. Interest includes interest on debt incurred or continued to carry the position, and carrying charges include the cost of insuring, storing, or transporting the personal property that makes up the position, as well as charges for the temporary use of the property in a short sale. Hedging transactions (see ¶25,258) are excluded from this rule (.50).

To allow for the fact that a lender of securities to be used in a short sale may receive compensation from a borrower in lieu of interest or other amounts, it is provided that the amount of interest and carrying costs required to be capitalized is reduced by any compensating payments to a lender of securities used in a short sale that are includible in gross income. Compensating payments include dividends, interest, fees, income from collateral security and income from investment of collateral security.

.05 Code Sec. 1092(c)(1).

.10 *B.S. Glass*, 87 TC 1087, CCH Dec. 43,495, aff'd *sub nom. E. Bohrer*, CA-10, 91-2 USTC ¶50,462.

.15 Code Sec. 1092(a)(1)(A).

.20 Temp. Reg. § 1.1092(b)-5T(n).

.25 Temp. Reg. § 1.1092(b)-1T(a).

.30 Code Sec. 1092(b)(2)(A)(i)(I).

.35 Code Sec. 1092(b)(2)(A)(i)(II).

.40 Temp. Reg. § 1.1092(b)-3T(b).

.45 Temp. Reg. § 1.1092(b)-4T(b).

.50 Code Sec. 263(g).

Mutual Funds

¶25,269 Distributed Income Taxed Once. Investors desiring to invest in stocks and securities often buy shares in mutual funds that invest the pooled funds. Mutual funds are also available that invest pooled funds in bonds, money market instruments, and tax-exempt securities. Recognizing this fact, Congress has provided that a mutual fund that distributes at least 90 percent of its ordinary income is taxed only on its undistributed income (.05). The shareholders are taxed on the amounts distributed to them. Thus, unlike the earnings of an ordinary corporation, which pays tax on income distributed to shareholders, who in turn pay tax on the dividends they receive, earnings of a mutual fund are, in general, taxed only once.

In order to secure this favorable tax treatment, a qualified mutual fund must elect to be taxed as a regulated investment company (RIC). The election is made by computing taxable income as a RIC on the income tax return for the first tax year for which the election is applicable. An election is irrevocable.

.05 Code Sec. 851, Code Sec. 852; Reg. §1.851-2(a), Reg. §1.852-2.

¶25,270 Taxing Mutual Fund Shareholders. Shareholders of mutual funds (regulated investment companies) are taxed on dividends from the fund in the year that the dividends are received (.05). There are four basic types of dividends that shareholders receive: ordinary dividends, capital gain dividends, return-of-capital dividends, and tax-free income dividends. The tax treatment of each type of dividend should be considered when investing in a mutual fund, because the treatment does vary.

Ordinary dividends

An ordinary dividend is a distribution by a mutual fund from its earnings and profits. Ordinary dividends are reported to shareholders on the 2004 Form 1099-DIV, in Box 1a.

Qualified dividends

Qualified dividends are taxed at a maximum rate of 15% (5% for individuals in a 10% or 15% bracket). Qualified dividends are reported to taxpayers on the 2004 1099-DIV, in Box 1b.

Capital gain dividends

A capital gain dividend is a distribution by a mutual fund from its net realized long-term capital gains or profits. Capital gain dividends are taxed as long-term capital gains, regardless of how long the shareholder has owned stock in the fund. Capital gain distributions (i.e., those eligible for the 5% or 15% capital gains rates) are reported to investors on the 2004 Form 1099-DIV, in Box 2b. Total capital gain distributions for the year are shown in Box 2a.

Return of capital

A return of capital is a distribution by a mutual fund that is not derived from earnings and profits. This dividend is a return of the shareholder's investment in the company. A return of capital reduces the basis in a shareholder's stock and is taxable only when the basis in the stock is fully recovered. Any gain realized (after the basis has been recovered) is taxable as either short-term or long-term capital gain, depending on how long a shareholder has held the stock.

> ***Example:*** Ken Hogan bought shares in a mutual fund in 2003 for $2,000. In 2004, he received a return of $5 in capital. Hogan then reduced his basis in the stock by $5—the amount of the distribution—to $1,995. In 2004, he received another return of $4 in capital. He reduced his basis in the stock by $4, to $1,991. Even though it is unlikely that the return of capital distributions will exceed the remaining basis of $1,991, if that does occur, Hogan would report the excess as a long-term capital gain.

Tax-free dividends

Tax-free dividends are distributions by mutual funds from tax-exempt interest earned on tax-exempt obligations of a state or one of its political subdivisions, the District of Columbia, or a U.S. possession or one of its political subdivisions. These dividends retain their tax-exempt status and are not included in a shareholder's income.

To qualify for this favorable tax treatment, the fund must have at least 50 percent of its total assets invested in these tax-exempt obligations at the close of each quarter of its tax year. Also, the fund must pay out annually at least 90 percent of its net tax-exempt interest. Then, the fund must designate the amount of the tax-free dividend in a notice to its shareholders within 60 days after the fund's tax year.

Undistributed capital gains

Shareholders must also include in income as capital gain their shares of undistributed capital gain designated by the fund. Form 2439 is issued to shareholders when they must report undistributed capital gains. The shareholder is considered to have paid his share of the tax paid by the fund on these gains and thus may claim a tax credit on Form 1040. The basis of his shares is increased by the amount of the undistributed capital gain included in his income.

.05 Code Sec. 852(a)(1) and 854(b)(1), (2); Reg. §§1.852-4, 1.854-1.

¶25,271 Sale of Mutual Fund Shares. The treatment of gain or loss on the sale or exchange of mutual fund shares is similar to the treatment of gain or loss on dispositions of other capital assets (see ¶25,232). A taxable disposition occurs when an investor sells shares of a mutual fund or switches money among the various funds a mutual fund company manages (.05). In general, gain or loss is the difference between the amount realized on the sale and the investor's adjusted basis in the shares sold (see ¶25,270 for special adjustments to mutual fund shares).

Identification of shares sold

As is the case with other securities (see ¶25,234), an investor who has purchased shares in a mutual fund at different times or at different prices must identify which shares are sold. This is important in determining both the holding period of the shares and their basis. If no identification is made, the first-in, first-out rule will be applied, with the result that the earliest acquired shares will be deemed to have been sold.

Average basis

If certain requirements are met, however, the IRS permits mutual fund shareholders to make an election to determine the basis of mutual fund shares by using either of two methods to compute an "average basis" for the shares sold—the "double-category" method or the "single-category" method. The mutual fund shareholder may elect either average basis method if:

(1) the mutual fund shares were left in the custody of a custodian or agent in an account maintained for the acquisition or redemption of shares of such fund, and

(2) the mutual fund shares held in the account were acquired at different prices.

In order to determine the average basis of mutual fund shares under the double-category method, all shares held in an account at the time of sale are divided into two categories:

(1) shares held more than 12 months (long-term shares), and

(2) shares held 12 months or less (short-term shares).

The average basis of the shares in each category is equal to the total adjusted basis of all shares in that category divided by the total number of shares in the same category.

The seller may specify the category from which the shares are to be sold to the custodian or agent holding the shares in the account. The custodian or agent must confirm in writing that such specification was made. If such a specification is not made or confirmation is not received, the IRS will consider that the shares sold came first from the long-term category.

Example 1: Over a period of time, Eugene Stone acquired a number of shares in "Nifty-Fifty," a mutual fund. The shares were held by a custodian.

Acquisition Date	*Number of Shares*	*Cost per Share*	*Total Cost*
7/15/90	100	$ 18.80	$ 1,880
10/20/90	20	20.00	400
3/1/04	20	20.50	410
4/25/04	7	20.00	140

On December 1, 2004, Stone directs the custodian to sell 40 shares of the mutual fund. Stone elects to use the double-category method. Because he does not direct the custodian to sell the shares from either the long-term or short-term category, the IRS treats the sale as having been made from the long-term category.

His average basis for the shares sold is $19 per share (total cost of the shares in the long-term category $2,280 ($1,880 + $400) divided by 120 shares in that category).

In order to determine the average basis of mutual fund shares under the single-category method, all shares in an account at the time of the sale are considered to be part of a single category. The average basis of each share in the account is equal to the total adjusted basis of all shares in the account divided by the number of shares in the account. For purposes of determining the holding period of the shares sold, they are considered to be those shares that were acquired first.

> ***Example 2:*** Assume the same facts asset forth in Example (1), except that Stone elected to use the single-category method of determining the average basis of the shares sold. The average basis of the 40 shares sold is \$19.25 (the total cost of shares in the account, \$2,830 (\$1,880 + \$400 + \$410 + \$140), divided by the 147 shares in the account).

If a taxpayer wishes to elect either one of the averaging methods, it must clearly be indicated on the tax return for each year in which the election is applicable that an average-basis method has been used to report gain or loss from the sale of mutual fund shares. In addition, the method used (double-category or single-category) must also be specified on the tax return. Once an average-basis method is elected for the shares of a particular mutual fund, it cannot be revoked without the permission of the IRS.

.05 Reg. §1.1012-1(e).

¶25,272 Foreign Taxes. Mutual funds that invest in international stocks generally pay foreign taxes on the investors' behalf. Investors have two options for claiming these foreign taxes. They may claim the foreign taxes as an itemized deduction on Schedule A of Form 1040 or they may claim a foreign tax credit on Form 1116. Keep in mind that a deduction results in only a percentage tax savings based on the investor's tax bracket, while a tax credit results in a dollar-for-dollar savings. If certain requirements are met, the individual need not file Form 1116 and may claim the credit directly on Form 1040.

Real Estate

¶25,274 Sales of Investment Property. Real estate held as an investment is a capital asset. Thus, gain or loss on its sale or exchange must be reported as a capital gain or loss. Investment property may be held for the production of income without loss of its capital asset status (.05). In such a case, depreciable real property is treated as being used in the taxpayer's trade or business and is considered "section 1231 property." If gains exceed the losses from sales of such property, all the gains and losses are treated as capital gains and losses. If the losses exceed the gains, all the losses and gains are treated as ordinary losses and gains (.10).

Whether property is held for investment or for sale depends upon a number of factors such as: (1) continuity of sales over a period of time, (2) frequency of sales as opposed to isolated transactions, (3) general activities of the seller or those acting under his instructions, (4) the extent or substantiality of the transactions, and (5) the purpose for which the property was acquired.

Depreciation

Most real property used in a taxpayer's trade or business and placed in service after December 31, 1980, and before March 16, 1984, was depreciable over 15 years (18 years if placed in service after March 15, 1984, and before May 9, 1985, and 19 years if placed in service after May 8, 1985, and before 1987) under the accelerated cost recovery system (ACRS) method or, at the taxpayer's election, under a statutory straight-line method over the regular recovery period or an optional, longer recovery period of 35 or 45 years and without regard to useful life or salvage value (.15). Under MACRS, the cost of property placed in service after 1986 and before May 13, 1993, is recovered over 31.5 years under the straight-line method. Property placed into service on or after May 12, 1993, has a 39-year recovery period. Land is never depreciable.

Recapture

Generally, *excess* depreciation is recaptured as ordinary income under the following rules (.20):

Rule 1 Post-1975 excess depreciation is 100 percent recaptured. No further computation is necessary if the recapture equals or exceeds the gain on the sale of such property. All of the gain will be ordinary income.

Rule 2 Excess depreciation after 1969 and before 1976 may be partially recaptured or fully recaptured if the post-1975 recapture under Rule 1 is less than the gain. The amount of this recapture will be a percentage of the 1970-1975 excess depreciation or the unrecaptured gain (gain less recapture under Rule 1), whichever is less. The percentage is 100 percent for housing held more than 12 months and less than 101 months. The percentage decreases by one percent for each month that the property has been held over 100 full months, and there is no recapture under this rule after 16 years and eight months.

Rule 3 Excess depreciation after 1963 and before 1970 may be partially or fully recaptured if the amounts recaptured under Rules 1 and 2, above, are less than the gain. The amount of this pre-1970 recapture will be a percentage of the 1964-1969 excess depreciation or the unrecaptured gain (gain less amounts recaptured under Rules 1 and 2), whichever is less. The percentage is 100 percent for realty held for more than 12 months and less than 21 months. The percentage decreases by one percent for each full month that the property has been held over 20 months. Thus, there is no Rule 3 recapture if the property is held for more than 10 years. Certain categories of low-income housing are excluded from Rule 1 recapture.

Taxation of "Unrecaptured Section 1250 gain."

Under MACRS (used for real property placed in service after 1986), all depreciation is computed under the straight-line method. When the real property is sold, the amount of gain equal to the MACRS depreciation that had been claimed, is termed "Unrecaptured Section 1250 gain" and is subject to a maximum tax rate of 25%. The balance of any gain is taxed under the rates that generally apply to long-term capital assets (e.g., 15% for sales after May 5, 2003). See ¶25,232 for more information concerning the capital gains tax rates.

.05 Code Sec. 57, 167, 1231 and 1250.
.10 Code Sec. 1231.
.15 Code Sec. 168.
.20 Code Sec. 1250(a).

¶25,275 Tax-Free Exchanges. Real property held for investment or for productive use in a trade or business can be exchanged tax free for "like kind" property that is also to be held either for investment or for productive use in a trade or business (.05). Owners of land and improved real estate frequently use this type of exchange as an effective tax-minimizing device where their normal procedure upon disposing of one piece of real property would be to reinvest the proceeds in other property.

With respect to real estate, it is not necessary that the property be of the same type or quality. The requirement is only that the investment or business property be exchanged for other property to be held for investment or for productive use in a trade or business. Thus, there may be a tax-free exchange of unimproved city land for a factory building or of farm land for a rental building.

Nonrecognition of gain or loss on a like-kind exchange is mandatory. Hence, if an investor wishes to claim a loss on property he is disposing of, he must not exchange it for other real estate.

Another reason for not using a like-kind exchange is to obtain a higher basis for depreciation. In a tax-free like-kind exchange, each taxpayer transfers his basis in the surrendered property to the acquired property. However, in a non-like-kind exchange, where the full amount of gain must be recognized, the taxpayer usually takes a market value basis in the acquired property.

Somewhat similar to a tax-free exchange, total or partial nonrecognition of gain on the disposition of a low-income housing project is permitted if replacement property is acquired within a specified time (.10).

.05 Code Secs. 1031 and 1039; Reg. §1.1031(a)-1.

.10 Code Sec. 1039.

Real Estate Investment Trusts (REITs)

¶25,277 Tax-Saving Election. A real estate investment trust (REIT) that otherwise would be taxable as a corporation can make an election that will save taxes for both itself and its shareholders. An electing REIT is taxed only on its retained earnings. The distributed earnings are taxed to the shareholders (.05). Thus, distributed earnings are taxed only once. If the election is not made, the earnings are taxed twice—at the corporate level and again when distributed to the shareholders as dividends.

This tax treatment of REITs puts investments in real estate on somewhat of a par with investments in stocks and securities through purchase of shares in regulated investment companies, e.g., mutual funds (see ¶25,269). It also gives small investors an opportunity to pool their investments in a real estate investment trust and thereby receive the same tax treatment that those of greater wealth receive by direct investments. The advantages of pooling their funds include the spread of risk through diversification of investments, the benefits of expert investment counsel, and the collective financing of projects that one investor alone could not undertake.

The election must be made by the trust by computing taxable income as a real estate investment trust on its return for the first tax year for which the election is applicable. An election can be revoked for any tax year after the first tax year it was effective.

.05 Code Secs. 856-858.

¶25,278 Taxation of Shareholders of REITs. A shareholder or holder of a beneficial interest in a real estate investment trust (REIT) must include dividends in gross income for the tax year in which they are received, except to the extent that dividends are excludable or deductible from gross income (.05). Dividends distributed after the close of the REIT's tax year for which it is allowed a deduction are taxable to the beneficiary in the year in which the distribution is actually received.

Taxation of dividends. Not all the dividends distributed by an REIT may be eligible for the 5% or 15% tax rates on dividends. The REIT is required to notify the shareholders the amount of the distributed dividends that do qualify for the 5% or 15% maximum tax rates (.10)

Capital gains distributions. Capital gain distributions are treated as long-term capital gains in the year received. Loss on the sale or exchange of a share or beneficial interest held for six months or less is a long-term capital loss to the extent of any capital gain dividend received with respect to such share or beneficial interest (.15).

Capital gains that a REIT passes through to its stockholders are treated as their tax-preference items rather than as tax-preference items of the real estate investment trust for purposes of the minimum tax. All tax-preference items other than capital gains (and accelerated depreciation) are apportioned between the REIT and its shareholders according to the ratio between the dividends (other than capital gains dividends) paid each shareholder and the taxable income of the real estate investment trust (ignoring the dividends-paid deduction).

Dividends received for a year during which a trust is not a qualified REIT do not qualify (.20) for the dividends-received deduction allowed corporations.

.05 Code Sec. 857(b)(3), (4), 858(b); Reg. §§1.857-4, 1.858-1.

.10 Code Sec. 854(b)(2).

.15 Code Sec. 857(b)(7).

.20 Code Sec. 857(c).

Real Estate Mortgage Investment Conduits (REMICs)

¶25,280 Qualification as a REMIC. A special set of tax rules are available for a tax entity called a Real Estate Mortgage Investment Conduit (REMIC). In general, a REMIC is an entity that holds a fixed pool of mortgages and issues multiple classes of interests in itself to investors. A REMIC is treated basically like a partnership, with its income allocated to, and taken into account by, holders of the interests in the REMIC.

An entity can be a REMIC if it satisfies requirements relating to the composition of the entity's assets and the nature of the interests of the investors in the entity and if it elects REMIC status for its first and all subsequent years. A REMIC must use the calendar year as its tax year.

Substantially all of a REMIC's assets at the close of the third month ending after the start-up day and at all times thereafter must consist of "qualified mortgages" and "permitted investments." A "qualified mortgage" is any obligation that is principally secured by an interest in real property and that is transferred to the entity on the start-up day in exchange for regular or residual interests in the REMIC, or is purchased by the REMIC within the three-month period beginning on the start-up day, provided that the purchase is under a fixed price contract in effect on the start-up day. "Permitted investments" can be cash flow investments, qualified reserve assets, and foreclosure property.

In addition, in order to qualify as a REMIC, all of the interests in the REMIC must be either regular interests or a single class of residual interests.

¶25,281 Taxation of REMICs. In general, a REMIC is not taxed on its income. Instead, the income is taxed to the holders of the interests in the REMIC (.05). Tax treatment varies depending on whether the holder has a regular or a residual interest in the REMIC.

.05 Code Secs. 860A-860G.

Life Insurance and Annuities

¶25,283 Endowment Deferral Election. Under an endowment policy, the insured usually can elect to take the proceeds in installments or to leave the proceeds with the insurance company and receive interest. If the insured elects the installment option, it should be made within 60 days after maturity of the policy. If made more than 60 days after maturity, the entire gain (excess of face value over premiums paid) is taxed at maturity, even though the proceeds are not received until later years. If the election is made within the 60-day period, the gain is taxed over a period of years under the annuity rules (.05).

If the insured elects to leave the proceeds with the insurance company and receive interest, the time of making the election is immaterial if the proceeds are available to the insured at maturity and if, under the settlement agreement, he can withdraw the proceeds at any future interest payment date. Any gain (the excess of face value over premiums paid) generally is taxable in the year the policy matures or at least in the year of the first interest payment. However, if the insured does not retain any right to withdraw the proceeds at any interest payment date, the gain is not taxable in the year of maturity of the policy if the election is made before maturity. If the election is made at or after maturity of the policy, the gain is taxable in the year of maturity.

Interest payments, regardless of how the gain on the proceeds is taxed, are fully taxable in the year received.

.05 Code Sec. 72(e) and (h); Reg. §§1.72-11 and 1.72-12.

¶25,284 Sales and Exchanges of Insurance Policies and Annuities. Certain life insurance, endowment and annuity contracts may be exchanged tax free. The following exchanges are exempt from taxation (.05):

(1) A life insurance contract for another life insurance contract or for an endowment or annuity contract.

(2) An endowment contract for another endowment contract (provided the endowment contract received provides for regular payments beginning at a date not later than the date payments would have begun under the contract exchanged) or for an annuity contract.

(3) An annuity contract for another annuity contract.

Other exchanges are taxable. For example, tax cannot be avoided at maturity of endowment or annuity contracts by exchanging them for life insurance policies, the proceeds of which, payable at death, are tax exempt.

Sale before maturity

A taxpayer realizes ordinary income on the sale of an endowment or annuity contract before maturity. Ordinary income treatment resulted in similar situations where there was a guaranteed and predictable interest rate and most of the policies had been paid up for some time before the sale (.10).

Surrender of policy or contract

The surrender of an insurance policy, endowment contract or annuity contract for its cash surrender value, as distinguished from an exchange of policies or contracts, results in taxable income where the amount received on surrender exceeds the premiums or other consideration paid.

Loss realized upon the surrender or sale of a life insurance or endowment contract is not recognized. However, loss realized upon the surrender or forfeiture of an annuity contract, is generally recognized as an ordinary loss (.15).

.05 Code Sec. 1035; Reg. §1.1035-1.

.10 *H. Roff*, 36 TC 818, CCH Dec. 24,970, aff'd by CA-3, 62-2 USTC ¶9515, 304 F2d 450; *G.H. Crocker Est.*, 37 TC 605, CCH Dec. 25,303.

.15 Rev. Rul. 61-201, 1961-2 CB 46.

¶25,285 Annuities. Annuities are another method of sheltering income when a taxpayer is in a high-income bracket because the interest earned on the annuity deposits is not taxed until the annuitant begins receiving annuity payments, and then the interest income may be reportable over a number of tax years.

Wrap-around annuities

One of the major drawbacks of annuities is often that the specified rates of return on such contracts do not match the rates of return that are available for other types of investments. In an effort to overcome this disadvantage, a number of tax-deferred annuities are marketed by life insurance companies, outside investment advisors, and mutual fund companies. These annuity plans come in various forms and under a plethora of names, including "wrap-around annuities," "variable annuity contracts coupled with insurance company separate accounts" (unit investment trusts), and "deferred variable annuities." However, a common feature in all of these annuities is that the annuitant is permitted to invest in securities and deposits that yield current rates of return, typically money market mutual funds, and in many cases the annuitant is permitted to select and dispose of the investments.

The IRS has established certain ground rules for determining whether the yields are deferrable or currently taxable (.05).

(1) Policyholders are considered the owners of mutual fund shares for federal income tax purposes if the shares are held by an insurance company as part of publicly offered "wrap-around annuity contracts" because the policyholders typically have direct or indirect investment control and other incidents of ownership in the shares. In such situations, the policyholder must include in gross income any earnings and gains from (or attributable to) the shares and may not defer the income under the normal annuity rules.

(2) The insurance company will be considered the owner of mutual fund shares for federal income tax purposes where the investment of the shares is controlled by the insurance company and the shares are available only through the purchase of an annuity from the company; in such a situation the earnings and gains will be deferred.

The purchaser of an investment annuity contract under which the purchaser individually selected and controlled one or more investments in a portfolio comprising a separate account of the life insurance company issuing the contract is considered the owner of the underlying investments for federal income tax purposes (.10). The purchaser of an annuity contract under which the purchaser selected and controlled specified certificates of deposit issued by a savings and loan association is considered to be the owner of the certificates for federal income tax purposes (.15).

Although the investments of the mutual fund must be controlled by the insurance company, the purchaser nevertheless can exercise a significant degree of investment discretion. The purchaser may choose to allocate the premium payments among mutual funds with different investment strategies as long as the shares of the mutual funds are not available for sale directly to the general public (.20). For instance, he may allocate a portion of the payment to a mutual fund that invests primarily in common stocks, a portion to another mutual fund that invests primarily in bonds, and the remainder in a fund that invests primarily in money market instruments. Moreover, he not only may allocate future payments in different proportions, but also may reallocate his previous allocations, provided that the annuity contract permits him to do so, without being treated as having investment control over the fund.

In addition, the contract may contain a number of features common to deferred annuity contracts, including the right of the purchaser to surrender the contract in part or in full for cash (subject to a surrender charge) and the right (at some future date to be determined by the purchaser) to convert the accumulated values under the contract into a stream of periodic payments under one of several settlement options (.25).

Withdrawal of annuity funds before starting date

Investors who withdraw funds from an annuity before the starting date of the annuity payments stand to lose all or most of the tax benefit because (1) this type of "nonannuity payment" is often fully taxable (to the extent of the accrued income in the contract for contracts entered into after August 13, 1982), which is unlike the partial taxability of normal annuity payments; and (2) the withdrawal is subject to a penalty. The amount of the penalty is 10 percent of the amount of the withdrawal that is includible in gross income (.30). The 10-percent penalty does not apply to a distribution that is (1) made on or after the date the policyholder reaches age 59½ ; (2) made on or after the death of the holder; (3) attributable to the holder's becoming disabled; (4) one of a series of substantially equal periodic payments made for life; (5) made from a qualified plan; (6) allocable to investment in the contract made before August 14, 1982; (7) made under a qualified funding asset; (8) made under an immediate annuity contract; or (9) purchased by an employer upon the termination of a qualified plan and held by the employer until the employee separates from service. The penalty and the "early" inclusion in income may nullify the advantage of deferring the tax on annuity payments.

.05 Rev. Rul. 81-225, 1981-2 CB 12, amplifying Rev. Rul. 76-281, 1976-2 CB 206.
.10 Rev. Rul. 77-85, 1977-1 CB 12.
.15 Rev. Rul. 80-274, 1980-2 CB 27.
.20 Rev. Rul. 82-54, 1982-1 CB 11.
.25 Rev. Rul. 81-225, 1981-2 CB 12, amplifying Rev. Rul. 76-281, 1976-2 CB 206.
.30 Code Sec. 72(q).

Retirement and Savings Incentives

¶25,287 Individual Retirement Accounts. Cash paid by or on behalf of an individual into an individual retirement account—commonly referred to as a traditional IRA—may be deducted from gross income if certain requirements are met (.05). IRAs and other qualified self-employed or employee benefit plans (see ¶25,288—¶25,289) can benefit their contributors in several ways: (1) contributions to these accounts and plans are not currently taxed; (2) interest or other income is not *recognized* until a later date, e.g., withdrawal on retirement; and (3) both contributions and earnings on such contributions are generally taxed at lower rates upon their withdrawal. Individuals should also consider the significant tax advantages that Roth IRAs hold over traditional IRAs.

Deduction limits

An individual is permitted to make deductible contributions to a traditional IRA of up to the lesser of $3,000 or 100 percent of compensation if: (1) the individual has adjusted gross income that does not exceed the "applicable dollar amount" or (2) the individual is not an active participant in an employer-maintained retirement plan for any part of the plan year ending with or within the individual's tax year. The maximum deduction will increase to $4,000 in 2005. Also, for 2004 and 2005, individuals who will be age 50 or over by the end of the year are entitled to make an additional catch-up contribution of $500.

For 2004, the "applicable dollar amount" is $45,000 for a single individual, $65,000 for a married couple filing jointly, and zero for a married couple filing separately. The IRA deduction limit is reduced by an amount that bears the same ratio to the applicable dollar limit as the individual's adjusted gross income in excess of the applicable dollar amount bears to $10,000. Thus, in the case of an active participant, the IRA deduction is eliminated for single individuals with adjusted gross incomes over $55,000, married couples filing jointly with adjusted gross incomes above $75,000, and marrieds filing separately if a spouse has adjusted gross income above $10,000 (.10).

Spousal IRAs

An individual is not considered an active participant in an employer plan merely because the individual's spouse is an active participant. However, the maximum deductible IRA contribution for the individual who is not an active participant, but whose spouse is, is phased out at an adjusted gross income between $150,000 and $160,000 (jointly computed).

Nondeductible contributions

Individuals are permitted to make nondeductible contributions to a traditional IRA to the extent that they are ineligible to make deductible IRA contributions (.15). Earnings on nondeductible IRA contributions are not subject to tax until they are withdrawn. The limit on designated nondeductible contributions for 2004 is the lesser of 100 percent of compensation or $3,000 ($3,500 if the individual is over age 49). However, before making nondeductible contributions to a traditional IRA, an individual should certainly consider making the contributions to a Roth IRA.

Rollover rules

Generally, a distribution from an employer's qualified plan may be rolled over tax free to a traditional IRA or to another qualified plan that permits it on a nondiscriminatory basis. Generally, an individual may rollover funds from a qualified plan into most types of employer plans (e.g., 457 plans). However, the plan provided by the new employer must provide for such rollovers.

Time for making contributions

In order to be deductible for a given tax year, contributions to an IRA (traditional or Roth) may be made through the due date (not including extensions) for that year's income tax return. A taxpayer is deemed to have made a voluntary contribution to a qualified employer or government plan for a calendar year if the contribution is made by April 15 of the following calendar year or by an earlier time provided for by the plan administrator.

Limits on IRA investment in collectibles

An IRA participant may generally direct the investment of the assets in an IRA account even though those assets are under the control of the IRA trustee or custodian (bank, insurance company, or other qualifying financial institution). However, an IRA participant (or a participant in a qualified plan that allows individually directed accounts) who directs IRA contributions into collectibles (art works, rugs, antiques, metals, gems, stamps, coins, alcoholic beverages, or any other tangible personal property characterized by the IRS as a "collectible") may be penalized for making such investments. Generally, if any IRA assets are used to acquire a collectible, the amount is treated as a distribution from the account and is taxed to the participant (.20). However, certain U.S.-minted gold and silver coins and bullion may be used as IRA investments.

Miscellaneous rules

Traditional IRA contributions cannot generally be made for or after the tax year in which an individual (other than a simplified employee pension (SEP) plan participant) reaches age 70½. This rule does not apply to Roth IRAs. However, a deduction is permitted for contributions to a spousal IRA in a year in which the benefitting spouse has not reached age 70½ before the close of the tax year, even though the contributing spouse is age 70½ or older. Also, no amount rolled over from another qualified plan or IRA can be deducted as a qualified retirement contribution. Further, if an IRA invests in an endowment policy, no IRA contribution deduction can be taken for amounts that are allocable to the cost of life insurance.

An individual who is covered under a simplified employee pension (SEP) plan (see ¶25,289) is eligible to establish and maintain an IRA (and a spousal IRA).

.05 Code Sec. 219 and 408.
.10 Code Sec. 219(g).
.15 Code Sec. 408(o).
.20 Code Sec. 408(m).

¶25,288 Retirement Plans for the Self-Employed (Keogh Plans). In addition to deferring income by making deductible IRA contributions, a self-employed individual may make deductible contributions to a qualified Keogh plan up to a specified amount (.05). This is beneficial because the use of both retirement plans raises the amount that can be deducted from gross income and the use of the latter type of retirement plan allows greater flexibility. An owner-employee may:

(1) make direct cash contributions to a trust or custodial account created for retirement purposes (with the trustee or custodian being a bank, building and loan association, insured federal credit union, or another entity or person that can demonstrate an ability to administer the account in accordance with the law),

(2) purchase nontransferable annuity contracts from a life insurance company (and such annuity need not be held by a trustee or custodian), or

(3) directly purchase "face amount certificates," as defined in the Investment Company Act of 1940, from an investment company.

Thus, the plan may be trusteed or nontrusteed, depending on the method of funding.

An owner-employee is a self-employed individual who is a sole proprietor of an unincorporated trade or business or a partner who owns more than 10 percent of either the capital interest or the profit interest in the partnership (.10).

.05 Code Sec. 404.

.10 Code Sec. 401(c)(3).

¶25,289 Simplified Employee Pension Plans. A simplified employee pension (SEP) plan is essentially a traditional IRA to which an employee and his employer may contribute (see ¶25,287). The employee must include any employer contributions in income but is permitted an offsetting deduction from his income (.05).

The employer's contribution to an SEP plan is governed by the same contribution limit that applies to contributions made by a self-employed individual to a Keogh plan (see ¶25,288). An employee who is covered by an SEP plan can make contributions to an IRA, subject to the limitations discussed at ¶25,287, independently of the employer's SEP contributions.

.05 Code Sec. 219.

Incorporated Pocketbooks

¶25,291 Holding Investment Property in a Corporation. Because of the relatively low tax rates for individuals, investors may not find it desirable to form C corporations in order to hold investments. Although qualifying corporations may be eligible for a 70% or 80% dividends-received deduction on dividends received from other corporations, the dividends are not be tax free (.05). The remaining percentage of such dividends are subject to taxation at the corporate rate. Distributed dividends are tax again to the shareholders. Dividends received by individuals are generally taxed at a maximum rate of 15%. Income from other investments also be subject to double taxation, first at the corporate level and then at the individual level.

In addition to being exposed to double taxation, investor-owners of personal holding companies may lose some of the profits from their corporations if such corporations fail to make distributions so as to avoid the personal holding company tax. Also, such corporations may risk exposure to the accumulated earnings tax for accumulating earnings and profits beyond the reasonable needs of the business.

.05 Code Sec. 531, 541 and 543; Reg. §§1.531-1, 1.541-1.

¶25,292 S Corporations. An S corporation is a corporation with 75 or fewer shareholders (100 or fewer after December 31, 2004) that has elected, under Subchapter S (by unanimous consent of its shareholders), to have the shareholders pay taxes on its income in much the same way that they would have if the income had been received directly by them (.05).

Whether a corporation should elect to be an S corporation depends upon the tax advantages to be derived from having its income taxed directly to the shareholders.

Generally, an S election may be desirable during the early years of a corporation when it has losses and large deductions that can be passed through to its shareholders.

S corporations with Subchapter C earnings and profits and passive investment income (excluding gain or loss realized by options and commodities dealers on any Code Sec. 1256 contract or property related to such contract (.10)) totalling more than 25 percent of gross receipts are subject to a tax on excess passive investment income (.15). Moreover, the S corporation will be terminated where:

(1) the corporation has passive investment income of more than 25 percent of its gross receipts for each of three consecutive tax years, and

(2) the corporation has accumulated Subchapter C earnings and profits at the end of each of the three tax years in question (.20).

.05 Code Secs. 1361-1379.

.10 Code Sec. 1362(d)(3)(E).

.15 Code Sec. 1375(a) and (b).

.20 Code Sec. 1362(d)(3).

OWNERS AND DEVELOPERS OF MINERAL PROPERTIES

Introduction

¶25,294 The federal income tax provisions concerning income derived from the ownership and development of mineral properties are complex. Owners and developers of mineral properties have often been involved in litigation over the tax treatment of income and expenses relating to such properties. Generally, the owners or operators receiving income from natural resources are entitled to a deduction in the form of a depletion allowance from gross income derived from the properties. The depletion allowance, either cost or percentage, is based on the wasting nature of the natural resource. Depletion is allowable only to the person or entity who possesses an economic interest in the mineral.

Percentage depletion of oil and gas wells or of mining properties is limited to a certain percentage of the taxable income derived from the property. Consequently, it must be determined what constitutes taxable income. Other tax and financial considerations concerning mineral properties are the proper handling of the depreciation of physical properties; the expensing or capitalization of exploration and development expenses and intangible drilling expenses; the handling of carved-out mineral production payments and so-called ABC transactions; and the control of operating expenses such as fees, interest, contributions, taxes, abandonment losses, overhead expenses, and lifting costs.

Depletion

¶25,296 Nature of Depletion Allowance. Because mineral deposits are assets that waste away over time, the Code permits taxpayers to a deduction for the depletion of such assets in order to compensate the owner for the part of the minerals used up in production. In other words, the depletion deduction allows the owner of mineral deposits a pro rata return of their capital investment over the production life of the resource. The proper amount of depletion that may be deducted in a particular tax year is limited to that year. The deduction cannot be increased in a later tax year because an inadequate amount of a deduction was taken in a prior year. When the taxpayer takes no deduction for a year, or takes an incorrect allowance for a year, his remedy is to file an amended return for that year (.05).

There are two methods for calculating depletion on mineral property: cost depletion and percentage depletion. There is no election to choose either depletion method. Instead, the Code requires a taxpayer to use the method that will result in the greater deduction allowance. Consequently, both cost and percentage depletion must be calculated, and the one allowing the greater deduction must be used. Even though the basis of depletable property is reduced by the amount of percentage depletion currently deductible, the percentage depletion deduction will not be denied simply because the basis of the property has been reduced to zero. On the other hand, cost depletion is not applicable once the basis of the property has been reduced to zero.

A depletion allowance may not be increased where a mineral property is under a threat of condemnation (.10). A threatened condemnation does not constitute a fixed and certain event that decreases the size of a property for mining purposes. A taxpayer must wait until the time of an actual condemnation before reallocating his basis in mineral deposits recoverable in land remaining after the condemnation.

Where reported on return. An individual reports depletion either on separate Schedule C or on Schedule E (Form 1040), depending on whether the depletable property is used in trade or business or whether it is held as an investment. A schedule should be attached showing how the depletion deduction was determined in the case of depletion incurred in a business. A corporation reports its depletion allowance on Form 1120, and should attach a separate schedule. The depletion deduction is allowed in determining an individual's adjusted gross income regardless of whether the depletable property is used in trade or business.

Taxpayers who claim a deduction for worthlessness of mineral rights or geothermal deposits need to identify the deduction and enter the amount on their returns (i.e., enter on line for "Other deductions" on corporate returns and line for "Other expenses" on Schedule C of Form 1040). They must also keep the necessary records used to figure the amount of the deduction and documents evidencing value.

.05 Code Sec. 611; Reg. §1.611-1.

.10 *Martin Marietta Corporation*, ClsCt, 85-1 USTC ¶9284, 7 ClsCt 586.

¶25,297 Cost Depletion. The basic method of computing depletion is known as "cost depletion." Determination of cost depletion requires an estimate of the number of units, such as tons or barrels, that make up the deposit (.05). The basis of the property that is allocable to the depletable reserve is then divided by the number of units. For cost depletion purposes, the basis of the mineral or timber property is the adjusted basis that would be used for determining gain or loss upon the sale or other disposition of the property. However, the adjusted basis for cost depletion does not include:

(1) amounts recoverable through depreciation deductions, deferred expenses, and deductions other than depletion; or

(2) the residual value of land and improvements at the end of the mineral or timber operation (.10).

The quotient of the basis of the property divided by the number of units that make up the deposit is the cost depletion per unit. This cost-depletion-per-unit amount is multiplied by the number of units *sold* during the year to determine the cost depletion deduction for the year. Each year the basis of the property is reduced, but not below zero, by the amount of the depletion deducted for that year. The remaining basis is used in computing cost depletion for the following year.

Where the fair market value of the mineral property and improvements is determined for the purpose of ascertaining the basis, no revaluation is permissible except in the case of misrepresentation, fraud, or gross error. Where, as a result of operations or of development work, or any other cause, it is ascertained by the taxpayer or the IRS that the remaining recoverable units are materially greater or less than the prior estimate of such units, the estimate of the remaining recoverable units (but not the basis for depletion) must be revised. The cost-depletion allowance for the current tax year and subsequent tax years must then be based upon the revised estimate. However, a change in reserve estimate is *not* permitted due solely to a change in current oil or gas prices (.15). On the other hand, owners of domestic oil and/or gas properties are provided a safe harbor over what constitutes the appropriate amount of probable or prospective reserves (.20).

Example: In 2003, Mary Hastings purchases a mine and estimates that there are 200,000 tons of ore to be extracted. The adjusted basis of the mineral property is $20,000. During the year, she mines 11,500 tons and *sells* 10,000 tons. Depletion for 2003 is computed as follows:

Rate of depletion per ton ($20,000/200,000)	10¢
Depletion for 2003 (10¢ X 10,000)	$1,000

In 2004 Hastings mines and sells 9,000 tons. However, a revised estimate at the end of 2004 indicates that there are 371,000 tons of unextracted ore. Depletion for 2004 is computed as follows:

Revised estimate of unextracted tonnage	371,000
Tons mined during 2004	9,000
Total tonnage to be used in computing new rate	380,000
Adjusted basis	$ 20,000
2003 depletion	1,000
Remaining basis	$ 19,000
New rate of depletion per ton ($19,000/380,000)	5¢
Depletion for 2004 (5¢ X 9,000)	$ 450

It is assumed that the salvage value of the property (i.e., the value of the property after extraction of all the minerals) is negligible. If this is not the case, the basis to be recovered must be reduced by the salvage value.

.05 Code Sec. 611; Reg. §1.611-1.

.10 Code Sec. 612; Reg. §1.612-1.

.15 Industry Specialization Program (ISP) Coordinated Issue Paper (Petroleum Industry–Cost Depletion Recoverable Reserves, 1-13-97).

.20 Rev. Proc. 2004-19, I.R.B. 2004-10, 563.

¶25,298 Percentage Depletion in General. In order to encourage the development of natural resources and to compensate owners, producers, and investors for the financial risks inherent in developing such resources, a special method of computing depletion, known as percentage depletion, is provided. Use of the method ordinarily results in a substantial reduction of taxes. Percentage depletion is a flat percentage of gross income from the property. The maximum percentage depletion deduction is 50 percent (100 percent in the case of oil and gas properties for tax years beginning after 1990) of the taxable income from the property computed without the depletion deduction and the manufacturers' deduction under Code Sec. 199 (.05).

A deduction for percentage depletion is not available if it is less than depletion based on cost. Nor is percentage depletion available for the depletion of timber. Additionally, percentage depletion is not available on lease bonuses, advance royalties or other amounts payable without regard to actual production from the property. Coal and iron ore royalties are eligible for percentage depletion for any tax year in which the maximum rate of tax imposed on any net capital gain is equal to or greater than the maximum rate for ordinary income (.10).

Rates of depletion

Percentage depletion is allowed at varying percentages of gross income from the property. The rates are as follows: (.12):

(1) *22 percent:*

(a) sulphur (including sulphur chemically converted from hydrogen sulfide) (.13) and uranium; and

(b) if from deposits in the United States—anorthosite, asbestos, bauxite, block steatite talc, celestite, chromite, clay, corundum, fluorspar, graphite, ilmenite, kyanite, laterite, mica, nephelite syenite (to the extent that alumina and aluminum compounds are extracted therefrom), olivine, quartz crystals (radio grade), rutile, zircon, and ores of the following metals: antimony, beryllium, bismuth, cadmium, cobalt, columbium, lead, lithium, manganese, mercury, molybdenum, nickel, platinum, platinum group metals, tantalum, thorium, tin, titanium, tungsten, vanadium, and zinc.

(2) *15 percent:* If from deposits in the United States —

(a) gold, silver, copper, and iron ore

(b) oil shale (except shale covered in the 7 ½ percent rates),

(c) geothermal deposits.

(3) *14 percent:*

(a) metal mines (if not covered in the 22 percent and 15 percent rates), rock asphalt, and vermiculite; and

(b) if the 22 percent rate, the 7½ percent rate, or the 5 percent rate for clay used or sold for use in the manufacture of drainage and roofing tile, flower pots and kindred products does not apply, then ball clay, bentonite, china clay, sagger clay, and clay used or sold for use for purposes dependent on its refractory properties.

(4) *10 percent:* Asbestos (if from deposits from without the United States), brucite, coal, lignite, perlite, sodium chloride, wollastonite and certain geopressured natural gas.

(5) *7½ percent:* Clay and shale used or sold for use in the manufacture of sewer pipe or brick, and clay, shale, and slate used or sold for use as sintered or burned lightweight aggregates.

(6) *5 percent:*

(a) gravel, peat, pumice, sand, scoria, shale (except oil shale), and stone (except stone used as dimension or ornamental stone);

(b) clay used, or sold for use, in the manufacture of drainage and roofing tile, flower pots, and kindred products;

(c) if from brine wells—bromine, calcium chloride, and magnesium chloride;

(d) lava rock that is crushed, ground, and used or sold for use in the molding of figurines (.15); and

(e) magnesium hydroxide chemically extracted from brine (.20).

Depletion at 14 percent is allowable for all minerals not listed in (1)-(6) (.25). For the special percentage depletion rules that apply to oil and gas production, see ¶25,299.

.05 Code Sec. 613, as amended by the American Jobs Creation Act of 2004 (P.L. 108-357).

.10 Code Sec. 631(c).

.12 Reg. §1.613-2.

.13 *Louisiana Land and Exploration Co.,* 90 TC 630, CCH Dec. 44,681.

.15 Rev. Rul. 79-382, 1979-2 CB 245.

.20 *Martin Marietta Corporation,* ClsCt, 85-1 USTC ¶9219, 7 ClsCt. 586.

.25 Rev. Rul. 84-87, 1984-1 CB 142; Rev. Rul. 82-17, 1982-1 CB 95.

¶25,299 Percentage Depletion for Oil and Gas. Percentage depletion for oil an gas properties is allowed only for the following (.05):

(1) regulated natural gas

(2) natural gas sold under a fixed contract;

(3) any geothermal deposit in the United States or in a possession of the United States that is determined to be a gas well; and

(4) independent producers and royalty holders of oil and gas wells.

Natural gas

For regulated natural gas and natural gas sold under a fixed contract there is a 22-percent depletion rate. For this purpose, natural gas sold under a fixed contract is domestic natural gas sold under a contract:

(1) that is in effect on February 1, 1975, and at all times thereafter before such sale; and

(2) that does not permit the price of the gas to be adjusted in order to reflect the increased federal income tax liability of the seller, due to the repeal of percentage depletion for gas sold after 1974.

Under a fixed contract for natural gas, price increases after February 1, 1975, are presumed to be based on increased federal income tax liabilities unless the seller can show by clear and convincing evidence that such increases were not based on increased tax liabilities. Examples of clear and convincing evidence that price increases under a fixed contract are entirely attributable to a reason unrelated to the repeal of percentage depletion for gas include (.10):

- increases to reflect additional state and local real property or severance taxes;
- increases for additional operating costs;
- adjustments for inflation;
- increases for additional drilling and related costs;
- increases to reflect changes in the quality of gas sold.

Gas sold after a such a price increase is treated as not sold under a fixed contract if the price adjustment provided for in a contract permits:

- the possible increase in federal income tax liability of the seller to be taken into account,
- an increase in the price of the contract equal to the highest price paid for natural gas produced in the area, or
- a renegotiation of the contract price.

Geothermal deposits

Geothermal deposits in the United States or U.S. possession are subject to a 15 percent depletion rate. In addition, there is a 10-percent depletion rate for an unlimited amount of natural gas from geopressured brine produced from any well the drilling of which began after September 30, 1978, and before January 1, 1984. Natural gas from geopressured brine produced from a well drilled after 1983 is eligible for percentage depletion only if it meets the requirements of another exception to the percentage depletion restrictions on natural gas.

Independent producers and royalty owners

Percentage depletion for a small independent producer or a royalty owner for domestic production is limited to 15 percent of the gross income from the property, subject to a maximum depletable quantity of 1,000 barrels of domestic crude oil per day or 6 million cubic feet of gas per day. The allowable percentage depletion is restricted to the lesser of 65 percent of the taxpayer's taxable income or 100 percent of the taxable income from the oil- or gas-producing property. However, the 100-percent taxable income limit on percentage depletion has been temporarily suspended for marginal properties for tax years beginning after December 31, 1997, and before January 1, 2006 (.15). For this purposes, an independent producer of crude oil is any producer or related person who is not treated as a refiner or retailer. For purposes of percentage depletion, the determination of who is an independent producer is based on a refining and a retailing limitation for a tax year.

For interests in marginally producing oil and gas wells held by independent producers or royalty owners, the statutory percentage depletion rate (15 percent) is increased by one percent for each whole dollar that the reference price for crude oil for the immediately preceding calendar year is less than $20 per barrel (not to be adjusted for inflation) (.20). The increased percentage depletion rate applies for the taxpayer's tax year that immediately follows a calendar year for which the average crude oil price falls below the $20 floor. The percentage depletion rate for oil and gas produced from marginal production for the calendar years 2001 through 2004 calendar years is 15 percent (.25).

Refiners excluded

If a taxpayer or a person related to the taxpayer is a refiner of crude oil, that taxpayer does not qualify as an independent producer eligible for percentage depletion of oil or gas. A "refiner" is a taxpayer or related person who refines more than 50,000 barrels of crude oil during a tax year. The amount of oil refined by a related person is added to the amount refined by the taxpayer for purposes of the 50,000-barrel limit. A refinery run is the volume of inputs (as opposed to outputs) of crude oil into the refining stream. The inputs of crude oil into the refining process are exclusive of any product derived from oil (feedstock). Crude oil refined outside the United States is taken into account (.30).

Retailers excluded

If a taxpayer or a person related to the taxpayer is a retailer of oil or natural gas, the taxpayer does not qualify as an independent producer eligible for percentage depletion of oil or gas. A "retailer" is a taxpayer or related person who has combined gross receipts exceeding $5 million from the sales (excluding sales for resale) of oil or natural gas, or from the sale of by-products of such oil or gas:

(1) through any retail outlet operated by the taxpayer or related person; or

(2) to any person:

(a) obligated under an agreement or contract with the taxpayer or related person to use a trademark, trade name, or service mark or name owned by such taxpayer or related person, in marketing or distributing oil or natural gas, or by-products, or

(b) given authority under a contract with the taxpayer or related person to occupy any retail outlet owned, leased, or controlled by the taxpayer or related person.

Proceeds from bulk sales by a taxpayer or related person to the Department of Defense are not included in the $5-million limitation on retail sales. Also, proceeds from sales of oil, natural gas, or by-products that have occurred outside the United States are not included in the $5-million limitation if the taxpayer or related person does not export any of its domestic production during its current tax year or the immediately preceding tax year (.35).

Where a taxpayer sells lubricating oils to distributors under a contract that does not explicitly require the buyer to use the taxpayer's trademark in marketing or distribution, the taxpayer is not required to include the proceeds from those sales in the $5-million retail sales limitation. Moreover, if the taxpayer's sales offices handle sales to business and industry, the sales to distributors for resale and sales to political subdivisions are not treated as retail sales.

The term "retail sales" is limited to sales of small quantities of oil or gas (or their by-products) made to ultimate consumers (.40).

Related persons

For purposes of determining whether a taxpayer is a "refiner" or a "retailer," a person is related to the taxpayer if the taxpayer holds a significant ownership interest in such person (or vice versa), or if a third person has a significant ownership interest in both the taxpayer and such person. Significant ownership interest means:

(1) with respect to a corporation, five percent or more in value of the outstanding stock of such corporation;

(2) with regard to a partnership, five percent or more interest in the profits or capital of such partnership; and

(3) with regard to an estate or trust, five percent or more of the beneficial interests in such estate or trust (.45).

In determining whether a significant ownership interest is held, an interest owned by or for a corporation, partnership, trust, or estate is treated as owned directly both by itself and proportionately by its shareholder, partners, or beneficiaries.

Average daily production

A taxpayer's average daily production of domestic crude oil or natural gas for any tax year is determined by dividing the aggregate production of domestic crude oil or natural gas to which gross income from the property is attributable during the tax year by the number of days in that tax year. The production of a taxpayer holding a partial interest in the production from any property, including an interest held in a partnership or an S corporation, is determined by multiplying the total production, to which gross income from the property is attributable, of that property by the taxpayer's percentage of participation in the revenues from that property (.50).

If the taxpayer's average daily production exceeds the maximum depletable quantity (1,000 barrels of oil/day or 6 million cubic feet of gas/day), the maximum depletable quantity must be allocated among all of the domestic properties in which the taxpayer has an interest. The allocation is made by totaling the production from all of the properties and allocating to each property the same proportion of the maximum depletable quantity as that property's total production bears to the total production from all of the properties.

Where an independent producer or royalty owner has both oil and gas production, the oil is depletable without an election. If, however, a taxpayer wants to claim a percentage depletion for the gas, he must elect to do this. The election may be made on an original or amended tax return or a claim for credit or refund and at any time before the due date for filing the return, claim, or refund.

A taxpayer may elect to treat as his depletable natural gas quantity an amount equal to 6,000 cubic feet for each barrel of oil that may be depleted. Because the maximum depletable quantity of oil is an average daily production of 1,000 barrels, the maximum depletable quantity of natural gas is an average daily production of 6 million cubic feet.

The election to claim percentage depletion for natural gas does not increase the overall depletable quantity of oil or gas. A taxpayer who produces both oil and gas and who makes the election to claim a percentage depletion for natural gas must allocate the maximum depletable quantity between the two types of production, unless he elects to claim the entire depletable quantity as natural gas.

Partnership or S corporation

A partnership's or S corporation's basis in oil or gas properties must be allocated to the partners or shareholders proportionately. Thereafter, each partner or shareholder must maintain an individual basis account and compute his own allowance for either percentage depletion or cost depletion on all his oil and gas properties. For this purpose, a partner or shareholder must adjust his basis for his individual deductions for depletion, and he must separately compute gain or loss on the proceeds from the sale or exchange of an oil or gas property.

Fiscal-year taxpayer

When a fiscal-year taxpayer applies these rules to a tax year that is less than 12 months, each portion of such tax year that occurs during a single calendar year must be treated as if it were a short tax year.

Controlled group and family members

Persons who are members of the same controlled group of corporations are treated as one taxpayer (.55). If 50 percent or more of the beneficial interest in two or more corporations, trusts, or estates is owned by the same or related persons (taking into account only persons who own at least five percent of such beneficial interest), the 1000 barrel per day exemption must be allocated among all the entities in proportion to the respective production of domestic crude oil or natural gas.

In determining whether a significant ownership interest is held, an interest owned by or for a corporation, partnership, trust, or estate is treated as owned directly both by itself and proportionately by its shareholders, partners, or beneficiaries. If individuals are members of the same family, the exemption is allocated among them in proportion to the respective production of domestic crude oil or natural gas during the period in question by such individuals.

A person is "related to" another person if they are members of the same controlled group of corporations or if the relationship between them could result in a disallowance of losses. However, for this purpose, the family of an individual includes only his spouse and minor children.

Taxable income limitation

In the case of independent producers and royalty owners, the percentage depletion deduction may not exceed 65 percent of the taxpayer's taxable income from all sources, computed without regard to the depletion allowance, any net operating loss carryback to the tax year, and any capital loss carryback to the tax year (.60). An unused depletion allowance disallowed as a deduction by reason of this 65-percent taxable income limitation may be carried over to the following tax year. There is also a 100 percent limitation on the amount of percentage depletion an independent producer or royalty holder may claim during a tax year. This limitation applies to all taxpayers and restricts percentage depletion to 100 percent of taxable income from the oil- or gas-producing property. However, the 100-percent taxable income limit on percentage depletion deductions has been temporarily suspended for marginal properties for tax years beginning after December 31, 1997, and before January 1, 2006 (.65).

The taxable income of a trust is computed without a deduction for distributions to beneficiaries during the tax year. Also, percentage depletion is not treated as a deduction from the taxable income of the trust.

If gas-producing property is exempted from the restrictions on percentage depletion, then taxable income must be reduced by the amount of percentage depletion taken. Also, if the cost depletion deduction allowance on one or more of the taxpayer's oil or gas properties is greater than the percentage depletion deduction allowed under this provision (without regard to the limitation based on taxable income), then the entire amount of allowable cost depletion must be deducted in computing taxable income for purposes of the 65-percent limitation.

A corporation that is eligible for deductions for both percentage depletion and dividends received may take the depletion deduction first (.70).

.05 Code Sec. 613A.
.10 Reg. §1.613A-7(c) and (d).
.15 Code Sec. 613A(c), as amended by the Working Families Tax Relief Act of 2004 (P.L. 108-311).
.20 Code Sec. 613A(c)(6)(C).
.25 Notice 2004-48, I.R.B. 2004-30,88.
.30 Code Sec. 613A(d)(4); Reg. §1.613A-7(s).
.35 Code Sec. 613A(d)(2); Reg. §1.613A-7(r).
.40 *Witco Chemical Corp.*, CA-FC, 84-2 USTC ¶9751, 742 F2d 615, aff'g ClsCt, 83-1 USTC ¶9371.
.45 Code Sec. 613A(d)(3).
.50 Reg. §1.613A-7(f).
.55 Code Sec. 613A(c)(8).
.60 Code Sec. 613A(d)(1).
.65 Code Secs. 613(a) and 613A(c)(6)(H), as amended by the Working Families Tax Relief Act of 2004 (P.L. 108-311).
.70 *Lastarmco, Inc.*, CA-5, 84-2 USTC ¶9719, 737 F2d 1440, aff'g TC, 79 TC 810, CCH Dec. 39,483.

Who May Deduct Depletion

¶25,301 Owners of Economic Interest. Only a person who has an economic interest in mineral deposits is entitled to a depletion allowance (.05). Usually, a person is considered to have an economic interest in mineral deposits where the payments received by him from an interest in the mineral deposits:

(1) are dependent upon the extraction of the deposits; and

(2) are determined by the output of the deposits.

The right to a depletion allowance requires the ownership of a capital investment (economic ownership) in the natural resource in place. "Investment" does not simply mean a direct investment in the minerals in place (.10). An investment that is a practical prerequisite to successful exploitation of the right to mine the minerals in place is sufficient to satisfy the economic interest requirement, provided the taxpayer effectively acquires at least a share in the minerals in place. The legal form of the acquisition is not important.

Extraction of minerals

A depletion deduction for minerals must be based on an extraction of minerals from a property. For example, a farmer whose farm produced valuable top soil (peat) was not entitled to a depletion allowance where the peat subsided and was consumed through ordinary farming processes (.15).

However, even where there is an extraction of minerals, a taxpayer must have the requisite economic interest in the extracted minerals in order to claim a depletion allowance (.20). A roadbuilder who extracted minerals from a state-owned pit was not entitled to a depletion deduction because he did not have an economic interest in the pit (.25).

Output of deposits

In addition to the extraction of minerals, a depletion deduction must be based on an actual production of minerals. Thus, the depletion allowance is determined by the output of the mineral deposit. A taxpayer who does not retain an economic interest in the mineral output is not entitled to a depletion allowance.

Generally, a taxpayer who reserves a royalty (¶25,304) on the future production of a mineral has retained an economic interest in the mineral. A taxpayer who grants operating rights in oil and gas or mineral property and who retains fractional shares of production that constitute overriding royalty interests retains an economic interest in the property even if he does not receive any royalty payments during a given tax year (.30).

.05 Code Secs. 611 and 691(b)(2); Reg. §§1.611-1 and 1.691(b)-1(b).

.10 *L. Weaver*, 72 TC 594, CCH Dec. 36,152.

.15 *A. Duda & Sons, Inc.*, CA-5, 77-2 USTC ¶9678, 560 F2d 669.

.20 *Missouri River Sand Co.*, CA-8, 85-2 USTC ¶9732, 774 F2d 334, aff'g TC, 83 TC 193, CCH Dec. 41,404.

.25 IRS Letter Ruling 8427003, 3-20-84, CCH IRS LETTER RULINGS REPORTS.

.30 IRS Letter Ruling 8508058, 11-27-84, CCH IRS LETTER RULINGS REPORTS.

¶25,302 Lease of Mineral Property. A lease of property for mineral production permits the lessee to enter the lessor's property and extract the minerals subject to the lease (.05). A lessee often pays the lessor a bonus as consideration for the economic interest in the mineral deposit (¶25,303). In addition, the lessee usually makes royalty payments to the lessor as compensation for the actual extraction and sale of the mineral (¶25,304).

Lease agreement

In a typical lease of property for mining or drilling purposes, the lessee obtains a fee interest in the mineral (including oil and gas) deposit, and he has an easement over the surface of the land for the purposes of exploring and drilling for and removing the minerals. His interest entitles him to build or use roads on the land to reach his mines or wells and to transport any extracted mineral deposits. The rights to ingress and egress are usually spelled out in the lease agreement. However, such rights are appurtenant to the lease and exist even if not specifically mentioned in the lease. Any depletion allowance must be equitably apportioned between the lessor and lessee. Thus, the lessor and lessee must share the depletion allowance available with respect to the leased mineral property (¶25,311).

Lease v. sale

Where an owner (or other assignor, such as a sublessor) of mineral property transfers the development rights to such property, the owner must retain an economic interest in the property in order to claim a depletion allowance (¶25,301).

Generally, the owner may claim a depletion allowance only if the payments he receives from transferring the mineral rights are dependent upon actual mineral production. The transfer of mineral rights based on mineral production is treated as a lease (.10). If the consideration paid to an owner (or other assignor) for transferring mineral rights is not dependent upon actual mineral production, but must be paid regardless of whether any production occurs, the owner is not entitled to a depletion allowance. The transfer of mineral rights for consideration not based on production is treated as a sale.

The determination of whether a transfer or assignment of mineral rights is a lease or a sale does not depend upon the words used to describe the contract or upon peculiarities of the local law (.15). The important consideration is whether proceeds from the transfer are dependent upon production.

.05 Code Sec. 611; Reg. §1.611-1.

.10 *J.J. Perkins*, SCt, 37-2 USTC ¶9315, 301 U.S. 655, 57 SCt 911.

.15 *H. Harmel*, SCt, 3 USTC ¶990, 287 U.S. 103, 53 SCt 74.

¶25,303 Bonuses. A taxpayer who leases to another person the right to extract minerals often receives a bonus for granting the lease. The bonus is essentially a down payment for the granting of the economic interest in the mineral deposit. The bonus may be paid as a fixed sum per acre, in a lump sum, or in installments (.05). Generally, such bonuses are taxed in the same manner as advanced royalties (¶25,304).

Recipient of bonus

When a taxpayer (generally, a lessor) receives a bonus, he may take a cost depletion deduction for the proportional amount of his basis for depletion that the entire bonus bears to the sum of the bonus and expected royalties (¶25,304). That depletion allowance is then deducted from the taxpayer's basis for depletion and the remainder of the basis is recoverable through depletion deductions when royalties are received.

> ***Example 1:*** John Qualls leases coal-mining rights to Scoupex Corporation, reserving a \$1/ton royalty for each ton of coal Scoupex extracts from the property. Scoupex also pays Mr. Qualls a \$10,000 bonus for the right to extract the coal. Mr. Qualls has a \$21,000 basis in the coal property and the royalties he expects to receive equal \$20,000.
>
> The depletion deduction for the bonus is computed as follows:
>
> $$\frac{\$10{,}000 \text{ (bonus)}}{\$30{,}000 \text{ (bonus + estimated royalties)}} \times \underset{\text{(basis)}}{\$21{,}000} = \underset{\text{(depletion deduction)}}{\$7{,}000}$$
>
> The remaining \$14,000 will be recovered by Mr. Qualls through depletion deductions when he receives royalties.

Payor of bonus

Where a taxpayer (generally, a lessee) pays a bonus, payment of the bonus is a capital investment made for the acquisition of an economic interest in a mineral deposit and is recoverable through the depletion allowance. The amount paid as a bonus is neither excluded nor deducted from the payor's gross income, but is capitalized as part of the amount to be recovered through depletion deductions when the mineral is sold.

Expiration, termination, or abandonment of economic interest

If the grant of an economic interest in a mineral deposit with respect to which a bonus was received expires, terminates, or is abandoned before there has been any income derived from the extraction of the mineral, the bonus recipient must adjust his basis of the mineral property by adding the depletion deduction previously taken on the bonus, and he must include a corresponding amount in his income for the tax year in which the expiration, termination, or abandonment occurs.

> ***Example 2:*** Assume the same facts as those in Example (1) above. Scoupex Corporation has a two-year lease from Mr. Qualls to mine coal, but fails to extract any coal by the end of the lease. Mr. Qualls must readjust his basis for the coal property from \$14,000 to \$21,000, adding the \$7,000 depletion deduction previously taken on the \$10,000 bonus. In addition, Mr. Qualls must include \$7,000 in his income.

.05 Reg. §§1.612-3, 1.613-2(c) and 1.613A-3(j)(2).

¶25,304 Royalties. The term "royalty," as applied to a mineral lease, means compensation paid to the owner of the premises for the privilege of producing a mineral from the leasehold, and a share in the mineral produced. Royalties are payments that are to be made during the entire future production of a mineral, as contrasted with payments that terminate upon reaching a specified sum. The holder of a royalty interest is deemed to have an economic interest in the mineral in place and is entitled to a depletion allowance. The royalty interest may be created by the owner of the land either by reservation when a lease is entered into or by a direct grant to a third person (.05).

> ***Example 1:*** Alfred Alloy, the owner of land, enters into an oil and gas lease between himself, as lessor, and Mark Miner, as lessee. In consideration for the lease, Alloy is to receive ⅛ of the market price of oil and gas produced. Alloy subsequently sells ¼ of the ⅛ fractional interest to Carl Caret for $20,000. Both Alloy and Caret have royalty interests.

A landowner who leases a mineral interest typically retains a royalty interest of between one-eighth and three eighths of the interest. A royalty interest entitles its owner to share in the production from the mineral deposits, free of development and operating costs and extends over the productive life of the property leased. The lessee in the transaction usually acquires the balance of the mineral rights in the form of a working interest. A working interest not only entitles its owner to share in the production, but also requires the owner to bear their share of the developing and operating costs (.10). Coal and iron ore royalties are eligible for percentage depletion for any year in which the maximum rate of tax imposed on any net capital gain is equal to or greater than the maximum rate for ordinary income (.15).

Overriding royalties

An overriding royalty is an interest carved out of the lessee's share of the mineral, as distinguished from the owner's interest. An overriding royalty can be created in a number of ways. It can be created by reservation when the original lessee transfers his interest by a sublease, or it can be created by grant when the original lessee conveys a fractional share to a third person.

> ***Example 2:*** Assume the same facts as in Example (1) above, except that Miner subleases his mineral leasehold to Derrick Tower, reserving ⅛ of his ⅞ interest in the oil and gas produced. Miner has reserved an overriding royalty for himself.

> ***Example 3:*** Assume the same facts as in Example (1) above, except that Miner enters into an agreement with Tower to assign to him 1⁄16 of his ⅞ interest in oil and gas produced under the terms of the lease. Tower's fractional interest is an overriding royalty.

An overriding royalty is also known as the "working interest" of a mineral lease.

Advanced royalties

An advanced royalty refers to the payment of royalties, whether or not any minerals have been extracted. Where a taxpayer pays advanced royalties and is entitled to offset those payments against royalties required to be paid when the mineral is actually extracted, the recipient of those advanced royalties must compute depletion on the amount paid in advance of actual extraction and must treat that amount as a depletion deduction for the tax year in which the payments are made. No depletion deduction may be taken in a subsequent year for previously deducted advanced royalties that are to be applied to minerals extracted in a subsequent year.

Percentage depletion is not available for lease bonuses, advanced royalty payments, or any other amount payable without regard to actual production from oil and gas properties, or for amounts received or accrued after August 16, 1986. For lease bonuses, advanced payments, or other amounts received or accrued before August 17, 1986, lessors of oil or gas properties are allowed to deduct percentage depletion on those amounts in the year the amounts are includible in gross income. In order to apply the barrel limitation on percentage depletion, lessors must convert bonuses or royalties to barrels of production (.20).

A taxpayer who pays advanced royalties generally may not deduct those payments from his gross income unless there is a sale of an extracted mineral. The taxpayer may also not deduct advanced royalties paid or accrued if the royalties are in reality a loan or the cost of acquiring an economic interest, which must be capitalized.

Minimum royalties

In the case of advanced mineral royalties paid or accrued in connection with a minimum royalty provision, the payor of the royalties, at his option, may treat the minimum royalties as deductions from gross income for the year in which the minimum royalties are paid or accrued, regardless of any mineral production.

A minimum royalty provision requires annual advanced royalty payments of a substantially uniform amount over the life of a mineral lease or for a period of at least 20 years. An arrangement that provides, over the life of a sublease, for annual royalties, payable through the issuance of promissory notes, the principal of which was due after termination of the sublease, fails to meet the requirement that a substantially uniform amount of royalties be paid at least annually over the life of the sublease. Thus, the arrangement does not qualify as an advanced minimum royalty (.25).

A taxpayer may not deduct any amount as a minimum royalty where his obligation to pay such amount is based on a nonrecourse promissory note that is to be repaid out of the proceeds from the sale of the mineral (.30). A liquidated damage clause to guarantee repayment of the promissory note does not eliminate the contingent nature of the note, where the liquidated damages may also be paid with nonrecourse notes.

A taxpayer must make an election as to the tax treatment of advanced minimum royalties for the first tax year in which such amounts are paid or accrued (.35). A failure to deduct minimum royalties for the first tax year is deemed an election to have all payments of advanced royalties treated as deductions for the tax year in which the mineral is actually sold.

.05 Reg. §§1.612-3 and 1.613-2(c).

.10 Market Segment Specialization Program (MSSP) (Audit Technique Guide for Oil and Gas Industry, May 1996)

.15 Code Sec. 631(c).

.20 Code Sec. 613A(d)(5); Reg. §1.613A-3(j)(2).

.25 *S.E. Wing*, 81 TC 17, CCH Dec. 40,262.

.30 *J. Maddrix*, CA-11, 86-1 USTC ¶9189, 780 F2d 946, aff'g TC, 83 TC 613, CCH Dec. 41,572; see also *D. Vastola*, 84 TC 969, CCH Dec. 42,102; *Est. of C.P. Blay*, 48 TCM 1463, CCH Dec. 41,574(M), TC Memo. 1984-565; *R.G. Hershenhorn*, 50 TCM 135, CCH Dec. 42,155(M), TC Memo. 1985-286.

.35 Reg. §1.612-3(b)(3); Rev. Rul. 79-386, 1979-2 CB 246.

¶25,304A Delay Rentals. A delay rental is an amount paid for the privilege of deferring development of a property which could have been avoided by abandonment of the lease, by starting development operations, or by obtaining production. A delay rental is ordinary income to the payee (lessor). The payor (lessee) may treat a delay rental as a deductible expense or elect to charge it to a depletable capital account as a carrying charge under Code Sec. 266 (.05). Proposed regulations clarify that the election to expense or capitalize a delay rental as a carrying charge under Code Sec. 266 is only available to the extent that the delay rental is not required to be capitalized under the uniform capitalization rules.

.05 Reg. §1.612-3(c).

¶25,305 "In-Oil" or "In-Mineral" Payments. A production payment, commonly referred to as "in-oil payment," "gas payment," or "mineral payment," is the right to a specified share of the production from mineral in place or from the proceeds of such production. A production payment may be limited by a dollar amount, a quantum of mineral, or a period of time. It may burden more than one mineral property, and the burdened mineral property need not be an operating mineral interest (.05). Regardless of the language used to describe the right, the method of creation of such right, or the form in which such right is cast (even though such form is that of an operating mineral interest), a right which is in substance economically equivalent to a production payment will be treated as a production payment. Whether or not a right is in substance economically equivalent to a production payment is to be determined from all the facts and circumstances.

.05 Code Sec. 636; Reg. §1.636-1.

¶25,306 Net-Profits Interest. A net-profits interest is a right to a percentage of the net proceeds derived from the production of an oil and gas or mineral property (.05). In some cases, the assignor may be entitled to receive, in addition to or in lieu of the lump-sum payment or period royalties, a percentage of the assignee's net profits. A depletion deduction may be applied by the assignor to his share of such net profits, as long as he has retained an economic interest. The holder of a net-profits interest receives no income unless there is a profit from the production of oil and gas or minerals. A depletion deduction may be taken by the owner on his share of such net profits provided he has an economic interest.

Not all net-profits arrangements create an economic interest (.10). A net-profits interest created through a leasing agreement by those who held an economic interest in the minerals before the creation of such interest is depletable. However, depletion might not be allowed if a net-profits interest is created by a taxpayer who did not previously hold an economic interest in the mineral before the creation of such an interest.

.05 Code Sec. 611.

.10 *Kirby Petroleum Co.*, SCt, 46-1 USTC ¶9149, 326 U.S. 599, 66 SCt 409; *Burton-Sutton Oil Co.*, SCt, 46-1 USTC ¶9243, 328 U.S. 25, 66 SCt 861; and *Southwest Exploration Co.*, SCt, 56-1 USTC ¶9304, 350 U.S. 308, 76 SCt 395.

¶25,307 Carried Interest. In a typical carried interest arrangement, one of the parties receiving or owning an operating interest in an oil and gas property will agree to advance the funds necessary to drill, complete, equip and operate a well on that property, and to look only to the other owner's share of production for the other owner's contribution to such costs. The party who advances the funds necessary to develop and operate the property is referred to as the "carrying party," and the other owner is referred to as the "carried party." Once the carrying party has reached the point of "complete payout" (that is, he has recouped all of his expenditures, including operating expenses, during the payout period), both parties will share income and expenses in accordance with their permanent shares of the operating interest (.05).

If the carrying party owns the entire operating interest during the complete payout period, he may capitalize and depreciate all equipment costs and deduct all domestic intangible drilling costs (IDC) (¶25,323). For this purpose, the complete payout period ends when the gross income attributable to all of the operating mineral interests in the well equals all expenditures for drilling and development (tangible and intangible) of such well plus the cost of operating the well to produce such an amount (.10). Once the complete payout period ends, the carrying party is required to capitalize, as a depletable capital cost, that portion of his undepreciated basis in the equipment attributable to the operating interest held by the carried party (.15).

If the carrying party is not entitled to complete recoupment, the fractional interest rule comes into play. That rule provides, in effect, that, if a drilling or development project is undertaken for a fraction of the operating rights, that portion of the costs of equipment and IDC attributable to the fractional operating interests held by others must be capitalized as the depletable cost of the interest acquired. If the carrying party holds the entire operating interest for less than the complete payout period, he has undertaken the drilling or development project for a fraction of the operating rights and must capitalize, as depletable costs, a portion of his expenditures for equipment and IDC.

.05 Code Sec. 611; Reg. §1.612-4.

.10 Rev. Rul. 71-207, 1971-1 CB 160.

.15 Rev. Rul. 69-332, 1969-1 CB 87.

¶25,308 Casinghead Gas Contracts. Wet gas is a very volatile mixture that comes from the well in the form of gas mixed with a more stable gas known as natural or dry gas. In this form, it is not a salable commodity. After separation, the merchantable products consist of casinghead gasoline and dry gas. Accordingly, an owner of casinghead gas contracts who operates a casinghead gasoline plant under contract with the owner of the oil lands, by treating wet gas by the extraction of gasoline, is a processor and not a producer and has no interest in the gas in place. The taxpayer was not entitled to a depletion allowance because the taxpayer took no part in the production of the wet gas, conducted no drilling operations upon any of the producing premises, did not pump oil or gas from the wells, and had no interest as lessor or lessee, or as sublessor or sublessee, in any of the producing wells (.05).

.05 *Bankline Oil Co.*, SCt, 38-1 USTC ¶9154, 303 U.S. 362.

¶25,309 Coal-Stripping Contractors. Coal-stripping contractors are entitled to a depletion deduction where, under the stripping contract, a capital interest is obtained in the coal in place and the contractor must look to severance and sale of the coal for the return of capital consumed in that process. If the contractor lacks this interest in the coal, he cannot properly claim a deduction for depletion.

Regardless of the technical ownership of the mineral in place, a contract to strip-mine a bed of coal may give the contractor an interest that is ultimately exhausted in the productive process (.05). For purposes of depletion, an economic interest does not grant title to the coal in place, but rather the possibility of profit dependent solely upon the extraction and sale of the coal.

Not all stripping contracts warrant a depletion deduction. If the contractor receives no binding right to extract the coal, he has failed to obtain a capital interest therein. This is the case where the coal company may terminate the contract at will and has the absolute right to do so (.10). Similarly, reservation of the right of the coal company to terminate entirely or at its discretion without liability for damage or loss to the contractor carries this implication. A contract that may be arbitrarily terminated upon nominal notice is likewise regarded as one that may be canceled at will (.15).

The U.S. Court of Appeals for the Third Circuit has held that the contractor acquires no economic interest where he receives a stated price per ton of coal mined regardless of whether or not the coal is sold, rather than a percentage of the selling price or profit (.20). The U.S. Court of Appeals for the Fourth Circuit, on the other hand, has been more lenient and has allowed depletion to the contractor where his rights were dependent upon the extraction of coal (.25).

The cost of back-filling credited to a reserve during the tax year to cover the cost of refilling acreage mined during such year may be held to be deductible on the accrual basis, although the back-filling is not done until the following year, in instances where both state law and the contract require the work to be done and where the cost can be accurately estimated (.30).

.05 G.C.M. 22730, 1941-1 CB 214; *Alworth-Stephens Co.*, SCt, 1 USTC ¶117, 267 U.S. 364.

.10 *E.W. Parsons*, SCt, 59-1 USTC ¶9366, 359 U.S. 215.

.15 *E. Swank*, SCt, 81-1 USTC ¶9426, 101 SCt 1931.

.20 *Denise Coal Co.*, CA-3, 59-2 USTC ¶9769, 271 F2d 930.

.25 *Gregory Run Coal Co.*, CA-4, 54-1 USTC ¶9342, 212 F2d 52, cert. denied, 348 U.S. 828.

.30 *P. Harrold*, CA-4, 52-1 USTC ¶9107, 192 F2d 1002.

¶25,310 Assignments of Operating Rights, Royalty Interests, and Payments. The treatment by an assignee of his payments to an assignor under a contract transferring mineral operating rights depends upon exactly the same consideration as those that determine the nature of the payments in the hands of the assignor. Thus, if the payments are dependent upon the assignee's production, they represent income derived from an economic interest held by the assignor in the oil or minerals in place. The payments to the assignor, therefore, are excludable from the gross income of the assignee. On the other hand, if the payments are not dependent upon production but must be made in any event, they represent the price paid for purchase of an asset. Such payments do not represent an exclusion or deduction to the assignee even though he pays them out of his proceeds from mineral production (.05).

An assignment of oil payment rights for a stated period or until an agreed amount is collected is not a transfer of capital assets resulting in capital gains, even though the oil payment rights are interests in land under local law. There is merely an assignment of anticipated future income, and the consideration is ordinary income to the assignor, subject to depletion allowance. It is immaterial whether the oil payments are carved out of the royalty interest retained by the lessor or are part of the lessee-operator's working interest (.10). However, see ¶25,329 for the treatment of oil production payments under the mineral production payment rules.

.05 *J.J. Perkins*, SCt, 37-2 USTC ¶9315, 301 U.S. 655.

.10 *P.G. Lake, Inc.*, SCt, 58-1 USTC ¶9428, 356 U.S. 260.

¶25,311 Apportionment. Where a natural resource is leased, the depletion deduction must be equitably apportioned between the lessor and the lessee (.05). In the case of cost depletion, the lessee does not deduct depletion as such but deducts the royalties. Since the royalties constitute his cost, deduction of the royalties allows him to recover his cost. The lessor applies a depletion deduction to the royalty payments and recovers his cost by means of the depletion deductions.

If the only consideration to the lessor under the lease consisted of periodic royalties payable if and when oil is produced, there would be little difficulty. In practice, however, an oil lease usually requires an advance lump-sum payment that may be applied by the lessee against future royalties. In such a case, the lessor must apply a proportionate part of his depletion allowances to this lump-sum payment when it is received. In the case of cost depletion, the lessor must then estimate the royalties to be received, and allocate the cost accordingly (.10).

> ***Example 1:*** A lessor paid $2,000,000 for mineral property. The lessee is required to make an advance payment of $1,000,000. The lessor estimates that he will receive $3,000,000 more in royalties. Since the advance payment of $1,000,000 constitutes 25% of the total expected payments, the lessor must allocate 25% of his cost to the advance payment. Therefore, he can deduct $500,000 from the advance payment as depletion. Because the lessor's cost ($2,000,000) is 50% of the total expected payments ($1,000,000 plus $3,000,000), he may deduct 50% of the royalties as depletion when received, until he recovers the remaining $1,500,000 ($2,000,000 minus $500,000) of his cost.

It may happen that the lease will expire before the lessee has extracted as many mineral units as he paid for by means of the bonus. In such a case, the lessor must restore part of the previous depletion deduction by reporting a corresponding amount as income.

> ***Example 2:*** A lessor transfers mineral-producing property under a lease that requires the lessee to pay royalties of 10¢ per unit of mineral extracted. The lessee is required to make an advance payment of $50,000 which may be applied against royalties falling due as the mineral is extracted. At 10¢ per unit, $50,000 would represent the royalties on 500,000 units. Assume also that depletion of $10,000 (computed as shown in Example (1)) was allocated to the bonus and deducted when the lease was executed. When the lease expires in a subsequent year, the lessee has extracted only 400,000 units of minerals. Since this is only 4/5 (400,000/500,000) of the mineral on which the lessor received advance royalties, he

is entitled to only 4/5 , or $8,000, of the $10,000 depletion that he deducted. The remaining 1/5, or $2,000, must be reported as income.

Also, even though a lessee must exclude a proportionate part of the bonus from the "gross income from the property" in later years, it does not follow that a lessee may deduct from his gross income that portion of advanced royalties allocable to that particular year. While advanced royalties are treated as income to the lessor, they are treated as a capital cost to the lessee. In the case of cost depletion, this capital cost is added to the lessee's cost basis and recovered through depletion (.15).

.05 Code Sec. 611; Reg. §1.611-1(c).

.10 *Murphy Oil Co.*, SCt, 3 USTC ¶1002, 287 U.S. 299.

.15 *Sunray Oil Co.*, CA-10, 45-1 USTC ¶9181, 147 F2d 962, cert. denied, 325 U.S. 861.

Gross Income from Depletable Property

¶25,313 Gross Income Defined. Percentage depletion is based on the gross income from a mineral or oil and gas producing property. Consequently, when gross income is higher, percentage depletion will also be higher (.05).

Gross income from oil and gas properties

Gross income from an eligible oil and gas producing property (¶25,299) for the purpose of computing percentage depletion is the amount for which the taxpayer sells the oil and gas in the immediate vicinity of the well. If the oil and gas is not sold on the premises but is manufactured or converted into a refined product before sale, gross income is computed by use of a representative market or field price (.10).

Gross income from mineral properties other than oil and gas properties

Gross income from mining is the actual price for which the ore or mineral is sold where the taxpayer sells the ore or mineral as it emerges from the mine before application of any processes other than a mining process or any transportation, or after application of only mining processes, including mining transportation. If a taxpayer sells his ore or mineral in more than one form and if only mining processes are applied, gross income is the price for which the various forms of ore are sold after adjustments for discounts and transportation. If a taxpayer processes ore or mineral before sale by the application of nonmining processes, gross income must be computed by use of the representative market or field price (.15). The objective in computing gross income from mining by the representative market or field price method is to ascertain, on the basis of an analysis of actual competitive sales by the taxpayer or others, the dollar figure or amount which most nearly approximates price at which the taxpayer, in the light of market conditions, could have sold the ores or minerals to which the nonmining processes were applied.

In determining the representative market or field price, consideration is given only to prices of ores or minerals of like kind and grade as those of the taxpayer with which, under commercially accepted standards, the taxpayer's ore or mineral would be considered to be in competition. A weighted average of the competitive selling prices of ores or minerals of like kind and grade as the taxpayer's, benefitted only by mining processes, if any, in the relevant markets, is an important factor used in determining the taxpayer's representative market or field price. Sales or purchases, including the taxpayer's, of ores or minerals of like kind and grade as the taxpayer's are taken into consideration in determining the representative market or field price of the taxpayer's ore or mineral only if those sales or purchases are the result of competitive transactions. Exceptional, insignificant, unusual, tie-in, or accommodation sales are to be disregarded (.20).

If there is no representative market or field price for a mineral of like kind and grade as the taxpayer's, representative or field prices for an ore or mineral which is of like kind but which is not of like grade may be used, but appropriate adjustments for differences in mineral content must be made. In such cases the adjustments must be readily ascertainable (.25).

A taxpayer who computes his gross income from mining by use of a representative market or field price must attach to his return a summary statement setting forth the prices used in computing gross income from mining and the source of information as to those prices. Relevant supporting data must be assembled, segregated, and made readily available at the taxpayer's principal place of business (.30).

It will be presumed that a price is not a representative market or field price for the taxpayer's ore or mineral if the sum of such price plus the total of all costs of the nonmining processes (including nonmining transportation) which the taxpayer applies to his ore or mineral regularly exceeds the taxpayer's actual sales price of his product. For example, if on a regular basis the total of all costs of nonmining processes applied by the taxpayer to coal for the purpose of making coke is $12.00 per ton, and if the taxpayer's actual sale price for such coke is $18.00 per ton, a price of $7.00 per ton would not be a representative market or field price of the taxpayer's coal which is used for making coke (.35).

Proportionate profits formula

Where it is impossible to determine a representative market or field price, gross income from mining must be computed by use of the proportionate profits method (.40). The object of the proportionate profits method is to ascertain gross income from mining by applying the principle that each dollar of the total costs paid or incurred to produce, sell, and transport the first marketable product or group of products earns the same percentage of profit.

The proportionate profits formula is based on the assumption that each dollar of the total costs paid or incurred to produce, sell, and transport the first marketable product or group of products earns the same percentage of profit. Sales income is allocated on the basis of a breakdown of costs into mining and nonmining categories. Once this breakdown has been made, income is allocated to mining based upon the ratio of mining costs to total costs. The proportionate profits formula is illustrated by the following equation:

$$\frac{\text{Mining Costs}}{\text{Total Costs}} \times \text{Gross Sales} = \text{Gross Income from Mining}$$

"Finished products"

Percentage depletion is not to be computed on the basis of the gross income from the sale of "finished products." For example, where an integrated miner-manufacturer of burnt clay products from fire clay and shale claimed percentage depletion allowance on the basis of its gross income from the sale of vitrified clay sewer pipe and other related finished products, the allowance was disallowed (.45). Instead, the miner-manufacturer was entitled to a percentage depletion allowance on the basis of gross income from the value of its raw fire clay and shale, after the application of ordinary treatment processes applied by nonintegrated miners engaged in the recovery of those minerals. A nonintegrated miner is a miner who is not also a manufacturer of mineral products.

Specific treatment processes

Treatment processes included in "gross income from the property" relate to coal, sulfur, iron ore, bauxite, ball and sagger clay, rock asphalt, and ores or minerals customarily sold in the form of a crude mineral product, lead, zinc, copper, gold, silver, uranium, fluorspar ores, potash, and ores or minerals not customarily sold in the form of a crude mineral product, talc, magnesite, phosphate rock, quicksilver ores, calcium carbonates and other minerals used in making cement, and clay used or sold for use in the manufacture of certain products (.50).

Treatment processes that, generally, are not part of "mining" are electrolytic deposition, roasting, calcining, thermal or electric smelting, refining, polishing, fine pulverization, blending with other materials, treatment effecting a chemical change, thermal action, and molding or shaping.

Treatment processes considered to be mining in the case of calcium carbonates and other minerals used in making cement are limited to all processes (other than pre-heating of the kiln feed) applied prior to the introduction of the kiln feed into the kiln. All later processes are not considered to be mining (.55). In the case of clay used or sold for use in the manufacture of building or paving brick, drainage and roofing tile, sewer pipe, flower pots, and kindred products, the processes are limited to crushing, grinding, and separating the mineral from waste. All later processes are excluded.

Depletion for waste or residue

A deduction for percentage depletion extends to deposits of waste or residue which are worked by the mine owner or operator. In this respect the definition of "gross income from the property" has been expanded to include gross income from the extraction by mine owners or operators of ores or minerals from the waste or residue of prior mining. The extraction must be by the mine owner or operator, and not by a purchaser of the mine tailings or of the right to extract ores or minerals therefrom.

The term "purchaser" does not include a person who acquires the whole mine property, including the waste or residue, in a tax-free exchange, as for example, under a tax-free corporate reorganization from a person who was entitled to depletion on the waste or residue. Nor does the term "purchaser" apply to a lessee, upon the renewal of a mineral lease, if the lessee was entitled to depletion with respect to the waste or residue prior to the renewal of the lease.

.05 Code Sec. 613(c); Reg. §§1.613-3 and 1.613-4.

.10 Reg. §1.613-3.

.15 Reg. §1.613-4(c)(1).

.20 Reg. §1.613-4(c)(3).

.25 Reg. §1.613-4(c)(4).

.30 Reg. §1.613-4(c)(5).

.35 Reg. §1.613-4(c)(6).

.40 Reg. §1.613-4(d).

.45 *Cannelton Sewer Pipe Co.*, SCt, 60-2 USTC ¶9553, 364 U.S. 76.

.50 Reg. §1.613-4(f).

.55 *Standard Lime and Cement Co.*, CtCls, 64-1 USTC ¶9311, 329 F2d 939.

¶25,314 Aggregation of Mineral Properties. When computing the depletion allowance for mines, wells and other natural deposits, the term "property" generally means each separate interest owned by the taxpayer in each mineral deposit in each separate tract or parcel of land (.05). A taxpayer may aggregate and treat as one property any number of *mines* (for oil or gas wells, see ¶25,316) within an operating unit made up of several mineral interests. If the taxpayer owns two or more separate "operating mineral interests" that make up part or all of one operating unit, they may elect:

(1) to aggregate and treat as one property all the interests that make up any one mine or any two or more mines; and

(2) to treat as a separate property any interest that is not included in (1).

The aggregation may be made whether the interests that are part of one operating unit are included in a single tract or parcel of land or in contiguous tracts or parcels. More than one aggregation of interests may be formed within one operating unit. However, no aggregation may include an interest that is part of a mine without including all the operating interests that are a part of that mine in the first tax year for which the election to aggregate is effective. Also, any subsequent interest in that mine must be included in the aggregation.

> ***Example 1:*** Within a single operating unit, Carol Stream owns 25 operating mineral interests and such interests comprise five mines of five interests each. Stream may elect to aggregate the 15 interests within mines one, three, and four and treat them as one property; to aggregate her five interests in mine two and treat them as one property; and to treat each of the five interests comprising mine five as a separate property. Alternatively, she may elect to aggregate all 25 interests in the five mines and treat them as a single property.

Definitions

"Operating mineral interest" means an interest in respect of which the taxpayer must take into account the costs of production of the mineral for the purpose of the limitation of percentage depletion to 50 percent of the taxpayer's taxable income from the property. If the mine or other natural deposit is not in the production stage, the interest must be such that the taxpayer would be required to take the costs into account in computing taxable income from the property if it were in production. Consequently, a royalty or similar interest cannot be aggregated with operating interests.

> ***Example 2:*** Martin Fairchild owns a large tract of mineral property on which he operates two mines as one operating unit. He leases a part of the tract to another operator and retains a royalty interest under which he is not required to take the costs of production into account. Fairchild owns three separate properties. He may elect to aggregate the two mines and to treat the aggregation as one property. But he cannot aggregate the royalty interest with the other two separate properties, or with either of them, because the royalty interest is not an operating mineral interest.

"Nonoperating mineral interests" are interests for which the taxpayer is *not* required to take costs of production into account in determining the 50-percent-of-taxable-income limitation on percentage depletion. Thus, royalty and similar interests are "nonoperating mineral interests." A taxpayer who owns two or more separate nonoperating mineral interests in a single tract or parcel of land, or in two or more adjacent tracts or parcels, may be permitted to treat such interests in each separate kind of mineral deposit as one property upon a showing that a principal purpose is not the avoidance of tax. However, in no case can a nonoperating interest be aggregated with an operating interest.

The U.S. Supreme Court has ruled that in determining the amount of depletion that was a tax preference item for alternative minimum tax (AMT) purposes (¶1400), taxpayers in the business of oil and gas exploration and production were not entitled to include the unrecovered costs of depreciable drilling and development equipment in computing the adjusted basis of their properties (.10). In so ruling, the Court reversed a decision by the U.S. Court of Appeals for the Federal Circuit that allowed unrecovered costs of depreciable tangible items to be included in computing adjusted basis.

The Supreme Court emphasized that the rules for making adjustments to basis in determining the amount of gain or loss a taxpayer must recognize when selling or disposing of property have been incorporated into the Code section requiring taxpayers to reflect the excess of percentage depletion over the adjusted basis of the property as a preference item in determining AMT income (.15). Under the recognition rules, a depletable mineral deposit and depreciable associated equipment that are sold together must be separated and treated as different properties by the seller because each property is subject to different tax treatment.

According to the Court, depletion and depreciation are two of the major categories of tax treatment with virtually impassable boundaries.

.05 Code Sec. 614(c); Reg. §§1.614-0—1.614-8.
.10 *W.F. Hill*, SCt, 93-1 USTC ¶50,037, rev'g CA-FL, 91-2 USTC ¶50,475.
.15 Code Sec. 57(a)(1).

¶25,315 Separation of Mineral Properties. If a single tract or parcel of land contains a mineral deposit (excluding oil or gas) that is being extracted, or will be extracted, from two or more mines, then the taxpayer may elect to allocate to each of the mines a portion of the tract or parcel, and to treat that portion of the tract and the mineral deposit contained therein as a separate property (.05). A separate property so formed may be included as part of an aggregation, but the election may not be made for any property that is part of an aggregation without the consent of the IRS.

.05 Code Sec. 614(c) and (d); Reg. §1.614-3.

¶25,316 Aggregation of Oil and Gas Wells. For purposes of computing percentage depletion on qualifying oil and gas properties (¶25,299), all operating mineral interests in oil or gas wells or geothermal deposits within a separate tract or parcel of land are combined and treated as one property unless the taxpayer elects to separate them (.05). An operating interest in one tract cannot be combined with an operating interest in another tract or with a nonoperating interest in the same or another tract (¶25,314).

If a taxpayer elects to treat one or more operating interests in a single tract as separate properties, the remaining interests in the same tract are automatically combined and treated as one property. Only one combination of operating interests is allowed in each tract. If there is a combination of operating interests in a tract, any operating interest discovered or acquired after the taxable year of election is added to the combination unless an election is made to separate the new interest. Similarly, if no combination exists in the tract, the newly acquired or discovered interest will be considered separate property unless an election is made to combine it with another operating interest.

> ***Example:*** Oilman Oliver Jones has three operating interests in lease A, interests one, two, and three, and two operating interests in lease B, interests four and five. Jones makes no election with respect to interests one, two, and three, so they are automatically combined into one property for depletion purposes. However, in lease B, he elects to separate interests four and five, so they are treated as separate properties.
>
> In the tax year following the election, Jones acquires interest six in lease B. Interest six automatically becomes separate property unless Jones elects to combine it with either interest four or five. In the same year, Jones discovers interest seven in lease A. Interest seven automatically is combined with interests one, two, and three, unless Jones elects to treat it as a separate property.

The election to treat operating interests as separate properties must be made by the return due date for the first tax year in which any expenditure for development or operation of the operating interest is made by the taxpayer after the acquisition of such interest. The election is made by attaching a statement to the income tax return for the year the election is made. The statement must identify by name, code number, or other means the operating mineral interests within the same tract or parcel of land which the taxpayer is electing to treat as separate properties or combined properties. It must also identify by name, code number, or other means the tract or parcel and state the facts upon which its treatment as a single and entire tract or parcel is based.

If a taxpayer is electing to treat all of his operating mineral interests in a tract or parcel as separate properties, a blanket election with regard to all interests in that tract or parcel that are owned by him at the time of the election is sufficient and only the tract or parcel itself need be identified. The taxpayer must maintain and have available records and maps sufficient to clearly define the tract or parcel and all of his operating mineral interests.

Although the depletion allowance for oil and gas properties must be computed separately by each partner of a partnership, only the partnership can elect to treat separate mineral operating interests in a parcel of land as separate depletable properties (.10).

Exception

An exception to nonaggregation of operating interests occurs where one or more of the taxpayer's operating interests (in the same or different tracts) participate under a voluntary or compulsory unitization or pooling arrangement in a single cooperative or unit plan of operation. In such case, the operating interests are treated as one property for the period of the participation, if the following tests are met:

(1) all of the operating interests must be in the same deposit or in two or more deposits, the joint development of which is logical from the standpoint of geology, convenience, economy or conservation; and

(2) all participating interests must be in tracts which are contiguous or in close proximity.

However, these tests are not applicable to compulsory arrangements (¶25,328).

Allocating adjusted basis of operating interests

Two rules apply for allocating the adjusted basis of operating interests that previously formed part of an aggregation under the repealed "operating unit" rule and that now form new properties. The "fair market value" rule generally applies with respect to any aggregation unless the taxpayer elects the "allocation of adjustments" rule (.15).

.05 Code Sec. 614(b); Reg. §§1.614-6—1.614-8.
.10 Rev. Rul. 84-142, 1984-2 CB 117.
.15 Reg. §1.614-6(a)(2).

Taxable Income From the Property

¶25,318 Taxable Income Defined. The percentage depletion allowance of 15 percent for oil and gas wells generally applies only to independent producers and royalty owners (¶25,299). In the case of these independent producers and royalty owners, percentage depletion is subject to a limitation based on 65 percent of the taxpayer's taxable income from all sources. In addition, in the case of oil and gas properties, the maximum depletion deduction is limited to 100 percent of the taxable income from the property (.05). However, the 100-percent taxable income limit on percentage depletion deductions for oil and gas properties has been temporarily suspended for marginal properties for tax years beginning after December 31, 1997, and before January 1, 2006 (.10).

Costs of exploiting a natural resource (including maintenance of geological and land departments), if properly deductible in computing taxable income, are also deductible in computing the taxable income limitation on percentage depletion. Where such costs have been properly capitalized, any loss deduction resulting therefrom, taken in computing net income, must also be included as a deduction in computing taxable income from the property for the purpose of the taxable income limitation (.15).

Deductible mining expenses are decreased by any gain on the sale or other disposition of the mining property treated as ordinary income to the extent of depreciation deductions previously taken (.20). This reduction of deductible mining expenses increases taxable income and, as a result, increases the base against which the percent limitation applies. The increase in taxable income, however, is made *only* for the purpose of computing taxable income from the property for the percent limitation. Other items that have been held to reduce the taxable income to which the percent limitation is applied are interest on money borrowed to develop mines (.25), premiums paid on prepayment of outstanding bonds (.30), silicosis claims (.35), and state income taxes (.40).

Separate property

The taxable income from the property must be separately computed for each depletable economic interest or property held by the taxpayer. Deductible items directly attributable to a specific interest or property are deductions only in computing the taxable income from that interest or property, and overhead or general items of deduction must be fairly allocated between depletable properties and the activities relating thereto and all other properties and activities. The part allocable to depletable properties must then be fairly apportioned to the several specific properties.

.05 Code Secs. 613 and 613A(d)(1); Reg. §§1.613-3 and 1.613-4.

.10 Code Secs. 613(c)(6)(H), as amended by the Working Families Tax Relief Act of 2004 (P.L. 108-311).

.15 *Wilshire Oil Co., Inc.*, SCt, 39-2 USTC ¶9743, 308 U.S. 90.

.20 Code Sec. 1245.

.25 *Mirabel Quicksilver Co.*, 41 BTA 401, CCH Dec. 11,006.

.30 *St. Mary's Oil and Gas Co.*, 42 BTA 270, CCH Dec. 11,242.

.35 *Montreal Mining Co.*, 41 BTA 399, CCH Dec. 11,005.

.40 *Grison Oil Corp.*, 42 BTA 1117, CCH Dec. 11,366.

¶25,319 Foreign Income and Foreign Taxes. U.S. shareholders of controlled foreign corporations are taxed on foreign oil and gas nonextraction income derived within a foreign country where the oil is extracted (.05). Foreign oil-related income includes income from such sources as processing, transportation, distribution, sale or provision of service (but only if the service provider is engaged in extraction). It also includes, under certain conditions:

(1) income from the sale or exchange of certain assets used for oil-related activities; and

(2) dividends, interest and other amounts to the extent that they are attributable to foreign oil nonextraction income.

Foreign tax credit

For purposes of the foreign tax credit limitation (¶17,235), a net loss in one country resulting from extraction activities reduces the amount of foreign oil-related income from other countries and correspondingly reduces the amount of the foreign tax credit available.

The amount of foreign taxes on foreign oil-and-gas-extraction income that qualifies for the credit with respect to corporations is determined by multiplying the corporation's oil-and-gas-extraction income by 35 percent. For individuals, the extraction income must be multiplied by a fraction the numerator of which is their total U.S. income tax against which the foreign income tax credit is taken and the denominator of which is their worldwide income.

Generally, when the amount of creditable foreign taxes paid or accrued by a taxpayer during the tax year exceeds the limitation above, the excess may be carried back to the two preceding tax years and then carried forward to the five succeeding tax years. However, the carryback period will be limited to one year for excess credits arising in tax years after October 22, 2004. Additionally, the carryfoward period is expanded to ten years for excess credits that may be carried to any tax year ending after October 22, 2004 (.10).

The terms "foreign oil and gas extraction income" (FOGEI) and "foreign oil related income" (FORI) do not include interest or dividend income that is passive income for purposes of the separate foreign tax credit limitation. As a result, the income is excluded for purposes of calculating the special foreign tax limitation on both FOGEI and FORI (.15). Dividends and interest, however, received from a foreign corporation in respect of which taxes are "deemed paid" under Code Sec. 902 remain FOGEI or FORI, to the extent attributable to such income.

.05 Code Secs. 907 and 954.

.10 Code Sec. 907(f), as amended by the American Jobs Creation Act of 2004 (P.L. 108-357).

.15 Code Sec. 907(c)(1) and (2).

Capital Expenditures, Expenses, Losses and Recaptures

¶25,321 Depreciation. A taxpayer is entitled to a depreciation deduction from his gross income for the wear and tear of property used in the operation of mineral properties (.05). Currently, a taxpayer is entitled to recover the costs of depreciable mineral property through the modified accelerated cost recovery system (MACRS) for property generally placed in service after 1986 and through the accelerated cost recovery system (ACRS) for property generally placed in service before 1987.

Cost recovery of property under post-1986 MACRS

The modified accelerated cost recovery system (MACRS) applies to most tangible depreciable property placed in service after 1986, or, if elected, to property placed in service after July 31, 1986, and before 1987. Personal property is recovered over a 3-year, 5-year, 7-year, 10-year, 15-year, or 20-year period. The cost of real property is recovered using the straight-line method over 39 years for non-residential real property. An alternative depreciation system based on Asset Depreciation Range class lives is established for certain assets.

Cost recovery of assets under pre-1987 ACRS

The Accelerated Cost Recovery System (ACRS) is mandatory for most tangible depreciable property placed in service after 1980 and before 1987 for which MACRS is not elected. Recovery of capital costs under ACRS is made by applying statutory percentages to the unadjusted basis of the property. The cost recovery methods and periods are the same for both new and used property. Salvage value is disregarded in computing ACRS allowances. The cost of eligible property is recovered over a 3-year, 5-year, 10-year, 15-year, 18-year, or 19-year period, depending upon the type of property. Included as 5-year property are storage facilities used in connection with the distribution of petroleum and its primary products.

Deduction of exploration, development, and intangible drilling expenses

Instead of capitalizing and recovering mining or drilling costs through depreciation deductions, a taxpayer may elect to deduct currently certain costs, such as domestic intangible drilling and development costs of oil and gas wells (¶25,323) and exploration costs of mineral deposits other than oil and gas (¶25,322). A taxpayer is permitted to deduct development costs of mineral deposits other than oil and gas, but he may elect to defer a current deduction and capitalize such costs (¶25,324). Intangible drilling costs paid or incurred outside the United States are recovered over a 10-year, straight-line amortization schedule or added to the adjusted basis of the property for cost depletion. Dry hole expenses incurred outside the U.S. are currently deductible, however (¶25,325).

.05 Code Sec. 168.

¶25,322 Exploration Expenditures. Taxpayers other than corporations may elect to deduct all exploration expenses incurred for the purpose of ascertaining the existence, location, extent or quality of any deposit of ore or any mineral other than oil or gas, provided that the amount deducted is recaptured once the mine reaches the production stage or is sold (.05). Recapture is accomplished by the taxpayer's election either:

(1) to include in income for that year the previously deducted exploration expenditures chargeable to the mine, increase the basis of the property by the amount included in income, and subsequently recover this amount through depletion; or

(2) to forgo depletion from the property (which includes or comprises the mine) until deductions that have been forgone equal exploration expenditures previously deducted.

Expenditures not recaptured by this method are recaptured on the sale or other disposition of the mining property, in much the same way as the recapture rules for depreciable property operate, with the amount recaptured treated as ordinary income.

Limit on corporations

The deductions otherwise allowable for mineral exploration costs to a corporation (other than an S corporation) must be reduced by 30 percent (.10). The 30-percent reduction must be deducted using the straight-line method over a 5-year period. The investment tax credit that was previously allowed for the former 20-percent reduction amount is no longer available since the investment tax credit has generally been repealed for property placed in service after 1985. The 30-percent amount is permitted as a deduction ratably over the 60-month period beginning with the month that the costs are paid or incurred.

Gain on the disposition of mining property for which exploration costs have been capitalized may lead to the recapture of such costs as ordinary income (.15). The portion of the adjusted basis of any property that is attributable to mining exploration and development costs is not considered for purposes of determining cost depletion. The recapture rules do not apply to:

(1) transfers of mining property by gift;

(2) transfers of mining property at death;

(3) contributions of mining property to a partnership in exchange for a partnership interest or distributions of mining property in partial or complete liquidation of a partnership interest; or

(4) certain dispositions of mining property involving tax-free transactions where the basis of the property in the hands of the transferor is carried over into the hands of the transferee (.20).

Development and production expenses

Exploration-type expenditures that are incurred during the development or production stage of a mine are treated as development expenses that are deductible currently and are not subject to recapture. Such expenditures include drilling, crosscutting, and other expenditures to determine the location, extent or quantity of a known deposit in a mine or to locate another vein of ore in the mine. If the exploration project is for the discovery of a new mine, then the expenditure is to be treated as an exploration expense subject to recapture, rather than as a development expense. This is true even though the exploration is conducted from underground workings of an existing mine.

Ten-year amortization

Where corporate or noncorporate taxpayers have incurred exploration expenditures, they may elect either to deduct them currently or amortize them over a 10-year period beginning with the year the expenditure occurs. If they elect to deduct the expenses, the deduction will constitute an item of preference for the imposition of the alternative minimum tax. In the case of a partnership, any election is made separately by each partner with respect to the partner's allocable share of any qualified expenditure (.25).

Foreign exploration

Taxpayers are required to recover foreign mining exploration and development costs over a 10-year, straight-line amortization schedule beginning with the tax year the costs were paid or incurred, or, at the election of the taxpayer, by including the costs in the adjusted basis of the property for purposes of computing cost depletion (.30).

.05 Code Sec. 617; Reg. §§1.617-1—1.617-4.
.10 Code Sec. 291(b)(1).
.15 Code Sec. 617(d).
.20 Code Sec. 617(d); Reg. §1.617-4(c).
.25 Code Secs. 56(a)(2) or 59(e).
.30 Code Sec. 616(d).

¶25,323 Intangible Drilling and Development Costs. In the case of oil and gas wells, the taxpayer may elect to deduct currently, instead of capitalizing and recovering through depletion, the class of items known as "intangible drilling and development costs" (IDC). Such costs include labor, fuel and power, materials and supplies, tools, truck and auto rental, repairs to drilling equipment, and depreciation upon drilling equipment (.05). The cost of these items, incurred during the drilling of wells and during the preparation of wells for production, would have to be capitalized if it were not for this elective treatment permitted by the law. The election, once made, is binding for future years (.10). Tax benefits resulting from the deduction of intangible drilling costs must be recaptured (¶25,327).

The election to expense intangible drilling costs does not permit a taxpayer unlimited control of the timing of the deduction. If the deduction would result in a substantial distortion of the taxpayer's income for the year of payment, the taxpayer will be required to capitalize the costs (.15). Where payments made by an oil and gas limited partnership to the parent of its general partner for drilling services at a fixed rate were made for beneficial income tax purposes rather than a legitimate business purpose, a current deduction is denied to the extent that such drilling services have not yet been provided (.20).

The election to expense currently intangible drilling and development costs is limited to wells located within the United States. Such costs are recovered over a five-year straight-line amortization schedule (10-year amortization for tax years beginning before 1990) beginning with the month in which they were paid or incurred (.25). Intangible drilling and development costs paid or incurred with respect to oil and gas wells located outside the United States may be included in the adjusted basis of the property, at the election of the taxpayer, for purposes of computing cost depletion, or, if that does not apply, they may be amortized over a 10-year period beginning with the tax year in which such costs were paid or incurred (.30).

Reporting requirements

Intangible drilling and development costs, such as wages, fuel, repairs and supplies, may be recovered as capital expenditures or the taxpayer may elect to deduct these costs currently. Expensed costs of a sole proprietor are reported on Schedule C of Form 1040. Form 4562, Depreciation and Amortization, is utilized to claim depreciation and amortization relating to IDC.

Offshore platforms

Expenditures that are incurred in the course of fabricating, transporting, and installing an offshore oil and gas drilling and production platform and the related facilities are within the option to expense intangible drilling and development costs: (1) if the platform is incident to and necessary for the drilling of wells (even though subsequently used for production); (2) if the platform is designed and constructed for use at a specific site; and (3) if the platform is of a type not ordinarily reused or otherwise salvaged as a unit (.35).

Several restrictions apply to limit the scope of the IDC option as it relates to offshore operations. First, without regard to salvageability, the option to expense IDC is not available for the costs of items acquired by purchase. Second, costs of fabricating drilling equipment, machinery, and similar items installed on offshore platforms, even though necessary for drilling, are not eligible for the IDC option, because, as a class, they can ordinarily be used or reused at another site without significant and expensive modification. Third, the IDC option excludes costs relating to production structures, facilities, and equipment, such as service facilities for production personnel and pumping equipment.

Geothermal wells

Intangible drilling costs incurred with respect to geothermal wells may also be deducted. Taxpayers having properties containing geothermal deposits and other properties containing oil and gas must make separate elections for the different properties. Deductions claimed with respect to geothermal wells are limited to the aggregate amount to which the taxpayer is at risk (.40). In addition, if a taxpayer claims deductions for intangible drilling costs on wells, the tax benefits resulting from such deductions must be recaptured (.45).

Integrated oil companies

Corporations that are integrated oil companies (other than S corporations) must reduce by 30 percent the amount otherwise allowable as a current expense deduction. The 30-percent amount disallowed as a current expense deduction must be written off ratably over a 60-month period beginning with the month in which the costs are paid or incurred. In addition, the ratable deductions are subject to recapture if the property to which they are allocable is disposed of (.50). This provision does not affect the option to expense dry hole costs in the year the dry hole is completed (¶25,325).

Exploratory drilling costs

Exploratory drilling costs incurred for the sole purpose of obtaining geological and geophysical information qualify as intangible drilling and development costs (.55). The IRS considers exploratory costs, as well as development costs, to be eligible for the election to deduct intangible drilling costs.

Tax Court's deductibility test for prepaid IDC

The Tax Court has developed a two-part test for determining the proper tax year in which prepaid intangible drilling and development costs (IDC) are to be deducted by cash-basis taxpayers (.60):

(1) the expenditure must be a payment rather than a refundable deposit, and

(2) the deduction must not result in a material distortion of income.

This deductibility test is based on the following fact situation. An individual limited partner claimed a loss equal to his investment, in the year in which it was made, because the deduction of all prepaid expenses created a net operating loss for the partnership. Prepayments were made for drilling and service contracts under which estimated costs were prepaid but refundable, for turnkey contracts that did not provide for refund of prepayments, and for services of the common general partner as program manager and drilling operator in a two-tier partnership arrangement.

Under its two-part test, the Tax Court determined that only IDC prepayments on the turnkey contracts were fully deductible in the year made since the liability for payment in that year could not later be excused and no distortion of income would result from taking the full deduction. However, since the partnership retained a unilateral right to a return of its payments on the other contracts, amounts transferred were deposits rather than payments unless services contracted for were completed by year end. Proration of the IDC deduction for contracts begun but not completed would be required. As to nonrefundable well charges prepaid to the general partner-operator, no motive existed for such transfer other than an acceleration of the deduction, and this would result in a distortion of income.

.05 Code Sec. 263(c); Reg. §1.612-4.

.10 Rev. Rul. 80-2, 1980-1 CB 61.

.15 Code Sec. 446(b); Reg. §1.461-1(a).

.20 Rev. Rul. 80-71, 1980-1 CB 106, distinguishing Rev. Rul. 71-252, 1971-1 CB 146.

.25 Code Sec. 59(e).

.30 Code Sec. 263(i).

.35 Rev. Rul. 89-56, 1989-1 CB 83, modifying and superseding Rev. Rul. 70-596, 1970-2 CB 68.

.40 Code Sec. 465(c).

.45 Code Sec. 1254(a).

.50 Code Secs. 291 and 1254.

.55 *Sun Co., Inc.*, CA-3, 82-1 USTC ¶9336, 677 F2d 294, aff'g TC, 74 TC 1481, CCH Dec. 37,293 (Acq.); *Gates Rubber Co.*, CA-10, 82-2 USTC ¶9702, 694 F2d 648, aff'g TC, 74 TC 1456, CCH Dec. 37,292 (Acq.); *Standard Oil Co. (Indiana)*, 68 TC 325, CCH Dec. 34,442 (Acq.).

.60 *S.A. Keller*, CA-8, 84-1 USTC ¶9194, 725 F2d 1173, aff'g TC, 79 TC 7, CCH Dec. 39,169.

¶25,324 Development Expenditures. Expenditures paid or incurred for the development of mines or of other natural deposits (other than an oil or gas well), after the existence of ores or minerals in commercially marketable quantities are discovered, may be currently deducted (.05). Development costs include depreciation allowances, but not the amount paid or incurred for the acquisition or improvement of depreciable property. Development expenditures do not stop when the mine reaches the production stage but continue until it reaches a level of full production.

Development costs are to be deducted currently unless the taxpayer elects to defer them and deduct a ratable portion as the ore or mineral is produced and sold. However, in this instance, the election to defer the deduction must be made for the total amount of the development costs affected (reduced by net receipts from the ores or minerals produced from the mine or deposit). The amount of the development expenditures treated as deferred expenses must be taken into account in computing the adjusted basis of the mine or deposit, but such amounts are disregarded for purposes of computing the depletion deduction.

In the case of a partnership, any election to defer the current deduction of development costs shall be made separately by each partner with respect to the partner's allocable share of any qualified expenditure (.10). However, the partnership must have elected to be excluded from the provisions governing partnership status (.15). Even though one partner elects to defer development costs, other partners may currently deduct their share of such costs (.20).

Corporate taxpayers are subject to a special 30-percent reduction in the amount currently deductible as development expenditures (.25). Also, expensed exploration and development expenditures are subject to recapture as ordinary income to the extent that they would have been included in the adjusted basis of the property if they had not been deducted. The 30-percent reduction amount is deducted ratably over a 60-month period beginning with the month in which the costs are paid or incurred (.30).

A mine development expense deduction is not allowed for that portion of expenses financed by a contingent nonrecourse note (.35). Also, a taxpayer may not deduct mine development expenditures if he does not have an interest in the property for which he claims the deduction (.40).

.05 Code Sec. 616; Reg. §§1.616-1—1.616-3.

.10 Code Sec. 59(e)(4)(C).

.15 Code Sec. 761(a).

.20 Rev. Rul. 83-129, 1983-2 CB 105.

.25 Code Sec. 291(b)(1).

.30 Code Sec. 291(b)(2).

.35 *E.J. Saviano*, CA-7, 85-2 USTC ¶9475, 765 F2d 643, aff'g TC, 80 TC 955, CCH Dec. 40,124.

.40 *M.E. Anderson*, 83 TC 898, CCH Dec. 41,650.

¶25,325 Abandonment Losses. An amount paid into an oil or gas well drilling operation that results in a dry hole is usually an investment that qualifies as a transaction entered into for profit and can be deducted as an abandonment loss in the year of abandonment (.05). This rule also applies to a well that had produced oil or gas but is a dry hole when abandoned (.10). If a taxpayer is in the trade or business of drilling oil and gas wells, a business loss deduction is allowable.

The amount of the loss deduction is usually the depreciated cost of the abandoned physical equipment plus the intangible drilling and development costs (wages, fuel, repairs, hauling, supplies, etc.) of the well. If the operator has elected to capitalize intangible drilling and development costs, and the well later proves to be nonproductive (a dry hole), the operator may still elect to deduct such costs as an ordinary loss under the regulations.

The election to take the ordinary loss deduction must be made in the operator's return for the first taxable year in which the nonproductive well is completed. The election, when made, is binding for all later years. The absence of a clear indication in such return of an election to deduct as ordinary losses intangible drilling and development costs of nonproductive wells will be deemed to be an election to recover such costs through depletion to the extent that they are not represented by physical property, and through depreciation to the extent that they are represented by physical property or cost recovery.

Loss deductions on oil and gas royalty interests are also allowable. For instance, a loss deduction based on the worthlessness of an oil interest was allowed in the year that the oil company lessee decided that there was no reasonable prospect of finding oil in the land and cancelled its lease (.15). In determining the worthlessness of oil interests, the same rule is applied as with other types of property: that an oil interest becomes worthless and is deductible as a "closed and completed" loss upon the happening of some identifiable event which results in the loss of sale value in the ordinary channels of trade. A formal release or relinquishment of the interest during the taxable year in which the loss is claimed is not necessary.

Abandonment of development by the operator in the tax year is not conclusive of worthlessness where the operator still retains the lease. Unless abandonment of development also results in termination of the lease, worthlessness will have to be established by other evidence. For instance, a loss was allowed upon proof that dry holes were drilled on or in the immediate vicinity of royalty interests during the tax year, thus demonstrating the improbability of oil and gas production in commercial quantities (.20). A deduction was allowed in the year that the lease was delivered to another person without any consideration, this fact being evidence of abandonment of the lease (.25). Intention to abandon the lease was also present in a case where the lessee withdrew from the premises, removing all the equipment, and not returning (.30). A deduction was allowed for the cost of a lease in the year it was determined that it would no longer be commercially profitable to operate, even though the lessee retained title to the lease and recouped several hundred dollars by way of rental to another oil company and a small royalty from the company's operations (.35).

The same principles that govern the deductibility of abandonment losses for oil and gas interests govern mineral interests as well.

.05 Reg. §1.612-4(b)(4); *B. F. Crabbe*, 15 TCM 216, CCH Dec. 21,603(M), TC Memo. 1956-52; *Belridge Oil Co.*, 11 BTA 127, CCH Dec. 3735 (Acq.).

.10 *United Oil Co.*, 25 BTA 101, CCH Dec. 7368 (Nonacq.).

.15 *E. S. Pool*, CtCls, 54-1 USTC ¶9263, 119 FSupp 202.

.20 *Harmon and Moore (E. H. Moore)*, 1 TCM 239, CCH Dec. 12,918-E.

.25 *A. L. Huey*, 4 BTA 370, CCH Dec. 1516.

.30 *A.H. Fell*, 7 BTA 263, CCH Dec. 2517 (Acq.).

.35 *Chaparral Oil Co.*, 43 BTA 457, CCH Dec. 11,636 (Acq.).

¶25,326 Tax Credits. The regular 10-percent investment tax credit (ITC) has been generally repealed for property, other than ITC transition property, placed in service after 1985. Where the ITC is allowed for transition property or for carryovers from pre-1986 tax years, the amount of the ITC is reduced by 35 percent for tax years beginning after June 30, 1987 (.05)

Although no longer part of current Code Sec. 49, the transition rules continue to apply to qualifying transition property and entitle taxpayers to claim a regular investment tax credit with respect to such property (.10).

.05 Code Sec. 49.

.10 Act Sec. 11813(c) of the Revenue Reconciliation Act of 1990 (P.L. 101-508).

¶25,327 Recaptures. Gains on the disposition of oil or gas property are treated as ordinary income. Gain is recognized on the lower of: (1) the amount of adjusted intangible drilling and development costs with respect to the property; or (2) the amount by which the fair market value of the property or the amount realized on the sale exceeds the adjusted basis of the property. The term "adjusted intangible drilling and development costs" means the aggregate amount of expenditures allocable to the oil or gas property that have been deducted under Code Sec. 263(c) and that, but for being deducted, would have been included in the adjusted basis of the property reduced by the amount by which the depletion deduction relating to the property would have been increased had the costs been charged to the capital account rather than deducted. Intangible drilling and development costs are subject to recapture without reduction for the additional depletion that could have been deducted if the costs had been capitalized.

Depletion is subject to recapture as ordinary income upon the sale of oil or gas property at a gain. Recapture is limited to the amount by which the depletion deduction reduced the adjusted basis of the disposed property.

Pre-1987 oil, gas or geothermal property

Intangible drilling and development costs expensed after 1975 in connection with oil or gas property placed in service before 1987 are generally recaptured as ordinary income to the extent of gain realized upon the disposition of such property. This recapture rule also applies to such costs expensed regarding geothermal property commenced on or after October 1, 1978, and before 1987. Specifically, the amount recaptured as ordinary income is the lower of:

(1) the aggregate amount of expenditures deducted that are allocable to such property and that have been deducted as intangible drilling and development costs by the taxpayer or any other person and that (but for being so deducted) would have been reflected in the adjusted basis of the property; the total amount of these costs, however, is reduced by the amounts that would be deductible as cost depletion (if any) if such costs had been charged to a capital account instead of being deducted; or

(2) the excess of (a) the amount realized (in the case of a sale, exchange, or involuntary conversion) from the disposition, or the fair market value of the interest (in the case of any other disposition), over (b) the adjusted basis of the property.

Unitization and Joint Ventures

¶25,328 Pooled Interests. In many oil-producing areas, the interests of several owners and lessees of oil-producing properties are pooled for the best economic results. In some states such unitization, or unit operation, is required by law as a conservation measure. The classification of an organization derived from such a unitized agreement is of immediate importance to the participants for federal income tax purposes. In general, such unitization agreements contain the following typical features (.05):

(1) The costs of development and expenses of operation are prorated among the parties in accordance with their respective interests.

(2) Division of the oil proceeds is usually accomplished by payment of the purchase price by the pipeline company or other purchaser directly to the several parties in accordance with their respective shares as indicated by division orders signed

by them. Generally, any party may take his share of the oil in kind. Where that right exists, any authority given the operator to market the oil may be revoked upon proper notice. Sometimes, however, the operator is authorized without qualification to market the product.

(3) The operator is required to carry adequate insurance and to make an accounting.

(4) Operating agreements remain in force until the mineral is exhausted or for the term of the lease or leases or renewals thereof. Sometimes an express provision is made for withdrawal of one of the parties by assignment of his rights to the others.

(5) The parties have voting power proportionate to their interests to choose and advise the operator (in a case where only one lease is involved, broad powers are commonly vested in the operator named in the agreement), to change the operator, to determine drilling and operating plans, to audit and pass on the operator's accounting, and to pass on transactions for disposal of surplus equipment.

(6) Any partner may sell or encumber his entire interest, but may not subdivide or sell without giving the others preferential option. (In the case of agreements covering single leases, the contract may not contain express provisions to that effect.)

(7) The liabilities of the parties are to be separate and not joint.

An association will be classified as a corporation rather than as a partnership for tax purposes if it has more corporate characteristics than noncorporate characteristics. Therefore, to prevent an association from being taxed as a corporation, the agreement should be drawn up to eliminate the joint profit motive through the reservation by each individual of the right to take his share of the mineral in kind or provide for the sale of the respective shares under revocable agency powers. Other corporate characteristics, such as continuity of life, centralized management, and limited liability, may be eliminated through proper drafting of the agreement if necessary to accomplish the desired result.

The IRS can exclude from partnership status, at the election of the members, certain unincorporated organizations used for investment or for the joint production, extraction or use of property (except where such organizations are involved in sales of services or property which has been produced or extracted) (.10). It is possible for unit participants to remove themselves from treatment as a partnership by properly drafting the unitization or joint-venture agreement to provide that the organization was not created for the purpose of selling the extracted product, and the marketing function was not undertaken by the group operator or other representatives for joint profit. Of course, the requirement of filing the election with the IRS must be fulfilled.

Unitization

A unitization agreement providing for production of oil and gas on a cooperative basis, with each participant receiving an agreed percentage of oil and gas on the basis of previous production, was not an exchange by the participants of their separate interests for a single depletable undivided interest in the oil lands (.15).

The Tax Court has ruled that a compulsory unitization under state law also was not an exchange (.20). However, on appeal, the U.S. Court of Appeals for the Fifth Circuit held that the cost adjustments received under the oil and gas unitization agreements were a nontaxable return of capital, so that it was not necessary to decide whether the unitization was a cross-conveyance of properties (.25). Further, the sums received by the owners from the purchasers of the production to compensate the owners for amounts contributed by them to the costs of development and facilities, for which they were entitled to reimbursement from other owners, were not depletable income from a retained economic interest in the oil and gas in place. The sums received as an adjustment of costs under the unitization agreement were merely repayment of a debt and, therefore, a nontaxable return of capital. The payments represented a return of capital and were not "oil payments," because the other owners were personally liable for the payments if the oil production was not sufficient.

Legal fees and survey expenses incurred in defining the units, preparing the pooling agreements and filing designations may be deducted currently and need not be capitalized (.30).

.05 Code Secs. 761 and 7701; Reg. §§301.7701-1—301.7701-4.

.10 Code Sec. 761.

.15 *Belridge Oil Co.*, CA-9, 59-1 USTC ¶9460, 267 F2d 291.

.20 *E.V. Whitwell*, 28 TC 372, CCH Dec. 22,374.

.25 *E.V. Whitwell*, CA-5, 58-2 USTC ¶9658, 257 F2d 548.

.30 *E. Campbell*, CA-5, 56-1 USTC ¶9233, 229 F2d 197.

Mineral Production Payments

¶25,329 Mineral Production Payments. A mineral production payment is entitled to special tax treatment in that it is treated as a nontaxable mortgage loan rather than as an economic interest in the mineral property to which the production payment is attributable (.05). The term "production payment" generally means a payment for the right to a specified share of the production from the mineral in place when produced, or to the proceeds from such production. Such right must be an economic interest in the mineral in place (¶25,301). At the time of its creation, the production payment must have an economic life shorter than that of the mineral property it burdens. Generally, contracts that do not require any delivery of a mineral ("take or pay" contracts) to the purchaser of a mineral interest do not create an economic interest with respect to the purchaser (.10). For example, taxpayers who sold an interest in gas production to a utility under a fixed-payment contract that did not require the delivery of gas to the utility were not entitled to treat advance payments for the gas as mineral production payments (.15).

A carved-out production payment is created when the owner of a mineral property sells—or carves out—a portion of his future production. It is usually sold for cash to an outside party, often a financial institution. It may be for a specific dollar amount and usually bears interest. The payment is secured by an interest in the minerals and the known mineral reserves available are often greatly in excess of those required to pay off the production payment.

A carved-out mineral production payment is treated as a mortgage loan on the mineral property rather than as an economic interest in the property. Thus, the seller of a carved-out production payment is required to match the income from the production payment with the expenses incurred to generate that income. However, a production payment carved out for the exploration or development of a mineral property is not subject to this treatment.

> ***Example 1:*** A, the owner of a lease, carves out a production payment in favor of X in consideration for X's drilling a well on the lease. Gross income is not realized by A on the transaction and A is not entitled to deduct the drilling costs incurred by X.

> ***Example 2:*** A carves out a production payment for $100,000, sells it to X for $90,000 and agrees to use the proceeds to drill development wells on the lease to which the carve-out relates. The $90,000 is not income to A, and A cannot deduct the $90,000 incurred in drilling the wells.

Since the seller of a carved-out production payment is required to treat the transaction as a loan, he is required to match the income from the production payment with the expenses incurred to generate that income. Therefore, in the year of sale of the production payment, the owner of the working interest does not take the proceeds into income. In the year(s) in which the production payment is paid off, the income used to make the payment is from a depletable resource in the hands of the operator, who is allowed a deduction for the expenses incurred to produce the income. The purchaser of the production payment does not have an economic interest in the mineral production, and the income he receives is not subject to depletion.

ABC transactions and retained production payments

A retained production payment is created when the owner of a mineral interest sells the working interest but reserves a production payment for himself (.20). Such payments are treated as a purchase money mortgage rather than as an economic interest in the mineral property. Accordingly, the income derived from the property which is used to satisfy the retained production payment is taxable to the owner of the property, subject to the depletion allowance. The production costs attributable to producing the mineral used to satisfy the production payment are deductible by the owner of the working interest in the year incurred.

A production payment retained in a mineral property by the lessor in a leasing transaction is to be treated by the lessee or his successor in interest as a bonus granted by the lessee to the grantor, payable in installments. The lessee is required to capitalize the payments and then recover them through depletion. In the hands of the lessor the production payments are to be treated as derived from an economic interest in the mineral property and, thus, are includible in his income subject to the percentage depletion deduction.

A retained production payment should be distinguished from payments received under a "take or pay" contract, in which a party purchases a specified amount of a mineral each month, but is not obligated to take such monthly production. To the extent that the seller receives payments from the purchaser in excess of the production taken, a deficiency in the "take" exists. The purchaser has the right during any of the subsequent years of the contract life to make up any deficiency by taking production in excess of the specified monthly production. The payments received for the mineral to be taken in the future are not mineral production payments and, consequently, are includible in the seller's gross income (.25).

The ABC transaction is the same as a retained production payment, except that after selling the working interest the initial owner then sells the retained production payment. In an ABC transaction, A, the owner of oil and gas property, sells it to B, an operator and developer, who secures financing from C, who receives an oil payment for the amount of his advance, payable out of production at a fixed interest rate.

The production payment is treated as a purchase money mortgage rather than as an economic interest in the mineral property. The purchaser of the working interest (B) is required to treat as depletable income the amounts used to pay off the production payment in the year of payment. Expenses attributable to that income are deductible in the year incurred. The tax treatment of A remains unchanged—he realizes capital gain on his sale. Also, the tax result to C, the purchaser of the production payment, remains the same. C treats the payments as the receipt of a nontaxable return of principal plus taxable interest.

.05 Code Sec. 636; Reg. §§1.636-1—1.636-4.

.10 Rev. Rul. 80-48, 1980-1 CB 99.

.15 *H.J. Freede,* CA-10, 88-2 USTC ¶9581, rev'g 86 TC 340, CCH Dec. 42,918.

.20 *L.W. Brooks, Jr.,* CA-5, 70-1 USTC ¶9326, 424 F2d 116.

.25 Rev. Rul. 80-48, 1980-1 CB 99.

FARMERS

Introduction

¶25,332 Farmers and ranchers are generally subject to the same rules that apply to other taxpayers, but they are also affected by a variety of unique nontax considerations, such as federal subsidy programs, special inventory needs, and intensive land use. To help remove some of the tax inequities that might result from these nontax considerations, the tax laws provide farmers and ranchers with certain tax-saving opportunities.

The purpose of the material at ¶25,334–¶25,423 is to highlight the tax choices available to farmers and ranchers. In addition to an explanation of various tax provisions, the material provides guidance in determining the consequences of making a particular tax election. However, while these elections can provide opportunities for tax savings, each farmer and rancher should consider his or her own financial circumstances and the general economic conditions before making an election.

For tax purposes, a distinction is usually not made between "farmer" and "rancher". Because the following discussion about farmers and ranchers is predominantly tax-related, the term "farmer" is also used to describe both farmers and ranchers, even when the term "rancher" may be more descriptive of the fact situation.

What is Farming?

¶25,334 Types of Farming. The definitions of "farm" and "farming" are not the same in every tax provision relating to farms and farming. However, as a general definition, the term "farm" means farm in the ordinarily accepted sense. (Special definitions of a "farm" are discussed where applicable.) For instance, a farm includes the land and other assets used in the following operations (.05):

Dairy farms

Fish farms

Fruit farms

Nurseries

Orchards	Ranches
Oyster farms	Ranges
Plantations	Stock farms
Poultry farms	Truck farms

Farmer: The business and risks

The term "farmer" includes all forms of business organizations, including individuals, partnerships and corporations. Thus, tax considerations relating to income, deductions, credits, exemptions, tax rates, and filing requirements should be considered whenever selecting the business organization most advantageous and appropriate for each taxpayer's circumstance, needs and goals. For example, a sole proprietor's payments for personal expenses, such as groceries and utilities, are not deductible. However, the same payments by a farming corporation for the farm "employee" may be a deductible business expense, even though the employee may be the sole shareholder of the farm corporation (.10).

In order to be considered as engaged in the business of farming, a taxpayer must assume the risks of farming. Therefore, an assistant or manager employed by a farm operation at a straight salary is not a farmer carrying on a business. The term "farmer," however, includes both the owner and the tenant where the farm is rented on the basis of a share-crop agreement based on crop production; it also includes a farm manager whose compensation is based in whole or in part on production. An individual need not necessarily live on a farm to be a farmer. For example, a poultry raiser was a farmer, even though he lived on the outskirts of a city (.15).

The term "farmer" includes a taxpayer engaged in the business of breeding and raising chinchillas, mink, foxes, or other fur-bearing animals, which are also livestock (.20). A corporation operating a commercial feedlot that sold cattle to meat-packers was considered to be a farmer for purposes of the accounting regulations and was entitled to file tax returns on the cash method (.25). A company that slaughtered and processed ducks and that bore a substantial risk of loss from a duck-raising process was engaged in farming, even though the majority of the ducks were raised by others (.30).

As to persons operating farms for pleasure and not for profit, see ¶25,335, below.

Primary occupation

The term "farmer" is limited to those engaged primarily in the business of farming. Generally, a farming business involves the cultivation of land or raising or harvesting any agricultural or horticultural commodity (.35). For example, a taxpayer was not considered to be a farmer because, due to his wife's separate nonfarm income, less than two-thirds of the aggregate gross income reported on the couple's joint return was from farming (.40). Thus, the taxpayers could not take advantage of the special estimated tax filing date for farmers (see ¶25,416), and they were assessed a penalty for the underpayment of estimated tax. Where only one spouse has substantial nonfarm income, married taxpayers can avoid the two-thirds farm income rule by filing separate returns, although doing so will generally subject their separate incomes to higher tax rates and increase their overall tax liability.

.05 Code Sec. 61; Reg. §1.61-4(d).

.10 *D.L. Johnson*, 49 TCM 1203, CCH Dec. 42,017(M), TC Memo. 1985-175; *J. Grant Farms, Inc.*, 49 TCM 1197, CCH Dec. 42,016, TC Memo. 1985-174; *J.M. Harrison*, 41 TCM 1384, CCH Dec. 37,869(M), TC Memo. 1981-211; *M.A. Tougher*, CA-9, 71-1 USTC ¶9398, 441 F2d 1148.

.15 *L.A. Chemell*, CA-5, 57-1 USTC ¶9679, 243 F2d 944.

.20 Rev. Rul. 57-588, 1957-2 CB 305.

.25 *Hi-Plains Enterprises, Inc.*, 60 TC 158, CCH Dec. 31,956, aff'd by CA-10, 74-1 USTC ¶9431, 496 F2d 520.

.30 *Maple Leaf Farms, Inc.*, 64 TC 438, CCH Dec. 33,273 (Acq.).

.35 Reg. §48.6420-4(b).

.40 IRS Letter Ruling 7813073, 12-29-77, CCH IRS LETTER RULINGS REPORTS.

¶25,335 Hobby Farming. A person operating a farm for pleasure and without a profit motive is not engaged in the business of farming (.05). This type of farming is commonly called hobby farming. In general, a hobby farmer may not deduct any loss from the operation of the farm as an offset against non-farming income. This means that, if expenses exceed receipts, the receipts are not taxable but the expenses are not allowable deductions (.10). Thus, the loss from a hobby farm is not considered a loss incurred in a trade or business.

Specifically, a hobby farmer is entitled to deduct the following amounts in the following order:

(1) Amounts allowable as deductions without regard to a profit motive, such as interest, taxes and casualty losses. These amounts are fully deductible, after taking into account any limitations or exceptions to the deduction of such amounts. For example, a deduction for interest on an individual hobby farmer's investment indebtedness is subject to the investment interest limitation (Code Sec. 163(d)) and is, therefore, generally deductible only to the extent of investment income.

(2) Amounts that would be allowable as deductions if the hobby farm was operated for profit and that would not result in an adjustment to the basis of property. These amounts are deductible only to the extent that the gross income attributable to the hobby farm exceeds the deductions allowed or allowable under (1), above. These types of expenses include fertilizer, utilities, and wages

(3) Amounts that would be allowable as deductions if the hobby farm were an activity engaged in for profit, and that would result in an adjustment to the basis of property. These amounts are deductible only to the extent that the gross income attributable to the hobby farm exceeds the deductions allowed or allowable under (1) and (2), above. Deductions falling into this category include such items as depreciation, partial losses with respect to property, partially worthless debts, amortization, and amortizable bond premiums.

The question of a taxpayer's intention to operate for profit or to operate for pleasure is to be determined from the facts and circumstances of each case (.15). For example, a taxpayer who owned his own lumber business and invested in a cattle-breeding operation was entitled to a depreciation deduction and investment credit for the cattle operation because he was motivated by profit, even though his cattle investment activity was secondary in size and importance to his lumber business and his need for tax write-offs (.20).

Factors to be considered in determining whether the hobby rules apply to a specific case include:

(1) the farmer's business-like manner, expertise, and experience;

(2) the degree of time and effort expended;

(3) the history of losses and/or profits;

(4) the presence of recreational facilities; and

(5) the appreciated value of assets (.25).

For-profit presumption

Farming is generally presumed not to be a hobby if profits are made in three out of five consecutive years. If the farm activities consist primarily of breeding, training, showing, or racing of horses, a profit motive is presumed if profits are made in two out of seven consecutive years (.30). Once the for-profit presumption arises, the burden of proof shifts to the IRS to show that a farm is not being operated on a for-profit basis (.35).

☐ For further treatment of hobby losses, see ¶10,001. See, also, the discussion of tax shelters at ¶25,422.

.05 Code Sec. 183; Reg. §§1.162-12, 1.183-1.

.10 *A.G. Thacher*, DC N.Y., 1 USTC ¶70,288 F2d 994; *W.B. Morton*, CA-2, 49-1 USTC ¶9254, 174 F2d 302; *R.C. Coffey*, CA-5, 44-1 USTC ¶9233, 141 F2d 204; *A.W. Hemphill*, 10 TCM 1080, CCH Dec. 18,658(M).

.15 *J. Frazier*, 49 TCM 715, CCH Dec. 41,875(M), TC Memo. 1985-61; *R.M. Shumaker*, CA-9, 81-2 USTC ¶9508, 648 F2d 1198.

.20 *G.B. Lemmen*, 77 TC 1326, CCH Dec. 38,510 (Acq.).

.25 Reg. §1.183-2(b), *M. Nickerson*, CA-7, 83-1 USTC ¶9217, 700 F2d 402; *H. Faulconer, Sr.*, 45 TCM 1084, CCH Dec. 39,994(M), TC Memo. 1983-165; *W.G. Daugherty*, 45 TCM 1224, CCH Dec. 40,018(M), TC Memo. 1983-188.

.30 Code Sec. 183(d); Rev. Rul. 74-28, 1974-1 CB 67.

.35 *H. Faulconer, Sr.*, CA-4, 84-2 USTC ¶9955, 748 F2d 890, reversing and remanding TC, 45 TCM 1084, CCH Dec. 39,994(M), TC Memo. 1983-165.

Accounting Methods

¶25,337 Cash v. Accrual Method. Farming income is generally treated in the same way as income from any other business. As a general rule, the accrual method of accounting is more accurate than the cash method in reflecting true business income because the accrual method results in a more even distribution of income over a period of years. This more equal distribution of income and expenses may result in reduced tax liability in profitable years (.05).

However, most farmers, particularly those who raise and sell livestock for dairy, draft, or breeding purposes, may find it more advantageous to use the cash receipts and disbursements method of accounting. In addition to simpler record-keeping requirements, there are several other factors that may make the cash method more advantageous to use than the accrual method (see "Cash method," below).

Under either accounting method, taxable income must be computed on the basis of the taxpayer's annual accounting period (fiscal year or calendar year) in accordance with the method of accounting regularly employed in keeping the taxpayer's books. If no books are kept, income must be computed on the basis of the calendar year and must be reported on the cash method, unless the taxpayer is not eligible to use such method.

Farming partnerships in which a corporation is a partner *must* (1) use the accrual method of accounting and (2) capitalize preproductive period expenses (see ¶9860) (.10). Where a farming partnership is required to use the accrual rules, the noncorporate partners may also have to report their respective shares of partnership income under the accrual method (.15)

Farming corporations (with three exceptions) also must use the accrual method of accounting and capitalize preproductive period expenses (.17). The exceptions are:

(1) any S corporation,

(2) any corporation (other than a family farming corporation) with gross annual receipts not exceeding $1 million, and

(3) any family farming corporation with gross annual receipts not exceeding $25 million.

Farming tax shelters may not use the cash method of accounting (.20). For this purpose a tax shelter includes a farming syndicate, which is a partnership or any other enterprise (not including a corporation that does not elect S corporation status) that is engaged in the trade or business of farming if: (.25)

(1) any interests of the partnership or enterprise have been offered at any time for sale in an offering that is required to be registered with any federal or state agency that regulates security sales, or

(2) more than 35 percent of the losses during any period are allocable to limited partners or limited entrepreneurs (i.e., an investor who does not actively participate in the management of the farming enterprise).

An individual who has an interest in a farming partnership or enterprise is not treated as a limited partner or as a limited entrepreneur if:

(1) the interest is attributable to the individual's active participation in the management of a farming business for at least five years;

(2) the individual lives on the farm where the business is conducted;

(3) the individual actively participates in the management of a business involving the raising of livestock (or is so treated under (1) or (2)), and the partnership or enterprise further processes the livestock raised in that business; or

(4) the individual is a member, or a spouse of any such member, of the family of a grandparent of an individual who is not treated as a limited partner or limited entrepreneur in situations (1) through (3), above.

For purposes of the definition of a farming syndicate, "farming" means the cultivation of land, or the raising or harvesting of any agricultural or horticultural commodity (.30). This includes the raising, shearing, feeding, caring for, training, and management of animals. With regard to trees, however, only those bearing fruit or nuts are treated as agricultural commodities. Hence, a syndicate raising livestock, fish, poultry, bees, dogs, flowers, vegetables, etc., is engaged in farming.

The rules relating to the required use of the accrual method of accounting are discussed in detail at ¶15,200 and following. For a discussion of farm inventory valuation, see ¶25,340—¶25,343.

Cash method

Under the cash method of accounting, income is generally reported in the year received, whether in cash or trade. Inventories are not used to figure income (unless farm items have been purchased for resale). Expenses are deducted when paid for in cash or in farm products. For cash-method farmers, the basis of crops or livestock raised is zero; costs of raising them are deductible currently. Thus, when such crops or livestock are sold, the entire proceeds are taxable. The basis of livestock or crops purchased for resale is cost.

A farming corporation that uses the cash method of accounting for its purchases and sales of livestock may not determine its cost of livestock as if it used an inventory method. This applies unless the taxpayer is subject to the uniform capitalization rules (.35).

An individual cash-method farmer generally has a tax advantage over an accrual-method farmer in raising livestock that are held for dairy, draft, breeding, or sporting purposes. This tax advantage arises from the current deduction of expenses to raise such livestock by cash-method farmers. While the cash-method farmer's cost of *raising* livestock (draft, breeding, or dairy) is currently deductible, and, therefore, no depreciation deduction is allowable, the cost of *purchasing* such livestock is not currently deductible and must be capitalized and recovered through depreciation deductions. See ¶25,379. An exception to this "capitalizing of cost" rule applies to the cost of hens purchased for egg-laying and baby chicks purchased for raising and resale. Farmers who use the cash method may deduct the cost in the year of payment (.40).

A cash-method farmer who receives insurance proceeds as a result of destruction or damage to crops may elect to include these proceeds in income in the year after the year of damage or destruction upon showing that the income from the crops would normally have been reported in the following year (.45) (see ¶25,385 for details).

Another advantage of operating on the cash method is the opportunity to defer income by purchasing at the end of the current year feed to be consumed in the following year. The cost of feed for raising animals is generally a currently deductible expense even though it may not be used until the next year. See ¶25,366.

A farmer can change from the accrual to the cash method by obtaining the IRS's consent (see ¶15,655) (.50). Application for permission to change the accounting period (calendar or fiscal year) is explained at ¶15,055.

A farmer who uses the cash method and whose only business consists of farming does not have to keep permanent books or records. However, this does not constitute a waiver of the customary rule that any determination by the IRS is presumptively correct. Thus, a farmer who wants to challenge an IRS determination will need books and records to meet the burden of proving that the IRS is incorrect.

Planning Note

CCH Analysts note that farm operations can be quite varied as to the products, operating cycles, and degree of sophistication. Accordingly, the task of recordkeeping also runs the continuum of sophistication with some farmers relying solely on checkbooks and ledgers, while others use intricate computer systems. In light of all of this, compliance is a constant battle for farmers and their advisers. There are several reasons why farming lends itself to underreporting income, including (.55):

(1) Most income is received from non-information return sources. Only cash rent, machine hire, patronage dividends, and most government payments will have Forms 1099 issued.

(2) Income is received in an irregular manner. Crops are not sold on a daily basis. They may be sold immediately after harvest or held and sold later in the year or in a subsequent year.

(3) The books maintained may be very elementary, for example, a single entry accounting method. A basic system could be merely a checking account deposit and check spread.

(4) There is usually a lack of internal control since the farmer is responsible for receiving, recording, and depositing all income.

(5) There are usually no internal controls that can be used to test income reporting (for example, numbered sales invoices or customer accounts).

Accrual method

Under the accrual method of accounting, all items of gross income from farming operations are included in gross income when they are earned, even though payment may be received in another tax year. Farm business expenses incurred for property or services are not deductible until economic performance occurs. Economic performance generally occurs when the farmer is provided with the property or services, rather than when the farmer pays for them. An exception for recurring items allows certain expenses to be treated as incurred in a tax year even though economic performance has not occurred.

Farmers who use the accrual method are generally required to use inventories taken at the beginning and end of the tax year. In this way, increases and decreases in inventory values of livestock, produce, feed, and other items during the course of the year are reflected through closing inventories. For the valuation of farm inventories, see ¶25,340 and following. Accrual-method farmers are not required to inventory crops (see ¶25,341).

The method of calculating net farm profit under the accrual method is similar to that for calculating net profit from businesses in which the production, purchase or sale of merchandise is an income-producing factor. Thus, net farm income equals total sales less cost of livestock or crops sold, plus miscellaneous farm receipts and income less expenses incurred during the year (whether or not paid), including depreciation allowances. Although deductible expenses include the cost of feed and other expenses of raising crops and livestock, the deduction for such costs is offset by the inclusion in the closing inventories of crops and animals raised during the year.

Farming corporations, farming partnerships in which a corporation is a partner, and farming syndicates generally must (1) use the accrual method and (2) capitalize certain "preproductive period" expenses. This rule does not apply to S corporations, certain family-controlled corporations, and corporations with gross annual receipts not exceeding $1 million (.60).

For additional details also applicable to computations and records of farmers, see ¶25,340.

Annual accrual method of accounting

A special rule permits certain corporations to use the annual accrual method of accounting, under which expenses incurred during the preproductive period are not capitalized but are deducted currently (.65). This rule applies to corporations that raise crops that are harvested at least 12 months after planting (including qualified corporate sugar cane joint ventures). In addition, the corporation must have used the annual accrual method for the 10-year period ending with its first tax year beginning after 1975 and must have continued to use such method for each tax year after its first tax year beginning after 1975.

Preproduction period costs

Generally, the uniform capitalization rules apply to crops with preproduction periods of more than two years (.70). These rules generally require the capitalization of the direct costs and an allocable portion of the indirect costs that benefit or are incurred in the production of plants or animals. However, some farmers may make an irrevocable election not to have the rules apply to plants produced in their farming operations. A taxpayer who makes the election must use an alternative depreciation method to compute depreciation on all farm property placed in service when the election is in effect.

The election may be made by a farming business, including a nursery, a sod farm or a farm engaged in the raising or harvesting of trees other than fruit and nut trees. Corporations, partnerships and tax shelters required to use the accrual method must use the uniform capitalization rules, even for crops with a preproduction period of less than two years (.75). See ¶25,344.

Income averaging

Wide variations in farm income can occur from year to year due to weather and other uncontrollable factors. To help mitigate the tax consequences of these income fluctuations, an individual engaged in a farming business may elect to average farm income over three years, allocating income from one year over the prior three years (.80). Schedule J is used to compute the tax under the farm income averaging method. The tax imposed in any tax year will equal the sum of the tax computed on taxable income, reduced by the amount of farm income elected for averaging plus the increase in tax that would result if taxable income for each of the three prior tax years were increased by an amount equal to one-third of the elected farm income.

Planning Note

CCH Analysts note that the income averaging election will not always be beneficial. For example, a farmer who had a high profit year after low-income years will benefit from averaging because farm income that would be taxed at the higher rate is shifted to a lower tax bracket for the prior years. In contrast, a farmer who consistently falls into the higher bracket would not be any better off by averaging farm income.

Income averaging requires the following calculations:

(1) Determine the amount of elected farm income, which is the amount of taxable income attributable to any farming business that is designated in the farmer's election;

(2) Calculate the tax for the election year on taxable income for the year less elected farm income;

(3) Add one-third of the elected farm income to taxable income for each of the three prior tax years and calculate the amount of tax for each year using the appropriate tax table or schedule;

(4) Add the results in (2) and (3) to arrive at the tentative tax on averaged farm income;

(5) Add together the actual tax reported for the three prior tax years to determine the total tax for the base period; and

(6) Subtract the result in (5) from the result in (4).

If the amount in step (6) is higher than the tax determined on Form 1040 without income averaging, then income averaging is not beneficial and should not be elected. If this amount is lower than the tax determined on Form 1040 without income averaging, then income averaging is beneficial and the lower tax should be reported on Form 1040. The election is made by attaching a Schedule J showing these computations to the taxpayer's return. The election can be made on a late or amended return, as long as the limitations period for filing a claim for credit or refund has not expired. An individual can also change the amount of elected farm income in a previous election or revoke a previous election if the limitations period for filing a claim for credit or refund has not expired for the election year (.85).

For purposes of income averaging, a farming business is defined in Code Sec. 263A(e)(4) as the trade or business of farming, including operating a nursery or sod farm, or the raising or harvesting of trees bearing fruit, nuts or other crops, or ornamental trees. Gain from the sale or disposition of property, other than land, that is regularly used for a substantial period in the farming business may be treated as elected farm income (.95).

The allocation of elected farm income among tax years applies for purposes of any election in a subsequent tax year. However, it does not require the recalculation of the tax liability of any other taxpayer, including a minor child required to use the tax rates of his or her parents under the Code Sec. 1(g) kiddie tax.

.05 Code Sec. 61(a), 162(a), 441, 446(b), and 471; Reg. §§1.61-4(a), 1.162-12, 1.441-1T, 1.446-1, and 1.471-6(a).
.10 Code Sec. 447(a) and (b).
.15 House Committee Report on P.L. 94-455.
.17 Code Sec. 447(a) and (b).
.20 Code Sec. 448(a)(3) and (b)(1).
.25 Code Secs. 464(c) Code Sec. 464(i)(4).
.30 Code Sec. 464(c) and (e).
.35 Rev. Rul. 88-60, 1988-2 CB 30.
.40 Rev. Rul. 60-191, 1960-1 CB 78.
.45 Rev. Rul. 74-145, 1974-1 CB 113
.50 Code Sec. 442; Reg. §1.442-1.
.55 Market Segment Specialization Program (MSSP) Audit Technique Guide for Grain Farmers (12-5-95).
.60 Code Sec. 447 and 471. IRS Letter Ruling 8245009, 7-30-82, CCH IRS LETTER RULINGS REPORTS.
.65 Code Sec. 447(g).
.70 Code Sec. 263A.
.75 Code Sec. 263A.
.80 Code Sec. 1301; Reg. §1.1301-1.
.85 Reg. §1.1301-1.
.95 Code Sec. 1301(b)(1)(B).

¶25,338 Crop Method of Computing Income. If an accrual-method or cash-method farmer produces crops (other than timber) that take more than a year from the time of planting to the time of harvesting, the income from the crops may be computed under the crop method with the consent of the IRS. Under this method, the entire cost of producing the crop must be deducted in the year the income from the crop is realized (.05).

The advantage of using the crop method is that it permits a farmer to deduct expenses attributable to the planting and growing of the crops in the year income is realized from the crops, thereby reducing taxable income for that year. However, the disadvantage of using this method is that a current expense may not be deductible until a subsequent tax year. Consequently, election of the method may be unwise if the farmer's income during the years the crops are planted and grown is sufficient to offset the related expenses.

> ***Example:*** Samuel Long is a farmer in Hawaii who uses the crop method of reporting. He planted a crop of sugarcane in the spring of 2003. He brought the crop under cultivation in the fall of 2004 and finally harvested and sold it for $10,000 in 2005. Under the crop method of accounting, Long may report the $10,000 and all his expenses for the crop on his 2005 income tax return.

A farmer (including a nursery operator) who does not compute income using the crop method may deduct the cost of seeds, young plants and shrubs purchased for growing to salable sizes in the tax year of purchase, regardless of when they are actually sold, provided the farmer or nursery operator follows a consistent practice of deducting such costs as an expense from year to year.

For use of the crop method of accounting for the cost of a new crop that replaces an involuntarily converted standing crop, see ¶25,385.

.05 Code Sec. 61 and 162; Reg. § §1.61-4, 1.162-12.

Farm Inventory Valuation

¶25,340 Choice of Methods. Like other taxpayers, a farmer who uses the accrual method of accounting may value inventories by either of the two common methods—cost or lower of cost or market (.05). These methods are explained at ¶15,625 and ¶15,640.

Cost under both methods includes the price of purchased animals and crops and the expenses of raising such crops or livestock. Consequently, the cost of a purchased, mature animal is its purchase price. The cost of animals born and raised on the farm is the expense of raising them to maturity. The cost of a purchased, immature animal is the sum of its purchase price and the expense of raising it to its present age or maturity.

The market value of purchased livestock, crops or other farm produce to be included in inventory is, under normal market conditions, the prevailing current bid price for the particular inventory item in the volume in which a farmer usually purchases the item. "Bid price" means replacement cost or the price a farmer would have to pay on the open market to purchase or produce the inventory item (.10). The market value of raised farm livestock, crops and other produce is based on the current price of feed and other supplies required to raise or produce the inventory item.

A farmer using either the cost or the lower-of-cost-or-market method may include livestock held for draft, breeding or dairy purposes in inventory, or capitalize their cost and cost recover or depreciate them. See ¶25,379. For rules covering the basis for gain or loss on the sale of such animals, see ¶25,402.

Because of the practical difficulty of determining cost of livestock and crops raised, however, two additional methods are permitted: (1) the farm-price method (¶25,342) and (2) the unit-livestock-price method (¶25,343).

.05 Code Sec. 471; Reg. §§1.471-1—1.471-4.

.10 *Thor Power Tool Co.*, SCt, 79-1 USTC ¶9139, 439 U.S. 522.

¶25,341 Accrual-Method Taxpayers. Generally, a farmer who uses the accrual method of accounting must maintain inventories (.05). However, this is not always the case. See "Growing crops," below.

A farmer who keeps inventories should maintain complete inventory records showing an inventory by actual count or measurement, as well as all the factors that have been used to value the inventory, such as quality and weight.

Items required to be included in inventory

A farmer's inventory must include:

(1) All harvested and purchased farm products held for sale or for feed or seed, such as grain, hay, ensilage, concentrates, cotton and tobacco. However, hay grown by a cattle raiser solely for feeding a herd is not required to be inventoried if the unit-livestock-price method of valuing cattle inventories is used. See ¶25,343.

(2) Eggs in the process of incubation (where a farmer is in the hatchery business).

(3) Raised or purchased livestock held for draft, breeding, dairy, or sporting purposes, unless a farmer capitalizes (and then depreciates) the cost of the livestock. A farmer who elects to use the unit-livestock-price method (see ¶25,343) must include all raised livestock in inventory. If livestock is included in inventory, no deduction may be taken for depreciation.

(4) Supplies, unless only small amounts are on hand.

Growing crops

Generally, farmers, nursery operators or florists who utilize the accrual method of accounting, and who are not subject to the provisions applicable to farming corporations requiring the capitalization of preproductive period expenses, need not inventory growing crops, trees, or plants (.10). The term "growing crops," however, does not include trees grown for lumber, pulp, or other products.

.05 Code Sec. 471; Reg. § §1.471-3—1.471-6.

.10 Sec. 352 of the Revenue Act of 1978 (P.L. 95-600); Rev. Rul. 79-102, 1979-2 CB 184.

¶25,342 Farm-Price Method. Under the farm-price method of accounting, each item, whether purchased or raised, is valued at the market price on the date of inventory less the estimated direct cost of marketing (disposition), such as expenses for freight, trucking or other transportation, broker's commission, feeding of animals en route, and handling (.05). Under normal conditions, market value is the prevailing current bid (selling) price on the date of inventory in the volume in which the item is usually purchased or sold by the farmer.

If a current bid price is unobtainable, the best available evidence of fair market value must be used. In such case, specific purchases or sales by the farmer or other persons may be used as evidence of fair market value. Local market prices are a determining factor, rather than the prices of some distant market.

Example: At the end of the year, a calendar-year farmer's inventory of produce raised for sale consisted of the following kinds and quantities, together with the market value per bushel:

Kind	*Quantity*	*Market value per bushel*
Produce raised for sale:		
Wheat	200 bu.	$ 3.00
Rye	100 bu.	2.10

The cost of marketing the wheat and rye is 20 cents per bushel at the end of the year.

The farmer's inventory of breeding cattle and livestock raised for sale consists of the following kinds and quantities, together with the average weight and market value per hundredweight of each animal:

Kind	*Quantity*	*Average weight per animal*	*Market value per cwt.*
Livestock raised for sale:			
1-year-old steers	300	500 lbs.	$ 100.00
1-year-old heifers	250	500 lbs.	90.00
Steer calves	600	300 lbs.	110.00
Heifer calves	350	300 lbs.	95.00
2-year-old steers	150	800 lbs.	120.00
Breeding cattle:			
Cows	500	800 lbs.	75.00
Bulls	20	1,000 lbs.	80.00

The cost of marketing the livestock and breeding cattle is $10.00 per hundredweight.

Accordingly, the farmer's total inventory value under the farm-price method is as follows at the end of the year:

Kind	*Quantity*	*Average value per bu. and per head*	*Total inventory value*
Produce raised for sale:			
Wheat	200 bu.	$ 2.80	$ 560
Rye	100 bu.	1.90	190
Livestock raised for sale:			
1-year-old steers	300 hd.	450.00	135,000
1-year-old heifers	250 hd.	400.00	100,000
Steer calves	600 hd.	300.00	180,000
Heifer calves	350 hd.	255.00	89,250
2-year-old steers	150 hd.	880.00	132,000
Breeding cattle:			
Cows	500 hd.	520.00	260,000
Bulls	20 hd.	700.00	14,000
Total inventory value			$ 911,000

If the farm-price method is used, it must be applied to the entire inventory with the exception of livestock that the farmer has elected to inventory under the unit-livestock-price method (see ¶25,343) (.10). Permission to change from the farm-price method to the unit-livestock-price method must be obtained from the IRS.

The opening inventory value must be used as the basis for computing the gain or loss on the sale of animals held for draft, breeding or dairy purposes. No adjustments are permitted for the costs incurred in raising the animals to maturity in the year of sale.

Chicken flocks are treated as livestock and may be valued under the farm-price method (.15).

.05 Code Sec. 471; Reg. §1.471-6(d); Farmer's Tax Guide, IRS Publication No. 225.

.10 Reg. §1.471-6(d).

.15 Rev. Rul. 75-37, 1975-1 CB 148.

¶25,343 Unit-Livestock-Price Method. The unit-livestock-price method of valuing inventories can be used only to value livestock raised, or livestock purchased before maturity and raised to maturity. Unit prices and classifications must be a reasonable estimate of the cost of producing the animal, and are subject to approval by the IRS upon an examination of the taxpayer's return. A taxpayer elects the unit-livestock-price inventory method by filing returns using the method (.05).

Raised livestock

Under the unit-livestock-price method, raised livestock is valued at standard unit prices depending on the age and the kind of the animal. Reasonable classifications of animals must be made so that the unit prices assigned to each class will reasonably account for the normal costs of producing the animals in that class. Thus, a cattle raiser should have age classifications for calves, yearlings, two-year-olds, and mature animals. It might also be wise to have separate classifications for steers, heifers, cows and bulls, and perhaps even a further breakdown into those held for sale, breeding, draft, and dairy purposes.

> ***Example 1:*** If it costs a cattle rancher about $100 to produce a calf and $150 a year to raise it to maturity, the following unit prices and classifications could be used: calves, $100; yearlings, $250; two-year-olds, $400; and mature animals, $550.

As its name implies, the unit-livestock-price method is generally used by livestock raisers. Where the operator of a slaughter plant that placed cattle in its own feed lots until they were slaughtered or sold consistently had used the unit-livestock-price method, the Tax Court held that the IRS could not require a change to another method (.10). Although the IRS agreed with the result in this case, it has ruled that it may refuse to allow the unit-livestock-price method to slaughter-plant operators that do not consistently use the method (.15).

Cattle raisers using the unit-livestock-price method do not have to inventory hay raised solely for feeding to the cattle (.20).

Purchased livestock

Purchased livestock must be included in inventory at cost. If an animal is immature when purchased, its cost must be increased each year by the amount added to the inventory in accordance with the established unit-livestock-price increases. But no increase will be made in the year of purchase if the animal is acquired during the last six months of the year.

> ***Example 2:*** Assume that the cattle rancher in Example (1) is a calendar-year taxpayer who purchased a calf for $125 on April 5 and another calf for $150 on August 23. These calves are included in the yearling inventory on December 31. The calf purchased April 5 is valued at $275 ($125 + $150 unit-livestock-price increase), and the calf purchased August 23 is inventoried at its $150 cost.

Option to capitalize and depreciate

A livestock raiser using the unit-livestock-price method can elect to remove from inventory after maturity an animal raised or purchased for draft, breeding or dairy purposes, and treat the inventoried cost of the animal as an asset subject to depreciation.(.25) Prior to 2002, this option to capitalize and depreciate was limited to purchased animals; raised livestock had to be included in the unit-livestock-price inventory, regardless of whether the animals were held for sale or for breeding, draft or dairy purposes (.30). Depreciation and the cost recovery of livestock are discussed at ¶25,379.

Change in method

The consent of the IRS is generally required to change the method of inventory valuation used. A taxpayer who has been using the farm-price method (see ¶25,342) must obtain the consent of the IRS before switching to the unit-livestock-price method. A taxpayer who has valued livestock inventory at cost or at the lower of cost or market, may change to the unit-livestock-price method without the IRS's consent. A taxpayer who has filed returns based on a constant unit-price method of valuing livestock inventories is considered to have elected the unit-livestock-price method (.35).

A taxpayer that elects to use the unit-livestock-price method must reevaluate unit prices each year and make any adjustments necessary to reflect increased or decreased costs. These annual cost-based adjustments do not require IRS approval, but the IRS must consent to any other changes in unit prices and classifications (.40).

.05 Code Sec. 471; Reg. §1.471-6(c)-(h); Farmer's Tax Guide, IRS Publication No. 225.

.10 *Auburn Packing Co., Inc.*, 60 TC 794, CCH Dec. 32,103 (Acq.).

.15 Rev. Rul. 74-505, 1974-2 CB 154.

.20 Rev. Rul. 74-527, 1974-2 CB 42.

.25 Reg. § 1.471-6

.30 *J. Catto*, SCt, 66-1 USTC ¶9376, 384 U.S. 102.

.35 Reg. §1.471-6(h).

.40 Reg. § 1.471-6.

¶25,344 Uniform Capitalization Rules. The uniform capitalization rules do not apply to costs (including interest) incurred in producing crops with a preproductive period of two years or less (.05). Animals are also exempt from the UNICAP rules (.10).

These exceptions to the uniform capitalization rules for taxpayers engaged in a farming business do not apply to entities (corporations, tax shelters, or partnerships) that are required to use the accrual method of accounting by reason of Code Secs. 447 or 448. The capitalization rules also do not apply to the costs that are attributable to the replanting, cultivation, maintenance, and development of any plants bearing an edible crop for human consumption that were lost or damaged while in the hands of the taxpayer by reason of freezing temperatures, disease, drought, pests, or casualty (see "Replacement of damaged crops," below).

For purposes of these rules, a farming business includes the operation of a nursery or a sod farm, or the harvesting or raising of fruit- or nut-bearing trees or ornamental trees—except for evergreen trees that are more than six years old when cut (e.g., Christmas trees). The raising or harvesting of Christmas trees and other excluded trees (e.g., timber) is exempt from the uniform capitalization rules altogether.

Caution

CCH Analysts note that the term "harvesting" does not apply to taxpayers that engage in contract harvesting of an agricultural commodity grown by another (.15).

Farmers not required to use an accrual method of accounting may elect to exclude crops with a preproductive period in excess of two years (.20). The election comes at a price. Deducted expenses are subject to recapture as ordinary income and any farming property placed in service while the election is in effect must be depreciated using the straight-line MACRS alternative depreciation system. See below, "Preproductive period expenses."

General capitalization rules

Generally, the uniform capitalization rules apply to the preproductive period costs of crops that have a preproductive period of more than two years and to livestock. Interest is subject to these capitalization rules.

Plants. For purposes of applying these rules, the preproductive period of plants is deemed to begin when seed is first planted or the plant first acquired by the taxpayer and to end when the plant either becomes productive or is sold. In the case of the crop or yield of a plant that will have more than one crop or yield, the preproductive period begins when the plant has become productive in marketable quantities and the crop or yield first appears in the form of a sprout, bloom, blossom, or bud. If a plant will have more than one crop or yield, the preproductive period includes only the period before the first marketable crop or yield. In the case of other plants (including the crop or yield of a plant that will have more than one crop or yield), the preproductive period is the period up to the time the plant is reasonably expected to be disposed of (.25).

The preproductive period of plants grown in commercial quantities in the United States is based on a nationwide weighted average, determined by the IRS using available statistical data. The following plants are considered to have a preproductive period in excess of two years: almonds, apples, apricots, avocados, blueberries, blackberries, cherries, chestnuts, coffee beans, currants, dates, figs, grapefruit, grapes, guavas, kiwifruit, kumquats, lemons, limes, macadamia nuts, mangoes, nectarines, olives, oranges, papayas, peaches, pears, pecans, persimmons, pistachio nuts, plums, pomegranates, prunes, raspberries, tangelos, tangerines, tangors, and walnuts. This list is not exclusive and is updated periodically. (.30).

For all other plants, at or before the time the seed or plant is acquired or planted the taxpayer must reasonably estimate the preproductive period of the plant. If the taxpayer estimates a preproductive period in excess of two years, the taxpayer must capitalize preproductive period costs (.35).

Animals. The period for which an animal's preproductive period expenses must be capitalized is determined by that animal's actual preproductive period. The preproductive period of an animal begins at the time of acquisition, breeding, or embryo implantation. For an animal that will be used in the trade or business of farming, such as a dairy cow, the preproductive period generally ends when the animal is or would be considered placed in service for depreciation purposes. For an animal that will have more than one yield (offspring), such as a breeding cow, the preproductive period ends when the animal produces its first yield. For any other animal, the preproductive period ends when the animal is sold or otherwise disposed of. For an animal that will have more than one yield, the costs incurred after the beginning of the preproductive period of the first yield but before the end of the preproductive period of the animal must be allocated between the animal and the yield on a reasonable basis; any depreciation allowance on the animal may be allocated entirely to the yield; and the taxpayer's allocation method is a method of accounting that must be used consistently (.40).

A taxpayer may use reasonable inventory valuation methods to compute the amounts that have to be capitalized in the case of plants and animals subject to the uniform capitalization rules (.45). The costs can be capitalized by using the current simplified inventory methods, such as the farm-price (see ¶25,342) or unit-livestock-price method (see ¶25,343) in lieu of "tracing" and accumulating costs applicable to each separate animal. For instance, farmers may use the unit-livestock-price method to account for the costs of raising livestock that will be used in the trade or business of farming even though the livestock is not inventory property (.50).

Certain persons and entities that are required to use the accrual accounting method must capitalize preproductive costs without regard to whether the productive period is more than two years. These are the farming corporations and farming partnerships with corporate partners who must use the accrual method and must capitalize preproductive period costs (.55) and tax shelters that must use the accrual method (.60).

Replacement of damaged crops

Taxpayers are allowed to deduct the costs of replacing crops for human consumption that are lost or damaged because of freezing, disease, drought, pests or other casualty so long as the replacement plants bear the same type of crop as was destroyed or damaged (.65). The land on which the replanting takes place does not have to be the same land on which the lost or destroyed plants were located, and the replanting can take place on any parcel of land of the same acreage located anywhere in the United States. This tax benefit can be claimed by any person who has a majority interest (more than 50 percent) in the plants that were affected by the casualty. It is also available to a person who has a minority interest and who materially participates in the planting, maintenance, cultivation or development of the plants during the tax year in which the replacement costs were paid or incurred (.70).

Preproductive period expenses

Certain farmers may irrevocably elect to disregard the preproductive period capitalization rules and claim current deductions for preproductive period costs of plants (.75). The election is made by not applying the UNICAP rules on the original return for the first tax year in which the taxpayer is otherwise required to capitalize section 263A costs. A taxpayer who does not make the election on the original return must obtain consent to make the election by filing Form 3115 (.80). It may be revoked only with IRS consent. If the election is made, gain from disposition of the product is recaptured (that is, taxed as ordinary income) to the extent of prior deductions that otherwise would have been required to be capitalized. In addition, the electing taxpayer or related person must use the alternative MACRS depreciation system (ADS) for all farm assets used in any farming business and placed in service in tax years for which the election is in effect. A taxpayer who fails to use ADS is not considered to have made the election on an original return.

Farmers who can make this election include producers of nursery stock and ornamental trees, and the traditional growers of agricultural crops. Farming corporations, partnerships with corporations as partners, and tax shelters cannot make this election if they are required to use the accrual method of accounting under Code Secs. 447 and 448. The election to deduct preproductive period costs is not available for any cost that is attributable to the planting, cultivation, maintenance or development of a citrus or almond grove that is incurred before the end of the fourth year after the year in which the trees were planted.

.05 Code Sec. 263A(c) and (d).
.10 Code Sec. 263A(d)(1).
.15 Reg. §1.263A-4(a)(3).
.20 Code Sec. 263A(d)(3).
.25 Reg. §1.263A-4(b)(2).
.30 Notice 2000-45, I.R.B. 2000-36, 256.
.35 Reg. §1.263A-4(b)(2)(i)(B).
.40 Reg. §1.263A-4(b)(2)(ii).
.45 Reg. §1.263A-4(c)(1).
.50 Reg. §1.263A-4(c)(1).
.55 Code Sec. 447 or 448.
.60 Code Sec. 448(a)(3).
.65 Reg. §1.263A-4(e).
.70 Code Sec. 263A(d)(2)(B).
.75 Code Sec. 263A(d)(3).
.80 Reg. §1.263A-4(d).

Special Income Sources

¶25,345 Gross Income from Farming. A farmer's gross income includes the cash or fair market value of property received from the sale, trade or exchange of livestock or farm products raised or purchased and resold by the farmer. It also includes such miscellaneous items as breeding fees and rent received for the use of teams, machinery or land (.05). Income from farming is subject to certain special rules and must be accounted for separately from other income.

An exclusion from gross income is provided for certain conservation grants (cost-sharing payments) received under specified programs (see ¶25,362). However, a farmer must generally include in gross income all subsidy and conservation payments received from the government, whether received in cash or materials.

Cash method

For a farmer on the cash method (¶25,337), gross income for the tax year includes:

(1) the amount of cash or the market value of merchandise or other property received from the sale or exchange of livestock and produce that were raised during the tax year or prior years,

(2) profits from the sale of livestock or other purchased items, and

(3) total receipts from all other sources, such as—

(a) agricultural program payments (¶25,356),

(b) breeding fees,

(c) commodity credit loans (if so elected) (see ¶25,354),

(d) crop insurance proceeds (cash or equivalent, but cash-basis farmers may elect to defer certain crop insurance proceeds or disaster payments) (see ¶25,385),

(e) machine work earnings,

(f) patronage dividends, rebates, or refunds (see ¶25,355), and

(g) rent received in crop shares if reduced to money or its equivalent.

Wheat Stabilization and Feed Grain Program payments are taxable on the cash basis when received or when made available by the Agricultural Stabilization and Conservation Service Committee, whichever is earlier (.10). However, if these items were consistently reported as income in the tax year of actual, rather than constructive, receipt, and such income reflects payments for two crop years, the farmer may, with the IRS's consent, report a pro rata portion of such income for each of 10 tax years, beginning with the year that reflects payments for two crop years (.15).

Accrual method

On the accrual method, gross income must be determined by reference to inventory valuations, accounts receivable, and other inventory-related income items (see ¶25,337). The items listed in (3), above, are included for the year in which the farmer is unconditionally entitled to receive them, irrespective of when they are actually paid.

Accrual-method farmers must treat inventory protection payments and first handler payments accrued under a cotton equalization program of the Commodity Credit Corporation as a reduction of inventory costs to the extent such costs include the cost of cotton giving rise to the payments. Any payment in excess of the cost of cotton is treated as an item of gross income (.20). See, also, ¶25,354, which discusses all Commodity Credit Corporation price support loans.

Destruction of crops

See ¶25,385.

Forced sales of livestock

Income from forced sales of livestock resulting from drought, flood or other weather-related conditions in an area designated for assistance by the federal government may be partially deferred until the next tax year. A farmer may elect to defer until the next tax year income from forced sales of livestock (other than that held for draft, dairy, breeding or sporting purposes, qualifying as property held in a trade or business) in excess of the number that would have been sold under the farmer's usual business practices. See ¶25,402 (.25).

Futures or options contracts

A farmer's trades in commodity futures contracts within the range of the farmer's production generally are considered hedges. A hedging transaction involves trading in commodities that are an integral part of the taxpayer's business itself for price-insurance purposes, rather than for speculative purposes. Therefore, any profit realized is ordinary income and any loss is deductible as a business expense (.30).

However, a futures contract will not serve as a hedging transaction unless it is designed to protect against (offset) a risk of loss. A contract in the long position (a contract to buy) cannot serve as a hedge against unfavorable movements in the price of a crop where the farmer has not attained a balanced (offsetting) position (.35).

Discharge of indebtedness

Income arising from the discharge of qualified farm indebtedness is treated in the same manner as the discharge of an insolvent taxpayer's debt, even if the farmer is solvent. Thus, realized income is excluded from the taxpayer's gross income, but the farmer's tax attributes and basis in qualified property are reduced.

However, the amount of income excluded cannot exceed the taxpayer's total tax attributes and basis in the qualified property. Income will be recognized to the extent of any excess (.40). Further, income from the cancellation of debt owed by an insolvent taxpayer on a Farmers Home Administration loan resulted in taxable income to the extent the excess of discharged indebtedness exceeded her negative net worth (.45). The discharged amount was not excludable as qualified farm indebtedness because less than 50 percent of her aggregate gross receipts for the three years prior to the year of debt discharge were attributable to farming.

.05 Code Sec. 61; Reg. §1.61-4.

.10 Rev. Rul. 65-97, 1965-1 CB 211; Rev. Rul. 65-98, 1965-1 CB 213.

.15 T. I. R. No. 762, 9/20/65.

.20 Rev. Rul. 88-95, 1988-2 CB 28.

.25 Code Sec. 451(e).

.30 Code Sec. 1256(e).

.35 *N. Patterson*, 41 TCM 807, CCH Dec. 37,658(M), TC Memo. 1981-43; *R. Day*, CA-8, 84-1 USTC ¶9475, 734 F2d 375.

.40 Code Sec. 108 and Code Sec. 1017.

.45 *M.A. Lawinger*, 103 TC 428, CCH Dec. 50,106.

¶25,346 Adjusted Gross Income. Net profit from farming (gross profit less allowable depreciation or cost recovery and other expenses or losses shown on Schedule F of Form 1040) is entered on Form 1040. It becomes a part of gross income, to be offset by any other losses or deductions allowable against gross income. It is only where the taxpayer has no other income and no other deductions attributable to a trade or business or to the production of rents or royalties that the net profit from farming is the same as adjusted gross income.

¶25,347 Barter Income. The fair market value of property or services received in exchange for a farmer's property or services is included in the farmer's gross income as ordinary income. For example, if a farmer helps a neighbor build a barn and receives a cow in payment for the work, the fair market value of the cow is ordinary income to the farmer.

¶25,348 Income Received in Crops. Income in the form of goods or commodities received is usually includible to the extent of fair market value (¶25,345 and ¶25,347). The principle does not apply, however, to rents received in crop shares. These rents must be reported by a taxpayer using either the cash or accrual method as income in the year in which the crop shares are reduced to cash or its equivalent (.05).

Conversion into cash or its equivalent occurs when the taxpayer/lessor sells or exchanges the crop shares for cash or other commodities, or uses the crops to feed livestock in the taxpayer's farming operation. The cash or value of the commodities received at such time represents rental income for income tax purposes reduced to cash or its equivalent (.10). The cash or value of the commodities received, minus any amount treated as compensation for personal services (up to 30 percent of the net rental income), is rental income at the time of conversion for income tax purposes (including the credit for the elderly) as well as for self-employment tax purposes (.15).

By using crop shares to feed breeding, draft or dairy livestock eligible for capital gain treatment (see ¶25,395), ordinary income is, in effect, converted to capital gain to the extent that capital gain is realized upon the sale of these animals. This can offer an advantage when the tax rate applicable to capital gain is lower than the tax rate applicable to ordinary income (.20). The taxpayer may claim a trade or business deduction for livestock feed at the same time and in the same amount as the gross rental income included in income. Even though the amount of the income inclusion and deduction generally cancel each other out for purposes of calculating taxable income and net earnings from self-employment, a taxpayer who uses the optional farm or optional nonfarm method to determine net earnings from self-employment (see ¶25,418 and following) must accurately calculate the amount of the income inclusion (.25).

Crop shares received as rent and donated to a charity represent rental income in an amount equal to their fair market value at the time of the contribution and not at the time the charity converts them to cash (.30).

☐ For a discussion of when rental income is subject to self-employment tax, see ¶25,418.

.05 Code Sec. 61; Reg. §1.61-4(a).

.10 Rev. Rul. 56-496, 1956-2 CB 17, as modified by Rev. Rul. 75-11, 1975-1 CB 27.

.15 Rev. Rul. 58-257, 1958-1 CB 9.

.20 Code Sec. 1.

.25 Rev. Rul. 75-11, 1975-1 CB 27.

.30 Rev. Rul. 63-66, 1963-1 CB 13, as modified by Rev. Rul. 75-11, 1975-1 CB 27; *C.G. Tatum*, CA-5, 68-2 USTC ¶9563, 400 F2d 242.

¶25,349 Gifts of Farm Property. The general rule is that a gift of property does not result in income to the donor, so the excess of the fair market value of the donated property on the date of the gift over the basis of the property to the donor is not taxable gain (.05). Thus, if a farmer paid $5,000 for land and gave it his daughter a few years later when it was worth $7,500, the $2,500 appreciation would not be taxable income to the father. For gifts of crop shares to a charity, see ¶25,348.

If a taxpayer makes a gift of an item that is no longer used in the taxpayer's business, the cost of the item is no longer a business cost. If livestock or farm products that are transferred as gifts are raised or grown in the year of the gift, the donor-farmer cannot deduct the costs. If part of the raising or growing occurred in earlier years, the costs and expenses incurred or paid in the year of the gift cannot be deducted (.10).

Like other taxpayers, farmers are entitled to a gift tax deduction for charitable contributions in cash or property (see FTG ¶20,260). A farmer who donates property to a religious, educational, charitable, scientific or literary organization, is entitled to deduct the fair market value of the property at the time of the donation (subject to reduction for certain interest paid or to be paid on indebtedness connected with the property) (.15).

Appreciated property

Special rules apply, however, to the donation of appreciated ordinary income property. If a farmer donates property that, if sold at its fair market value at the time of the contribution, would result in ordinary income or short-term capital gain, the contribution deduction is limited to the fair market value of the property, reduced by the amount that would have been treated as ordinary income or short-term capital gain if the farmer had sold the contributed property. In effect, this rule limits the allowable deduction to the farmer's basis in the contributed property.

Ordinary income property includes items held for sale in the ordinary course of a farmer's business, such as poultry, livestock, livestock products and crops. A cash-basis farmer who donates raised crops or produce to a charitable organization usually is not entitled to a charitable deduction because the fair market value of these items reduced by the amount of ordinary income that the farmer would have realized from the sale of such items is zero. (A farmer generally has a zero basis in raised crops and produce; thus, the amount realized from a sale of such items is equal to their fair market value.)

If a farmer donates purchased items held for sale in the ordinary course of the farming business, the charitable deduction is reduced by the amount that would have been ordinary income or short-term capital gain if the contributed property had been sold. If a farmer donates property used in the farming business that is subject to the recapture rules (see ¶25,405 and following), the charitable deduction must be reduced by the amount recaptured as ordinary income.

Special rules also apply in the case of the donation of appreciated capital gain property. Where a farmer donates to a charitable organization property that, if sold at its fair market value, would result in long-term capital gain, the amount of the contribution may have to be reduced by a percentage of the amount that would be capital gain, depending on the nature of the property (tangible personal property) and of the charitable organization (for example, private foundation). Property used in a farmer's trade or business (Code Sec. 1231 property), such as depreciable farm equipment, is treated as a capital asset. The charitable contribution deduction for such property is reduced by the amount that would normally have been recaptured as ordinary income had the property been sold at its fair market value. The amount of gain realized that would normally be recaptured as ordinary income is equal to the depreciation, cost recovery or amortization deductions claimed with respect to the property (.20).

Inventories

When a taxpayer uses inventories, costs paid or incurred in earlier years are reflected in the cost of goods carried in the opening inventory for the year in which the gift is made. An inventory adjustment must therefore be made at the time of the gift to reflect the removal from the business of the donated asset and its cost. The cost must be eliminated in order to counterbalance the reduction of income caused by removal of the goods from the business. Items of cost of the current year applicable to the property are not deductible by the donor, as is the case if inventories are not used (.25).

> ***Example 1:*** In 2004, Joan Black, a dairy farmer, bought 25 heifers for $200 each. Her cost of raising them in 2004 was $2,500. In 2005, she gave 10 of the animals to her son. Her cost of raising these 10 animals in 2005 was $1,000. Her cost of raising the remaining 15 animals in 2005 was $1,500. Her 2004 closing inventory for the 15 heifers is as follows, assuming she used the "Lower of Cost or Market" method in inventorying livestock:

On Hand Beginning of Year		Donated Animals Eliminated		On Hand End of Year	
Quantity	*Inventory Value*	*Quantity*	*Cost*	*Quantity*	*Inventory Value*
25	$ 7,500	10	$ 3,000	15	$ 7,000
Adjustment for donated animals					$ 1,000
Adjusted closing inventory					$ 6,000

The basis in the hands of the donee of a gift that has not been inventoried is the same as the basis in the hands of the donor—the cost that is not allowable to the donor as a deduction in the current year, plus items of cost that have not been deducted by the donor in prior years. In the case of property that has been inventoried, the basis in the hands of the donee is the last inventoried basis plus the current year's cost applicable to the gift. For the purpose of determining loss, the donee's basis is either this amount or the fair market value at the time of the gift, whichever is lower. If a gift tax is paid by the donor, the donee's basis may be increased by the amount of the gift tax but the basis may not exceed the fair market value of the property at the time of the gift.

> ***Example 2:*** Based upon the facts shown in Example (1), the basis of the 10 heifers in the hands of the donee is the sum of $3,000 ($2,000 cost + $1,000 2000 expenses) plus $1,000 (2003 costs), or $4,000.

.05 Code Sec. 170, Code Sec. 501, and Code Sec. 1011. *G.S. Champlin*, DC R.I., 48-2 USTC ¶9332.

.10 Rev. Rul. 55-531, 1955-2 CB 520, as distinguished by Rev. Rul. 63-66, 1963-1 CB 13.

.15 Rev. Rul. 70-15, 1970-1 CB 20; IRS Letter Ruling 8305075, 11-3-82, CCH IRS LETTER RULINGS REPORTS.

.20 Reg. §1.170A-4.

.25 Rev. Rul. 55-531, see .15, above.

¶25,350 Personal Use of Farm Products. The same principle that applies in the case of gifts of farm property (see ¶25,349) applies in the case of personal use of farm products by a farmer and the farmer's family. The value of the products is not income, and the expenses attributable to raising or producing them are not deductible (.05).

.05 *P.P. Sweeten*, 3 BTA 37, CCH Dec. 1030 (Acq.).

¶25,351 Crop Insurance Proceeds. Proceeds from insurance—such as hail or fire insurance—on growing crops are included in gross income to the extent that they are received in cash or its equivalent. Such amounts merely replace the income that the crops would have produced (.05). But if standing crops are purchased to replace destroyed standing crops, the involuntary conversion rules apply (¶25,385), and the income from the insurance proceeds can be postponed until the replacement crops are sold (.10). In such case, the resulting gain is normally recognized only to the extent that the amount realized from the conversion exceeds the cost of the replacement property, e.g., to the extent the insurance proceeds representing payment for the destruction of a standing crop of wheat exceed the purchase price of another standing crop of wheat or other similar harvested crop.

However, insurance proceeds used to cover costs of planting a new crop are not considered part of a cash-basis farmer's replacement property as they are for farmers using the crop method of accounting.

A cash-basis taxpayer who receives insurance proceeds as a result of damage or destruction of crops (including amounts received under the Agricultural Act of 1949, Title II of the Disaster Assistance Act of 1988, or Title I of the Disaster Assistance Act of 1989) may elect to include the income in the year following the loss if it can be shown that the income from the crops would have been reported in that year (.15).

Crop insurance proceeds include federal payments received as a result of drought, flood or other natural disaster that destroys, damages or prevents the planting of crops. Thus, the farmer may elect to include the payments in gross income for the tax year following the tax year of the destruction or damage (.20).

.05 Code Sec. 61; Reg. §1.61-4(c).

.10 Code Sec. 1033; Rev. Rul. 59-8, 1959-1 CB 202, as modified by Rev. Rul. 81-279, 1981-2 CB 163.

.15 Code Sec. 451(d); Reg. §1.451-6.

.20 Treasury Decision 8429, 8-25-92, amending Temp. Reg. § 1.451-6(a)(1) and removing Temporary Reg. §1.451-6T.

¶25,352 Credits for Gasoline and Special Fuels. Farm owners, tenants and operators are permitted to claim the federal excise tax paid on gasoline and special fuels used on a farm for farming purposes as a credit against tax liability on their annual income tax returns (.05).

The individual who buys or bears the cost of the gasoline or special fuels is entitled to claim a fuel tax credit on the annual income tax return (whether or not a return would otherwise be required) in a manner similar to that used for the credit for tax withheld on wages. The credits are computed on Form 4136, "Credit for Federal Tax Paid on Fuels." As in the case of the credit for tax withheld on wages, any excess gasoline or special fuels tax credits will be refunded or applied against estimated tax for the following tax year.

The credit taken for gasoline and special fuels taxes must be included in a farmer's income if the entire cost of the gasoline or special fuels (including federal taxes) was deducted as a business expense (.15). Otherwise, the farmer would receive a credit against income tax for an amount that was already deducted as a business expense. A farmer who uses the cash method of accounting includes the credit in gross income for the tax year in which the credit was claimed on a timely income tax return. An accrual-method farmer must include the credit amount in income for the tax year in which the gasoline or special fuel is used.

> ***Example 1:*** A cash-method farmer files his 2004 income tax return on March 1, 2005. He deducts the entire cost of gasoline used on his farm, but he also claims a credit for the federal excise tax on the gasoline used on his farm for farming purposes during 2004. The amount of the credit taken on his 2004 return must be included in his gross income for the calendar year 2005.

> ***Example 2:*** An accrual-method farmer files a timely income tax return for the calendar year 2004, on which she deducts her gasoline costs and claims a tax credit for the gasoline used on her farm for farming purposes during 2004. The amount of the credit attributable to gasoline used during 2004 is included in her gross income for 2004.

Gasoline or a special fuel is considered as "used for farming purposes" if it is used:

(1) by the farmer or any other person in connection with cultivating the soil or raising or harvesting any agricultural or horticultural commodity, including the raising of livestock, poultry, etc., on the farmer's own farm,

(2) by the farmer in handling, drying, packing, grading, or storing any agricultural or horticultural commodity in its unmanufactured state, but only if the farmer produced more than one-half of that commodity during the period for which the claim is filed,

(3) by the farmer in connection with the planting, cultivating, caring for, or cutting of trees, or the preparation (other than sawing into lumber, chipping, or other milling) of trees for market, but only if the planting, etc., is incidental to his farming operations, or

(4) by the farmer in the operation, management, conservation, improvement, or maintenance of the farm or its tools or equipment.

State taxes

State taxes on gasoline used in operating farm machinery or vehicles may be deducted as a farm expense. The cost of gasoline, fuel, and oil (excluding taxes) used by a farmer in the farming business is also deductible as a business expense.

.05 Code Sec. 4081 and 6420.

.15 Rev. Rul. 67-2, 1967-1 CB 13.

¶25,353 Alcohol Fuels Credit. Farmers who use alcohol as a fuel in their trade or business are entitled to claim (on Form 6478) an income tax credit of 60 cents for each gallon of alcohol rated 190 proof or greater and 45 cents for each gallon for alcohol that is at least 150 proof but less than 190 proof. The rates for ethanol (a particular type of alcohol), however, are 54 cents (190 proof or greater) and 40 cents (150 to 190 proof). To qualify for this credit (the straight alcohol credit), the alcohol generally may not be mixed with other fuels, but alcohol with denaturants added is not treated as a mixture. If alcohol purchased by a farmer at retail is placed in the vehicle's fuel tank by the seller, the seller may claim the credit; the farmer may not (.05).

An alcohol credit (mixture credit) is available for alcohol blended with gasoline or with other liquid fuels suitable for use in an internal combustion engine, provided that the farmer: (1) produces the mixture and sells it for use as a fuel directly to the user or to a buyer for resale to the user; or (2) uses it as a fuel in the farmer's own trade or business. The above rates apply to the alcohol (including ethanol) used in the mixture.

A 10-cent-per-gallon credit is available to eligible small ethanol producers on production of up to 15 million gallons per year of ethanol. Qualified ethanol fuel production is defined as alcohol produced by an eligible small ethanol producer and sold during the tax year to another person (the buyer) for use in the production of a qualified mixture in the buyer's trade or business (not including casual off-farm production), for use as a fuel in the buyer's trade or business, or for use for sale at retail by the buyer where such fuel is placed in the fuel tank of the retail purchaser by the buyer. The credit may also be claimed if the producer does not sell to a buyer but instead uses the ethanol for any of the above purposes.

Farmers who claim any of these alcohol fuel credits must include the amount of the credit in gross income in the tax year in which the credit is claimed (.10). Unused alcohol fuels credits may be carried forward for three tax years after the credit expires.

A farmer is not required to claim the credit. A farmer can change the choice made on a prior return to claim or not claim the credit by filing an amended return within the limitations period.

.05 Code Sec. 40.

.10 IRS Publication No. 378, "Fuel Tax Credits and Refunds."

¶25,354 Commodity Credit Corporation Loans. Generally, the receipt of a loan is not a taxable event because the borrower's repayment obligation cancels out the income from the loan. However, a nonrecourse crop support loan from the Commodity Credit Corporation (CCC) is more in the nature of a guaranteed sale because if the market price for the crop falls below the loan amount, the farmer can simply relinquish the crop to satisfy the loan. If the market price is higher than the loan amount, the farmer can sell the commodity and use the proceeds to repay the loan. Thus, the sale or relinquishment of the crop is normally a taxable event that produces income. Alternately, however, the farmer can elect to include the loan proceeds in income in the year the loan is actually received (.05).

If the farmer elects to include the loan in income when received, the receipt of the certificate of interest from the Commodity Credit Corporation (which the farmer takes to a bank for redemption) is not an event giving rise to taxable income. According to the IRS, it is the receipt of the actual loan proceeds upon presentation of that certificate that gives rise to taxable income (.10).

Gain and Loss

A farmer who pledges a commodity to the CCC as security for a loan and elects to include the face amount of the loan proceeds in income for that year realizes no gain or loss when the loan is repaid. Gain is realized only when the commodity is later sold for more than the certificate amount. The amount the farmer reported as income from the loan becomes the farmer's basis in the commodity; thus, sales proceeds in excess of the loan amount are included in income (.15).

If the farmer forfeits the commodity to the CCC in payment of the loan, the forfeiture is treated as a sale. If the farmer did not elect to include the loan proceeds as income in the year they were received, they are included in income for the year they are forfeited. If the farmer included the loan proceeds in income when received and the amount of the forfeited loan is less than the farmer's basis in the commodity, the difference can be reported as a loss (.20).

Making the election

A farmer makes the election by including on Schedule F, Form 1040, the amount of the loan as income in the year it is received. The farmer should attach a statement to the return indicating that the election has been made and showing the amount of the loan, the year the loan was received, the commodity on which the loan was received, and the quantity of the commodity. The election may also be made on an amended return filed within six months of the due date of the original return (excluding extensions). The farmer should write "Filed pursuant to section 301.9100-2" at the top of the amended return and attach a statement indicating the election is being made.

The Court of Appeals for the Fifth Circuit has held that a cash-basis farmer who elected to treat loans received from the Commodity Credit Corporation as income did not have to include in income loans that were received and repaid in the same tax year (.25). However, the Court of Appeals for the Ninth Circuit expressly refused to follow that Fifth Circuit decision, holding that a Commodity Credit Corporation loan transaction is analogous to a sale, with the receipt of the loan proceeds constituting the taxable event (.30).

Once an election is made to treat a Commodity Credit Corporation loan as income in the year in which it is received, the farmer must continue to follow this method for succeeding years unless the IRS grants permission to change to a different method of accounting. The farmer can obtain automatic consent to the change by attaching a Form 3115 to the timely filed (including extensions) original income tax return for the year of change. A copy of the application must also be filed with the National Office (.35). See FTG ¶15,655 for further discussion of automatic IRS consent to accounting method changes.

.05 Code Sec. 77 and 1016(a)(8); Reg. §§1.77-1, 1.77-2, 1.1016-5(e).

.10 Rev. Rul. 60-211, 1960-1 CB 35.

.15 Rev. Rul. 87-103, 1987-2 CB 41, revoking Rev. Rul. 87-17, 1987-1 CB 20; "Farmer's Tax Guide," IRS Publication 225.

.20 "Farmer's Tax Guide," IRS Publication No. 225.

.25 *F. Thompson*, CA-5, 63-2 USTC ¶9676, 322 F2d 122.

.30 *H.C. Isaak*, CA-9, 68-2 USTC ¶9598, 400 F2d 869.

.35 Rev. Proc. 2002-9, 1-7-01, I.R.B. 2002-3, 327.

¶25,355 Cooperatives' Patronage Dividends. A cooperative is an association in which a number of business people join together to buy products, sell products, or otherwise operate a business collectively. Farmers that buy farm supplies through a cooperative may receive income from the cooperative in the form of patronage dividends. Farmers that sell farm products through a cooperative may receive either patronage dividends or a per-unit retain certificate. Cooperative profits are shared on a patronage basis, not on the basis of equity ownership. A patron is any person with whom or for whom the cooperative association does business on a cooperative basis, whether a member or a nonmember of the cooperative association, and whether the person is an individual, a trust, estate, partnership, company, corporation or another cooperative association. Generally, a patron must either market a product through the cooperative or purchase items from it.

Cooperatives are generally taxed in the same manner as regular corporations except that they are allowed to take the following special deductions from gross income (.05):

(1) patronage dividends that were paid in money, qualified written notices of allocation or other property related to patronage occurring during the tax year;

(2) amounts that were paid in money or other property to redeem nonqualified written notices of allocation, and that were paid as patronage dividends during the payment period for the tax year in which the patronage occurred;

(3) per-unit retain allocations that were paid in money, qualified per-unit retain certificates, or other property (except nonqualified per-unit retain certificates) with respect to marketing (see material under "Per-unit retain certificates," below); and

(4) amounts paid in money or other property (except per-unit retain certificates) to redeem a nonqualified per-unit retain certificate that was paid as a per-unit retain allocation.

For tax purposes, these items are to be treated as items of gross income with a corresponding deduction.

All dividends that are deductible by cooperatives are included in the gross income of the patrons. An exempt cooperative may deduct both patronage and nonpatronage dividends. A nonexempt cooperative (taxable corporations operating on a cooperative basis) may deduct only patronage dividends.

An exempt cooperative's deductible nonpatronage distributions include amounts paid as dividends on capital stock and amounts paid out of earnings derived from business done for the United States or its agencies, or from other nonpatronage sources. An exempt cooperative may deduct such payments when paid in money, qualified written notices of allocation, or other property but not in nonqualified written notices of allocation.

Patronage dividends are amounts paid by the cooperative to its patrons under the following circumstances:

(1) The amount must be based on the quantity or the value of the business that was done with or for the patron.

(2) The cooperative must have been under an obligation to pay this amount, and the obligation must have existed before the cooperative received the amount that was paid to the patron.

(3) The amount paid must be determined by reference to the cooperative's net earnings from the business that it has done with or for its patrons.

Generally, in order to claim a deduction for patronage dividends, a cooperative must allocate such dividends to its patrons on the basis of the amount of patronage business done during the year of allocation. However, a nonexempt cooperative that allocated to its patrons patronage dividend income earned by them in prior years was permitted to deduct such patronage dividends because the stability of the cooperative's membership, the difficulty of tracing current patronage income to prior patrons, and the apparent approval of the cooperative's allocation method demonstrated that such allocation was equitable (.10).

A nonexempt marketing cooperative was permitted by the U.S. Claims Court to take deductions for patronage dividends paid to its members, even though only 24 percent of the cooperative's entire sales resulted from produce purchased from its members (.15). According to the IRS, an organization that conducts more than half of its business with nonmembers may still qualify for cooperative status (.20).

Netting of losses

A cooperative may, at its option, offset the earnings and losses of its various allocation units in computing its net earnings for the purpose of determining the amounts to be distributed or allocated to patrons (.25). However, losses that are attributable to one or more allocation units, including a loss that is carried over from another year, may be offset against earnings of one or more other allocation units only to the extent such earnings and losses are derived from business done with or for patrons. The offsetting of earnings and losses may also be used, at the cooperative's option, for computing its net earnings in determining the amount of patronage dividends to be paid or allocated to patrons. However, if a cooperative acquires the assets of another cooperative in a qualifying transaction, and exercises its option to offset earnings and losses, it may not thereafter offset losses of one or more of the allocation units of the acquiring units of the acquiring or the acquired cooperative against earnings of the acquired or acquiring cooperative to the extent that the earnings that are offset are not properly allocable to periods after the date of acquisition and such earnings and losses could not have been offset if derived from allocation units of the same cooperative.

A cooperative that exercises the netting option must inform its patrons in writing of the netting on or before the 15th day of the ninth month following the close of the tax year for which earnings and losses are netted.

Caution

CCH Analysts note that the IRS may consider a farm cooperative arrangement as a sham if the arrangement is organized to resemble a cooperative solely for the purpose of getting tax-favored cooperative status for its members. In determining whether a farming business is operated on a cooperative basis, the IRS considers whether the members are instrumental in generating the cooperative's income.

For instance, the IRS could not find the requisite membership involvement among poultry farmers who merged their production activities into a corporation (.30). Ostensibly, the corporation was created for the purpose of running the poultry operation on a cooperative basis. However, the arrangement was structured so that the farmers no longer participated in the poultry operations on a day-to-day basis. Consequently, the corporation was subject to tax at the corporate level on amounts distributed to the farmers.

Patrons and members of cooperative

Patrons (members of the cooperative and nonmembers doing business with it) are required to include in income the patronage dividends and the nonpatronage distributions in the year in which they are received, or, in the case of nonqualified distributions, in the year in which they are redeemed. The amount that the patron is required to include in income is the amount that is deductible or excludable by the cooperative—that is, the stated face amount of qualified allocations or the fair market value of other property. This rule does not apply to patronage dividends paid for purchases of personal, living, or family items, capital assets, or depreciable property, since they represent downward adjustments of the purchase price.

Patronage dividends paid in cash by exempt marketing cooperatives are taxable in full and are not entitled to the benefit of the dividend exclusion. Dividends on business purchases can either be reported as income or offset against the related purchase price.

Per-unit retain certificates

Per-unit retain certificates are issued on the basis of units of a product marketed for the patron—so much per bushel of corn, for example. The tax treatment of per-unit retain certificates is similar to patronage dividends.

There are two types of per-unit retain certificates, and the tax rules differ for each type. A qualified certificate is one issued to patrons who have consented to include the stated dollar amount of their per-unit retain certificates in current income. All other per-unit retain certificates are nonqualified certificates.

A patron who receives a qualified per-unit retain certificate is required to include its stated dollar amount in income in the year in which the certificate is received. On the other hand, a patron who receives a nonqualified certificate includes nothing in income for the year of receipt, but when the patron disposes of the certificate—by having it redeemed by the cooperative or by selling it to some other person—the amount received is included in income.

☐ The rules governing cooperatives, patronage dividends, and per-unit retain certificates are set out in further detail at ¶16,750 and following.

.05 Code Sec. 1382(b).

.10 *Kingfisher Cooperative Elevator Association*, 84 TC 600, CCH Dec. 41,997.

.15 *The Columbus Fruit and Vegetable Cooperative Association, Inc.*, ClsCt, 85-1 USTC ¶9314, 7 ClsCt 561.

.20 Rev. Rul. 93-21, 1993-1 CB 188, modifying Rev. Rul. 72-602, 1972-2 CB 510.

.25 Code Sec. 1388(j).

.30 Rev. Rul. 82-51, 1982-1 CB 117. See, also, *Mississippi Valley Portland Cement Co.*, CA-5, 69-1 USTC ¶9277, 408 F2d 827, cert. denied, 395 U.S. 944, 89 SCt 2015.

¶25,356 Agricultural Program Payments. Any payment received from the government—cash or the fair market value of materials—such as those for approved conservation practices must be included in income. However, see ¶25,362 for an exclusion for certain conservation grants. To the extent that materials received, such as lime or fertilizer, represent current expenses, they are offset by a corresponding expense deduction (.05).

However, if the material is used to increase productivity over a period of years, the offsetting deduction cannot be taken; instead, the "expenditure" must be capitalized and amortized over the years in which there is increased productivity. See, however, the election relating to the current deduction of expenses incurred for lime and certain other fertilizers at ¶25,372.

If any cash is expended for capital improvements, the expenditure is "recovered" through depreciation or amortization. Because the government payments are included in income, they do not reduce the basis for cost recovery or depreciation purposes. Also, if any of these capital expenditures do not "last" as long as anticipated, any remaining unamortized cost would be deductible.

Agricultural program payments to joint payees and agents are reported by the U. S. Department of Agriculture to the IRS as having been paid to the persons whose identifying numbers appear on the payment drafts. A payee of record who receives cash program payments actually belonging to others should attach Form 1099-G (Statement for Recipients of Certain Government Payments) to the income tax return to advise the IRS of the identity of the actual owners of the payments. Such information should also be furnished to the owners.

Cropland adjustment program payments received by a farmer must be included in gross income. Under the cash receipts and disbursement method, such payments must be included for the earlier of the tax year in which received or the tax year in which they are made available. Under the accrual method, the payments must be included for the earlier of the tax year in which they are received or the tax year in which a right to receive them arises (see ¶25,337).

Landowners, producers and tobacco quota owners who receive money from the National Tobacco Growers' Settlement Trust must report these payments as income each year. The payments compensate farmers for lost revenue due to decreased demand for tobacco and therefore constitute gross income taxable as ordinary income. Farmers in Alabama, Florida, Georgia, Indiana, Kentucky, Maryland, Missouri, North Carolina, Ohio, Pennsylvania, South Carolina, Tennessee, Virginia and West Virginia are receiving the payments over a 12-year period that began in 1999. A farmer who receives payments also receives a Form 1099-MISC each year, showing the payment amount to be reported as income. A farmer that produces a tobacco crop reports the payments as income from farming on Schedule F. A landowner or tobacco quota owner that leases tobacco-related property but does not produce the crop reports the payments as farm rental income on Form 4835 (.10).

.05 Code Sec. 61; Reg. §1.61-4.

.10 Internal Revenue News Release 2003-07, January 21, 2003; "Farmer's Tax Guide", IRS Publication 225.

¶25,357 Decedent's Income. The last tax year of a decedent is a short tax year that ends on the date of death. In general, the income of a decedent for the last tax year includes only those amounts that would be includible in a tax year not terminated by death (.05).

The return on behalf of a deceased farmer includes only income items, deductions, and credits that would be included under the farmer's normal method of accounting. Thus, if the decedent used the cash basis of accounting, crops or cattle raised and not sold are not income. Upon the subsequent sale of the crops or cattle by the executor or legatee, the stepped up basis rules (see ¶5180—¶5192) apply, and gain or loss is ordinary or capital, depending upon the type of gain or loss the decedent would have realized upon making the sale before death. If the decedent used the accrual method of accounting, the unsold crops and raised cattle are reflected in the increased inventory valuation at the date of death (the date used in lieu of the normal closing date).

In fixing inventory values at the date of death, care must be taken to follow the valuation method previously used by the taxpayer (that is, cost method, farm-price method, etc.). It is not sufficient merely to adopt the valuation made for estate or inheritance tax purposes, or to use other outside property appraisals.

.05 Code Sec. 691, Code Sec. 1014, Code Sec. 6012; Reg. §§1.691(a)-1—1.691(a)-3, 1.1014-1 and 1.6012-3.

¶25,358 Easements and Rights-of-Way. The granting of an easement or a right-of-way on a farm or ranch, such as for flooding land, laying pipelines, or putting up utility lines, may cause the farmer to realize taxable income or reduce the farmer's basis in the land. If the payment received represents compensation for lost income, it is included in income. Where the payment reduces basis, if only a portion of the property is affected by the easement and the basis for that portion is determinable, the amount received is offset against only that portion of the taxpayer's basis. If the easement affects the entire property or allocation of the basis is impractical, the payment reduces the basis for the entire property.

> ***Example:*** Colin owns a 600-acre farm with a basis of $60,000. He received $5,000 for an pipeline easement that affects only 20 acres of the farm. $2,000 of his $60,000 basis can be allocated to the 20 acres affected by the easement, so only $2,000 is offset against the amount received. Thus, Colin realizes a gain of $3,000 ($5,000 - $2,000) and his basis in the 20 acres is reduced to zero. If, however, the easement affected the entire property, none of the $5,000 payment would be included in income, and Colin's basis in the property would be reduced to $55,000. If Colin also received a $250 payment as compensation for damage done to growing crops while the pipeline was laid, the entire $250 would be taxable income because it would compensate him for anticipated profits.
>
> If Colin had sold a part of the farm land and he had held the land for more than 12 months, the resulting gain or loss would have to be included in a "Code Sec. 1231" comparison (see ¶25,394).

¶25,359 Payment Received in Year After Sale. The doctrine of constructive receipt, whereby income is charged to a taxpayer with the legal right to control the disposition of a transaction's proceeds or payments, may result in a cash-method farmer's income including items that have not yet actually been received, particularly in the case of year-end sales (.05). The farmer's request that the buyer delay payment for a sale does not take the transaction outside the constructive receipt doctrine and delay the taxation of the sale proceeds. However, if payment in the following year is a provision in the contract of sale, and the seller has consistently so contracted, the deferral of income may be permitted (.10). A deviation from such a consistent practice for even one year might result in later deferrals being held to be ineffective for tax purposes (.15).

No distortion of income occurred where a cash-method farmer sold cotton grown in one year under a valid and enforceable deferred payment contract calling for payment in the following year and the seller had no legal right to receive payment before the stipulated date (.20). Similarly, a farmer did not constructively receive income when he sold cattle to a marketing company because the sales contract legitimately provided that he would not be paid by the company until the company collected the proceeds from its resale of the cattle in the next tax year (.25). However, a cash-method cotton farmer was not entitled to defer the realization of income from the sale of his crops by a middleman (a cotton ginner) because the farmer had control over the disposition of the sale proceeds, and the middleman was merely the agent of the farmer (.30). Also, the entire income realized from the sale of cattle at an auction through a livestock market was recognized by the cattle breeder in the year of sale even though a portion of the proceeds was paid to the breeder in a later year (.35).

A deferred-payment contract between a marketing company and a cash-method farmer who retains ownership of the cattle until they are sold at auction and agrees to receive payment in a later year is a consignment. Thus, any gain realized by the marketing company upon the sale of the cattle must be recognized by the farmer in the year in which the proceeds are received by the marketing company and may not be deferred to the year the proceeds are actually received by the farmer (.40).

Proceeds received in January by a cash-method farmer under a deferred payment contract entered into with a cooperative before the delivery of the cotton in the prior year are includible in the farmer's gross income in the year received, even though, under a preexisting marketing agreement with the cooperative, he would have been entitled to an advance payment equal to the governmental loan on his cotton upon delivery (.45).

Payments received by a cash-method farmer for losses sustained as a result of cattle feed contamination may not be deferred (.50). The IRS states that the special disaster income deferral rule applies only when the losses were due to a natural disaster; contaminated feed does not qualify as such.

Arranging the contract

In arranging deferred payment contracts, care should be taken to execute the contracts before delivery of the crops in order to avoid control over a right to receive payment in the year of delivery. A provision should also be included stating that the contracts are nonnegotiable, nonassignable, or null and void if assigned, as a safeguard against the IRS argument that the marketing contract has a fair market value and should be taxed in the year that the contract is executed. A two-year deferred grain sale contract was considered to have a fair market value and such amount was includible in income in the year that the contract was executed where the grain was delivered to the grain elevator before the contract was signed, the seller's contractual rights were deemed assignable in the absence of evidence to the contrary, and local lending institutions would accept such contracts as collateral for loans (.55). Finally, the contract must make it clear that the buyer of the farmer's products is not acting as the farmer's agent when reselling the products.

.05 Code Sec. 451.

.10 Rev. Rul. 58-162, 1958-1 CB 234 (this ruling is limited to the fact situation stated therein and does not govern tax treatment for sales under contracts calling for payments in two or more tax years, T. I. R. No. 1264, November 29, 1973, distinguished by Rev. Rul. 70-294, 1970-1 CB 13, in which an opposite result was reached because the contract demonstrated that the relationship between the taxpayer and the livestock market was one of principal and agent); *J.D. Amend,* 13 TC 178, CCH Dec. 17,122 (Acq.).

.15 *M.J. Hineman,* DC Kan., 51-2 USTC ¶9403, 99 FSupp 582.

.20 *C.B. Schniers,* 69 TC 511, CCH Dec. 34,800; *J.H. Busby,* CA-5, 82-2 USTC ¶9443, 679 F2d 48.

.25 *H.C. Crimmins,* CA-8, 81-2 USTC ¶9576, 655 F2d 135.

.30 *B.E. Arnwine*, CA-5, 83-1 USTC ¶9179, 696 F2d 1102.

.35 Rev. Rul. 70-294, 1970-1 CB 13.

.40 Rev. Rul. 72-465, 1972-2 CB 233. But see *H. C. Crimmins*, CA-8, 81-2 USTC ¶9576, 655 F2d 135, involving a bona fide deferred payment contract sale of cattle to a marketing company in which the farmer's delayed recognition of gain from the subsequent sale to a third party until the proceeds were actually received by the farmer was upheld.

.45 Rev. Rul. 73-210, 1973-1 CB 211.

.50 IRS Letter Ruling 7807002, 9/15/77, CCH IRS LETTER RULINGS REPORTS.

.55 IRS Letter Ruling 8001001, 9/4/79, CCH IRS LETTER RULINGS REPORTS.

¶25,360 Pasture Income and Pasture Rental. If a farmer takes someone else's cattle to pasture and assumes responsibility for furnishing water, salt, and other related items for a fee, the income is reported as income from farming on Schedule F of Form 1040 (or on Form 1120 if a corporate farmer). But if a farmer only rents out the pasture land, the income is reportable as rent on Schedule E, Form 1040 (.05).

.05 "Farmer's Tax Guide," IRS Publication No. 225.

¶25,361 Prizes. Prizes won with respect to farm livestock or products at contests, exhibitions, and fairs are income. If received in cash, the amount received must be included in income. If received in produce or other property, the fair market value of the property received must be included in income (.05).

.05 Code Sec. 74; Reg. §1.74-1.

¶25,362 Cost Sharing Payments. An exclusion from gross income is provided for certain conservation grants received under the following programs: (1) rural clean water program, (2) rural abandoned mine program, (3) water bank program, (4) emergency conservation program, (5) agricultural conservation program, (6) great plains conservation program, (7) resource conservation and development program, (8) forestry incentive program, (9) small watershed program, and (10) state programs (including programs of U.S. possessions) where payments are made to individuals primarily for certain conservation or environmental purposes (.05).

The exclusion applies to the extent that the Secretary of Agriculture determines that the payment is made primarily for conservation or related purposes, and only to the extent that the Secretary of the Treasury (or a delegate) determines the payment does not substantially increase the annual income of the recipient. Thus, recipients of cost-sharing payments under the Colorado River Basin Salinity Control Program could exclude the payments from their gross income because the Department of Agriculture determined that the payments were made primarily for purposes of soil and water conservation, protecting or restoring the environment, or providing a habitat for wildlife (.10).

Consistent with the exclusion from income, the taxpayer may not claim a current deduction, depreciation, amortization, depletion or the investment credit for the excluded amount. Further, the basis of any property acquired or improved with such payments is not increased to reflect the amount of the payments.

Ordinary income must be recaptured if the property or improvement purchased with the payments is disposed of before the expiration of 20 years. The amount to be recaptured is reduced by 10 percent per year after the first 10 years. See ¶25,412.

A farmer may elect not to apply the exclusion rules within the time for filing an income tax return for the tax year (including extensions), for the year in which the payment was received, or the year the payment was accrued.

.05 Code Sec. 126; Temporary Reg. §§16A.126-1 and 16A.126-2.

.10 U.S. Department of Agriculture Notice of Determination, 10-24-90.

Special Farming Deductions

¶25,363 In General. Because farming is a business, all ordinary and necessary expenses incurred in the farm business are deductible. The deductibility of an expenditure may be affected by the type of business organization adopted (sole proprietor, partnership, or corporation). Operating losses, bad debts, and rental expenses (except where paid in crop shares) are all deductible. The following is a partial listing of typical farm expenses that are currently deductible (.05):

(1) Ginning
(2) Farm organization dues
(3) Trucking
(4) Tenant house expenses
(5) Labor hired
(6) Feeds purchased
(7) Feed grinding
(8) Seed and plants purchased
(9) Machine hire (threshing, silo filling, combining, etc.)
(10) Supplies (barrels, bags, twine, etc.)
(11) Minor maintenance repairs (of buildings other than dwellings, machines, fences)
(12) Breeding fees
(13) Fertilizers and lime
(14) Terracing land
(15) Soil and water conservation
(16) Veterinary and medicine
(17) Gas and oil for farm work
(18) Storage and warehousing
(19) Taxes
(20) Insurance, except on dwelling
(21) Interest on farm debt
(22) Water, electricity and telephone
(23) Rent of farm, pasture, etc.
(24) Freight, yardage, express trucking
(25) Small tools with a life of 1 year or less
(26) Office supplies and stamps
(27) Travel expense (farm share)
(28) Advertising of farm products
(29) Auto upkeep (farm share)
(30) Spraying materials

The costs of constructing such items as tanks, reservoirs, dams, and ditches during the preparatory period of a farm, orchard or ranch are generally capital in nature and, therefore, nondeductible as ordinary business expenses, but such costs are recoverable or depreciable.

Note: Under the American Jobs Creation Act of 2004, a new deduction is allowed for certain U.S. production activities (.10). This new provision applies to tax years beginning after December 31, 2004. It appears that some farming operations (i.e., those that involve "production activities") will qualify for this deduction. The IRS is expected to spell-out the details in future regulations.

The IRS generally treats a repair as a capital expenditure rather than a business expense if the repair adds to the value of the property or appreciably prolongs its useful life (.15).

However, the costs of constructing earthen dams and ditches for conservation purposes are eligible for a current deduction as soil or water conservation expenditures if consistent with a conservation plan approved by the USDA or a state agency (¶25,369). Expenditures made by a farmer for repairs to a dam and reservoir located on his farm were deductible as ordinary and necessary business expenses and were not capital expenditures where the purpose of the repairs was to return such items to the condition they were in before water seepage occurred (.20). Although the repairs increased the capacity of the dam and reservoir and increased their value and prolonged their use, the court employed a subjective rather than an objective test in determining the deductibility of the expenditures. In other words, the court placed the most emphasis on the actual purpose for which the repairs were made.

Interest on notes and mortgages

Interest on farm notes and mortgages is a deductible business expense, but interest allocable to indebtedness on a farmhouse is allowed only as an itemized deduction on Form 1040.

Rent and utilities

Rent and water, electricity, and telephone costs are deductible to the extent allocable to farm purposes, as opposed to personal use.

Rent for the farm, part of the farm, or pasturage paid in cash is deductible, but rent paid in the form of crops or other farm produce is not, although the expense of raising them may be deducted.

Personal expenses—Allocation between business and personal expenses

Normally, no deduction is allowed for personal, living, and family expenses. These include rent and insurance premiums paid on property used as a farm residence, premiums on life insurance for the farmer or the farmer's (unless the insured individual is employed by a farm corporation), the cost of maintaining automobiles or horses for personal use, allowances to minor children, attorney's fees and legal expenses incurred in connection with personal matters, household expenses, and personal effects. Likewise, the cost of purchasing or raising produce or livestock consumed by the farmer or the farmer's family is not deductible. Allocation between business and personal expenses is frequently made in connection with some of these expenses since some qualify as business expenses and are deductible to that extent.

> ***Example 1:*** On June 1, Brown purchased 10 shoats (young hogs) for resale. On December 1, Brown sold 8 of them and had the other 2 slaughtered for family consumption. Brown's expenditures for purchasing, raising and fattening the 10 hogs were:

1.	Purchase cost	$ 750
2.	Corn and other feed purchased-fed to the 10 hogs	200
3.	Hired labor for raising the crops which were fed to the 10 hogs	400
4.	Machinery expense in harvesting the crops which were fed to the 10 hogs	40
5.	Gasoline expense in using tractors for cultivating crops that were fed to the 10 hogs	50
6.	Rent for pasturage for the 10 hogs	40
7.	Vaccinations	50
	Total	$ 1,530

> Since ⅕ (2 of 10) of the hogs were slaughtered for family use, ⅕ of these expenditures may not be deducted by Brown on his return.

A farmer may not depreciate or obtain a depreciation deduction for the farmer's dwelling or charge to business expense the household costs allocable to personal use (.25). The fact that a residence is used for the farm bookkeeping and other incidental business purposes does not justify a deduction for rental, depreciation, or miscellaneous operating expenses. In addition, no deduction is allowed for any expenses attributable to the use of the taxpayer's home for business purposes except to the extent that they are attributable to a portion of the home used exclusively and on a regular basis as the taxpayer's principal place of business or as a place of business used by customers to meet or deal with the taxpayer in the normal course of business.

Planning Note

CCH Analysts note that generally, no deduction is allowed for a farmer's personal, living, and family expenses. However, a farm employee who resided on his employer's farm at all times was permitted to exclude the value of his lodging and utilities from his income, even though his employer was his wholly owned farm corporation, because the lodging had to be accepted as a condition of his employment (.30). The farming operation (which consisted of breeding and farrowing sows and planting, cultivating, harvesting, drying, storing, and selling corn and soybeans) was sufficiently complex to require constant monitoring and attention. The farm employee established that it was unlikely that a farmer would maintain such an operation on its premises without having a resident manager overseeing the farm activities. Also, because the farm employee's lodging facilities were used in the corporation's business, i.e., as a residence for its manager, the corporation could deduct depreciation and utility expenses related to the residence.

Car and its operating costs

The cost of a car is capital in nature and, therefore, not currently deductible. Car operating expenses, such as for gas, oil, grease and repair parts, and other similar costs, are deductible if the vehicle is used entirely for farm purposes. If it is also used for personal travel, certain restrictions as to previously taken depreciation or cost recovery deductions apply. Essentially, when a farmer places in service and uses an automobile or other transport property over 50 percent for business purposes in a tax year and, in a subsequent tax year, the property is no longer used predominantly for business purposes, all or part of any depreciation or cost recovery deductions must be recaptured as ordinary income (.35). For further details, see ¶8110.

A farmer must substantiate car expenses by adequate records (.40) in order to ensure IRS acceptance of deductions or credits for those expenses. A farmer who uses property for both business and personal purposes should carefully document or record the business use of the property. Vehicles that are generally not susceptible to personal use, such as tractors and combines, are exempt from the adequate recordkeeping requirements.

A farmer may use "adequate records" or "sufficient evidence" to substantiate business use of cars and pick-up trucks. Sufficient evidence can include oral substantiation of a business use. However, the IRS may discount or reject totally evidence that has little or no probative value. The farmer's tax return must also provide information regarding the total number of miles the car or truck was driven; whether the vehicle was available for personal use, and if so, the percentage of the total use that was personal; and whether there is written substantiation of any car-related credits or deductions claimed on the tax return.

Equipment expenses

Expenditures for durable or permanent equipment are capital expenses. Where a period of useful life is one year or less—that is, where the asset is worn out and discarded within one year of its purchase—the entire cost is deductible for that year. However, tractors, plows, threshing machines, milking apparatus and other large tools are capital items, the costs of which are recoverable through cost recovery or depreciation (see ¶25,377).

□ As to the tax treatment of the cost of repairs, see FTG ¶7396. For a discussion of the tax treatment of farm equipment leases—particularly the rules relating to financed, leveraged, and fixed price-purchase option leases—see FTG ¶7388.

Expensing election

Farmers may elect under Code Sec. 179 to treat the cost of qualified property placed in service as a currently deductible expense rather than as a capital expenditure. The annual dollar limitation on the aggregate cost that may be expensed under this election for tax years beginning in 2004 is $102,000. See ¶9130.

Travel expenses

The expense of travel incurred in connection with farm business is deductible. However, travel or other expenses incurred while investigating the desirability of establishing a farm or livestock business are not deductible (unless the taxpayer can allocate them to some other business), since the taxpayer is not engaged in that trade or business during the tax year (.45). See FTG ¶8220.

Farm labor

Wages paid to hired farmhands are deductible. Items purchased for board and lodging for hired labor or furnished to sharecroppers and salaries paid for household work in boarding and housing farm laborers are deductible, but the portion of the payments expended in connection with the farmer's own household is nondeductible. An employer may not deduct the rental value of living quarters furnished to employees if the employer charges no rent, but the employer can depreciate the portion of the building that is used to provide the quarters, along with a proportionate part of other related maintenance expenses. Similarly, the value of farm products used in providing board and lodging for employees is not deductible, but the expense of raising the products is deductible.

Insurance premiums

Most types of insurance premium payments are deductible if they are incurred in connection with the taxpayer's trade or business, as opposed to being personal in nature. Premiums on fire, storm, crop, theft, and other casualty insurance on farm business items or assets (exclusive of the farmer's dwelling) are deductible on Schedule F as business expenses. Deductions can also be claimed on Schedule F for health and accident insurance premiums the farmer pays for employees.

The deductibility of life insurance premiums for the farmer and the farmer's family may depend on the form of the farm business. A farmer doing business as a sole proprietor or partner generally cannot deduct such insurance expenses since they are considered personal in nature (although certain group insurance policies are a notable exception). However, a farm corporation is generally a separate entity for tax purposes, even if it is controlled by one person. Thus, it may deduct the cost of insurance premiums for its employees (including the shareholder-farmer) provided the premiums are an ordinary and necessary business expense for the corporation, the employer is not directly or indirectly a beneficiary under the insurance policy, and the premiums and other compensation constitute reasonable payment for services rendered.

When insurance premiums are paid in advance, the deductible premiums are limited to the portion allocated to the taxpayer's current tax year. The balance is apportioned and deducted in the later years covered by the insurance policy. This is true whether the farmer uses the cash or the accrual method.

> ***Example 2:*** A farmer pays a fire insurance premium of $3,000 on her barn on July 1 of Year 1, with the policy covering a period of three years beginning on that

date. Only the portion applicable to the last 6 months in Year 1 is deductible as an insurance expense on her return for Year 1. The amount deductible is $500, which is 6/36 of $3,000 (6 months of the 36-month premium). The farmer may then deduct $1,000 (12/36 of $3,000) in Year 2 and $1,000 in Year 3. The remaining $500 is deductible in Year 4. If the policy took effect on January 1 of Year 1, the deductible expense would be $1,000 for each of Year 1, Year 2 and Year 3, based on the use of one-third of the premium each year.

Taxes and assessments

State and local taxes are generally deductible from income, either on Schedule F (Form 1040) as farm expense or on Form 1040 as personal taxes paid by the farmer. However, farmers may not deduct state sales tax that they have paid in connection with the purchase of farm equipment (even though the tax is separately stated and charged to them on the purchase invoice) whenever their state law imposes such a sales tax on the seller of farm equipment, who, in turn, merely passes the tax cost on to the purchaser. In such cases, the state sales tax must be treated as a cost of acquiring a capital asset so that the purchasing farmer must capitalize rather than expense the sales tax paid—regardless of how the transaction is structured (.50).

Property taxes on the farmland, machinery, livestock and other production items are deductible as farm expenses. However, special taxes and assessments, such as assessments for levee drainage and certain irrigation taxes, are not deductible if they increase the value of the property against which they are assessed (but see ¶25,369).

Where an irrigation district assesses farm property for the purpose of purchasing water from an irrigation project, the assessment is not deductible as a tax, but the portion of such assessment attributable to operation and maintenance, administration, and water purchase costs is deductible as a business expense (.55).

.05 Code Sec. 162; Reg. §1.162-12.

.10 Code Sec. 199, as added by the American Jobs Creation Act of 2004 (P.L. 108-357).

.15 Reg. §1.162-4.

.20 *S.C. Evans*, CA-5, 77-2 USTC ¶9596, 557 F2d 1095.

.25 *J. Frazier*, 49 TCM 715, CCH Dec. 41,875(M), TC Memo. 1985-61.

.30 *J. Grant Farms, Inc.*, 49 TCM 1197, CCH Dec. 42,016(M), TC Memo. 1985-174.

.35 Code Sec. 280F.

.40 Code Sec. 274(d).

.45 *G.C.W. Westervelt*, 8 TC 1248, CCH Dec. 15,850.

.50 *G.W. Maack*, 45 TCM 553, TC Memo. 1983-37, CCH Dec. 39,840(M).

.55 Rev. Rul. 67-337, 1967-2 CB 92.

¶25,364 Wages Paid to Family Members. While the value of services gratuitously performed by members of a farmer's family cannot be deducted, wages actually paid to the farmer's children or spouse for farm work are deductible to the extent that the payments are reasonable and so long as a true employer-employee relationship exists (.05). Wages paid to the farmer's child are included in the child's income and may result in the child's having to file an income tax return. The child's use of the money to purchase clothes or to buy other necessities that a parent is normally obligated to furnish does not prevent the farmer from deducting the wages. However, if the child provides at least half of his or her own support, the child would not qualify as a dependent of the parent. The value of meals and lodging furnished to a minor child is not deductible as wages, since a parent is legally liable for the child's support and, therefore, such cost is a personal expense (.10).

.05 Rev. Rul. 72-23, 1972-1 CB 43.

.10 Rev. Rul. 73-393, 1973-2 CB 33, superseding Rev. Rul. 59-110, 1959-1 CB 45.

¶25,365 Operating Losses. Losses incurred in the operation of a farm are deductible in the same manner as any other net loss from a business. Generally, a loss sustained from a farm operated for profit may be deducted from the farmer's gross income from all other sources (.05). (However, see the discussion on at-risk loss limitations at ¶10,200.) The farm loss then appears as a minus item in a computation of net farm profit on Schedule F (Form 1040) and is also entered on Form 1040 as a minus item. See ¶25,422 for a discussion of passive farm losses.

Shrinkage

If farm products are stored, no loss deduction is allowed for shrinkage in weight or for deterioration. If a farmer keeps inventories, these losses are reflected by the reduced amount of the product included in the inventory.

.05 Code Sec. 165; Reg. §1.165-6.

¶25,366 Feed Prepayments. As a general rule, farmers may deduct prepaid expenses, such as those for rent or insurance, ratably only over the period to which they apply (.05). However, for cash-method farmers, advance purchases of feed or other supplies may be restricted as a current deduction (see below). Accrual-method farmers reflect the cost of the extra supplies in a higher ending inventory (.10).

In order to obtain an advance deduction for prepaid feed and other supplies, a cash-method farmer must pass the following tests (.15):

(1) the expenditure must be a payment and not a refundable deposit;

(2) it must be made for a business purpose and not merely for tax avoidance; and

(3) the deduction must not materially distort income.

Test 1: Payment v. refundable deposit

The IRS noted the following factors as evidence, though not necessarily conclusive, that a payment represented a refundable deposit rather than an advance payment: (1) the absence of specific quantity terms; (2) the right to a refund of any unapplied credit at termination of the contract; (3) the treatment of the expenditure as a deposit by the seller; and (4) a provision permitting substitution of other goods or products for the feeds specified in the contract.

The Court of Appeals for the Eighth Circuit (.20) has placed the most emphasis on a deposit's refundability. It ruled that a nonrefundable deposit was actually a deductible prepayment from the cash-basis taxpayer.

The Court of Appeals for the Fifth Circuit has held that a cash-basis farmer's substantial year-end prepayments to his wholly-owned supplier for specific quantities of fertilizer and herbicides was not a currently deductible business expense because those quantities bore little relationship to items actually charged against the farmer's account, and the farmer could have refunded the prepayments to himself (.25).

Test 2: Business purpose v. tax avoidance

Under test 2, a payment is more likely to qualify as a deductible prepayment rather than a refundable deposit if it is intended to produce some business benefit, such as to fix maximum prices, secure an assured feed supply, or obtain preferential treatment over other customers. Business purpose is a question of fact. Generally, if an expenditure is appropriate and helpful to the taxpayer's business, the courts are reluctant to override the taxpayer's judgment as to when the expense should paid. The fact that a farmer also receives tax benefits from prepaying an expense does not mean the farmer lacked a business purpose for the prepayment.

In order for a prepayment to serve a business purpose, it generally must be a binding contract to acquire particular goods (.30). If the prepayment is refundable or can be used for other goods or expenses, it probably is a deposit rather than a deductible prepayment. For instance, advance payments for cattle feed were nondeductible deposits because the prepayment did not give the taxpayers any price advantage or preferential treatment, and they could receive refunds of credit balances in their feed accounts (.35). Similarly, a farmer's purported prepayment for fertilizer was actually a nondeductible deposit because he was not obligated to take delivery of the fertilizer and he had the option of using the balance in his fertilizer account to purchase other items (.40).

Test 3: Material distortion of income

Some of the factors to be considered in connection with the material distortion-of-income test are: (1) the useful life of resulting assets during and beyond the tax year paid; (2) the amount of the expenditure in relation to past purchases; and (3) comparison of the taxes paid by a taxpayer consistently deducting prepaid feed costs over a period of years with the taxes that would have been paid had the same taxpayer consistently not paid in advance. However, the distortion-of-income test should be considered in light of the following:

(1) The language of Reg. §1.162-12(a) unconditionally permits current deduction for the costs of raising livestock: "[t]he purchase of feed and other costs connected with raising livestock may be treated as expense deductions insofar as such costs represent actual outlay. . ."

(2) The U.S. Supreme Court has stated that farmers have been given the option of using a method that could, and probably would, materially distort income: "It is clear that application of the cash method of accounting to sales of breeding livestock would substantially distort the economic picture of the respondents' ranching operations. The sacrifice in accounting accuracy under the cash method represents an historical concession by the Secretary and the Commissioner to provide a unitary and expedient bookkeeping system for farmers and ranchers in need of a simplified accounting procedure" (.45).

(3) Courts have tolerated prepayment deductions that can distort income. The Tax Court has held that "a substantial legitimate business purpose satisfies the distortion of income test" (.50). The Court of Appeals for the Tenth Circuit has ruled in favor of a cash-basis farmer on the question of whether or not a material distortion of income would prevent deduction of a feed prepayment (.55).

The U.S. Court of Appeals for the Fifth Circuit may have summarized best the judicial attitude toward the "distortion-of-income" test when it stated that some distortion may be warranted (and even inevitable) depending upon the authorized method of accounting employed by the farmer—particularly where a "prepayment is in line with normal business practices and is not unreasonable" (.60).

Expected consumption period

The expected consumption period at the time of purchase, rather than the actual consumption period, controls the deductibility of feed prepayments (.65). Thus, a deduction by a cash-basis farmer for the purchase of a one-year supply of feed was allowed even though the actual consumption period extended over more than one year (payment was made in December and feed was exhausted in the beginning of the second tax year following the year of purchase) because of weather and economic conditions—these were considered to be "legitimate business purposes."

Moreover, the IRS's argument that the cost of cattle feed had to be capitalized over the period used was rejected. Cattle feed is not considered an asset having a useful life extending substantially beyond the close of a tax year. Its character is that of an inventory item that is reduced when consumed by cattle, and its cost becomes part of the cost of goods sold (the cattle sold). It is a product cost that varies with the magnitude of the production process, and its consumption does not rest upon the mere passage of time as is the case with period costs, such as overhead. Although cattle feed is akin to an inventory item, cash-method farmers are not required to use inventories to reflect the cost of such feed (.70).

Farming syndicates

Farming syndicates are required to capitalize amounts paid for feed, seed, fertilizer, or other similar farm supplies and are allowed to claim deductions for these items only in the tax year in which the feed, seed, fertilizer or other supplies are actually used or consumed or, if later, in the tax year when the item is allowable as a deduction under the syndicate's accounting method.

Farming syndicates come within the definition of "tax shelters" (see ¶15,210) and, therefore, they must use the accrual method of accounting (.75). As a result, the timing of their deductions is determined under the rules for accrual-method taxpayers (see ¶25,337). However, it appears that the costs of feed, seed, fertilizers and supplies on hand at the end of a tax year, because consumption or use was prevented by fire, storms, floods, or other casualties, or by drought or disease, are deductible in that year (.80).

Farming syndicate defined. For purposes of these prepaid farming expense rules, "farming" means the cultivation of land, or the raising or harvesting of any agricultural or horticultural commodity (.85). This includes the raising, shearing, feeding, caring for, training, and management of animals. With regard to trees, however, only those bearing fruit or nuts are treated as agricultural commodities. Hence, a syndicate raising livestock, fish, poultry, bees, dogs, flowers, vegetables, etc., is engaged in farming.

A farming syndicate is a partnership or any other enterprise (not including a corporation that does not elect S corporation status) that is engaged in the trade or business of farming if:

(1) any interests of the partnership or enterprise have been offered at any time for sale in an offering that is required to be registered with any federal or state agency that regulates security sales, or

(2) more than 35 percent of the losses during any period are allocable to limited partners or limited entrepreneurs (i.e., an investor who does not actively participate in the management of the farming enterprise).

An individual who has an interest in a farming partnership or enterprise is not treated as a limited partner, or as a limited entrepreneur if:

(1) the interest is attributable to the individual's active participation in the management of a farming business for at least five years;

(2) the individual lives on the farm where the business is conducted;

(3) the individual actively participates in the management of a business involving the raising of livestock (or is so treated under (1) or (2)), and the partnership or enterprise further processes the livestock raised in that business; or

(4) the individual is a member, or a spouse of any such member, of the family of a grandparent of an individual who is not treated as a limited partner or limited entrepreneur in situations (1) through (3), above.

Certain cash-basis farmers

Cash-basis farmers may be limited in their current deductions for prepaid farm supply expenses. Prepaid supplies expenses that exceed 50 percent of the total deductible farming expenses (excluding prepaid supplies for the current tax year) may be deducted only in the year in which the supplies are actually used or consumed (.90). For purposes of the 50-percent test, expenses include farm business expenses, interest and taxes paid, depreciation on farm equipment and other deductible expenses. However, if either of two exceptions is met, the prepaid supplies are deductible even though they exceed 50 percent of the total deductible farming expenses for the tax year (.95). First, the supplies expense are currently deductible if the total prepaid supplies of a farm-related taxpayer for the three preceding years is less than 50 percent of the total deductible farming expenses. The second exception allows the current deduction if, due to a change in business operations attributable to extraordinary circumstances, a farm-related taxpayer will fail to satisfy the 50-percent test. A "farm-related taxpayer" includes any person whose principal residence is on a farm, or whose principal occupation is farming, or any individual who is a member of the family of such person.

.05 Code Sec. 162(a), Code Sec. 461(a); Reg. §§1.162-12(a), 1.461-1(a)(1).

.10 *J. Ernst*, 32 TC 181, CCH Dec. 23,554. (Acq.) The court noted in a footnote that an IRS agent recommended that the taxpayer take delivery in the year of prepayment.

.15 Rev. Rul. 79-229, 1979-2 CB 32.

.20 *R. Mann*, CA-8, 73-2 USTC ¶9618, 483 F2d 673.

.25 *B. Stice*, CA-5, 76-2 USTC ¶9700, 540 F2d 1077.

.30 *Golden Rod Farms, Inc.*, DC Ala, 87-1 USTC ¶9312, 652 FSupp 972; *J. Ernst*, 32 TC 181, CCH Dec. 23,554 (Acq.).

.35 *T.W. Lillie*, CA-9, 67-1 USTC ¶9146, 370 F2d 562.

.40 *L. Schenk*, CA-5, 82-2 USTC ¶9594, 686 F2d 315.

.45 *J. Catto, Jr.*, SCt, 66-1 USTC ¶9376, 384 U.S. 102.

.50 *Van Raden*, 71 T.C. 1083, CCH Dec. 35,964, affd CA-9, 81-2 USTC ¶9547], 650 F.2d 1046.

.55 *R.D. Cravens*, CA-10, 60-1 USTC ¶9139, 272 F2d 895.

.60 *R. Frysinger*, CA-5, 81-1 USTC ¶9463, 645 F2d 523.

.65 *R. Frysinger*, CA-5, 81-1 USTC ¶9463, 645 F2d 523; *J.F. Haynes*, 38 TCM 950, CCH Dec. 36,145(M), TC Memo 1979-240; *H.J. Heinold*, 39 TCM 685, CCH Dec. 36,490(M), TC Memo. 1979-496. The Court of Appeals for the Ninth Circuit reached the same result on the basis of its rule that allows a full deduction in the year of payment when an expenditure creates an asset having a useful life of one year or less (*K.H. Van Raden*, CA-9, 81-2 USTC ¶9547, 650 F2d 1047).

.70 *D. Bandes*, 44 TCM 243, CCH Dec. 39,133(M), TC Memo. 1982-355.

.75 Code Sec. 464(a), (b) and (g).

.80 Code Sec. 464(d).

.85 Code Sec. 464(c) and (e).

.90 Code Sec. 464(a).

.95 Code Sec. 464(f).

¶25,367 Cost of Items Purchased for Resale. The cost of any item purchased for resale by a cash-method farmer can be deducted only in the year of disposition. Thus, if cattle were purchased for resale in 2003 but the resale did not take place until 2004, the cost of the cattle could not be deducted until 2004. See ¶25,373, however, for optional treatment in the case of a purchase of young plants, hens or baby chicks.

¶25,368 Farm Development Costs. The life of a farm, ranch or orchard is generally considered to be divided into three periods for purposes of deducting development costs. There is a preparatory, a developmental, and a productive period (.05).

Any capital expense incurred during the preparatory and developmental periods (with the exception of those expenses which qualify for the elective current deduction treatment afforded soil and water conservation expenditures) *must* be capitalized and may be depreciated. The following are examples of typical preparatory and developmental expenses:

(1) clearing brush, trees and stumps;

(2) leveling and conditioning land;

(3) purchasing and planting trees;

(4) building irrigation canals and ditches;

(5) laying irrigation pipes;

(6) installing drain tile;

(7) straightening or modifying creek beds;

(8) constructing earthen, masonry, or concrete tanks, reservoirs or dams;

(9) building roads; and

(10) drilling and equipping wells.

During the preproductive period, the farmer has the option of either deducting developmental expenses that are ordinary and necessary business expenses (expenses that are not capital expenses) or capitalizing them. (But see ¶25,337 for special rules applicable to corporations.) Typical developmental expenses to which this option applies are those incurred for upkeep, spraying, water for irrigation, fertilizer used up each year, taxes, interest, and controlling undergrowth. While the option does not apply to true capital expenditures, it is available for those capital expenses incurred for soil and water conservation (see ¶25,369 for added limitations for soil and water conservation expenditures).

The option to deduct or capitalize noncapital developmental expenses is confined to the developmental period preceding the time when the farm, orchard, or ranch reaches its productive state. For instance, in the case of an orchard that has been planted during the preparatory period but that does not yet produce income, the taxpayer must cultivate and spray the trees, pay for water for irrigation, and buy fertilizer each year. In any of these cases, the taxpayer has the option either of deducting these expenditures as ordinary and necessary business expenses or of capitalizing them.

Certain farmers may not deduct the costs of producing long-term crops and livestock in the year of payment. A crop with a preproductive period of more than two years is subject to the uniform capitalization rules. However, expenses related to the production of animals in a farming business, other than those expenses incurred by a taxpayer required to use the accrual method, are exempt from the uniform capitalization rules (.10). Farmers not required to use the accrual method of accounting may elect not to have the uniform capitalization rules apply to the production of certain farm property, a so-called Code Sec. 263A election. Generally, the election may be made by not applying the UNICAP rules on the original return for the first tax year in which the taxpayer is otherwise required to capitalize section 263A costs. A taxpayer that does not make the election on the original return must obtain consent to make the election by filing Form 3115 (.15). Cash-basis taxpayers may elect to deduct all preproductive costs of plants and animals currently if they recapture the costs as ordinary income upon disposition of the product. The alternative MACRS method to depreciate all farm assets must be used for any year that the election is in effect. Those eligible for the election include producers of livestock, nursery stock, and ornamental trees, as well as agricultural crops. See ¶25,344.

When the farm, orchard, or ranch reaches its productive period, the farmer loses the capitalization option available during the developmental period. Ordinary and necessary expenses may no longer be capitalized. Instead, the farmer must deduct these expenses each year, either when they are incurred by an accrual method farmer, or when they are paid by a cash method farmer. However, the elective treatment for soil and water conservation expenditures described at ¶25,369 still applies during the productive period.

See the special rules for planting trees under the heading "Trees or tree planting," below; those for farm syndicates are at ¶15,520.

Leveling and conditioning of land

Costs incurred to level and condition land for farming purposes are nondeductible capital expenses. However, expenses for ordinary maintenance activities (brush clearing) related to property already used in farming are currently deductible to the extent that they constitute ordinary and necessary business expenses. The annual cost of releveling irrigated land to maintain the proper land level and to prevent water from standing in ponds or flowing off too rapidly is currently deductible (.20). See, also, ¶25,369.

Roads

The cost of constructing a private road on business property is a capital expenditure, but the cost of maintaining such a road is currently deductible (.25). Plank roads have been held to be depreciable over a 10-year useful life (.30).

Taxpayers have been allowed to amortize the cost of paving roads on their own property (.35). If the roads are formally converted to public use, however, they are not depreciable. The cost is simply added to the basis of the taxpayer's remaining property.

Assessments for local improvements are capital expenditures to be added to the basis of the property (.40). Similarly, the cost to a farmer of voluntarily paving a public road might increase the basis of the farmland but are not amortizable. If the county government agrees to maintain the road, depreciation is probably not allowable, even though the original cost is incurred by the farmer and the pavement is on the farmer's own land, since the farmer will not bear any loss resulting from wear and tear. But the original cost of the pavement would be added to the basis of the farmland in computing gain or loss.

Straightening creek beds

The cost of straightening creek beds for the purpose of preventing erosion is a nondeductible capital expense, unless it can qualify as a soil or water conservation expense described at ¶25,369 or a leveling and conditioning of land expense described above.

Trees or tree planting

Costs incurred in the preparatory period in the life of a farm, orchard, or ranch and the cost of planting trees are generally capital in nature and nondeductible, except as to (1) nut tree seedlings and (2) soil or water conservation expenditures (see ¶25,369).

According to the IRS, most costs of planting and raising seedlings are preparatory expenditures that must be capitalized (.45). The IRS does not generally follow decisions (.50) that have allowed deductions for payments to a nursery for the care and preparation of seedlings before replanting them in an orchard where the risk of loss from growing the seedlings was borne by the taxpayer and not by the nursery. However, the IRS has issued a ruling consistent with the precedent set by numerous court decisions that the cost of caring for nut tree seedlings before they are permanently planted—that is, maintaining and transplanting them before and after the first budding of the trees in the field—is a deductible business expense. Although the ruling is addressed specifically to growers of pistachio nut tree seedlings, the IRS noted that it also applies to growers of most other types of nut tree seedlings.

The farmer has the option of capitalizing or deducting ordinary and necessary expenses incurred during the development period of trees. Thus, after planting trees in an orchard during the preparatory period, and before the orchard starts to produce, the farmer may incur expenses for cultivating and spraying the trees, for water to irrigate, and for fertilizer that must be replaced annually. Such expenses during the development period may be capitalized or deducted at the farmer's election.

Orchard trees: Orchard trees may be depreciated by a farmer in the fruit-growing business. This depreciation is based on the cost at the time the orchard has reached the income-producing stage, including not only the initial, but also the actual, capitalized expenditures incurred in bringing the trees to maturity (.55).

Under MACRS, fruit- or nut-bearing trees or vines placed in service after 1988 are treated as 10-year property depreciable using the MACRS straight-line method (.60).

Christmas trees: A grower of Christmas trees must capitalize the cost of planting and stump culture and add it to the basis of the trees (.65). However, costs incurred for shearing and basal pruning are deductible as business expenses (.70). Maintenance costs, such as weeding or cleaning, are also currently deductible.

Wells

The costs of drilling and equipping wells are depreciable capital expenditures. Well equipment includes pumps, piping, casing, and similar types of equipment.

Depreciation of a well was disallowed in one case because no useful life of the well was established (.75). A 25-year useful life was determined in another case, however (.80).

The cost of drilling test holes for water to be used for agricultural purposes is also a capital expenditure. If the test holes prove unproductive and are abandoned, a deductible loss results. However, if the test holes do prove productive and are then abandoned, no loss deduction is allowed (.85).

.05 Code Sec. 162, 175, 263, 263A; Reg. §§1.162-12, 1.175-2, 1.263(a)-1.

.10 Code Sec. 263A(d)(1).

.15 Reg. §1.263A-4(d).

.20 *Union Packing Co.*, CA-9, 59-1 USTC ¶9317, 265 F2d 712.

.25 *Pennock Plantation, Inc.*, 10 TCM 1077, CCH Dec. 18,649(M).

.30 *Lord & Bushnell*, 7 BTA 86, CCH Dec. 2480 (Acq.).

.35 *Clinton Cotton Mills, Inc.*, CA-4, 35-2 USTC ¶9449, 78 F2d 292.

.40 *Hubbell Son & Co., Inc. v. Burnet*, CA-8, 2 USTC ¶785, 51 F2d 644.

.45 Rev. Rul. 75-405, 1975-2 CB 63; IRS Letter Ruling 8005001, 11-10-79, CCH IRS LETTER RULINGS REPORTS.

.50 *R.L. Maple*, 27 TCM 944, CCH Dec. 29,115(M), TC Memo. 1968-144, aff'd by CA-9, 71-1 USTC ¶9348, 440 F2d 1055; *Wagner Mills, Inc.*, 33 TCM 1267, CCH Dec. 32,817(M), TC Memo. 1974-274, aff'd by CA-8, 76-1 USTC ¶9298, 530 F2d 827.

.55 *Ribbon Cliff Fruit Co.*, 12 BTA 13, CCH Dec. 3977 (Acq.).

.60 Code Sec. 168(e)(3)(D)(ii) and (b)(3)(E).

.65 Rev. Rul. 66-18, 1966-1 CB 59, as modified by Rev. Rul. 71-228, 1971-1 CB 53.

.70 Rev. Rul. 66-18, 1966-1 CB 59, as modified by Rev. Rul. 71-228, 1971-1 CB 53. *G. Ransburg*, DC Ind., 67-2 USTC ¶9672, 281 FSupp 324; *D.D. Kinley*, 51 TC 1000, CCH Dec. 29,503 (Acq.).

.75 *P. Dietz*, 7 BTA 1048, CCH Dec. 2694.

.80 *M.K. Patch*, BTA Memo., CCH Dec. 12,225A.

.85 Rev. Rul. 61-206, 1961-2 CB 57, amplifying Rev. Rul. 56-599, 1956-2 CB 122.

¶25,368A Reforestation Expenses. Taxpayers, other than trusts, can elect to amortize up to a total of $10,000 ($5,000 for married individuals who file separate returns) of "reforestation expenses" made during a tax year that are related to the reforestation or forestation of qualified timber property held for commercial production (.05). These expenses must be amortized over an 84-month period that begins on the first day of the first month of the second half of the tax year (July 1 for calendar-year taxpayers) in which the amortizable basis (i.e., that portion of the basis of the qualified timber property attributable to reforestation expenditures) is acquired. Thus, expenses can be amortized only for a half year in the tax year in which they were incurred.

Note: Under the American Jobs Creation Act of 2004, and effective for expenses paid or incurred after October 22, 2004, $10,000 in reforestation expenses may be deducted currently ($5,000 for married filing separately) (.10). Annual expenses in excess of $10,000 may be amortized over 84-months. The reforestation tax credit has been repealed for expenses paid or incurred after October 22, 2004.

The amortization for a given month can be computed by dividing the amortizable basis by the number of months (including the month for which the deduction is taken) remaining in the 84-month amortization period (.15). The maximum annual amortization deduction for expenditures incurred in any tax year is $1,428.57 ($10,000 ÷ 7 years). For the first and eighth tax years of the amortization period the maximum deduction is $714.29 ($1,428.57 ÷ 2), due to the half-year convention. For individuals, this deduction may be taken from gross income, rather than as an itemized deduction (.20).

No carryover or carryback of expenditures in excess of $10,000 ($5,000 for married individuals filing a separate return) is permitted.

Reforestation expenses

Reforestation expenses are direct costs incurred for forestation or reforestation by planting or by artificial or natural seeding (.25). They include costs for:

(1) site preparation,

(2) seeds or seedlings, and

(3) the costs of labor and tools, considering depreciation on equipment (tractors, trucks, tree planters, and similar machines) used in planting or seeding.

The costs must be capital expenditures that are includible in the basis of the property.

Amortization is not allowed for expenses that are reimbursed under any governmental reforestation cost-sharing program unless the taxpayer includes the reimbursements in income (.30).

Qualified timber property

Qualified timber property is a woodlot or other site (an acre or more in size) located in the United States that will contain trees in significant commercial quantities and that is held by the taxpayer for the planting, cultivating, caring for, and cutting of trees for sale or use in the commercial production of timber products (.35). Qualified timber property does not include property on which shelter belts or ornamental trees, such as Christmas trees, have been planted.

A taxpayer need not own this property; therefore, a lessee of qualified timber property may elect to amortize reforestation expenses.

Allocation of deduction and limitations

The $10,000 limit applies to reforestation expenses paid or incurred by a taxpayer with respect to all of the taxpayer's qualified timber properties (.40). The taxpayer may select the properties for which the amortization election will be made and the manner in which the $10,000 limitation is to be allocated among such properties.

For controlled groups of corporations (based on 50-percent ownership), the $10,000 limitation applies to all of the members, and it must be apportioned among the members. For partnerships and S corporations, the limitation applies at the partnership or S corporation level and also to each partner or shareholder.

The amortization deduction must be apportioned between the estate and the beneficiaries. Such apportionment is made on the basis of income that is allocable to the estate and the beneficiaries, respectively.

If there is a remainder interest in qualified timber property, the amortization deduction may be claimed only by the life tenant. The remainder interest is ignored for purposes of the amortization election.

Basis adjustment

The basis of the taxpayer's interest in the qualified timber property for which an amortization is made must be adjusted to reflect the amount of the amortization deduction allowable to the taxpayer (.45).

Recapture

If a taxpayer disposes of qualified timber property within 10 years of the year in which the amortizable basis was created and amortization deductions have been claimed, all or part of any gain may have to be recaptured as ordinary income (.50).

Election

To make the election to amortize forestation or reforestation expenses, a taxpayer must attach Form 4562 (Depreciation and Amortization) to a timely filed return (including extensions) for the tax year in which such expenses were incurred and include a statement describing the expenses and indicating the dates on which they were incurred (.55). In addition, the type of timber being grown and the purpose for which it is being grown must be included. The election may be revoked only with IRS consent.

Reforestation investment credit

To claim the investment credit for reforestation expenses, the taxpayer should attach Form 3468 (Investment Credit) to the tax return for the year in which the election to amortize is made (.60). This credit may be taken regardless of whether the expenses are also amortized. However, the amortizable basis is reduced by 50 percent of the amount of the claimed credit.

.05 Code Sec. 194(b)(1).

.10 Code Sec. 194(b), as amended by the American Jobs Creation Act of 2004 (P.L. 108-357).

.15 Reg. §1.194-2(a) and (b).

.20 Code Sec. 62(a)(11).

.25 Code Sec. 194(c)(3); Reg. §1.194-3(c).

.30 Rev. Rul. 84-67, 1984-1 CB 28.

.35 Code Sec. 194(c)(1); Reg. §1.194-3(a).

.40 Code Sec. 194(b) and (d); Reg. §1.194-2(b) and (c).

.45 Reg. §1.194-2(b)(3).

.50 Reg. §1.194-1(c).

.55 Reg. §1.194-4.

.60 Internal Revenue News Release 80-130, December 16, 1980.

¶25,369 Soil and Water Conservation Expenses. A farmer has the option of currently deducting (generally, up to a maximum of 25 percent of gross income from farming, see ¶25,371), rather than capitalizing, certain soil and water conservation expenses (including those incurred to prevent erosion), regardless of the period of development in the life of the farm during which the expenses are incurred (.05). Deductions for soil and water conservation expenditures are limited to those costs that are consistent with a conservation plan approved by the Soil Conservation Service of the U.S. Department of Agriculture, or a comparable state agency. Expenditures related to the draining or filling of wetlands or land preparation for the installation or operation of center pivot irrigation systems may not be deducted under this expensing provision.

In order for soil and water conservation expenditures to be deductible, the land must be used in farming. This means that it must have been used by the taxpayer or by the taxpayer's tenant, prior to or when the expenses were incurred, for the production of crops, fruits or similar agricultural products, including fish, or for the sustenance of livestock. A horticultural nursery is considered as a farm for this purpose, as are stock, dairy, poultry, fruit and truck farms, and ranches, plantations, ranges and orchards. However, a taxpayer is not considered to be farming when engaged in forestry or the growing of timber, or when cultivating or operating a farm for recreation or pleasure.

For purposes of currently deducting soil and water conservation expenditures made for newly acquired land, the taxpayer need only continue to use it in farming, but does not have to continue the previous owner's particular farming use.

> ***Example 1:*** Farmer Carter purchases a farm from farmer Jackson after farmer Jackson has harvested his crops. At the time the land is suitable for farmer Carter's particular farming use without making initial preparations. While the ground is idle because of the season, farmer Carter makes certain soil and water conservation expenditures. They can be currently deducted under the election since the land is considered as being used for farming at the time farmer Carter made her expenditures.
>
> ***Example 2:*** Farmer Carter acquires uncultivated land, not previously used in farming, which she intends to develop for farming. Any soil and water conservation expenditures incurred in preparing the land for production is not deductible under this election because the land was not being used for farming before or at the time that the expenditures were made.
>
> ***Example 3:*** Farmer Carter acquires land which had been used for grazing cattle. She intends to use the land for a citrus grove. The soil and water conservation expenditures incurred in preparing the land for use as a citrus grove are

deductible under this election, since the newly acquired land was used in farming by farmer Carter at the time she made the expenditures.

An allocation must be made if it was reasonable to believe, when the expenditures were made, that they would substantially benefit nonfarming as well as farming land. The amount otherwise deductible is proportional to the amount of the expenditures that the taxpayer could reasonably believe would substantially benefit farming land (unless the taxpayer can establish that another allocation method is reasonable under all the facts and circumstances).

A taxpayer is engaged in farming if the taxpayer receives rentals in cash or in crop shares that are based upon production. In contrast, a taxpayer who receives fixed rentals that are not based upon production is not in the business of farming unless the taxpayer participates to a material extent in the operation or management of the farm. (See ¶25,418 for a discussion of material participation in connection with self-employment income).

Deductible expenses include the cost of leveling, grading, terracing, and contour furrowing land; construction, control and protection of diversion channels, drainage ditches, earthen dams, watercourses, outlets and ponds; and the eradication of brush, the planting of windbreaks, and other treatment or moving of earth.

The election is not available, however, in the case of expenditures made by a farmer for depreciable property. No deduction is allowed for expenditures paid or incurred for the purchase, construction, installation or improvement of depreciable masonry, tile, metal or wood structures, appliances, or facilities such as tanks, reservoirs, pipes, canals, dams and pumps.

Also, the election to currently deduct soil and water conservation expenses is generally not applicable to the cost of lime or fertilizer that is effective for substantially longer than one year. These expenses must be capitalized, unless they qualify for the fertilizer expense election (see ¶25,372). However, the cost of lime or fertilizer used in gully stabilization or in the stabilization of severely eroded areas in order to obtain a soil-binding stand of vegetation on infertile land may be currently deducted under the conservation election.

Generally, it is more desirable to deduct soil and water conservation expenses, since, if they are not deducted, they are ordinarily added to the basis of the land. Because land is nondepreciable, expenses that are added to the basis are not recovered until the land is sold.

Electing the deduction

A farmer may elect to deduct soil and water conservation expenses without the consent of the IRS for the first tax year for which the expenditures are paid or incurred. Once made, the election is binding for all subsequent years unless the IRS authorizes a change. A farmer who wants to start deducting a type of expense that was previously capitalized must obtain the consent of the IRS.

If the farmer who does not elect to deduct soil and water conservation expenses, they are added to the basis of the land.

The soil and water conservation expenses eligible for the election are expenditures that would ordinarily be considered to be capital expenditures, and thus not currently deductible, if it were not for this special provision. As noted at ¶25,371, however, the deduction allowed for such expenses is limited to 25 percent of gross income.

The ordinary and necessary expenses for the maintenance and repair of items that have been constructed for conservation purposes or for the prevention of erosion are deductible in full and are not subject to the 25-percent limitation. A farmer who has both conservation expenditures and maintenance and repair expenditures should keep separate records of the two types of expenditures.

To meet the reporting requirements for claiming soil and water conservation expenses, Schedule F of Form 1040, Form 4835 "Farm Rental Income and Expense," or Form 1040-SS "US Self Employment Tax Return," may be used and must be attached to income tax returns of taxpayers.

□ The recapture of soil and water conservation expenses upon the sale of a farm is discussed at ¶25,409 and following. Also, see ¶25,412 for a discussion of the recapture of certain cost-sharing conservation payments and the exclusion from gross income of designated conservation grants.

.05 Code Sec. 175; Reg. § §1.175-1—1.175-7;
"Farmer's Tax Guide," IRS Pub. 225.

¶25,370 Assessments by Conservation or Drainage Districts. Deductible expenses also include assessments levied by a soil or water conservation or drainage district in order to defray expenditures made by the district. This deduction applies to the extent that the assessment covers expenditures made by the district that would have been deductible by a farmer who incurred them directly (but see below for a discussion of expenditures for depreciable property) (.05).

Assessment for depreciable assets

A farmer is also permitted to deduct the portion of an assessment by a soil or water conservation or drainage district that is attributable to the district's acquisition of depreciable assets. This depreciable property includes pumps, locks, concrete structures such as dams and weir gates, draglines, and similar equipment. However, the depreciable equipment must be used in the district's soil or water conservation or drainage activities.

A farmer's deduction may not exceed 10 percent of the total amount of the assessment attributable to the acquisition of depreciable assets. For example, if an assessment by a district against its members in the total amount of $1 million includes $100,000 that is attributable to the acquisition of depreciable property, no one member may deduct a more than $10,000 with regard to the portion of the assessment for depreciable property.

Any portion of the assessment for acquiring depreciable property that exceeds the 10-percent limit is a capital expenditure that must be added to the basis of the farm property involved. If an assessment that exceeds the 10-percent limit is payable in installments, each installment is to be divided between a deductible portion and a capitalized portion.

Generally, if the amount of the assessment paid (attributable to the acquisition of depreciable property by the district) is in excess of an amount equal to 10 percent of the total amount that has been and will be assessed as the farmer's share of the cost to the district in acquiring the property, only 10 percent of the assessment is deductible in the year when paid by the farmer, and the remaining 90 percent is to be deducted ratably over the following nine tax years. But where the amount that otherwise would have to be spread over the nine-year period is $500 or less, the full assessment is allowed as a deduction in the year of payment. Thus, amortization is not necessary where the amounts involved are relatively small.

Soil or water conservation or drainage district

The term "soil or water conservation or drainage district" includes nonprofit mutual irrigation companies exempt from tax, as well as soil and water conservation districts, drainage districts, irrigation districts, watershed improvement districts, flood control districts, and conservancy districts. However, it does not include irrigation or drainage companies operated for profit.

.05 Code Sec. 175(c)(1); Reg. §1.175-2(c).

¶25,371 Limitations on the Conservation Deduction. The total deduction for soil and water conservation expenses of a capital nature is limited to 25 percent of the gross income from farming during the tax year. The excess is deductible in succeeding tax years, without time limitation, but in each year the entire deduction is limited to 25 percent of the gross income from farming in the year of the deduction. The excess amount carried over is treated as the first expenditure in each later year (.05).

> ***Example:*** In Year 1 Mr. Linden had gross income of $16,000 from two farms. During the year he made deductible soil and water conservation expenditures totaling $5,300 for one of the farms. However, his deduction is limited to 25% of $16,000, or $4,000. The excess of $1,300 is carried over to Year 2 and added to deductible soil and water conservation expenditures, if any, made in that year. The total of the Year 1 carryover plus Year 2 expenditures is deductible in Year 2, subject to the limitation of 25% of his gross income from farming in Year 2. Any excess expenditures over the limitation in Year 2 are carried to succeeding years.

An unused carryover cannot be added to the basis of the land if a farmer sells the land and discontinues farming. However, if the farmer subsequently goes into the business of farming at any time and at any place, the farmer may "pick up" the unused deduction from previous operations and deduct it.

Gains derived from the sale of assets, such as farm machinery, or from the disposition of land, may not be included in gross income from farming in computing the limitation.

The ordinary and necessary expense of maintaining and repairing completed structures built for conservation purposes or for the prevention of erosion is separately deductible and is not subject to the 25-percent limitation. For example, the removal of sediment from a drainage ditch or interest and maintenance charges assessed by a drainage or conservation district is fully deductible. Such expenses should be segregated in the farmer's records to insure full deductibility.

.05 Code Sec. 175(b); Reg. §1.175-5.

¶25,372 Fertilizers and Lime. Farmers may elect to deduct currently (1) expenditures for fertilizer, lime, ground limestone, marl, and other materials for enriching, neutralizing, or conditioning land used in farming and (2) the costs of applying the materials to the land (.05). This is true even where the period of benefit or effectiveness of such materials extends beyond the tax year.

If the farmer does not elect to currently deduct the costs of materials whose benefits extend beyond the tax year, the costs must be treated as capital expenditures and amortized over the period of benefit or effectiveness (.10). The election is effective only for the tax year for which the deduction is claimed and may be revoked only with the consent of the IRS.

A taxpayer engaged in the business of growing and selling sod was eligible for the election to deduct currently expenses incurred in the acquisition of fertilizer because the growing and selling of sod is a farming activity (.15).

Expenditures for preparing land not previously used for farming by the taxpayer are ineligible for the election.

☐ See, also, the rules for farm syndicates at FTG ¶15,520.

.05 Code Sec. 175, Code Sec. 180; Reg. §§1.175-2(b)(2), 1.175-3, 1.175-4, 1.180-1, 1.180-2.

.10 Reg. §1.263(a)-1; *E.B. Swaney*, 5 BTA 990, CCH Dec. 2038 (Acq.).

.15 IRS Letter Ruling 8440003, 5-22-84, CCH IRS LETTER RULINGS REPORTS.

¶25,373 Young Plants, Hens and Baby Chicks. A cash-basis farmer who purchases seeds and young plants for further development before reselling them (except plants for Christmas trees and timber) may deduct the purchase price in the year paid (.05). The same is true of the cost of hens bought for commercial egg production and of baby chicks bought for raising and selling (.10).

A cash-method purchaser of seeds and young plants that have already been planted and that constitute growing crops is not entitled to a current deduction for the cost of such crops (.15). The cost of the crops must be added to the purchaser's basis. When the purchaser sells the crops, profit (or loss) is the difference between the basis of the crops and their sale price.

If the farmer elects to deduct currently the purchase cost of seeds, young plants, hens, and baby chicks, the entire selling price of the item is taxable. If the election is not made, the purchase price is offset against the sales price in the year of sale. See ¶25,367.

The cost of poultry, including egg-laying hens and baby chicks, purchased for use in the trade or business of a farming syndicate must be capitalized and deducted ratably over the lesser of 12 months or the poultry's statutory recovery period or useful life in the trade or business.

.05 Code Sec. 162; Reg. §1.162-12(a).

.10 Rev. Rul. 60-191, 1960-1 CB 78.

.15 Rev. Rul. 85-82, 1985-1 CB 57; *R. Dodds*, 51 TCM 950, CCH Dec. 43,027(M), TC Memo. 1986-174.

¶25,374 Repairs and Improvements. Expenditures for repairs in the nature of replacements that appreciably prolong the life of the property, arrest its deterioration, or increase its value or usefulness are ordinarily capital expenditures for which deductions are allowed only through the depreciation/cost recovery allowance (.05). However, incidental repairs that merely keep property in an ordinary operating or usable condition are deductible current expenses rather than capital expenditures (.10). Thus, when parts of a machine are replaced with other parts that will last for several years but do not increase the useful life or value of the machine, the cost is deductible as repair expense. However, a major overhaul prolonging the useful life of the machine but including the same replacement of parts would ordinarily be a capital expenditure.

.05 Code Sec. 162; Reg. §1.162-4.

.10 *L.E. Vogel*, 47 TCM 1360, CCH Dec. 41,090, TC Memo. 1984-149.

¶25,375 Marketing Quota Penalties. Deductions for farm business expenses include marketing quota penalties paid for marketing crops in excess of farm marketing quotas. However, a separate deduction for the penalty is not allowed if the purchaser of the crop offsets such amount against the amount paid to the farmer, and the farmer includes in income only the amount actually received (.05).

.05 Farmer's Tax Guide, IRS Publication No. 225.

Depreciation, Depletion and Investment Tax Credit

¶25,377 Depreciation. Costs incurred to increase a farm's value must be distinguished from costs incurred to keep the farm in operating condition. Expenses incurred in increasing a farm's value are a capital expenditure or an investment, while expenses incurred to keep the farm in operating condition is an ordinary expense. Thus, the cost of improving a farm is not deductible in one lump sum in the year when the expenditure is made (.05).

The Modified Accelerated Cost Recovery System (MACRS) is used for depreciating farm property placed in service after 1986. The MACRS deduction is computed by applying the applicable recovery period, depreciation methods, and averaging convention to the basis of the property. However, the IRS has provided optional percentage tables that may be used in lieu of using the prescribed method and convention over the applicable recovery period (see ¶9180). In the case of property placed in service after 1980 and, generally, before 1987, the Accelerated Cost Recovery System (ACRS) applies. In this case, depreciation is computed by applying statutory percentages for the respective class of property to the unadjusted basis of the property (see ¶9200). For property placed in service before 1981, the cost of machinery, equipment, farm buildings and other property with a useful life of more than one year is generally capitalized and recovered through depreciation deductions over the period of the property's useful life (see ¶9300) or under the Asset Depreciation Range (ADR) system (see ¶9400).

Depreciation under MACRS or ACRS for assets placed in service after 1980

Under MACRS or ACRS the cost of most tangible depreciable property used in a trade or business or held for the production of income and placed in service after 1980 (including farm property) is recovered over a predetermined statutory period that is generally shorter than the useful life of the asset or the period during which the asset is used to produce income. The cost recovery methods and periods are the same for both new and used property. Salvage value, like useful life, is disregarded in computing MACRS or ACRS allowances.

In order to qualify for the MACRS or ACRS allowance, the property must be used in a trade or business or held for the production of income. Depreciable items used in farming include:

(1) all farm buildings, including tenant houses (but excluding the residence occupied by the farmer);

(2) machinery and equipment;

(3) livestock used for work, dairy, or breeding purposes if its cost has been capitalized rather than inventoried (if the cost of raising livestock has been currently deducted, there can be no depreciation, since there is no basis);

(4) fences and tile drains;

(5) orchards, groves, and vineyards when they reach producing age;

(6) automobiles and trucks (business portion);

(7) corrals and loading pens;

(8) tanks and vats; and

(9) water wells (business portion), including drilling costs.

Nonresidential real property placed in service after May 12, 1993, is generally depreciated over a 39-year recovery period under MACRS using the straight-line method. Under ACRS, real property is depreciated over a 15-, 18- or 19-year recovery period, depending on when it was placed in service, using statutory recovery percentages (see ¶9210 and following).

The basis of property for depreciation is its cost or other basis. However, for tax years beginning after 1982 and before 1986, the basis for depreciation was reduced generally by one-half of the investment tax credit. For property placed in service after 1985 and qualifying for the investment tax credit as transitional property, the depreciation basis must be reduced by the full amount of the allowable investment tax credit.

For any class of property, farmers and other taxpayers may elect to claim straight-line depreciation deductions (instead of the regular MACRS deductions) over the recovery period (see ¶9115).

☐ See ¶9180 for a list of types of properties and their classifications for MACRS.

Depreciation on assets placed in service before 1981

With regard to pre-1981 depreciation allowances, the cost of depreciable property is spread over its useful life to the extent that the property is used up in the production of farm commodities. The cost must be ratably depreciated over the period of years that constituted the useful life of the property. The property may not be entirely deducted before the end of the useful life.

Expensing election

An expense deduction is available under Code Sec. 179 to farmers (and other taxpayers) who elect to treat the cost of qualified property as an expense rather than as a capital expenditure. Generally, the maximum expense a farmer may elect to deduct for property placed in service in 2004 is $102,000. See ¶9130.

Recapture

For a discussion of the farm-related depreciation recapture provisions, see ¶25,405.

.05 Code Sec. 167, Code Sec. 168, and Code Sec. 179; Reg. §1.167(a)-6.

¶25,378 Trade-Ins. If a depreciable item, such as a threshing machine, is traded for a new machine to be used in the farming business, the gain, if any, is limited to the "boot" (cash or property) received. A loss is not recognized on the trade-in, even though the farmer both pays cash and trades in the old machine (.05).

The basis of the new machine is the same as the adjusted basis of the old machine, minus the amount of money received and plus the amount of cash paid and the amount of gain included in the farmer's income.

> ***Example 1:*** Daniel Black trades a plow used in his farming business for another plow worth $250. The plow traded in cost $1,950 and depreciation allowed or allowable to the date of the trade was $1,875. Since no boot was received, no gain is included in income. The basis for the acquired plow is the same as the adjusted basis of the plow traded in, $75 ($1,950 cost of plow traded in, less $1,875 depreciation allowed or allowable).
>
> If Black had paid $200 cash in addition to his trade-in, his basis in the acquired plow would be $275 ($75 adjusted basis of plow traded in, plus $200 cash difference).
>
> ***Example 2:*** Mary White trades a harvester with an adjusted basis of $1,500 for another harvester worth $1,600 and $300 in cash. There is a $400 gain on the trade ($1,600 plus $300 minus $1,500), but only $300 (cash received) is included in income. The basis of the acquired harvester is $1,500 ($1,500 adjusted basis of harvester traded, minus $300 cash received and plus $300 gain recognized).
>
> If the acquired harvester had a value of $1,450, instead of $1,600, White's gain would be $250 ($1,450, plus $300, minus $1,500), all of which would be included in income. The basis of the acquired harvester would be $1,450 ($1,500 adjusted basis of harvester traded minus $300 cash received and plus $250 gain recognized).
>
> If the acquired harvester had a value of $1,000, instead of $1,600, White would have a loss of $200 ($1,500, minus $1,000 and minus $300), which is not recognized. The basis of the acquired harvester would be $1,200 ($1,500 adjusted basis of harvester traded minus $300 cash received).

The carryover basis of property acquired in a trade-in and placed in service after January 2, 2000, is depreciated as if the trade-in had not occurred. The remaining portion of the basis is treated as newly acquired MACRS property(.10).

☐ See ¶5293 and following for general rules involving the exchange of like-kind property.

.05 Code Sec. 1031; Reg. §1.1031(a)-1.

.10 Notice 2000-4, 2000-3 I.R.B. 313.

¶25,379 Livestock. There are special rules regarding depreciation of livestock, depending on the year the livestock was placed in service (.05).

Livestock placed in service after 1980

Included in the three-year MACRS class are race horses that are more than two years old when placed in service and breeding or work horses that are more than 12 years old when placed in service. Breeding hogs are three-year recovery property. However, breeding or dairy cattle and breeding sheep and goats are five-year property under MACRS, while breeding or work horses less than 12 years old when placed in service are seven-year property.

The above classes of livestock have the same recovery period for ACRS purposes, except that breeding or work horses (other than those in the three-year class) are five-year property (rather than seven-year property).

Livestock placed in service before 1981

Pre-1981 livestock is depreciable only if it was acquired or used for work, breeding, or dairy purposes and only if it is not included in inventory. As noted at ¶25,377, prior to 1981 and the ACRS (cost recovery) method of depreciation, such depreciation had to be determined with reference to the cost or other basis, salvage value, and estimated useful life of the livestock.

It is necessary to consider the salvage value of animals just as in the case of other types of property placed in service prior to 1981. Thus, in computing pre-1981 depreciation on foxes used by a fur rancher for breeding purposes, failure to consider salvage value resulted in denial of depreciation where the fur pelts exceeded the depreciable cost basis of the foxes (.10).

.05 Code Sec. 167 and Code Sec. 168; Reg. §1.167(a)-6.

.10 *Cedarburg Fox Farms, Inc.*, CA-7, 60-2 USTC ¶9760, 283 F2d 711; Rev. Rul. 61-42, 1961-1 CB 751.

¶25,380 Depletion. Farmers who own economic interests in timber, coal, or another depletable mineral, including topsoil, gravel, and sand, are entitled to an allowance for depletion of such resources (.05). The purpose of a depletion allowance is to compensate owners of a mineral or timber resource for the consumption of the resource.

Depletion may be computed on a cost-per-unit basis, such as $1 per ton of coal extracted and sold, or on a percentage-of-gross-income basis, such as five percent of all income from a coal-producing property. However, the depletion allowance for timber must be computed on the cost-per-unit basis.

For minerals, the depletion allowance is generally computed and deducted in the tax year in which the mineral resource is sold. For timber, the depletion allowance is computed when the timber is cut; the depletion allowance on cut timber that remains unsold at the end of a tax year is included as an item of cost in a farmer's closing inventory of the timber products (.10). A farmer who keeps no timber inventories treats the depletion allowance as an addition to the cost basis of the unsold cut timber and, when the timber is sold, the addition to the basis serves as a deduction to offset any gain realized from the sale.

Groundwater

Generally, a farmer is not entitled to a depletion allowance for groundwater. However, water is a depletable natural resource in the Ogallala Formation (also known as the High Plains Aquifer), which runs under much of the western plains states, if the farmer must pay a premium to obtain land under which there is groundwater (.15).

.05 Code Sec. 611; Reg. §1.611-1.

.10 Reg. §1.611-3(b)(1).

.15 *M. Shurbet*, CA-5, 65-2 USTC ¶9474, 347 F2d 103; Rev. Rul. 82-214, 1982-2 CB 115.

¶25,381 Investment Tax Credit. The investment credit is a component of the general business credit (.05). The investment credit is the sum of the following three credits (.10): (1) the rehabilitation credit; (2) the energy credit; and (3) the reforestation credit. For more information, see ¶2653.

.05 Code Sec. 38.

.10 Code Sec. 46.

Casualty Losses and Involuntary Conversions

¶25,383 Casualty Losses in General. The general casualty and theft loss rules apply to farming just as they do to any other business, and a farmer treats nonbusiness casualty losses in the same way other taxpayers do. A casualty loss is not permitted for damage to insured property that is not used in a trade or business or in a transaction entered into for profit unless the taxpayer files a timely insurance claim with respect to the damage to the property (.05).

If casualty losses—whether business or nonbusiness—exceed income, the excess can be carried back or forward as a net operating loss.

Casualty and theft losses to property used in the farming business are reported on Form 4684. Casualty losses from nonbusiness property are reported on Schedule A of Form 1040.

Business casualty losses

Losses on farm buildings, machinery, and other depreciable property from fire, storm, drought, or other casualty are deductible to the extent of cost, less depreciation allowed or allowable, if any, and less compensation received by way of insurance or otherwise. The general rules as to the time and amount of the deduction are the same as for other business property. Also, the loss can be included in the computation of a net operating loss.

A netting of gains and losses resulting from the casualty or theft of any property used in the business of farming is required. If there is a net gain, both gains and losses are covered by the capital gain and loss rules for such property (.10). On the other hand, if there is a net loss, neither gains nor losses are covered by the business property rules (¶5702 and following). In effect, this means that net gains are treated as gains from the disposition of property used in a trade or business, while net losses are ordinary losses. These rules apply only to business and investment property.

Personal casualty losses

An individual farmer may deduct personal casualty and theft losses only to the extent that the losses (less casualty gains from insurance or other sources) exceed $100 and 10 percent of the farmer's adjusted gross income. The 10-percent restriction on personal casualty losses is applied to an individual farmer's combined personal casualty losses after the $100 floor is subtracted from each single loss.

> ***Example:*** Edward Hanks has a $1,500 casualty loss to his personal car and a $5,000 casualty loss to his personal residence. His casualty gains from insurance are $500 from the damage to the car and $2,000 from the damage to the residence. Mr. Hanks has an adjusted gross income of $20,000.
>
> To determine if he may deduct any part of his personal casualty losses, Mr. Hanks must first reduce his losses by the insurance compensation. This results in a

$1,000 casualty loss to the car and a $3,000 casualty loss to the residence. Next, he must reduce each loss by the $100 floor, which lowers the $1,000 loss to $900 and the $3,000 loss to $2,900, for a combined loss of $3,800.

Because Mr. Hanks has an adjusted gross income of $20,000, combined casualty losses that exceed 10% of $20,000, or $2,000, may be deducted. Thus, Mr. Hanks has an $1,800 deductible personal casualty loss.

For individual farmers there is a special rule for personal casualty (and theft) gains (.15). If the personal casualty gains for any tax year exceed the personal casualty losses for that tax year, the net gain from the personal casualty losses is either a long-term or short-term capital gain, depending upon how long the farmer held the casualty property.

Disaster loss election

A taxpayer who, at any time during the tax year, sustains a loss from a disaster that occurred in an area later determined by the President of the United States as warranting federal disaster assistance has the choice of (1) deducting the loss for the tax year in which the disaster occurred or (2) electing to claim it on the original or amended return or a refund claim for the preceding year. See ¶25,389.

.05 Code Sec. 165 and Code Sec. 1231; Reg. §1.165-7.

.10 Code Sec. 1231.

.15 Code Sec. 165(h)(2)(B).

¶25,384 Amount of Casualty Loss. The casualty loss deduction on property used in the business of farming is determined in the same manner as for other business property. Thus, a farmer could deduct the unrecovered cost of certain itemized depreciable farm assets, including a brooder, destroyed by fire (.05). Similarly, if a barn is damaged or destroyed in the fire, loss is deductible to the extent of cost or other adjusted basis, reduced by salvage value and any compensation received by way of insurance or otherwise.

The same rule is applicable to a farmer on the cash basis who purchases depreciable animals for draft, breeding or dairy purposes. Therefore, if these animals were in the barn at the time it was destroyed by fire, the farmer can also claim a deduction for their loss based on the cost, less depreciation allowed or allowable (.10). The same rule applies to an accrual-basis taxpayer who raises or purchases such animals.

☐ For the special rules applicable to the amount of loss resulting from damage to or destruction of the residence or other personal property, see ¶6320.

.05 *V. Treanor*, 10 TCM 336, CCH Dec. 18,242(M).

.10 *D.G. Tenney*, 42 BTA 1049, CCH Dec. 11,358.

¶25,385 Casualty to Crops. No deductible casualty loss results from the destruction of a growing or standing crop by disease, pests, storm, drought, frost, flood, or other casualty. This is because current deductions for seed, labor, and other costs have made the farmer "whole" as far as actual expenses are concerned, so the only loss is for anticipated profits, for which no deduction may be taken. Thus, deductions were disallowed for the destruction of an onion crop by disease (.05) and an alfalfa crop by fire (.10). Loss deductions were permitted, however, to the extent of capitalized expenses incurred in preparing and developing cranberry bogs, orchards and vineyards destroyed by, or as the result of, flooding or disease (.15).

Crop disaster and insurance payments are generally includible in a farmer's gross income in the year received. However, a cash-basis farmer can defer inclusion of the crop disaster or insurance proceeds to the following tax year if the farmer can show that income from the damaged crop would normally have been reported in the following year (.20). See ¶25,390.

By virtue of the so-called partial-recognition-of-gain rule involving property that is involuntarily converted and replaced within the statutorily prescribed period with similar property, any gain recognized is generally limited, at the election of the farmer, to the excess of the amount realized from the converted property over the cost of the replacement property (.25).

If a standing crop is lost after the farmer has elected to apply the crop method of accounting rules (see ¶25,338), the costs of planting and raising a new crop qualify as replacement costs in computing gain under the above partial-recognition-of-gain rule because the IRS considers such crop-method expenses as capital in nature and, thus, treats them as part of the cost or basis of the replacement property (.30). A separate election must be made for each damaged crop that represents a separate trade or business. If a trade or business has more than one damaged crop, a single election can be made for all crops of that trade or business.

Feed contamination

A cash-basis farmer could not defer income recovered in connection with losses sustained as a result of cattle feed contamination because the losses were not considered to be due to a natural disaster and the proceeds were not considered insurance proceeds (.35).

Orchards and fruit groves

A farmer in the fruit-growing business whose fruit trees are damaged as the result of a storm, flood, fire, hurricane, drought, or other casualty is entitled to a casualty loss deduction (.40). Where the loss is from frost damage, the damage to the trees must be determined separately from the land on which they are located (.45).

.05 *Horr-Warner Co.*, 3 BTA 277, CCH Dec. 1106.

.10 *V. Treanor*, 10 TCM 336, CCH Dec. 18,242(M).

.15 *J.B. Hadaway*, 13 BTA 986, CCH Dec. 4460 (Acq.); *H.B. Hooper*, 8 BTA 397, CCH Dec. 2835 (Acq.); *F.H. Wilson*, 12 BTA 403, CCH Dec. 4043 (Acq.).

.20 Code Sec. 451(d); Reg. §1.451-6.

.25 Code Sec. 1033.

.30 Rev. Rul. 81-279, 1981-2 CB 163.

.35 IRS Letter Ruling 7807002, 9-15-77, CCH IRS LETTER RULINGS REPORTS.

.40 Code Sec. 165.

.45 *Carloate Industries, Inc.*, CA-5, 66-1 USTC ¶9159, 354 F2d 814.

¶25,386 Casualty to Land. Actual damage to the land itself, such as loss of topsoil during a flood, is deductible if adequate proof of the amount of the loss is presented and a “closed transaction” is shown (.05). This closed transaction requirement will, as a practical matter, prevent the deduction of losses for soil erosion, due to the problem of proving that the soil erosion has stopped and is, therefore, a closed transaction (.10).

Sinking of the land as the result of a sudden shifting of the layers beneath the surface is allowed as a deductible loss (.15).

.05 *W.M. Ferguson*, CA-10, 3 USTC ¶975, 59 F2d 893.

.10 *Texas & Pacific Ry. Co.*, 1 TCM 863, CCH Dec. 13,110(M).

.15 *H.J. Grant*, 30 BTA 1028, CCH Dec. 8613 (Acq.).

¶25,387 Condemnations and Severance Damages. If a portion of a farmer’s land is involuntarily converted by a condemnation proceeding or is sold under threat or imminence of condemnation, the farmer can elect to postpone the recognition of gain (if any) by using the condemnation award or sale proceeds to buy “like-kind” property (.05).

However, where the money is not reinvested in like-kind property, the determination of the gain recognized requires consideration of the expenses incurred, special assessments against the property retained, and severance damages (payments to compensate for the impairment of the use of the property retained).

Severance damages

Severance damages play an important part in postponing the recognition of gain from a condemnation award because they are first applied to reduce the basis of the retained (noncondemned) property to the extent that they exceed

(1) the expenses incurred in obtaining the damages,

(2) the expenses incurred in making the retained property usable, and

(3) any special assessments against the retained property.

If severance damages, after the above reductions, exceed the basis of the retained property, the excess damages are taxable as ordinary income.

> ***Example 1:*** Janet Black owns a 1,000-acre farm. Her adjusted basis in the farm is $100 an acre. The state condemns a strip of land through her farm for a new highway. The total area condemned is 25 acres. The condemnation award is $5,000. There is a special assessment of $3,500 against the property retained; severance damages of $7,500 are also awarded. Black incurs $750 in legal fees in securing the total $12,500 award ($5,000 condemnation award and $7,500 severance damages). She also spends $1,500 in refencing the retained property adjoining the condemned property, with $250 in fencing being destroyed from the construction of the highway.
>
> For tax purposes, the $7,500 severance damages (3⁄5 of the total award) are offset by $450 in legal fees (3⁄5 of $750), the $3,500 special assessment, and the $1,500 spent for new fencing. The $2,050 of the severance damages remaining reduces the basis of the property retained. Thus, the retained property has a basis of $5,450 ($7,500–$2,050). The $5,000 condemnation award is reduced by $300 in legal expenses (2⁄5 of $750), the $2,500 basis of the land condemned, and the $250 basis of the destroyed fence. The difference, $1,950, is taxable as long-term capital gain.
>
> ***Example 2:*** Assume the same facts as in Example (1), except that the condemnation award is for a lump sum of $12,500, with no allocation of severance damages. Janet Black now has taxable long-term capital gain of $4,000, since the $2,050 in severance damages used to reduce the basis of the retained property in Example (1) is now a part of the gain on the "sale" of the condemned portion of the farm.

It may not be enough merely to prove that severance damages were considered in the process of negotiating. They can be separated only where both parties have agreed upon the portion of an award that is allocable to severance damages. Thus, it is extremely important to ensure that the eventual contract of sale spells out the elements of the award.

.05 Code Sec. 1033(g); Reg. § §1.1033(a)-1 and 1.1033(a)-2; IRS Letter Ruling 8226066, 3-30-82, CCH IRS LETTER RULINGS REPORTS.

¶25,388 Involuntary Conversions of Livestock. Special provisions treat the death of livestock from disease, the destruction of livestock because they are diseased, the sale or exchange of livestock because they are diseased, and the drought-, flood-, or other weather-caused sale or exchange of livestock held for draft, dairy or breeding purposes as involuntary conversions (.05). Consequently, the involuntary conversion nonrecognition-of-gain benefits that apply to condemnations also apply to involuntary conversions of livestock provided they are replaced within a statutorily prescribed period with property of a "like-kind." The livestock need not have been held for any minimum length of time to qualify for these benefits. However, only livestock sold in excess of the number normally sold under usual business conditions in the absence of drought, flood or other weather-related conditions are considered involuntarily converted. Note, however, livestock of different sexes are not treated as property of a like-kind (.10).

Recognized gain or loss on such involuntary conversions involving livestock used for draft, dairy or breeding purposes that have been held for the requisite holding period, is included in a "Code Sec. 1231" comparison (capital gain-ordinary loss treatment on the sale or exchange of certain property used in a trade or business) to determine whether it is capital or ordinary gain or loss (see ¶25,394).

The sale or exchange does not have to take place in the affected area, but it must be solely on account of the weather-related conditions, the existence of which affected the water, grazing, or other livestock needs, so as to necessitate the sale or exchange. For this purpose, drought is a condition that exists by reason of abnormally low rainfalls or snowfalls in the area. The fact that feed could have been purchased commercially does not affect the result if drought conditions exist (.15).

In the case of a sale or exchange by a partnership, the election not to recognize the gain and the purchase of the replacement property must be made by the partnership, and not the partners (.20).

A cash-basis farmer who is forced to sell livestock because of drought, flood or other weather-related conditions, may elect to defer to the tax year following the year of sale or other disposition income from these forced sales. See ¶15,295.

If, because of soil or other environmental contamination, it is not feasible for a taxpayer to reinvest the proceeds from involuntarily converted livestock in similar or related property, the taxpayer may invest the proceeds in other property, including real property, to be used for farming. Such property is then treated as similar or related property for purposes of the involuntary conversion nonrecognition-of-gain rules (.25). Under the American Jobs Creation Act of 2004, the sale of livestock may also be due to drought, flood or other related weather conditions (.30). This change is generally effective for returns with a due date after December 31, 2002. However, real property will still be treated as the only type of replacement property in situations involving soil or other environmental contamination.

.05 Code Sec. 451, 1031, 1033(e), 1033(f), and 1231; Reg. §§1.1033(e)-1, 1.1231-1 and 1.1231-2.

.10 Reg. §1.1031(e)-1.

.15 Rev. Rul. 66-191, 1966-2 CB 300.

.20 *M. Demirjian*, 54 TC 1691, CCH Dec. 30,321, aff'd, CA-3, 72-1 USTC ¶9281, 457 F2d 1; see Reg. §1.703-1(b).

.25 Code Sec. 1033(f).

.30 Code Sec. 1033(f), as amended by the American Jobs Creation Act of 2004 (P.L. 108-357).

¶25,389 Disaster Area Losses. Farmers who sustain a loss from a disaster that occurred in an area later determined by the President of the United States to warrant federal disaster assistance may elect to deduct the loss on their returns for the immediately preceding tax year (.05). If the election is made, the loss is considered as having occurred in the preceding year.

.05 Code Sec. 165(i); Reg. §1.165-11.

¶25,390 Deferral of Crop Insurance Proceeds. A cash-method farmer who receives insurance proceeds as a result of destroyed or damaged crops may elect to include those proceeds in income in the year following the year of damage or destruction upon showing that the income from the crops would normally have been reported in a following year (.05). This treatment is also available for payments authorized under the Agricultural Act of 1949, title II of the Disaster Assistance Act of 1988 (.10) or title I of the Disaster Assistance Act of 1989 (.15) and received by a farmer as a result of destruction or damage to crops caused by drought, flood, or other natural disaster, or as a result of the inability to plant crops because of such a natural disaster. Proceeds received by cash-method farmers from insurance companies for losses sustained as a result of cattle feed contamination cannot be deferred, however. These losses are not caused by a natural disaster (.20). Federal payments received as a result of destruction or damage to crops caused by drought, flood, or any other natural disaster or due to the inability to plant crops because of such a disaster are treated as insurance proceeds for this purpose (.25).

The election can be made by attaching a separate statement to the return for the year of destruction or damage (.30). The statement should indicate that the taxpayer is making the election, name the crops destroyed or damaged, declare that income from them would have been included in a following tax year under the taxpayer's normal practice, state the cause of destruction or damage, itemize the total amount of insurance payments received, and name the insurance carriers from whom payments were received. Disclosure on the return that insurance proceeds were deferred is insufficient to effect an election.

This election may be made on an amended return filed within the period of limitations. Once made, however, the election is binding and may not be revoked without the consent of the IRS.

.05 Code Sec. 451(d), Reg. §1.451-6.

.10 Notice 89-55, 1989-1 CB 696.

.15 Rev. Rul. 91-55, 1991-2 CB 321.

.20 IRS Letter Ruling 7807002, 9-15-77, CCH IRS Letter Rulings Reports.

.25 Reg. §1.451-6.

.30 Rev. Rul. 74-145, 1974-1 CB 113.

¶25,390A Deferral of Adverse Weather Related Livestock Sale Income. A cash-method farmer who is forced to sell livestock because of drought conditions, flood or other weather related conditions, may elect to defer a portion of the income to the tax year following the year of sale or other disposition (.05). The income that may be deferred from these forced sales is that portion of the proceeds in excess of the amount that would have been received for such livestock if sold under the farmer's usual business practices.

The election is available only if:

(1) The farmer (i.e., a taxpayer whose principal trade or business is farming) uses the cash method of accounting;

(2) The farmer can establish that, under usual business practice, the sale of the livestock would not have occurred in that tax year but for drought or other weather related conditions; and

(3) The drought, flood or other weather related conditions resulted in the area's being designated as eligible for assistance by the federal government.

The amount of income that may be deferred is determined as follows:

$$\frac{\text{total income from sales of livestock}}{\text{total number of livestock sold}} \times \text{excess number of livestock sold} = \text{amount that may be deferred}$$

This election also applies to foundation herds, such as cattle and horses, that are held for draft, breeding, dairy, or sporting purposes for 24 or more months, or to other livestock that are held for similar purposes for 12 or more months.

> ***Example:*** Marty Stone is a cash-method livestock producer who sells about 400 to 500 yearlings each year. He normally keeps the calves from his foundation herd, pastures them for a year, and then sells them in the following year. In Year 1, a drought in his disaster-declared area forces him to sell 200 of his calves, in addition to his normal quota of yearlings. Stone can elect to defer the income from the sale of the calves until Year 2.

Time and manner of making the election

The election, which must be made by the due date for filing the farmer's return, including extensions, is made by attaching a statement to the return or amended return for the tax year involved. The statement must contain the name and address of the taxpayer and the following information for each classification of livestock for which the election is made:

(1) A declaration that the taxpayer is making an election under section 451(e);

(2) Evidence of the existence of the drought or other weather related conditions that forced the early sale or exchange of the livestock and the date, if known, on which the area was designated as eligible for assistance by the federal government as a result of the drought or other weather related conditions;

(3) A statement explaining the relationship of the drought or other adverse weather related area to the taxpayer's early sale or exchange of the livestock;

(4) The total number of animals sold in each of the three preceding years;

(5) The number of animals that would have been sold in the tax year had the taxpayer followed normal business practice in the absence of drought or other adverse weather;

(6) The total number of animals sold, and the number sold on account of drought or other adverse weather, during the tax year; and

(7) A computation of the amount of income to be deferred for each such classification.

The election must be made separately for each tax year to which it is to apply and may be revoked only with the approval of the IRS.

.05 Code Sec. 451(e); Reg. §1.451-7.

Sales and Exchanges

¶25,391 In General. Sales and exchanges (other than tax-deferred, like-kind exchanges) made in the ordinary course of the business of farming may result in a capital gain or loss or an ordinary gain or loss. A farmer who exchanges property for services, or services for property must report the fair market value of the property or services received (.05). This includes such exchanges as livestock or produce for services, groceries, feed, or other items, or the exchange of services for livestock, produce, feed, or other items (see ¶25,347).

In order to determine whether sales and exchanges have resulted in ordinary or capital gain or loss, property must first be classified as (1) capital assets (¶5610), (2) noncapital or ordinary assets, or (3) assets used in a trade or business for more than one year (the so-called "Code Sec. 1231 assets") (see ¶5702 and following).

A sale or exchange of a true capital asset results in a capital gain or loss, and a sale or exchange of a true noncapital or ordinary asset results in ordinary income or loss. Whether a sale or an exchange of a "Code Sec. 1231 asset" results in capital or ordinary gain or loss must be determined from a comparison of the recognized gains and losses from all sales and exchanges involving "Code Sec. 1231 assets" within a given tax year. See ¶25,394. Generally, capital gains are taxed at lower rates than ordinary income (see ¶5580 an following).

Recapture

For a discussion of the special rules relating to the recapture of depreciation, cost recovery, and farm land expenditure deductions through the subsequent sale of farm property, see ¶25,405 and following.

Basis reduction

For a discussion of the basis reduction rules for depreciation deductions and investment tax credits claimed, see ¶25,392.

.05 Code Sec. 1231; Reg. §1.1231-1.

¶25,392 Buildings, Land or Equipment. Whether a sale of farmland, buildings or equipment results in a capital or ordinary gain or loss depends primarily on the applicability of Code Sec. 1231 (¶5702 and following), and the various "recapture" provisions (Code Sec. 1245, 1250, and 1252 (¶5800 and following). A farmer's residence and other nonbusiness property are generally capital assets, unless they are used at least in part for business purposes. As to inclusion of a loss in the computation of a net operating loss, see ¶10,800 and following.

Depreciation deductions claimed during the life of depreciable farm assets reduce the basis of such assets proportionately and, to this extent, may result in taxable income upon a sale or exchange. The farmer's basis in such property must be reduced further by the full amount of commercial rehabilitation investment tax credits claimed. As to most farm property placed in service after December 31, 1982, farmers must also reduce the basis of farm assets by 50 percent of the amount of regular, energy, and certified historic investment tax credits claimed (see ¶25,381 for a discussion of the repeal of ITC) unless an election was made with respect to the regular investment tax credit to elect a two-percentage-point reduction in the credit. The basis of farm assets is reduced by 100 percent of the regular investment credit for property placed in service after 1985.

For further discussion of the basis reduction and transitional rules for investment tax credits, see ¶2653 and following.

¶25,393 Allocation of Basis or Selling Price Among Assets Sold. If more than one asset is sold, it may be necessary for the seller to apportion the selling price among the various types of assets sold in order to determine what portion is ordinary income or loss and what part is capital gain or loss (.05). Similarly, the purchaser is usually required to allocate the cost among the various assets acquired, in order to determine their cost or other basis to the purchaser (.10). In both cases, the allocation is made on the basis of market values at the time of the sale, which are not necessarily the same as the values fixed in the contract or used by either party as a basis for the negotiations leading to the sale.

☐ See ¶5160 for additional details.

.05 Code Sec. 1012; Reg. §1.1012-1.

.10 *L.H. Edwards*, CA-5, 57-1 USTC ¶9495, 242 F2d 142, aff'g IRS Letter Ruling 8421001, 1-25-84, CCH IRS LETTER RULINGS REPORTS.

¶25,394 Code Sec. 1231 Assets. Code Sec. 1231 (¶5702) contains a special provision for grouping long-term gains and losses from (1) depreciable property and real estate used in a trade or business, (2) involuntarily converted property used in a trade or business, and (3) involuntarily converted capital assets used in a trade or business or a transaction entered into for profit (.05). These items are called "Code Sec. 1231 assets."

The first step in grouping Code Sec. 1231 gains and losses is to compute the gains and losses from involuntary conversions of (1) business property held for more than 12 months and (2) capital assets held for more than 12 months. If the result is a net gain, all the gains and losses are treated as Code Sec. 1231 capital gains and losses. If the result is a net loss, however, the gains and losses are considered ordinary in nature (.10).

The second step is to net all the Code Sec. 1231 gains and losses (including involuntary conversion gains and losses treated as such under the first step). If a net gain results, Sec. 1231 gains and losses are treated as long-term capital gains and losses. If a net loss results, they are treated as ordinary gains and losses.

Recognized gains or losses

For purposes of the Code Sec. 1231 comparison of whether recognized gains exceed recognized losses, farmers must list recognized gains and losses from the sale, exchange, or involuntary conversion of

(1) cattle and horses held for 24 months or more for draft, dairy, breeding, or sporting purposes and other livestock held for 12 months or more for draft, dairy, breeding, or sporting purposes (see ¶25,402). Recognized gains or losses from involuntary conversions of livestock resulting from drought, flood, other weather-related conditions, or disease are also included if the animals have been held for the required period (see ¶25,388);

(2) depreciable property used in the farming business, such as farm machinery, trucks, barns, sheds, etc.;

(3) real estate used in the farming business;

(4) unharvested crops on land used in farming; the crops and land must be sold or exchanged at the same time and to the same person in one transaction (see ¶25,400), but a lease of the land with the standing crops is not included;

(5) timber where the election has been made to treat the cutting of timber as a sale, and timber held for more than 12 months in which an economic interest has been retained;

(6) coal or iron ore held more than 12 months in which an economic interest has been retained; and

(7) capital assets held for more than 12 months in connection with a trade or business or a for-profit transaction but only if these assets have been involuntarily converted.

When recognized gains and losses arising from a casualty or theft of the property listed above result in a net gain, the gains and losses are treated as gains and losses from Code Sec. 1231 assets. However, if there is a net loss, gains and losses are treated as ordinary gains and losses and are not part of the overall Code Sec. 1231 comparison.

Example: Rice Garland, a farmer, shows the following results for his current tax year:

Property	*Months Held*	*Gain*	*Loss*
25 acres of farm land	40	$ 2,000	—
Barn (insured in part) burned down	48	$ 2,300	—
Truck sold	4	—	$ 140
Extra tractor sold	13	—	$ 150
		$ 4,300	$ 290

All of these items are subject to Code Sec. 1231 except the sale of the truck, which was held for less than 12 months and a day. Since the involuntary conversion of the barn arising from a casualty loss resulted in a net gain of $2,300, it is treated as a Sec. 1231 transaction. The result of netting all the Sec. 1231 gains and losses is a $4,150 gain. Accordingly, those gains and losses are treated as long-term capital gains and losses. If the sale of the farm land had resulted in a $3,000 loss instead of a gain, the net result would have been an $850 loss and the gains and losses would have been treated as ordinary gains and losses.

Where there is an ordinary income recapture of previously taken cost recovery or depreciation deductions from the sale of farm assets, only the excess of the gain from the sale or exchange over the recapture amount is treated as a Code Sec. 1231 gain.

.05 Code Sec. 1231; Reg. §§1.1231-1, 1.1231-2.

.10 Code Sec. 1033(e); Reg. §1.1033(e)-1

¶25,395 Code Sec. 1231 Treatment on Return. Gains and losses from section 1231 assets are reported on Form 4797 (Sales of Business Property). The excess of these gains over any ordinary income recapture amounts (see ¶25,405 and following) is considered with all other Code Sec. 1231 items in determining whether there is a net Code Sec. 1231 gain or loss (.05). If there is a net Code Sec. 1231 gain, it is carried to Schedule D (Capital Gains and Losses) and combined with the other capital gains and losses. The net capital gain or loss from Schedule D is carried to Form 1040.

If there is a net Code Sec. 1231 loss, it is included with the other ordinary gains and losses (including the Code Sec. 1245, 1250 and 1252 ordinary income) on Form 4797. The net ordinary gain or loss from Form 4797 is entered on Form 1040.

Recapture of past Code Sec. 1231 losses

Net Code Sec. 1231 gains must be treated as ordinary income to the extent of net Code Sec. 1231 losses (ordinary losses) for the five immediately preceding tax years beginning after 1981. Therefore, a farmer must recapture post-1981 net Code Sec. 1231 losses when the farmer has net Code Sec. 1231 gains. However, past Code Sec. 1231 net losses may not be recaptured in excess of current net Code Sec. 1231 gains.

.05 Code Sec. 1231(c); Reg. §§1.1231-1 and 1.1231-2.

¶25,396 Installment Method of Reporting Gain. Sales of farm property are eligible for installment reporting, under which a portion of each installment is treated as taxable gain on receipt. The method applies to sales of real property and to certain sales of personal property (.05). For the installment method to apply to a transaction, at least one payment must be receivable after the close of the tax year in which the sale occurs. The installment method is automatic unless the taxpayer elects to the contrary. Farmers may also use the installment method for dispositions of stock in trade, inventory, or property held primarily for sale to customers for purposes of the alternative minimum tax (.10)

If the installment method is used, any depreciation recapture under Code Sec. 1245 and 1250 (see ¶25,405 and following) must be included in income in the year in which the property is disposed of even though the balance of the gain is included in income for subsequent tax years as payments are received. Thus, for purposes of determining the amount of ordinary income recaptured, the payments under an installment contract are treated as if they were all received in the year of disposition.

The use of the installment method is limited in certain instances involving the sale of real property or sales of personal property by a dealer in personal property that has received cash for borrowings related to its installment obligations, termed "allocable installment indebtedness." A deemed payment based on allocable installment indebtedness will accelerate the reporting of deferred income on the installment sales. However, this so-called proportionate disallowance rule does not apply to installment obligations arising from the disposition of any property used or produced in the trade or business of farming.

Example: An S corporation that was a dealer in farming equipment was not entitled to report gains from sales of irrigation equipment on the installment method of accounting because the farm property exception to the prohibition on the use of the installment method by dealers in personal property did not apply to the corporation. The contention by the corporation shareholders that "used in farming" includes equipment to be used by farmers was contrary to the language of the Code, which excepts only dealers of timeshare and residential lots from the prohibition. Additionally, since most equipment can be used in farming, the shareholders' interpretation of the statute would place an unreasonable burden on the IRS to determine if a purchaser was actually using the equipment for farming.(.15)

☐ For further details regarding accounting for installment sales, see ¶15,355 and following.

.05 Code Sec. 453; Reg. §1.453-1.
.10 Code Sec. 56(a)(6).
.15 *J.L. Thom,* CA-8, 2002-1 USTC ¶50,293, 283 F3d 939; Code Sec. 453(l)(2)(B).

¶25,397 Timber. There are some special tax rules to be observed by farmers who own timber. As a general rule, a farmer's standing timber is a capital asset because it is not usually held for sale in the ordinary course of farming operations. Thus, a sale of standing timber generally results in either long-term or short-term capital gain or loss, reported on Schedule D of Forms 1040, 1041 and 1065 (.05). However, if the timber is held for sale in the ordinary course of the business, the gain or loss is reported on Schedule F as ordinary farm income or loss.

The holding period for long-term capital gain or loss for timber is more than one year, and, for short-term capital gain or loss, one year or less (.10). If timber has been held for less than 12 months before it is cut and sold in the form of logs, pulpwood, firewood, or other products, the sale results in ordinary income or loss if the timber was held for sale, and short-term capital gain or loss if it was not held for sale.

If a farmer owned cut timber for a period of more than 12 months prior to cutting, the farmer will have ordinary income or loss or long-term capital gain or loss on its sale, depending upon the purpose for which it was held.

Election to treat cutting as sale

Ordinarily the gain or loss from the cutting of such timber is taxable in the year in which the sale is made. However, a farmer may elect to treat the cutting of timber as a sale if the farmer owned the timber or held a contract right to cut timber on the first day of the tax year in which the timber is cut and for more than 12 months before the cutting (.15). An election to treat the cutting of timber as a sale means that the gain or loss is reported in the year of the cutting rather than in the year of the actual sale. The gain or loss is the difference between the fair market value of the standing timber at the beginning of the tax year and its adjusted basis.

If the farmer elects to treat the cutting as a sale, the gain or loss is included in the "Code Sec. 1231" comparison of gains and losses from certain property used in the farm business (see ¶25,394). The fair market value of the timber becomes the basis of the cut timber, and the later sale of the cut timber generally results in ordinary gain or loss.

Once this election is made, it is binding for subsequent years unless permission to change is obtained from the IRS.

Involuntary conversion

Where the cutting of timber is necessitated by a natural disaster, such as a forest fire, and the taxpayer has elected to treat the cutting as a sale, the involuntary conversion nonrecognition-of-gain rules apply (¶25,387) (.20).

Sales and depletion allocation

If a farmer cuts timber and sells it in the form of logs, cordwood, lumber, or other products, the proceeds are included in income, as are the proceeds from the sales of other farm products. The costs of cutting and marketing the timber products, and also the timber depletion allocable to the timber sold, are deductible expenses. Depletion is computed as follows:

(1) determine the cost or other basis of the timberland, including the standing timber;

(2) allocate to the timber its proper portion of the combined basis of the land and the timber, using relative values at the time of acquisition; and

(3) determine the proportion of the basis of the timber that is allocable to the timber cut and sold during the tax year.

For example, if the allocated cost of the standing timber—item (2) above—is $2,000 and the amount of the timber cut and sold during the tax year represented one-tenth of the original standing timber—item (3) above—the depletion allocable to the timber cut and sold is $200. If a depletion deduction is taken for timber cut in the current tax year but not sold until the following year, the cost of the cut timber must be included in the current year's closing inventory.

> ***Example:*** Forest Green purchased a 1,000-acre timber tract for $3,000,000, of which $750,000 was allocable to the land and $2,250,000 was allocable to the timber. It was estimated that there were 500,000 board feet of timber on the tract. During the first year, Green felled 175,000 board feet of timber. His depletion allowance for the year in which the timber was sold (assuming all of the felled timber was sold in one year) is computed as follows: $2,250,000 (cost) ÷ 500,000 (board feet available) = $4.50 per board foot (rate of depletion). 175,000 (board feet of timber felled) × $4.50 (rate) = $787,500 (amount of depletion).

If the value of timber property as of any specific date has been determined and approved by the IRS, no revaluation will be made or allowed while it remains under the same ownership, except in the case of misrepresentation or fraud or gross error as to any facts known on the date as of which the valuation was made. Reg. §1.611-3(g) states that revaluation will be made only with the written approval of the IRS.

The adjusted basis of the timber for depletion computation purposes includes the cost of timber units acquired during the year and any proper additions to capital. The number of remaining units in the timber account is equal to the number of units on hand in the account at the beginning of the year, plus the number of units acquired during the year, plus or minus the number of units needed to be added or subtracted to correct the estimate of remaining units (.25).

If a taxpayer has elected under Code Sec. 631 to treat the cutting of timber as a sale or exchange, the allowable depletion (or cost of goods sold) on a later sale of the timber or its products is, generally, the fair market value of the timber cut during the tax year. The fair market value of the timber cut during the tax year is determined as of the first day of the year in which the timber was cut (.30).

Sale caused by clearing land

Presumably, the same depletion treatment explained above is proper even though the sale of the timber is a direct result of clearing the land, and the proceeds from the sale might be treated as salvage that reduces the cost of clearing. If there is only one contract for cutting and clearing, without specific charges for each, it is necessary to apportion a part of the contract costs to the cutting and use this allocated part in computing the gain on the sale of the timber. The balance of the clearing contract costs is a capital expenditure.

The result is different if the party contracting to clear the land is permitted to dispose of the timber and the clearance contract calls for payment of a net sum reflecting an estimate of the amount the contractor will realize from the timber. In this instance, since the situation is comparable to a trade-in that is absorbed in the cost of the new item, the amount paid on the contract would be a capital expenditure.

Depreciation

Buildings, machinery and equipment of a sawmill or timber plant may be written off by using the modified accelerated cost recovery system for property placed in service after 1986 or, alternatively, by electing out of MACRS by using the unit-of-production method. The latter method contemplates the writing off of the assets at a rate which varies each year, according to the current exhaustion of stumpage. Except when computing the MACRS deduction, due regard must be given to salvage value at the end of the estimated useful lives, and to equipment that can be moved to another location at the end of logging operations in the area. The unit-of-production method is the more widely used method of deducting depreciation, as it puts the heavy deductions in the years of extensive cutting.

.05 Code Sec. 631; Reg. §§1.631-1, 1.631-2.

.10 Code Sec. 1222.

.15 Code Sec. 631(a).

.20 IRS Letter Ruling 8212008, 12-18-81, CCH IRS LETTER RULINGS REPORTS.

.25 Reg. §1.611-3(b)(2).

.30 Reg. §1.631-1(e).

¶25,398 Retained Economic Interest in Timber. If a farmer disposes of timber under any form of cutting contract whereby the farmer retains an economic interest in the timber (such as in a pay-for-as-cut contract), and the farmer had previously held the timber for more than 12 months, the disposal is treated as a sale of property used in the farmer's business (.05). The resulting gain or loss is then included in the "Code Sec. 1231" comparison (see ¶25,394). This is a mandatory result, not an elective one. The farmer has no choice in the matter. For sales of timber after December 31, 2004, the requirement that the taxpayer retain an economic interest has been generally eliminated (.10).

The date that the timber is disposed of is the date on which the timber is cut except that, if the payment is received before the timber is cut, the date of the payment can be treated as the date of disposal. The date on which the timber is cut means the date when, in the ordinary course of business, the quantity of the felled timber is first definitely determined.

.05 Code Sec. 631(b); Reg. §1.631-2.

.10 Code Sec. 631(b), as amended by the American Jobs Creation Act of 2004 (P.L. 108-357).

¶25,399 Evergreen ("Christmas") Trees. Evergreen trees that are more than six years old when severed from their roots for sale for ornamental purposes (such as Christmas trees) are included in the term "timber" for purposes of the provisions described at ¶25,397 (.05).

.05 Reg. §1.631-1(b)(2).

¶25,400 Unharvested Crops. When a farm is sold with an unharvested crop, the unharvested crop is considered as property used in the trade or business, and Code Sec. 1231 capital gain treatment (see ¶25,394) applies to the entire sales proceeds if the land has been held for more than 12 months. Expenses related to the crop must be capitalized in computing the overall gain. This applies to fruit as well as to other crops (.05).

Code Sec. 1231 does not apply to a sale, exchange or involuntary conversion of an unharvested crop if the taxpayer retains any right or option to reacquire the land on which the crop is growing (other than the right incident to a mortgage or other security transaction). The length of time for which the crop, as distinguished from the land, is held is immaterial. Nor does Code Sec. 1231 apply to the sale of crops growing on leased land, since a leasehold is not considered land for this purpose (.10).

Any expenses incurred in connection with the crop must be removed from the farmer's current deductions, both for the year of the sale and for previous years, and added to the farmer's basis. Amended returns are required for all open years, but expenses can still be used to increase basis even though no adjustment is made for closed year.

.05 Code Sec. 268, Code Sec. 1231; Reg. §§1.268-1, 1.1231-1(f).

.10 *Bidart Bros.*, CA-9, 59-1 USTC ¶9193, 262 F2d 607, cert. denied, 359 U.S. 1003.

¶25,401 Topsoil and Gravel. Soil and loam in place are natural deposits eligible for depletion (.05). Therefore, a landowner is entitled to claim an allowance for cost depletion, but not percentage depletion, if soil and loam in place are severed and sold (.10). Gravel and sand are eligible for percentage depletion or cost depletion, whichever produces the larger allowance (.15).

The gradual consumption of topsoil through ordinary farming processes does not qualify for a depletion allowance (.20). However, cost depletion of topsoil is allowable upon the sale of sod or balled nursery stock if the amount of depletable soil can be determined (.25).

If the amount of naturally occurring soil depleted with each sod harvest cannot be established, no deduction for cost depletion is allowed. For example, where a sod farmer removes a certain amount of soil with each harvest and partially replenishes it through the decomposition of grass roots remaining in the soil, the periodic addition of fertilizer and lime, and the decomposition of a leguminous cover crop grown and plowed under after each second harvest, a cost depletion deduction is improper because the amount of natural soil depletion cannot be determined (.30).

If the farmer sells soil in place with the buyer to sever and remove it in bulk, the gain is treated as capital gain taxable at ordinary income rates. The farmer must apportion a part of the cost of the land to the topsoil, and the allocation might be made in substantially the same manner as that outlined for sales of timber at ¶25,397. If this allocation cannot be made, the proceeds (reduced by expenses of sale) are not income but a return of capital, which reduces the basis of the land.

The effect of the sale on the farming business should be considered. The owner of land used in dairy farming realized long-term capital gain from the sale to a contractor of all the usable topsoil down to the top of the water table (to be used by the contractor as fill (.35)). The farmer no longer retained an economic interest in the soil in place, and the removal of the soil rendered the land useless for dairy farming.

.05 Code Sec. 611-617.

.10 Rev. Rul. 79-411, 1979-2 CB 246.

.15 Code Sec. 613(b).

.20 *A. Duda*, CA-5, 77-2 USTC ¶9678, 560 F2d 669.

.25 Rev. Rul. 79-411, 1979-2 CB 246; Rev. Rul. 77-12, 1977-1 CB 161; *J. W. Meyers*, 66 TC 235, CCH Dec. 33,807 (Acq.); *Flona Corp.*, DC Fla., 63-2 USTC ¶9544, 218 FSupp 354.

.30 Rev. Rul. 79-267, 1979-2 CB 243.

.35 *R. M. Dann*, 30 TC 499, CCH Dec. 23,011; *Vance Est.*, 19 TCM 904, CCH Dec. 24,314(M), TC Memo. 1960-167.

¶25,402 Culls, Dairy, Draft, Sporting and Breeding Animals. The income tax basis for gain or loss on the sale of breeding, draft, dairy, or sporting livestock by farmers depends on whether the animals have been depreciated, whether they are qualified-investment-tax-credit property for which an investment tax credit was claimed, or whether they have been inventoried (.05). If the animals have been depreciated, the basis for gain or loss is the cost or other basis reduced by allowed or allowable depreciation. If they were pre-1986 qualified-investment-tax-credit property, their basis must be reduced by 50 percent of the amount of the investment tax credit (see ¶25,381 for post-1986 ITC repeal) claimed unless the farmer elected to lower the claimed credit percentage by two points (four percent instead of six percent in the case of 3-year cost recovery property). Basis must be reduced by the full amount of the credit for periods after 1985. If there is a recapture of the credit, there is an upward basis adjustment immediately prior to the disposition of the property by an amount equal to 50 percent of such recapture amount (for property placed in service before January 1, 1991) (.10).

If the animals are mature and part of an inventory, the basis for gain or loss is their inventory value.

Immature animals

Where immature draft, breeding, dairy, or sporting animals that have been inventoried are sold during the year, their basis for gain or loss is the beginning inventory value plus any additional normal raising costs incurred to the date of sale that would be reflected under the taxpayer's method of inventorying (.15). Thus, under the cost or the lower-of-cost-or-market method (¶15,640), the basis of an immature animal sold during the year is the beginning inventory value plus the actual costs of raising it that were incurred during the year. Under the unit-livestock-price method (see ¶25,343), the basis is the beginning inventory value plus a pro rata portion of the unit-livestock-price increase for the year. Under the farm-price method (see ¶25,342), the basis is the animal's opening inventory value without any increase for normal raising costs since the inventory values under this method are determined without taking raising costs into consideration.

> ***Example 1:*** Gwen Roper is a rancher using the unit-livestock-price method of inventorying her cattle, with standard unit prices of $100 for calves, $150 for yearlings, $200 for two-year-olds, and $250 for mature animals. On July 1, she sells an animal that was classified in the January 1 inventory as a yearling and held for breeding purposes. The animal's basis for gain or loss on the sale is $175—$150 opening inventory value plus one half of the $50 annual unit-livestock-price increase. Roper must reduce her opening inventory by the $150 inventory value of the animal sold and she must reduce the farm expense deduction for the year by the $25 increase in basis of the animal during the year.

When inventoried immature draft, breeding, dairy or sporting animals are sold during the year, their inventory value must be eliminated from the opening inventory and the additional normal raising costs for the year that are included in the basis for gain or loss (the pro rata portion of the price increase under the unit-livestock-price method) must be eliminated from the deduction for farm expenses for the year. Because there are no additional normal raising costs included in basis under the farm-price method, there is no corresponding reduction of the farm expense deduction.

Sec. 1231 capital gain-ordinary income loss treatment

Gain or loss on the sale of a cull from a dairy, draft, breeding, or sporting herd, or from the sale of any animals from such herds, may qualify for the capital gain-ordinary loss treatment under Code Sec. 1231 (¶25,394 and ¶25,395). The following classes of livestock qualify for Code Sec. 1231 treatment:

(1) cattle and horses, regardless of age, held for draft, breeding, dairy or sporting purposes for 24 months or more from the date of acquisition and

(2) other livestock, regardless of age, held for draft, breeding, dairy or sporting purposes for 12 months or more from the date of acquisition.

The capital gain from the sale of depreciated or qualified-investment-tax-credit livestock is generally reduced by the application of the depreciation and investment tax credit recapture provisions explained at ¶5800 and ¶25,411.

Purpose for which animal was held

A key problem in qualifying for capital gain treatment under Code Sec. 1231 lies in proving that the animal was held for dairy, draft, breeding, or sporting purposes, or that it is a cull. Whether livestock is held for dairy, draft, breeding or sporting purposes, and the propriety of a classification as a cull, depends on the facts of each case.

The actual use to which the animal is put will ordinarily establish the purpose for which the animal is held. Even though an animal is part of a breeding herd, if the breeding herd itself is held by the taxpayer for ultimate sale to customers in the ordinary course of trade or business, Code Sec. 1231 treatment will not generally apply (.20). However, capital gain and not ordinary income was realized on the sale of mink pelts from animals removed from a breeding herd and slaughtered (.25). Also, the advertising of animals culled (identified and separated) from a breeding herd for sale did not change the character of culls, and a taxpayer was entitled to capital gains on their sale (.30).

An animal is not held for dairy, draft, breeding, or sporting purposes simply because it is suitable for such purposes, or because it is held for sale to other persons to be used by them for dairy, draft, breeding or sporting purposes.

Even though the *ultimate* purpose for which an animal is held is for sale in the ordinary course of business, it may still be considered as having been held for breeding purposes, under certain circumstances.

> ***Example 2:*** Farmer Jones raises hogs for slaughter. He makes it a practice to breed his sows once before selling them (to produce offspring to be held for sale). These brood sows can be treated as having been held for breeding purposes.

> ***Example 3:*** Farmer Jones also raises breeding cattle for sale. To prove their fitness for breeding purposes, he breeds them once before selling them. These cattle are not considered to be held for breeding purposes, since the breeding in this case is an ordinary and necessary incident for their sale for breeding purposes.

Where the actual use for dairy, draft, breeding, or sporting purposes has not begun before the sale (and is not prevented by accident, disease, or other occurrence), proving the purpose for which the livestock were held becomes more difficult. While Code Sec. 1231 benefits are generally not available if the animals are sold before reaching maturity (the age at which they become suitable for dairy, draft, breeding, or sporting purposes), the availability of such benefits must be determined on a case-by-case basis after a consideration of the circumstances surrounding the farmer's purpose for holding the livestock (.35).

Code Sec. 1231 benefits are not necessarily denied when the actual use of the animal for dairy, draft, breeding, or sporting purposes is prevented, as by accident, weather-related conditions, or unfitness (sterility for instance), so long as the farmer can prove the purpose for which the animal was intended and provided such animals are disposed of within a reasonable time.

Breeding purpose determination. Although a decision as to an animal's quality for breeding purposes is not affirmatively determinable before it has offspring, the breeder can judge in advance if an animal is unsatisfactory for breeding. The following are some of the factors that have been considered in concluding whether young animals not yet capable of breeding were being held for that purpose or were held for sale:

(1) quality of the herd;

(2) reasons for disposing of immature animals, if related to their value for draft, breeding, dairy or sporting purposes rather than merely to the size of the herd;

(3) absence of a limit on size of the herd;

(4) adequacy of facilities to keep all animals if they should all meet the standards of the herd;

(5) adequacy of records to identify each animal, its status as a member of the herd, and its desirable or undesirable characteristics; and

(6) absence of extensive efforts to sell immature animals, although some advertising is acceptable.

Inventory. Capital gain treatment, under Code Sec. 1231, is allowed on sales of draft, breeding, dairy, or sporting livestock that have been included in inventory. They are property used in a trade or business, even though they have been inventoried (.40). Capital gains resulted from the sale of animals by livestock raisers and breeders who used the unit-livestock-price method and the farm-price method of inventorying the animals (.45). However, the basis of each animal is its inventory valuation at the time of sale (.50).

Livestock investment programs

There is some conflict as to the tax consequences of livestock investment programs. In a typical program, an investor purchases animals from a professional livestock breeder and then pays the breeder a management fee to care for the animals. The breeder guarantees a certain number of offspring from each animal, the purchase of the offspring at a specified price, and the repurchase of the animals originally sold. Risk of loss due to death of the animals or their offspring remains with the livestock breeder.

According to the IRS, the investors cannot be treated as owning any of the animals. Thus, livestock purchase agreements under these programs do not constitute purchases of animals for tax purposes (.55). The livestock breeder must capitalize, rather than deduct, expenses relating to the animals, and the investors cannot claim depreciation deductions or investment credits on the animals. However, the Tax Court holds that investors can be treated as owners of animals that are not specifically assigned to them if there are valid reasons for the nonassignment—such as spreading the risk of loss due to death of calves and ensuring that investors received calves of equal value (.60).

The IRS does not permit maintenance fee deductions under livestock-breeding agreements that give an investor the option of purchasing animals at a future date. From the IRS standpoint, the investor has not incurred any risk in the raising of the livestock, even when the investor actually purchases the livestock and maintenance fees for raising the livestock are added to the purchase price. Because there is no actual ownership of the livestock until the investor purchases them, the investor undertakes no risk in the raising of the livestock. To claim maintenance fee deductions for livestock, an investor must incur the risk of raising the livestock. Without actually owning the livestock, that risk is usually absent, and the entire purchase price and maintenance expense for the livestock must be capitalized (.65).

.05 Code Sec. 1231(b)(3); Reg. §1.1231-2.

.10 Code Sec. 48(q), prior to amendment by the Revenue Reconciliation Act of 1990 (P.L. 101-508).

.15 Rev. Rul. 55-188, 1955-1 CB 226, as amplified by Rev. Rul. 55-736, 1955-2 CB 522.

.20 *M. P. Moore*, 31 TC 735, CCH Dec. 23,406 (Acq.); *L. D. Hancock*, 31 TC 752, CCH Dec. 23,408 (Acq.).

.25 *Cedarburg Fox Farms, Inc.*, CA-7, 60-2 USTC ¶9760, 283 F2d 711; *C.F. Cook*, CA-8, 59-2 USTC ¶9706, 270 F2d 725; *B. Edwards*, 32 TC 751, CCH Dec. 23,652 (Acq.); Rev. Rul. 61-42, 1961-1 CB 751.

.30 *L. D. Hancock*, 31 TC 752, CCH Dec. 23,408 (Acq.).

.35 *Biltmore Co.*, CA-4, 56-1 USTC ¶9129, 228 F2d 9; *J. M. McDonald*, CA-2, 54-2 USTC ¶9488, 214 F2d 341; *J. M. McDonald*, 23 TC 1091, CCH Dec. 20,939 (Acq.); *R. B. Gotfredson*, CA-6, 55-1 USTC ¶9119, 217 F2d 673; *C. A. Smith Est.*, 23 TC 690, CCH Dec. 20,828 (Acq.); *A. Duda*, CA-5, 77-2 USTC ¶9678, 560 F2d 669.

.40 *Fawn Lake Ranch Co.*, 12 TC 1139, CCH Dec. 17,061 (Acq.).

.45 *Diamond A Cattle Co.*, 21 TC 1, CCH Dec. 19,927.

.50 *E. Sorelle*, 22 TC 459, CCH Dec. 20,372 (Acq.).

.55 Rev. Rul. 78-411, 1978-2 CB 112 (reasoning based on *H. D. Wiener*, 58 TC 81, CCH Dec. 31,388, aff'd by CA-9, 74-1 USTC ¶9403, 494 F2d 691). See, also, Tax Court discussion of the livestock investment rules in *M.O. Houchins*, 79 TC 570, CCH Dec. 39,387.

.60 *P. N. Duggar*, 71 TC 147, CCH Dec. 35,518 (Acq.).

.65 Rev. Rul. 84-35, 1984-1 CB 31.

¶25,403 Residence Sold with Farm. The sale of a farm usually involves the disposition of both nonbusiness property (residence) and business property (the land, buildings used for farm operations, machinery, livestock, and other farm items). Tax on gain realized on the sale of the residence may be postponed or eliminated. See ¶5416 and ¶5543.

Recapture of Farm Depreciation

¶25,405 Gain from Depreciable Personal Property. Gain from the sale or other disposition of depreciable property (known as "Code Sec. 1245 property" is taxable as ordinary income to the extent of depreciation or cost recovery deductions previously taken (.05). Property classified as Code Sec. 1245 property is personal property, such as machinery, equipment, and vehicles. Property that is contained in or attached to a building is also subject to this recapture rule, as are livestock (see ¶25,411) and single-purpose agricultural and horticultural structures.

> ***Example:*** Mr. Malcolm Holz owns and sells a tractor and a livestock-feeding machine. He realizes a $5,000 gain from the tractor and a $200 loss from the feeding machine. Mr. Holz had previously taken cost recovery deductions on the tractor and feeding machine.
>
> Because there was a loss from the feeding machine, only the tractor is subject to recapture as Code Sec. 1245 property. Therefore, Mr. Holz must treat as ordinary income an amount of the gain from the tractor equal to his cost recovery deductions previously taken for the tractor as ordinary income. The amount that may be recaptured as ordinary income is limited to the amount of gain realized from the sale of the tractor.

Land and inherently permanent improvements on land, such as buildings and their structural components, are not considered Code Sec. 1245 property. Those assets are considered realty and are subject to recapture as Code Sec. 1250 realty property (see ¶25,406).

For purposes of recapture, an election to expense certain depreciable business property under Code Sec. 179 is treated as a depreciation deduction. Moreover, the amount of the basis adjustment for the investment tax credit is treated as a depreciation deduction. Therefore, the expensing election and credit adjustment are both subject to ordinary income recapture.

☐ For a detailed explanation of the recapture rules for Code Sec. 1245 property, see ¶5800 and following.

.05 Code Sec. 1245; Reg. §1.1245-1.

¶25,406 Gain from Depreciable Realty. Part or all of the gain from the sale or other disposition of depreciable or cost recovery realty known as Code Sec. 1250 property is taxable as ordinary income (.05). Generally, when a farmer disposes of Code Sec. 1250 property, the recapture amount is equal to the cost recovery or depreciation deductions allowed in excess of the deductions that would have been permitted under straight-line depreciation.

☐ For a detailed explanation of the recapture rules for Code Sec. 1250 property, see ¶5810 and following.

.05 Code Sec. 1250; Reg. §1.1250-1.

Recapture of Farm Land Expenditures

¶25,409 Recapture of Farm Land Expenditures on Sale. If farm land held for less than 10 years is disposed of at a gain, a percentage of the total post-1969 deductions for soil and water conservation expenditures (see ¶25,369) and land clearance expenditures is subject to recapture as ordinary income (.05). If the land is held for five years or less, the recapture percentage is 100 percent. The recapture percentage is 80 percent if the land is disposed of within the sixth year after acquisition. If disposal is within the seventh, eighth or ninth year after acquisition, the recapture percentage is 60 percent, 40 percent or 20 percent, respectively. There is no recapture after the ninth year.

> ***Example:*** A calendar-year farmer acquired farm land on October 1, 1992. On January 18, 2003, he sold the land at a $40,000 gain. Between January 1 and October 1, 1996, he made soil and water conservation expenditures of $15,000 that were fully deductible in 1996. The recapture percentage is 20%, since the land was sold within the ninth year after acquisition. Thus, $3,000 (20% of $15,000) of the $40,000 gain is treated as Sec. 1252 ordinary income. (The $37,000 balance is treated as Sec. 1231 gain.)

The recapture of farm land expenditures covers only deductible soil and water conservation and land-clearing expenditures. If deduction of these expenditures is limited because of the 25 percent-of-gross-farming-income ($5,000 for land-clearing expenditures) limitation they are not subject to recapture. Also, there is no recapture if these expenditures are capitalized.

There are a number of exceptions under which the gain from the transfer of farm land does not have to be recognized; for these exceptions, see ¶25,410.

.05 Code Sec. 1252; Reg. §1.1252-1.

¶25,410 Exempt Transfers. There are a number of exceptions to the rule that ordinary income is recognized on dispositions of farm land on which soil and water conservation expenditures (Code Sec. 175) and land clearing expenditures (former Code Sec. 182) have been deducted (¶25,409) (.05). This is done indirectly by stating in the various sections of the Code that rules similar to those under the Code Sec. 1245 depreciation recapture provisions (see ¶25,407) will apply. In general, these exceptions apply to—

(1) gifts,

(2) transfers at death,

(3) like-kind exchanges (see ¶5293),

(4) involuntary conversions (see ¶5350),

(5) complete liquidations of subsidiaries (see ¶12,256),

(6) transfers to a controlled corporation for stock (see ¶12,301),

(7) reorganization transfers (see ¶12,302),

(8) transfers in certain receivership and bankruptcy proceedings (see ¶12,303), and

(9) transfers between partners and partnerships (see ¶14,415).

.05 Code Secs. 1245(b) and 1252(b); Reg. §1.1252-2.

Recapture of Livestock Depreciation

¶25,411 Depreciation Recapture. To prevent the conversion of ordinary income into capital gain through depreciation and sale of draft, breeding, dairy, or sporting livestock, post-1969 depreciation is recaptured as ordinary income on the sale under Code Sec. 1245 (see

¶5800). Of course, since this provision was enacted, the preferential treatment of capital gains has been repealed and the original intent behind its enactment has been voided (.05).

This recapture provision affects mainly the sale of breeding and other livestock that were purchased and not included in inventory. Raised livestock generally will not have a basis for depreciation (raising costs are currently expensed on the cash basis), but, to the extent it does have a basis and is depreciated, recapture is required.

The gain recognized is ordinary income to the extent of prior depreciation or cost recovery deductions under (1) ACRS or MACRS after 1980 and 1986, respectively, and (2) depreciation deductions taken before 1981 under the pre-ACRS depreciation rules (see ¶25,377).

.05 Code Sec. 1245(a)(2) and (3).

Recapture of Cost-Sharing Payments

¶25,412 Cost-Sharing Recapture. An exclusion from gross income is provided for conservation grants received under programs determined by the Secretary of Agriculture to have been made primarily for conservation or related purposes (see ¶25,362) (.05). Gain on the disposition of property or improvements purchased with such payments may be recaptured as ordinary income where the disposition of such property occurs before the expiration of 20 years after the date of receipt of the payments. The amount subject to recapture is reduced by 10 percent for each year the property is held after the first 10 years. An election may be made to decline application of the exclusion-recapture rules (.10). The election is made on or before the due date (including extensions) for filing the return for the tax year in which the payment was received or accrued.

.05 Code Sec. 126 and 1255.

.10 Code Sec. 126(c).

Returns

¶25,414 In General. A farmer, like other individuals, must file an income tax return if the gross income exceeds the filing threshold for the tax year. Gross income from farming is defined at ¶25,345, but the farmer must also include all other income that is not specifically exempt in determining whether the gross income test is met.

The return of an individual farmer must be made on Form 1040. The requirements for farmers in using and filing Form 1040 are the same as for other taxpayers, except insofar as the reporting of farm income or loss is concerned. For this purpose, see ¶25,415, below.

Income from farming is not subject to withholding tax.

¶25,415 Schedule F. While net farm income is reported on Form 1040, Schedule F (Form 1040) must be used with Form 1040 to generally report farm income, expenses and depreciation. Income and deductions not related to farm operations are reported on other schedules (.05).

Farm income and expenses are accounted for by cash-basis farmers in Parts I and II of Schedule F (Form 1040), except for sales or exchanges of property such as livestock, machinery and other items eligible for capital gain treatment under Code Sec. 1231. These sales transactions are computed and reported on Form 4797 (Sales of Business Property). (See ¶25,383 for the reporting of farm casualty and theft losses.) Farm income also must be carried to Schedule SE (Self Employment Tax) for computing self-employment tax. All non-farm income and deductions are accounted for on Form 1040.

Farmers who use an accrual or inventory method of accounting must enter their business names and addresses, employer identification numbers, and the location and number of acres in each farm and use the schedule of "Farm Deductions," Part II, Schedule F, but will also use Part III, in addition to computing self-employment tax on Schedule SE. Capital transactions, including sales or exchanges of farm property eligible for Sec. 1231 capital gain-ordinary loss treatment, are computed and reported on Form 4797, and other non-farm income and deductions are reported on Form 1040.

Both cash-basis and accrual-basis farmers report net gain from sales and exchanges of property subject to Sec. 1231 treatment on separate Schedule D (Capital Gains and Losses) and on Form 4797.

Farm corporations

If a farm is operated by a corporation, the farm profit or loss is reported on the corporation income tax return (Form 1120).

Farm partnerships

If a farm is operated by a partnership, the profit or loss is reported on the partnership return (Form 1065). Schedule L, a balance sheet, must be filed with the partnership return on Form 1065 (.10).

A penalty is imposed where a partnership fails to file a timely or complete Form 1065 (.15). The penalty is assessed for each month, or fraction of a month (but not to exceed five months) that the failure continues. The penalty for any month is an amount equal to the sum of $50 times the total number of partners that are in the partnership during the tax year. The penalty is imposed on the partnership, rather than on the partners. It will not be imposed in cases where reasonable cause is established for the failure to file a timely or complete partnership return.

However, a domestic farming partnership composed of 10 or fewer non-corporate partners of a type that has not historically filed a partnership return, such as a family farm partnership, will be considered to have met the reasonable cause test and will not be subject to the penalty for the failure to file a partnership return, provided that the partnership or any of the partners establishes, if so requested by the IRS, that all partners have fully reported their shares of the income, deductions, and credits of the partnership on their timely filed income tax returns (.20).

Information returns

Payments of $600 or more made by a farmer in the course of business are reported on information return Form 1099-MISC. Wage payments to individual workers and other forms of compensation subject to withholding are reported on Form W-2.

.05 Code Sec. 6011—6013; Reg. §§1.6011-1—1.6013-4.

.10 Rev. Rul. 59-169, 1959-1 CB 627.

.15 Code Sec. 6698.

.20 Rev. Proc. 84-35, 1984-1 CB 509, modifying and superseding Rev. Proc. 81-11, 1981-1 CB 651.

¶25,416 Payment of Estimated Tax. An individual farmer is not required to file a declaration of estimated tax, although other provisions of the estimated tax rules—including payment requirements and penalties for failure to pay estimated income tax—apply as though a declaration were filed (.05). Individual farmers must earn or receive at least two-thirds of their total gross income from farming in order to qualify for special estimated tax rules. Those rules permit individual farmers on a calendar tax year to defer payment of their estimated tax until January 15 (or the 1st business day after if the 15th falls on a Saturday, Sunday or holiday) of the following tax year. At that time (January 15), the farmer must pay all the estimated tax that is due for the prior tax year (66 ⅔ percent of the tax shown on the return for the tax year).

Alternately, the farmer may simply file a Form 1040 by March 1 of the following tax year and pay the actual tax that is due for the prior tax year.

For example, here is how the estimated tax rules apply to a farmer who began the tax year on January 1, 2003. The farmer may

(1) pay all the estimated tax due by January 15, 2004, and file the Form 1040 (along with payment for the remainder of the tax due) by April 15, 2004, or

(2) file the Form 1040 by March 1, 2004, and pay all the tax that is due at that time (no penalty for failure to pay estimated tax will be imposed).

Farmers who do not start their tax years on January 1 may

(1) pay all the estimated tax due by the 15th day after the end of the tax year and file Form 1040 (along with payment for the remainder of the tax due) by the 15th day of the 4th month after the end of the tax year, or

(2) file Form 1040 by the first day of the third month after the end of the tax year and pay all the tax due at that time.

Corporations

A calendar-year corporation must pay its estimated tax on April 15, June 15, September 15, and December 15 (or, in the case of a fiscal-year corporation, the 15th day for the 4th, 6th, 9th, and 12th months of its year) (.10). Form 1120-W (Corporate Estimated Tax) may be used to compute the estimated tax payments due in any quarter. Penalties are computed on Form 2220 (Underpayment of Estimated Tax by Corporations).

.05 Code Sec. 6654.

.10 Code Sec. 6655.

Self-Employment Tax and Retirement Plans

¶25,418 Self-Employment Tax. The self-employment tax is imposed upon farmers and other self-employed persons to provide them with social security and hospital insurance coverage. Farmers who operate their own farms on land they either own or rent are self-employed, even though they may employ someone to do the farm work and do not live on the farm (.05).

Whether, and to what extent, income from farm operations will be considered self-employment earnings (for purposes of the self-employment tax) usually depends on the manner in which the farm is operated. The most common situations are:

(1) sole proprietorship operation of the farm by the owner,

(2) tenant operation on shares,

(3) tenant operation for a salary plus bonus,

(4) owner-tenant joint operation,

(5) operation by a professional management company or agent,

(6) operation by joint owners, and

(7) use of purchasing or marketing cooperative's facilities.

In situations (1), (3), (4), and (6), the net farm profit, or share of net profit, received by the owner or owners of the farm property qualify as net earnings from self-employment. In the case of tenant operation on shares (situation (2)), crop shares received by the owner or tenant of the land under a share-farming arrangement are treated as self-employment income if the owner or tenant participates materially with the share-farmer working the land in the production or management of the production of an agricultural or horticultural commodity.

The tenant or share-farmer realizes self-employment income from the operation of the farm only if the tenant's share of the crops, livestock, or produce (or the proceeds from the sale thereof) is based upon actual production or if the tenant is not subject to the landowner's direction and control (.10).

Material participation

There are basic guidelines for determining whether a landowner is materially participating in the production, or management of production, of farm products under a share-farming rental arrangement (.15). A landowner must include the income derived under the arrangement in computing net earnings from self-employment if any one of the following four tests is met:

(1) The landowner does any three of the following: (i) advances, pays, or stands good for at least half the direct costs of producing the crop; (ii) furnishes at least half the tools, equipment, and livestock used in producing the crop; (iii) advises and consults with the tenant periodically; and (iv) inspects the production activities periodically.

(2) The landowner regularly and frequently makes or takes an important part in making management decisions substantially contributing to or affecting the success of the enterprise.

(3) The landowner works 100 hours or more over a period of five weeks or more in activities connected with producing the crop.

(4) The landowner does things that show in their overall effect that the landowner is materially and significantly involved in the production of the farm commodities.

Share-cropping arrangement

For self-employment tax purposes, the share-farmer, under the ordinary crop-sharing arrangement, is considered to be a self-employed individual and not an employee. Therefore, net earnings from self-employment include the share-farmer's share of the proceeds from the sale of the crops and livestock. An ordinary crop-sharing arrangement is one where an individual undertakes to produce a crop or livestock on land owned or leased by another person; the crop or livestock produced, or the proceeds thereof, are divided between the individual and such other person; and the amount of the individual's share is dependent on the amount of the crop or livestock produced.

Professional management

Where a farm is operated under an agreement between the landowner and a professional management company or other person who has the responsibility of choosing a tenant and of managing and supervising the farm operation (situation (5), above), the activities of the company or other person are not attributable to the landowner if the landowner does not personally participate in the operation of the farm. In these cases, the farm rental income realized by the landowner under the agreement is not includible as income from farm self-employment.

Cooperative's facilities

If a purchasing or marketing cooperative's facilities are used, the cash advances and patronage dividends that are received by the landowner from the cooperative association, less the landowner's expenses of operation, are net earnings from farm self-employment. Patronage dividends received from the landowner's purchase of supplies, however, are not included in net earnings from farm self-employment since they ordinarily represent a reduction of cost of the supplies purchased.

> ***Example:*** Mr. and Mrs. Avril are retired from farming, but they are still active profit-seeking members of an agricultural cooperative that processes and sells corn. Because the value-added payments received by the couple directly relate to the volume of corn acquired and delivered by the Avrils to the cooperative, (and are paid in consideration for the Avril's patronage), the payments have a direct nexus to the Avrils' trade or business and are derived from that trade or business. The Avrils

cannot classify this income as proceeds from the sale of capital assets, because the capital asset purportedly sold is separate and distinct from the property actually sold. The payments are not generated by the sale of the Avrils' shares in the cooperative, but instead result from the sale of corn. Therefore, the payments must be included in the Avrils' calculation of earnings as self-employment income. (.20)

Joint ownership

Mere ownership or joint ownership of farm property does not qualify a spouse as self-employed. Accordingly, if a farmer and his wife are personally operating a farm on property that they hold as joint tenants, the net farm profit is, generally speaking as self-employment income earned by the person who actually operates the business (.25). On the other hand, if the property is rented out on a share-crop basis, and both the farmer and his wife materially participate in producing income (or in managing the production of it), the rental received can be split for self-employment tax purposes (.30).

Tax rate

The self-employment tax rate is 15.3% (12.4% Social Security (OASDI) and 2.9% Medicare (HI)). The OASDI portion of the tax applies to the first $87,900 in net earnings from self-employment in 2004. The HI tax is imposed on all net earnings from self employment. A farmer and other self-employed individuals may deduct one-half of their self-employment tax liability for the year as a business expense in arriving at adjusted gross income (.35). They may also reduce self-employment income by an amount equal to the product of their net earnings multiplied by one-half of the self-employment tax rate for the year (.40).

Net earnings

Ordinarily, a farm operator's net earnings from farm self-employment are net farm profits adjusted for the items of income and deduction specifically excluded in the definition of "net earnings from self-employment.".

Agistment fees (amounts received for taking in, pasturing, feeding and caring for another's cattle on the farmer's own land) (.45) and grain storage fees (.50) are also subject to the tax. The canceled portion of an emergency loan granted by the Farmers Home Administration to a farmer who suffered an uninsured drought loss to his growing crops, in which the farmer had no adjusted basis at the time of the loss, was includible in computing his net earnings from self-employment (.55).

Excluded items include real estate rentals (including cash and crop shares received under the ordinary crop-sharing arrangement (but see ¶25,419, below)), gains and losses from sales and exchanges of capital assets, and the deduction for net operating losses of other years.

Farmers, whether on the cash or accrual basis, are also entitled to an optional method of computing net earnings from self-employment (see ¶25,420).

.05 Code Secs. 1402 -1403, Code Sec. 3121; Reg. §§1.1402(a)-1—1.1403-1; Market Segment Specialization Program (MSSP) Audit Technique Guide for Grain Farmers (12-5-95).

.10 IRS Publication No. 225, "Farmers' Tax Guide."

.15 IRS Publication No. 225, "Farmers' Tax Guide."

.20 *R.J. Bot*, CCH Dec. 54,652, 118 TC 138.

.25 IRS Publication No. 225, "Farmers' Tax Guide."

.30 Rev. Rul. 57-58, 1957-1 CB 270.

.35 Code Sec. 164(f).

.40 Code Sec. 1402(a)(12).

.45 Rev. Rul. 56-677, 1956-2 CB 564.

.50 Rev. Rul. 65-149, 1965-1 CB 434.

.55 Rev. Rul. 76-500, 1976-2 CB 254, amplifying Rev. Rul. 73-408, 1973-2 CB 15.

¶25,419 Farmers' Self-Employment Income. The following is a list of farmers' income items that must be included in determining net earnings from self-employment (.05):

(1) taxable patronage dividends from cooperatives;

(2) agricultural program payments, including wheat and cotton program payments and similar government payments received by farm operators;

(3) taxable Commodity Credit Corporation loans;

(4) storage fees by Commodity Credit Corporation under a "resale" agreement if paid to farmer for storing the farmer's own grain;

(5) refunds and rebates, if they represent a reduction in a deductible expense item, including the credit for gasoline and lubricating oil tax;

(6) prizes or awards on farm produce or livestock;

(7) crop damage payments;

(8) value of merchandise received for farm products; and

(9) standing crop sales, if not sold with land held for more than one year.

The following is a list of items (both income and deductions) that must not be taken into account in computing self-employment income even though they may be included for purposes of figuring income tax liability:

(1) rents from real estate or personal property leased with real estate (unless received as a real estate dealer), whether in the form of crop shares, cash or other property, unless the landlord has materially participated in the production (see ¶25,418);

(2) gain or loss from sales or exchanges of livestock held for draft, dairy, breeding, or sporting purposes;

(3) gain or loss from sales or exchanges of depreciable property, such as machinery or trucks, used in a trade or business;

(4) gain or loss from the sale of a standing crop with land held for more than one year;

(5) gain or loss from (a) the sale of timber that qualifies as a capital asset (see ¶25,397), (b) the cutting of timber that is treated as capital gain or loss, and (c) the disposal of timber, coal or iron ore held more than six months in which an economic interest had been retained;

(6) gain or loss from sale, exchange, or involuntary conversion (including casualty losses), or other disposition of property that is neither stock in trade nor held primarily for sale to customers;

(7) capital gains or losses from capital assets, such as gain or loss from the sale of investment property or a personal residence;

(8) wages received as an employee;

(9) dividends on shares of stock;

(10) interest (unless received in connection with the conducting of a trade or business);

(11) any other income, gains, losses, or expenses not resulting from the conduct of a trade or business;

(12) net operating loss deductions;

(13) nonbusiness deductions or the standard deduction;

(14) deductions for personal exemptions and dependents;

(15) income or loss of a limited partner, as such, other than guaranteed payments for services actually rendered; and

(16) income received by a retired partner under a written plan of the partnership that provides for lifelong periodic retirement payments if the retired partner no longer has any interest in the partnership and did not perform any services for it during the year.

.05 IRS Publication No. 225, "Farmers' Tax Guide.".

¶25,420 Optional Method of Computing Net Earnings from Farm Self-Employment. Both cash- and accrual-basis farmers can elect to use an optional method of determining net earnings from farm self-employment (.05).

If gross income from farming is $2,400 or less, a farmer can treat two-thirds of it as net earnings from farm self-employment. If gross income from farming is more than $2,400, but net earnings from farm self-employment are less than $1,600, a farmer can report $1,600 as net earnings from farm self-employment.

This election can be used both ways, that is, to increase or decrease actual net earnings from self-employment. The greater the net earnings from self-employment, the greater the self-employment tax is, and the greater the eventual benefits will be. Even though actual net earnings might exceed $400, the option can be used even if it reduces the net earnings below $400 and no tax would be due.

> ***Example 1:*** David Chandler has gross income from farming of $1,800. His actual net earnings from farming self-employment are only $350, however. He can use either his actual net earnings of $350 and pay no self-employment tax, or he can report $1,200 (two-thirds of $1,800) as his net earnings.

> ***Example 2:*** Jenny Brown has gross income from farming of $585. Her actual net earnings are $410. Brown can report her actual net earnings of $410, or she can treat $390 (two-thirds of $585) as her net earnings and pay no self-employment tax.

> ***Example 3:*** Frances Green has gross income from farming of $2,500. Her actual net earnings are $1,000. She can report either the actual net earnings of $1,000 or the $1,600 optional amount.

The following table summarizes the effect of the optional method of figuring the amount of self-employment income to be reported when there are no nonfarm earnings from self-employment.

		The self-employment income to be reported is:	
If the gross farm income is:	*And the net farm profit is:*	*Regular method*	*Optional method*
Under $600	Under $400	None	None
Under $600	$400 to $599	Actual net	None
$600 to $2,400	Under $400	None	Two-thirds of gross
$600 to $2,400	$400 to $2,400	Actual net	Two-thirds of gross
More than $2,400	Under $400	None	$1,600
More than $2,400	$400 to $1,599	Actual net	$1,600
More than $2,400	$1,600 and over	Actual net	Actual net (Option cannot be used)

A deduction of 7.65% (one-half of self-employment tax rate of 15.3%) (see ¶25,418) of net earnings is taken when figuring self-employment tax. This deduction may be arrived at by multiplying net earnings by .9235 (100% – 7.65% = 92.35%, or .9235). Therefore, if gross income from farming is more than $2,400 and actual net earnings from farm self-employment are less than $1,733 (.9235 × $1,733 = $1,600.43), then the $1,600 figure can be reported as net earnings from farm self-employment (.10).

.05 Reg. §1.1402(a)-15.

.10 IRS Publication No. 533, "Self-Employment Tax."

¶25,421 Self-Employed Retirement Plans and Individual Retirement Savings Accounts. Self-employed farmers have access to retirement plans on a basis similar to that given to employees whose employers have established pension, profit-sharing or stock bonus plans. Self-employed farmers, including partners, have the benefit of current tax deductions for contributions to a qualified retirement plan. Contributions that are nondeductible may also be made within specified limits. Plans providing such benefits are commonly called "Keogh plans." For details, see ¶ 11,300 and following.

Farmers may also be able to establish their own individual retirement savings programs. Employees may establish individual retirement accounts or annuities (IRAs) even though they are covered by employer plans. For details, see ¶11,400. Individuals who are active participants in employer-maintained retirement plans are restricted in the deductible contributions that may be made to their traditional IRAs (.05).

.05 Code Sec. 219; Reg. §1.219-1.

Farming as a Tax Shelter

¶25,422 Tax Shelter. Some investors have invested in farming ventures for the purpose of generating net losses in the initial years of the investment, thereby permitting them to reduce the tax liability on their regular income, often from a business or professional activity.

A number of provisions are aimed at curbing the tax abuses created by such farming shelters:

(1) To prevent the deduction by investors of farming losses generated through nonrecourse loans for which the investors are not personally liable, the investor is permitted to deduct farming losses only to the extent that the investor has funds at risk in the farming activity (.05).

(2) Farming syndicates, as a form of tax shelter, are restricted to the use of the accrual method of accounting (.10). Basically, a farming syndicate for this purpose is a partnership or other enterprise, other than a corporation not electing Subchapter S status, that is engaged in the business of farming if at any time there has been a regulated sale offering of interests in the partnership or other enterprise or if more than 35 percent of the losses are allocable to investors with limited liability (.15). See ¶25,337.

(3) Farming corporations and partnerships with farming corporation partners are required to use the accrual method of accounting and must capitalize preproductive period expenses (expenses preceding disposition or preceding the first marketable crop or yield where the property has a life of more than one year and will produce more than one crop or yield) (.20). Three types of corporations are excluded from these requirements: S corporations, family corporations, and corporations with gross receipts not in excess of $1 million a year (.25). See ¶25,337.

(4) Certain losses that may be deductible for purposes of computing the regular tax are denied for purposes of computing alternative minimum taxable income. These

include losses from a tax shelter farm activity, which is a farming syndicate as defined in Code Sec. 464(c) or a passive farming activity (under the passive activity rules of Code Sec. 469(c). Losses from a tax shelter farm activity are treated as a preference item for post-1986 tax years to the extent that such treatment is not already denied for minimum tax purposes under any of the other preference provisions (.30).

A tax shelter that computes its taxable income on the cash method generally may not deduct an expense any earlier than the time that an accrual-basis taxpayer would treat the expense as having been incurred. Thus, a cash-basis tax shelter may not deduct an expense until the expense is paid and economic performance occurs (.35).

.05 Code Sec. 465.
.10 Code Secs. 448(a)(3), 448(d)(3) and (4), 461(i)(3) and (4), and 464(e).
.15 Code Sec. 464(c).
.20 Code Sec. 447.
.25 Code Sec. 447(c).
.30 Code Sec. 58(a).
.35 Code Sec. 461(i).

Special Estate Tax Valuation

¶25,423 Valuation. Under certain conditions, an estate may elect to value real property and other farm property that consists of a family farm or a closely held business on the basis of its actual (farm) use rather than its highest and best use (.05). However, this special use valuation election may not be used to reduce a gross estate by more than $850,000 in 2004. (.10).

Whether property is of the type for which the special use valuation is available is not always clear. The property must be a farm and be used for farming purposes. While “farming purposes” covers a wide spectrum of agricultural activities, some limitations apply. In addition, the activities must amount to a “trade or business,” which is defined differently for purposes of Code Sec. 2032A than for purposes of Code Sec. 162. The term applies only to an active business, such as a manufacturing, mercantile or service enterprise, or to the raising of agricultural or horticultural commodities.

A parcel of real property may qualify for special use valuation if it is devoted to either use as a farm for farming purposes or use in a trade or business other than farming. In either case, there must be a trade or business use. To qualify:

(1) the decedent must have been a resident of the United States and the property must be located in the United States;

(2) the adjusted value of the real and personal property used in the farm or closely held business must make up at least one-half the adjusted value of the gross estate;

(3) the real property qualifying for the special use valuation must pass to a qualified heir;

(4) a requisite agreement must be filed;

(5) the decedent or a member of the decedent’s family must have owned the qualifying property and have materially participated in the operation of the business for five of the eight years preceding the earliest of: (a) the date of the decedent’s death; (b) the date the decedent became disabled; or (c) the date the decedent retired; and

(6) at least 25 percent of the adjusted value of the gross estate must be qualified real property.

Once elected, the property must actually be put to a qualified use or risk being subject to additional estate taxes. The duty of consistency requirement precludes heirs from denying the validity of a special use valuation election (.15).

☐ For details, see FTG ¶ 20,350.

.05 Code Sec. 2032A(a); Reg. §20.2032A-3.

.10 Rev. Proc. 2003-85, 2003-49 I.R.B. 1184.

.15 *W. LeFever*, CA-10, 96-2 USTC ¶ 60,250, 100 F3d 778.

SALESPERSONS

Introduction

¶25,425 The tax situations faced by salespersons are usually more complex than those faced by other types of employees. As an employee, the salesperson engages in a business and receives compensation for services. However, unlike most other employees, the salesperson usually incurs special expenses in connection with activities in selling and promoting the employer's product or service.

All unreimbursed employee business expenses, including car expenses and travel, must be claimed by a salesperson as miscellaneous itemized deductions. These deductions are subject to the two-percent-of-adjusted-gross-income floor. Unreimbursed employee business expenses are deducted on Form 2106, "Employee Business Deductions," or Form 2106-EZ, "Unreimbursed Employee Business Expenses." Special rules apply to "statutory employees" (see ¶25,428).

The material at ¶25,427 and following illustrates how a salesperson can best handle these special expenses and reimbursements. In addition, it sets out the manner in which these items must be substantiated and provides forms for maintaining adequate records.

Deductible Expenses

¶25,427 Tax Treatment of Expenses. All salespersons may deduct entertainment, transportation, office, and other customary business expenses provided such expenses are ordinary and necessary in carrying on sales activities (.05). Certain restrictions apply to some of these ordinary and necessary expenses. For example, only 50 percent of entertainment and meal expenses are deductible (see ¶25,454 and following). Moreover, substantiation requirements apply to all business expenses (see ¶25,475).

The specific treatment of these expenses depends upon whether they are reimbursed by the salesperson's employer and, if they are reimbursed, whether they are considered reimbursed under an accountable plan (see ¶25,468) (.10) or a nonaccountable plan (see ¶25,467).

In most situations, a salesperson claims unreimbursed expenses as a miscellaneous itemized deduction that is subject to the two-percent-of-adjusted-gross-income floor (.15). If a salesperson is reimbursed for expenses under an accountable plan (¶25,468), the reimbursement is not included in gross income of the salesperson. The employer, in this situation, is entitled to the deduct the amount of the reimbursed expenses. It should be noted, however, that the employer's deduction is also subject to the 50 percent limitation imposed on any reimbursed meal and entertainment expenses.

If a salesperson is reimbursed for expenses under a nonaccountable plan (¶25,467), the reimbursement is included in gross income and is subject to withholding for taxes. Additionally, the unreimbursed meal and entertainment expenses are subject to the 50-percent limitation before being subject to the two-percent-of-adjusted-gross-income floor of miscellaneous itemized deductions (.20).

The only major exception to these general rules concerning reimbursed and unreimbursed employee business expenses is the tax treatment of moving expenses. Deductible moving expenses incurred that are not reimbursed by the employer may be deducted directly from gross income.

Reduction for meal and entertainment expenses

Generally, only 50 percent of meal and entertainment expenses are deductible by either the employee or the employer.

The effect of the reduction rule cannot be avoided by virtue of the absence of separate charges for meals and entertainment and charges for business expenses that may be claimed in full. Thus, if a hotel charges $200 per night for a room and two meals, and the price of the meals is not separately stated, a determination must be made as to the price of the meals and the price of the room. If it is determined that the price of the meals was $50 and the price of the room was $150, the deductible amount for the salesperson, if it is not reimbursed, would be $175 ($150 room + $25 meals) as a miscellaneous itemized deduction subject to the two-percent-adjusted-gross-income floor. If the amount is reimbursed, the deductible amount for the employer remains the same, $175. However, the employer's deduction is not subject the additional two-percent-of-adjusted-gross-income floor.

This same allocation rule holds true when an employer pays a fixed per diem amount to cover its salespersons' lodging and meal expenses while away from home.

Forms 2106 and 2106-EZ

Salespersons and other types of employees who claim employee business expenses are generally required to file Form 2106 "Employee Business Expenses", with their Form 1040 tax return. On the Form 2106, the salesperson lists his expenses and also indicates whether he was reimbursed, if so, how much and how this reimbursement was treated by his employer. The salesperson need *not* file Form 2106 if reimbursement is received under an accountable plan and business expenses are equal to the reimbursement.

After the Form 2106 is completed, the salesperson is directed to either report any excess reimbursements as gross income on page 1 of Form 1040 or to deduct any expenses in excess of reimbursements on Line 20, Schedule A of Form 1040.

An employee might be able to file Form 2106-EZ, "Unreimbursed Employee Business Expenses," instead of Form 2106. Generally, Form 2106-EZ may be filed if the employer did not pay for any of deductible business expenses and the employee is using the standard mileage rate for claiming vehicle expenses.

.05 Code Sec. 62; Temp. Reg. § 1.62-1T.
.10 Code Sec. 62(a)(2)(A).
.15 Code Sec. 67(a).
.20 Code Sec. 274(n)(1).

¶25,428 Employment Status. Salespersons must determine whether they have employee or independent contractor status. If classified as independent contractors, they are liable for the self-employment tax and cannot rely on anyone else to withhold tax on their wages. However, as independent contractors, salespersons are not subject to the rules that require all unreimbursed employee business expenses to be claimed as miscellaneous itemized deductions. As self-employed individuals, salespersons may claim all their ordinary and necessary business expenses as deductions from gross income. Income and expenses are reported on Schedule C, "Profit or Loss From Business (Sole Proprietorship)," or C-EZ, "Net Profit From Business (Sole Proprietorship)."

A salesperson is *not* treated as an employee if:

(1) there is a reasonable basis for not treating him as an employee,

(2) the employer (or a predecessor employer) has never so treated the salesperson, and

(3) the employer filed all post-1978 tax returns that had to be filed on the basis that the salesperson was not an employee (.05).

The reasonable-basis test can be met by reliance on judicial precedents, on published rulings, or on a letter ruling addressed to that employer. However, an employer must treat an individual as an employee if that employer (or a predecessor employer) has treated *any* individual holding a substantially similar position as an employee for employment tax purposes for any period beginning after 1977. Thus, a salesperson is deemed an employee if he is associated with a company that has treated similarly situated salespersons as employees.

Statutory employees

A salesperson who is classified as a "statutory employee" is treated as an independent contractor, not as an employee, for purposes of Code Sec. 62 and Code Sec. 67 (.10) (see, also, ¶25,834 and following). Accordingly, he is entitled to deduct his trade or business expenses from gross income to arrive at adjusted gross income. Ordinary and necessary expenses are claimed on Schedule C or C-EZ.

Direct sellers and real estate agents

In addition, salespersons who qualify as direct sellers or real estate agents are treated as self-employed persons for federal income and employment tax purposes (.15).

In order to be treated as a direct seller, a salesperson must be engaged in the selling of consumer products (goods used in the home or in a place other than a permanent retail establishment) either directly to the consumer or to any buyer on a buy-sell basis, a deposit-commission basis, or similar basis for resale to the consumer. Substantially all of the salesperson's remuneration (regardless of the form of payment) for the selling activity must be based on the amount of sales or on the performance of services, rather than on the number of hours worked. The direct seller must engage in the activity pursuant to a written contract between himself and the person for whom he performs the services, and the contract must state that the direct seller will not be treated as an employee with respect to the activity for tax purposes.

Individuals, such as sales managers, who are responsible for increasing the direct sales activities of direct sellers also qualify as direct sellers, providing that their remuneration is dependent on the productivity of the direct sellers under their control. These individuals need not deal personally with customers.

In order to qualify as a real estate agent, a salesperson must be a licensed real estate agent and meet the same remuneration and contractual requirements imposed on direct sellers. In addition, an individual who is engaged in appraisal activities connected with real estate sales and who receives remuneration dependent on sales or output will be treated as a real estate agent (.20).

.05 Sec. 530(a) of the Revenue Act of 1978; Rev. Proc. 85-18, 1985-1 CB 518.

.10 Rev. Rul. 90-93, 1990-2 CB 33; Reg. §31.3121(d)-1(d)(3)(ii).

.15 Code Sec. 3508; IRS Publication 911, Direct Sellers, CCH IRS PUBLICATIONS.

.20 Conference Committee Report on P.L. 97-248 (Code Sec. 3508).

Importance of "Tax Home"

¶25,430 Travel and Transportation Expenses Distinguished. Travel and transportation expenses, although quite similar in nature, are different for tax purposes. Travel expenses are those ordinary and necessary business expenses incurred in the pursuit of employment duties *while away from home* (.05). They include expenses for both domestic and foreign travel; fares for air, rail, bus, etc.; the cost of operating and maintaining a car; and the costs of meals and lodging.

Transportation expenses on the other hand, are *local* travel expenses directly attributable to the actual conduct of the salesperson's business while not away from home, but they do not include meals and lodging (for a discussion of when these costs are deductible as entertainment expenses, see ¶25,454) or the cost of commuting between a personal residence and a local place of employment.

.05 Reg. §1.162-2.

¶25,431 Salesperson's Tax Home. In order for travel expenses to be deductible, they must not only be reasonable and necessary and incurred in the pursuit of business, but must also have been incurred *while away from home* (.05).

A salesperson's tax home is considered located at either:

(1) his regular or principal (if more than one) place of business, or

(2) if he has no regular or principal place of business because of the nature of his trade or business, then at his regular place of abode in a real and substantial sense (.10).

An individual's tax home is not limited to a particular building or property but includes the entire city or general area in which his place of employment is located.

If the salesperson's tax home cannot be described by either (1) or (2), above, he is considered an itinerant and cannot be "away from home" for purposes of the travel expense deduction. Because his tax home is wherever he happens to work, he is never "away from home" (.15).

Regular place of abode

If a salesperson claims that his tax home is his regular place of abode in a real and substantial sense, the following three factors are used to determine the bona fide nature of that assertion:

(1) whether the salesperson performs a portion of his business in the vicinity of the claimed abode and utilizes the abode while performing business there;

(2) whether the salesperson's living expenses incurred at his claimed abode are duplicated because his business requires him to be away there from; and

(3) whether the salesperson—

(a) has not abandoned the vicinity in which his historical place of lodging and his claimed abode are both located,

(b) has a member or members of his family (marital or lineal only) currently residing at his claimed abode, or

(c) uses his claimed abode frequently for purposes of his lodging.

If all three questions, considered objectively, are answered affirmatively, a salesperson is treated as having his tax home at his regular place of abode. If two of the questions are answered affirmatively, all of the facts and circumstances will be considered in determining the status of the salesperson's tax home. If only one condition is answered affirmatively, the salesperson will be deemed an itinerant. As such, he cannot deduct any travel expenses (.20).

> ***Example 1:*** Mike Tripper has a sales territory covering several states. His employer has its main office in Henderson, Kentucky, and Tripper returns there for approximately one month each year for business and nonbusiness reasons. Tripper's work assignments are temporary and he has no way of knowing where future assignments will be located. He has lived in Henderson for 14 years, first with his wife in his own house until their divorce, and presently with his married sister in her house. Tripper pays his sister $500 per month for a room in her house where he stays when he is in Henderson and where he also keeps his furniture and any clothing that he does not take on his out-of-town business trips.
>
> Because all three objective factors of the test are met, including historical lodging, Tripper is entitled to deduct expenses incurred while away from Henderson, his tax home.
>
> ***Example 2:*** Bill Travel has a sales territory covering several states. His employer has its main office in Indianapolis, Indiana, but Travel does not go there for business reasons. His work assignments are temporary, and he has no way of knowing where future assignments will be located. He has a room in his married sister's house in East Lansing, Michigan, where he keeps the things he does not need on his business trips. He stays at his sister's house for one or two weekends each year, but he performs no work in the vicinity of East Lansing. He makes no payment to his sister for the use of the room in her house. He has abandoned his historical and other family contacts that are in the vicinity of Eldorado, Arkansas.
>
> Because none of the three objective factors has been satisfied, Travel is an itinerant and his tax home is wherever he happens to work. Thus, he cannot be away from home and cannot deduct travel expenses.

"Tax Home" defined

Although the IRS, the Tax Court, and most other federal courts follow the view that "tax home" is synonymous with "business situs," the U.S. Court of Appeals for the Second Circuit rejects this view, refusing to believe that Congress intended to attribute any unusual or novel meaning to "tax home" in the tax law. The Second Circuit interprets an individual's "tax home" as the place where he votes, pays his taxes, and resides between periods of employment away from the home (.25).

Although the U.S. Court of Appeals for the Fourth Circuit has not specifically embraced the tax home concept, that court has ruled that expenses incurred by a salesperson in traveling from his personal residence to the area of his greatest sales activity were not deductible as business expenses where his reasons for living in an area different from the center of income-producing activity were personal (.30). Because a salesperson's reason for choosing to live in a locale other than his major sales territory will almost always be personal, the logic followed by the Fourth Circuit leads to the same result as the IRS position.

Two tax homes

Although a salesperson's tax home is where his principal place of business is located, complications may arise if the salesperson has two places of business. In such a case, a salesperson's tax home is the general area where his main place of business is located. To determine which is the principal business, the following factors are taken into account:

(1) the length of time spent in each location performing duties;

(2) the degree of business activity in each location; and

(3) the relative amount of income derived from each location (.35).

.05 Reg. §1.162-2.

.10 Rev. Rul. 60-189, 1960-1 CB 60, amplified by Rev. Rul. 83-82, 1983-1 CB 45; Rev. Rul. 71-247, 1971-1 CB 54.

.15 Rev. Rul. 73-529, 1973-2 CB 37.

.20 Rev. Rul. 83-82, 1983-1 CB 45, amplifying Rev. Rul. 60-189, 1960-1 CB 60, and clarifying Rev. Rul. 73-578, 1973-2 CB 39.

.25 *R. Rosenspan*, CA-2, 71-1 USTC ¶9241, 438 F2d 905, cert. den., 404 U.S. 864; *R.F. Six*, CA-2, 71-2 USTC ¶9694, 450 F2d 66.

.30 *L.E. Daly*, CA-4, 81-2 USTC ¶9721, 662 F2d 253, rev'g after rehearing en banc, CA-4, 80-2 USTC ¶9719, 631 F2d 351.

.35 *F.J. Markey*, CA-6, 74-1 USTC ¶9192, 491 F2d 1249.

¶25,432 Temporary v. Indefinite Assignment. A salesperson retains his tax home (see ¶25,431) even though he may be temporarily assigned to another locale. Thus, he may deduct travel expenses incurred while temporarily employed away from home (.05).

A temporary assignment is one whose termination can generally be foreseen to last one year or less (.10). Employment away from home that lasts more than one year is treated as indefinite and related travel expenses, such as meals and lodging, are not deductible (.15).

Travel expenses from home may be deductible

There are some situations in which expenses that would otherwise be classified as nondeductible commuting expenses become deductible as transportation expenses. It has been held that an individual who maintained a home office to manage his business could deduct transportation costs incurred between his home office and outside business activities when his residence was also his principal place of business (.20). However, a physician could not deduct car expenses incurred in traveling from his home to his clinic office because the office at home was used merely for ministerial functions and was not his principal place of business (.25). Police captains were able to deduct costs arising from the use of their patrol cars to travel between their residences and police headquarters because the special nature of their employment transformed commuting expenses into deductible business expenses (.30).

The IRS has ruled that a taxpayer may deduct daily transportation expenses incurred in traveling between the taxpayer's residence and work location in the following three situations (.35):

(1) The travel is between the taxpayer's residence and a temporary work location outside the metropolitan area where the taxpayer lives and normally works. (Expenses incurred to travel to a temporary work location inside the metropolitan area are not deductible unless situation (2) or (3), below, apply).

(2) The travel is between the taxpayer's residence and a temporary work location in the same trade or business, regardless of the distance, if the taxpayer has one or more regular work locations away from the residence.

(3) The travel is between the taxpayer's residence that is a principal place of business for purposes of the home office deduction and another work location in the same trade or business, regardless of whether the work location is temporary or regular and regardless of the distance.

.05 *J.E. Peurifoy*, SCt, 58-2 USTC ¶9925, 358 U.S. 59.

.10 Code Sec. 162(a).

.15 Rev. Rul. 93-86, 1993-2 CB 71.

.20 *E.R. Curphey*, 73 TC 766, CCH Dec. 36,753; *Wisconsin Psychiatric Services, Ltd.*, 76 TC 839, CCH Dec. 37,923; *J.J. Adams*, 43 TCM 1203, CCH Dec. 38,971(M), TC Memo. 1982-223.

.25 *J. Lary, Jr.*, DC Ala., 85-1 USTC ¶9306, 608 FSupp 258, aff'd on other grounds, CA-11, 86-1 USTC ¶9376.

.30 *J.R. Pollei*, CA-10, 89-1 USTC ¶9389, rev'g 87 TC 869, CCH Dec. 43,464.

.35 Rev. Rul. 99-7 I.R.B. 1999-5, 4.

¶25,433 Local Transportation Expenses. A salesperson is entitled to deduct as business expenses local transportation costs incurred in traveling;

(1) between his principal place of business and his clients or potential customers and

(2) between various clients or potential customers.

Transportation expenses include car expenses (see ¶25,446) and subway, bus, and cab fares (.05).

The costs incurred by a salesperson in traveling between his home and his principal place of business are not deductible even if work is done during the trip; these are considered commuting expenses. A business call made on a car phone while a taxpayer is commuting to work does not transform the character of the trip from commuting to business. Use of a car to display advertising material does not make the expense of the car deductible, either (.10).

> ***Example:*** Peter Stone, a sales representative, commutes by car from his home to his sales office. Stone uses his cell phone to make business calls while en route. Use of the cell phone does not alter the character of the trip from commuting to business. The commuting expenses are not deductible, but the cost of the cell phone may be deductible.

.05 Code Sec. 162; Reg. §1.162-2.

.10 Conference Committee Report on P.L. 98-369 (Code Sec. 280F).

Travel Expenses

¶25,435 Qualifying Expenses. Deductible travel expenses include, but are not limited to, transportation costs incurred while away from home on business (.05). These include the cost of fares charged for travel by air, rail, water, bus, taxi, etc., and the cost of renting a car, or of operating and maintaining one's own car, for business travel (see ¶25,446). Additionally, a salesperson who used a private airplane to cover and service his six-state sales territory was entitled to a business expense deduction for the airplane expenses paid by him, even though his employer did not reimburse him for those expenses (.10).

Taxi and bus fares for trips between an airport or railway station and the hotel at which a salesperson is staying (.15) and for trips from one customer to another are deductible travel expenses if the costs are reasonable and are incurred while the salesperson is away from home on business.

Miscellaneous expenses

The costs of nonextravagant lodging and meals (even meals eaten alone) are deductible as travel expenses (.20). However, all unreimbursed meal expenses must be reduced by 50 percent before any deduction may be claimed. For rules relating to the deductibility of the cost of business meals, see ¶25,459. Expenditures for laundry or other cleaning and pressing of clothing are deductible travel expenses if they are reasonable in amount and are incurred while the taxpayer is away from home on business (.25). Reasonable tips (.30), baggage charges, and the cost of transporting sample cases, display material, etc., fall within the same classification. Also included are telephone and telegraph costs and the expenses of stenographic services.

.05 Reg. §1.162-2.

.10 *W.F. Sherman, Jr.*, 44 TCM 1324, CCH Dec. 39,404(M), TC Memo. 1982-582.

.15 Rev. Rul. 55-109, 1955-1 CB 261, modified by Rev. Rul. 76-453, 1976-2 CB 86, and Rev. Rul. 90-23, 1990-1 CB 28.

.20 Rev. Rul. 75-432, 1975-2 CB 60.

.25 Rev. Rul. 63-145, 1963-2 CB 86.

.30 *J.C. Henricks*, 8 TCM 993, CCH Dec. 17,279(M).

¶25,436 One-Day Trips. A salesperson's expenditures for his own meals and lodging on a trip of less than 24 hours, although otherwise qualifying as travel expenses, may not be claimed as deductions unless they also meet the "overnight" rule (also known as the "sleep and rest" rule) (.05). Under this rule, a salesperson may claim meal and lodging expenses on a business trip away from home only if:

(1) the trip lasts substantially longer than an ordinary day's work,

(2) the salesperson cannot reasonably be expected to make the trip without being released from duty for sufficient time to obtain substantial sleep or rest, and

(3) the release from duty is with the employer's tacit or express acquiescence or is required by governmental regulations.

> ***Example:*** George Grant, a salesperson, was on a 16-hour round-trip between two cities and stopped for six hours at his turnaround point, where he ate two meals and rented a hotel room to sleep before starting the return trip. Grant is considered as being away from home overnight and may claim his unreimbursed costs of lodging and 50% of his meal expenses as miscellaneous itemized deductions, subject to the two-percent-of-adjusted-gross income floor (.10).

.05 Rev. Rul. 75-432, 1975-2 CB 60; *H.O. Correll*, SCt, 68-1 USTC ¶9101, 389 U.S. 299; Reg. §1.162-2.

.10 Rev. Rul. 75-170, 1975-1 CB 60.

¶25,437 Conventions and Meetings. Expenditures incurred by salespersons in attending business conventions and meetings in the United States may be deductible as ordinary and necessary expenses where the agenda of the convention is so related to the individual's position that his attendance is required for business purposes (.05). A business purpose exists if the convention is structured so that its primary purpose is to improve the business skills and effectiveness of the salesperson.

However, when, incidental to a convention trip, a salesperson engages in some personal activity, such as social entertaining and sight-seeing, the expenses allocable to that activity are not deductible. (For rules regarding foreign conventions and conventions on cruise ships, see ¶25,444.) If the trip is primarily a vacation, only that portion of the salesperson's expenses that is ordinary and necessary and directly related to business is deductible (see ¶25,438).

Use of videotapes at conventions

Travel expenses are not deductible if incurred in connection with conventions if a salesperson does not participate in seminars, discussions or workshops, but is merely furnished individually with videotapes of lectures that are viewed at his convenience. This disallowance rule applies only when no other significant business-related activities occur during the time allotted for the convention. Thus, the use of videotapes or televised material will not cause the expenses to come under the disallowance rule if the participants are required to attend a convention session in order to view the materials (.10).

Even if a taxpayer's travel expenses are disallowed under this rule, he may still be able to claim a deduction for purchasing or renting the videotape materials.

Employer-sponsored conventions

Expenses incurred by a salesperson in attending a convention held by his employer are not automatically deductible. In determining whether a convention sponsored by a salesperson's employer is primarily for business purposes or is a reward for the salesperson, the following factors are given consideration:

(1) the amount of time devoted to business at the convention in comparison with the time devoted to recreational and social activities;

(2) the place at which the convention is held, such as at a resort hotel;

(3) the attitude of the employer holding the convention; and

(4) whether the salesperson was required to attend the convention by his employer (.15).

However, when it is determined that the convention is primarily a reward in the form of a vacation, the fair market value of the trip to and from the convention is includible in the salesperson's gross income (.20).

Expenses incurred in attending conventions and meetings will not be disallowed merely because these activities are held at a resort area, if it can be clearly shown that the expenses were incurred for business purposes (.25). Only those local expenses incurred at the site of the convention that are directly related to the salesperson's business and that are incurred by him are deductible under these circumstances (see ¶25,438).

☐ For a discussion of deductible foreign convention expenses, see ¶25,444.

.05 Rev. Rul. 63-266, 1963-2 CB 88; Reg. §1.162-2.

.10 Conference Committee Report on P.L. 99-154 (Code Sec. 274).

.15 *J.C. Thomas v. Patterson*, CA-5, 61-1 USTC ¶9310, 289 F2d 108, cert. denied, 368 U.S. 837; *C.J.D. Rudolph*, CA-5, 61-2 USTC ¶9539, 291 F2d 841, cert. dismissed, 62-2 USTC ¶9543, 370 U.S. 269.

.20 *E.R. McCann*, CA-FC, 83-1 USTC ¶9153.

.25 Internal Revenue News Release 394, August 3, 1961.

¶25,438 Combined Business and Personal Trips. If a salesperson makes a trip within the United States that is primarily for business and he incidentally engages in some personal activity, such as sight-seeing, visiting family or friends, etc., the travel expenses to and from the destination are deductible (.05). However, if the purpose of the trip is primarily personal, the travel expenses to and from the destination are nondeductible. Regardless of whether the trip is primarily for business or pleasure, any expenses that are properly allocable to the salesperson's trade or business are deductible.

Whether a trip is made primarily for business or for personal reasons depends on the individual facts and circumstances. The amount of time during the period of the trip that is spent on personal activity compared to the amount of time spent on activities directly relating to the salesperson's trade or business is an important factor in determining whether the trip is primarily personal. If, for example, a salesperson, while at a destination, spends one week on activities that are directly related to his trade or business and subsequently spends an additional five weeks for a vacation or other personal activities, the trip will be considered primarily personal in nature in the absence of a clear showing to the contrary.

Spouse's expenses

No deduction is allowed for travel expenses paid or incurred that are attributable to a spouse, dependent or other person accompanying a salesperson whose travel is deductible as an ordinary and necessary business expense unless specific conditions are met. These conditions require the spouse or other individual accompanying a salesperson on business travel to be a bona fide employee of the person paying or reimbursing the expenses. Further, the travel must serve a bona fide business purpose and the expenses must be otherwise deductible (.10).

☐ For the allocation of foreign travel expenses between those that are for business and those that are personal, see ¶25,441.

.05 Reg. §1.162-2.

.10 Code Sec. 274(m)(3).

¶25,439 Luxury Water Travel. Deductions for the costs of travel by ocean liner, cruise ship, and other form of luxury water transportation are subject to limitations (.05). Allowable deductions are limited to a daily amount equal to twice the highest per diem travel amount allowable to employees of the federal government while on official business away from home but serving within the United States. Thus, if a salesperson paid $750 per day for passage on an ocean liner at a time when the highest federal per diem rate was $275 per day, he would only be able to claim $550 per day as an employee business expense assuming he met all of the other requirements of business travel.

Separately stated meal and business entertainment expenses that are incurred on the ocean liner or other form of luxury water transportation must be reduced by 50 percent (see ¶25,443). However, if business meals or entertainment expenses are not separately stated, no allocation for these expenses need be made and no portion of the package price need be reduced.

This limitation applies only to luxury water transportation used for travel. Convention expenses aboard cruise ships are subject to separate rules (see ¶25,444).

.05 Code Sec. 274(m).

Foreign Travel Expenses

¶25,441 When Allocation Is Required. Although a salesperson may claim all reasonable and necessary business expenses in connection with a foreign trip, the transportation costs to and from the business destination may have to be allocated when the trip involves some nonbusiness activities (.05). However, no allocation is required if:

(1) the foreign trip lasts less than one week (seven consecutive days counting the day of return but excluding the day of departure); or

(2) the time spent on personal pursuits is less than 25 percent of the total time away from home.

If a salesperson is away on a foreign trip for more than a week, both the day of departure and the day of return are counted as "business" or "nonbusiness" days in determining whether he spent 25 percent or more of his time on nonbusiness activities and in making the allocation (see ¶25,442).

> ***Example 1:*** Tony Milano, a salesperson, flies to Rome on a business trip. He spends 2 days flying, 2 days on business, and 2 days sight-seeing. Because the trip is for less than a week, no allocation of transportation costs is required.
>
> If the trip had been for 10 days (including flying time) and he spent 2 days sight-seeing and 6 days on business, no allocation would have been required because only 20 percent of the time was spent for personal reasons.
>
> ***Example 2:*** Martha Lee, a salesperson, planned and arranged a 10-day trip. She spent 2 days flying, 5 days on business, and 3 days sight-seeing (30 percent of total time). She must make an allocation of the transportation expenses.

Even though a salesperson does not meet either of the two exemptions mentioned above, no allocation is required in any case if:

(1) the salesperson has no substantial control over the arranging of the business trip, *or*

(2) a personal vacation was not a major consideration in making the trip (.10).

A salesperson traveling under a reimbursement or expense-account-allowance arrangement is not considered as having substantial control over the arranging of a business trip unless he is a managing executive (an employee who can, without being vetoed, decide on whether and when to make the trip) or owns at least 10 percent of the business.

☐ For a discussion of substantiation of travel expenses, see ¶ 25,476.

.05 Reg. §1.274-4. **.10** Reg. §1.274-4(f)(5)(i).

¶ 25,442 Making the Allocation. If an allocation of foreign transportation expenses is required, the allocation is made on the basis of time spent on business and personal affairs (.05).

Business days

Days spent traveling to or returning from the place where the salesperson engages in his business are considered as "business" days, unless he does not travel by a reasonably direct route or he interrupts his travel by engaging in substantial diversions for nonbusiness reasons (in which case, the number of days it would normally take to travel by a direct route without the interruptions would be considered "business" days). If a salesperson must, and does, attend a specific business meeting on a particular day, it is considered a "business" day even though the rest of the day is spent sight-seeing or used for personal pleasure.

A Saturday, Sunday, legal holiday, and other reasonably necessary days that intervene between "business" days away from home are treated as "business" days, unless they are tacked onto the end of a trip.

The places where nonbusiness activities occur on a trip are a factor in determining how much of the foreign travel expense is subject to allocation. Thus, if a salesperson takes a business trip from New York to London and then travels to Switzerland for a vacation before returning to New York, the cost of the round-trip from New York to London is the amount subject to allocation.

> ***Example:*** Sheila Smith, a sales representative, flies to London. She engages in business for 4 days. She next flies to Switzerland for a 14-day vacation and then flies home. The total transportation expense for the whole trip is $1,200 and a round-trip to London costs $900. Generally, only 30% (the 6 days spent on business (2 days flying and 4 days in London) over the total trip time of 20 days (2 days flying, 4 days in London, and 14 days in Switzerland)) of the $900 portion of the transportation expense, or $270, would be classified as a business expense.

.05 Reg. §1.274-4(d).

¶ 25,443 Meals and Lodging. The cost of meals and lodging on a trip abroad of more than a week and on which more than 25 percent of the time is spent on personal affairs must be allocated between amounts that are attributable to business and those that are personal (.05). The deduction for the cost of meals and lodging away from home on business is limited to amounts that are not extravagant under the circumstances (.10). In addition, only 50 percent of unreimbursed meal expenses may be claimed as miscellaneous itemized deductions, subject to the two-percent-of-adjusted-gross-income floor (.15). In the case of reimbursed expenses, the salesperson is subject to the 50-percent reduction if the reimbursement is treated as compensation subject to withholding; otherwise, the employer is subject to the reduction (see ¶ 25,427).

.05 Reg. §1.274-4. **.15** Code Sec. 274(n).
.10 Code Sec. 162(a)(2).

¶25,444 Expenses of Attending Foreign Conventions. Generally, no deduction is allowed for expenses allocable to a convention, seminar, or similar meeting held outside the North American area (.05), unless the salesperson establishes that the meeting is directly related to the active conduct of his trade or business and that, after taking certain factors into account, it is "as reasonable" for the meeting to be held outside the North American area as within it. The factors taken into account in determining reasonableness are:

(1) the purpose of the meeting and the activities taking place at the meeting;

(2) the purposes and activities of the sponsoring organization or group;

(3) the places of residence of the active members of the sponsoring organization or group and the places at which other meetings of the organization or group have been held or will be held; and

(4) such other relevant factors as the taxpayer may present.

North American area

The North American area includes the United States and the District of Columbia and (.10):

American Samoa
Antigua and Barbuda
Aruba
Baker Island
Barbados
Bermuda
Canada
Costa Rica
Dominica
Dominican Republic
Grenada
Guam
Guyana
Honduras
Howland Island
Jamacia
Jarvis Island
Johnston Island
Kingsman Reef
Marshall Islands
Mexico
Micronesia
Midway Islands
Northern Mariana Islands
Palau
Palmyra
Puerto Rico
Saint Lucia
Trinidad and Tobago
U.S. Virgin Islands
Wake Island

Cruise ships

A limited business expense deduction is permitted for the cost of attending business conventions, seminars, and similar meetings on a U.S.-flag cruise ship, provided the salesperson:

(1) establishes that the meeting is directly related to the active conduct of his trade or business,

(2) establishes that the cruise ship is a vessel registered in the United States and that all ports of call of the cruise ship are located in the United States or its possessions, and

(3) attaches to his income tax return written information statements concerning the cruise (.15).

The maximum deduction for qualifying cruise ship conventions per year is $2,000 ($4,000 if a joint return is filed and both spouses attend qualifying cruise ship conventions).

☐ For a more detailed discussion of the requirements, limitations, and method of allocating the cost of attending foreign conventions, see ¶8260.

.05 Code Sec. 274(h).

.10 Rev. Rul. 2003-109, I.R.B. 2003-42, 839; Treasury Department News Release JS-1914, effective as of September 13, 2004.

.15 Code Sec. 274(h)(2).

Car Expenses

¶25,446 General Rules. Car expenses are deductible if the car is used in connection with a salesperson's trade or business (.05). However, any portion of car expenses attributable to personal use is nondeductible.

The amount of deductible car expenses may be computed under either the standard mileage rate method (see ¶25,447) or the actual cost method (see ¶25,448). Generally, a salesperson is free to use the method that produces the largest deduction. In addition to deductible car expenses, there are also energy conservation incentives available. For clean-fuel vehicles, the incentive takes the form of a deduction of up to $2,000 in the year the vehicle is placed in service (.10). For electric vehicles, the incentive is a credit of 10 percent of the cost of any qualified electric vehicle, not to exceed $4,000. The full amount of the credit may be claimed for vehicles place in service before December 31, 2005. For vehicles placed into service in 2006, the maximum amount of this credit is reduced by 75 percent to $1,000. The electric vehicle credit is unavailable for vehicles placed into service after December 31, 2006 (.15).

.05 Code Sec. 162.

.10 Code Sec. 179A.

.15 Code Sec. 30, as amended by the Working Families Tax Relief Act of 2004 (P.L. 108-311).

¶25,447 Standard Mileage Rate. In lieu of deducting all actual operating and fixed costs, a salesperson may use the standard mileage rate method to determine the deductible expenses of his car used for business purposes (.05). Parking fees, tolls, interest and taxes may be deducted in addition to the amount determined under the standard mileage rate method. If the salesperson operates his car for both personal and business purposes, an allocation between the business and nonbusiness portion of his expenses for the car is required to determine his business deduction (.10). The standard mileage rate may also be used for leased cars (.15).

The salesperson may use either the standard mileage rate method or the actual cost method (see ¶25,448) each year. However, if he failed to choose the standard mileage rate method for the first year the car is placed in service, he may *not* use the standard mileage rate method in subsequent years. If the salesperson chooses the standard mileage rate method, the IRS will treat it as an election to exclude the automobile from the modified accelerated cost recovery system (MACRS) of depreciation (.20).

For 2004, the rate is 37.5 cents for each business mile (.25), up from the 36 cents per business mile for 2003 (.30).

Multiple cars

Beginning in 2004, the IRS allows businesses who use four or less automobiles simultaneously to use the standard mile rate (.35). Thus, if a salesperson uses four or fewer cars simultaneously in one business, he should be to combine the mileage of all the cars and apply the standard mileage rate in determining his business expense deduction.

In 2003, the standard mileage rate method could not be used by a business that used two or more cars simultaneously (.40). Accordingly, if a salesperson uses different cars on different occasions in a single business, he is not allowed to combine the mileage of both cars and apply the standard mileage rate in determining his business expense deduction. Rather, he is required to use the actual cost method (see ¶25,448) (.45).

Husband and wife

If a salesperson and his wife both use the same car for separate businesses, they are allowed to combine the mileage and use the standard mileage rate method to figure their business expense deduction whether they file a joint or separate income tax return (.50). However, a husband and wife who drive separate cars for use in their respective businesses are not required to combine the mileage of both cars in computing their car expenses (.55). Because the cars are used by separate individuals in different business capacities, each spouse can compute his or her car expense for the year using the standard mileage rate based on the mileage of his or her own car.

.05 Reg. §1.162-1 and Reg. §1.162-2.
.10 Reg. §1.274-5T(g).
.15 Rev. Proc. 2003-76, I.R.B. 2003-43, 924.
.20 Rev. Proc. 2003-76, I.R.B. 2003-43, 924.
.25 Rev. Proc. 2003-76, I.R.B. 2003-43, 924.
.30 Rev. Proc. 2002-61, I.R.B. 2002-39, 616.
.35 Rev. Proc. 2003-76, Sec. 5.06(1), I.R.B. 2003-43.
.40 Rev. Proc. 2002-61, I.R.B. 2002-39, 616.
.45 *W.K. Shroyer*, 42 TCM 233, CCH Dec. 38,013(M), TC Memo. 1981-327; see also *C.H. West*, 63 TC 252, CCH Dec. 32,852, and *S.R. Dillon*, CA-5, 90-1 USTC ¶50,307.
.50 Rev. Rul. 77-147, 1977-1 CB 41.
.55 IRS Letter Ruling 8343005, 7-15-83, CCH IRS LETTER RULINGS REPORTS.

¶25,448 Actual Cost Method. Instead of the standard mileage rate method, salespersons may be able to use the actual cost method to determine their allowable car expenses (.05). Under this method, all the costs of owning and operating the car are taken into consideration. However, the total car expense must be allocated between business and personal use in order to determine the portion that can be classified as employee business expenses. The percentage of business use is determined by dividing the business miles driven during the year by the total miles driven during the year.

The actual cost method should be used if the actual operating costs are in excess of the deduction allowed under the standard mileage allowance method, or if the taxpayer does not qualify to use the standard mileage allowance.

The cost of operating a car includes expenditures for the following: gas and oil, lubrication, cleaning and washing, repairs, garage and parking fees, insurance, depreciation (see ¶25,450), and tires and supplies. It does not include the cost of the car itself; nor does it include the cost of replacement parts that prolong the useful life of the car or increase its value. These items are "capitalized," which means that they are added to the cost of the car and recovered by way of depreciation (see ¶25,450). The cost of a new radio, heater, or other accessory is typical of expenditures that have to be capitalized, assuming that the item purchased has a life in excess of one year.

A salesperson who uses a car extensively in business may be entitled to claim a current deduction for the cost of tires if he is able to show that they have a useful life of less than one year (.10). Capitalization of tire costs is required when business mileage is low and the tires can be expected to last more than a year.

Fines for violation of traffic regulations are not deductible (.15).

.05 Reg. §1.162-2.

.10 Rev. Rul. 68-134, 1968-1 CB 63.

.15 Code Sec. 162(f); *Hoover Motor Express Co., Inc.*, SCt, 58-1 USTC ¶9367, 356 U.S. 38, 78 SCt 511.

¶25,449 Actual Cost/Standard Mileage Methods Compared. The actual cost method of computing deductions for car expenses will usually produce a greater deduction if the car is above average in cost and the salesperson uses the basic MACRS percentages discussed at ¶25,450. However, the standard mileage rate may be more advantageous for some high-mileage drivers. Further, the salesperson must consider which method to use—actual cost or standard mileage—when the car is purchased. Using the standard mileage allowance means that the salesperson has elected not to use the MACRS system in claiming deductions for the car (.05).

Example: Mary Scott, a book publisher's representative, purchased a car on April 1, 2004, for $17,500. During the year, she drove it 25,000 miles, 80% of which were for business purposes. Her deductible expenses, including depreciation (see ¶25,450), were as follows:

Gas, oil and lubrication	$ 1,705
Repairs	500
Supplies	190
Insurance	400
State and city licenses	95
Motor club membership	110
Total expenses	$ 3,000
Less: 20 percent personal use	600
Deductible business expenses	$ 2,400
Add: Section 179 expense election ($2,960[1] × 80%)	2,368
Deductible car expenses under actual cost method	$ 4,768

[1]Rev. Proc. 2004-20, I.R.B. 2004-13, 642. Mary elected out of claiming any additional bonus depreciation for cars placed into service before January 1, 2005.

If Mary computed her deduction using the standard mileage rate method discussed at ¶25,447 her deduction would amount to $7,500 (25,000 miles × 80% × 37.5 cents per mile).

As a result, it would be more advantageous for Mary to use the standard mileage rate method in computing the deduction.

.05 Rev. Proc. 2003-76, I.R.B. 2003-43, 924.

¶25,450 Depreciation. A salesperson using the actual cost method (¶25,448) of computing car business expense is able to claim a depreciation deduction based upon the *business* cost of the car (.05). The business cost of a car is generally its purchase price multiplied by the business use percentage (.10). Self-employed salespersons compute their depreciation deduction on Form 4562, "Depreciation and Amortization (Including Information on Listed Property)." Salespersons who are employees compute their deduction in Section D of Form 2106.

Determining the allowable amount of depreciation for a particular car has become increasingly complex over the past few years due to the fact that the rules have been changed a number of times. These rules control the methods of depreciation and the maximum amount of depreciation that can be claimed in the first year, as well as the succeeding years, of operation. The date that a car was placed into service determines what set of rules applies.

The Job Creation and Worker Assistance Act of 2002 (P.L. 107-147) has added to this complexity by allowing for the election of an additional depreciation amount to be claimed in the first year. For automobiles acquired new after September 10, 2001, and placed into service before January 1, 2005, taxpayers are allowed to elect to claim a 30-percent bonus depreciation amount. This bonus depreciation is addition to the regular MACRS depreciation deduction. The bonus depreciation amount is claimed after any Code Sec. 179 deduction but before the MACRS deduction after any appropriate basis adjustments (.15).

Planning Note

CCH Analysts note that the claiming of the 30-percent bonus depreciation is an election. The IRS will assume you are making the election unless one affirmatively elects out. For assets that were acquire after September 10, 2001, and reflected on returns filed before the enactment date of March 9, 2002, these returns should be reviewed and amended accordingly. However, a benefit of electing to claim the bonus depreciation, is that no AMT adjustment is necessary.

Another layer of complexity for claiming depreciation in the first year has been added by the Jobs and Growth Tax Relief Reconciliation Act of 2003 (P.L. 108-27) (JGTRRA). For qualified property acquired after May 5, 2003, and placed into service before January 1, 2005, the additional first-year depreciation percentage is increased to 50 percent (.20). As with the 30-percent additional depreciation amount, the 50-percent additional depreciation amount is in additional too the regular MACRS depreciation deduction, claimed after any Code Sec. 179 deduction and there is no alternative minimum tax adjustment required.

Planning Note

Taxpayers may have to figure the depreciation amounts claiming Code Sec. 179 deduction, using regular MACRS depreciation rates, with the 30-percent additional depreciation amount and with the 50-percent depreciation amount to determine the most effective depreciation method to minimize their tax liability over the life of the automobile for those placed into service after May 6, 2003 and before January 1, 2005. Should a taxpayers decide not to claim the 50-percent additional depreciation amount, they must affirmatively make an election out of claiming this additional amount. However, they still may claim the 30-percent additional first-year depreciation amount. Alternatively, a taxpayer may decide to affirmatively elect out of all additional first-year depreciation and simply claim the regular MACRS depreciation amount.

Sports utility vehicles (SUVs)

The maximum amount of expenses for new equipment placed into service that a taxpayer may claim under Code Sec. 179 was increase from $25,000 to $100,000 for tax years 2003 through 2007. The $100,000 is to be inflation adjusted and for 2004 is $102,000. The amount of depreciation, including any expenses claimed under Code Sec. 179, is limited for vehicles that are considered luxury automobiles. The basic definition of a luxury automobile is a vehicle that weighs 6000 pounds or less. This meant that in 2004 the maximum amount of depreciation, include Code Sec. 179 amounts, that could be claimed for the business use of a luxury automobile is $2,960. Since most SUVs weigh more than 6,000 pounds, they are not subject to the luxury car depreciation limitation. This meant a taxpayer putting a SUV into service in 2004 in a trade or business, by expensing the maximum amount under Code Sec. 179, claiming the 50-percent additional bonus depreciation amount and regular MACRS, could claim almost the entire purchase price in the first year. However, the American Jobs Creation Act of 2004 (P.L. 108-357) amended the Code Sec. 179 limitation for SUVs placed into service after October 22, 2004. The maximum amount of Code Sec. 179 expenses and depreciation that may be claimed for a SUV is $25,000. A SUV is defined as a vehicle between 6,000 and 14,000 pounds (.25).

Leased cars

Salespersons who lease a passenger automobile for business use for a term of 30 days or more are required to include in gross income an inclusion amount for each tax year during which the automobile is leased (.30). This provision, which is an attempt to achieve parity between leasing and purchasing a car, is aimed at limiting a salesperson's lease payment deductions to the amounts that would have been deducted had the salesperson purchased the car.

The inclusion amount is a percentage of part of the fair market value of the leased car multiplied by the percentage of business and investment use of the car for the tax year. This amount is prorated for the number of days of the lease term included in the tax year (.35).

.05 Code Sec. 280F(a)(1).

.10 Code Secs. 280F(d)(5)(A) and 280F(d)(6)(A); Rev. Proc. 2004-20, I.R.B. 2004-13, 642.

.15 Code Sec. 168(k), as amended by the Jobs Creation and Worker Assistance Act of 2002 (P.L. 107-147) and the Jobs and Growth Tax Releif Reconciliation Act of 2003 (P.L. 108-27)

.20 Code Sec. 168(k), as amended by the Jobs and Growth Tax Relief Reconciliation Act of 2003 (P.L. 108-27).

.25 Code Sec. 179(b)(6), as added by the American Jobs Creation Act of 2004 (P.L. 108-357).

.30 Code Sec. 280F(c).

.35 Reg. §1.280F-7(a); Rev. Proc. 2004-20, I.R.B. 2004-13, 642.

¶25,451 Interest and Taxes. How the payment of interest, sales taxes and personal property taxes is treated depends upon whether a salesperson is an employee or is self-employed (.05). If a salesperson is an employee, the interest paid on the business portion of his automobile is not deductible because the interest is considered nondeductible personal interest. Additionally, sales taxes and any personal property taxes cannot be deducted but must be added to the car's basis and recovered through depreciation. If the salesperson is self-employed, interest, sales taxes and personal property taxes paid on the business portion of his automobile is deductible as a business expense on Schedule C or Schedule C-EZ.

.05 Code Secs. 163(h) and 164(a); Reg. §§1.162-1 and 1.162-2.

¶25,452 Substantiation. A salesperson who claims a deduction for car expenses on his tax return must be able to substantiate certain items pertaining to the expenses. The substantiation may either be by adequate records or sufficient written or oral evidence that corroborates the salesperson's own statements (.10).

The items that must be substantiated are:

(1) The amount of each separate expense for the car (e.g., gas, oil, and depreciable basis).

(2) The business mileage and the total mileage for the year.

(3) The dates of the expense or dates of business use.

(4) The business reason for the use of the car.

A simplified rule has been issued under which an employee's expenses for local travel or transportation away from home will meet the substantiation requirements if an employer provides a mileage allowance under a reimbursement or other expense allowance arrangement (.30). An additional method by which employee car expenses may be deemed substantiated has been provided (.35). This method—known as FAVR (fixed and variable rate allowance)—appears to primarily affect employers that are able to generate through computer or data processing capabilities the information necessary to determine an acceptable FAVR rate.

☐ See ¶8110 and ¶8285 for a discussion of these two simplified methods for substantiating employee car expenses.

☐ See ¶25,476 for a discussion of substantiating travel expenses.

.10 Code Sec. 274(d).

.30 Rev. Proc. 2004-20, I.R.B. 2004-13, 642.

.35 Rev. Proc. 2004-20, I.R.B. 2004-13, 642.

Entertainment Expenses

¶25,454 Entertainment Expenses Defined. Fifty percent of amounts spent for entertaining customers and clients are deductible if the amounts are ordinary and necessary expenses incurred in the salesperson's business and are "directly related to" *or* "associated with" business or the production of income (.05). Additionally, the expenses must be adequately substantiated (see ¶25,477).

Entertainment

Entertainment activities include those of a type generally considered to be entertainment, amusement, or recreation. Thus, going to nightclubs, restaurants, social clubs, theaters, and sporting events and on hunting, fishing, vacation, and similar trips would be entertainment activities, but see ¶25,457 for the deductibility of entertainment facilities. The furnishing of food and beverages, a hotel suite, a vacation cottage, a car or a private airplane for business guests would also be considered entertainment.

When a salesperson invites customers to his home for the purpose of transacting business, only the additional expenses incurred by reason of their presence can be considered entertainment expenses. If the customers are accompanied by their spouses, the occasion would probably be considered a social gathering among friends rather than an entertainment activity, and, thus, the costs of the event would not be deductible (.10).

A salesperson's business may determine if an activity constitutes entertainment (.15).

> ***Example 1:*** Margo Blake, a sales representative for a dress manufacturer, sponsors a fashion show in order to introduce the manufacturer's new fashion line. The show is not considered entertainment.

> ***Example 2:*** Sid Potts, a sales representative for a machine parts distributor, sponsors a fashion show for his clients' spouses; the show is considered entertainment.

A salesperson may claim allowable expenses for entertainment incurred in the course of his employment whether or not he is reimbursed by his employer. If unreimbursed, 50 percent of the allowable expense is claimed as a miscellaneous itemized deduction and is thus subject to the two-percent floor imposed on such deductions. If reimbursed, entertainment expenses may or may not be subject to the 50 percent reduction depending upon whether the reimbursement is treated as compensation subject to withholding (see ¶25,427) (.20).

Limitations on entertainment tickets/skyboxes

The allowable deduction for the cost of a ticket for any entertainment activity or facility is limited to 50 percent of the face value of the ticket.

In addition, if a luxury skybox at a sports arena is leased by a salesperson for more than one event, the deduction for the rental or other use of the skybox is disallowed to the extent that the cost exceeds the cost of the most expensive nonluxury box seat tickets generally held for sale to the public for the same event multiplied by the number of seats in the skybox (.25). All seats in the skybox are included in the calculations, even if the skybox is not fully occupied.

.05 Code Secs. 62 and 274(a); Reg. §§1.274-1 and 1.274-2.

.10 Compare *J.R. Howard*, 41 TCM 1554, CCH Dec. 37,921(M), TC Memo. 1981-250, with *P.H. Leon*, 37 TCM 1514, CCH Dec. 35,407(M), TC Memo. 1978-367.

.15 Reg. §1.274-2(b)(1)(ii).

.20 Code Sec. 274(e).

.25 Code Sec. 274(l)(2).

¶25,455 "Directly Related" Test. No deduction is allowed for entertainment expenditures unless the salesperson establishes that the expenditures are *directly related to or associated with* (see ¶25,456) the active conduct of his trade or business (.05). Thus, for example, an insurance salesperson could deduct dues paid to a Mardi Gras club that had as one of its purposes the improvement of tourism in New Orleans because the expenditures were directly related to the taxpayer's business (.10). The taxpayer's commission income from sales to tourism-related businesses that were also club members was directly impacted by tourism.

For entertainment expenditures to be considered directly related:

(1) the salesperson must have more than a general expectation of deriving some income or other specific business benefit (other than goodwill) at some indefinite future time from the expenditure;

(2) the salesperson must engage in active conduct of business during the entertainment with the person being entertained;

(3) the active conduct of business must be the *principal* aspect of the combined business and entertainment; and

(4) the expenses must be allocable to the salesperson and the person with whom business is conducted during the entertainment or with whom business would have been conducted had unexpected circumstances not intervened.

It is not necessary that more time be devoted to business than to entertainment in order to meet requirement (3).

Entertainment expenditures made in a clearly business setting are treated as directly related entertainment expenses. Examples of this type of entertainment include:

(1) entertainment in a hospitality room at a convention that creates business goodwill through a display or discussion of business products;

(2) the entertainment of civic and business leaders at the opening of a new hotel or theatrical production; and

(3) entertainment that has the main effect of a price rebate in the sale of the salesperson's products.

Also considered as directly related entertainment expenditures are expenditures made by the salesperson on behalf of an individual (not an employee) that either constitute compensation for services rendered or are paid as a prize or award.

Excluded entertainment

Certain types of entertainment expenses are generally considered not directly related to a salesperson's trade or business, unless the salesperson produces proof that they are directly related, such as by showing that a business discussion took place during the entertainment. Excluded expenses include those for entertainment:

(1) at which the salesperson is not present;

(2) at night clubs, theaters, sporting events, or social gatherings, such as cocktail parties;

(3) at cocktail lounges, country clubs, golf and athletic clubs or vacation resorts if the group entertained includes persons other than business associates;

(4) on hunting or fishing trips; or

(5) aboard yachts or other pleasure boats.

☐ See ¶25,456 for an explanation of substantial business discussions.

.05 Reg. §1.274-2(c).

.10 *R.J. Hymel, Jr.*, CA-5, 86-1 USTC ¶9419, 794 F2d 939, rev'g TC per curiam, 49 TCM 1313, CCH Dec. 42,048(M), TC Memo. 1985-198.

¶25,456 "Associated With" Test. Salespersons may deduct the cost of entertainment associated with the active conduct of a trade or business and occurring directly before or after a bona fide and substantial business discussion (.05).

Substantial business discussion

The business discussion that the entertainment precedes or follows must represent an active effort by the salesperson to obtain a sale or other business benefit. Moreover, the active conduct of business must be the principal aspect of the combined entertainment and business, although it is not necessary to spend more time on business than on entertainment.

Meetings at conventions or similar general assemblies, or at bona fide trade or business meetings sponsored and conducted by business or professional organizations, are considered as substantial and bona fide business discussions if they are on the program scheduled by the sponsoring organization and the expenses of attending the meeting are ordinary and necessary business expenses.

Directly before or after business discussion

Entertainment is considered to immediately precede or follow the business discussion if both events occur on the same day. If they do not occur on the same day, the facts and circumstances of each case must be examined. Situations in which entertainment expenses are associated with the salesperson's business include the following:

(1) A salesperson conducts a lengthy business meeting with business associates and they go with their spouses to a night club in the evening.

(2) Out-of-town business guests and their spouses are entertained in the evening before holding substantial business discussions.

(3) A salesperson entertains business associates or prospective customers attending business meetings at a convention between, or in the evening after, such meetings.

Goodwill

Expenditures for entertainment to keep or create goodwill are deductible when all other requirements are met and either;

(1) the entertainment consists of a business meal which is nonreciprocal in nature, or

(2) the entertainment is associated with the active conduct of business and directly precedes or follows a substantial business discussion, or

(3) the entertainment takes place in a clear business setting (.10).

Spouses

If the cost of entertaining a customer is deductible either as directly related entertainment or as associated entertainment, the cost of entertaining the spouse of the salesperson and of the customer is deductible as associated entertainment (.15).

.05 Reg. §1.274-2(d).
.10 Rev. Rul. 63-144, 1963-2 CB 129.
.15 Reg. §1.274-2(d)(4).

¶25,457 Entertainment Facilities. Salespersons are generally not allowed to deduct any expense paid or incurred with respect to an entertainment, recreational, or amusement facility that they own, rent, or use for entertainment, such as 50 percent of the cost of meals provided on a yacht (.05). These facilities include yachts, hunting lodges, fishing camps, swimming pools, tennis courts, and bowling alleys. However, a salesperson may deduct expenses incurred for the business use of an entertainment facility that is used for purposes other than entertainment (.10). A facility that is used only incidentally for entertainment is not considered an entertainment facility.

.05 Code Sec. 274(a); Reg. §1.274-2.
.10 Reg. §1.274-2(e)(3)(iii)(b).

¶25,458 Club Dues and Fees. Club dues are generally not deductible regardless of whether the salesperson uses the club primarily for business (.05). However, dues paid to certain service organizations (e.g., Kiwanis) and professional groups for business reasons, are generally deductible.

.05 Code Sec. 274(a)(3).

¶25,459 Business Meal Rules. Deductions claimed for food and beverage expenses are subject to the same business-connection requirement applicable to other entertainment expenses (.05). Thus, a meal expense is not deductible unless the taxpayer establishes that the expense is directly related to the active conduct of his trade or business. In the case of a meal expense directly preceding or following a substantial and bona fide business discussion, the taxpayer must establish that the expense is associated with the active conduct of his trade or business. A business discussion, however, is not required in the case of an individual who is traveling away from home on business and claims a deduction only for his own meal expenses.

The expense is not deductible unless the taxpayer substantiates the deduction. Two further restrictions are placed on meal expenses:

(1) they are not deductible if neither the taxpayer nor an employee of the taxpayer is present at the meal, and

(2) the disallowance of the deduction of meal expenses to the extent that the meals are lavish or extravagant applies to all business meals, with certain exceptions (.10).

If it is not reimbursed, 50 percent of the allowable expense is claimed as a miscellaneous itemized deduction and is thus subject to the two-percent floor imposed on such deductions. If reimbursed, business meal expenses are subject to the 50 percent reduction if the reimbursement is treated as compensation subject to withholding (see ¶25,427) (.15).

In determining the amount of meal expenses that must be reduced, expenses for taxes and tips are included. Thus, if a salesperson spends a total of $120 for a business meal ($90 for the food and drinks, $10 in tax and $20 in tips) for which he is not reimbursed, the maximum amount that he may claim as a miscellaneous itemized deduction is $60 ($120 × 50%).

Expenses such as cover charges paid for admission to a night club, the amount paid for a room that the salesperson rents for a dinner, or the amount paid for parking at a sports arena in order to attend an entertainment event are examples of the types of expenses that are included as part of a meal or entertainment expense and that are thus subject to the 50 percent reduction. However, expenses for transportation to and from a business meal, for example cab fares, are not subject to the reduction (.20).

.05 Code Sec. 274(e).
.10 Code Sec. 274(k).
.15 Code Sec. 274(e).
.20 General Explanation of the Tax Reform Act of 1986, Staff of the Joint Committee on Taxation, p. 64.

Business Gifts

¶25,461 Limited Deduction. Salespersons are allowed a deduction for business gifts made directly or indirectly to individuals to the extent that the expense is limited to a total of $25 per year for each donee (.05). If the total amount of business gifts to any one person during the year exceeds this amount, the amount in excess of $25 may not be deducted.

A business gift is considered made to a specific person if the gift is intended for his eventual use or benefit but is made initially to some member of his family. This includes situations where the gift is made to the spouse of a business customer or contact. However, if a business gift is made to a husband and wife who are partners in a business, the $25 limitation applies to each individually because each is a business customer or contact.

Incidental costs, such as wrapping, insurance, and mailing, need not be included in determining whether the $25 limit has been exceeded, provided the value of the container does not exceed the value of the contents.

If a salesperson makes business gifts that he wishes to claim as deductions, adequate records must be kept (see ¶25,478).

.05 Code Sec. 274(b); Reg. §1.274-3.

¶25,462 Business Gifts Defined. A business gift is any item excludable from the recipient's gross income (.05) that is designed to promote the salesperson's business. However, the following items are not considered business gifts (.10):

(1) promotional items purchased in bulk for broad distribution, with the salesperson's name imprinted on each item, provided the cost per item does not exceed $4;

(2) a sign, display rack, or other promotional material used on the business premises of the recipient; and

(3) gifts of tangible personal property awarded to employees under certain circumstances (see "Gifts to employees," in ¶8270).

Although the above gifts are tax deductible, they are not counted in determining the $25 annual maximum gift deduction. The value of the awards described in (3), above, are includible in the employee's gross income unless the award was given because of the employer's detached generosity and did not represent compensation for services rendered.

.05 Code Sec. 102.

.10 Code Sec. 274(b); Reg. §1.274-3.

¶25,463 Gift or Entertainment. Generally, any expense that might be considered to be for either a gift or for entertainment or for either travel or for entertainment is considered to be for entertainment (.05). However, expenses for certain items are deemed gifts. Thus, if a salesperson gives a customer packaged food or beverages intended for later use, such as a cheese, nut, or fruit assortment, the expense is for a gift. If a salesperson provides a customer with tickets to the theater or a sporting event and does not accompany him to the event, the salesperson, at his election, may treat the tickets as either a gift or entertainment. However, if the salesperson accompanies the customer to the event, he must treat the cost of the tickets as entertainment (.10).

.05 Reg. §1.274-2(b)(1) (iii).

.10 Reg. §1.274-2(b).

Reimbursements and Expense Allowance

¶25,465 Reimbursements and Allowances as Income. The tax treatment of business expenses paid or incurred by a salesperson for travel, transportation, entertainment, gifts and other ordinary and necessary expenses depends upon whether the expenses are reimbursed by the salesperson's employer (its agent or a third party), and, if so, under what type of reimbursement or expense allowance arrangement the expenses are paid (.05).

A salesperson's arrangement with his employer can be classified as either an accountable or a nonaccountable plan. However, a salesperson may be treated as having more than one arrangement with his employer, so that some business expenses are considered paid under an accountable plan while other expenses are considered paid under a nonaccountable plan (.10).

.05 Reg. §1.62-2.

.10 Reg. §1.62-2(c)(1).

¶25,466 Accountable and Nonaccountable Plans Defined. A plan is an accountable plan only if the following three conditions are satisfied:

(1) there must be a business connection for the expenses;

(2) the employee must either substantiate or be deemed to have substantiated the expenses, and

(3) the employee must return to the employer amounts in excess of the substantiated (or deemed substantiated) expenses within a reasonable period of time (.10).

A plan that fails to meet one or more of the three conditions listed above is considered a nonaccountable plan, and any amounts paid pursuant to the plan are treated as paid under a nonaccountable plan. A salesperson who receives payments under such a plan cannot compel his employer to treat the payments as paid under an accountable plan by voluntarily substantiating the expenses and returning any excess payments to his employer (.15). The above three requirements are applied on an employee-by-employee basis. Accordingly, the failure by one salesperson to substantiate expenses under an arrangement does not cause amounts paid to another salesperson to be treated as paid under a nonaccountable plan (.20).

.10 Reg. §1.62-2(c)(1).
.15 Reg. §1.62-2(c)(3).
.20 Reg. §1.62-2(i).

¶25,467 Reimbursements Under Nonaccountable Plans. Amounts treated as paid under a nonaccountable plan are included in the salesperson's gross income, are reported as wages or other compensation on the salesperson's Form W-2, and are subject to withholding and payment of FICA, FUTA, and income tax (.05). However, the amounts included in a salesperson's gross income may be deducted, provided that the salesperson can substantiate the full amount of the expenses, as an itemized deduction subject first to the 50 percent limitation on meal and entertainment expenses and then the two-percent-of-adjusted-gross-income floor for itemized deductions.

.05 Reg. §1.62-2(c)(5).

¶25,468 Reimbursements Under Accountable Plans. Amounts treated as paid under an accountable plan are excluded from the salesperson's gross income, are not reported as wages or other compensation on the salesperson's W-2, and are exempt from the withholding and payment of employment taxes (FICA), federal unemployment tax (FUTA), and income tax (.05).

.05 Reg. §1.62-2(c)(4).

¶25,469 No Reimbursement or Expense Allowance Plan. If a salesperson's employer does not maintain a reimbursement or expense allowance plan, the salesperson may deduct ordinary and necessary business expenses as a miscellaneous itemized deduction, provided that he can substantiate the expenses. However, these items are subject first to the 50 percent limitation on meal and entertainment expenses and then the two-percent-of-adjusted-gross-income floor for itemized deductions (.05). A salesperson uses Form 2106, "Employee Business Expenses," or Form 2106-EZ, "Unreimbursed Employee Business Expenses," to claim his expenses, and his allowable deduction is determined on Schedule A of Form 1040.

.05 Code Sec. 62; Reg. §1.62-2(c)(5).

Reporting of Business Expenses

¶25,471 Nonreportable Expenses. An employee need not report on his income tax return the business expenses he pays or incurs for travel, transportation, entertainment, gifts, etc., if he is required to, and does, make an adequate accounting to his employer (.05). As long as the expenses are charged directly or indirectly to the employer (for example, through credit cards) or reimbursed to him, and the total amount of the reimbursement or allowance is equal to the amount of the expenses, no reporting is required.

.05 Temp. Reg. § 1.274-5T(f).

¶25,472 Reportable Expenses. If a salesperson is *not* required to make an adequate accounting to his employer for business expenses, or, although required to make an accounting, he fails to do so, he must submit as part of his tax return a completed Form 2106, including information concerning the business use of passenger automobiles and other listed property (such as yachts, airplanes or certain computers) (.05). For automobiles, a salesperson is required to provide information as to mileage, percentage of business use, date placed in service, use of other vehicles, after-work use, whether evidence exists to support the business use claimed, and whether the evidence is written (.10). For listed property other than automobiles, a salesperson is required to provide information as to the date the property was placed in service, the percentage of business use, whether evidence exists to support the business use claimed, and whether the evidence is written (.15). In addition, the salesperson is required to maintain records and other supporting evidence to substantiate the claimed expenses (see ¶25,475).

.05 Temp. Reg. § 1.274-5T(f).
.10 Temp. Reg. § 1.274-5T(d)(2).
.15 Temp. Reg. § 1.274-5T(d)(3).

¶25,473 Adequate Accounting Requirement. In order to make an adequate accounting to his employer, a salesperson must submit his account book, diary, log, trip sheet, statement of expense or similar record in which he lists each element of an expenditure or use, recorded at or near the time of the expenditure or use, together with supporting documentary evidence in a manner which conforms to all the adequate records requirements (discussed at ¶25,475 (.05). Further, the salesperson must account for all amounts received from his employer during the tax year as reimbursements or allowances (including those charged directly or indirectly to the employer through credit cards or otherwise) for travel, entertainment, and gifts.

Adequate accounting

The methods of substantiating expenses (see ¶25,475 and following) are considered to constitute adequate accounting if the employer accepts a salesperson's substantiation and establishes that the substantiation meets the necessary requirements. However, adequate accounting does not include the salesperson's written or oral statements concerning the expenses (.10).

When a salesperson makes an adequate accounting to his employer, he will ordinarily not again be required to substantiate his expense account information unless (.15):

(1) his business expenses exceed the total amounts charged to his employer and reimbursement received from the employer, and he claims a deduction on his income tax for the excess expenses;

(2) the salesperson is related to his employer—where the employer is the salesperson's spouse, parent, children, or controlled corporation, or works for a corporation in which he owns, directly or indirectly, more than 10 percent of the value of the outstanding stock of the corporation; or

(3) the accounting procedures used by the employer for the reporting and substantiation of expenses by employees are not adequate, or it cannot be determined that the procedures are adequate.

Standard mileage rate

Salespersons who receive an allowance or reimbursement of not more than the standard mileage rate for the year (see ¶25,447) and whose travel expenses have been substantiated (see ¶25,476) will be deemed to have made an adequate accounting (.20).

Per diem allowances

The IRS has provided per diem allowances under which the *amount* of the away-from-home meals, incidental and lodging expense may be deemed to be substantiated by a salesperson (.25). Per diem allowances may be used only if a salesperson substantiates by adequate records or other evidence the time, place, and business purpose of the travel (see ¶25,475).

The per diem method can be used to substantiate a salesperson's reimbursement expenses only if the arrangement is considered an accountable plan and the allowance is:

(1) paid with respect to expenses incurred or which the employer reasonably expects to be incurred by a salesperson for lodging, meal and/or incidental expenses while traveling away from home in connection with the performance of services as an employee;

(2) reasonably calculated not to exceed the amount of the expense or the anticipated expenses; and

(3) paid at the applicable federal per diem rate, a flat rate, or a stated schedule (.30).

There are two types of per diem allowances:

(1) meal and incidental expenses (M&IE) only, which provides a per diem allowance for either meals and incidental expenses only or incidental expenses only, and

(2) lodgings plus M&IE, which provides a per diem allowance to cover lodging as well as meals and incidental expenses.

Incidental expenses, effective for travel on or after October 1, 2004, are now given the same meaning as found in the Federal Travel Regulations, 41 C.F.R. Part 300-3.1 (2004) (.35). The Federal Travel Regulation define the term "incidental expenses" to include fees and tips given to porters, baggage carriers, bellhops, hotel maids, stewards or stewardesses and others on ships, and hotel servants in foreign countries, and transportation between places of lodging or business and places where meals are taken. This definition apparently did not include expenses for laundry, cleaning and pressing of clothes, lodging taxes or telephone calls. The General Services Administration amended the Federal Travel Regulation to clarify that the term "incidental expenses" did include expenses for laundry, cleaning and pressing of clothes for travel of less than four days. Lodging taxes for travel within the continental United States and non foreign areas are not include in either the lodging per diem rate or incidental expenses but were eligible reimbursable expenses. Lodging taxes for travel in foreign areas are still included in lodging per diem amounts. Additional, energy surcharges for lodging are considered a separate reimbursable expense. The costs of telephone calls continues to be a separate reimbursable expense.

If expenses are substantiated using a per diem amounts, and the reimbursement exceeds the relevant federal rates for that type of allowance, then the salesperson is required to include the excess in gross income. The excess portion is treated as paid under a nonaccountable plan (see ¶25,467).

.05 Temp. Reg. § 1.274-5T.

.10 Temp. Reg. § 1.274-5T(f)(4).

.15 Temp. Reg. § 1.274-5T(f)(5).

.20 Temp. Reg. § 1.274-5T(g).

.25 Rev. Proc. 2003-80, I.R.B. 2003-45; Rev. Proc. 2004-60, I.R.B. 2004-42.

.30 Rev. Proc. 2003-80, I.R.B. 2003-45; Rev. Proc. 2004-60, I.R.B. 2004-42.

.35 Rev. Proc. 2004-60, I.R.B. 2004-42.

Substantiation of Business Expenses

¶25,475 Elements to Be Proved. A salesperson must substantiate business travel, local transportation, entertainment, and gift expenses by adequate records or sufficient written or oral evidence corroborating his own statements as to (.05):

(1) amount,

(2) time,

(3) place,

(4) business purpose, and

(5) business relationship of the person entertained (or receiving a gift).

Documentation required

Should a salesperson choose to maintain written evidence for substantiation purposes, adequate records or sufficient written evidence includes:

(1) account books, diaries, and logs;

(2) documentary evidence (receipts, paid bills, etc.);

(3) trip sheets;

(4) expense reports; and

(5) written statements of witnesses.

A salesperson may not approximate or estimate his expenditures for travel, entertainment, and gift expenses. In general, the records should be retained for three years from the date on which the return reflecting the deduction was filed.

.05 Code Sec. 274(d); Temp. Reg. § 1.274-5T.

¶25,476 Proof of Travel Expenses. When travel expenses away from home are incurred, a salesperson must record—

(1) the cost of each expenditure for transportation, meals and lodging, and incidentals (telephone, telegraph, sample rooms, etc.);

(2) the dates of departure and return for each trip away from home, and the total number of days spent away from home on business;

(3) the place or places of travel, including the name or location of each destination; and

(4) the business purpose of the travel, meaning the business reason or the nature of the business benefit expected to be derived (.05).

A salesperson does not have to separately state each *miscellaneous* expenditure (parking, local telephone calls, local taxi fares, public transportation, gasoline, and oil) if he lists the total of miscellaneous items for each one-day period in reasonable categories. Further, although expenditures for breakfast, lunch, and dinner are generally treated as separate expenditures, he may record daily totals of them under the category of meals.

Just how much detail must be recorded as to business purpose depends on the circumstances in each case. For example, a salesperson who travels on an established sales route each month to call on his customers is not ordinarily required to make a written statement of the business purpose of such travel.

Per diem rates

When a salesperson is traveling on a per diem and/or mileage allowance, he will be considered as having kept adequate records or provided other sufficient evidence of the travel expenses if the rates his employer pays him do not exceed the maximum per diem allowance for the appropriate locality (.10) (see ¶25,473).

☐ For the specific amounts for localities within the continental United States, see ¶8282; for nonforeign localities outside the continental United States, see ¶8283; and for foreign localities outside the continental United States, see ¶8284.

A salesperson seeking to take the away-from-home business mileage deduction must meet the same substantiation requirements that apply to other away-from-home travel expenses (.15). However, due to the nature of this expense deduction, the substantiation requirements are relatively easy for a salesperson to meet. The amount of mileage can be substantiated by any reasonable means, such as the use of a log of business travel.

Documentary evidence should be retained to support all expenses for lodging while traveling away from home and for any other expenditure of $75 or more. Documentary evidence, such as a receipt, paid bill, or similar document, is ordinarily considered adequate to support an expense if the document discloses the amount, date, place, and essential character of the expenses.

Standard daily meal allowance

Salespersons have the option of electing a standard daily meal allowance rather than keeping records of meal expenses (.20). However, election of the standard meal allowance does not relieve salespersons of the necessity of substantiating the time, place, and purpose of the business travel, or of the need to substantiate other travel expenses such as lodging expenses.

Under this election, salespersons may use the federal meals and incidental expense (M&IE) rate for the locality of travel. Deductions claimed by employees using the optional method are itemized deductions subject to the two-percent-of-adjusted-gross-income floor on miscellaneous itemized deductions.

Optional method for incidental expenses deduction

Rev. Proc. 2002-61 created a new option for computing the amount of allowable incidental expenses only for travel on or after January 1, 2003. This method may be used instead of actual expenses to determine the deductible amount from income for ordinary and necessary incidental expenses. An employee or self-employed may use the amount of $3 per day for incidental expenses only incurred or paid while traveling away from home after October 1, 2004 (.25).

There was no increase from the $3 per day for incidental expenses only for travel on or after November 1, 2003 (.30).

Local travel expenses

To be deductible, local travel expenses must be ordinary and necessary to the salesperson's business. Local travel expenses must be substantiated by adequate records or sufficient oral or written evidence (.35) (see ¶25,479).

.05 Temp. Reg. § 1.274-5T.

.10 Rev. Proc. 2002-61, I.R.B. 2002-41; Rev. Proc. 2003-80, I.R.B. 2003-45.

.15 *C.F. Smith*, 80 TC 1165, CCH Dec. 40,245.

.20 Temp. Reg. § 1.274-5T(j).

.25 Rev. Proc. 2004-60, I.R.B. 2004-42..

.30 Rev. Proc. 2003-80, I.R.B. 2003-45

.35 Code Sec. 274(d).

¶25,477 Entertainment Expense Records. To establish a deduction for an entertainment expense, a salesperson must keep a record of

(1) the amount of each separate expenditure for entertainment;

(2) the date the entertainment took place;

(3) the name, address or location, and the type of entertainment, if the information is not apparent from the designation of the place;

(4) the reason for the entertainment or the business benefit to be gained and, except for business meals, the nature of any business discussion or activity that took place; and

(5) the name, title, and business relationship of the person entertained (.05).

Incidental expenditures, such as taxi fares or telephone calls, may be totalled on a daily basis and do not need to be recorded separately. Tips may be considered as separate expenditures in determining whether the salesperson has exceeded the $75 limit (see ¶25,476), but they do not have to be recorded on the expense account records separately.

The business purpose of an expenditure need not be stated if it is evident from the business relationship of the persons entertained.

Business discussion

If a salesperson claims a deduction for entertainment expense incurred before or after a business discussion on the ground that the entertainment was associated with the active conduct of a trade or business, he must, in addition to the items noted at ¶25,475 reflect:

(1) the date and duration of the business discussion;

(2) the place of business discussion;

(3) the nature of the business discussion and the business reason for the entertainment; and

(4) the names of those persons entertained who participated in the discussion.

.05 Temp. Reg. § 1.274-5T(b)(3) and (4).

¶25,478 Proof of Business Gifts. Business gifts are generally limited to $25 per donee during the tax year. If a salesperson makes business gifts for which he wishes to claim a deduction, he must keep a record of:

(1) the cost;

(2) the date of the gift;

(3) a description of the gift;

(4) the business purpose for making the gift or the benefit expected to be reaped; and

(5) the name of the donee, his occupation or title, or some other designation that will establish his business relationship to the salesperson (.05).

.05 Temp. Reg. § 1.274-5T(b)(5).

¶25,479 Other Sufficient Evidence. If adequate records are not maintained, expenses must be proved by a salesperson's own statement in writing and by other corroborating evidence, either oral or written (.05). Circumstantial evidence may be used to establish the business relationship or business purpose of an expense item.

Weight of oral evidence

However, it should be noted that different weight will be given to written evidence than to oral evidence. Oral evidence alone has less probative value than written evidence; the probative value of written evidence is greater the closer in time it is to the expenditure. Further, salespersons cannot utilize the *Cohan* expense estimation rule (.10) to determine the amount of the allowable deduction where insufficient records have been kept to substantiate a deduction.

Written evidence

If a salesperson chooses to maintain written evidence for substantiation purposes, adequate records or sufficient evidence includes:

(1) account books, diaries, and logs;

(2) documentary evidence (i.e., receipts, paid bills);

(3) expense reports; and

(4) written statements of witnesses.

Additional evidence may be required, even though adequate records are kept or sworn statements (or oral testimony) of persons entertained are provided.

> ***Example:*** A salesperson keeps a diary of all his travel expenses, but none of these expenses exceeds the $75 limit. Thus, he has kept adequate records and need not produce additional corroborating evidence (including documentary or circumstantial evidence) except for his lodging expenses. For example, a salesperson might supply a copy of a commission statement showing commissions on sales made to certain customers in certain locations on specific dates to substantiate his claim for a deduction.

.05 Temp. Reg. § 1.274-5T(c).

.10 *G.M. Cohan*, CA-2, 2 USTC ¶489, which adopted the rule that, if the evidence indicates that a taxpayer incurred a deductible expense but the exact amount cannot be determined, the court should make an approximation and not disallow the deduction entirely. The approximation rule of *Cohan* is inadequate and unacceptable for purposes of the substantiation rules of Code Sec. 274(d). Its use in other areas of tax law, such as computing reasonable compensation, etc., is still permitted.

¶25,480 Separate Expenditures. For purposes of the substantiation requirements, each separate payment made by a salesperson is considered a separate expenditure (.05). Recurring expenses of a similar nature during a single event, however, are treated as a single expenditure.

> ***Example 1:*** A salesperson entertains a business guest at dinner and takes him to a baseball game. Payments for the dinner and the tickets to the game are two separate expenditures and each must be substantiated by adequate records or other sufficient evidence.

> ***Example 2:*** Payments for breakfast, lunch, and dinner on a day of business travel are three separate expenditures (although a salesperson has the option of lumping these three expenditures into one daily total for meals).

Example 3: Separate payments for each round of drinks while entertaining at a cocktail lounge can be totalled and treated as one expenditure.

Example 4: A salesperson takes a business guest to lunch. The lunch is $73.50 and the tip is $11.00. Since the cost of the lunch is less than the $75 limit, the salesperson does not need to obtain documentary evidence of the expenditure. Further, the tip may be added to the cost of the lunch and $84.50 recorded on the salesperson's expense account record as the amount spent for the lunch plus tip.

If a salesperson has established the amount of an expenditure for two or more persons, the amount will be allocated among the persons on a pro rata basis, unless the salesperson is able to prove the cost for each person.

Example 5: A salesperson takes three customers to lunch at a total cost of $75. If the salesperson fails to indicate how much his own lunch cost, it will be assumed to be one-fourth of $75, or $18.75.

.05 Temp. Reg. § 1.274-5T(c)(6).

¶25,481 Loss of Records. If a salesperson demonstrates to the IRS that his records have been destroyed or lost through circumstances over which he had no control, such as destruction by fire, flood, earthquake, or other casualty, the IRS will permit him to make a reconstruction of his expenditures (.05).

Also, if, because of the inherent nature of the situation in which an expenditure is made, a salesperson could not obtain proper evidence of an element of the expenditure under the above rules, he may prove the element by presenting other evidence where available.

.05 Temp. Reg. § 1.274-5T(c)(4) and (5).

Sample Expense Account Forms

¶25,483 Purpose of Forms. At ¶25,485 and ¶25,486 two sample forms are reproduced that can be used by salespersons for reporting or recording expenses. One deals with travel and business (reimbursable) expenses generally (see ¶25,485); the other provides detailed information about entertainment expenses (see ¶25,486). These forms provide information, details and the grouping of expenses needed in preparing a salesperson's income tax return.

Although salespersons and other employees who must submit an adequate accounting to their employers (see ¶25,473) are relieved of responsibility for reporting either their expenses or their reimbursements on their income tax returns, there may still be many occasions when it will be helpful for them to keep records and have them available. For example, a salesperson might be reimbursed only for certain types of expenses, or his allowance may not cover all the expenses he has actually incurred or paid. In addition, there is always the possibility that the IRS will ask to see the types of records that the employee submits to his employer in order to make a determination that an adequate accounting has been made.

¶25,484 How to Use Forms. The expense account form at ¶25,485 is only a suggested sample. A salesperson can adopt variations as to size or arrangement of materials to fit his or her employer's particular needs. Alternatively, a salesperson may obtain a copy of the CCH *2005 Business Expense Log* by calling 1-800-449-8114 or by logging onto http://tax.cchgroup.com and click on "Store" icon.

The suggested type of expense account form is one that covers a daily period. If a trip covers more than one day, a separate sheet should be prepared for each day and the totals for each day should be carried over to the next day's sheet. In this way, a cumulative total will be available at the end of the trip. In the space marked "Business Reason," a salesperson should record his day's activities so that the business purpose of the trip may be shown.

> ***Example:*** From April 1, 2004 through the balance of the year, John Jones, a salesperson, receives a 37.5 cents-per-mile car allowance from his employer. In addition, he is reimbursed for entertainment expenses upon approval of his expense account by the employer. He keeps daily records on his own set of forms (using the "Tax Record" column), then accumulates them, and submits the expense accounts weekly. During the week of October 18-22, 2004, he traveled 800 miles. For October 18 through October 21 he spent $800 for lodging, meals, gasoline, parking, and telephone calls. On October 22, the last day of his work week, he incurred the following expenses:

Meals	$ 55.00
Gasoline	25.00
Parking	10.00
Telephone calls	5.00
Entertainment	75.00
Total	$ 170.00

> In filling out his daily expense form for October 18, Mr. Jones would carry over his previous four days' expenses and place $800 in the "Tax Record" column opposite the "carryover" line. In the same "Tax Record" column, he would list all of his expenses for October 18, on the appropriate lines. The entertainment expenses of $75 (to be reimbursed by the employer) should be listed in both the "Amount" column and the "Tax Record" column. In the "Expense Details" column, Mr. Jones lists his car allowance under the "Car" entry, where he shows 800 miles at 37.5 cents and enters $300 in the "Amount" column.

> After totaling both columns, Mr. Jones knows that he is entitled to $375 from his employer—$300 car allowance plus $75 entertainment reimbursement. Periodically, Mr. Jones must also record items such as insurance, repairs, etc., with supporting computations, receipts, and adjustments for personal use of the car. Any excess expense will be claimed on his own return as a miscellaneous itemized deduction, in which case the "Tax Record" information he keeps is essential. If the amounts received from the employer exceed his expenses, the excess is included in gross income.

> At the bottom of the expense account form for the first day, Mr. Jones should indicate the general business purpose for the trip and list customer contacts for that day. On the daily forms for the rest of the trip, he should list the customer contacts for each day. On the form for the last day of the trip, he should fill out the dates of departure and return, the total days away and the number of days spent on business.

> The $75 entertainment expense details should be explained on the entertainment expense form, such as appears at ¶25,486. In Mr. Jones's case, he took Mr. Rogers, a purchasing agent of a customer firm, to dinner and a night club where business was discussed and orders were taken for supplies. Mr. Jones should list the guest's name and his connection with the employer's business. He should also list the name and address of the night club and the time and duration of the entertainment. Mr. Jones should also give a brief description of the business purpose for the entertainment.

¶25,485 Sample Travel Expense Account Form. The following form illustrates the type of form that may be used for accounting for travel expenses.

EMPLOYEE'S COPY

Name .... **Date** ....
Address ....

Use the **"Tax Record"** column to record unreimbursed expenses or additional items or details you will need in preparing your income tax return.

Expense Details	Place	Amount	Tax Record
Carryover (from preceding page, if any)		$	$
Lodging			
Meals			
Transportation:			
From			
To			
Mode			
Car:			
From			
To			
........miles at.........cents.			
Gas, oil, lubrication, etc.			
Repairs, tires, supplies, etc.			
Explanation:			
....			
....			
....			
....			
....			
....			
....			
....			
Entertainment (explain on attached "entertainment record" (¶25,486))			
Miscellaneous: (Taxi, car rental, telephone calls, etc.)			
....			
....			
....			
....			
....			
....			
....			
....			
	TOTAL	$	
	Credit Card (employer)		
	BALANCE (for reimbursement)		

Business Reason:

Departure ....
Return ....
Total days away ....
No. of business days ....

¶25,486 Sample Entertainment Expense Record. The following is a sample entertainment expense record.

EMPLOYEE'S COPY

Name . . . .
Date . . . . (Show date of entertainment)

Amount $ . . . .

	Use one copy of this form to provide details for each entertainment. Cover all items charged to or to be paid by the employer.
Guests:	Give business relationship to your employer of each person entertained for whom deduction is claimed, including his name, title, or the nature of his activities as they relate to employer's business. Also, give total number of persons entertained, including other employees. And designate those who partook in business discussion before or after entertainment. . . . .
Place:	Give name, address, or location. . . . .
Type:	Give description of entertainment. . . . .
Business Purpose:	Give nature of the business benefit expected to be derived by employer as result of the entertainment. . . . .
Business Discussion:	Give date, duration, place, and nature of business discussion which preceded or followed entertainment. . . . .
Tax record (Employee):	. . . . Use the "tax record" section on the "employee's copy" to provide details of amounts you will need in preparing your own return, to support deductions for amounts not reimbursed.

SCHOOLTEACHERS

Introduction

¶25,487 The tax position of a teacher is generally the same as that of other employed persons. All ordinary and necessary expenses incurred in the trade or profession as an employee are deductible as employee business expenses (see ¶7298). However, unlike many employees, a teacher must meet requirements for continuing professional training and education. Expenses related to this purpose are deductible so long as they are qualifying educational expenses. Special rules also apply to teachers regarding classroom expenses, scholarships and grants, tax-sheltered annuities and income earned foreign teachers.

Educational and Research Expenses

¶25,489 Qualifying Educational Expenses. Education expenses incurred by a taxpayer (including a teacher) may be deducted as ordinary and necessary business expenses if the education:

(1) maintains or improves skills required by the individual in his employment or other trade or business; or

(2) meets the express requirements of the individual's employer, applicable law or regulations, or is imposed as a condition on the individual in retaining his job, status, or rate of compensation (.05).

Education may meet these requirements and still be considered nonqualifying education, for which expenses are not deductible, if the education is to meet minimum education requirements (¶25,490) or to enter into a new trade or business (¶25,491).

To claim the deduction, the taxpayer must be engaged in a trade or business at the time the education expenses are incurred. Mere membership in good standing in a profession will not suffice. A person must be actively carrying on a trade or business. Thus, for a teacher to deduct educational expenses, he must be presently involved in actual teaching or related duties. Temporary cessation of employment is permitted for enrollment for study, but only if it is temporary and an employment relationship continues, such as a leave granted by the employing school. The IRS has held that this cessation must not be for more than one year in order to claim the deduction. The courts, however, have not accepted this time limitation. Instead, they have looked at the facts and circumstances of each case seeking evidence of more than a subjective intent to resume employment. In some cases, deductions were allowed when the taxpayer hiatus from employment was for two years.

To claim the deduction, a taxpayer must be engaged in a trade or business at the time the education expenses are incurred. For example, a teacher must be presently involved in actually teaching (and related duties) during the period of study. Merely maintaining membership in good standing will not suffice. Cessation of employment is permitted, but only if such cessation is temporary and an employment relationship continues (e.g., leave granted by employing school). The IRS has held that any cessation must not be for more than one year (.10). However, the Tax Court has rejected any time limitation but instead has ruled that a fact and circumstance test of the subjective intent of the taxpayer to resume employment (.15).

Types of expenses. Educational expenses must be related to the taxpayer's current employment in order to be deductible. Such expenses include: (1) tuition, books, supplies, lab fees and similar items; (2) certain transportation and travel costs (¶25,492); and (3) other educational expenses, such as costs of researching and typing when writing a paper as part of an educational program (¶25,493). Educational expenses do not include any personal or capital expenses.

.05 Reg. §§1.162-5(a) and (c).

.10 Rev. Rul. 68-591, 1968-2 CB 73.

.15 *S.G. Sherman*, 36 TCM 1191, CCH Dec. 34,261(M), TC Memo 1977-301.

¶25,490 Minimum Educational Requirements. If a taxpayer is required to meet minimum education requirements in order to qualify for employment or another trade or business, any expenses for that education are considered personal in nature and nondeductible (.05). The minimum education necessary to qualify an individual for a position, trade or business depends on factors such as the employer's requirements, applicable laws and regulations, and the standards of the profession, trade or business involved. The fact that an individual is already employed does not mean that the individual has met the minimum educational requirements.

For teachers, minimum qualification requirements are typically specified as an aggregate number of hours or a degree obtained, as determined at the time the teacher is hired. If a teacher meets the requirements but they are subsequently changed after the date of hire, the teacher will be treated as continuing to meet the minimum requirements. Any expenses incurred for education beyond the minimum requirements will be deductible so long as the general requirements are met. This includes any expenses a teacher incurs to meet the minimum qualification requirements in a second state (.10). It does not include the expenses of a teacher's assistant because such individuals by definition have not met the minimum qualification requirements to be a teacher (.15).

> ***Example 1:*** State X requires a bachelor's degree for beginning secondary school teachers which must include 30 credit hours of professional educational courses. However, an individual may be hired by a school if the individual has a bachelor's degree and completes 30 credit hours of professional educational courses within three years. Helen Smith is hired as a teacher in State X. She has a bachelor's degree but has only completed 20 credit hours of educational courses. After one year of employment, Helen incurs expenses to complete an additional 10 credit hours of educational courses. Helen may deduct the expenses because they do not constitute education required to meet the minimum educational requirements, which is a bachelor's degree. The course will also not lead Helen to qualifying in a new trade or business.

> ***Example 2:*** Assume the same facts as in Example (1), above, except that because of a shortage of applicants, Helen is hired before she completes her bachelor's degree. The expenses incurred by Helen in completing her bachelor's degree are not deductible because obtaining the degree constitutes meeting the

minimum requirements. This is true even though she may be employed as a teach prior to completing her degree.

If there are no requirements as to the minimum level of education for a teacher, then an individual will be deemed to have met the minimum requirements for qualification as a teacher when he becomes a member of the faculty of an educational institution (.20). Becoming a member of the faculty of an educational institution means: (a) the teacher obtains tenure or has years of service counted toward obtaining tenure; (b) the institution makes contributions to a retirement plan (other than Social Security) on behalf of the teacher; or (3) the teacher has a vote in faculty matters.

.05 Reg. §§1.162-5(b)(1) and (2).

.10 Rev. Rul. 71-58, 1971-1 CB 55.

.15 *L.C. Diaz*, 70 TC 1067, CCH Dec. 35,436.

.20 *L.M. Toner*, CA-3, 80-2 USTC ¶9507, 623 F2d 315.

¶25,491 New Trade or Business Expenses. Any educational expenses incurred which qualify a taxpayer for a new trade or business are considered personal in nature and nondeductible (.05). A new trade or business is involved when the educational expenses enable the taxpayer to perform substantially different tasks and activities in various occupations or employment. It does not matter whether the taxpayer has any intention to enter a new trade or business or whether the motive in incurring the educational expenses was to improve skills for his current trade or business. It also does not matter whether the taxpayer actually works in the new trade or business. In this sense, it may be all but impossible to prove that a bachelor of liberal arts or science degree program does not qualify a taxpayer for a new trade or business (.10).

On the other hand, a change of duties does not constitute a new trade or business if the new duties involve the same general type of work as is involved in the taxpayer's current trade or business. For this purpose, all teaching and related duties are considered to involve the same general type of work. Thus, changing from an elementary to a secondary school teacher or from teaching one subject to another does not constitute entering a new trade or business. Similarly, a change from a classroom teacher to a principal or guidance counselor does not constitute a new trade or business. Any educational expenses incurred in order to make such changes would be deductible.

.05 Reg. §§1.162-5(b)(1) and (3).

.10 *D.N. Bodley*, 56 TC 1357, CCH Dec. 30,997; *J.R. Meredith*, 65 TCM 2876, CCH Dec. 49,082(M), TC Memo. 1993-250.

¶25,492 Travel and Transportation Expenses. If any individual, including a teacher, travels away from home primarily to obtain an education, his expenditures for travel, meals and lodging while away from home are deductible (.05). The rules for deducting education-related travel expenses are the same as for other business-related travel expenses (¶8201). Generally, expenses attributable to personal activities are not deductible. If travel is primarily personal, only meal and lodging expenses attributable to the educational pursuit are deductible. Whether travel is primarily personal or for education is dependent upon the facts and circumstances.

> ***Example:*** A high-school English teacher incurs travel expenses in connection with university courses taken in Greece. The expenses are deductible if her foreign study serves clear business needs such improving her teaching ability because the school that employs her devotes a sizeable of time of its English curriculum studying Greek mythology. Another factor to determine deductible would be if a majority of her time was spent in educational activities, rather than personal activities (.10)

Local transportation expenses incurred in connection with deductible educational activities may be deducted in certain circumstances. For example, a taxpayer may deduct the cost of going directly from work to school. If the taxpayer is regularly employed and goes to school on a temporary basis, the cost of return from school to home is also deductible. Temporary for this purpose means one year or less (.15).

Travel as a form of education. In general, no deduction is allowed for expenses for travel as a form of education (.20). However, expenses for travel as a form of education are deductible but only if such expenses are directly related to a taxpayers employment duties or other trade or business (.25). Travel will be considered directly related if a major portion of the activities during the period of travel maintains or improves skills of the taxpayer in his current employment. Approval of the travel by the taxpayer's employer is not determinative.

.05 Code Sec. 162(a)(2); Reg. §1.162-5(e).
.10 *A. Jorgensen*, 79 TCM 1926, CCH Dec. 53,855(M), TC Memo. 2000-138.
.15 Rev. Rul. 99-7, 1991-1 CB 361.
.20 Code Sec. 274(m)(2).
.25 Reg. §1.162-5(d).

¶25,493 Research Expenses. For many teachers, their duties encompass not only the usual lecture and teaching duties but also the communication and advancement of knowledge through independent research and publication. Research expenses incurred by a teacher for this purpose may be deductible as ordinary and necessary expenses if it can be shown that the research is directly related to the general field of expertise in which he is performing services as an educator (.05). The teacher must also show that the research was undertaken without an expectation of profit but instead with a view to scholarly publication. In the event that income does directly result from teaching, lecturing, or writing based on the research, any expenses already deducted may be taken into account to offset the taxable income received by the teacher. Examples of research expenses include typing or stenographic expenditures, as well as travel expenditures related to the work (.10). Research expenses connected with nontaxable or partially nontaxable fellowship grants are discussed at ¶25,504.

.05 Rev. Rul. 63-275, 1963-2 CB 85; see also *R.L. Feldman*, 26 TCM 444, CCH Dec. 28,441(M), TC Memo. 1967-91.
.10 Rev. Rul. 67-421, 1967-2 CB 84.

¶25,494 Educational Provided Benefits. An employer may help to finance the education of its employees. How an employee, such as a teacher, treats such benefits depends on how the benefits are provided. For example, a teacher who receives benefits under an educational assistance program (¶4550) may exclude up to $5,250 of such benefits from his gross income per year so long as the education is work-related. An employer could also provide direct reimbursements to a teacher for educational expenses related to work. The proper tax treatment depends on whether the employer's reimbursement arrangement is an accountable or nonaccountable plan (¶7301). Employer provided educational assistance that does not satisfy the requirements for either of these arrangements could also be considered a working condition fringe benefit (¶4664).

Miscellaneous Expenses

¶25,497 In General. Teachers are generally subject to the same rules regarding employee expenses as apply to all other employees (¶7298). Expenses that are reimbursed under a qualified accountable plan are deductible from the teacher's gross income (¶7301). However, in actual practice, this deduction is given effect by the exclusion of the reimbursement from a teacher's taxable wages reported on Form W-2. Unreimbursed expenses incurred by a teacher are generally only allowed as miscellaneous itemized deductions (¶6501).

¶25,498 Classroom Expenses. For tax years 2003 through 2005, eligible educators are permitted an above-the-line deduction of up to $250 per year for any unreimbursed expenses incurred in supplying books, supplies (other than nonathletic supplies for courses in health or physical education), computer equipment (including related software and services) and other supplementary materials used in the classroom (.05). To be deductible, the expenses must otherwise qualify as a deductible trade or business expense under Code Sec. 162. Thus, a teacher must demonstrate that the expense was ordinary and necessary, and that it was not capital in nature. The $250 per year deduction is permitted only to the extent that the amount of the expenses incurred exceeds the amount excludable for the tax year for: (1) United States Savings Bonds used to pay education expenses (Code Sec. 135); (2) distributions and earnings from qualified tuition programs Code Sec. 529(c)(1); or (3) distributions from education savings accounts (Code Sec. 530(d)(2)) (.10).

For this purpose, an eligible teacher is any individuals who, for at least 900 hours during the school year is a kindergarten through grade 12 teacher, instructor, counselor, or principle, or aide (.15). A school is defined as an organization that provides elementary or secondary education, as determined under state law.

Comment

CCH Analysts note that since most school systems run on a 180-day school year, teachers that work half-time will most likely have to proof that they worked at least 10 hours a day in order to be eligible for the deduction. The same is true for teachers that ended their teaching career in June or started their teaching career in September.

.05 Code Sec. 62(a)(2)(D), as amended by the Working Families Tax Relief Act of 2004 (P.L. 108-311).

.10 Code Sec. 62(d)(2).

.15 Code Sec. 62(d)(1).

¶25,499 Dues, Journals, and Books. The dues paid by teachers to professional societies and the price of subscriptions for educational journals connected with their profession are deductible as trade or business expenses if unreimbursed. The cost of technical books purchased by a teacher specifically for use in connection with his or her professional work is also deductible if the useful life of the book is one year or less. A teacher must keep adequate records to substantiate the claimed deductions.

¶25,501 Strike Fines. In general, no deduction is allowed for any fine or similar penalty payment paid to a government for the violation of any law (.05). This include any fine or penalty assessed against any public employee (including a teacher) for engaging in a strike which is illegal under state law (.10)

.05 Code Sec. 162(f).

.10 Rev. Rul. 76-130, 1976-1 CB 16; *A. Tucker*, 69 TC 675, CCH Dec. 34,963.

Scholarships and Fellowship Grants

¶25,504 Inclusion in Gross Income In general, a taxpayer who is a degree candidate at a qualified educational organization may exclude from gross income the amount of any scholarship or fellowship grant received during the tax year (¶4325). However, the exclusion does not apply to any portion of a scholarship or grant that represents payment for teaching, research or other services as a condition for receiving the funds (or any reduction in tuition) (.05). This is true whether or not all degree candidates are required to perform the same services.

For this purpose, a scholarship or grant will represent a payment for services when the grantor requires the taxpayer to perform services in return for the granting of the scholarship or fellowship (.10). For example, any requirement that the recipient pursue studies, research or other activities primarily for the benefit of the grantor would be treated as a requirement to perform services. However, a requirement that the recipient provide periodic reports to the grantor as to his general progress would not be considered a requirement to perform services. A scholarship or grant conditioned upon past, present or future teaching, research or other services by the recipient would represent a payment for services.

The determination of whether an activity is primarily for the benefit of the grantor or the recipient is based on the facts and circumstances of each case. For example, payments made by a state grant program to bring about a better understanding between teachers and students in inner-city schools primarily benefited the state (.15). Thus, even though the program provided the opportunity for recipients to obtain credits toward a degree in teaching, payments to recipient's constituted compensation and therefore were required to be included in the recipient's gross income.

Exclusion amount

If only a portion of a scholarship or fellowship grant represents a payment for services, then it is the grantor that must determine the amount to be allocated for that payment (.20). A number of factors may be taken into account in making this determination including the compensation paid to similarly situated students or other employees of the grantor and other education organizations. Amounts that are allocated for the payment of services must be included in the recipients gross income, any additional amounts of the scholarship or grant would be excluded. That portion allocated for the payment of services is considered wages for withholding purposes (.25). The nature of the services provided and the status of the organization will determine whether such amounts are subject to FICA and FUTA requirements (¶18,301).

.05 Code Sec. 117(c)(1); Proposed Reg. §1.117-6(d)(1).
.10 Proposed Reg. §1.117-6(d)(2).
.15 *J.M. Jaeger*, 32 TCM 732, CCH Dec. 32,047(M), TC Memo. 1973-151; but see also *M.D. Olick*, 73 TC 479, CCH Dec. 36,500.
.20 Proposed Reg. §1.117-6(d)(3).
.25 Proposed Reg. §1.117-6(d)(4).

Tax-Sheltered Annuities

¶25,507 Exclusion of Employer Contributions. A tax-sheltered annuity (TSA) arrangement is a special type of retirement or deferred compensation plan covering employees of public schools and certain tax-exempt organizations. If a TSA meets certain qualification requirements (¶11,600 and following), then any employer contributions made to the plan on behalf of a teacher will be excludable from the teacher's gross income if the contributions are substantially vested when made (.05). This exclusion, however, is limited to the lesser of:

(1) the employer's contributions (including elective contributions of employees, but not rollovers from IRAs or other TSAs, or contributions allocable to purchase of life insurance protection for the employee);

(2) the annual limit on employer contributions for the year (for 2004 the lesser of $41,000 or 100% percent of the teacher's includible compensation); or

(3) the annual limit on elective deferrals for the year under a salary reduction agreement ($13,000 for 2004).

Caution

CCH Analysts note that for tax years prior to 2002, the exclusion was limited to the lesser of the above limitations or the maximum exclusion amount (MEA), which was determined by multiplying the number of years of service of the teacher by 20 percent of his includible compensation (see example below) (.10). Deductions from this amount were then taken for any employer contributions that were excluded from the teacher's gross income for prior tax years. Any amount left was the MEA.

For this purpose, a teacher's interest in a TSA is substantially vested when that interest is either freely transferable or not subject to a substantial risk of forfeiture (.15). If only part of a teacher's interest in a TSA is substantially vested during the tax year, then the amount treated as an employer contribution is calculated by determining the total amount that would treated as an employer contribution if the teacher's entire interest is substantially vested during the year and multiplying that amount by the percent of the interest that actually did become substantially vested during the tax year (.20).

Includible compensation

Includible compensation is the amount of compensation received by a teacher from a public school for the most recent period constituting a full year of service (.25). Generally, this includes all wages that a teacher reports as gross income including any income earned abroad (regardless of whether or not it is excluded for federal income tax purposes). Includible compensation does not include the amount of any employer contributions made to the plan for the year, even if they are in excess of the exclusion limits. A year of service does not necessarily mean a 12-month calendar year, but instead refers to the usual annual work period of a full-time teacher (.30). For part-time teachers (or full-time teachers working only half-time), this means that the amount of includible compensation is the aggregate amount of compensation received for the period until they have completed a full-year of service.

> ***Example 1:*** Ellen Foster is a calendar-year taxpayer. She has been employed full-time for the past four years as a teacher in a public school. The regular academic year of the school is the period September through June. For purposes of determining Ellen's exclusion limit, the amount of includible compensation she receives for her most recent one-year period of service is the compensation she received for her services during the 10-month period covering January through June and September through December.
>
> Assume the same facts as in Example 1, except that Ellen is employed on a part-time basis and only works the last three months of the academic year (April-through-June). Her includible compensation for 2004 would be the compensation she received for her services during 2004 (3/10 year of service), 2003 (3/10 year of service), 2002 (3/10 year of service) and June 2001 (1/10 year of service).

Calculating the maximum exclusion amount

The following example applies to tax years prior to 2002 and shows how to calculate the exclusion limit using the maximum exclusion amount.

> ***Example 3:*** Jane Quigley is a calendar-year taxpayer. She has been employed since January 1, 1998, as a full-time teacher at a private school which is a tax-exempt Code Sec. 501(c)(3) organization. Her yearly salary is $20,000. However, Jane entered into a salary reduction agreement with the school to have 10 percent of her salary used each year to purchase an annuity contract on her behalf. In addition, each year the school contributed an amount equal to 18 percent of her salary (before reduction) to a qualified pension trust on Jane's behalf. If Jane's

salary remains the same for years 1999, 2000 and 2001, then the amount of the premiums for the annuity contract that is excludable from Jane's income is computed as follows: (.35)

	Year 2000	
(1)	Amount contributed by employer for annuity contract	$2,000
(2)	Amounts contributed by employer in prior years to qualified plan	None
(3)	Includible compensation ($20,000 –$2,000)	$18,000
(4)	20 percent X includible compensation	$3,600
(5)	Number of years of service	1
(6)	Item (4) X item (5)	$3,600
(7)	Employer's contributions excludable in prior years	None
(8)	Amount excludable for 2000 under Code Sec. 403(b); lesser of either (1) or ((6) – ((7)	$2,000
(9)	Amount includible in gross income for 2000 ((1) – (8))	None
	Year 2001	
(10)	Amount contributed by employer for annuity contract	$2,000
(11)	Amount contributed in prior years to qualified plan (line (6)) (excludable from employee's gross income under Code Sec. 402(a))	$3,600
(12)	Includible compensation ($20,000 – $2,000)	$18,000
(13)	20 percent X includible compensation	$3,600
(14)	Number of years of service	2
(15)	Item (13) X item (14)	$7,200
(16)	Employer's contributions excludable in prior taxable years ((8) + (11))	$5,600
(17)	Amount excludable for 2001 under Code Sec. 403(b); lesser of either (10) or ((15) – (16))	$1,600
(18)	Amount includible in gross income for 2001 ((10) – (17))	$400
	Year 2002	
(19)	Amount contributed by employer for annuity contract	$2,000
(20)	Amount contributed in prior years to qualified plan (line (15)) (excludable from employee's gross income under Code Sec. 402(a))	$7,200
(21)	Amount contributed by employer in prior years for annuity and excludable under Code Sec. 403(b) ((8) + (17))	$3,600
(22)	Includible compensation ($20,000 – $2,000)	$18,000
(23)	20 percent times includible compensation	$3,600
(24)	Number of years of service	3
(25)	Item (23) X item (24)	$10,800
(26)	Employer's contributions excludable in prior taxable years ((20) + (21))	$10,800
(27)	Amount excludable for 2002 under Code Sec. 403(b); lesser of either (19) 0r ((25) – (26))	None
(28)	Amount includible in gross income for 2002 ((19) – (27))	$2,000

.05 Code Sec. 403(b).
.10 Code Sec. 403(b)(2) prior to repeal by P.L. 107-16.
.15 Reg. §1.83-3(b).
.20 Reg. §1.403(c)-1(b)(3).
.25 Code Sec. 403(b)(3).
.30 Code Sec. 403(b)(4).
.35 Rev. Rul. 84-149, 1984-2 CB 97.

¶25,508 Excess Contributions. Employer contributions to a tax-sheltered annuity (TSA) that exceed the exclusion limit (¶25,507) in any tax year, must be included in the teacher's gross income if the teacher's interest in the TSA is substantially vested (.05). If that interest is not substantially vested at the time of the contribution, but becomes substantially vested in a later tax year, any excess amount will ordinarily be included in the teacher's gross income in the later year.

If the excess contribution is due to any excess deferrals from a salary reduction agreement, then such excess may be distributed to the teacher if there was a reasonable error in calculating the elective deferral for the tax year. The qualified annuity plan must permit the distribution of the excess deferral and the distribution must be labeled as a corrective distribution. If the distribution occurs no later than April 15, then it will be included in the teacher's gross income for the year it was contributed. All earnings on such excess contributions are also included in the teacher's gross income in the year the distribution occurs.

In addition to inclusion in gross income, a teacher will also be subject to an excise tax on any excess contributions made during the tax year (.10). The rate of tax is six percent on the amount of the excess contributions for the year. However, the tax cannot exceed six percent of the value of the account at the close of the taxable year, thus avoiding imposition of the tax on excess contributions that may have disappeared because of the decline in value of account assets. See ¶21,415.

.05 Code Sec. 403(c).

.10 Code Sec. 4973(a).

¶25,509 Distributions. Distributions to a teacher from a tax sheltered annuity plan are treated no differently than distributions to any individual from any other qualified retirement plan. They can be made lump-sum, in annuity form or rolled over into other qualified retirement plans (see ¶11,060 and following).

Exclusions from Income

¶25,512 In General. A teacher is eligible to exclude items from gross income to the same extent as every other individual taxpayers. This includes amounts received under an accident, health and disability plan, employer contributions to a tax-sheltered annuity (¶25,507), amounts received under a educational assistance program (¶25,494) or a qualified scholarship or fellowship grant (¶25,504). A teacher may also exclude from gross income amounts received under a workers' compensation regulation having the effect of a state law (.05).

.05 *M.G. Dyer*, 71 TC 560, CCH Dec. 35,825 (Acq.).

¶25,516 Visiting Foreign Teachers. Income tax treaties between the United States and certain foreign countries contain articles that set forth the conditions for the exemption from income tax any remuneration earned by visiting professors or teachers for teaching (.05). Income is generally exempted for two or three years, whichever period is applicable under the treaty, even though the total period of the visiting teacher's presence in the United States extends beyond such period. The exemption will also apply to any income earned during a second teaching assignment if it is completed within the appropriate period. This is true even if the second assignment is not arranged until after the visiting professor or teacher's arrival in the United States for the first assignment.

The exemption generally applies to pay received during a second teaching assignment if both are completed within the specified time, even though the second assignment was not arranged until after arrival in the United States on the first assignment. The exemption applies to schoolteachers from the following countries: Belgium, China, Commonwealth of Independent States (formerly the Union of Soviet Socialist Republics), Czech Republic, Denmark, Egypt, France, Germany, Greece, Hungary, Iceland, India, Indonesia, Israel, Italy, Jamaica, Japan, Korea (Republic of), Luxembourg, the Netherlands, Norway, Pakistan, Philippines, Poland, Portugal, Romania, Slovak Republic, Thailand, Trinidad and Tobago, Turkey, Ukraine, the United Kingdom, and Venezuela.

.05 Rev. Rul. 69-236, 1969-1 CB 193.

MILITARY SERVICE MEMBERS

Introduction

¶25,518 For federal income tax purposes, members of the Armed Forces benefit from special rules regarding their income and deductions and the filing of their returns. The income tax laws take into account the fact that persons in military service may not be able to comply with the time requirements imposed on other taxpayers. The IRS also has special rules relating to the income of veterans and persons engaged in active combat duty and to the travel and per diem allowances furnished to service members.

Returns, Income and Deductions

¶25,520 Definition of "Armed Forces." In order to deal with the special benefits afforded members of the Armed Forces and to determine who qualifies for the benefits, it is necessary to know the parameters of the Armed Forces. For these federal tax purposes, the term "military or naval forces of the United States" and the term "Armed Forces of the United States" each include all regular and reserve components of the uniformed services subject to the jurisdiction of the Secretary of Defense, the Secretary of the Army, the Secretary of the Navy, the Secretary of the Air Force, and the Coast Guard (.05). The members of such forces include commissioned officers and personnel below the grade of commissioned officers. Members of the U.S. Coast and Geodetic Survey and its successor, the National Oceanic and Atmospheric Administration, are included as members of the military (.10), but members of the U.S. Merchant Marine are not (.15).

.05 Code Sec. 7701(a)(15); Reg. §301.7701-8.

.10 *C. King*, CtCls, 53-1 USTC ¶9415, 112 FSupp 804.

.15 Rev. Rul. 70-537, 1970-2 CB 17.

¶25,520A IRS Website for Armed Forces Personnel. The IRS has created a section on its website to help servicemen and women in combat zones secure all the tax benefits available to them. The section can be accessed by going to "Armed Forces Tax Benefits," at irs.gov.

¶25,521 Tax Forgiveness for Combat Zone Decedents. Income taxes of service members who die while in active service in a combat zone as a result of wounds, disease or injuries incurred in a combat zone are forgiven (.05). The term, combat zone, includes a qualified hazardous duty area, which includes (1) as part of Operation Joint Endeavor, Bosnia and Herzegovina, Croatia and Macedonia (.10) and (2) as part of Operation Allied Force, the Federal Republic of Yugoslavia, Albania, the Adriatic Sea and the northern Ionian Sea (.15). Further, effective January 17, 1991, the "Arabian Peninsula Combat Zone" was declared (.20).

This area covers the land and airspace of Bahrain, Iraq (therefore, covering participants in Operation Iraqi Freedom), Kuwait, Oman, Qatar, Saudi Arabia, the United Arab Emirates, Gulf of Aden, Gulf of Oman, Persian Gulf, Red Sea and part of the Arabian Sea. In addition, effective September 19, 2001, Afghanistan has been declared a combat zone (.25), along with neighboing nations in which American Armed Forces personnel are serving in direct support of Afghanistan military operations. A Vietnam MIA whose death is determined while in such status likewise is forgiven his taxes. The forgiveness applies to the entire calendar year in which the service member dies, not just to the tax year shortened by death. For example, income taxes were abated on a deceased serviceman's share of his partnership's income from the date of death to the end of the partnership's fiscal year (.30).

Forgiveness of taxes for military personnel under the above rules also extends to any prior year ending on or after the first day of service in a combat zone. Tax liabilities for those years will be forgiven, assessments for those years will be abated, and taxes paid for those years will be credited or refunded. However, refund of any taxes collected is subject to the statute of limitations (.35).

Terroristic or military action

In addition, forgiveness extends to service members who die as a result of wounds or injuries sustained in "terroristic or military action" (.40). "Terroristic or military action" means:

(1) any terroristic activity that a preponderance of the evidence indicates was directed against the United States or any of its allies; and

(2) any military action involving the Armed Forces of the United States and resulting from violence or aggression against the United States or any of its allies (or threat thereof).

Income tax is forgiven for such individuals for the tax year in which the death occurs, and for any earlier year in the period beginning with the last year ending before the year in which the injury occurred.

Astronauts

Tax forgiveness has also been extended with respect to astronauts who die in the line of duty (including those who died in the space shuttle Columbia disaster) after December 31, 2002 (.45)

Specified terrorist victims

As part of the Victims of Terrorism Relief Act of 2001 (P.L. 107-134), relief is additionally granted to a "specified terrorist victim," namely anyone who died as a result of wounds or injury incurred as a result of the terrorist attacks against the U.S. on April 19, 1995 (Oklahoma City bombing), or September 11, 2001 (New York and Washington, DC attacks), or anyone who died as a result of illness incurred as a result of an attack involving anthrax occurring on or after September 11, 2001 and before January 1, 2002 (.50).

.05 Code Sec. 692; Reg. §1.692-1.

.10 P.L. 104-117, sec. 1(a) and 1(b).

.15 P.L. 106-21, sec. 1(a) and 1(b).

.20 Executive Order 12744, 1-17-91.

.25 Executive Order 13239, 12-12-01.

.30 Reg. §1.692-1(a); *R. Lupia Est.*, SCt, 55-1 USTC ¶49,097, 348 U.S. 956, aff'g CA-2, 54-2 USTC ¶49,049, 214 F2d 942.

.35 Rev. Rul. 69-301, 1969-1 CB 183.

.40 Code Sec. 692(c).

.45 Code Sec. 692(d)(5).

.50 Code Sec. 692(d)(4).

¶25,522 Payroll Withholding. Military compensation of members of the Armed Forces generally is subject to withholding (.05). This includes amounts received by a service person in addition to his regular monthly pay, such as sea and foreign duty pay, hazardous duty pay, and diving duty pay (.10). However, combat zone compensation is not subject to withholding, to the extent it is excludable from gross income (.15).

Since members of the Armed Forces Reserves are taxed on compensation as are other members of the Armed Forces, military compensation received by them is subject to withholding. Moreover, the difference between regular wages and the amount paid by the National Guard that is paid by an employer to employees who are temporarily serving in the National Guard is subject to withholding (.20).

Withholding also applies to retirement pay, except for amounts received for personal injuries or sickness resulting from active service in the Armed Forces (.25).

.05 Code Sec. 3401; Reg. §1.61-2(a), Reg. §1.61-2(b) and Reg. 31.3401(a)-1.
.10 Rev. Rul. 58-532, 1958-2 CB 879.
.15 Code Sec. 3401(a)(1).
.20 Rev. Rul. 68-238, 1968-1 CB 420.
.25 Code Sec. 104(a)(4).

¶25,523 Returns. Generally, members of the Armed Forces are subject to the same filing requirements as other taxpayers, except that the due date may be postponed in certain cases. Currently, the duty to file is triggered by the income-filing-level provisions.

The general rules applicable to refunds and credits apply to all service members in much the same way they apply to all other taxpayers. If the taxpayer is overseas and desires that a family member claim his refund, he should execute a power of attorney in favor of that person.

Special extensions

Service members who are on duty outside the United States or Puerto Rico may be granted an extension of time for filing their returns up to and including the 15th day of the sixth month following the close of the tax year (e.g., June 15 for calendar-year taxpayers). However, interest will accrue from the due date until the time of payment.

If a member of the Armed Forces is serving in a designated combat zone (see ¶25,521 for a list of current areas designated as combat zones) or is deployed in a contingency operation (as defined in 10 U.S.C. Sec. 101(a)(13)) or is hospitalized outside the United States due to injury received while serving in a combat zone or in a contingency operation, the due date of the member's return is postponed for the period of the combat service or hospitalization *plus* 180 days, and no interest or penalties will be assessed (.05). This extension is also available to the spouse of such service member wishing to file a joint return. However, the extension to the spouse is not available more than two years after termination of combatant activities in combat zones (.10). The combat zone/contingency operation exception (which also includes service in qualified hazardous duty areas) also applies to other tax acts for which a time limit is prescribed, i.e., paying tax, instituting Tax Court proceedings, filing refund claims, making contributions to qualified retirement plans, making distributions from IRAs, etc. (.15).

Persons missing in action in Vietnam

Three tax relief provisions relating to returns apply to persons missing in action in Vietnam and their spouses, effective for tax years beginning after 1982:

(1) Under the definition of a surviving spouse, the date of death of a person in MIA status is the date determined by the Armed Forces under 37 U.S.C. 556 or 5 U.S.C. 5566 (.20);

(2) For any tax year during which an individual is in MIA status, the spouse of the individual may elect to file a joint return (.25);

(3) The rule that covers the performance of certain acts, such as filing of a return or payment of taxes, that were postponed by reason of service in a combat zone applies to the spouse of an individual who is in MIA status (.30).

Hostages

No return or payment of tax by a civilian employee of the U. S. government or a member of the Armed Forces involuntarily detained, i.e., held hostage, in a foreign country is due until the 15th day of the third month following release (.35). No interest will accrue upon tax paid on or before the deferred date, and further extensions may be granted where necessary. Spouses of hostages may take advantage of the postponement or may file a joint return to obtain a refund by indicating hostage status on the line provided. Returns may also be filed on behalf of hostages for whom a spouse or another party holds a valid power of attorney (.40).

.05 Code Sec. 7508(a).
.10 Code Sec. 7508(c).
.15 Rev. Proc. 2004-13, I.R.B. 2004-4, 335.
.20 Code Sec. 2(a)(3)(A) and Code Sec. 2(a)(3)(B).
.25 Code Sec. 6013(f)(1).
.30 Code Sec. 7508(c).
.35 Rev. Rul. 69-246, 1969-1 CB 300.
.40 IRS News Release, Mar. 1980.

¶25,524 Income. Service members compute their income, deductions and losses much the same as other taxpayers. Exceptions are noted in the paragraphs below. The following items of income received by service members are classified as taxable income:

(1) active duty pay (.05);

(2) reserve training pay;

(3) attendance at a designated service school;

(4) back wages;

(5) drills and training duty;

(6) enlistment and reenlistment bonuses (.10);

(7) incentive pay;

(8) lump-sum payment for accrued leave;

(9) severance pay, including payments on release to inactive duty;

(10) readjustment pay (.15);

(11) travel and per diem allowances (see ¶25,530);

(12) lump-sum payments on separation or release from active duty;

(13) payments received from a former employer, even though paid directly to dependents (.20);

(14) remuneration for duties performed as chaplain (.25);

(15) personal allowances (cash) for the discretionary use of high-ranking officers (.30);

(16) military retirement pay based on age or length of service;

(17) amounts received by ROTC instructors;

(18) scholarships, such as the Armed Forces Health Professions Scholarship Program (AFHPSP) and similar programs, granted after August 16, 1986; and

(19) student loan repayment from programs such as the General Educational Loan Repayment Program.

Community property

State community property laws apply to active military pay. Generally, the character of the pay as separate or community income is determined by the marital status and domicile of the Armed Forces member and spouse during the time the member is in active military service. Thus, the member's active military pay while married and domiciled in a community property state is community income. This income is considered to be received half by the member and half by the spouse (.35).

☐ For treatment of regular and retirement military pay received by a resident of a community property state, see ¶25,534 and ¶25,559.

Combat zone compensation

There is an exemption from taxation for all compensation received for active service as a commissioned warrant officer, warrant officer, enlisted member or commissioned officer in the Armed Forces of the United States for any month during any part of which such member served in a combat zone (see ¶25,521 for a list of current areas designated as combat zones) (.40). However, the exclusion for a commissioned officer is limited to the highest rate of enlisted pay for each month. The constitutionality of the monthly ceiling on the combat zone compensation (formerly referred to as "combat pay" (.45)) exclusion has been upheld by the U.S. Claims Court (.50). The exclusion for commissioned officers also applies to enlisted members and warrant officers serving as temporary commissioned officers in a combat zone (.55).

The exclusion also applies for any month during any part of which the service member is hospitalized anywhere as a result of wounds, disease or injury incurred while serving in a combat zone. The exclusion ceases for any month beginning more than two years after termination of combatant activities.

A member of the Armed Forces performing service in a noncombat zone in direct support of military operations in a combat zone and qualifying for Hostile Fire Pay is entitled to the combat zone compensation exclusion. However, Armed Forces members who:

(1) are present in a combat zone while on leave from a duty station located outside a combat zone,

(2) pass over or through a combat zone during the course of a trip between two points both of which lie outside such a zone, or

(3) are present in a combat zone solely for their own personal convenience

are not considered to have served in a combat zone and are not entitled to the combat zone compensation exclusion (.60).

Accrued leave payments attributable to active service in a combat zone paid to members of the Armed Forces at the time of their discharge from the service are excludable from gross income subject to the combat exclusion rules above (.65). Also, service members serving in a combat zone while on detail to the Agency for International Development (AID) are entitled to the combat pay and withholding tax exclusions (.70).

An early separation payment that an individual who had served in the Navy became entitled to receive while on active duty in a combat zone was held to be includible in gross income (.75). The U.S. Court of Appeals for the Fourth Circuit concluded that the payment did not constitute compensation for military service; instead, it was made in exchange for the taxpayer's agreement to leave the Navy. Therefore, it was irrelevant that the individual became entitled to the payment while on active duty in a combat zone.

Earned income and child tax credits. In an effort to provide assistance to military families in combat zones, the earned income credit (EIC) (¶2275) and refundable child credit (¶2222) amounts have been increased for military families by giving them the option to include combat zone compensation when calculating the EIC and the child tax credit. Effective for tax years ending after October 4, 2004, and before January 1, 2006, any taxpayer may elect to treat combat zone compensation that is otherwise excluded from gross income as earned income for purposes of the earned income credit (.77). Also, effective for tax years beginning after December 31, 2003, combat zone compensation that is otherwise excluded from gross income is treated as earned income that is taken into account in computing taxable income for purposes of calculating the refundable portion of the child tax credit (.78).

Compensation during missing-in-action status

In addition to the combat zone compensation exclusion, there is a total exclusion for compensation received for active service for any month during any part of which a member of the Armed Forces or a civilian government employee is in a prisoner-of-war or other "missing" status as a result of the Vietnam conflict (.80), except for a member of the Armed Forces officially absent from his post of duty without authority. Refunds that are otherwise precluded by the statute of limitations are permitted if refund claims are filed within two years after the date on which the individual's "missing" status has terminated.

Miscellaneous nontaxable items

Miscellaneous items of income received by service members and regarded as nontaxable include (.85):

(1) living allowances (see ¶25,531):

(a) Basic Allowance for Quarters (BAQ)

(b) Basic Allowance for Subsistence (BAS)

(c) Housing and cost-of-living allowances abroad (paid by U.S. or foreign government)

(d) Variable Housing Allowance (VHA)

(2) family allowances:

(a) certain educational expenses for dependents

(b) emergencies

(c) evacuation to a place of safety

(d) separation

(3) death allowances:

(a) burial services

(b) death gratuity payment ($12,000, as of September 11, 2001) to eligible survivors (.90)

(c) travel of dependents to burial site

(4) moving allowances (see ¶25,525 and ¶25,541):

(a) dislocation

(b) moving household and personal items

(c) moving trailers or mobile homes

(d) storage

(e) temporary lodging

(5) travel allowances (see ¶25,530):

(a) annual round-trip for dependent students

(b) leave between consecutive overseas tours

(c) reassignment in dependent-restricted status

(d) transportation for serviceperson or dependents during ship overhaul or inactivation

(6) combat zone compensation for commissioned officer under executive order up to the maximum enlisted amount (.95) per month

(7) combat zone compensation for enlisted personnel, if under executive order

(8) defense counseling

(9) disability (see ¶25,533)

(10) medical benefits

(11) group-term life insurance

(12) professional education (see ¶25,542)

(13) ROTC allowances

(14) survivor and retirement protection plan premiums

(15) uniform allowances paid to officers (see ¶25,540)

(16) uniforms furnished to enlisted personnel (see ¶25,540)

(17) effective for payments made after November 11, 2003, amounts received under the Department of Defense Homeowners Assistance Program (see ¶25,536).

There is no exclusion from income for the fair market value of a serviceperson's use of a government-provided vehicle.

.05 IRS Publication No. 3, "Tax Information for Military Personnel (Including Reservists Called to Active Duty)" (for 2003 returns), CCH IRS PUBLICATIONS.

.10 I. T. 3473, 1941-1 CB 192.

.15 Rev. Rul. 58-496, 1958-2 CB 20, amplified by Rev. Rul. 67-350, 1967-2 CB 58.

.20 Rev. Rul. 69-104, 1969-1 CB 33; *S. Amoroso*, CA-1, 52-1 USTC ¶9135, 193 F2d 583, cert. denied, 343 U. S. 926; Rev. Rul. 69-136, 1969-1 CB 252.

.25 Rev. Rul. 79-132, 1979-1 CB 62, amplifying Rev. Rul. 77-290, 1977-2 CB 26.

.30 Rev. Rul. 77-350, 1977-2 CB 21.

.35 IRS Publication No. 555, "Federal Tax Information on Community Property" (Rev. June 2003), CCH IRS PUBLICATIONS.

.40 Code Sec. 112; Reg. §1.112-1.

.45 Code Sec. 112.

.50 *J.P. Bruinooge*, CtCls, 77-1 USTC ¶9244, 550 F2d 624.

.55 Rev. Rul. 68-11, 1968-1 CB 54.

.60 Reg. §1.112-1(k).

.65 Rev. Rul. 73-187, 1973-1 CB 51, amplifying Rev. Rul. 71-343, 1971-2 CB 92; *A. E. Baker, Jr.*, 70 TC 460, CCH Dec. 35,219.

.70 Rev. Rul. 69-353, 1969-1 CB 49.

.75 *R.P. Waterman*, CA-4, 99-1 USTC ¶50,569.

.77 Code Sec. 32(c)(2)(B), as amended by the Working Families Tax Relief Act of 2004 (P.L. 108-311).

.78 Code Sec. 24(d)(1), as amended by the 2004 Working Families Tax Act (P.L. 108-311).

.80 Code Sec. 112(d).

.85 IRS Publication No. 3, "Tax Information for Military Personnel (Including Reservists Called to Active Duty)" (for 2003 returns), CCH IRS PUBLICATIONS.

.90 10 U.S.C. Sec. 1478(a), as amended by the Military Family Tax Relief Act of 2003 (P.L. 108-121).

.95 Code Sec. 112(b) and Code Sec. 112(c)(5).

¶25,525 Moving Expenses and Reimbursements. U.S. Armed Forces personnel receive special tax treatment under the tax law for their moving expenses and reimbursements (.05). Members of the Armed Forces are entitled to deduct moving expenses without meeting the distance and time requirements.

This special tax treatment applies to personnel on active duty who move pursuant to a military order that results in a permanent change in station. A permanent change in station includes:

(1) a move from the taxpayer's home to the area of his first post of duty;

(2) a move from the taxpayer's last post of duty to his home or a place in the United States that is nearer to the last post of duty, if the move is made within one year of completion of active duty, as a result of

(a) retirement,

(b) discharge,

(c) resignation,

(d) separation under honorable conditions,

(e) transfer,

(f) relief from active duty,

(g) temporary disability retirement,

(h) transfer to a Fleet Reserve; or

(3) a move from the taxpayer's permanent post of duty to another post of duty (.10).

If a member of the Armed Forces dies, deserts, or is imprisoned, a permanent change of station for his spouse or dependent(s) includes a move to the place of enlistment, to the member's home, to the spouse's home, to the dependent's home, or to any closer point in the United States (.15).

Moving expenses no longer must be itemized and, instead, are deductible from gross income; however, meals are no longer deductible as moving expenses.

Spouses and dependents

The spouse and dependent(s) of an Armed Forces member receive the same tax treatment as does the military member of the family. They need not meet the time and distance requirements when they move to the new post of the military family member or when they themselves move to some other job location, regardless of whether or not the military spouse has a job there.

Reimbursements

Armed Forces personnel are given favorable tax treatment regarding reimbursement for their moving expenses. They are not subject to the same restrictions on their deductions, and they need not include in their gross income as much of the reimbursement-of-expense amounts as civilians are required to include. The value of any moving or storage services provided by the United States directly, or by a third party compensated directly by the government, is not included in the gross income of Armed Forces personnel or in their moving expenses for the purpose of determining the maximum deduction (.20).

.05 Code Sec. 217(g).
.10 Reg. §1.217-2(g)(3).
.15 Reg. §1.217-2(g)(5).
.20 Reg. §1.217-2(g)(4).

¶25,526 Reservists' Continued Health Care Coverage. Group health plans are required to offer continuation of group health coverage under COBRA to qualified beneficiaries upon the occurrence of a qualifying event (.05). The IRS has stated that the call-up of military reservists to active duty was a qualifying event (.10).

.05 Code Sec. 4980B.
.10 Notice 90-58, 1990-2 CB 345.

¶25,527 Deductions. The deductibility of various miscellaneous itemized deductions related specifically to service members has been determined. These items, if unreimbursed, are generally classified as miscellaneous itemized deductions and are deductible only to the extent that the total of such expenses exceeds two percent of adjusted gross income.

Deductible

The following items are deductible from the adjusted gross income of members of the military or veterans:

(1) contributions by enlisted members and officers to "company" funds (.05);

(2) expense of obtaining increased retirement pay (.10);

(3) professional dues (but not paid to officers' or noncommissioned officers' clubs) (.15);

(4) recruiting officer's unreimbursed traveling expenses;

(5) uniform cost and expense of cleaning and maintenance if uniform is required and not adaptable to personal use (see ¶25,540);

(6) educational expenses properly deductible, with reduction for the amount of nontaxable benefits received during the year from the Department of Veterans Affairs (.20);

(7) meal (subject to 50% limitations) and lodging expenses incurred at a military post by a member of the U. S. Armed Forces for himself (but not his family) while serving on temporary active duty in the Ready Reserve if such member has a principal or regular place of business which he has not abandoned and to which he intends to return after his service duty (.25) (see, also, ¶25,530);

(8) travel and temporary quarters expenses incurred by a retired army officer in his move to a new location, despite his failure to remain employed at the new location for 39 weeks, because he was involuntarily terminated from his job (.30); and

(9) mortgage interest and real property taxes incurred by military personnel even though they receive a military allowance that is excluded from gross income (.35).

Nondeductible

The following items are not deductible by members of the military:

(1) daily transportation cost between home and station;

(2) damage to household equipment in moving;

(3) expense of visiting home while on furlough, leave or liberty;

(4) fines (as distinguished from forfeited pay) imposed by court-martial;

(5) living expenses of naval officer stationed in one locality;

(6) mess bills of a naval officer assigned to permanent duty aboard a ship that has regular eating and living facilities (.40);

(7) cost of professional textbooks and school equipment purchased to pursue education in military academies, such as the Coast Guard Academy (.45); and

(8) uniform cost and expense of cleaning and maintenance if uniform is not required or is adaptable to personal use (see ¶25,540).

.05 Rev. Rul. 73-296, 1973-2 CB 67.

.10 Rev. Rul. 72-169, 1972-1 CB 43.

.15 IRS Publication 3, "Tax Information for Military Personnel (Including Reservists Called to Active Duty)," (for 2003 returns),CCH IRS PUBLICATIONS.

.20 Rev. Rul. 83-3, 1983-1 CB 72, corrected by Announcement 83-100, I.R.B. 1983-22, 26, and modified by Rev. Rul. 87-32, 1987-1 CB 131.

.25 Rev. Rul. 63-64, 1963-1 CB 30, distinguishing Rev. Rul. 55-572, 1955-2 CB 45.

.30 *J.A. Lyle*, 76 TC 668, CCH Dec. 37,852 (Acq.), aff'd by CA-5 in an opinion unpublished under rules of that court, 4/1/82, cert. den., 13 SCt 83.

.35 Code Sec. 265(a)(6).

.40 Rev. Rul. 67-438, 1967-2 CB 82, modifying Rev. Rul. 55-571, 1955-2 CB 44.

.45 Rev. Rul. 62-122, 1962-2 CB 12.

Allowance and Other Payments

¶25,529 Qualified Military Benefits. Benefits for military personnel other than qualified military benefits are includible in gross income (.05). Qualified military benefits are amounts received that were excludable from gross income as of September 9, 1986, under any provision of law in effect on that date (other than a Code provision). These benefits continue to be excludable.

Military dependent care assistance provided to members of the Armed Forces is excludable from gross income as a qualified military benefit (.10).

.05 Code Sec. 134.

.10 Code Sec. 134(b)(4).

¶25,530 Travel and Per Diem Allowances. The cash value of transportation furnished a service member in kind need not be included in gross income (.05). Neither is he required to include in income cash reimbursements of his actual travel or transportation expenses. If the government pays him on a mileage basis for transportation, or on a per diem basis for expenses while in a travel status in the United States, the mileage allowance does not have to be reported as gross income if it does not exceed the standard mileage rate (37.5 cents per mile in 2004) and the per diem allowance is not reportable if it does not exceed the federal per diem rate or the high-low rate ($207 for high-cost localities and $126 for all other localities from November 1, 2003 through September 30, 2004; $199/$127 from October 1, 2004 through September 30, 2005 (or when updated by the IRS) (.10).

The exemption of travel and transportation allowances for a service member applies whether the allowances were made for enlistment, transfer or separation from the service, or temporary travel in the interests of the government.

However, where the cost of transporting families and dependents upon a change of station is paid by the government, such cost is not deductible from the service member's gross income.

"Away from home"

A service member is not considered "away from home" while at his permanent duty station and, thus, may not deduct traveling expenses, including those for meals and lodging, incurred at such location (.15). This rule applies even when it is not feasible or even permissible for the member's family to join him at his permanent duty station. Similarly, naval officers' mess bills incurred while on shipboard are not deductible as travel expenses incurred away from home (.20).

Meals, subject to the 50% limitation, and lodging taken on shore when assigned to a ship, such as an aircraft carrier, battleship, cruiser, destroyer, submarine, or supply ship, may be deductible. Commonly called a "boomer deduction," this may be allowed since home is defined as the service member's permanent duty station, which could be a ship or base, regardless of where the member or his family live. The member of the service is away from home if he is away from his permanent duty station long enough to need significant rest or sleep to be able to complete his duties. For naval personnel of a dry-docked submarine, the tax home is not the submarine itself, but is the area or vicinity of the person's principal place of employment or shore assignment (.25).

National Guard and Reserve travel

National Guard and Reserve members are entitled to deduct from gross income (above-the-line deduction) the cost of overnight transportation, meals and lodging incurred in order to attend National Guard or Reserve meetings that are more than 100 miles away from home (.30). The amount of deductible expenses cannot exceed the general federal per diem rate applicable to the locality.

.05 Code Sec. 61; Reg. §1.61-2.

.10 Rev. Proc. 2004-60, I.R.B. 2004-42, 682; Rev. Proc. 2003-80, I.R.B. 2003-45, 1037.

.15 *H. Stidger*, SCt, 67-1 USTC ¶9309, 386 U. S. 287; *J. McDonald*, 33 TCM 274, CCH Dec. 32,486(M), TC Memo. 1974-57; *M.R. Mayne*, 65 TCM 2522, Dec. 49,019(M), TC Memo. 1993-193.

.20 Rev. Rul. 67-438, 1967-2 CB 82, modifying Rev. Rul. 55-571, 1955-2 CB 44.

.25 *R.B. Griffin*, 63 TCM 2582, Dec. 48,111(M), T.C. Memo. 1992-186.

.30 Code Sec. 162(p).

¶25,531 Quarters and Subsistence Allowances. Subsistence and uniform allowances and the basic allowance for quarters (BAQ) or the value of quarters or subsistence provided in kind to members of the armed forces are all excludable from income (.05). These include: amounts for temporary lodging pending assignment of permanent quarters at a new post of duty outside the continental United States; housing and cost-of-living allowances abroad; uniform allowances; quarters, heat and light furnished in kind; and evacuation allowances. These allowances are excludable whether they are paid by the U.S. government or by the government of the country in which the service person is stationed.

Basic allowances for subsistence (BAS), including ROTC subsistence and rations furnished in kind to enlisted service members, are excludable from gross income also, as are allowances furnished to National Guard members (.10). However, quarters and subsistence allowances received by junior ROTC instructors are not excludable because these instructors are not considered as being on active duty (.15).

Members of the armed forces may deduct interest and property taxes for housing, even if they received tax-free allowances for housing expenses (.20).

Although military quarters and subsistence allowances are excludable from gross income, they are includible in earned income for purposes of computing the earned income credit (.25)

.05 IRS Publication No. 3, "Tax Information for Military Personnel (Including Reservists Called to Active Duty)" (for 2003 returns), CCH IRS PUBLICATIONS.

.10 Rev. Rul. 60-65, 1960-1 CB 21.

.15 *J. Lyle*, 76 TC 668, CCH Dec. 37,852 (Acq.), aff'd by CA-5 in an opinion unpublished under rules of that court, 4/1/82, cert. den., 13 SCt 83.

.20 Code Sec. 265(a)(6).

.25 *M.C. Neff*, FedCl, 99-1 USTC ¶50,571.

¶25,532 Mustering-Out Payments. Mustering-out payments are included in gross income. The payments were only excludable from gross income if received before November 5, 1990 (.05).

.05 Code Sec. 113, repealed by the Revenue Reconciliation Act of 1990 (P.L. 101-508).

¶25,533 Disability Retirement Pay. Amounts received as pension, annuity or similar allowances for personal injury or sickness incurred while the recipient was in the armed forces of any nation or in the U. S. Foreign Service, National Oceanic and Atmospheric Administration, or Public Health Service are excludable from gross income only for persons who (.05):

(1) were entitled to receive such allowances on or before September 24, 1975;

(2) were in such Armed Forces or other services on that date;

(3) are receiving disability retirement payments for combat-related injury or sickness; or

(4) are receiving (or would be entitled to receive on application therefor) Veterans Administration disability compensation (see ¶25,537).

If the disability retirement pay is based on years of service, it is included in income, but the portion that is based on percentage of disability is excluded (.10). Also, lump-sum payments are excludable if the disability was physical in nature (.15).

In order to be excludable, payments received by members of the armed services must have been paid *because of* military injuries or on-the-job injuries. Thus, a serviceman who was classified as unfit to serve in the U.S. Nay after suffering a heart attack could not exclude the payments from gross income because, as a member of the armed services, he had a right to the payments regardless of whether or not the illness was caused by his job (.20). Similarly, social security disability benefits received by a former serviceman because of cancer brought about by exposure to Agent Orange during service in Viet Nam were not excludable from the individual's gross income (.25). Social security disability payments do not take into consideration the nature or cause of the disability or the extent of the injury.

Caution

CCH Analysts note that a retired Armed Forces member in the process of challenging a decision by the Veterans Administration (VA) that retirement benefits were not excludable disability pay should make protective claims on any tax returns filed during such period in order to protect potential refund rights. In one case, a retired Navy captain was not entitled to a refund of taxes paid on retirement benefits more than three years before he filed his refund claim (.30). The decision by the VA to retroactively recognize him as totally disabled converted the retirement benefits from taxable income to excludable disability compensation. However, because he had failed to make protective claims on filed tax returns, the three-year statute of limitations on refund claims was not affected.

.05 Code Sec. 104; Reg. §1.104-1.

.10 10 USC 1403; Reg. §1.104-1(e); IRS Publication No. 525, "Taxable and Nontaxable Income" (for 2003 returns), CCH IRS PUBLICATIONS.

.15 *R.C. St. Clair,* DC Va., 91-2 USTC ¶50,457, 778 FSupp 894.

.20 *R.B. Lonestar,* 47 TCM 1118, CCH Dec. 41,004(M), TC Memo. 1984-80.

.25 *W.D. Reimeis,* 123 TC 245, CCH Dec. 55,727.

.30 *J.G. Sullivan,* FedCl, 2000-1 USTC ¶50,402.

¶25,534 Nondisability Retirement and Severance Pay. Nondisability retirement pay received by service members is subject to income tax in the same manner as other income.

Retirement v. disability pay

Whether or not pay is considered retirement pay or disability retirement pay does not depend on the determination of the Veterans Administration. Where a former Air Force officer was found by the Air Force to qualify for normal retirement and not disability retirement, the Veterans Administration finding that the taxpayer was disabled did not change the nature of the retirement benefits paid to the taxpayer for tax purposes. The payments were ordinary retirement pay and includible in his gross income (.05).

The U.S. Court of Claims has held that retirement pay is exempt, even though based on length of service, where the taxpayer could have received retirement pay based on disability had he requested disability retirement pay (.10), but the Tax Court has held to the contrary (.15). Where a retired Army veteran failed to prove that he could have retired on disability or that payments made to him were in lieu of wages paid pursuant to an accident or health plan, his retirement pension was not exempt (.20).

Separation pay recoupment

A former member of the Armed Forces was denied a refund of taxes paid on the lump-sum separation benefit that she received as a retirement incentive, even though her nontaxable Veterans Affairs disability benefits were withheld until the full amount of her separation benefit was recouped (.25). The separation pay recoupment statute (.30) permits the government to recoup the total amount of separation pay issued, without providing tax relief. According to the court, the statute makes no reference to the retroactive reclassification of separation pay as nontaxable disability compensation upon the awarding of such compensation by the Veterans Administration.

Readjustment pay

Similarly, readjustment allowances received by reservists involuntarily released from active duty were taxable in the year received, even though the Veterans Administration later awarded retroactive disability compensation that was reduced by the amount of such allowances (.35). Reservists who receive lump-sum readjustment payments and later qualify for retirement pay must repay the readjustment pay before they can receive retirement pay (.40). They may either (1) repay the readjustment payment in full or in installments or (2) have a monthly amount withheld from the retirement payments until the full amount is recouped. If a reservist elects to repay the readjustment pay in full upon retirement, he may exclude from gross income that portion of the retirement pay he receives up to the amount of readjustment pay he was paid (.45). If he elects, instead, to repay the readjustment payment by having installments deducted from his retirement payments, he may exclude from gross income that portion of the retirement payments equal to the repayments of readjustment pay withheld each month (.50).

Community property

Armed Forces retirement pay that is based on age or length of service is regarded as additional compensation for past services. Thus, such retirement pay is community income if it is attributable to the member's active military service performed while married and domiciled in a community property state. This is true even if the retirement pay is received in a noncommunity property state.

Even though the community has been subsequently terminated, i.e., by divorce, the spouse formerly married to the Armed Forces member must include in gross income amounts received out of military retirement benefits that otherwise would be classified as community income. Thus, the amount of naval retirement benefits awarded to an ex-wife under a New Mexico divorce judgment and one-half of such benefits paid into an educational trust for the children of her former marriage were includible in her gross income (.55).

.05 *P. Sidoran*, CA-9, 81-1 USTC ¶9226, 640 F2d 231.

.10 *G.S. Prince Est.*, CtCls, 54-1 USTC ¶9264, 119 FSupp 421.

.15 *E. Pangburn*, 13 TC 169, CCH Dec. 17,119.

.20 *D.D. Guernsey*, 39 TCM 446, CCH Dec. 36,421(M), TC Memo. 1979-444.

.25 *M.J. Palm*, DC Ala., 96-1 USTC ¶50,017.

.30 10 U.S.C. Sec. 1174(h).

.35 Rev. Rul. 80-9, 1980-1 CB 11, distinguishing Rev. Rul. 78-161, 1978-1 CB 31.

.40 P.L. 96-513, §1174.

.45 Rev. Rul. 67-350, 1967-2 CB 58.

.50 *J.L. Connelly*, 82 TC 608, CCH Dec. 41,140.

.55 *A. Lowe*, 42 TCM 334, CCH Dec. 38,044(M), TC Memo. 1981-350.

¶25,535 Payments to Service Member's Beneficiary. The following payments to service members' beneficiaries are excludable from gross income (.05):

(1) payments to a service member's beneficiary under a life insurance policy, government or otherwise (.10);

(2) payments to a service member's beneficiary under the Servicemen's Indemnity Act of 1951 (.15);

(3) payments made under the World War Veterans Act of 1924 to dependents of persons who died as a result of disability (.20); and

(4) death-gratuity pay to the beneficiary of a deceased officer or enlisted member. Beneficiaries of members of the Armed Forces listed as missing in action at the end of hostilities in Vietnam in 1973 may exclude those payments from gross income, even though the Department of Defense made no official finding of death (.25).

.05 Code Sec. 101; Reg. §1.101-1.

.10 Code Sec. 101.

.15 Rev. Rul. 55-622, 1955-2 CB 385; Veteran's Benefits Act of 1957, P.L. 85-56, 71 Stat. 83, 158.

.20 Rev. Rul. 55-622, 1955-2 CB 385; Veteran's Benefits Act of 1957, P.L. 85-56, 71 Stat. 83, 158.

.25 Rev. Rul. 78-372, 1978-2 CB 93, clarifying Rev. Rul. 76-468, 1976-2 CB 202.

¶25,536 Homeowners Assistance Payments. The Department of Defense operates a special program, the Homeowners Assistance Program (HAP) (42 U.S.C. Sec. 1013), to assist military homeowners when a military base closes and housing values in the area decline. Military homeowners may be reimbursed for losses incurred from the private sale of their homes after a base closure or reduction in operations. Such payments are excludable from gross income to the extent they do not exceed the limitation imposed under HAP (.05).

.05 Code Sec. 132(a)(8) and 132(n).

Veterans

¶25,537 Miscellaneous Exempt Income of Veterans. Payments to veterans for benefits administered by the Veterans Administration are tax free (.05). Among the tax-exempt Veterans Administration payments are the following:

(1) education, training, or subsistence allowances;

(2) grants for motor vehicles to provide transportation for veterans who lost their sight or the use of their limbs;

(3) veterans' pensions paid either to veterans or to their families;

(4) veterans' insurance proceeds and dividends paid either to the veteran or to the beneficiaries, including the proceeds of a veterans' endowment policy paid prior to death;

(5) grants to seriously disabled veterans for homes designed for wheelchair living; and

(6) disability compensation and pensions received by veterans because of service-connected and nonservice-connected disabilities.

Bonuses paid by states to or on behalf of their qualified veterans of the Spanish-American War, the Philippine Insurrection, World War I, World War II, the Korean War and the Vietnam Conflict are gifts and exempt from tax (.10).

Although Veterans Administration educational assistance allowances are exempt from taxation, an additional educational assistance (work-study) allowance paid to a student-veteran employed by the Veterans Administration under a work-study/outreach agreement constitutes compensation for services and, therefore, is includible in his gross income (.15).

A veteran cannot deduct educational expenses for courses to maintain and improve his job skills if he is reimbursed for those expenses by a tax-exempt Veterans Administration educational payment. An amount cannot be deducted by a taxpayer if it is allocable to a class of tax-exempt income other than interest (.20).

.05 38 USC 3101; IRS Publication No. 525, "Taxable and Nontaxable Income" (for 2003 returns), CCH IRS PUBLICATIONS.

.10 Rev. Rul. 68-158, 1968-1 CB 47.

.15 IRS Letter Ruling 8337008, 5-20-83, CCH IRS LETTER RULINGS REPORTS; General Counsel Memorandum 39031, 4-27-83, CCH IRS POSITIONS REPORTS.

.20 *J. Manocchio*, CA-9, 83-2 USTC ¶9478, aff'g TC, 78 TC 989, CCH Dec. 39,097; Rev. Rul. 83-3, 1983-1 CB 72, corrected by Announcement 83-100, I.R.B. 1983-22, 26, and modified by Rev. Rul. 87-32, 1987-1 CB 131.

¶25,538 Interest on G.I. Insurance Dividends. Interest earned on G.I. life insurance policy dividends left on deposit with the Veterans Administration is not subject to federal income tax (.05). In reversing long-standing precedent, the IRS stated that the ruling applies to interest on dividends accumulated by the Veterans Administration on a converted U.S. Government Life Insurance policy or on a National Service Life Insurance policy.

.05 Rev. Rul. 91-14, 1991-1 CB 18, revoking Rev. Ruls. 57-441, 1957-2 CB 45, and 71-306, 1971-2 CB 76 (with respect to the interest income portion only), and modifying Rev. Rul. 72-604, 1972-2 CB 35.

Miscellaneous

¶25,540 Cost of Uniforms and Equipment. Allowances received by personnel of the Armed Forces for uniforms are not taxable. If the service member purchases his own uniform, a miscellaneous itemized deduction is allowed only in accordance with the general rules that it be required and not adaptable to personal use. Thus, where an army officer was required to purchase dress uniforms that were adaptable to civilian wear (e.g., a blue dress uniform could be worn at formal occasions, such as weddings and funerals), no deduction was allowed (.05).

If the cost of a uniform is deductible, the cleaning and maintenance costs are also deductible. The cost and maintenance of fatigue uniforms are deductible by service members on active duty where local military regulations prohibit their off-duty wear (.10). The expenses are deductible to the extent they exceed the allowance therefor. Even if the cost of the uniform itself, or the maintenance thereof, is not deductible, miscellaneous required items would be deductible, including gold lace, chin straps, gilt buttons, insignia of rank, corps devices, Sam Browne belts, epaulettes, campaign bars and aiguillettes (.15).

The cost of uniforms and equipment is a miscellaneous itemized deduction. Such deductions are allowable only to the extent that their total exceeds two percent of the taxpayer's adjusted gross income (.20).

.05 *E.R. Motch, Jr.*, 11 TC 777, CCH Dec. 16,663, N.A., rev'd on another issue by CA-6, 50-1 USTC ¶9239, 180 F2d 859; *B.F. Hatch*, 35 TCM 1737, CCH Dec. 34,155(M), TC Memo. 1976-384; IRS Letter Ruling 8120036, 2/18/81, CCH IRS LETTER RULINGS REPORTS.

.10 Rev. Rul. 67-115, 1967-1 CB 30.

.15 IRS Publication No. 3, "Tax Information for Military Personnel (Including Reservists Called to Active Duty)" (for 2003 returns), CCH IRS PUBLICATIONS.

.20 Code Sec. 67.

¶25,541 Cost of Moving to New Station. Armed Forces service members on active duty who receive moving and storage expense benefits (including both in-kind benefits and reimbursements for such expenses) for permanent changes of station pursuant to military orders are not required to include the amount of such benefit in income (.05). A permanent change of station includes a move in connection with retirement or other termination of active duty made within one year of such separation from service (.10). A graduate student, however, could not deduct as a moving expense those costs incurred to complete work on his Ph.D. after returning from military service to school because he was considered to be a student rather than an employee (.15).

If the allowances are more than the actual cost of moving, the difference must be included in gross income.

.05 Code Sec. 217; Reg. §1.217-2.
.10 Reg. §1.217-2.
.15 *B. Taylor*, 71 TC 124, CCH Dec. 35,502.

¶25,542 Educational Expenses. A service member, like other taxpayers, can deduct, as employee business expenses, the cost of education undertaken for the purpose of maintaining or improving skills required in his employment or other trade or business or of meeting the express requirements of his employer (.05). However, a veteran cannot deduct educational expenses for courses to maintain and improve his job skills if he is reimbursed for those expenses by a tax-exempt Veterans Administration educational payment (¶25,537) (.10).

Moreover, expenses are not deductible by a service member if the course of study pursued qualifies him for a new trade or business. Thus, a general accounting specialist in the Air Force was not entitled to a deduction for expenses incurred in pursuance of a degree of Master of Science in Business Administration since the courses were only remotely related to his duties in the Air Force (.15). But a Navy captain whose duties primarily involved commanding and administering personnel could deduct the expenses he incurred in obtaining a master's degree in personnel administration (.20).

Educational expenses are claimed as miscellaneous itemized deductions. They are allowable only to the extent that their total exceeds two percent of the taxpayer's adjusted gross income (.25).

Regular military pay and allowances received by a member of the Armed Forces while on active duty and while attending college as a full-time student are not excludable from gross income because they represent compensation for services (.30).

Service academy appointments

Penalty-free withdrawals are allowed from Coverdell Education Savings Accounts (ESAs) and qualified tuition programs made on behalf of a beneficiary attending the United States Military, Navy, Air Force, Coast Guard, and Merchant Marine Academies (.35). The amount of savings that can be withdrawn penalty free is limited to the costs of advanced education, as defined in 10 U.S.C. Sec. 2005(E)(3).

.05 Code Sec. 162; Reg. §1.162-5.
.10 *J. Manocchio*, CA-9, 83-2 USTC ¶9478, 710 F2d 1400, aff'g TC, 78 TC 989, CCH Dec. 39,097.
.15 *J.R. Heffernan*, 39 TCM 86, CCH Dec. 36,301(M), TC Memo. 1979-363.
.20 Rev. Rul. 69-199, 1969-1 CB 51.
.25 Code Sec. 67.
.30 General Counsel Memorandum 39128, CCH IRS POSITIONS REPORTS.
.35 Code Sec. 530(d)(4)(B)(iv).

¶25,543 Exclusion of Gain on Sale of Residence. All taxpayers may exclude up to $250,000 of gain from the sale or exchange of their principal residence (married taxpayers filing jointly may exclude up to $500,000 of gain (.05). The exclusion is subject to an ownership and use test. Gain may be excluded only if the taxpayer owned and used the property as his or her principal residence for at least two years during the five-year period that ends on the date of sale of the property.

A special exception to the two-out-of-five-year rule is provided for uniformed and foreign service personnel called to active duty away from home on "qualified official extended duty" (.10). They may elect to suspend the five-year test period. The maximum length of the suspension is 10 years, and it may only be made with respect to one property. If the election is made, the five-year period ending on the date of the sale of a principal residence does not include any period up to 10 years during which the serviceman or woman, or his or her spouse, is on qualified official extended duty. An election may be revoked at anytime.

"Qualified official extended duty" is defined as any "extended duty" while serving at a duty station that is at least 50 miles from the taxpayer's principal residence or while residing in government quarters under government orders. "Extended duty" is any period of active duty pursuant to a call or order to such duty for a period in excess of 90 days or for an indefinite time.

Reduced maximum exclusion rule. A taxpayer who fails to meet the ownership and use requirements as a result of a change of place of employment, health, or unforeseen circumstances (including military assignments) is able to exclude an amount equal to the fraction of the maximum $250,000 ($500,000 for joint filers) limitation that is equal to the fraction of the two years that the ownership and use requirements are met (.15). In applying this provision, the five-year period is suspended during the time that the taxpayer or the taxpayer's spouse is on qualified official extended duty (.20)

.05 Code Sec. 121.
.10 Code Sec. 121(d)(9).
.15 Code Sec. 121(c); Reg. §1.121-3.
.20 Code Sec. 121(d)(9)(A).

¶25,544 Stay of Tax Actions Against Servicemembers. The Servicemembers Civil Relief Act includes provisions to stay tax actions against members of the military during, and immediately after, military service.

The Act expands the Soldiers' and Sailors' Civil Relief Act of 1940 to temporarily suspend legal proceedings and transactions that could interfere with military service. It prevents the sale of personal or real property to collect taxes unless a court determines that military service does not "materially affect" a servicemember's ability to pay. If property is sold, the servicemember has the right to redeem it within 180 days after the end of military service. Courts can stay tax collections during the same period, although the tax would accrue interest at a yearly rate of six percent.

In addition, the Act suspends the collection of federal and state taxes on the income of servicemembers during and up to 180 days after the performance of military service. To qualify, the servicemember's ability to pay the tax must be materially affected by service in the military. No interest or penalty will accrue during nonpayment. However, the statute of limitations in a tax action would be suspended during and up to 270 days after the period of service.

The legislation also clarifies that income or personal property of servicemembers cannot be taxed by a local jurisdiction if the individual is present in it to fulfill military service. Personal property used in a trade or business is exempt.

RESIDENTS OF COMMUNITY PROPERTY STATES

Domiciles

¶ 25,546 Community Property Jurisdictions. In certain states—Arizona, California, Idaho, Louisiana, Nevada, New Mexico, Texas, Washington and Wisconsin (.05)—each spouse has community property rights in the income earned by the marital community (the husband and wife).

Spouses can acquire separate interests in their marital community regardless of whether they live in a community property state or a noncommunity property state. However, in community property states, each spouse has a present, automatic one-half interest in the property and income of the marital community. By contrast, in noncommunity property states, each spouse's separate interest is generally established only when the marriage terminates, and it is measured in terms of an equitable distribution that does not automatically equate to a one-half interest. Thus, if a husband and wife file separate returns in a noncommunity property state, neither spouse must report one-half of the other spouse's income. In a community property state, however, one-half of the community income must be reported on a separate return without regard to which spouse actually generated the income.

Community property laws affect federal income tax liability when a husband and wife elect or are required to file separate returns. The effect can be disadvantageous because each spouse is taxed on one-half of the income earned by each (but see ¶ 25,570). However, with planning, this can be advantageous, as where tax is reduced by maximizing medical, casualty, theft loss and miscellaneous itemized deductions (see ¶ 25,567).

.05 Rev. Rul. 87-13, 1987-1 CB 20.

¶ 25,547 "Domicile" Defined. Taxpayers must take community property laws into account if they are domiciled in one of the following states during their marriage: Arizona, California, Idaho, Louisiana, Nevada, New Mexico, Texas, Washington or Wisconsin (although not traditionally a community property state, Wisconsin is classified as a community property state by virtue of its enactment of the Uniform Marital Property Act). In addition, community property laws must be taken into account with respect to any property that the taxpayers acquire while domiciled in a community property state. A taxpayer has only one domicile for federal income tax purposes, even though the taxpayer may have more than one home (.05). Domicile is determined by intent: it is the place that one believes is one's true, fixed, permanent home, the place to which one intends to return even if one does not currently reside there (.10).

Generally, the domicile of the parties determines whether their income is to be classified as community property or as separate property. However, income from real property is community income if so treated under the laws of the state in which the real property is located, regardless of whether the owners are domiciled in noncommunity property states (.15).

.05 *L.B. Peeples*, 27 BTA 879, CCH Dec. 7955.

.10 *P. Crespi*, 44 BTA 670, CCH Dec. 11,845 (Acq.); *S.W. Weis*, 30 BTA 478, CCH Dec. 8526 (Acq.).

.15 *M.S. Hammonds*, CA-10, 39-2 USTC ¶ 9679, 106 F2d 40; *W.F. Horsting*, 5 TCM 421, CCH Dec. 15,206(M).

¶25,548 Factors Considered in Determining Domicile. If domicile is questioned by the IRS, the taxpayer must be able to show that a given place or state was intended to be the taxpayer's permanent home (.05).

The following are significant factors or activities (.10) for evaluating a person's declaration of intention to make a given place the permanent home (.15):

(1) payment of local and state taxes,

(2) exercise of right to vote,

(3) location of property owned and investments made,

(4) business and social affiliations,

(5) length of residence, and

(6) citizenship.

The length of time a taxpayer spends in one location does not always determine a domicile. A temporary home may continue for months or years, while a domicile may be established at the first moment the property is occupied (.20) because a person's intent is the controlling factor.

.05 *P. Grafe,* 5 TCM 81, CCH Dec. 14,988(M); *R.M. Gooding,* CA-DC, 57-2 USTC ¶10,009, 250 F2d 765.

.10 IRS Publication No. 555, "Community Property".

.15 *K.H. Francis,* 8 TCM 346, CCH Dec. 16,918(M).

.20 *G. Okamoto,* 41 TCM 857, CCH Dec. 37,682(M), TC Memo. 1981-59.

Community Property and Income

¶25,550 State Law Effect. Neither the state community property laws nor any other state laws govern taxation of income by the federal government. However, they do fix the ownership of income and of the property from which income flows (.05); even federal penalty taxes are affected by state ownership law (.10).

State law also controls whether a couple is married and, thus, whether they have a "community estate." In some states a legal marriage is required, while in others a valid common-law marriage brings the community property laws into play (.15). The death of either spouse ends the community estate (see ¶25,576). An absolute decree of divorce always ends the community estate although, in Louisiana, it ends by a "separation from bed and board." In some cases, separation of the parties may terminate the community (see ¶25,573).

If a husband and wife file separate returns (see ¶25,581), the laws of the community property state in which they are domiciled (see ¶25,547) govern the classification of their income as separate or community income. The income, expenses, deductions, exemptions, and credits of the husband and wife are also identified according to the law of their domicile state.

.05 *Gallagher v. Smith,* CA-3, 223 F2d 218; *Poe v. Seaborn,* SCt, 2 USTC ¶611, 282 U.S. 101.

.10 General Counsel's Memorandum 38927, 2-26-82.

.15 *M.A. Schmidt,* 41 TCM 793, CCH Dec. 37,652(M), TC Memo. 1981-38.

¶25,551 Community Property. As noted at ¶25,550, both real and personal property located in community property states are identified as community or separate property in accordance with the law of the owner's domicile (.05).

Community property may be generally defined as all property, both personal and real, that (1) does not fall within the definition of separate property and (2) is acquired by the husband and wife during their marriage (.10). However, since the laws vary from state to state, the relevant state law must be consulted in each case.

Property that cannot be identified as separate property is treated as community property. This is particularly important in that income from community property is considered to be community income in some community property states and must be so treated for tax purposes (.15) (see ¶25,553).

Removal of personal property to a noncommunity property state does not negate its community property status (.20). Real property is treated differently. The law of the state in which real property is located determines whether it is community or noncommunity property. Similarly, income from real estate is community income if it is community income under the laws of the state in which the property is located. Real property will retain the form of ownership assigned to it regardless of changes in the taxpayer's domicile.

.05 Cal. Civ. Code §§4800.5 and 5110; *Rosan v. Rosan,* Cal. Sup Ct, 317 P2d 11; *Perkins Est.,* Cal. Sup Ct, 134 P2d 231; *M.C. Fink,* Cal. Sup Ct, 603 P2d 881.

.10 *A. Weeks,* 31 BTA 627, CCH Dec. 8789 (Acq.).

.15 Code Sec. 66, Code Sec. 1402(a), Reg. §1.1402(a)-8.

.20 *T.C. Phillips,* 9 BTA 153, CCH Dec. 3085 (Acq.).

¶25,552 Separate Property. Separate property (property that is not community property -see ¶25,551) is all property, both personal and real, owned separately by each of the taxpayers before their marriage. It also includes property received separately after marriage by one spouse as a gift, devise, bequest, or inheritance. Separate property may also be acquired during marriage by purchase with separate funds or in exchange for separate property (.05). Also, money earned while domiciled in a noncommunity property state is separate property (.10). In some community property states, a spouse's award for personal injuries, other than the part awarded as compensation for loss of earnings, is that spouse's separate property.

Generally, once property is classified as separate property, it remains separate property as long as it can be identified (.15). However, separate property may be changed to community property by an agreement between the parties (see ¶25,561) or by operation of law (.20). In one instance, separate property inherited by an individual became community property when both he and his wife were listed as sellers of the property by the mortgage company conducting the settlement of the sale (.25). Each spouse was responsible for the taxes on only one-half of the sales proceeds.

.05 *M.E. Trapp,* CA-10, 49-2 USTC ¶9398, 177 F2d 1, *cert. denied* 339 U.S. 913; *M.E. Trapp,* CA-10, 51-1 USTC ¶9116, 186 F2d 951; *K.E. Merren,* CA-5, 2 USTC ¶767, 51 F2d 44.

.10 *H. Veit,* 8 TC 809, CCH Dec. 15,718 (Acq.).

.15 *R.M. Drysdale,* CA-6, 56-1 USTC ¶9508, 232 F2d 633.

.20 *J.L.C. McFaddin,* CA-5, 45-1 USTC ¶9262, 148 F2d 570.

.25 *T. Cowan,* 71 TCM 2649, CCH Dec. 51,269(M), TC Memo. 1996-161.

¶25,553 Community Income. If a husband and wife file separate returns (see ¶25,581), half of all community income must be reported by each spouse (.05). Community income is all income from community property, salaries, wages, and other compensation for the services of either the husband or wife or both. In addition, in Idaho, Louisiana, Texas and Wisconsin, all income earned from separate property is generally community income.

However, there are exceptions to the general rule. For instance, in most community property states, a husband and wife may, prior to marriage, enter into a valid agreement providing that any income earned by either of them for personal services is his or her separate property, although the requirements vary widely from state to state (see ¶25,561). Then, the income earned by either of them after the agreement is entered into is treated, for federal tax purposes, as the separate income of the spouse earning the income, not as community income (.10). Taxpayers may also be able to avoid community property laws if they are separated (see ¶25,573) or if they are entitled to innocent spouse relief (see ¶25,571). The IRS can deny the benefits of community property law to a taxpayer who abandons a spouse (see ¶25,570) or who conceals community property from a spouse and treats it as separate property (see ¶25,572).

If a taxpayer moves into a community property state during the year, income is prorated between community property and noncommunity property periods (.15).

.05 *Poe v. Seaborn,* SCt, 282 U. S. 101; *Helene Simmons Est.,* 26 TC 409, CCH Dec. 21,764 (Acq.); *S.G. Chapman,* 45 TCM 238, CCH Dec. 39,536(M), TC Memo. 1982-695.

.10 Rev. Rul. 73-390, 1973-2 CB 12.

.15 *H. Veit,* 8 TCM 919, CCH Dec. 17,240(M).

¶25,554 Separate Income. Generally, income earned before marriage is separate income, even if collected after marriage (.05). Also, income earned before moving into a community property state is separate income (.10).

In community property states other than Idaho, Louisiana, Texas and Wisconsin (see ¶25,553), income from separate property (see ¶25,552) is generally treated as the separate income of the spouse who owns the property.

.05 *A.J. Houston,* 31 BTA 188, CCH Dec. 8705.

.10 *M. Asher v. Welch,* DC Cal., 39-1 USTC ¶9279.

¶25,555 Income from Property Acquired with Commingled Funds. If, during their marriage, taxpayers domiciled (see ¶25,547) in a community property state acquire property partly with community funds and partly with separate funds, the income from such property must be divided. Income from the portion of property bought with community funds is generally considered community income (see ¶25,553). Income from the portion bought with separate funds is community income or separate income (see ¶25,554), depending on the laws of the state in which the taxpayers are domiciled.

Where taxpayers domiciled in a community property state use assets to purchase property that are so commingled that they cannot be traced and divided between separate and community property, the whole may be classified as community property (.05). If community property and noncommunity property is commingled by taxpayers domiciled in a noncommunity property state, it may lose its community character (.10).

.05 *W.F. Horsting,* 5 TCM 421, CCH Dec. 15,206(M).

.10 *W.D. Johnson,* 1 TC 1041, CCH Dec. 13,168 (Acq. and Nonacq.). Cross appeals dismissed, 139 F2d 491.

¶25,556 Apportionment of Earnings Between Capital and Compensation. A problem arises in community property states where one spouse receives a payment that includes both compensation for personal services in a business and a return on a capital investment. The payment must be apportioned between compensation and return on capital, using a formula devised by the Tax Court (see "Example," below), which requires the choosing and application of a percentage as a fair return on the investment. Seven percent was used in a 1934 case (.05), eight percent was used in a 1944 case (.10) and 12 percent was used in a 1960 case (.15).

Example: The average investment of a husband, from his separate property, in a business in California was $70,000 during the tax year. He rendered full-time services to the business, for which reasonable compensation was $14,400. Assuming that 10 percent is a fair rate of return on his investment and that net profits from the business were $25,000, allocation is as follows:

(1) $\dfrac{\$\,7{,}000\ (10\%\text{ of }\$\,70{,}000)}{\$\,21{,}400\ (\$\,7{,}000\text{ plus }\$14{,}400)} \times \$\,25{,}000$, or $ 8,178
is attributable to the investment and is his separate income.

(2) $\dfrac{\$\,14{,}400}{\$\,21{,}400} \times \$\,25{,}000$, or $ 16,822
is attributable to personal service and, therefore, is community income; if separate returns are filed, one-half of this amount would be reported on each return.

.05 *C.B. Parker*, 31 BTA 644, CCH Dec. 8794.
.10 *Karpe v. Riddell*, DC Cal, 56-2 USTC ¶10,016.
.15 *D. Fowler*, 26 TCM 175, CCH Dec. 28,357(M), TC Memo. 1967-36.

¶25,557 Income of Partnerships. Generally, the income or loss from a trade or business carried on by a partnership of which one spouse is a member is treated as community income or loss and, therefore, must be divided between spouses if they elect to file separate returns (see ¶25,581). However, under California and Washington laws (.05), if separate property is invested in a partnership, the distributive share in excess of salary is separate income to the extent attributable to the separate property.

Even if a husband and wife cannot legally be partners under state law, this does not necessarily prevent recognition of their partnership for federal income tax purposes (.10). On the other hand, the fact that a partnership is valid under state law does not necessarily require it to be recognized for federal tax purposes (.15).

The IRS will accept a couple's characterization of an entity that is owned solely by a husband and wife as community property, if no person other than one or both spouses would be considered an owner for federal tax purposes and the entity is not treated as a corporation. Thus, if the couple treats the entity as a disregarded entity for federal tax purposes, the IRS will accept the position that it is a disregarded entity for federal tax purposes. If the entity is treated as a partnership for federal tax purposes and the appropriate partnership returns are filed, the IRS will accept the position that the entity is a partnership for federal tax purposes. A change in reporting position will be treated for federal tax purposes as a conversion of the entity (.20).

☐See ¶14,057 for partnerships and disregarded entities.

.05 *Julius Shafer*, 2 BTA 640, CCH Dec. 777; *J.Z. Todd*, CA-9, 46-1 USTC ¶9108, 9144, 153 F2d 553; *J.Z. Todd*, 7 TC 399, CCH Dec. 15,288, aff'd per curiam by CA-9, 48-1 USTC ¶9145, 165 F2d 781.
.10 *F.A. Parker*, 6 TC 974, CCH Dec. 15,135 (Acq.).
.15 Rev. Rul. 58-243, 1958-1 CB 255.
.20 Rev. Proc. 2002-69, I.R.B. 2002-44.

¶25,558 Income of Decedents' Estates. In all the community property states, one-half of the community property, upon the death of a spouse, vests immediately in the surviving spouse. For federal income tax purposes, therefore, income flowing from the community property during administration of the estate is divided equally between the estate and the surviving spouse (.05).

If at least half of the community property interest is includible in the decedent's estate, the fair market value of the community property at the date of death, or the alternative valuation date if chosen, becomes the basis of the entire property (even the portion belonging to the surviving spouse) (.10).

☐See ¶20,330 for treatment of property held at death. See ¶20,340 for treatment of estate valuation.

.05 *S.W. Bishop*, CA-9, 46-1 USTC ¶9107, 152 F2d 389; *H. Henderson Est.*, CA-5, 46-1 USTC ¶9258, 155 F2d 310; Rev. Rul. 75-79, 1975-1 CB 184; *B.L. Sneed Est.*, CA-5, 55-1 USTC ¶9271, 220 F2d 313; *R.D. Merrill*, CA-9, 54-1 USTC ¶9275, 211 F2d 297; Rev. Rul. 55-726, 1955-2 CB 24.

.10 Code Sec. 1014(b)(6), Reg. §1.1014-1, Reg. §1.1014-2.

¶25,559 Treatment of Armed Forces Pay. State community property laws apply to active military pay. Generally, the character of the pay as separate income (see ¶25,554) or community income (see ¶25,553) is determined by the marital status and domicile (see ¶25,547) of the Armed Forces member and spouse during the time the member is in active military service (.05). Thus, the member's active military pay earned while married and domiciled in a community property state is community income. This income is considered to be received half by the member and half by the spouse.

State community property laws also apply to military retirement pay if, at the time the required period of service is completed, the retiree was married and domiciled in a community property state. For instance, an Army member's military retirement pay was community income because he and his wife resided in a community property state when he became entitled to the payments, even though the couple had lived in noncommunity property states during most of his military career (.10).

.05 *R.J. Sivalls*, CA-5, 53-2 USTC ¶9492, 205 F2d 444, cert. den., 346 U.S. 898; *R. Pentland, Jr.*, 11 TC 116, CCH Dec. 16,516.

.10 *C.R. Wilkerson*, CA-9, 66-2 USTC ¶9715, 368 F2d 552.

¶25,560 Treatment of Foreign-Source Income. Community income earned by a spouse whose tax home is a foreign country and who therefore is exempt from income tax (.05) is exempt income for both spouses (.10).

.05 Code Sec. 911.

.10 Rev. Rul. 55-246, 1955-1 CB 92.

¶25,561 Contracts Altering Community Property Rights. The community property system is imposed on spouses domiciled in community property states (see ¶25,547). However, persons contemplating marriage in some states may enter into an prenuptial contract that governs their post-marriage accumulations and bypasses the community property rules of the state (.05). After marriage, spouses may contract between themselves as to their separate and community property rights in most of the community property states.

Such contracts entered into orally may be difficult to prove and enforce (.10) and, therefore, should be reduced to written form. Further, prenuptial and post-marriage agreements will be given effect for federal income tax purposes only if it they are valid under state law; therefore, the relevant state law must be consulted and followed carefully (.15).

.05 *J. Crail Est.*, 46 BTA 658, CCH Dec. 12,462 (Acq.).

.10 *S.L. Schwartz*, DC Calif., 47-1 USTC ¶9140, 70 FSupp 437.

.15 *In re Prasch*, BC-DC Calif., 90-2 USTC ¶50,537.

¶25,562 Effect of Renouncing Community Property Rights. The ability to renounce community property debts depends upon the applicable state law. However, a married taxpayer domiciled in a community property state does not escape federal tax liability on a one-half interest in the community income realized during the existence of the marital community by subsequently renouncing or revoking community status pursuant to state law. Thus, a wife was liable for income taxes, interest and penalties for years in which her husband filed no income tax returns, despite her subsequent attempt to renounce her community status (.05). Although renouncing the community status under state law does not relieve a spouse from federal tax liability, a spouse may be relieved if not timely notified by the other spouse of community income (see ¶25,570).

.05 *A.G. Mitchell,* SCt, 71-1 USTC ¶9451, 403 U.S. 190.

Community Expenses and Deductions

¶25,564 Expenses as Community or Separate Deductions. Community deductions must be accounted for in the same manner as community income. Thus, taxes, interest, salaries and miscellaneous office expenses in managing the separate property of one spouse are community deductions if the income from the property is community income, even though the expenses are actually paid from the separate funds of the spouse who owns the property (.05). The same rule applies to foreign taxes paid by one spouse on community income.

If there is no community income, the Tax Court has held that expenses paid or incurred in connection with one spouse's property are that spouse's separate deductions (.10).

.05 *M.E. Stewart,* CA-5, 38-1 USTC ¶9246, 95 F2d 821.

.10 *I.J. Hunt,* 47 BTA 829, CCH Dec. 12,849 (Nonacq.).

¶25,565 Losses Attributable to Separate Property. When spouses governed by community property laws file separate returns, a loss on the sale of separate property is allocable in its entirety to the spouse who owned the property, even though income from the property would have been community income (.05). Similarly, a bad debt loss growing out of the investment of one spouse's separate property is deductible in full on the separate return of that spouse (.10).

.05 *C.C. Harmon,* 1 TC 40, CCH Dec. 12,886.

.10 *M.E. Stewart,* CA-5, 38-1 USTC ¶9246, 95 F2d 821.

¶25,566 Community Charitable Contributions. If charitable contributions are paid from community property, a spouse is not entitled to claim the full deduction on a separate return (.05).

However, charitable contributions paid from separate property are chargeable against the separate income of the spouse making them (.10). And where the charitable contributions are paid out of an account in which community funds are commingled with separate funds, the full deduction may be properly taken on the separate return (.15).

.05 *J.A. Lesoine,* DC Calif., 51-2 USTC ¶9457, rev'd on another issue, CA-9, 53-1 USTC ¶9273, 203 F2d 123.

.10 *M.E. Stewart,* 35 BTA 406, CCH Dec. 9570 (Acq.), aff'd on another issue, CA-5, 38-1 USTC ¶9246, 95 F2d 821.

.15 *E.W. Clemens,* 8 TC 121, CCH Dec. 15,559 (Nonacq.).

¶25,567 Maximizing Certain Deductions by Filing Separate Returns. In some instances, the filing of separate returns will reduce taxes because the spouse with the smaller amount of income will obtain a larger deduction if that deduction is limited to the amount by which it exceeds a percentage of adjusted gross income.

Medical expense deduction

The medical expense deduction is limited to amounts exceeding 7.5 percent of adjusted gross income (AGI). Therefore, in both community property and noncommunity property states, two spouses who both have income might be able to increase their total medical deductions by filing separate returns. In community property states there are additional advantages where only one spouse has income or where one spouse earns considerably more than the other. These advantages can be maximized with proper planning.

A spouse in a community property state who files separately reports one-half of the community income. Therefore, if only one spouse works, the nonworking spouse reports one-half of the income. This alone affords an advantage to the community property state resident because, in effect, the 7.5-percent threshold is applied against only half of the couple's income. Normally, that spouse deducts one-half of the medical expenses as well, but if a spouse pays the medical expenses out of *separate* funds (see ¶25,552, ¶25,554, and ¶25,556), that spouse can take the full deduction (.05), thus maximizing the medical expense deduction.

If the payor spouse ensures that separate funds are used to pay the medical expenses, then one spouse may report half of the community earnings while claiming the full medical deduction. A commingling of separate funds with community funds in a joint bank account may give rise to a presumption that the community debt for medical expenses was paid by community funds (.10). For that reason, a prudent taxpayer, upon learning that medical expenses will be incurred for which there will not be any reimbursement, would be wise to open a separate checking account and clearly identify the account as separate property.

☐ See ¶6503 and following for treatment of medical expense deductions.

Miscellaneous itemized deductions

Miscellaneous itemized deductions can be claimed only to the extent that the total of such deductions exceeds two percent of adjusted gross income. If one spouse in a community property state has most or all of the miscellaneous itemized deductions, the deduction will be increased because the two-percent floor will be reduced (two percent of half of the community income).

☐ See ¶6035 for treatment of miscellaneous itemized deductions.

Casualty and theft loss deduction

Casualty and theft loss deductions are limited to those amounts that exceed 10 percent of adjusted gross income subject to a $100 floor. Provided that a taxpayer's casualty or theft relates to separate property, a taxpayer in a community property state may find it worthwhile to file a separate return (.15).

☐ See ¶6305 an following for treatment of casualty and theft loss deductions.

Lost advantages

When the time comes to make the actual decision whether to use the above planning factors or to file jointly and take advantage of the married-filing-jointly rates, there are additional factors that should not be overlooked. A married person who files separately is precluded from claiming a variety of credits and deductions, including the child and dependent care credit and the earned income credit.

.05 Rev. Rul. 55-479, 1955-2 CB 57.

.10 *E.W. Clemens,* 8 TC 121, CCH Dec. 15,559 (Nonacq. on another issue).

.15 Code Sec. 165(h).

¶25,568 Alimony in Community Property States. Community property laws have no effect on the reporting of alimony once the marital community is terminated, whether by divorce or another method permitted under state law. Thus, the full amount of each alimony payment is deductible by the payor and includible in the income of the payee, provided that all the usual requirements for deductibility are met. However, community property laws do have an effect on payments made before the marital community is terminated. These laws also have an effect on the tax treatment of payments made to a former spouse after the taxpayer remarries (.05).

Alimony before termination of the community

If taxpayers have separated but the marital community has not been terminated, the amount of the deduction for alimony paid is limited to the amount, if any, by which the payments exceed the recipient-spouse's share of the community income. The theory behind this rule is that one-half of the income earned by the payor is not the payor's property—it belongs to the recipient by virtue of the community property laws. It is analogous to the rule disallowing an alimony deduction on a joint return filed by separated spouses in a noncommunity property state.

Alimony after payor remarries

If a remarried taxpayer in a community property state pays alimony to a former spouse, the alimony deduction may be considered a community deduction that must be shared with the new spouse, depending upon state law and whether the alimony payments are made out of community or separate income. This will generally have an effect for tax purposes only if the taxpayer and the new spouse file separate income tax returns. If alimony paid is treated as a community deduction, then one-half of the amount paid is deductible on each spouse's separate return.

☐ See ¶3401 and following for treatment of alimony.

.05 *R.A. Sharon*, CA-5, 49-2 USTC ¶9411; *D. Newcombe*, CA-9, 53-1 USTC ¶9241; *W.F. Miller*, 42 TCM 654, CCH Dec. 38,146(M), TC Memo. 1981-427.

Estranged Spouses

¶25,570 Relief for Abandoned Spouses. An abandoned or estranged spouse can be relieved of liability for federal income tax on community income that is earned by the other spouse and is not received (directly or indirectly) by the abandoned spouse (.05). The community property laws are disregarded with respect to, and the abandoned spouse is not taxed on, income that meets the conditions discussed below. Furthermore, the spouse who has produced and benefited from the income, whether from personal services, business or partnership income, is fully liable for the federal income tax on the community income.

Requirements for relief

To qualify for relief,

(1) the taxpayer must have had a spouse during the calendar year;

(2) the taxpayer must have lived apart from the spouse at all times during the calendar year;

(3) the taxpayer must not have filed a joint return with the spouse for a tax year that began or ended during the calendar year;

(4) the taxpayer and/or the spouse must have had earned income for the calendar year that was community income; and

(5) no portion of the earned income may have been transferred (directly or indirectly) between the spouses before the close of the calendar year.

Transfers of *de minimis* amounts and payments made to or on behalf of the couple's child are not counted as a transfer of income (.10).

Taxation rules

If the five elements above are satisfied, the community income is taxed to each spouse in accordance with the following rules:

(1) Earned income (other than trade or business income and a partnership's distributive share of partnership income) is taxed to the spouse who rendered the personal services.

(2) Trade or business income is treated as income of the spouse who operates the business unless the other spouse exercises substantially all of the management and control of the trade or business.

(3) A partner's distributive share of ordinary income from a trade or business is taxed to the spouse who is the partner and is not attributed to the partner's spouse.

(4) Community income not covered in categories (1)-(3), above, that is derived from the separate property of one of the spouses is taxed to that spouse.

(5) The taxation of all other income (dividends, interest, rents, royalties and gains) is determined in accordance with applicable community property laws.

.05 Code Sec. 66(a).

.10 Senate Finance Committee Report on P.L. 96-605; Proposed Reg. §1.66-2(b).

¶25,571 Relief from Community Property Laws. The Code has a relief measure designed to prevent a taxpayer from being liable for federal income tax on community income that is earned by the taxpayer's spouse and that is not received (directly or indirectly) by the taxpayer (.05). This is a completely different relief from the innocent spouse provisions that apply to all married taxpayers filing joint returns whether or not they live in community property states (.10). If the conditions are met, the taxpayer is not taxed on the spouse's income, and the community property laws for taxing the income are disregarded.

Two types of relief are available. To qualify for specific relief, the taxpayer must satisfy the following conditions:

(1) the taxpayer must not file a joint return with the spouse for the tax year at issue (.15);

(2) the item of community income at issue must have been omitted from the taxpayer's gross income and be attributable to the taxpayer's spouse (.20);

(3) the taxpayer must establish that he or she did not know or have reason to know of the omitted item of community income; and

(4) taking into account all of the facts and circumstances, it must be inequitable to include the item of community income in the taxpayer's gross income.

The requirement that the taxpayer seeking relief has no knowledge or reason to know of the unreported income is construed very strictly. It is not enough that the taxpayer has no knowledge of the *amount* of the income; he or she must have no knowledge of the existence of the item of income itself. Thus, if a taxpayer knows a spouse has a job or receives distributive income from a partnership, it is highly unlikely the taxpayer will be protected from liability for tax on one-half of the spouse's income (.25).

The taxpayer seeking relief must also establish that it is inequitable to include one-half of the spouse's income in the taxpayer's gross income. In making this determination, the court will consider whether or not the taxpayer has benefited from the untaxed income. It may also consider whether the taxpayer raised the defense of innocent spouse relief promptly enough to prevent the statute of limitations from running in favor of the "non-innocent" spouse (.30).

Under proposed regulations, a taxpayer knows or has reason to know of an understatement of community income if he or she actually knew of the understatement, or if a reasonable person in similar circumstances would have known of the understatement. All of the facts and circumstances are considered in determining whether it is inequitable to deny relief, including whether the omitted income provided the taxpayer with a significant benefit in excess of normal support, and whether the taxpayer has been deserted or abandoned by the spouse. Specific relief is generally available only after a deficiency has been asserted, and the taxpayer must request relief no later than six months before the statute of limitations on assessment expires with regard to the nonrequesting spouse. The IRS will not consider premature requests that are filed for a tax year prior to the date that a deficiency for the year is asserted (.35).

The second type of relief, equitable relief, is available when it would be inequitable to deny relief to a taxpayer who does not meet the conditions listed above (.40). The IRS has suggested that the primary purpose of equitable relief is to expand relief beyond deficiencies arising from understatements of community income, and include deficiencies arising from underpayments related to community income (.45). Under proposed regulations, the IRS will determine whether equitable relief should be granted after considering relevant factors, including the spouses' current marital status, the requesting spouse's knowledge of the understatement or underpayment, and the threat of economic hardship if relief is denied (.50).

Innocent spouse relief also is granted under TEFRA partnership proceedings. If the spouse of a partner in a TEFRA partnership asserts that the innocent spouse rules apply with respect to a liability attributable to any adjustment to a partnership item, the spouse may file with the IRS a request for an abatement of the assessment. The spouse may also file a petition in the Tax Court. In addition to this relief, the spouse may file a claim for refund on the ground that the IRS failed to relieve the spouse under the innocent spouse rules (.55).

.05 Code Sec. 66(c).

.10 Code Sec. 6015.

.15 Note, this is a very significant difference from the well-known "innocent spouse" relief under Code Sec. 6015, which is available only for spouses who did file a joint income tax return.

.20 The standards set forth in Code Sec. 879(a), governing community income for nonresident aliens, are used to determine whether an item of income is attributable to one spouse.

.25 *G.D. Bozek*, 51 TCM 350, CCH Dec. 42,844(M), TC Memo. 1986-37; *R. Sanders*, 51 TCM 317, CCH Dec. 42,830(M), TC Memo. 1986-26.

.30 Report of the House Ways and Means Committee on the Tax Reform Act of 1984 (P.L. 98-369).

.35 Proposed Reg. §1.66-4.

.40 Code Sec. 66(c).

.45 IRS Chief Counsel Advice 200050002, August 31, 2000.

.50 Proposed Reg. §1.66-4(b).

.55 Code Sec. 6230.

¶25,572 Denying the Benefits of Community Property Law. In addition to the relief provisions available to a wronged spouse discussed at ¶25,570 and ¶25,571, the law also allows the IRS to deny the benefits of community property laws to a culpable spouse (.05). Community property laws do not apply to an item of community income and the culpable spouse will be solely responsible for reporting it if that spouse acts as if he or she is solely entitled to that income and fails to notify the other spouse before the filing deadline (including extensions) of the nature and amount of the income.

.05 Code Sec. 66(b).

¶25,573 Decrees of Divorce, Annulment and Separation Generally. When the marital community is ended, the community assets (money and property) are divided between the spouses (see ¶25,575). Any income or property received after the community is ended is separate income. State law governs what event ends the community. Generally, separation alone does not dissolve the community (.05). In all community property states, an absolute decree of divorce or annulment ends the community (although, depending on the applicable state law, an annulment may or may not negate community property effects during the "marriage") (.10). In Louisiana, the community may end by a "separation from bed and board."

Depending upon the applicable state law, a decree of separate maintenance may or may not end a community interest. For instance, in New Mexico, a decree of legal separation ends the community unless the decree states otherwise. Termination of a marriage by other than absolute decree ends the community status in the state of Washington (.15), where spouses show an intent to terminate it by

(1) living apart,

(2) giving no support to the other spouse,

(3) giving no information to the other spouse about income received,

(4) making no claims for income or property the other spouse acquires after the separation,

(5) managing affairs without the interference of the other spouse,

(6) filing a divorce complaint or not fighting a divorce action, or

(7) entering into a property settlement.

In some community property states, personal earnings prior to termination of the community continue to be community income even though the spouses have separated. However, in other states, the earnings and property acquired by either spouse while living apart are separate property (.20).

For the year in which the community is ended, each spouse is generally taxable on half the community income for the part of the year before the community was ended (.25).

.05 *T.R. Jones,* 38 TCM 599, CCH Dec. 35,996(M), TC Memo. 1979-136.

.10 IRS Publication No. 555, "Community Property."

.15 *Knodle v. Warren,* DC Wash., 67-1 USTC ¶9261.

.20 IRS Publication No. 555, "Community Property."

.25 See, e.g., *S.G. Chapman,* 45 TCM 238, CCH Dec. 39,536(M), TC Memo. 1982-695, where an estranged spouse residing in Louisiana was held personally liable for, and taxable on, one-half of her husband's earnings, even though the couple were subsequently legally separated and both filed separate returns.

¶25,574 Community Separation Agreements. Generally, separation of the parties of itself does not dissolve the community (see ¶25,573); therefore, community income continues to be allocated between a husband and wife during the period prior to the entry of a final divorce decree (.05). However, a valid separation agreement may affect the character of the property (.10). State law will control the requirements of a valid agreement. For instance, in Texas, an oral agreement is sufficient (.15), while New Mexico law requires a written one.

Separation agreements may deal with the disposition of property and/or future income. An agreement that purports to settle rights in community property and determine the character of property acquired in the future may make a spouse's future income separate income from the time the agreement becomes effective (.20). A settlement agreement that deals exclusively with property rights and is silent regarding future earnings cannot affect the community nature of income earned pending the divorce (.25).

.05 *D. Sullivan,* CA-5, 58-2 USTC ¶9563, 256 F2d 4; *B.J. Brady,* 24 TCM 313, CCH Dec. 27,289(M), TC Memo. 1965-58; *C.K. Hill,* 32 TC 254, CCH Dec. 23,569.

.10 *E. SoRelle,* 22 TC 459, CCH Dec. 20,372 (Acq.).

.15 *Coburn v. Collins,* 244 SW2d 526 (Civ.App.Tex., 1951), rehearing denied.

.20 *F.E. Boland,* CA-9, 41-1 USTC ¶9371, 118 F2d 622.

.25 *E.S. Sherman,* CA-9, 35-1 USTC ¶9308, 76 F2d 810.

¶25,575 Division of Community Property. No gain or loss is recognized on a property transfers between spouses incident to their divorce (.05). This rule applies whether there is an equal or unequal division of community property. A property transfer is incident to a divorce if the transfer occurred within one year after the date on which the marriage ends or if the transfer is related to the termination of the marriage. However, gain is recognized on the transfer of property in trust to the extent that the sum of the amount of the liabilities assumed plus liabilities to which the property is subject exceeds the total of the transferor's adjusted basis (.10).

.05 Code Sec. 1041.

.10 Code Sec. 1041(e).

¶25,576 Death of a Spouse. Upon the death of a spouse, the community is terminated and a division of the community property occurs (see ¶25,558).

The Nonresident Alien Spouse

¶25,578 Election to Treat Nonresident Alien as U.S. Resident. A U.S. citizen or resident married to a nonresident alien may choose to treat the nonresident alien spouse as a U.S. resident if the nonresident alien spouse agrees (.05). If the U.S. citizen or resident is domiciled (see ¶25,547) in a community property state (see ¶25,546), community property laws apply.

Effect of making the election

If the couple chooses to treat the nonresident alien spouse as a U.S. resident, the alien spouse's income worldwide becomes subject to U.S. income tax. For the year of election, the spouses must file a joint return; therefore, only a few community property concepts, for example those applicable to calculating the self-employment tax (see ¶25,586) and estimated tax (see ¶25,587), will be relevant. For subsequent years, the spouses may file separate returns, at which time all the community property concepts would apply.

Effect of not making the election

If the spouses choose not to treat the nonresident alien spouse as a U.S. resident, community property is handled as set forth in "Taxation rules" at ¶25,570, but the requirements for abandoned spouse relief do not have to be met (.10).

Where both spouses are nonresident aliens

If both spouses are nonresident aliens who live in a community property law country and one spouse's income is effectively connected with a U.S. trade or business, the spouse's income effectively connected with a U.S. trade or business will be treated as separate income of that spouse, regardless of community property law.

.05 Code Sec. 6013(g); Reg. §1.6013-6(a).

.10 IRS Publication No. 555, "Community Property."

Preparing the Federal Income Tax Return

¶25,580 Overview. In preparing the federal tax return, the community property rules apply to income and expenses. Note, however, that in calculating the earned income credit, self-employment tax and the IRA deduction, community property rules are *not* to be applied.

To classify taxable income, taxpayers must follow state law as discussed at ¶25,550 - ¶25,562, above, as it relates to community income and separate income.

Itemized deductions

Itemized deductions, such as charitable contributions, interest, taxes, and medical expenses, generally are considered paid from community funds, and one-half is deductible by each spouse, unless it can be shown that such amounts were actually paid from separate funds of the husband or wife. In that case, they are deductible on the return of the spouse who paid them (.05). See ¶25,564-¶25,567, above.

If one spouse itemizes deductions on a separate return, the other should also itemize (.10).

☐ See ¶6501 and following for treatment of itemized deductions.

.05 *L.L. Powell,* 26 TCM 161, CCH Dec. 28,348(M), TC Memo. 1967-32.

.10 IRS Publication No. 555, "Community Property."

¶25,581 Decision to File Separately. The Internal Revenue Code encourages married taxpayers to file joint returns. For couples filing separate returns, tax brackets are higher, standard deductions are lower, and many credits are disallowed completely. Thus, most married taxpayers benefit from filing joint returns, regardless of whether they live in community property or noncommunity property states.

However, in a few situations, a couple may benefit from filing separate returns. For instance, when allowable deductions are limited by the taxpayer's income, a couple in a community property state may pay less total tax by filing separate returns (see ¶25,567). Also, a spouse cannot be held jointly and severally liable unless a joint return has been filed (.05). Thus, a taxpayer who files a separate return is not responsible for a spouse's tax problems.

Relief from liability for spouse not notified of community income

If certain requirements are met, unreported community income will be included in the gross income of the spouse to whom the income is attributable (.10). See ¶25,570 and following.

.05 Code Sec. 6013.

.10 Code Sec. 66.

¶25,582 Personal Exemptions. When a married couple domiciled in a community property state (see ¶25,547) files separate returns, each spouse must claim his or her own exemption (.05). Neither may claim any part of the other spouse's exemption.

Exemptions for dependents

If a dependent child or other relative is supported from community income, the dependency exemption may be claimed by either the husband or the wife on a separate return, depending on their agreement, but it cannot be divided for any one dependent.

Where the community income is inadequate to provide for the support of the dependent as well as the other charges against it (see ¶25,564), it may be proper to allocate the exemptions for dependents to the spouse whose separate income was actually or probably charged with the principal part or with all of the support, depending on the facts and adequacy of proof (.10).

.05 Code Sec. 151(b); Reg. §1.151-1(b).

.10 *E.G. Maley,* 17 TC 260, CCH Dec. 18,490 (Acq.).

¶25,583 Tax Credit for the Elderly and the Disabled. In computing the income of married individuals filing joint returns, if there is income from a public retirement system, the couple should disregard community property laws in making any determination or computation required for the tax credit for the elderly or the disabled. Each item of income is attributed in full to the spouse whose income it would have been in the absence of community property laws. Thus, if a 67-year-old individual files a joint return with a 62-year-old spouse, and the only income of the couple is from a public pension of the older spouse, that public pension is attributed in full to the older spouse, even though the applicable community property law may treat one-half of the pension as the income of the 62-year-old spouse (.05).

.05 Reg. §1.37-3.

¶25,584 Earned Income Credit. Earned income for purposes of the earned income credit (.05) (see ¶25,706 and following) is computed without regard to community property laws. Thus, there is no allocation of taxable wages, salaries, tips, other compensation (excluding pensions and annuities, but including union strike benefit payments (.10)), and net earnings from self-employment (.15).

.05 Code Sec. 32.
.10 Rev. Rul. 78-191, 1978-1 CB 8.
.15 Reg. §1.43-1.

¶25,586 Self-Employment Tax. If any income from a trade or business is community income under the laws of the state of domicile, all the gross income and related deductions are treated as those of the spouse exercising substantially all the management and control over the business. To be a self-employed person, the spouse must have a separate business or be a member of a partnership (.05).

Where the business is a partnership and only one spouse is a partner, the distributive share of partnership income is included in computing that spouse's net earnings from self-employment, and no part of the share is treated as net earnings from self-employment of the non-partner spouse. If both spouses are partners, each may claim his or her distributive share in figuring net earnings from self-employment for income tax purposes (.10).

.05 See Code Sec. 1401 and Code Sec. 1402; Reg. § 1.1401-1 and Reg. §1.1402(a)-8(a); Rev. Rul. 82-39, 1982-1 CB 119.
.10 Reg. §1.1402(a)-8(b).

¶25,587 Estimated Tax. Community property state residents may make estimated tax payments on a joint or separate basis. In calculations on a separate basis, each spouse takes into account (1) one-half the community income and deductions, (2) all separate income and deductions, and (3) each spouse's own exemption and exemptions for any dependents he or she may claim. The way in which estimated payments are made does not affect the choice as to filing a joint or separate income tax return. Jointly paid estimated tax may be divided for separate returns in any manner to which the spouses agree. If no agreement can be reached, the estimated tax for each is:

$$\text{Total estimated tax} \quad \times \quad \frac{\text{tax on separate return}}{\text{sum of tax on both spouses' returns}^{1}}$$

[1] IRS Chief Counsel Advice 200130036, 5-25-2001.

¶25,588 Individual Retirement Arrangements. The calculation of the IRA deduction is made without regard to community property laws. Thus, a taxpayer must compute the allowable deduction solely on the basis of his or her own earnings. Further, the distribution provision of the tax law says that it is to be applied without regard to any community property laws (.05). However, the IRS has privately ruled that a husband's IRA was community property, and, upon his wife's death, her legatees were entitled to one-half of his IRA account (.10).

.05 Code Sec. 408(g).
.10 IRS Letter Ruling 8040101, 7-15-80.

U.S. CITIZENS ABROAD

Introduction

¶25,590 With the growth of multinational corporations, it is not uncommon for U.S. citizens to be employed and to reside overseas. Not surprisingly, a number of unique tax rules apply to such persons. These rules are necessary not only from a common-sense point of view, but also from an economic one—they are often designed to place the U.S. taxpayer in a position to successfully compete with his foreign counterpart. The following paragraphs examine these rules, focusing on the exclusions and deductions available to U.S. citizens living abroad, the foreign tax credit, and the effects of tax treaties. They also deal with such miscellaneous matters as filing requirements, special rules that apply when both husband and wife are abroad, and the effect of "blocked income."

Exclusions and Deductions

¶25,592 Foreign Earned Income Exclusion. One of the most significant benefits afforded qualified individuals who live and work abroad is the exclusion from gross income of certain amounts of foreign earned income. A qualified individual (¶25,594) who works abroad may elect (¶25,595) to exclude from gross income up to $80,000 of "foreign earned income." The actual amount that a taxpayer may exclude is the lesser of: (1) the qualified individual's foreign earned income for the tax year in excess of any foreign housing expenses excluded (¶25,593); or (2) the maximum exclusion amount for the tax year reduced ratably for each day during the tax year that the individual is not a bona fide resident of, or physically present in, a foreign country (.05). No deduction or credit attributable to the excluded income is allowed (¶25,596). Moreover, the amount of foreign earned income and foreign housing expenses excluded combined cannot exceed the amount of the taxpayer's foreign earned income (.10). The exclusion is calculated and reported on Form 2555 or Form 2555-EZ.

> ***Example:*** Robert Ames, a U.S. citizen, has made his tax home and been a bona fide resident of a foreign country for the past few years. However, on September 1, 2004, Robert flies back to the United States on permanent assignment for his employer. During the first eight months of 2004, Ames has $100,000 of foreign earned income. His employer does not provide him with any reimbursement for foreign housing expenses. The maximum amount of foreign earned income that Ames can exclude for 2004 is $53,333 ($80,000 maximum annual exclusion multiplied by 244/366).

The exclusion is separately computed for each spouse in the case of married taxpayers. In the case of a husband and wife with community income, the exclusion is determined as if the income were not community income.

Foreign earned income defined

For purposes of the exclusion, foreign earned income includes any wages, salaries, professional fees and other amounts received as compensation for personal services actually rendered when the taxpayer's tax home was located in a foreign country and met either the bona fide residence test or the physical presence test (.15). If the taxpayer engages in a trade or business where both personal services and capital are material income-producing factors, no more than 30 percent of the taxpayer's share of net profits can be treated as foreign earned income. Amounts that do not qualify as foreign earned income for purposes of the exclusion include (.20):

- compensation received in the form of corporate earnings and profits (.25);
- payments from pensions and annuities (including social security payments), nonexempt employees' trusts and nonqualified annuities;
- amounts paid to an employee of the United States or its agencies (even though the foreign country reimburses the United States for the amounts paid to the employee) (.30);
- amounts received after the end of the tax year following the tax year in which the income was earned;
- income earned in any foreign country in which travel by U.S. citizens and residents has been generally restricted by regulations issued under the Trading with the Enemy Act and the International Emergency Economic Powers Act (.35);
- amounts included in income as a recaptured unallowable moving expense (¶25,598); and
- amounts for meals and lodging furnished by an employer and excluded from the employee's gross income (¶25,597).

.05 Code Sec. 911(a)(1) and (b)(2); Reg. §1.911-3(d)(2).

.10 Code Sec. 911(d)(7).

.15 Code Sec. 911(b)(1) and (d)(2); Reg. §1.911-3.

.20 Code Sec. 911(b)(1)(B); Reg. §1.911-3(c).

.25 Reg. §1.911-3(b)(1).

.30 *J.T. Smith*, CA-9, 83-1 USTC ¶9255, 701 F2d 807, aff'g TC, 77 TC 1181, CCH Dec. 38,460; Rev. Rul. 85-29, 1985-1 CB 223.

.35 Code Sec. 911(d)(8).

¶25,593 Foreign Housing Exclusion. In addition to the election to exclude foreign earned income (¶25,592), a qualified individual (¶25,594) may elect ¶25,595) to exclude from gross income a certain amount of employer-provided foreign housing expenses (.05). The amount of the exclusion is the excess of: (1) the taxpayer's reasonable foreign housing expenses for the tax year; over (2) a base housing amount equal to 16 percent of the salary of a federal employee at grade level GS-14 (step 1) as of January 1 of the calendar year, multiplied by the percentage of days during the year that the taxpayer has his tax home in the foreign country. For this purpose, the 2004 GS-14 (step 1) salary is $72,381, 16 percent of which is $11,581, or $31.64 per day. The exclusion is calculated and reported on Form 2555 or Form 2555-EZ.

For purposes of computing the exclusion, a taxpayer's housing expenses include the reasonable costs paid or incurred during the tax year for providing housing for the taxpayer and his or her family if they reside with the taxpayer. Eligible expenses include rent, utilities (other than telephone charges), real or personal property insurance, household repairs, furniture, and necessary improvements. Housing expenses do not include expenses that are otherwise deductible (i.e., interest, taxes) or that are extravagant. On the other hand, housing expenses may include the costs of maintaining a separate foreign household for the taxpayer's family if they do not reside with the taxpayer because of adverse conditions.

Self-employed taxpayers

A self-employed taxpayer is entitled to deduct from gross income a certain amount of his foreign housing expenses in lieu of the exclusion (.10). The deduction is limited to the amount by which the taxpayer's foreign earned income for the tax year exceeds his foreign earned income exclusion. Any amount that exceeds the deduction limit can be carried forward to the next tax year. If the taxpayer has foreign earned income that consists of both employer provided amounts and self-employment amounts, then the taxpayer may elect to exclude that part of their housing expenses that are provided by their employer and also claim a deduction for any remaining housing expenses attributed to his self-employment income.

.05 Code Sec. 911(a) and (c). **.10** Code Sec. 911(c)(3).

¶25,594 Eligibility for Exclusions. In order to qualify for the foreign earned income exclusion (¶25,592) and the foreign housing exclusion (¶25,593), an individual's tax home must be in a foreign country and he or she must establish qualified residence either through the bona fide residence test or the physical presence test (.05). A foreign country is any territory, including airspace and territorial waters, under the sovereignty of a government other than the United States. However, the exclusions will be denied if the taxpayer is present in a foreign country in which travel is generally restricted under the Trading with the Enemy Act or the International Emergency Powers Act.

Tax home

Tax home for this purpose has the same meaning as it does for determining the deductibility of traveling expenses away from home (¶8220). An individual's tax home is where his principal place of business is located, regardless of where he maintains a family home (.10). The location of a taxpayer's tax home often depends on whether a work assignment is temporary or indefinite. An individual is not considered to have a tax home in a foreign country for any period during which his abode is in the United States. Temporary presence in the United States, or maintenance of a dwelling in the United States, does not necessarily mean that an abode is in the United States during that time.

Bona fide residence

A taxpayer may qualify for the foreign income exclusions if he is a bona fide resident of a foreign country (or countries) for an uninterrupted period that includes a full tax year (.15). This determination is based on all of the facts and circumstances including the taxpayer's intentions regarding the length and nature of his stay. It is not determined by the taxpayer's status under the laws of the foreign country. Nor does a taxpayer automatically acquire bona fide residence status by merely living a foreign country for a year. Once the bona fide residence requirement is met, the taxpayer is permitted the exclusions for any tax year in which the period of residence began or ended.

> ***Example 1:*** A calendar-year taxpayer, whose salary is $100,000 per year, establishes bona fide residence in a foreign country on January 1, 2003. If his residence lasts until March 31, 2004, he qualifies for an exclusion of $80,000 in 2003 under the bona fide residence test since residence was established for a full tax year. He also qualifies for the exclusion of $19,891 ($80,000 × 91/366) for the partial tax year of 2004.

Physical presence

As an alternative to the bona fide residence test, a taxpayer may qualify for the foreign income exclusions if he is present in a foreign country (or countries) for 330 days out of any consecutive 12-month period. The taxpayer does not have to be present in the foreign country solely for business purposes to meet this test. Some of the qualifying foreign presence can be vacation time (.20).

Example 2: A calendar-year taxpayer, whose salary is $100,000 per year, is physically present in a foreign country from July 1, 2003, though June 15, 2004. He meets the physical presence test, but to determine the number of qualifying days the taxpayer has in 2004 (in order to calculate his exclusion amount), he must count back 330 days (to July 22, 2003) from the last full day the taxpayer was in the foreign country. Thus, the total number of qualifying days for 2004 that fall within the 12-month period beginning on July 22, 2003, is 167. The taxpayer may elect to exclude $36,503 of his foreign earned income (167/366 × $80,000).

Waiver of time limits

Relief from the residence requirements is provided for taxpayers who would otherwise satisfy the bona fide residence or the physical presence tests except for the fact that they were forced to flee a foreign country because of civil unrest, war, or other adverse conditions (.25). The IRS publishes the names of foreign countries where such conditions exist. To qualify, the taxpayer must:

- be a bona fide resident of, or present in, a foreign country for any period;
- establish that he left the foreign country during the period when adverse conditions existed; and
- establish that he could reasonably have expected to have satisfied the bona fide residence or physical presence test had the adverse conditions not arisen.

.05 Code Sec. 911(d)(1); Reg. §1.911-2.
.10 Code Sec. 911(d)(3).
.15 Code Sec. 911(d)(5).
.20 Reg. §1.911-2(d).
.25 Code Sec. 911(d)(4); Reg. §1.911-2(f).

¶25,595 Electing the Exclusions. A qualified individual (¶25,594) must make a separate election with respect to the foreign earned income exclusion (¶25,592) and the foreign housing exclusion (¶25,593). The elections are made by filing Form 2555 (or Form 2555-EZ) with the taxpayer's timely-filed income tax return (including extensions), amended return or a late-filed return if filed within one year after the due date for the first year for which the election is to be effective (.05). Once made, an election will remain in effect for the tax year in question and all subsequent years unless revoked with approval from the IRS. If the taxpayer revokes an election without IRS approval, he will be prohibited from making a new election for at least five years. A self-employed taxpayer does not have to make an election in order to claim the foreign housing deduction. However, sufficient information must be provided to determine the correct amount of tax.

Generally, a taxpayer must file Form 1040 by April 15 of the following tax year. However, an automatic two-month extension (June 16) will be granted to qualifying U.S. citizens or residents if on the normal due date his or her tax home and abode, in a real and substantial sense, are outside of the United States and Puerto Rico (.10). The automatic extension also applies to the payment of tax but interest will be charged from the original due date.

An individual that claims either the foreign earned income or foreign housing exclusion may not claim the foreign tax credit for any income excluded. Similarly, a taxpayer eligible for the earned income tax credit may not claim both the credit and either of the exclusions. Claiming the foreign tax credit or earned income credit may result in the revocation of the elections.

.05 Code Sec. 911(e); Reg. §1.911-7.
.10 Reg. §1.6081-5.

¶25,596 Deductions. In general, the deductions available to U.S. citizens living abroad are the same as those available to citizens who live in the United States. However, if a taxpayer excludes foreign earned income (¶25,592) and/or foreign housing expenses (¶25,593), no deduction is allowed for an item that is properly allocable to, or chargeable against, the excluded amount of income.

Charitable contributions

While charitable contributions are generally deductible by U.S. citizens living abroad, no deduction is permitted for contributions made directly to foreign charitable organizations (e.g., churches). Contributions made to a U.S. organization that transfers funds to a foreign charity may be deducted if the U.S. organization controls the use of the funds by the foreign entity or if the foreign entity is merely an administrative arm of the U.S. organization (.05). Moreover, under the tax treaty with Canada, direct contributions to certain Canadian charitable organizations may be deductible. In addition to be being subject to the limits for U.S. charitable contributions, the allowable amount of such contributions cannot be more than the amount that would be allowable under the Canadian income tax law, figured as though the taxpayer's Canadian-source income was his adjusted gross income.

Foreign taxes

A U.S. citizen living abroad may take either a tax credit (¶25,601) or an itemized deduction for foreign income taxes paid (.10). However, all foreign incomes taxes must be treated similarly (i.e., either as a deduction or as a credit) (.15). Other foreign taxes may be deducted as well, such as real property taxes, and personal property or sales taxes if they are incurred in a trade or business.

Moving expenses and reimbursements

The rules relating to the deduction of moving expenses resulting from a new job location outside the United States and its possessions are similar to those governing domestic moving expenses (.20). In general, moving expenses are deducted from gross income in arriving at adjusted gross income if the expenses are incurred in connection with the commencement of work at a new principal place of employment. The distance between the taxpayer's new principal place of employment and his former residence must be 50 miles greater than the distance between his former principal place of employment and his former residence. In addition, an employee must be a full-time employee for at least 39 weeks during the 12-month period following the move. The moving costs must have been incurred within one year from the time the taxpayer first reported to his new job or business. In the case of a self-employed individual, the deduction may be claimed only if, in addition to meeting the 50 mile limitation, the taxpayer, during his first 24 months in the foreign country, performs services on a full-time basis for at least 78 weeks, 39 of which fall within the 12 months immediately following his arrival.

With regard to foreign moves, deductible moving expenses include the following:

(1) the cost of moving household goods and personal effects, including the cost of moving such goods to and from storage and storing them for all or part of the period during which the new place of work continues to be the taxpayer's principal place of work; and

(2) the cost of transportation and lodging for one trip from the taxpayer's former home to his new home (.25).

Taxpayers claiming a foreign moving expense must file Form 3903-F (Foreign Moving Expenses).

A foreign move does not generally include a move back to the United States or its possessions. However, persons who work abroad and retire while abroad qualify for a moving expense deduction in connection with moving to a new residence in the United States (.30). The same rule applies to the spouse or any dependent of a decedent who at the time of his death had a principal place of work outside the United States. However, in this latter instance, the move to the United States must occur within six months of the decedent's death and must be from a foreign residence that was the residence of the decedent and the person paying or incurring the moving expenses.

Special rules describe the interaction between the foreign earned income exclusion and moving expense deduction (.35). Moving expenses reimbursements may qualify for the foreign earned income exclusion in certain cases. In the absence of a written agreement or similar evidence to the contrary, moving expense reimbursements shall be attributable to future services to be performed at the new principal place of work under what is known as "the forward attribution rule." Thus, a reimbursement received by an employee from his employer for the expenses of a move to a foreign country will generally be attributable to services performed in the foreign country and could be eligible for the foreign earned income exclusion. However, a reimbursement received by an employee from his employer for the expenses of a move from a foreign country to the United States will generally be attributable to services performed in the United States.

If a reimbursement for moving expenses is determined to be from foreign sources, then for the purpose of determining the amount eligible for exclusion, the reimbursement shall be considered attributable to services performed in the year of the move as long as the individual is a qualified individual for a period that includes 120 days in the year of the move. If the individual is not a qualified individual for such period, then the individual shall treat a portion of the reimbursement as attributable to services performed in the year of the move, and a portion as attributable to services performed in the succeeding tax year, if the move is from the United States to a foreign country, or to the prior taxable year if the move is from a foreign country to the United States. The portion of the reimbursement treated as attributable to services performed in the year of the move shall be determined by multiplying the total reimbursement by a fraction, the numerator of which is the number of qualifying days in the year of the move, and the denominator of which is the number of days in the tax year of the move.

The IRS has provided examples of the interaction between the foreign earned income exclusion and moving expense deduction, and provided withholding advice for common encountered situations (.40). The examples cover moving to a foreign country and moving back to the United States to work for the same employer, to work for a different employer, and to retire. In general, the IRS ruled that: (1) expenses incurred in moving to a foreign country are allocable to or chargeable against foreign earned income in the year of the move; (2) expenses incurred in moving from a foreign country to work in the United States are allocable to U.S.-source income and not to foreign earned income; and (3) where the employee moves to the United States and is no longer employed after the move, the moving expense reimbursement will be viewed as attributable to compensation for past services performed by the employee for the employer

.05 Code Sec. 170(c)(2)(A); Reg. §1.170A-9; Rev. Rul. 66-79, 1966-1 CB 48, amplifying Rev. Rul. 63-252, 1963-2 CB 101.

.10 Code Sec. 164(a); Reg. §1.164-2.

.15 *M. Marsman*, 54-2 USTC ¶9628, 216 F2d 77, *cert. denied*, 348 U.S. 943.

.20 Code Sec. 217; Reg. §§1.911-3(e)(5) and 1.911-6(b); IRS Publication No. 54, "Tax Guide for U.S. Citizens and Resident Aliens Abroad," CCH IRS PUBLICATIONS.

.25 Code Sec. 217(b) and (h).

.30 Code Sec. 217(i).

.35 Reg. §§1.911-3(e)(5) and 1.911-6.

.40 Rev. Rul. 75-84, 1975-1 CB 236, amplified by Rev. Rul. 76-162, 1976-1 CB 197.

¶25,597 Employees Living in Foreign Camps. An employee can exclude the value of meals and lodging furnished to him, his spouse, and his dependents by or on behalf of his employer if the meals are furnished on the business premises of the employer, or the employee accepts any lodging on the business premises of the employer as a condition of his employment (.05). Where an individual is furnished lodging by or for his employer in a camp located in a foreign country, the camp is considered to be part of the employer's premises if the following requirements are met:

• the lodging is furnished for the convenience of the employer because the place at which services are to be performed is in a remote area without satisfactory housing;

• the camp is located as near as is practicable to the worksite, although the camp need not be in a hardship area nor must it be substandard housing; and

• the camp is operated as a common area that accommodates at least 10 employees and that is not available to the general public (.10).

Taxpayers who must leave a camp because of adverse conditions in the foreign country are entitled to pro rata benefits.

.05 Code Sec. 119(a).

.10 Code Sec. 119(c).

¶25,598 Residents of U.S. Possessions. A U.S. citizen who is a bona fide resident of a U.S. possession during the entire tax year, may exclude from gross income any income derived from sources within the possession (.05). The taxpayer may also exclude income that is effectively connected with the conduct of a trade or business by the individual within the possession. The exclusion shall not apply to income that is received for services performed by the individual as an employee of the United States or agency thereof. The individual may also not claim any credit against tax or deduction from gross income which is attributable to the amount of excluded income. Depending upon the individual's residency status, a tax return may have to be filed with the United States, the possession, or both. For this purpose, a U.S. possession includes Guam, American Samoa and the Northern Mariana Islands. However, the exclusion applies only if there is an effective implementing agreement between the United States and the possession. For 2004, only American Samoa has such an agreement. In order to exclude income from American Samoa sources, bona fide residents must complete Form 4563 and attach it to their tax return. Whether an individual is a bona fide resident of a U.S. possession is determined under a 183-day rule similar to that of the substantial presence test for resident aliens (.10).

.05 Code Sec. 931.

.10 Code Sec. 937, as added by the American Jobs Creation Act of 2004 (P.L. 108-357).

Tax Credits and Treaties

¶25,601 Foreign Tax Credit. A U.S. citizen or a domestic corporation who pays income or profits taxes to a foreign country on foreign-source income is entitled to either an itemized deduction or a tax credit for such taxes (.05). The result is that U.S. tax has to be paid on such foreign source income only if the foreign tax rate is less than the U.S. tax rate. No credit or deduction may be claimed for foreign income taxes paid on income that is excluded from U.S. taxation under the foreign earned income exclusion (¶25,592) or the foreign housing exclusion (¶25,593).

A taxpayer is free to choose between the credit and the deduction. However, it generally is more advantageous to credit qualified foreign taxes than to deduct them. A credit reduces the amount of tax due on a dollar-for-dollar basis, whereas a deduction reduces the amount of income subject to tax. In order to claim a credit, a taxpayer must complete Form 1116 (Computation of Foreign Tax Credit). The credit cannot be taken against a tax, such as the alternative minimum tax, that is not considered to be part of the taxpayer's regular tax liability (.10). Moreover, an individual is generally allowed a credit with respect to his proportionate share of any taxes of a partnership of which he is a partner (or of an estate or trust of which he is a beneficiary) that have been paid or accrued to a foreign country or to any possession of the United States , as the case may be.

To be creditable, a tax of a particular foreign country must be the substantial equivalent of an income tax or a tax assessed in lieu of an income tax. A foreign charge is treated as a creditable income tax if it is a tax and its predominant character is that of an income tax in the U.S. sense. A foreign levy is a tax if it requires a compulsory payment pursuant to the foreign country's authority to levy taxes. A charge for a specific economic benefit is not a tax. However, if a portion of a foreign levy is a compulsory payment pursuant to the foreign country's authority to levy taxes and a portion is a compulsory payment in exchange for a specific economic benefit, the levy is separable into two distinct elements and the portion of the levy that is a tax is creditable.

A foreign levy's predominant character is that of an income tax in the U.S. sense if the levy is likely to reach net gain in the normal circumstances in which the levy applies. A foreign tax payment that is returned to the taxpayer in the form of a subsidy, such as a refund or a credit, from a foreign country is not creditable (.15). A credit is also denied if the subsidy is given to persons related to the taxpayer or persons who participated in a transaction, or a related transaction, with the taxpayer.

Limitation on credit

In computing the amount of the foreign tax credit, taxpayers cannot use foreign tax credits to reduce U.S. tax liability on income from sources within the United States. The limitation on the amount of the credit must generally be computed under the overall method. This method bases the amount of the credit upon the total amount of foreign taxes paid to all foreign countries and U.S. possessions. An individual with $300 ($600 for joint filers) or less of creditable foreign taxes will be exempt from the FTC limitation, provided he has no foreign source income other than qualified passive income, and he/she elects the exemption (the election is annual) (.20). The credit may not exceed the same proportion of the U.S. tax against which the credit is taken as the taxpayer's taxable income from foreign sources bears to his entire taxable income for the year. The allowable foreign tax credit cannot exceed the taxpayer's actual foreign tax liability. Taxable income, for this purpose, is computed without any deduction for personal taxes.

A taxpayer is required to compute its foreign tax credit limitation separately for various categories of income, generally known as separate limitation categories or baskets (.25). For tax years prior to 2007, there are nine separate baskets of income including: passive income, high withholding tax interest, financial services income (i.e., banking and insurance income), shipping income, dividends from a noncontrolled Code Sec. 902 corporation, certain distributions from DISCs and FSCs, certain types of income earned by a FSC and all other types of income constitute the items of foreign income for which separate foreign tax credit limitations must be computed. For tax years beginning after December 31, 2006, the number of foreign tax credit baskets will be reduced to two: passive category income and general category income. Income which would be included in one of nine categories will be allocated to these two categories, as appropriate. Creditable foreign taxes imposed on amounts that do not constitute income under U.S. tax law ("base difference" items) will be treated as imposed on general category income. However, for tax years after 2004 and before 2007, the taxpayer may elect that such taxes be allocated to either the financial services basket or the general limitation basket.

When credit is taken

The credit may ordinarily be taken either in the year in which the taxes accrued or in the year in which they were paid, depending on whether the taxpayer is on the cash or the accrual basis. However, at the option of the taxpayer, the credit may be taken in the year in which the taxes accrued, irrespective of the accounting method employed by him, subject to certain adjustments. When the amount of creditable foreign taxes paid or accrued by a taxpayer during the tax year exceeds the overall limitation for that year, the excess may generally be carried back to the two preceding tax years and then forward to the five succeeding tax years. However, the carryback period will be limited to one year for excess credits arising in tax years after October 22, 2004 (.30). The carryforward period has been extended to 10 years for excess credits that may be carried to any tax year ending after October 22, 2004. The amount that may be carried back or forward is limited to the amount by which the credit limitation in the carryback or forward year exceeds the amount of foreign taxes paid or accrued in that year. A carryback to a year in which foreign taxes were deducted rather than credited may reduce the remaining carryover without resulting in a refund.

.05 Code Secs. 901, 903, 904 and 905.

.10 Code Sec. 26(b)(2).

.15 Code Sec. 901(i); Reg. §1.901-2(e)(3).

.20 Code Sec. 904(j).

.25 Code Sec. 904(d), as amended by the American Jobs Creation Act of 2004 (P.L. 108-357).

.30 Code Sec. 904(c), as amended by the American Jobs Creation Act of 2004 (P.L. 108-357).

¶25,602 Tax Treaties. Various benefits may be available under tax treaties between the United States and the country or countries in which the taxpayer resided during the year (.05). Thus, U.S. citizens abroad are advised to examine treaties carefully or to request assistance from competent authority, which can be done by filing a written request for consideration with the IRS (.10). Certain tax benefits are typically available under treaties. Every benefit is not afforded by every treaty. Therefore, pertinent treaties should be examined carefully. Typical treaty benefits include:

- exemption from foreign income tax of nongovernmental pensions and annuities;
- exemption, at least for a temporary period, of compensation received by U.S. residents who are teaching;
- exemption of all or part of the compensation received for personal services performed in the treaty country as an employee or independent contractor; and
- exemption of remuneration received from the United States for the purposes of study or research.

Disclosure of treaty-based position

A taxpayer who takes the position that any U.S. tax is overruled or otherwise reduced by a U.S. treaty (a treaty-based position), generally must disclose that position on Form 8833, (Treaty-Based Return Position Disclosure Under Section 6114 or 7701(b)), and attach it to the income return. If the taxpayer is not required to file a return because of the treaty-based position, the taxpayer must file a return anyway to report the position. The filing of Form 8833 does not apply to a reduced rate of withholding tax on noneffectively connected income, such as dividends, interest, rents or royalties, or to a reduced rate of tax on pay received for services performed as an employee, including pensions, annuities, and social security. A failure to file Form 8833, may subject a non-corporate taxpayer to a $1,000 penalty.

.05 Code Sec. 894; IRS Publication No. 901, "U.S. Tax Treaties," CCH IRS PUBLICATIONS.

.10 Rev. Proc. 2002-52, I.R.B. 2002-31, 242, modifying and superseding Rev. Proc. 96-13, 1996-1 CB 616 and Rev. Proc. 91-26, 1991-1 CB 543.

Miscellaneous Matters

¶25,604 Filing Requirements. The income tax return filing requirements for U.S. citizens and resident aliens in foreign countries generally are the same as those for citizens and residents living in the United States (.05).

Due date

If filing is on a calendar-year basis, the due date for filing a return is April 15 following the close of the tax year (if April 15 falls on a Saturday or Sunday, the due date is the first weekday thereafter). A taxpayer who files on a fiscal-year basis must file by the 15th day of the fourth month after the close of the tax year. All individual taxpayers may receive an automatic four-month extension of time to file their returns by filing Form 4868 (Application for Automatic Extension of Time to File U.S. Individual Income Tax Return) on or before the original due date of their returns. U.S. citizens and resident aliens whose tax homes and abodes are outside of the United States and Puerto Rico on the due date of their returns are entitled to an automatic two-month extension of time to both file and pay tax. The extension runs concurrently with the four-month extension (.10).

A taxpayer who needs an additional extension of time in order to qualify for the foreign earned income or housing exclusion and housing deduction must file Form 2350 (Application for Extension of Time to File U.S. Income Tax Return). If an extension is granted, it will generally be until 30 days after the date on which either the bona fide residence or physical presence test is met (¶25,594). However, if a taxpayer is allocating moving expenses, he may be granted an extension of 90 days beyond the close of the year following the year of first arrival in the foreign country. Form 2350 does not extend the time to pay any income tax due.

Information return

U.S. citizens who apply for passports are required to file an information return (.15). The information return will elicit the taxpayer identification number, the foreign residence of a passport applicant, and such other information as may be considered necessary. A $500 penalty is imposed on an individual for each failure to provide the information unless the failure is due to reasonable cause.

.05 Code Sec. 6012.

.10 Reg. §1.6081-5(a)(5).

.15 Code Sec. 6039E.

¶25,605 Nonresident Alien Spouse. Where one spouse is a U.S. citizen or resident and the other is a nonresident, most income that the latter receives from foreign sources is not subject to U.S. tax unless both spouses elect to treat the nonresident alien as a resident alien (¶25,816) (.05).

A nonresident alien whose only income is from sources outside the is not liable for any U.S. taxes unless the income is effectively connected with the conduct of a U.S. trade or business. However, if the election to treat the nonresident alien spouse as a resident alien is made (or if the spouse becomes a resident alien during the year), all income becomes taxable in the same manner as that of a U.S. citizen. If the election is made, the couple must file a joint return in that year but may file jointly or separately during later years.

The election is made by attaching a statement, signed by both spouses, to the joint return for the first tax year for which the election is in effect. It should contain:

(1) a declaration that one spouse was a nonresident alien and the other a U.S. citizen or resident on the last day of the tax year and that they choose to be treated as U.S. residents for the entire year, and

(2) the name, address and social security number of each spouse (.10).

The choice to be treated as a U.S. resident is not effective for any later year in which neither spouse is a U.S. resident or citizen at any time during the year. Moreover, the election can be formally revoked by either spouse in any later year by filing a statement to that effect. The statement is to be attached to the return if the "revoking" spouse is required to file a return (otherwise it is to be submitted to the IRS Center where the last joint return was filed). The death of a spouse or a legal separation under a decree of divorce or separate maintenance also terminates the election.

.05 Code Secs. 871 and 6013; Reg. §1.6013-6.

.10 IRS Publication No. 519, "U.S. Tax Guide for Aliens," CCH IRS PUBLICATIONS.

¶25,606 Exchange Rates. All federal income tax determinations must be made in the taxpayer's functional currency (.05). Generally, the functional currency of a U.S. taxpayer will be the U.S. dollar. However, in the case of a qualified business unit (QBU), the functional currency is the currency in which it conducts a significant part of its activities and which is used in keeping its books and records. For this purpose, a QBU is any separate and clearly identified unit of a trade or business of the taxpayer which maintains its own books and records (e.g., foreign subsidiary of a U.S. corporation or a foreign corporation). Special rules apply in determining when foreign income taxes and foreign earnings and profits must be translated into U.S. dollars (.10).

Any tax due must, with one exception, must also be paid in U.S. dollars (.15). Whatever exchange rate is used to translate foreign currency into U.S. dollars must be justifiable. The exception to the rule that federal income tax must be paid in U.S. dollars applies to the tax on Fulbright grants, provided at least 70 percent of the grant is paid in nonconvertible foreign currency. To the extent recipients are paid in such currency, they may pay federal income tax in the currency of the foreign countries involved.

.05 Code Sec. 985.

.10 Code Secs. 986 and 987, as amended by the American Jobs Creation Act of 2004 (P.L. 108-357)).

.15 Code Sec. 6316; Reg. §§301.6316-1—301.6316-9; IRS Publication No. 54, "Tax Guide for U.S. Citizens and Resident Aliens Abroad," CCH IRS PUBLICATIONS.

¶25,607 Blocked Income. If, because of restrictions in a foreign country, a taxpayer's income is not readily convertible into U.S. dollars or into other money or property (i.e., it is "blocked"), the taxpayer may either: (1) report the income and pay the tax with U.S. dollars that are in the or some other country; or (2) defer reporting of the income until it becomes unblocked (.05). Income becomes unblocked when it becomes convertible, or is converted, into dollars or other money or property that is convertible into U.S. currency. Moreover, it becomes unblocked when the taxpayer uses it for his personal expenditures or disposes of it by gift, bequest, or devise.

An election to defer the reporting of income is made by filing a second Form 1040 labelled "Report of Deferrable Foreign Income, Pursuant to Rev. Rul. 81-290," which must be attached to the taxpayer's first Form 1040. The taxpayer must declare that the deferred income will be included in taxable income in the year it ceases to be deferrable and that they waive any right to claim that the deferrable income was includible in income for any earlier year. A separate information return must be filed as to each country if the taxpayer has blocked income from more than one foreign country.

.05 Rev. Rul. 81-290, 1981-2 CB 108 modifying Rev. Rul. 74-351, 1974-2 CB 144; IRS Publication No. 54, "Tax Guide for U.S. Citizens and Resident Aliens Abroad," CCH IRS PUBLICATIONS.

MEMBERS OF THE CLERGY

Introduction

¶25,610 Members of the clergy are generally subject to taxation in the same manner as other members of the public. Taxable income includes any compensation received such as wages, salaries, honorariums and fees. Gifts to clergy may also constitute taxable income if the gift is from a church or its congregation. The major tax break granted to members of the clergy is exclusion from income of parsonage or housing allowances provided to them by the church or its congregation.

Even though members of the clergy may be employees, a church or congregation is not required to withhold income taxes on their salaries. Thus, members of the clergy are treated as self-employed persons and must pay self-employment taxes unless they meet certain exemption requirements. In addition, for purpose of the self-employment taxes, what constitutes income can vary from what it is for income tax purposes.

Taxable Income - General

¶25,612 Compensation for Services. The imposition of income taxes on the compensation of a member of the clergy does not violate his first amendment rights even if his religious tenets forbids the payment of taxes (.05). Thus, members of the clergy (e.g., priests, ministers and rabbis) are generally required to include in their gross income any amount that they receive in exchange for their services. This includes any salary, wages, or other amounts such as fees or stipends for performing marriages, baptisms or funerals (.10). However, if a member of the clergy is required to return any fees or stipends to a church or other organization, then such amounts are not included in his gross income (.15). Fees for such "outside" work must be reported on Form 1040, Schedule C, "Profit or Loss From Business," where they are retained by the minister.

Vows of poverty

Some members of religious orders take a vow of poverty and turn over amounts that they earn from teaching, nursing, or other employment to their order. Although such persons give up their earnings, they are still subject to federal income tax on such amounts unless they performed such services as agents of the order (.20). Whether an individual is treated as an employee (and thereby taxed) or as an agent of the religious order (and thereby not taxed) depends on the facts and circumstances of each case. Relevant factors to consider in making this determination include:

(1) the degree of control exercised by the order over the individual member;

(2) the ownership rights between the member and the order;

(3) the purposes or mission of the order;

(4) the type of work performed by the member as compared to the purposes or mission of the order;

(5) the dealings between the member and the third-party employer; and

(6) the dealings between the employer and the order (.25).

If the member of the religious order is an employee (and thereby taxed), he may be able to claim a charitable deduction for the amount of the income that he does turn over the the order, provided the order is an organization described in Code Sec. 170(c)(2) (.30).

.05 *L. Gonzales*, 91-1 USTC ¶50,100.

.10 Code Sec. 61; Reg. §1.61-2(a)(1).

.15 Rev. Rul. 76-341, 1976-2 CB 307.

.20 Rev. Rul. 79-132, 1979-1 CB 62; Rev. Rul. 77-290, 1977-2 CB 26.

.25 *G.P. Fogarty*, CA-Fed., 86-1 USTC ¶9139; *F. Schuster*, CA-7, 86-2 USTC ¶9664.

.30 Rev. Rul. 76-323, 1976-2 CB 18.

¶25,613 Gifts or Honorariums. In general, the value of any payment or property received by gift is not includible in a taxpayer's gross income. This rule has significant relevance in the case of payments from a church or its congregation to a member of the clergy because such payments may appear to be an ideal tax-avoidance situation. However, neither the IRS nor courts will generally view such payments as gifts. This is because if a church or congregation is making a payment to a member of the clergy primarily for moral or legal reasons, as is most often the case, it is not a gift. In order to for a payment to be properly considered a gift, it must proceed from a detached and disinterested generosity, that is out of affection, respect, admiration, charity or simple impulse. The payment must not be in exchange for services (in the past, present, or future) or for other valuable consideration (.05).

Sometimes, however, a church or its congregation will bestow on a minister a gift or honorarium upon a minister if the minister becomes ill, disabled or retires. Such payments may be made tax-free if the church specifies in the recorded actions of its authorizing body that the payments: (1) are made without consideration for past services; (2) have no relation to salary or length of service; and (3) are not conditioned on further services or on a consideration for an agreement to retire. Payments made under a legal agreement or an established plan, as an informal form of deferred compensation or due to a past practice, will be taxable (.10).

.05 *M. Duberstein*, SCt, 60-2 USTC ¶9515, 363 U.S. 278.

.10 Rev. Rul. 55-422, 1955-1 CB 14; *C. Schall*, CA-5, 49-1 USTC ¶9298, 174 F2d 893; *A.M. Hershman*, CA-6, 54-1 USTC ¶9267, 210 F2d 654; *A. Mutch*, CA-3, 54-1 USTC ¶9165, 209 F2d 390.

¶25,614 Deferred Compensation Arrangements. Tax-exempt organizations, such as a church or religious order, may set up deferred compensation arrangements for their employees. If the arrangement is a "qualified plan," then a limited portion of a clergy member's annual salary or wages may be deferred and excluded from his gross income until retirement (or until made available). In order to be qualified, the plan must meet certain participation, deferral, payout, trust and other requirements. Such plans are generally referred to as "Code Sec. 457 plans." For a detailed discussion of Code Sec. 457 plans, see ¶11,660 and following.

Code Sec. 401(k) plans

Prior to 1997, tax-exempt organizations such as churches and religious orders were prohibited from establishing deferred compensation arrangements known as Code Sec. 401(k) plans unless the plan was established before July 2, 1986. For plan years beginning in 1997, however, this prohibition is no longer applicable and tax-exempt organizations may establish Code Sec. 401(k) plans for their employees. For a detailed discussion of Code Sec. 401(k) plans, see ¶11,200 and following.

Keogh plans

Although members of the clergy are considered self-employed persons for social security purposes (see ¶25,625), they are generally not permitted to establish a qualified retirement plan for self-employed individuals, so called *Keogh* plans. This is because a member of the clergy is technically not self-employed. For example, a minister who performs services for which he is paid a salary is subject to right of control of the congregation. Thus, the salary paid is not really earnings from self-employment. It is only considered net earnings from self-employment for social security purposes, and not for income tax purposes. However, any amounts a member of the clergy receives directly from members of the congregation (such as fees for marriages, baptisms, etc.) are considered earnings from self-employment for all tax purposes.

Vow of poverty

Like compensation for services, retirement income received by a member of a religious order who is under a vow of poverty is not includible in the member's gross income where the member: (1) is employed at an institution associated with the church that exercises general and administrative supervision over the order; (2) performs services as an agent of the religious order; and (3) remits the income received to the religious order (.05). See ¶25,612.

.05 Rev. Rul. 83-126, 1983-2 CB 24.

¶25,615 Tax-Sheltered Annuities A tax-sheltered annuity (TSA) arrangement, also referred to as a Code Sec. 403(b) plan, is a special type of retirement or deferred compensation plan covering employees of public schools and certain tax-exempt organizations such as churches. A TSA is generally funded through a salary reduction agreement whereby an employee reduces his salary by a fixed amount to purchase an annuity contract or to establish a custodial account holding mutual fund shares. The annuity or custodial account may also be purchased by employer contributions. Like other retirement plans, if the TSA is a "qualified plan," then the employee may exclude from his gross income the amount deferred (or contributed by the employer) until retirement or until made available (.05). For a detailed discussion of the qualification requirements for TSAs, see ¶11,610.

Retirement income accounts

The rules relating to TSAs generally apply to "retirement income accounts." These are accounts established by a church or convention or association of churches (i.e., church pension board) for each of its employees. It is into each account that elective deferrals and employer contributions are made. However, unlike TSAs or custodial accounts, retirement income accounts do not have to be maintained by an insurer or custodian (.10).

In addition to retirement income accounts, a church-maintained retirement income program will not be considered as failing to satisfy the requirements for a TSA merely because the program is a defined benefit plan. If a church-maintained retirement income program that is otherwise a defined benefit plan provides a benefit that is based, in part, on the balance of a separate account of an employee, it is intended that the separate account can qualify as a defined contribution plan for purposes of the rules relating to retirement income accounts.

Self-employed clergy

Members of the clergy who are self-employed in connection with the exercise of their ministry are eligible to participate in "church plans" such as TSAs and retirement income accounts. This is because a church plan is any retirement plan established and operated by a church or convention or association of churches. Thus, a member of the clergy may not be an employee for income tax purposes, but will be treated as such for retirement plans purposes. All plans in which the self-employed clergy member participates in will be treated as one, for purposes of the applying any contribution limits.

Contribution limitations

The amount of contributions made to a TSA on behalf of employee that may be excluded from his gross income is subject to overlapping limitations. First, the amount that an employee may defer under a salary reduction agreement is limited to a certain dollar amount each year ($13,000 for 2004) (.15). Second, because a TSA is generally considered to be a type of defined contribution plan, the amount of annual contributions (annual additions) that the employer can make on behalf of an employee to the TSA is the lesser of: $41,000 (for 2004) or 100 percent of the employee's compensation. The total amount of compensation taken into account for this purpose is $205,000 (for 2004). A church may make contributions in excess of this limit, but only if the contribution is expressed as an annual addition and is limited to $10,000 for any one year and $40,000 for the employee's lifetime (.20)

Catch-up contributions. Employees who will be at least age 50 by the end of the year are able to make catch-up contributions to their plans. For 2004, the maximum contribution is $3,000 (.25).

Exclusion allowance. For tax years prior to 2002, a third limitation also applied, an "exclusion allowance" under Code Sec. 403(b)(2). The allowance was equal to 20 percent of the employee's includible compensation from the employer for the year, multiplied by the number of years of service, and then reduced by any amounts that were excluded from the employee's gross income in prior tax years (.30).

An employee could have made an election to choose alternative ways to calculate the exclusion allowance. One alternative would allow the employee to simply have the allowance determined under the limits on employer contributions to deferred compensation plans. This included the additional special election under which the annual additions limit could be increased to $10,000 per year and up to $40,000 for their lifetime (.35). A second alternative allowed qualified church employees to have the exclusion allowance equal the lesser of $4,000 or the employee's includible compensation for the year. This alternative was only available if the employee's adjusted gross income for the year did not exceed $17,000 (determined without regard to community property laws) (.40).

For this purpose, a qualified church employee included duly ordained, commissioned, or licensed ministers and lay employees of a tax-exempt organization controlled by or associated with a church. Thus, a qualified church employee was entitled to single-employer treatment under the exclusion allowance if he transferred from one organization to another within the same church. In addition, the includible compensation of a church employee who is a foreign missionary included the amount contributed by the church during the tax year for the purchase of a tax-sheltered annuity. A church employee is a foreign missionary for a tax year for which the employee's principal duties are the propagation of religious doctrine or the performance of sacerdotal functions or humanitarian good works for the church outside the United States.

Caution

CCH Analysts note that even though the Economic Growth and Tax Relief Reconciliation Act of 2001 (P.L. 107-16) eliminated the exclusion allowance limitation for tax years beginning in 2002, taxpayers must maintain proper record keeping in order to claim the exclusion allowance in tax years prior to 2002.

.05 Code Sec. 403(b).
.10 Code Sec. 403(b)(9).
.15 Code Sec. 402(g).
.20 Code Sec. 415(c).
.25 Code Sec. 414(v).
.30 Code Sec. 403(b)(2)(A).
.35 Code Secs. 403(b)(2)(B); 415(c)(7).
.40 Code Sec. 403(b)(2)(C).

Taxable Income - Housing Exclusion

¶25,618 Housing Exclusion - General. For income tax purposes, the gross income of a "minister of the gospel" does not include: (1) the rental value of a home, including utilities, furnished to him as a part of his compensation; or (2) the rental allowance paid to him as part of his compensation to the extent such allowance is used by him to rent or otherwise provide a home. The amount excluded cannot be more than the reasonable pay for the minister's services. In addition, such amounts are included as income for purposes of calculating self-employment taxes unless the clergy member is exempt from such taxes (see ¶25,624).

In order to qualify for the exclusion, the home or rental allowance must be provided as compensation for services which are ordinarily the duties of a minister of the gospel. This includes the performance of sacerdotal functions, the conduct of religious worship, the administration and maintenance of religious organizations and their integral agencies, and the performance of teaching and administrative duties at theological seminaries. In addition, the amount that may be excluded cannot be more than the reasonable pay for the clergy member's services (.05).

.05 Code Sec. 107; Reg. §1.107-1.

¶25,619 Housing Allowance. A minister of the gospel who receives a *housing allowance* may exclude the allowance from gross income to the extent it is used to directly pay expenses in providing a home. Any unused portion of the allowance must be included in the minister's gross income. For this purpose, expenses incurred in providing a home includes mortgage payments, rental payments, real estate taxes, and other costs of acquiring a home (i.e., insurance, legal fees, bank fees, title fees). It also includes any expenses incurred to maintain a home such as home improvements, minor repairs, the costs of utilities, and expenses for furnishing the home. The only expenses specifically excluded from the costs covered by the housing allowance are those for food and servants. These are considered as not directly related to providing a home (.05).

Ministers are allowed to deduct mortgage interest and real property interest on their homes even though they receive a parsonage allowance that is excludable from gross income. Ministers who were denied such deductions in prior years may apply for a refund for all open tax years (.10).

If a minister of the gospel does not incur any expenses in acquiring a home (i.e., mortgage, rent) but instead already owns a home, then he may still be eligible for the housing allowance so long as it is for actual expenses in maintaining the home. This not only includes utilities and minor repairs but also the cost of improving the home and the surrounding grounds. Thus, a minister could exclude from gross income the costs of building a new garage, constructing a new sidewalk or landscaping the area around the home (.15).

Caution

Prior to the clarification of the limit to the exclusion for payment of a housing allowance under Code Sec. 170(2), the IRS took the position that the exclusion was limited to the fair rental value of the minister's home, while the Tax Court concluded that it was not (.20). The Clergy Housing Clarification Act of 2002, however, provides that the exclusion may not exceed the fair market value of the home, including furniture, appurtenances, and the cost of utilities. This limit generally applies to tax years beginning after December 31, 2001. It does not apply retroactively to tax years beginning before January 1, 2002, unless the taxpayer filed a return after April 16, 2002, or filed before April 17, 2002, limiting the exclusion as clarified by the amendment (.25)

Designation of amount

A minister's church or other employing organization must designate any payment to the minister as a housing allowance. The designation must be made pursuant to an official action of the church and must be made advance of making the payment. If part of an allowance has not been officially designated, the minister must include the allowance in his gross income. If the minister is employed and paid by a local congregation, then the designation must come from the local congregation. Designation by a national church agency will not be effective unless the minister is directly employed by such agency (.30).

Regulations strongly imply that the designation must be in writing—that is, by means of an "employment contract . . . or in any other appropriate instrument evidencing such official action," such as the minutes of a church board meeting. However, the Tax Court has ruled that the regulations do not require the designation to be in writing. Instead, the court ruled that the designation requirement will be satisfied upon satisfactory proof of official action. For example, where a church retains its employees on an informal basis with no formal employment contract, an informal oral communication between the employer and the member of the clergy may suffice (.35).

However, if an exclusion is challenged by the IRS, the minister must be able to substantiate the housing allowance. Thus, the evidentiary problem may be avoided if a written document exists that shows the designation was made. A church board or congregation should record any designation and any action taken in making the designation. The record should also indicate the amount of the allowance and the dates when it will be paid. Adjustments in the amount may be made after the amount is fixed, but they must be made at the authorization of the board (.40).

Housing allowance examples

The following are some examples of the application of the housing allowance to ministers.

> ***Example 1:*** Anne is an ordained minister. She receives an annual salary of $36,000 and use of a parsonage which has a fair rental value (FRV) of $800 a month, including utilities. She has an accountable plan (see ¶25,468) for other business expenses such as travel. She may exclude the FRV of the parsonage from her gross income. However, the entire $9,600 ($800 × 12 months) must be included in income for self-employment tax purposes.
>
> ***Example 2:*** Burt, an ordained minister, is vice president of academic affairs at Holy Bible Seminary. His compensation package includes a salary of $80,000 per year and a $30,000 housing allowance. His housing costs for the year include mortgage payments of $15,000 and utilities of $3,000. The FRV of his home, as furnished, is $40,000 per year. Burt may exclude $18,000 ($15,000 + $3,000) from gross income but must include in income the other $12,000 of the housing

allowance. The entire $30,000 will be considered in arriving at net self-employment income.

Example 3: Carl is an ordained minister and has been in his church's employ for the last 20 years. His salary is $40,000 and his designated parsonage allowance is $15,000. Carl owns his own home with a FMV of $20,000. During the tax year he spends $3,000 on utilities, and $4,000 on real estate taxes and insurance. Carl may only exclude his actual expenses of $7,000 ($3,000 + $4,000) for income tax purposes. He may not exclude the FRV of his home. The entire $15,000 will be included in his income for self-employment tax purposes.

Example 4: Assume the same facts as in Example 3, except that Carl takes out a home equity loan and uses the proceeds to pay for his daughter's college tuition. The payments are $300 per month. Even though he has a loan secured by his home, the money was not used to "provide a home" and can't be used to compute the excludable portion of the parsonage allowance. The results are the same as for Example 3.

Example 5: Dan is an ordained minister and received $40,000 in salary plus a designated housing allowance of $12,000. He spent $12,000 on mortgage payments, $2,400 on utilities, and $2,000 on new furniture. The FRV of his home as furnished is $16,000. Dan's exclusion is limited to $12,000 even though his actual cost ($16,400) and the FRV of the home are more. He may not deduct his housing cost in excess of the designated allowance.

Example 6: Elaine is an ordained minister who receives $20,000 as a designated housing allowance. She and her husband live in one-half of a duplex which they own. The other half is rented. Mortgage payments for the duplex are $1,500 per month. Elaine's utilities are $150 per month for half of the duplex, her tenant pays his own from a separate meter. During the year, Elaine replaced carpeting throughout the structure at a cost of $6,000. Amounts allocable to the rented portion for mortgage interest, taxes, etc. would be reported on Schedule E. Her actual costs to provide a home were $13,800 ($9,000 for half the mortgage payments, $1,800 utilities, and $3,000 for half the carpeting and repairs). The FRV for her unit is the same as the rent she charges for the other half, which is $750 a month or $9,000. Elaine may exclude only $10,800, but the remaining $9,2000 of the housing allowance must be included gross income for income tax purposes.

.05 Code Sec. 107(2); Reg. §1.107-1(c)

.10 Code Sec. 265(a)(6).

.15 *J.L. Swaggart,* 48 TCM 759, CCH Dec. 41,394(M), TC Memo. 1984-409; IRS Letter Ruling 9115051, 1-16-91.

.20 Rev. Rul. 71-280, 1971-2 CB 92; *R.D. Warren,* 114 TC 343, Dec. 53,880.

.25 P.L. 107-181.

.30 Reg. §1.107-1(b).

.35 *M.L. Libman,* 44 TCM 370, CCH Dec. 39,161(M), TC Memo. 1982-377.

.40 *R.R. Eden,* 41 TC 605, CCH Dec. 26,637.

¶25,620 Minister of the Gospel. The parsonage and housing allowance exclusion is available only for "ministers of the gospel," which generally includes ministers, priests, and rabbis (i.e., those who have been ordained, commissioned or licensed by a church). However, the determination of who qualifies as a bona fide minister of the gospel is a fact and circumstances test, examining the type and characterization of the organization in combination with the nature of the ministerial duties. These duties or services generally include the performance of sacerdotal functions, the conduct of religious worship, the administration and maintenance of religious organizations and their integral agencies, and the performance of teaching and administrative duties at theological seminaries (.05).

If an ordained minister is not engaged in any ministerial services or duties, then he does not qualify for the parsonage or housing allowance exclusion. For example, a minister whose work primarily consists of preaching political tenets or who is an officer in a nonprofit corporation that assist churches with financial activities will be denied the exclusion (.10). Similarly, a minister who is a nursing home administrator is not eligible for the housing exclusion even if he is ordained (.15).

Teaching ministers

If a minister is not conducting religious worship ordinarily required in the exercise of his ministry, then the activities may be categorized as educational rather than religious and the minister will not qualify for the housing exclusion. However, if a ordained minister serves on the faculty of a school, college or university as a teacher or administrator, he may claim the housing exclusion if the school is an *integral part of a church.* It is not enough that the school is simply affiliated with a church, whether directly or indirectly. The school must be such an integral part of a church or religious organization that an ordained minister who serves on the faculty would be performing services in the exercise of their ministry. For example, a minister of music or education may not exclude a housing allowance if he only serves in an administrative function and does not perform the same religious functions as an ordained minister of the church (.20).

Factors to consider whether a school is an integral part of a church includes whether: (1) a religious organization continuously controls, manages, and maintains the school; (2) the trustees or directors of the institution must be approved or may be removed by the religious organization; (3) a religious organization incorporated the institution and any annual reports of finances and general operations are required to be made to the organization; and (4) in the event of dissolution of the institution its assets would be turned over to the religious organization (.25).

However, teachers and administrative staff who work for a school affiliated with a church do not qualify for the parsonage allowance. Such employees are hired as teachers and administrative staff and not as ministers of the gospel and none of the prescribed duties are equivalent to the services performed by a church minister (.30).

Theological students

A student of theology serving a required internship as an assistant pastor may not receive the housing exclusion unless he or she is ordained, commissioned, or licensed as a minister (.35).

Traveling ministers

An ordained minister who is a traveling evangelist may exclude amounts received from out-of-town churches visited if such amounts are designated as a housing allowance. The payments must actually be used to maintain the minister's *permanent* residence in order to qualify. If the minister rents out his permanent residence while traveling in the capacity of a traveling evangelist, he may exclude only the part of the housing allowance allocable to the time spent living at home (.40).

Retired ministers

Retired members of the clergy may also qualify for the parsonage or housing allowance exclusion for any amounts paid by a church for past service. These amounts are also not included in net earnings from self-employment. However, the surviving spouse of a retired ministers may not exclude any housing allowance provided. The designation of a payment to a retired minister as a housing allowance may be done by the general convention of a national religious domination. This rule applies so long as the local congregation authorizes the general convention to establish and maintain a unified pension system for all retired clergy members of the denomination (.45).

Cantors

The parsonage and housing allowance exclusion applies to Jewish cantors, even though they are not ordained. The cantor, however, must have a bona fide commission and must be employed by a congregation on a full-time basis to perform religious functions in observance of the Jewish faith (.50).

Chaplains

A qualified minister who is an employee of the United States or any political subdivision thereof (i.e, State, Territory, or possession of the United States) is considered to be in the exercise of his ministry provided the service performed includes such services as are ordinarily the duties of a minister. Thus, the minister is eligible for the parsonage or housing allowance exclusion. However, this rules does not apply to a chaplain in the Armed Forces of the United States, whose service is considered to be that of a commissioned officer, and not as a minister in the exercise of his ministry (.55). A chaplain of the Armed Forces may be able to exclude any quarters allowance (BAQ—Basic Allowance for Quarters), see ¶25,531.

.05 Code Sec. 107; Reg. §1.107-1(a).

.10 *J.D. Colbert,* 61 TC 449, CCH Dec. 32,410; Rev. Rul. 78-172, 1978-1 CB 35.

.15 Rev. Rul. 72-606, 1972-2 CB 78.

.20 Rev. Rul. 70-549, 1970-2 CB 16; Rev. Rul. 59-270, 1959-2 CB 44.

.25 Rev. Rul. 72-2606, 1972-2 CB 78.

.30 IRS Technical Advice Memorandum 200318002, 1-7-03.

.35 IRS Publication No. 525, "Taxable and Nontaxable Income."

.40 Rev. Rul. 64-326, 1964-2 CB 37; Rev. Rul. 72-588, 1972-2 CB 77.

.45 Rev. Rul. 75-22, 1975-1 CB 49; Rev. Rul. 72-249, 1972-1 CB 36.

.50 Rev. Rul. 58-221, 1958-1 CB 53.

.55 Reg. §1.170-1(a).

Employment Taxes

¶25,623 Tax Withholdings - General Whether an employer must withhold income and employment taxes for a given worker depends on whether a worker is classified as an employee or independent contractor. The distinction is generally made on common law grounds. The basic test is whether the employer controls the manner in which the work is performed. Actual control need not be exercised by the employer, provided the employer has the right to control the employee when it is appropriate and necessary. The control test must be applied by taking into account the nature of the work performed. When the worker is a professional, the extent of control necessary for the professional to qualify as an employee is less than that needed for a nonprofessional worker performing routine and mechanical duties.

Generally, a member of the clergy who is employed by a church or congregation for a salary is considered a common-law employee. Typically, this would mean that the church would be required to withholding both income and employment taxes from the clergy member's salary. However, special rules apply to members of the clergy, the most important of which is that for employment tax purposes, the clergy member is considered to be self-employed. As a practical matter, a member of the clergy and the church (or congregation) employing him can tailor their relationship in such a way that benefits both, while at the same time, complying with both the letter and spirit of the law. For example, if a church governing body wants to have significant control over its clergy, it should hire them as employees, while at the same time structuring its employee expense reimbursement plan in such a way that the minister does not suffer financially as a result of no longer reporting income and expenses on Schedule C.

¶25,624 Income Tax Withholding. Because a member of the clergy who is employed by a church or congregation for a salary is generally considered a common-law employee, any income from the exercise of the clergy member's ministry is considered wages for income tax purposes. However, the church or congregation that employs the clergy member is not required to withhold income taxes from his salary. Instead, the clergy member is required to pay his own income taxes to the IRS in the same manner as self-employed individuals (.05).

Alternatively, the clergy member may arrange to have income taxes withheld from his compensation by means of a voluntary withholding agreement with his employer. If the employer agrees to such an arrangement, the clergy member must furnish the church or congregation with a completed Form W-4, and the church will then withhold on the basis of the standard withholding tables. The agreement between the clergy member and the church must be in writing and must contain: (1) the name, address, and social security number of the clergy member; (2) the name and address of the church; and (3) a statement that the clergy member desires the withholding of income taxes from his wages. The agreement may be terminated at any time by means of a written statement (.10).

.05 Code Sec. 3401(a)(9); Reg. §31.3401(a)(9)-1.

.10 Code Sec. 3402(p); Reg. §31.3402(p)-1.

¶25,625 Self-Employment Taxes. For social security and medicare purposes, a member of the clergy is considered to be self-employed regardless of the determination under the common law rules. This means that a member of the clergy is subject to self-employment taxes on any wages received for services performed in the exercise of his ministry or in the exercise of his duties as required by a religious order (.05). However, self-employment taxes will not apply if the clergy member: (1) is a member of a religious order who has taken a vow of poverty; or (2) an exemption has been requested and received from the IRS (see ¶25,626).

A member of the clergy, for this purpose, includes any individuals who are duly ordained, commissioned, or licensed by a religious body constituting a church or church organization. If a church or denomination ordains some clergy and licenses or commissions others, anyone license or commissioned must be able to perform substantially all the religious functions of an ordained minister to be treated as a member of the clergy for self-employment tax purposes. Religious functions includes the authority to conduct religious worship, perform sacerdotal functions, and administer ordinances or sacraments according to the prescribed tenets and practices of that church or denomination.

Net earnings from self-employment

Self-employment taxes are calculated on the net earnings from self-employment. This means the gross income derived by the clergy member from his trade or business of being a member of the clergy less any allowable deductions. Gross income includes: (1) salaries and fees for ministerial services; (2) offering received for marriages, baptisms, funerals, etc.; (3) the value of meals and lodging provided for the convenience of the church; and (4) any amount the church pays toward the income tax or self-employment tax liability of the clergy member. Gross income from self-employment also includes the fair rental value of any parsonage or housing allowance provided, even when such amounts are excluded from gross income for income tax purposes.

A clergy member is allowed to deduct from gross income all allowable unreimbursed trade or business expenses that are incurred in performing ministerial services as a common-law employee of the church. Also, nonemployee ministerial expenses such as costs incurred in performing marriages or baptisms may be deducted. However, contributions to an individual retirement arrangement (IRA) are not deductible.

> ***Example:*** Michael receives a salary from the church of $20,000 and a parsonage allowance of $12,000. He has unreimbursed employee business expenses of

$5,200 (before excluding nondeductible amounts attributable to his exempt income). Michael's net earnings from self-employment are $26,800 ($20,000 + $12,000 – $5,200). All of Michael's unreimbursed business expenses are deductible for self-employment tax purposes. Code Sec. 265 requirement of allocating business expenses to exempt income applies to income tax computation, not self-employment tax computations.

Husband and wife missionaries

If a husband and wife are both duly ordained, commissioned, or licensed ministers of a church and have an agreement that each will perform specific services for which they are paid jointly or separately, they must divide self-employment income according to the agreement. If the agreement is with one spouse only and the other spouse is not paid for any specific duties, amounts received for their services are included in only the self-employment income of the spouse having the agreement.

.05 Code Sec. 1401; Code Sec. 1402.

¶25,626 Religious Exemptions from Self-Employment Tax. A member of the clergy may be exempt from the obligation to pay self-employment taxes if they meet certain requirements. These requirements are divided into two areas: those members of religious orders that have taken a vow of poverty, and those members of a religious order opposed to the acceptance of public insurance. The exemption only applies to amounts earned for performing religious services (see ¶25,625).

Vow of poverty

A member of a religious order who has taken a vow of poverty is automatically exempt from self-employment taxes for any amount earned for services performed as an agent of the order or its agencies. The earnings are considered the income of the religious order. Thus, no exemption application needs to be filed. However, any work performed for an organization outside the religious order or work not required or done on behalf of the order are subject to taxation. In these cases, the member of the order is considered an employee outside the organization (.05).

The religious order may elect certain members to be covered by the self-employment tax by filing Form SS-16. The coverage can be made retroactively for up to 20 calendar quarters before the quarter in which the order files the certificate. If the election is made, the order pays both the employer's and employee's share of the tax.

Opposed to insurance

Ministers, members of certain religious orders who have *not* taken a vow of poverty, and Christian Science practitioners are subject to the self-employment tax unless they specifically request an exemption. To qualify for the exemption, the taxpayer must be conscientiously opposed to the acceptance of any public insurance that makes payments because of death, disability, old age, or retirement, makes payments toward, or provides services for medical care (including social security benefits). The opposition must be based on the individuals religious consideration and because of the principles and discipline of the individual's particular religious denomination. (.10). Where an employer and an employee are both members and adherents of a recognized religious organization that is opposed to insurance and have both properly filed the required forms (see below), both are exempt from employment taxes (.15).

The exemption is limited to income with respect to services performed by the individual in his capacity as a minister, religious order member, or Christian Science practitioner. Accordingly, the individual's opposition need not extend to the acceptance of all public insurance payments, just those based on or measured by earnings from services performed in the capacity as a minister, religious order member, or Christian Science practitioner. Also, an individual may obtain an exemption even though he does not oppose purchasing private insurance from a commercial carrier (.20).

To request the exemption from self-employment tax, the taxpayer must file an application on Form 4361, "Application for Exemption from Self-Employment Tax for Use by Ministers, Members of Religious Orders and Christian Science Practitioners." The application must be filed by the due date (including extensions) for filing the individual's income tax return for the second year in which the individual has at least $400 of net earnings from self-employment for services performed in the exercise of his duties as a minister, religious order member, or Christian Science practitioner (.25).

On the application, the taxpayer must certify a statement proclaiming his religious or conscientious opposition to public insurance, as well as a statement that he has not previously elected social security coverage. A minister and religious order member (but not Christian Science practitioner) must also include a statement that he has informed the ordaining, commissioning, or licensing body of the church or order of his opposition. The application must be approved by the IRS before the exemption is effective. Approval occurs only when the IRS has verified that the applicant is aware of the grounds on which he may receive an exemption and indeed seeks an exemption on those grounds. Verification is completed on a certificate supplied by the IRS and which must be returned within 90 days after its issuance. Once, an exemption is granted it is generally irrevocable.

Second-faith ministers

A clergy member who is reordained in another faith as a result of having changed his religious beliefs regarding the acceptance of public insurance may file an application for exemption from self-employment taxes. The application must be filed by the due date (including extensions) for filing the individual's income tax return for the second year in which the individual has at least $400 of net earnings from self-employment for services performed in the exercise of his religious duties. The imposition of the two year time limit does not impermissibly burden the clergy member's right to freely exercise his religion. It is rationally related to a legitimate government interest. Moreover, the limitation period depends not only on the date of the clergy member's ordination, but also on the the amount of income he earns, which is a secular factor (.30).

.05 Code Sec. 1402(c).

.10 Code Sec. 1402(g)(1).

.15 Code Sec. 3127.

.20 Reg. §§1.1402(c)-5(a)(2); Reg. §1.1402(e)-2A(a).

.25 Reg. §§1.1402(e)-2(A) - 1.1402(e)-5(A).

.30 *J.M. Ballinger*, CA-10, 84-1 USTC ¶9286, 728 F2d 1287, aff'g TC, 78 TC 752, CCH Dec. 38,979.

Deductions for Ministers

¶25,628 General Deduction Rules. Members of the clergy can claim deductions on their income tax returns generally in the same manner as all other individual taxpayers. Thus, a clergy member may be able to deduct nonbusiness expenses that are itemized, the expenses incurred in earning any self-employment income, and unreimbursed business expenses of being an employee. With respect to business expenses, one exception applies. A special allocation is required of expenses attributable to any excluded parsonage or housing allowance.

Itemized deductions

Like all other taxpayers, clergy members can claim a deduction for certain expenses that are itemized on their tax returns. This includes medical expenses, casualty losses, charitable contributions, and unreimbursed employee expenses (see ¶25,629). Clergy members are also allowed to deduct mortgage interest and property tax on their homes even though they receive a parsonage allowance (.05). In the case of a clergy member who is required to turn over a portion of his secular earnings to a religious order, the amount that is turned over can be claimed as a charitable deduction. For a detailed discussion of itemized deductions, see ¶6501 and following.

Self-employment expenses

A clergy member may claim a deduction for all expenses incurred in earning any income from self-employment. For example, if in the exercise of his ministry a member of the clergy is self-employed, then all expenses incurred in earning his salary from the church would be deductible. On the other hand, if a clergy member is an employee, then only those expenses that are incurred in producing self-employment income (such as for baptisms, marriages, etc.), are deductible. Deductible self-employment expenses are reported on Schedule C of Form 1040.

A self-employed clergy may also claim a deduction for a portion of the amounts he pays for health insurance premiums and long-term care insurance for himself and his family (see ¶6440). The deduction is only allowed if the clergy member is not eligible to participate in his (or his spouse's) employer's plan. In addition, the expenses may not be taken as a medical expense deduction or be used to reduce net earnings from self-employment.

Business expenses

In general, the unreimbursed expenses of a clergy member of being an employee are deductible but only if the aggregate amount of these expenses and other miscellaneous itemized deductions exceeds two percent of the taxpayer's adjusted gross income (see ¶6035). Such business expenses include such things as: travel, meal, and lodging expenses; transportation expenses; home office expenses; and moving expenses. See ¶25,629 for a discussion of specific issues regarding these expenses and clergy members.

However, because a clergy member may receive business income exempt from income taxes (parsonage or housing allowance), a portion of business expenses related to the production of that income is not deductible. This is because if a deduction were allowed, the taxpayer would receive a double tax benefit by omitting the income and deducting the expenses incurred in the production of that income. The nondeductible portion of business expenses is calculated by multiplying the total business expenses by the following fraction: Exempt parsonage or housing allowance ÷ all income (taxable and nontaxable) earned from the clergy member's ministry. Income and expenses for this purpose includes items that relate to the ministerial services the taxpayer performs both as an employee and a self-employed person.

> ***Example:*** During his tax year, Alan, an ordained minister, receives a salary of $28,000 for his ministerial services, $10,000 as a tax-exempt housing allowance, and $2,000 for weddings and baptisms. He also incurred $4,000 in unreimbursed expenses connected with his ministerial services, $3,500 of which is related to his ministerial salary, and the remaining $500 related to the weddings and baptisms. The nondeductible portion of Alan's expenses related to his ministerial salary is $875 ($3,500 × ($10,000 ÷ $40,000)). The nondeductible portion of A's expenses related to weddings and baptisms is $125 ($500 × ($10,000 ÷ $40,000)). Thus, the amount of business expenses Alan may deduct is $3,000 subject to the general limitations on miscellaneous itemized deductions.

> ***Example:*** Assume the same facts as above, except that Alan's actual housing costs was only $6,000, which is less than both the housing allowance and the fair market value of his home. The nondeductible portion of Alan's expenses related to his ministerial salary would be $525 ($3,500 × ($6,000 ÷ $40,000). The nondeductible portion of Alan's expenses related to his ministerial salary would be $75 ($500 ×

($6,000 ÷ $40,000)). Thus, the total amount of business expenses Alan may deduct is $3,400 subject to the general limitations on miscellaneous itemized deductions.

The rule regarding the allocation of expenses to tax exempt income does not apply to a taxpayer's deduction of home mortgage interest or taxes on the home.

.05 Code Sec. 265(a)(6).

¶25,629 Business Deductions for Clergy. Subject to the rules discussed at ¶25,628, a variety of business deductions—some of which have been mentioned—are available to members of the clergy. These deductions should not be overlooked as they can save significant amounts of taxes.

Car costs

The most common type of deduction that clergy members may claim involves the cost of operating a car for church business. Frequently, clergy members must visit members of the church either at an individual's home or other institutions such as a hospital. An clergy member's ministry may also entail running errands for the church or even chauffeuring church guests. A clergy member may deduct the costs of operating and maintaining a car, truck, or other vehicle for such purposes. A clergy member may not deduct the cost of operating a vehicle for personal use, such as driving between his home and the church (.05). For a detailed discussion of deducting car expenses see ¶8101 and following.

Like other individual taxpayers, members of the clergy may compute their car expense deductions by using either the actual expense or standard mileage method. Under the actual cost method, a taxpayer may deduct the actual costs of operating a vehicle for business purposes including gas, oil, repairs, license fees, insurance, and depreciation. Under the standard mileage method, the taxpayer may deduct a set amount for each business mile put on a vehicle. The standard mileage rate is 37.5 cents a mile for 2004 (.10).

The deductions as computed under both methods are based on the number of miles that are driven on church business. Thus, it is advisable that members of the clergy keep accurate records of the business miles they use a vehicle for in order to obtain maximum deductions. If the actual expense method is used, this includes keeping any receipts for services performed in operating or maintaining a vehicle (.15).

Travel and entertainment

Like other taxpayers, members of the clergy may deduct the cost of any travel, meals, and entertainment for church incurred for business purposes. For example, the costs of traveling to and from church conventions or meetings held outside the clergy member's church is located are deductible. The same is true for any meals or lodging expenses incurred while attending such meetings. Entertainment expenses may also be deducted —such as providing meals for church guests and officials. For example, a clergy member was able to claim a deduction for the cost of meals he provided to individuals at the church's prayer meetings (.20). Travel, meal, and entertainment business costs are only deductible if they are substantiated. This includes a description of the business purpose of the expenditure, and in the case of entertainment expenditures, the name of the recipient. For a discussion of the deduction of travel, meal, and entertainment costs, see ¶8201.

Home office expenses

In many cases, a clergy member may spend part of his time working out of his home. If this is the case, the clergy member may be able to claim a deduction for the expenses of using a portion of his home for business purposes (.25). The home office must be used exclusively and regularly by the clergy member in order to claim deduction. Further, the deduction may not be available if the clergy member receives a parsonage or housing allowance. This is because the expenses incurred in earning tax-exempt income are generally not deductible. A deduction would permit the clergy member to have a double tax benefit. Moreover, the deduction may not be allowed if the taxpayer is reimbursed by his church for the expense — by means of an office allowance (.30).

Even though home office costs may not be deductible, the costs of items that are found in the office can still be deducted. These include: office equipment, typewriters, tables, file cabinets, and office equipment if the life of these items is less than one year. If the life of these items is more than one year, a depreciation deduction can be claimed. Generally, deductions can also be claimed for the full cost of periodicals, books, reference materials, machine rentals and dues paid to professional organizations, subject to the two-percent floor.

For a discussion of home office expenses see ¶7336 and following.

Moving expenses

Ministers who move from employment at one church to another church may be entitled to deduct moving expenses (.35). Any expenses that are reimbursed, of course, are not deductible. Some of the expenses that may be claimed include any costs incurred in the actual move; moving the minister, his family and his personal property, and transportation and lodging costs to the new residence. However, it should be noted that moving costs are deductible only if the new church is more than 50 miles farther from the minister's former residence than the former church. These expenses are taken as an "above-the-line" deduction, that is, a deduction from gross income, in arriving at adjusted gross income. See ¶25,004.

.05 Code Sec. 162(a).

.10 Rev. Proc. 2003-76, I.R.B. 2003-43.

.15 Reg. §1.162-17.

.20 *C.A. Onstott,* 41 TCM 827, CCH Dec. 37,668(M), TC Memo. 1981-50.

.25 Code Sec. 280A.

.30 Code Sec. 265; *M.H. Dalan,* 55 TCM 370, CCH Dec. 44,633(M), TC Memo. 1988-106.

.35 Code Sec. 217.

ACTORS, ARTISTS, AUTHORS AND MUSICIANS

Introduction

¶25,631 Authors, artists, actors and musicians encounter many tax situations faced by other taxpayers. However, situations involving business expense deductions or the estate and gift tax consequences of the transfer of an intangible asset are of special interest to creative persons. Other matters of special interest, such as charitable deductions for gifts of one's own creative work and incorporation, are also discussed herein.

Amounts Included in Income

¶25,633 Income on Sale of Creative Works. Generally, gain realized on the sale or exchange or property is included in a taxpayer's gross income. This includes the gain from the sale or exchange of work created by the personal efforts of an artist, author, musician, or other creative taxpayer such as copyrights, literary, musical or artistic compositions, letters, memos, or similar property. Because such property is created in whole or in part by the personal efforts of a taxpayer, any gain from the sale or exchange of such property is treated as ordinary income not a return of capital. For this purpose, the personal efforts of a taxpayer means that the individual affirmatively contributes to the creation of the property or directs and guides others in the performance of such work. However, this does not include any taxpayer, such as a corporate executive, who merely has administrative control of artists, authors, musicians, or other creative taxpayers. "Similar property" includes such property as a theatrical production, a radio program, a newspaper cartoon strip, or any other property eligible for copyright protection (whether under statute or common law), a manuscript, a diary, a log or journal, a drawing or a photograph. It also includes any royalties received from copyrights on literary, musical, artistic, or other similar work (.05).

.05 Code Sec. 61(a)(6); IRS Publication 544, "Sales and Other Dispositions of Assets for Use in Preparing 2003 Returns."

¶25,634 Foreign Earned Income. Taxpayers who live and work abroad may elect to exclude from gross income any "earned income" from sources outside the United States. Earned income for this purpose includes any income accrued to the taxpayer from the application of his personal skills, whether received in the form of wages, salaries, professional fees or otherwise. Thus, any gain from the sale or exchange of work by an artists, writer, actor, or musician to a foreign purchaser is foreign earned income eligible for the income exclusion. However, the exclusion is limited and the artist, writer, actor, or musician must meet the bona fide residence or physical presence tests discussed at ¶17,265 and following (.05).

.05 Code Secs. 911(a) -911(b); *M. Tobey*, 60 TC 227, CCH Dec. 31,971 (acq. Rev. Rul. 79-85, 1979-1 CB 246).

Deductions and Credits

¶25,636 Trade or Business Expenses. Generally, a taxpayer engaged in a "trade or business" may deduct from his gross income all the ordinary and necessary expenses in conducting that trade or business (see ¶7101 and following). A taxpayer is engaged in a trade or business if he is involved in the activity: (1) with continuity and regularity; and (2) with the primary purpose of making income or a profit. A sporadic activity, a hobby, or an amusement diversion does not qualify as a trade or business. Whether an artist, etc., engages in an activity with the requisite intention of making a profit is one of fact to be resolved on the basis of all the surrounding facts and circumstances of the case (.05).

The expectation of profit need not be a reasonable one, it is sufficient if the taxpayer has a bona fide expectation of realizing a profit. However, the burden of proving the requisite intent is on the taxpayer and the mere assertion of the taxpayer's expectation is not enough. On the other hand, actual profits are not necessary in order for a taxpayer to be engaged in a trade or business of being a writer, artist, actor, or musician (.10).

Writers

Courts have not been easily persuaded that individuals are engaged in the trade or business of being a writer. For example, a full-time pilot who had been writing for over 25 years was not considered to be engaged in the trade or business of being a writer because of the absence of any expectation by the taxpayer of a profit (.15). Similarly, a full-time employee who wrote two books was also not in the trade or business of being a writer because he failed to present evidence of participation in a business other than that of being an employee (.20). On the other hand, a full-time attorney who spent 30 hours a week taking photographs for a book was found to be engaged in a the trade or business of an author even though he was also in the trade or business of being a lawyer, and even though he had not yet produced a book (.25). In cases such as this, where a taxpayer is found to be engaged in the trade or business of being a writer or author, expenses such as supplies, travel costs, compensation for services (e.g., typing), and rentals (e.g., personal computers) are deductible whether or not itemized.

Artists

An artist's history of losses may not be as important a factor as in other fields in determining whether the taxpayer had a bona fide intention to derive a profit from his artwork. This is because the archetypal "struggling artist" must first achieve public acclaim before his work will command a price sufficient to provide him with a profit (.30). Thus, an artist who experienced six years of unprofitable artistic activities was nonetheless found to have had an intention to derive a profit when she set up an art gallery for her work and attempted to have her work shown in other galleries (.35). Among the expenses an artist may deduct include expenses for a studio, supplies and books, traveling costs, art classes, professional dues, subscription costs, and any other expenses for creating, exhibiting and selling art such as shipping charges.

Actors

The reasonableness of whether a taxpayer has an intention of making a profit can be an important factor in determining whether he is engaged in the trade or business of being an actor. For example, a full-time government employee was found to be engaged in the trade or business of being an actor where he devoted a significant amount of his time to acting classes, and attempting to obtain acting jobs, and joined a prestigious actor's union (.40). Among the expenses an actor may deduct includes acting lesson, resumes, photographs, costumes, wigs, and expenses to develop influential business contacts. Actors may also deduct a variety of medical expenses attributable to employment as an actor, including physical training or dental work.

Musicians

A taxpayer is considered to be in the trade or business of being a musician only if he is primarily motivated by the expectation of profit from his musical activity and can be reasonably expected to produce a profit. Among the expenses a musician may deduct include the cost of music lessons to maintain and improve skills, purchasing music, costumes for performances, and insurance, repairs, and transportation of the taxpayer's musical instrument (.45). If the useful life of the musical instrument is more than one year, its cost should be depreciated under the Modified Accelerated Cost Recovery System over the instrument's recovery period (see ¶9100).

.05 Code Sec. 162(a); Reg. §1.162-1(a).

.10 *R.P. Groetzinger*, SCt, 87-1 USTC ¶9191, 480 U.S. 23; *M.C. Dreicer*, 78 TC 642, CCH Dec. 38,948.

.15 *C.A. Nemish*, CA-9, 72-1 USTC ¶9135, 452 F2d 611.

.20 *M.L. Groder*, 19 TCM 1124, CCH Dec. 24,384(M), TC Memo. 1960-208.

.25 *P. Snyder*, CA-10, 82-1 USTC ¶9285, 674 F2d 1359.

.30 *C. West Churchman*, 68 TC 696, CCH Dec. 34,559.

.35 *B.E. Adams*, 25 TCM 1239, CCH Dec. 28,166(M), TC Memo. 1966-242.

.40 *J.M. Green*, 58 TCM 606, CCH Dec. 46,133(M), TC Memo. 1989-599.

.45 *C.W. Elliot*, DC N.Y., 66-1 USTC ¶9185, 250 FSupp 322.

¶25,637 Production-of-Income Expenses. Even if a writer, artist, actor or musician is not engaged in a trade or business, expenses for his activities may still be deductible if such expenses are incurred primarily for the production of income. Similar to determining whether an artist, etc., is engaged in a trade or business, the determination of whether a creative activity is carried on primarily for the production of income is based on all the facts and circumstances of each case (.05). The difference between the two standards, however, is in scope. Although an entire enterprise is considered when determining if a artist, etc., is engaged in the trade or business of being an artist, etc., a single transaction may be carried on for the production of income. Thus, qualification of an expense as incurred for the production of income is somewhat easier than qualifying a taxpayer as engaged in a trade or business. But as a consequence, expenses for the production of income do not have the same tax advantages as expenses incurred for a trade or business. Instead of deducting business expenses as an adjustment to income to arrive at adjusted gross income (AGI), expenses for the production of income may be taken only as miscellaneous deductions from AGI and then only if the taxpayer itemizes and meets the two-percent minimum (see ¶6035).

.05 Code Sec. 212; Reg. §1.212-1.

¶25,638 Hobby Loss Limitations. If a writer, artist, actor or musician is not considered engaged in a trade or business or engaged in an activity for the production of income, then the hobby loss rules apply. Under these rules, a taxpayer may still claim a deduction for expenses incurred while pursuing his activity, but only subject to strict limitations on the type of expenses involved and the amount of income earned from the activity. For a description of the hobby loss limitations, see (see ¶10,001 and following). The key factor that indicates that an artist, etc., is engaged in a hobby, and not in a trade or business, is the lack of a bona fide expectation of realizing a profit. If hobby expenses are deductible, then they are only deductible as miscellaneous itemized deductions subject to the two-percent adjusted gross income limit.

¶25,639 Employee Business Expenses. Many writers, artists, actors and musicians are employees and as such may deduct all the ordinary and necessary business expenses of being an employee. Generally, if such expenses are reimbursed by the employer, they are deductible from gross income but in general this deduction is given effect by the exclusion of the reimbursement from the employees taxable wages reported on Form W-2. Unreimbursed employee business expenses are deductible only as miscellaneous itemized deductions subject to the two-percent of adjusted gross income limit (see ¶7295).

However, unreimbursed employee business expenses may be deducted from the taxpayer's gross income (i.e., above the line) if the taxpayer is a "qualified performing artist." A qualified performing artist is an individual who: (1) performs services in the performing arts during the tax year for at least two employers; (2) has total business deductions attributable to the performance of such services that exceed 10 percent of the income received from such services; and (3) has adjusted gross income of $16,000 or less (determined prior to application of this provision). Employers from which an individual receives less than $200 for his services are not taken into account for purposes of meeting qualification (1), above (.05).

If the individual is married, the couple must file a joint return in order to deduct the performer's business expenses against adjusted gross income. If both spouses are performing artists, their expenses and income from performing services are applied separately. However, the $16,000 adjusted gross income limitation applies to the couple's combined income on their joint return.

.05 Code Secs. 62(a)(2)(B), (b).

¶25,640 Home Office Expenses. Like other taxpayers, an author, artist, actor or musician is permitted a limited deduction for expenses that relate to a portion of his home (or separate structure appurtenant to the home) used exclusively on a regular basis as the principle place of business (.05). For example, an artist who uses the attic to his home as a studio or a writer who uses a room in his home to write may deduct expenses related to the regular use of those rooms for the business purposes. On the other hand, an actor who uses a room in his house to learn lines or rehearse by himself, while he also rehearses at a theatre, would probably not be able to deduct expenses related to the use of the room. If the author, artist, actor or musician is an employee, then the business use of the home must be for the convenience of the employer (.10). For a detailed description of the home office expense rules, see ¶7336 and following.

If the taxpayer is an employee, then any allowable home office expenses may be taken only as miscellaneous itemized deductions subject to the two-percent adjusted gross income limit. However, if the taxpayer's employer rents the home office from the taxpayer, then the deduction is disallowed. If the taxpayer is not an employee, but is self-employed as an artist, etc., then any allowable home office expenses are deductible from the taxpayer's gross income (i.e., above-the-line).

Planning Note

CCH Analysts note that self-employed individuals who claim a deduction for business use of their home must file Form 8829, "Expenses for Business Use of the Home," along with their Schedule C.

.05 Code Sec. 280A.

.10 *K.V. Popov*, CA-9, 2001-1 USTC ¶50,353, rev'g in part and rem'd 76 TCM 695, CCH Dec. 52,920(M).

¶25,641 Charitable Contributions. An author, artist, or musician may be allowed a limited deduction for the contribution of original work created by him to a charitable, religious, educational, public or scientific organization, or a national, state or local governmental unit. An original work, such as a copyright or literary, musical, or artistic composition, is considered ordinary income property when donated. As such, the value of the original work is its fair market value less any amount that would be treated as ordinary income if the work was sold. In effect, this means that the amount of a charitable deduction for an artist, etc., of his original work is limited to the cost basis in the property (e.g., cost of materials, wages paid to assistants). Thus, when the artist's, etc., cost basis is small, as is often the case, there is little income tax incentive to make a charitable contribution of the original work. However, the artist, etc., may wish to make a charitable contribution for reasons other than tax savings, for example, to help a charity's fund-raising efforts (.05).

Charitable contributions are deductible from the taxpayer's gross income (i.e., above-the-line). However, the taxpayer must be sure prior to donating the original work to any organization, that contributions to that organization are deductible. If the value of the original work is $250 or more, the taxpayer must also must maintain a record of the contribution by a contemporaneous written acknowledgment from the donee organization of the contribution. For a detailed description of the requirements of charitable contributions, see ¶6575 and following.

Gifts of services

A charitable contribution deduction generally is limited to gifts of money or property. The value of professional or personal services rendered to a charity is not deductible as a charitable contribution (.10). For instance, a singer or actor who performs gratuitously at a benefit performance for a charity may not deduct the value of his performance. On the other hand, unreimbursed expenses incident to rendering services, such as travel, meals and lodging costs, may be deductible (.15).

.05 Code Sec. 170.

.10 *C.L. Etheridge,* 36 TCM 724, CCH Dec. 34,450(M), TC Memo. 1977-175.

.15 Reg. §1.170A-1(g).

¶25,642 Casualty and Theft Losses. An author, artist or musician who suffers a casualty or theft loss of his own creative work may be able to claim a deduction for the loss regardless of whether he is engaged in the trade or business of being an author, artist or musician. The amount of the deduction is generally limited to the lesser of: (1) the decrease in the fair market value of the property as a result of the casualty or theft; or (2) the adjusted basis of the property. Any amount of reimbursement such as insurance will reduce the amount of the deduction and may in fact produce a casualty or theft gain if the insurance exceeds the adjusted basis in the property (.05).

If the creative work was not used in the taxpayer's trade or business or for income-producing purposes, the deduction is reduced further by $100 for each casualty or theft loss plus 10 percent of the taxpayer's adjusted gross income. Adjusted gross income is determined without regard to gains, losses or involuntary conversions of property used in a trade or business. For this purpose, property used in a trade or business does not include copyrights, or literary, musical or artistic compositions, or similar property. If several items are destroyed in a single event, only one $100 reduction must be taken (.10).

Because an artist's, etc., adjusted basis is usually very small, there may be little tax benefit in deducting the loss of his creative work. However, any casualty or theft loss of the creative work (or any gain) may be netted with the taxpayer's other personal casualty and theft gains or losses for the year. For a detailed discussion of casualty or theft losses, see ¶6305 and following.

.05 Code Sec. 165.

.10 Code Sec. 165(h).

¶25,643 Depreciation. An author, artist, actor or musician who is engaged in the trade or business of being an author, artist, actor or musician may depreciate the cost of any capital expenditure (i.e., purchase an asset with a useful life of more than one year) over several tax years. For example, a musician may depreciate the cost of his musical instrument over the appropriate recovery period if he can establish that the instrument is used in his trade or business of being a musician (.05). In addition, an artist who uses a portion of his home for a studio may depreciate any portion of the cost of his home which is used regularly and exclusively for his trade or business of being an artist (see ¶25,640).

Tangible assets used in a trade or business are generally depreciated under the Modified Accelerated Cost Recovery System (MACRS). Purchased intangible assets may be depreciable under Code Sec. 197. See ¶25,100 and following.

.05 *B. P. Liddle*, 95-2 USTC ¶50,488; *C.W. Elliot*, DC-N.Y., 66-1 USTC ¶9185, 250 FSupp 322.

Self-Employment Taxes

¶25,647 Self-Employment Taxes. An author, artist, actor or musician is liable for any self-employment taxes on his income if he is engaged in the trade or business of being an author, artist, actor or musician, and is not engaged in the trade or business of being an employee. Income for this purpose includes any royalties received by the taxpayer. The determination of whether a taxpayer is engaged in the trade or business of being an author, artist, actor or musician is the same as for the deduction of business expenses (see ¶25,636). For a detailed discussion of self-employment taxes, see ¶25,701 and following.

Estate and Gift Taxes

¶25,649 Estate and Gift Taxes Generally. For federal estate tax purposes, the gross estate of an author, artist or musician includes the fair market value of his creative work which he owns at the time of his death. In addition, an author, artist or musician who transfers any of his creative work during his lifetime without receiving full and adequate consideration will be liable for federal gift taxes. Not all gifts, however, are taxable. A separate annual exclusion applies to each person to which a gift is made. For 2004, the annual exclusion is $11,000 (for 2003 and 2002, the exclusion was also $11,000; prior to 2002, the exclusion was $10,000). In addition, gifts of services, such as a gratuitous acting or musical performance, are not subject to the federal gift tax so long as the service does not involve the transfer of property that has value. Other gifts may also be exempt from taxation, see ¶20,260.

For tax years prior to 2004, the estate and gift taxes were linked through unified rates as well as a unified lifetime credit that individuals use to reduce their estate and gift tax liabilities. For example, if an individual currently uses a portion of the applicable credit amount against a gift tax liability, the amount of the individual's future estate tax liability may be increased because the total available applicable credit will have been reduced. After 1997, the unified credit was replaced with an "applicable credit amount," since the tax rates for gift and estate taxes are no longer unified. For 2004, the applicable credit amount is $555,800, which eliminates estate taxes on a total of $1.5 million (the "applicable exclusion amount") of taxable estates. The applicable exclusion amount for estate taxes will remain at $1.5 million for 2005, and will then be gradually increased to $3.5 million by 2009. However, the applicable exclusion amount for gift taxes is, and will remain at, $1 million, absent further modifications by Congress.

Planning Note

CCH Analysts note that the gradual increase in the applicable exclusion amount for estate taxes and the gradual reduction in the unified tax rates occurred as a result of the Economic Growth and Tax Relief Reconciliation Act of 2001 (EGTRRA) (P.L. 107-16). In addition, EGTRRA repealed the estate tax in 2010. However, due to a sunset provision in the law, the rates are scheduled to be reinstated to the same levels as before EGTRRA's passage (.05).

.05 Code Secs. 2001, 2010 and 2210, as amended and added by the Economic Growth and Tax Relief Reconciliation Act of 2001 (P.L. 107-16).

¶25,650 Estate or Gift Tax Charitable Deductions. The estate of an author, artist or musician is allowed a deduction for the value of any creative work transferred by the author, artist or musician either during his lifetime or at his death by will. The deduction is allowed without any percentage limitation so long as the creative work is transferred to or for the use of: (1) any corporation or association operated exclusively for religious, charitable, scientific, literary or educational purposes; (2) the United States or any state or political subdivision thereof, for exclusively public purposes; or (3) any veterans' organization, or its departments or local chapters, incorporated by an Act of Congress (.05). See ¶20,375.

Copyrighted artworks

Generally, if property is transferred for both charitable and noncharitable purposes, the charitable deduction to estate and gifts taxes will not be allowed unless the charitable remainder interest is in the form of a specified trust (see ¶20,375). This split-interest limitation does not apply in the case of a gift of a "work of art" and its copyright. For this purpose a work of art is any tangible personal property, such as literary, musical, dramatic or artistic work, with respect to which there is a copyright under federal law.

A work of art and its copyright will be treated as separate properties if the contribution of the work of art is a "qualified contribution." A qualified contribution is any transfer of property to a Code Sec. 501(c)(3) public charity or private operating foundation if the use of the property by the organization is related to its exempt purpose or function. Thus, a charitable deduction generally will be allowed for the transfer to charity of a work of art, even where the copyright is not simultaneously transferred to the charitable organization (.10).

Local law determines whether a transfer passes both the work of art and the copyright requirements. If, under local law, a transfer is treated as fully transferring both the work of art and the copyright interest to a charity, the contribution does not have to be a qualified contribution in order to be eligible for a gift or estate tax charitable deduction. On the other hand, if, under local law, the transfer is treated as transferring only the work of art to a charity, the contribution must be a qualified contribution to be eligible for an estate or gift tax deduction (.15).

> ***Example:*** Barney Gumble, an artist, dies during the tax year. Under the terms of his will, a work of art created by Barney is transferred to X, a public charity. X has no suitable use for the work of art and sells it. If under local law both the work of art and the copyright passes to X on the transfer, then Barney's estate is eligible for the gift and estate charitable deduction. However, if under local law only the work of art passes to X and the copyright remains an asset of Barney's estate, then no gift and estate charitable deduction may be taken as a qualified contribution has not occurred.

.05 Code Sec. 2055.

.10 Code Sec. 2055(e)(4) and Code Sec. 2522(c)(3).

.15 Reg. §20.2055-2(e) and Reg. §25.2522(c)-3.

¶25,651 Valuation of Creative Works. For estate and gift tax purposes, the value of a work of art or a manuscript created by an author, artist or musician is generally the price at which the object would change hands between a willing buyer and willing seller who both had knowledge of relevant facts and were not under any compulsion to buy or sell. The fair market value of creative works can be determined by means of an appraisal submitted by an expert. Such an appraisal is not binding on the IRS, however (.05).

Whatever the value placed upon a creative work, it is subject to review by the IRS. In the event that a valuation question reaches the courts, the testimony of expert witnesses is pertinent. For estates, the appraisal by an expert, or experts, is necessary in valuing art objects with a value of $3,000 or more. A copy of the appraisal made under oath must accompany the estate tax return. In addition, the appraisal must be accompanied by the executor's written declaration, made under penalties of perjury, that the itemized list of such property is complete and that the appraiser(s) was qualified and disinterested. Failure to obtain the services of a competent appraiser can result in an audit of the return, and can cause many difficulties and additional expenses if the IRS decides to challenge the valuation of the art objects shown on the estate tax return. The IRS is authorized to hire outside recognized appraisers to appraise any questioned art object (.10).

Information for appraisal report

Generally, a qualified appraisal is a document that (.15):

(1) relates to an appraisal that is made not earlier than 60 days prior to the date of contribution of the appraised property;

(2) is prepared, signed, and dated by a qualified appraiser;

(3) does not involve a prohibited type of appraiser fee, such as when part or all of the fee arrangement is based on a percentage of the appraised value of the property; and

(4) includes the following information:

(a) a description of the property,

(b) in the case of tangible property, the physical condition of the property,

(c) the date of contribution,

(d) the terms of any agreement entered into by the donor which relates to the use, sale or other disposition of the contributed property,

(e) the name, address, and taxpayer identification number of the qualified appraiser and the appraiser's employer or partnership,

(f) the qualifications of the qualified appraiser,

(g) a statement that the appraisal was prepared for income tax purposes,

(h) the date on which the property was valued,

(i) the appraised fair market value of the property on the date of contribution,

(j) the method of valuation used,

(k) the specific basis for valuation, if any, such as any specific comparable sales transactions, and

(l) a description of the fee arrangement between the donor and appraiser.

The IRS has indicated that the appraisal of art objects, and paintings in particular, should contain:

(1) a complete description of the object, indicating the size, the subject matter, the medium, and the approximate date the work was created;

(2) a photograph of a size and quality fully identifying the subject matter, preferably a 10" × 12" or larger print; and

(3) a statement of the factors upon which the appraisal was based, such as:

(a) sales of other works by the same artist, particularly on or around the valuation date;

(b) quoted prices in dealers' catalogs of the works of the artist or of other artists of comparable stature;

(c) the economic state of the art market at or around the time of valuation, particularly with respect to the specific property;

(d) a record of any exhibitions at which the particular art object had been displayed; and

(e) a statement as to the standing of the artist in his profession, and in the particular school or time period.

Artwork

Among the factors that are considered in determining the fair market value of a work of art, such as a painting or sculpture, for estate and gift tax purposes, are:

(1) the critical and popular recognition of the artist's work;

(2) the level of acceptability of his work in the marketplace;

(3) the number of sales by the artist in his career and the prices at which sales were made during the period immediately preceding and following the gift;

(4) whether a large number of items were donated, because the presence of a large number of pieces on the market at one time can depress the value of the artist's work;

(5) the period in the artist's life in which the work was created and its expression of the quality of his work;

(6) the size and general appeal of the work;

(7) the location of the item; and

(8) the size of the item and whether it is readily transported (.20).

Music manuscripts

In resolving the issue of fair market value of music manuscripts and related material of a prominent composer, for estate and gift tax purposes, one must consider:

(1) the composer's standing in his field and popularity of his works in general;

(2) the critical acclaim and popular appeal of the particular works;

(3) the relative place and importance of the works in the composer's career;

(4) the condition and content of the works;

(5) whether the works are originals, fair copies, or photo copies, are written in the composer's own hand, are signed, or are in ink, pencil, or typed;

(6) the length of the individual works and the sizes of the pages containing them;

(7) whether the mental processes of the composer are shown (i.e., working versus souvenir or finished manuscripts), including annotations;

(8) the demand in the marketplace for the type of works;

(9) the associative character of the works (such as a film, its actors and actresses, its director, or its subject);

(10) the quantity, or (conversely) the rarity, of the material (including whether the composer is dead or alive); and

(11) the length of time necessary to sell the works (.25).

Royalties

It is especially difficult to fix the value of royalty rights for estate and gift tax purposes. There is no strict formula that can be applied to determine whether a song will be a hit or whether a book will sell. Therefore, where possible, the following issues should be resolved:

(1) the amount of money to be received from royalties each year;

(2) how much longer the royalties will last;

(3) the risks involved, such as reduced sales, market conditions, etc.; and

(4) the relationship of royalties received in prior years to future royalties.

After a detailed consideration of these issues, a value can be assigned to royalty rights. In instances where there are no past sales or royalties to rely upon, however, the answer is even more difficult to ascertain. Sometimes, the best solution lies in consulting persons in the business of buying and selling music or books.

Penalty

When the creative work is substantially undervalued, a accuracy-related penalty of 20 percent of the underpayment of taxes may be imposed. There is a substantial valuation understatement if the value of any property claimed on any return is 50 percent or less of the correct value (.30). This penalty increases to 40 percent of the underpayment attributable to the understatement if the value claimed is 25 percent or less of the correct value (.35).

.05 Reg. §§20.2031-1 and 25.2512-1

.10 Reg. §20.2031-6.

.15 Reg. §1.170A-13(c)(3).

.20 *D. Smith Est.*, 57 TC 650, CCH Dec. 31,262, aff'd by CA-2, 75-1 USTC ¶13,046, 510 F2d 479, cert. denied, 423 U.S. 827.

.25 *M. Jarre*, 64 TC 183, CCH Dec. 33,177.

.30 Code Sec. 6662(g).

.35 Code Sec. 6662(h).

¶25,652 Marital Deduction. A copyright is a terminable interest and qualifies for the marital deduction if no other interest in the property passes from the decedent to another person for less than adequate and full consideration in money or money's worth and if, by reason of its not passing, no other person may possess or enjoy the copyright after termination of the spouse's interest (.05).

.05 Reg. §§20.2056(b)-1(b) and (c)(1)

¶25,653 Extension of Time to Pay Estate Taxes. Often, the estate of an author, artist or musician may be composed of non-liquid assets, such as unpublished manuscripts, copyrights, royalty contracts, works of art, and income in respect of a decedent. To the extent that the estate consists largely of such assets, it may face a liquidity problem for estate tax purposes. A forced sale of the works could result in their loss of value. A 14-year extension of time for the payment of estate taxes is available if more than 35 percent of a decedent's adjusted gross estate is an interest as a proprietor in a trade or business. The estate taxes attributable to that interest may be deferred for a maximum of 14 years, with the estate making annual interest payments only for the first four years and thereafter paying the balance in up to 10 installments of principal and interest (.05).

.05 Code Sec. 6166.

Incorporation

¶25,655 Incorporation. Authors, artists, actors and musicians are eligible to incorporate under many state corporation laws. In order to use the corporate form, the author, artist, actor or writer must respect the corporate entity and carry on business in the name of the corporation, keeping records in corporate form and observing state law requirements (.05).

.05 Rev. Rul. 70-101, 1970-1 CB 278, amplified by Rev. Rul. 82-213, 1982-2 CB 31, Rev. Rul. 74-439, 1974-2 CB 405, and Rev. Rul. 72-468, 1972-2 CB 647, and modified by Rev. Rul. 73-596, 1973-2 CB 384.

BANKRUPT INDIVIDUALS

Introduction

¶25,657 In many cases, the discharge of an individual's debt constitutes income just as if the debtor had received earnings in the amount of the forgiven debt. For example, an accrual-method taxpayer who has properly deducted amounts owed, even though unpaid, generally will recognize income if the debt is waived by the party to whom it is owed. The amount the taxpayer would have had to pay is no longer an account payable, but is treated by the taxpayer as income.

However, an individual's gross income does not include any amount that otherwise would be included as income resulting from the cancellation of a debt if the discharge: (1) occurs in bankruptcy (see ¶25,659), (2) occurs when the taxpayer is insolvent (see ¶25,659), (3) is of a qualified farm indebtedness (see ¶25,345) or (4) is of qualified real property business indebtedness.

The rules concerning the treatment of a debt discharged in bankruptcy are intended to balance bankruptcy policy—that a debtor should not leave bankruptcy saddled with debt or tax liability—and tax policy—that a taxpayer should pay income realized on the discharge of debt. To do this, the rules provide that a debt discharge, although excluded from income, must be used to reduce the taxpayer's net operating losses from business and certain other tax attributes (see ¶25,659) unless the taxpayer elects to apply the debt discharge amount first to reduce basis in depreciable assets or in realty held as inventory.

The attribute reduction rules give flexibility to the debtor to account for a debt discharge amount in the manner most favorable to the debtor's tax situation (see ¶25,660). The exclusion from gross income, the reduction of tax attributes, and the special rules concerning discharge of qualified farm indebtedness and qualified real property business indebtedness apply at the partner, not at the partnership, level.

Cancellation of Indebtedness

¶25,659 Discharges Through Bankruptcy or Insolvency. A discharge in bankruptcy includes release from debt under any of the chapters of Title 11 of the U.S. Code, "Bankruptcy." This includes, but is not limited to: (1) individuals who are declaring bankruptcy and liquidating their estates and (2) those who are seeking protection of the bankruptcy act to reorganize their debts and establish a plan for paying off their creditors. In the latter case, creditors often agree to accept less than the full amount owed them in order to prevent liquidation of a debtor's nonexempt assets to pay off creditors—an event that often would result in the creditors' being paid less than if they accepted a percentage of the total debt owed them to be paid over a period of time. In either of these events, the debtor is relieved of debt and must reduce the tax attributes of the remaining property.

The United States Supreme Court clarified that Chapter 11 (reorganization) proceedings are available to individual bankrupts who are not carrying on a going business (.05). Thus, the use of Chapter 11 proceedings is not limited to business insolvencies.

Although a discharge in bankruptcy prevents the IRS from taking any action to collect the debt as a personal liability of the debtor, the debtor's property may remain liable for a debt secured by a valid tax lien that had been perfected before the bankruptcy petition was filed (.10).

Where a taxpayer is insolvent, but is not involved in a court bankruptcy action, the amount excluded from current recognition cannot exceed the amount by which the debtor is insolvent (.15). For this purpose, the word "insolvent" means the excess of the debtor's liabilities over the fair market value of the debtor's assets (including, the IRS has ruled, property that is exempt from the reach of creditors under state law (.20)), both determined immediately before the discharge (.25). The excluded amount is applied to reduce tax attributes in the same manner as if the discharge had occurred in bankruptcy. Any amount that is not excluded from gross income because it exceeds the insolvency amount is treated in the same manner as debt cancellation in the case of a wholly solvent taxpayer. That is, the cancellation of debt must be included in the debtor's gross income.

Reduction of tax attributes

Debts that either are discharged through bankruptcy or are excluded by an insolvent taxpayer must be used to reduce the following tax attributes of the debtor's property in the following order:

(1) net operating losses or net operating loss carryovers;

(2) general business credit carryovers;

(3) minimum tax credit;

(4) capital losses or capital loss carryovers;

(5) basis in the remaining depreciable and nondepreciable assets;

(6) passive activity loss and credit carryovers; and

(7) foreign tax credit carryovers.

Reductions for discharged debts are to be made against a particular attribute in the order in which they would have been used; current year attributes are reduced first, and remaining attributes are reduced on a first-in, first-out basis. Generally, attributes are reduced on a dollar-for-dollar basis. However, the reduction in general business credit, minimum tax credit, foreign tax credit and passive activity loss and credit carryovers is made at a rate of 33⅓ cents per dollar of debt discharged.

.05 *Toibb v. Radloff*, SCt, 111 SCt 2197 (1991).

.10 *In re R.H. Isom*, CA-9, 90-1 USTC ¶50,216, 901 F2d 744, aff'g BAP-9, 89-1 USTC ¶9200.

.15 Code Sec. 108(a)(3).

.20 IRS Letter Ruling 199932013, 5-4-99, CCH IRS LETTER RULINGS REPORTS.

.25 Code Sec. 108(d)(3).

¶25,660 Election to Reduce Basis. In lieu of reducing tax attributes, a debtor in bankruptcy or an insolvent debtor can elect to reduce the basis in depreciable property (.05) by all or part of the amount of debt discharged. At the election of the taxpayer, the term "depreciable property" may include any real property that would be considered stock in trade and included in the taxpayer's inventory (.10). To make the election to reduce basis, the debtor must attach a completed Form 982, Reduction of Tax Attributes Due to Discharge of Indebtedness (and Section 1082 Basis Adjustment, to a timely filed (included extensions) income tax return for the tax year in which the debtor has excluded discharge of indebtedness income (.15).

If there is insufficient basis to absorb the full amount of debt, the remaining amount can be applied to reduce tax attributes in the order noted at ¶25,659. Where a taxpayer makes this election, the property is treated as Code Sec. 1245 property (depreciable personal property) or Code Sec. 1250 property (depreciable real property). Any gain on a subsequent disposition of this property is subject to recapture as ordinary income to the extent of the basis reduction (.20).

There are also ordering rules for reduction of basis of depreciable and nondepreciable assets, items in the fifth category of tax attributes listed in ¶25,659. The following ordering rules apply (.25):

(1) real property used in a trade or business or held for investment, other than real property described in Code Sec. 1221(a)(2), that secured the discharged indebtedness immediately before the discharge;

(2) personal property used in a trade or business or held for investment, other than inventory, accounts receivable, and notes receivable, that secured the discharged indebtedness immediately before the discharge;

(3) remaining property used in a trade or business or held for investment, other than inventory, accounts receivable, notes receivable, and real property described in Code Sec. 1221(a)(1);

(4) inventory, accounts receivable, notes receivable, and real property described in Code Sec. 1221(a)(1); and

(5) property not used in a trade or business or held for investment.

Instead of applying the above ordering rules, a debtor may elect to first reduce the adjusted bases of depreciable property, both real and personal, to the extent of the excluded debt discharge income (.30). If the adjusted bases of depreciable property are insufficient to offset the entire amount of excluded debt discharge income, the taxpayer must reduce any remaining tax attributes in the order above.

The possibility of electing to reduce basis rather than reducing existing tax attributes gives rise to planning possibilities. For example, where an expiring net operating loss would otherwise be wasted, a debtor taxpayer might opt for attribute reduction. On the other hand, a desire to preserve net operating losses to shelter future profits might suggest that the debtor reduce the basis of his depreciable property. These possibilities are illustrated in the following examples:

Example 1: At the time Leonard Long declares bankruptcy, he has $500,000 in net operating losses, which he can carry forward for another three years. He also has depreciable property with a basis of $1,000,000. Long's debts, which are discharged in bankruptcy, amount to $800,000. He expects to earn income following his declaration of bankruptcy and would like to preserve his losses. Instead of using the discharge of indebtedness to reduce tax attributes, Long elects to reduce the basis of his depreciable property. This leaves a basis of $200,000 ($1,000,000 – $800,000) for the property.

Example 2: Assume the same facts as Example (1), except that Long's net operating losses will expire in the year he declares bankruptcy. Rather than waste the losses, Long can use his discharge of indebtedness to reduce his tax attributes. Since losses are reduced on a dollar-for-dollar basis, Long's $800,000 of indebtedness discharged eliminates his $500,000 in net operating losses, leaving $300,000 to be applied against his other tax attributes.

.05 Code Sec. 108(b)(5) and Code Sec. 1017(b)(3)(B).

.10 Code Sec. 108(d)(5), Code Sec. 1017(b)(3)(E)(i) and Code Sec. 1221(a)(1).

.15 Reg. §1.108-4.

.20 Code Sec. 1017(d).

.25 Reg. §1.1017-1(a).

.30 Reg. §1.1017-1(c).

¶25,661 Related Party Debt. Acquisition of debt by a party related to, or under the control of, the debtor from an unrelated debtor is treated as acquisition of debt by the debtor (.05). This rule prevents debtors from avoiding cancellation of indebtedness income by having a related party purchase their outstanding debt.

Related parties include family members, certain interrelated corporations and partnerships, and fiduciaries (.10). For this purpose, a debtor's family includes the debtor's spouse, children, grandchildren, parents, and the spouse of any child or grandchild of the debtor; there is no attribution between siblings (.15).

.05 Code Sec. 108(e)(4).

.10 Code Sec. 267(b) and Code Sec. 707(b)(1).

.15 Code Sec. 108(e)(4)(B).

¶25,662 Unpaid Taxes. After the filing of a bankruptcy petition and during the period the assets of the bankrupt or the bankruptcy estate are under the jurisdiction of the bankruptcy court, assets are not subject to levy by the IRS. To collect taxes, the IRS must file a proof of claim in the bankruptcy court in the same manner as other creditors. This claim may be presented even though the taxes have not yet been assessed or are subject to a Tax Court proceeding.

After the filing of a proof of claim by the IRS, the pre-petition taxes set forth below must be paid out of the assets of the bankrupt or the bankruptcy estate to the extent that assets remaining after paying the claims of secured creditors and certain enumerated creditors having a higher priority are sufficient. Any portion remaining to be paid after the assets of the bankrupt or the bankruptcy estate are exhausted are not discharged by bankruptcy (.05). It should be noted that debt incurred to pay nondischargeable tax debts is nondischargeable (.10). Thus, debtors who use cash from their credit cards to pay taxes, then file for bankruptcy, cannot have those credit card debts discharged after satisfying the otherwise nondischargeable taxes.

Allocation of tax payments

The Bankruptcy Court has the authority to allocate payments made by trustees on behalf of corporations undergoing Chapter 11 reorganizations so that the corporations' trust fund taxes (unpaid withholding and employment taxes) are paid before other tax liabilities, provided that such action is necessary to the success of the reorganization plan (.15). Such allocations relieve "responsible persons" of liability for unpaid trust fund taxes and also deprive the IRS of an opportunity of seeking payment directly from the individuals whose duty it was to see that the trust fund taxes were paid. Thus, this rule creates an opportunity for "responsible persons" (usually corporate officers) to avoid being held personally liable for the unpaid employment and withholding taxes of an insolvent corporation.

This does not mean, however, that the Bankruptcy Court must make such a designation. The Court merely has the power to do so if it finds this to be necessary for the reorganization. Although the facts of the case deal with a debtor corporation, presumably the same rule could apply to employment taxes payable by businesses conducted through other types of entities that were in Chapter 11 proceedings. There has been a judicial conflict as to whether the rule may be applied to Chapter 11 "liquidations;" the U. S. Court of Appeals for the Eleventh Circuit has denied such application (.20), while a U. S. Bankruptcy Court in Mississippi has allowed it (.25).

Pre-petition taxes

The following federal taxes are pre-petition unsecured taxes of the government that have priority over the claims of general creditors (.30):

(1) Income taxes for tax years ending on or before the date of filing of the bankruptcy petition for which a return is last due, including extensions, after a date three years before the filing of the petition ("the three-year lookback period").

(2) Income taxes assessed within 240 days before the date of filing of the petition. This 240-day period is increased by any time during which an offer in compromise with respect to these taxes was pending (made within 240 days after the assessment) plus 30 days. The U.S. Court of Appeals for the Sixth Circuit has held that this tolling period applies only to offers made after assessment (.35).

(3) Income taxes, other than those for which no return, a late return (filed within two years of the filing of the bankruptcy petition), or a fraudulent return was filed, that were not assessed before but that were assessable after the filing of the petition.

(4) Any property tax that was assessed before bankruptcy proceedings were begun and that was last payable without penalty less than one year before the petition was filed.

(5) Income tax withholding for which the bankrupt is liable in any capacity.

(6) Employment taxes (FICA and FUTA) on the first $2,000 of wages, salaries, or commissions (including vacation, severance, and sick pay) earned by each individual employee from the bankrupt within the 90-day period before the earlier of the date of cessation of the bankrupt's business or the date of filing the bankruptcy petition (whether or not actually paid before that date), and employment taxes for which a return is last due (including extensions) after a date three years before the filing of the petition.

(7) Excise taxes on transactions occurring before the date of filing the bankruptcy petition, for which a return, if required, is last due (including extensions) after a date three years before the filing of the petition. If a return is not required, these excise taxes include only those on transactions occurring during the three years immediately before the date of filing the petition.

(8) Customs duties arising out of the importation of merchandise entered for consumption within one year before the date of the filing of the petition or covered by an entry liquidated or reliquidated within one year before the date of the filing. Also covered are duties imported within four years before the filing but unliquidated on the filing date where the IRS certifies that the failure to liquidate was due to an investigation pending on the filing date.

(9) Penalties related to claims related to one of the categories above and in compensation for actual pecuniary loss.

Since Congress added the three-year lookback provision to the Bankruptcy Code, controversy existed regarding when the three-year period would be tolled by a prior bankruptcy petition. The United States Supreme Court answered the question when it ruled that the three-year lookback period of Bankruptcy Code §507(a) is tolled during the pendency of a prior bankruptcy petition in cases where the taxpayer files back-to-back petitions (.40).

> ***Example:*** On May 1, 2003, Melvin Dwyer filed for Chapter 13 protection, but withdrew his petition on October 23, 2003. This was three years and one week after his 1999 taxes were due. Five months later, on March 12, 2004, Dwyer filed a Chapter 7 petition and was ultimately discharged on June 17, 2004. At the time of his discharge, Dwyer owed the IRS $13,000. This liability stemmed from underreported income on Dwyer's 1999 tax return, which Dwyer had filed on October 15, 2000. Dwyer refuses to pay, arguing that because the debt arose more than three

years before his Chapter 7 filing, it had been discharged under the three-year lookback period of Bankruptcy Code §507(a). Dwyer's argument will fail because, in light of the *C.P. Young* decision, the three-year lookback period was tolled during the pendency of Dwyer's Chapter 13 case.

Planning Note

CCH Analysts note that An IRS Chief Counsel Notice, which is in effect until incorporation in the Chief Counsel Directives Manual, clarifies that in light of the rationale of *C.P. Young*, the three-year lookback period of Bankruptcy Code §507(a)(8)(A)(i) should not be computed by including an additional six months based on Code Sec. 6503(h). Instead, the lookback period is tolled during the pendency of a prior bankruptcy petition. In addition, the automatic tolling rule adopted in *C.P. Young* will determine the priority or dischargeability of any tax debt unless a court has issued a final order on the priority or dischargeability of the debt and all applicable appeal periods have expired (.45).

.05 11 U.S.C. §523(a)(1).

.10 11 U.S.C. §523(a)(14).

.15 *Energy Resources Co., Inc.*, SCt, 90-1 USTC ¶50,281, 495 U.S. 545.

.20 *Kare Kemical, Inc.*, CA-11, 91-2 USTC ¶50,389

.25 *20th Century Enterprises, Inc.*, BC-DC Miss., 94-2 USTC ¶50,561.

.30 11 U.S.C. §507(a)(8).

.35 *G.E. Aberl*, CA-6, 96-1 USTC ¶50,151

.40 *C.P. Young*, SCt, 2002-1 USTC ¶50,257, aff'g CA-1, 2000-2 USTC ¶50,868

.45 Notice CC-2002-023, May 16, 2002

¶25,663 Choice to End Tax Year. The tax year in which a debtor declares bankruptcy under Chapters 7 or 11 may be divided into two "short" tax years (.05). If the debtor elects this treatment, the first tax year ends on the day before the filing of the bankruptcy petition, and the second tax year begins on the day that the debtor files the petition and ends on the last day of the normal tax year.

The debtor's income tax liability for the first tax year then becomes a claim against the bankruptcy estate, having arisen prior to bankruptcy, rather than becoming a post-bankruptcy liability of the debtor.

The debtor can elect to divide the tax year only if the estate includes assets other than exempt property (.10). A debtor who makes the election must annualize his income for each short tax year as though a change in accounting period has been approved (.15). If a debtor chooses not to make the election, the debtor's tax year is determined without reference to the filing of the bankruptcy petition (.20).

Once the choice is made, the individual bankrupt's income tax liability for the first short tax year becomes an allowable claim, as a claim arising before bankruptcy, against the bankruptcy estate. Any tax liability for that year is collectible from the estate so long as enough assets are available to pay off the estate's debts. However, to the extent that assets of the bankruptcy estate are not sufficient to pay any tax due for that year, the remaining liability is not dischargeable in the bankruptcy case and can be collected from the individual bankrupt after the case is settled.

If no choice is made to end the tax year, no part of the bankrupt's tax liability for the year in which bankruptcy proceedings begin can be collected from the estate.

Once made, the election is irrevocable.

Joint elections—joint returns

If the debtor is married, the debtor's spouse may join in the election, but only if the parties file a joint return for the first short year. No joint return need be filed for the second short year (.25).

Example 1: Harriet and Henry Howard are calendar-year taxpayers. Henry files a bankruptcy petition on May 1. If Henry makes the election, he will have two short tax years (January 1-April 30 and May 1-December 31). If Harriet joins Henry in the election and they file a joint return, her short tax years will correspond to his.

Example 2: Assume the same facts as in Example (1), except that Harriet does not join her husband in making the election. Although Henry will have two short tax years, Harriet's tax year will correspond to the calendar year. The couple cannot file a joint return at the end of the calendar year, because their tax years ending on December 31 are of differing lengths.

Even though a taxpayer has joined in an election made by his or her spouse, the taxpayer may declare bankruptcy later in the same year and make the election again. Under these circumstances, it is possible for a spouse to have three short tax years in the same calendar or fiscal year.

If the parties filed a joint return for the first short year when making the election, the original debtor can join the spouse in making the second election. However, if the couple did not file a joint return at the time of the first election, each will have a different tax year, and the debtor's spouse cannot join in the second election (.30).

Example 3: Betty and Bob Burnett are calendar-year taxpayers. Bob files a bankruptcy petition on April 1 and makes the election. Betty joins in the election, and then files her own bankruptcy petition on September 1. She makes her own election at that time. Since the parties joined in the earlier election, Bob can join in Betty's election. Both Betty and Bob have three short tax years (January 1-March 31, April 1-August 31, and September 1-December 31).

Example 4: Assume the same facts as in Example (3), except that Betty does not join in Bob's election. Consequently, when Betty makes her own election, Bob is not able to join her, since they have different tax years and are unable to file a joint return as of August 31. Bob has two short tax years (January 1-March 31 and April 1-December 31); Betty has two different short tax years (January 1-August 31 and September 1-December 31).

Making the election

An individual bankrupt who chooses to end the tax year does so by filing a return on Form 1040 for the first short tax year on or before the 15th day of the fourth full month after the end of that first short tax year. To avoid delays in processing the return, the bankrupt should write "Section 1398 Election" at the top of the return.

.05 Code Sec. 1398(d)(2).
.10 Code Sec. 1398(d)(2)(C).
.15 Code Sec. 443(b) and Code Sec. 1398(d)(2)(F).
.20 Code Sec. 1398(d)(1).
.25 Code Sec. 1398(d)(2)(D).
.30 Senate Finance Committee Report to the Bankruptcy Tax Act of 1980 (P.L. 96-589).

Individual's Bankruptcy Estate

¶25,665 Bankruptcy Estate. The property held by a trustee in bankruptcy for an individual is treated as a separate taxable entity under Chapter 7 (liquidation) or Chapter 11 (reorganization) of Title 11. The trustee of such a debtor is required to file a Form 1041 for any tax year in which the estate in bankruptcy has a gross income in excess of the "exemption amount" plus the basic standard deduction applicable to the individual bankrupt (.05). The exemption amount for 2004 is $3,100; for 2003, it was $3,050 (.10). For tax years beginning in 2004, the basic standard deduction, as adjusted for inflation, is $9,700 for married taxpayers filing jointly and surviving spouses; $7,150 for heads of household; $4,850 for single taxpayers; and $4,850 for married taxpayers filing separately. For tax years beginning after 2004, the standard deduction for married taxpayers and surviving spouses is twice the amount (200 percent) of the standard deduction for a single taxpayer (.15).

> ***Example:*** Thomas Kay, an individual using a calendar year, is declared bankrupt. This bankrupt's estate must file a return for 2004 if it has income in excess of $7,950 ($3,100 plus $4,850).

A separate taxable entity is not created if the case is brought under Chapter 13 of Title 11, which involves adjustment of debts of an individual with regular income.

The tax year for which the fiduciary files a return begins on the date of the filing of the petition in bankruptcy. The return may be for either a calendar or a fiscal year.

Transfers between debtor and estate

Although the debtor and the bankruptcy estate are two separate entities, transfers between a debtor and the bankruptcy estate are not "dispositions" for tax purposes. Therefore, the transfer of the bankrupt's property to the bankruptcy estate when the petition for bankruptcy is filed does not result in recognition of gain or loss, acceleration of income or deductions, or recapture of deductions or credits. Similarly, at the conclusion of the bankruptcy case, any transfers between the estate and the debtor are not treated as dispositions (.20).

These rules do not apply, however, if the transfer is an exchange or a sale.

.05 Code Sec. 6012(a)(9).

.10 Code Sec. 151(d).

.15 Code Sec. 63(c), as amended by the Jobs and Growth Tax Relief Reconciliation Act of 2003, P.L. 108-27, Act §103(a), and the Working Families Tax Relief Act of 2004, P.L. 108-311, Act §101(b)(1), and Code Sec. 1398(c)(3).

.20 Code Sec. 1398(f).

¶25,666 Tax Attribute Carryovers. A bankruptcy estate succeeds to certain tax attributes of the debtor (.05). These attributes include (but are not limited to) net operating loss carryovers; charitable contributions carryovers; basis, holding period and character of assets; method of accounting; capital loss carryovers; and credit carryovers (.10). Because the carryover of net operating losses is permissible, the estate is able to offset post-bankruptcy income by use of the debtor's pre-bankruptcy losses.

In addition, net operating losses of the estate may be carried back to the debtor's tax years preceding bankruptcy (.15). Post-bankruptcy losses, therefore, may be applied against pre-bankruptcy income, allowing the estate the possibility of obtaining tax refunds. Unlike the estate, however, the debtor may not carry post-bankruptcy losses back to pre-bankruptcy years (.20).

> ***Example 1:*** Darryl Davis has a net operating loss carryover of $500,000 at the time he declares bankruptcy. His bankruptcy estate realizes income of $700,000. Davis's estate can offset its post-bankruptcy income against Davis's pre-bankruptcy losses, leaving the estate with a net income of $200,000.

A debtor that is discharged from bankruptcy succeeds to the same tax attributes to which the estate succeeded upon the declaration of bankruptcy, provided those attributes are unexpired (.25).

> ***Example 2:*** When Alice Anderson declares bankruptcy, she has net operating loss carryovers of $75,000, credit carryovers of $200,000, and capital assets with a value of $600,000 that she has held for two years. Anderson's bankruptcy estate succeeds to these tax attributes. When Anderson is no longer in bankruptcy, she will succeed the bankruptcy estate to these same tax attributes, provided they have not expired or been used. The assets to which Anderson will succeed will retain their character as capital assets, just as they had remained capital assets in the hands of her bankruptcy estate.

The IRS has ruled that a surviving spouse filing a joint return with a decedent for the decedent's year of death may not use accumulated net operating losses (NOLs) arising pre-bankruptcy when the individual debtor dies before, but in the same calendar year as, his bankruptcy estate is terminated (.30). Since the decedent was not entitled to the NOL carryover before he died, his spouse cannot use it on the joint return. The decedent could have become entitled to the NOLs only had he survived the termination of the bankruptcy estate.

In contrast, a Tax Court has ruled that a debtor-in-possession whose bankruptcy case continued after his death succeeded, upon termination of that case, to any NOLs that were not used by the estate. The decedent had sustained the NOLs prior to his death, and his wife sought to use the NOLs on their joint return. The Tax Court determined that Code Sec. 1398(i) mandates that the debtor be the person who succeeds to, and takes into account, any NOLs from the bankruptcy estate. The debtor's death, in and of itself, did not alter his identity as the debtor in the bankruptcy proceeding. Per the Court, there was no statutory requirement that the NOLs be "vested" at the time of the debtor's demise in order to be claimed on the final return (.35).

A debtor's residence constitutes property of his bankruptcy estate, and, thus, the bankruptcy trustee may claim the exclusion under Code Sec. 121 of up to $250,000 of gain realized on the sale of the property (.40).

.05 Code Sec. 1398(g) and Code Sec. 1398(j).
.10 Code Sec. 1398(g).
.15 Code Sec. 1398(j)(2)(A).
.20 Code Sec. 1398(j)(2)(B).
.25 Code Sec. 1398(i).
.30 IRS Field Service Advice 200118003, 12-26-00, CCH IRS LETTER RULINGS REPORTS.
.35 A.M. *Lassiter*, 83 TCM 1139, CCH Dec. 54,629(M), TC Memo 2002-25
.40 IRS Chief Counsel Notice N(35)000-162

¶25,667 Deductions and Credits. The determination of whether amounts spent by the estate qualify for treatment as credits or deductions is made as if the amounts were incurred by the debtor (.05). The estate may take deductions and credits in the same way the debtor would have done had the debtor continued the trade, business, or activity in which the debtor was engaged before the declaration of bankruptcy.

Administration expenses are deductible from the bankruptcy estate (.10). These expenses include the costs of preserving the estate, taxes, certain fines, compensation for services rendered by the trustee and attorneys, expenses incurred by creditors, and court fees and costs (.15). However, deductions for administrative expenses are subject to the disallowance provisions for capital expenditures (.20) and for tax-exempt income (.25).

There is a two-percent floor on miscellaneous itemized deductions for estates (.30). The deductions for expenses incurred in connection with the administration of an estate that would not have been incurred if the property were not held in an estate are not subject to the two-percent floor. In addition, an exception to the full deduction of estates' administrative expenses has been enacted. The carryover deduction allowed beneficiaries of an estate that terminates with unused excess deductions for administrative expenses can be taken only if two percent of the beneficiary's adjusted gross income is exceeded.

Unused administrative expenses

Undeducted administrative expenses may also be carried back to the preceding three tax years, or carried over to the following seven tax years (.35). Carryovers and carrybacks can be made only to tax years of the estate, not to those of the individual debtor. Similarly, when the bankruptcy case is closed, the debtor cannot take advantage of the administrative expense carryovers. The carryback and carryover amounts are determined in accordance with the rules for carrying back and over the net operating loss deduction.

When the estate is terminated, the debtor must treat tax attributes such as deductions and credits in the same way the estate had treated them, even if they arose during bankruptcy.

.05 Code Sec. 1398(e).

.10 Code Sec. 1398(h).

.15 11 U.S.C. §503 and 28 U.S.C. §§1911-1929.

.20 Code Sec. 263(a).

.25 Code Sec. 265(a)(1).

.30 Code Sec. 67(e).

.35 Code Sec. 1398(h)(2)(B).

¶25,668 Computation of Tax. The gross income of a bankruptcy estate consists of the gross income of the debtor (excluding amounts received prior to the declaration of bankruptcy) and the gross income of the estate itself (.05). The estate succeeds to certain tax attributes of the debtor and is entitled to claim certain administrative expenses as deductions. Where the bankruptcy estate itself incurs net operating losses and the carryback year of the estate is a tax year before the estate's first tax year, the carryback is taken into account for the debtor's tax year corresponding to the carryback year (.10). (See also ¶25,666.) Excess credits may also be carried back to pre-bankruptcy tax years of the debtor.

The taxable income of a bankruptcy estate is computed in the same manner as for an individual. For 2004, the estate may claim a personal exemption of $3,100 as a deduction (.15). The applicable tax rate schedule for the estate is the same as for married individuals filing separate returns. The trustee must file a return for any year in which the estate's gross income exceeds a minimum amount (see ¶25,665) (.20).

A bankruptcy estate is entitled to one change of annual accounting period without IRS consent. The estate's federal income tax returns are open to inspection by, or disclosure to, the debtor (.25).

Planning Note

CCH Tax Analysts note that penalty relief is provided when debtors have failed to make timely payment of tax with respect to periods during which a bankruptcy case is pending. This relief is available provided:

(1) the tax was incurred by the estate, and the failure to pay followed a court order finding the funds of the estate probably insufficient to pay administrative expenses, or

(2) the bankruptcy petition was filed before either an order for relief was entered or a trustee was appointed, and either the bankruptcy petition was filed before the due date of the return, or the date a penalty would have been assessed occurs on or after the day on which the petition was filed.

This relief is not provided, however, for withholding taxes and taxes collected from others that are to be paid over to the IRS, for which the debtor remains liable (.30).

.05 Code Sec. 1398(e)(1).

.10 Code Sec. 1398(j)(2).

.15 Code Sec. 151 and Code Sec. 1398(c).

.20 Code Sec. 6012(a)(9).

.25 Code Sec. 6103(e)(5)(B).

.30 Code Sec. 6658.

¶25,669 Liens Against Estate. A system of priorities has been established for the satisfaction of liens against the estate that exist at the time bankruptcy is declared (.05). Generally, *secured claims* are satisfied first, followed by certain kinds of *unsecured claims. General claims* (unsecured claims not entitled to priority) are satisfied out of any assets that remain. Should there be insufficient assets to pay a class of claims in full, they are satisfied pro rata.

The priority given to unsecured claims is as follows (amounts provided were adjusted effective April 1, 2004, and are subject to such adjustment every three years, with respect to cases commenced on or after the adjustment date):

(1) Administrative expenses, including most taxes incurred during the estate's administration.

(2) Creditors' claims arising, in an involuntary case, in the ordinary course of business after the filing of the bankruptcy petition.

(3) Wage claims, including vacation, severance, and sick leave pay earned by an individual within 90 days before the date of the earlier of the bankruptcy filing or the date the bankrupt ceased business operations to the extent of $4,925 ($4,650 before April 1, 2004) per person.

(4) Claims for contributions to employee benefit plans, such as pension, life insurance, or health plans arising from services rendered within 180 days before the date of the earlier of the bankruptcy filing or the date the bankrupt ceased business operations, whichever occurs first.

(5) Special claims arising from grain farming and fishing up to the amount of $4,925 ($4,650 before April 1, 2004) per individual.

(6) Claims for alimony, maintenance or support.

(7) Unsecured claims of individuals up to $2,225 ($2,100 before April 1, 2004) arising from the deposit, before the commencement of proceedings, of money in connection with the purchase or rental of property or the purchase of services for the personal, family, or household use of such individuals, that were not delivered or provided.

(8) Taxes, including only:

(a) income taxes for which a return is due within three years of the commencement of the bankruptcy proceedings;

(b) property taxes for one year;

(c) employment and withholding taxes;

(d) excise taxes;

(e) customs duties; and

(f) tax penalties representing a pecuniary loss.

Trustees in bankruptcy have the status of judgment creditors and represent all general creditors (.10). Claims of a trustee in bankruptcy are superior to unfiled federal tax liens (.15). Liens (including tax liens) that are invalid as against a trustee in bankruptcy are also invalid as against all liens that are not discharged in bankruptcy.

Federal tax liens survive a debtor's bankruptcy and are fully enforceable against the debtor's exempt and nonexempt assets notwithstanding the discharge of the underlying tax liabilities (.20). A debtor's discharge in bankruptcy operates as a discharge only of personal liability and does not require a release of IRS pre-petition tax liens, so that the tax lien remains in force and property liability remains enforceable even against the debtor's exempt property (.25).

.05 11 U.S.C. §507.

.10 *R.F. Speers*, SCt, 66-1 USTC ¶9101, 382 U.S. 266.

.15 11 U.S.C. §110.

.20 *In re R.J. Holland*, BC-DC, 90-2 USTC ¶50,394.

.25 11 U.S.C. §522(c)(2)(B).

Trustees and Fiduciaries in Bankruptcy

¶25,671 Notice of Qualification of Trustee. Trustees in Title 11 bankruptcy cases are required to notify the IRS of their appointment as trustees within 10 days of being appointed (.05).

Notice of appointment may be made on Form 56, "Notice Concerning Fiduciary Relationship." Although the form is not required, disclosure of the social security number or taxpayer identification number of the entity represented by the trustee is required. Part IV of the form serves as the official form for notice of termination of fiduciary relationship. In addition, there is no requirement that notice be given on a year-to-year basis. Thus, one notice suffices.

The running of the period of limitations on the making of tax assessments against the bankruptcy estate is suspended from the date Chapter 11 bankruptcy proceedings are commenced until 30 days after the date upon which notice is received by the IRS; such period cannot, however, exceed two years (.10).

.05 Code Sec. 6036; Reg. §301.6036-1.

.10 Code Sec. 6872.

¶25,672 Power of Intervention. The commencement of a bankruptcy case results in an automatic stay of any proceedings in the Tax Court that concern the debtor's alleged tax deficiencies (.05). The U.S. District Court has the discretion to lift this stay in order to permit the debtor to institute a case before the Tax Court challenging the asserted deficiency. Should this happen, the trustee has the power to intervene in the Tax Court proceeding as a matter of right. This right of intervention extends to any Tax Court proceeding in which the debtor is a party. Should the automatic stay not be lifted by the District Court, that court will decide the tax issue, and its decision will bind all parties.

Although receivers in bankruptcy lack independent authority to enter into compromises of claims, they may do so with the approval of the District Court (.10). In addition, a District Court lacks jurisdiction over deficiencies that are the subject of Tax Court decisions entered prior to an adjudication of bankruptcy (.15). However, after the adjudication or declaration of bankruptcy, the District Court has the authority to resolve all disputes that interfere with the orderly administration of the estate (.20). This includes any questions as to the amount or legality of any tax owed to the federal government (.25).

.05 Code Sec. 7464; 11 U.S.C. §362(a)(8).

.10 *R.H. Long Co.*, CtCls, 36-1 USTC ¶9264, 14 FSupp 648.

.15 *S.P. Kelly*, CA-9, 37-1 USTC ¶9294, 90 F2d 73.

.20 *Major Dynamics, Inc.*, BC-DC, 81-2 USTC ¶9766, 14 BR 969.

.25 *General Film Corporation*, CA-2, 274 F 903.

¶25,673 Protection from Personal Liability. In order to avoid personal liability on a tax after the estate is closed, the trustee may submit a return requesting that the government make a determination as to any unpaid tax liability incurred during the bankruptcy proceedings (.05). Provided the return neither contains a material misrepresentation nor is fraudulent, the debtor and the trustee are discharged from further liability after paying:

(1) the tax determined by the government to be due;

(2) the amount determined by the court to be due after the government has completed its audit; or

(3) the amount shown on the return, if the government does not notify the trustee, within 60 days of the trustee's request for a determination, that the return is being audited, or if the government does not complete the audit and notify the trustee of any tax due within 180 days of his request for a determination.

By such means, the trustee is protected from governmental post-proceeding determinations that additional taxes have accrued during the administration of the bankruptcy estate.

.05 11 U.S.C. §505.

HANDICAPPED AND DISABLED TAXPAYERS

Introduction

¶25,676 The federal income tax laws afford advantages to taxpayers who are handicapped or disabled. Such taxpayers are eligible for certain deductions and exclusions from their taxable income as well as for credits applied directly against their taxes. In addition, taxpayers with handicapped or disabled dependents are allowed certain deductions and credits for the care of those dependents. Credits and deductions are also available to taxpayers who employ handicapped or disabled individuals or who make expenditures that enabie the handicapped or disabled to become an integral part of our society. These deductions, exclusions, and credits are intended to enable the handicapped or disabled individual to make a meaningful economic contribution to society and to gain self-respect in the process. These tax benefits are also intended to enable a taxpayer with handicapped or disabled dependents to be better able to pursue his or her own goals and shoulder the accompanying responsibilities.

Definition of a Handicapped or Disabled Individual

¶25,677 Definition of a Handicapped or Disabled Individual. The term "handicapped or disabled individual" means any individual who has—

(1) A physical or mental disability (including, but not limited to, blindness or deafness) that for such individual constitutes or results in a substantial impairment or functional limitation to employment, or

(2) A physical or mental impairment (including, but not limited to a sight or hearing impairment) that substantially limits one or more of such individual's major life activities, such as performing manual tasks, walking, speaking, breathing, learning, or working (.05).

The federal tax laws affecting such individuals are keyed to this definition. If it seems that such a definition is too restrictive or overly inclusive, it must be remembered that it is used specifically for tax purposes.

(For purposes of the following paragraphs, the terms "handicapped" and "disabled," or "handicap" and "disability," are used in tandem to define the group of individuals with disabilities or impairments that are accorded special tax treatment.)

.05 Reg. §1.190-2(a)(3).

Taxable Income

¶25,679 Gross Income of Handicapped or Disabled Taxpayers. The handicapped or disabled taxpayer may receive income, payments, or other items that may or may not be includible in gross income (.05). The following is a list of items of particular interest to the handicapped or disabled taxpayer and information on how they should be treated for tax purposes:

(1) *Work-training program income*—Wages and payments received from state or local work-training programs that enable handicapped or disabled individuals to obtain job skills are includible in gross income. These programs are established under the Economic Opportunity Act of 1964.

(2) *Medical insurance premiums*—Medical insurance premiums paid by an employer for an employee or the employee's spouse or dependents are not includible in gross income. If, upon retirement, the taxpayer has the option of continued coverage or receiving a lump-sum payment, receipt of that payment, if chosen, results in includible gross income.

(3) *Unemployment compensation*—Payments received in lieu of unemployment compensation because of a taxpayer's disability are treated as unemployment compensation. The entire amount of unemployment compensation is includible in gross income (.10).

(4) *Disability payments*—Amounts paid by the taxpayer's employer in lieu of wages for sickness or injury are fully includible in gross income, regardless of whether the payments are made directly by the employer or by a third party. If the payments are made under a plan to which both the taxpayer and his employer make contributions, then the payments made for sickness or injury are includible in income to the extent of the employer's contribution to the plan.

(5) *Gifts, bequests, and inheritances*—Generally, gifts, bequests, and inheritances are not includible in gross income although income received from, or generated by, these items may be includible.

(6) *Social Security benefits*—Amounts received as Social Security benefits may be includible in the taxpayer's gross income. A recipient may be taxed on a portion of those benefits if his income exceeds a certain base amount.

(7) *Welfare payments*—Payments, such as those made for blindness, received by taxpayers in the form of public assistance, are not includible in gross income. If a taxpayer receives welfare payments and also participates in a welfare agency-sponsored work-training program, any wages and payments made under the program that exceed welfare benefits received for the tax year are includible in the taxpayer's gross income.

(8) *Community service payments*—If a handicapped or disabled taxpayer is employed in community service under the Employment Opportunities for Handicapped Individuals Act, any wages, allowances, or reimbursements paid to the taxpayer are excludable from gross income. Examples of excludable reimbursements that enable such individuals to perform their jobs include transportation costs, interpreter services for the deaf, reader services for the blind, and services to help mentally retarded persons do their work.

(9) *Workers' compensation benefits*—Workers' compensation benefits, if received for sickness or injury, are excludable from gross income.

(10) *Military disability pensions*—Generally, disability payments to Armed Forces members are includible in gross income. An exclusion from gross income is provided for disability payments to Armed Forces members if: (a) the Armed Forces member was entitled to receive the payment before September 25, 1975, (b) the recipient was an Armed Forces member before that date, (c) the disability payments are for a "combat-

related injury," or (d) the recipient is eligible to receive Veterans Administration benefits.

.05 IRS Publication No. 907, "Tax Highlights for Persons with Disabilities" CCH IRS PUBLICATIONS.

.10 Code Sec. 85.

¶25,680 Standard Deduction—Blindness. The following basic standard deduction amounts (adjusted for inflation) are available to all individuals for 2004: married filing jointly and surviving spouses, $$9,700; married filing separately, $4,850; single filers, $4,850; and head-of-household filers, $7,150. To the basic standard deduction, an elderly or blind *married* individual or surviving spouse adds $950 or $1,900 if the individual is both elderly and blind in 2004. The increase for an elderly or blind *unmarried* individual is $1,200 or $2,400 if the individual is both elderly and blind in 2004.

Normally, an individual who is eligible to be claimed as a dependent on another's tax return must file his own tax return only if he has gross income in excess of the standard deduction, including the additional standard deduction for blind taxpayers, or if he has unearned income in excess of, for 2004, $800 plus the additional standard deduction allowance (.10).

.10 Code Sec. 63(c), *General Explanation of the Tax Reform Act of 1986,* Staff of the Joint Committee on Taxation, p. 24.

Medical Expenses

¶25,682 Deduction in General. A taxpayer is allowed to deduct the amounts paid for medical care for himself, his spouse, or his dependents (.05). Medical care is broadly defined to include amounts paid for the diagnosis, cure, mitigation, treatment, or prevention of disease, or for the purpose of affecting any structure or function of the body. Although the costs of transportation necessary to obtain medical care do not come under the literal definition of medical care, they are deductible as medical expenses, as are the costs of meals and lodging provided by a hospital or similar medical institution, as a necessary part of the medical care provided by those institutions. Likewise, payments of insurance premiums for medical care are deductible medical expenses. Amounts paid for qualified long-term care services and certain long-term care insurance premiums are also medical care. Although amounts paid for cosmetic surgery are not generally deductible, an exception applies if the procedure is necessary to ameliorate a deformity relating to a congenital defect or personal injury from an accident, trauma or disease and if the procedure promotes proper body function or prevents or treats illness or disease (.10).

Amount deductible

The deduction for medical expenses is limited to that portion of total medical expenses that exceeds 7.5 percent of the taxpayer's adjusted gross income and may only be taken as an itemized deduction. All deductible expenditures for medicine and drugs are pooled with other medical and dental expenses and are subject to the 7.5 percent limitation. Moreover, only costs for prescribed drugs and insulin are deductible as medical expenses.

Deductible medical care items

The following are lists of items payments for which are includible in calculating the medical expense deduction.

(1) Doctor's services, including services of:

(a) anesthesiologists

(b) chiropodists

(c) dermatologists

(d) gynecologists

(e) neurologists

(f) obstetricians

(g) ophthalmologists

(h) osteopaths

(i) pediatricians

(j) podiatrists

(k) psychiatrists

(l) surgeons

(m) Christian Science practitioners

(2) Hospital services, including:

(a) ambulance

(b) dental

(c) diagnostic

(d) laboratory

(e) nursing

(f) obstetrical

(g) surgical

(h) therapy

(i) X-ray

(3) Other items, including:

(a) Abortions

(b) Acupuncture

(c) Admission and transportation to medical conventions related to chronic illness

(d) Artificial limbs and teeth

(e) Birth control pills

(f) Certain lodging primarily for and essential to medical care

(g) Contact lenses

(h) Crutches

(i) Meals and lodging provided by a hospital or by an alcohol and drug treatment center during treatment

(j) Medical and hospital insurance premiums

(k) Prescription medicines and drugs and insulin

(l) Special dietary supplements, if prescribed

(m) Special equipment for the handicapped and disabled

(n) Special nursing or attendant care

(o) Stop-smoking programs

(p) Transportation for necessary medical care.

(q) Weight-loss programs (.15)

Handicapped and disabled taxpayers

Individual handicapped or disabled taxpayers, as well as handicapped or disabled spouses and dependents of taxpayers, incur medical expenses unique to their particular handicap or disability. Consequently, medical expense deductions are allowed for the cost of special items of medical care necessary to the well-being of the handicapped or disabled individual or instrumental in the alleviation of the handicap or disability. Generally, payments are deductible if they are made for items or treatment that helps the taxpayer, his spouse, or dependent compensate for, mitigate, or alleviate a handicap or disability unique to his personal situation, as the following paragraphs indicate.

.05 Code Sec. 213.

.10 Rev. Rul. 2003-57, I.R.B. 2003-22, 959.

.15 IRS Publication No. 502, "Medical and Dental Expenses", CCH IRS PUBLICATIONS.

¶25,683 Capital Expenditures as Medical Expense Deductions. Expenses paid for medical care are not necessarily rendered nondeductible merely because they also qualify as capital expenditures (.05). However, if the capital expenditures constitute permanent improvements to the taxpayer's property, they will be disallowed as medical expense deductions to the extent that they increase the value of that property (.10). In other words, a capital expenditure for medical care is deductible to the extent that the expenses paid exceed the fair market value increase in the taxpayer's property. This rule has been applied to allow partial deductions for expenses paid for the installation of elevators and swimming pools for therapeutic and medical care purposes (.15). Similarly, the installation of specialized equipment in the home or auto of a handicapped or disabled individual may give rise to a medical expense deduction.

Expenditures for removal of structural barriers

Capital expenditures that are incurred by a physically handicapped individual for the removal of structural barriers in his personal residence qualify for a medical expense deduction where the expenditures are necessary to accommodate the handicapped condition (.20). Examples of these types of expenditures include:

(1) the construction of entrance/exit ramps to the residence;

(2) the widening of doorways at the entrance/exit of the residence;

(3) the widening or other modification of hallways and interior doorways to accommodate wheelchairs;

(4) the installation of railings, support bars, or other modifications in bathrooms necessary to accommodate handicapped individuals;

(5) the lowering, or other modification, of kitchen cabinets and equipment to allow access by handicapped individuals; and

(6) the adjustment of electrical outlets and fixtures necessary to accommodate handicapped individuals.

The above list is not intended to be all-inclusive, and the IRS is free to identify similar expenditures that are necessary to accommodate handicapped individuals (.25). The types of expenditures described above do not add to the fair market value of a personal residence and, therefore, should be fully deductible as medical expenses.

.05 IRS Publication No. 907, "Tax Highlights for Persons with Disabilities," CCH IRS PUBLICATIONS.

.10 *R.A. Polacsek,* 42 TCM 1289, CCH Dec. 38,313 (M), TC Memo. 1981-569.

.15 Rev. Rul. 59-411, 1959-2 CB 100; *C.B. Mason,* DC Haw., 57-2 USTC ¶ 10,012.

.20 Senate and Conference Committee Reports to the Tax Reform Act of 1986 (P.L. 99-514).

.25 Rev. Rul. 87-106, 1987-2 CB 67.

¶25,684 Medical v. Business Expenses. At times, the issue of the deductibility of payments for services, procedures, or goods, apparently of a medical nature, can be a source of confusion to taxpayers. Thus, a business trip by a handicapped person who is accompanied by a companion who assists him in getting around can produce the following results: (1) no deduction at all for the meals and lodging provided for the companion if the companion is the taxpayer's spouse, since these costs would represent ordinary nondeductible living expenses; (2) a medical expense deduction for the cost of travel, meals, and lodging if the person providing the assistance is the handicapped person's neighbor, for instance, and the services provided are of the type that would be required in the taxpayer's personal life as well as incidentally in the conduct of business; or (3) a business expense deduction if the neighbor is providing services that would not be required in the taxpayer's personal activities but arise only because of business needs (.05).

Business expense deductions may be claimed where all of the following elements are present: (1) the nature of the taxpayer's work clearly requires that he incur a particular expense to satisfactorily perform such work; (2) the goods or services purchased are clearly not required or used, other than incidentally, in the conduct of the individual's personal activities; and (3) the federal income tax laws are otherwise silent as to the treatment of such an expense (.10). Another tax consequence of the delineation between medical expenses and business expenses is that, although medical expenses must be taken as itemized deductions, business expenses are deductible from gross income.

Accordingly, payments made by blind employees to readers for services performed in connection with the conduct of the blind employees' work were deductible as business expenses because the readers' services were required and used solely in the conduct of the work of the blind taxpayers (.10).

.05 Rev. Rul. 75-317, 1975-2 CB 57.

.10 Rev. Rul. 75-316, 1975-2 CB 119.

¶25,685 Special Transportation Equipment Costs. The cost of specialized equipment for the transportation of handicapped and disabled individuals is often deductible as a medical expense. The nature or the severity of the particular handicap or disability is not a controlling factor in determining deductibility of the cost of a particular item. For example, the tax laws have impacted heavily on the physically handicapped who must use extraordinary means of transportation when commuting to work. A handicapped taxpayer with a leg prosthesis was denied a deduction for the costs of using his car to commute to work (.05) even though he could not use public transportation, as was the case with a taxpayer afflicted with infantile paralysis (.10). However, a taxpayer who could not walk unaided due to a spinal cord injury was allowed a deduction for the cost of using his car in commuting to work because his doctor had recommended employment and commuting as therapeutic for the taxpayer. The use of the auto had to be primarily for and essential to the rendition of medical care to the taxpayer, and the fact that the handicapped individual's doctor had recommended the commuting as therapeutic was paramount in establishing that the use of the auto was necessary in rendering medical care to the taxpayer (.15).

The cost of hand controls and other equipment specially adapted to permit the operation or use of an automobile by a physically handicapped individual is a deductible medical expense (.20). Such costs are deductible, even though they are capital expenditures, because they are related only to the particular handicap or disability of the individual taxpayer and are not regarded as a permanent improvement of the taxpayer's property. Likewise, the excess cost of an automobile specially designed to accommodate wheelchair passengers is a capital expenditure that is related only to a person with a handicap or disability and is, therefore, deductible as a medical expense (.25). Excess cost is measured by subtracting from the cost of the specially designed automobile the cost of a comparable automobile of standard design. For example, if the specially designed vehicle cost $16,000 and the same model car not specially equipped is $14,500, then the amount that is deductible is $1,500 ($16,000 – $14,500). However, the operating and maintenance costs of such specially designed cars are not deductible as medical expenses.

Unlike specially designed cars, not only the entire purchase price, but also the maintenance and operating costs of wheelchairs and "autoettes" are fully deductible as medical expenses (.30). This is so because such items are used mainly for the alleviation of the taxpayer's handicap or disability and are not primarily used as transportation for the taxpayer.

.05 *A. Coopersmith,* 30 TCM 1203, CCH Dec. 31,057 (M), TC Memo 1971-280.

.10 *J. Donnelly,* 28 TC 1278, CCH Dec. 22,592, aff'd by CA-2, 59-1 USTC ¶9196, 262 F2d 411.

.15 *S.H. Weinzimer,* 17 TCM 712, CCH Dec. 23,100(M), TC Memo 1958-37.

.20 Rev. Rul. 66-80, 1966-1 CB 57.

.25 Rev. Rul. 70-606, 1970-2 CB 66.

.30 Rev. Rul. 58-8, 1958-1 CB 154 (modifying Rev. Rul. 55-261, 1955-1 CB 307), as amplified by Rev. Rul. 67-76, 1967-1 CB 70, and Rev. Rul. 56-280, 1958-1 CB 157.

¶25,686 Special Equipment Expenses of the Blind or Deaf. The costs of special items and equipment used by a blind or deaf taxpayer are deductible as medical expenses. The costs of purchasing, training, and keeping a seeing-eye guide dog and other service animals incurred by a blind taxpayer are deductible medical expenses (.05), as are the same costs incurred by a deaf taxpayer for a dog specially trained to aid the deaf to detect sounds (.10). The excess cost of braille books and magazines over the cost of the same printed material is deductible. For example, if the printed book or magazine costs $10.00 and the same material printed in braille costs $15.00, the $5.00 excess cost to print the braille material is the amount deductible as a medical expense (.15).

The cost of having someone accompany a taxpayer's daughter, who was blind from birth, in order to assist her in walking to her classes on campus was a deductible medical expense (.20), as was the cost of hiring someone to accompany the deaf child of a taxpayer to take notes during her classes (.25). The costs of special educational materials that prepared a child going blind to be able to cope with her eventual total blindness were also deductible.

Special equipment costs for the deaf that are deductible as medical expenses include the cost and repair of special telephone equipment that allows a deaf person to communicate over regular phones (.30). The excess cost of a specially equipped television set that provides captions for the hearing-impaired over the cost of a standard television set of the same model is also deductible (.35).

.05 Rev. Rul. 55-261, 1955-1 CB 307, modified by Rev. Rul. 58-8, 1958-1 CB 154, amplified by Rev. Rul. 67-76, 1967-1 CB 70, and Rev. Rul. 58-280, 1958-1 CB 157.

.10 Rev. Rul. 68-295, 1968-1 CB 92.

.15 Rev. Rul. 75-318, 1975-2 CB 88.

.20 Rev. Rul. 64-173, 1964-1 CB (Part 1) 121.

.25 *R.A. Baer Est.*, 26 TCM 170, CCH Dec. 28,352(M), TC Memo 1967-34.

.30 Rev. Rul. 71-48, 1971-1 CB 99, amplified by Rev. Rul. 73-53, 1973-1 CB 139.

.35 Rev. Rul. 80-340, 1980-2 CB 81.

¶25,687 Other Special Equipment Expenses. Other special equipment expenses are deductible as medical expenses. For instance, the costs of purchasing and operating an iron lung and associated equipment were deductible. However, the costs of construction in the taxpayer's home and a change in the taxpayer's home heating unit to accommodate the iron lung were not deductible (.05). Also, amounts paid for the purchase and installation of special bathroom equipment for a handicapped taxpayer were deductible (.10). However, the purchase and installation costs of a cellular phone in a taxpayer's automobile were disallowed as a medical expense deduction because the taxpayer could not prove that the phone was necessary to contact his doctor even though he was severely handicapped and had a heart condition (.15).

.05 Rev. Rul. 55-261, 1955-1 CB 307, modified by Rev. Rul. 58-8, 1958-1 CB 154, amplified by Rev. Rul. 67-76, 1967-1 CB 70, and Rev. Rul. 58-280, 1958-1 CB 157.

.10 Rev. Rul. 70-395, 1970-2 CB 65.

.15 *G.M. Womack*, 34 TCM 1009, CCH Dec. 33,323(M), TC Memo 1975-232.

¶25,688 Special Educational Needs for Handicapped and Disabled Dependents. Although ordinary education is not medical care, the cost of medical care for income tax purposes includes the cost of attending a special school by a mentally or physically handicapped individual, if the resources of the institution for alleviating the handicap or disability are a principal reason for his presence there. The costs of attending such a special school may include both the costs of meals and lodging and the cost of ordinary education that is incidental to the special services furnished by the school.

The cost of medical care includes the cost of attending a special school designed to compensate for, or overcome, a physical handicap in order to qualify the individual for future standard education or for social and economic intercourse, such as a school for the teaching of braille or lip reading. Likewise, the cost of care and supervision or the treatment and training of a mentally retarded or physically handicapped individual at an institution is included within the meaning of "medical care" (.05).

Special school

There are two parts to the "special school" requirement. Objectively, the school must have facilities to treat handicapped or disabled students. Subjectively, that treatment must somehow alleviate or compensate for the student's particular handicap or disability and must be the primary reason for the student's attendance at that school. However, the fact that a child is sent to a special school for an education as well as for medical care will not bar a medical expense deduction for the entire cost of the handicapped or disabled child's education (tuition, meals, and lodging) (.10).

Entitlement to the medical care expense deduction for special educational facilities requires that the institution rendering the special educational instruction qualify as a "special school." The primary reason for the handicapped or disabled dependent's attending the school must be because of its ability to treat the specific handicap or disability of the individual. A reputation of a school for strict discipline (.15) for being tolerant of and accommodating to handicapped or disabled individuals is not sufficient to qualify such institution as a special school. A doctor's recommendation that the handicapped or disabled dependent would do well to attend a certain school is also insufficient if that institution lacks the requisite facilities.

Private boarding schools attended by a hyperactive child (.20) and a deaf child (.25) were not considered special schools; therefore, no deduction was permitted for tuition costs, even though attendance at the schools was recommended by a physician. The taxpayer should be prepared to show that enrollment at a school for the physically handicapped or emotionally disturbed child is primarily for alleviation of the particular handicap. This would allow the entire cost at the school to be claimed as a medical deduction (.30).

Special services

In some instances, however, a child may be sent to a school that is not a special school, but that does provide special services for the handicapped or disabled child. For example, expenses of psychological counseling and tutoring for a learning disabled child received at a preparatory school were deductible as medical expenses, although the costs of tuition and room and board were not deductible (.35).

Transportation costs

Transportation costs incurred in sending a handicapped or disabled child to special schools or in obtaining special training or instruction are deductible as medical expenses (.40). Also deductible as medical expenses were costs of transporting a wheelchair-confined daughter of a taxpayer to a public school, even though she could have received instruction at home. This was because the girl's doctor had recommended that she attend school for therapeutic reasons (that is, to help her deal emotionally with her handicap) (.45).

.05 Reg. §1.213-1(e)(1)(v)(a).
.10 *H.J. Hendrick*, 35 TC 1223, CCH Dec. 24,772.
.15 *J. Giovengo*, 37 TCM 1551, CCH Dec. 35,420(M), TC Memo 1978-375.
.20 *Dr. E.M. Newkirk*, DC Ohio, 77-1 USTC ¶9452.
.25 *J.R. Martin*, CA-6, 77-1 USTC ¶9180, 548 F2d 633.
.30 *R.B. Donovan*, DC Tex., 61-1 USTC ¶9357.
.35 *A.J. Sims*, 39 TCM 700, CCH Dec. 36,493(M), TC Memo 1979-499.
.40 Rev. Rul. 70-285, 1970-1 CB 52.
.45 Rev. Rul. 65-255, 1965-2 CB 76.

¶25,689 Individualized Training for Handicapped and Disabled Children. The cost of individualized training of a handicapped or disabled child, whether inside or outside of an institutional setting, is usually deductible as a medical expense if it helps alleviate or compensate for the individual child's handicap or disability. For instance, "patterning exercises" administered by a non-professional and given to a mentally retarded child to enable the child to coordinate his physical movements qualified as deductible medical care costs (.05).

However, there have been mixed results for taxpayers who have endeavored to obtain special training for their children with dyslexia and other reading disorders. In one instance, individual training by a special tutor of a dyslexic child was medical care, the costs of the tutor's fees being deductible (.10). In contrast, dyslexic children sent to private schools that offered intensive remedial reading courses conducive to alleviating dyslexia were not deemed to have received medical care and the tuition costs were nondeductible (.15). In the latter cases, the schools may have helped the handicapped or disabled children alleviate their particular handicaps, but because the courses were available to both handicapped and nonhandicapped children, the costs for such courses were not deductible medical expenses. In the former case, the tutoring was specifically designed to alleviate a particular child's dyslexia.

.05 Rev. Rul. 70-170, 1970-1 CB 51.
.10 Rev. Rul. 69-607, 1969-2 CB 40.
.15 *R.G. Barnes*, 37 TCM 1408, CCH Dec. 35,370(M), TC Memo 1978-339; *L.J. Coyne*, 43 TCM 1351, CCH Dec. 39,017(M), TC Memo 1982-262.

¶25,690 Special Institutional or Home Care for the Handicapped and Disabled. The cost of institutional care for the severely handicapped or disabled is deductible as a medical expense. For instance, the costs of maintaining a mentally ill daughter at a specially equipped children's center, including room, board, and care by qualified personnel, were deductible as medical expenses, as were the transportation costs of the child's parents in travelling to visit her because such visits were therapeutic for the child (.05).

Advance payments made by parents required as a condition for enrolling their handicapped or disabled child in a special care institution in order to guarantee lifetime payments for the care of the child in case of the parents' untimely demise are fully deductible on a current basis if the future care is purchased in connection with obtaining specified types of lifetime care (.10). So are the costs of maintaining a child in a nonprofit therapeutic center for the purposes of helping a formerly mentally disturbed or mentally retarded child adjust from life in an institution to life in his community (.15). If it is deemed therapeutic for the handicapped or disabled child to live at home with his parents at his doctor's recommendation, costs incurred for that home care are also deductible.

Nursing care costs

Nursing home costs for the handicapped and disabled are deductible as medical expenses only if the nursing home has the special facilities to help alleviate, compensate for, or treat the handicapped or disabled dependent's particular handicap or disability (.20). This requirement is similar to the one mentioned at ¶25,689 for special schools. The costs of nursing care at the taxpayer's home are deductible as to the services themselves, including the costs of meals and lodging for the attendant nurse, but the costs of any work done by such an attendant that is unrelated to nursing the handicapped or disabled individual, such as household chores, is not deductible (.25), but may be eligible for a credit (see ¶25,694).

Legal fees

Legal fees and other related costs arising with respect to the confinement or commitment of a handicapped individual at an institution for special care are deductible as medical expenses (.30).

.05 Rev. Rul. 58-533, 1958-2 CB 108.

.10 Rev. Rul. 93-72, 1993-2 CB 77, clarifying Rev. Rul. 75-303, 1975-2 CB 87.

.15 Rev. Rul. 69-499, 1969-2 CB 39.

.20 *E.J. Ball*, 37 TCM 1573, CCH Dec. 35,433(M), TC Memo 1978-384; *H.W. Smith*, 79 TC 313, CCH Dec. 39,273 (Acq.).

.25 Rev. Rul. 76-106, 1976-1 CB 72.

.30 Rev. Rul. 71-281, 1971-2 CB 165.

Tax Credits for the Handicapped and Disabled

¶25,692 In General. The federal income tax laws offer credits that are to be applied directly against the tax liability of taxpayers who are handicapped or who have spouses or dependents who are handicapped or disabled. The following is an explanation of the credits available to taxpayers who are totally and permanently disabled and to individuals who have disabled dependents or spouses and who must incur expenses for their care with respect to those hours during which they are employed and unable to care for their spouses or dependents personally. These credits are often overlooked because they are part of credits available to taxpayers who neither are handicapped or disabled nor have disabled or handicapped spouses or dependents.

¶25,693 Credit for the Permanently and Totally Disabled. Taxpayers under age 65 who retire with a permanent and total disability and who received taxable disability income from a private or public employer are entitled to a credit against their taxes (.05). Married individuals generally must file a joint return to claim the credit. The credit may also be claimed by married individuals filing separate returns if such individuals did not live in the same household at any time during the tax year.

Permanent and total disability defined

An individual is permanently and totally disabled if he is unable to engage in any substantial gainful activity by reason of any medically determinable physical or mental impairment that can be expected to result in death or that has lasted, or can be expected to last, for a continuous period of not less than 12 months. It is up to the taxpayer to furnish proof to the IRS of such permanent and total disability in order to claim the credit.

"Substantial gainful activity" is defined as the performance of significant duties over a reasonable period of time in work for remuneration or profit, or in work of a type generally performed for wages or profit. A taxpayer who engages in full- or part-time work in competitive circumstances for at least the minimum wage is treated as having engaged in "substantial gainful activity."

Amount of credit

The maximum credit is equal to 15 percent of a taxpayer's "initial amount," which is:

(1) $5,000 in the case of a single individual,

(2) $5,000 in the case of married individuals filing a joint return where one spouse qualifies,

(3) $7,500 in the case of a married couple filing a joint return where both spouses qualify, and

(4) $3,750 in the case of a married individual filing separately.

If the disability payments received are less than the applicable initial amount, the taxpayer's initial amount is limited to the amount of disability income. The initial amount, however, is subject to reduction for certain excludable retirement-type benefits and for half of the taxpayer's adjusted gross income in excess of certain levels ($7,500 for single individuals, heads of households, and qualifying surviving spouses; $10,000 for married persons filing jointly; and $5,000 for married persons filing separately).

□ For further information, see ¶25,761 and ¶25,762.

.05 Code Sec. 22.

¶25,694 Dependent Care Credit for Employment-Related Expenses. Although primarily known as the child care credit, this tax credit is also available to taxpayers with handicapped or disabled dependents (.05). The function of this credit is to give taxpayers with disabled or handicapped dependents an incentive for seeking gainful employment. The taxpayer is allowed, as a credit against his taxes, a certain amount of the costs of procuring care for his handicapped or disabled dependent so that he can be employed.

Employment-related expenses

The expenses incurred for the care of the handicapped or disabled dependents must be employment-related, that is, they must be incurred to enable the taxpayer to maintain steady employment by relieving him of the responsibility of caring for the dependent while he is at work. Such expenses include those paid for household services and for the care of the handicapped or disabled dependent. They must be incurred during a period in which one or more qualifying handicapped or disabled individuals live in the taxpayer's household for at least eight hours a day (.10).

Household services qualifying for the credit include those for a maid or a cook who provides services to the taxpayer's dependent. They do not include the services of a gardener, bartender, or chauffeur.

To the extent that employment-related expenses are reimbursed by a state welfare agency, they may not be used in determining the credit (.15); however, to the extent that they exceed the reimbursement, such expenses are eligible for the credit (.20).

Qualifying individuals

The taxpayer's handicapped or disabled dependent must be classified as a "qualifying individual" in order for the taxpayer to be eligible for the credit. The term "qualifying individual" includes a taxpayer's dependent spouse who is physically or mentally incapable of caring for himself. Effective for tax years beginning after December 31, 2004, a disabled dependent or spouse must have the same principal place of abode as the taxpayer for more than one-half of the tax year (.25).

Amount of credit

If taxpayers have adjusted gross income of $15,000 or less, they are allowed a credit equal to 35 percent of employment-related expenses. For taxpayers with adjusted gross income over $15,000 and up to and including $43,000, the credit is reduced by one percentage point for each $2,000 of adjusted gross income, or fraction thereof, above $15,000. For taxpayers with adjusted gross income over $43,000, the credit is 20 percent of employment-related expenses.

The maximum amount of employment-related expenses to which the credit can be applied is $3,000 if one qualifying child or dependent is involved or $6,000 if two or more qualifying individuals are involved. However, the $3,000 or $6,000 limit (whichever one applies) must be reduced by the amount excludable from gross income for child and dependent care provided by an employer under a nondiscriminatory plan.

The following table outlines the *maximum* credit available at each adjusted gross income level.

Adjusted Gross Income Over — But Not Over:	*Applicable Percentage*	*Maximum Credits: One Qualifying Individual*	*Maximum Credits: Two or More Qualifying Individuals*
$ —0— $ 15,000	35%	$ 1050	$ 2,100
15,000 — 17,000	34%	1020	2,040
17,000 — 19,000	33%	990	1,980
19,000 — 21,000	32%	960	1,920
21,000 — 23,000	31%	930	1,860
23,000 — 25,000	30%	900	1,800
25,000 — 27,000	29%	870	1,740
27,000 — 29,000	28%	840	1,680
29,000 — 31,000	27%	810	1,620
31,000 — 33,000	26%	780	1,560
33,000 — 35,000	25%	750	1,500
35,000 — 37,000	24%	720	1,440
37,000 — 39,000	23%	690	1,380
39,000 — 41,000	22%	660	1,320
41,000 — 43,000	21%	630	1,260
43,000 —	20%	600	1,200

Married v. single taxpayer

If a taxpayer is married, the credit is available only if the couple files a joint return. A married taxpayer will not be considered married for purpose of the credit if he—

(1) has lived apart from his spouse for at least the last six months of the tax year,

(2) files a separate return,

(3) maintains the household in which the qualifying dependent lives for more than half the year, and

(4) furnishes more than half the cost of maintaining the household for the entire tax year.

A taxpayer who is legally separated from his spouse under a decree of divorce or separate maintenance is not considered married and can claim the credit on a separate return.

.05 Code Sec. 21; Reg. §§1.44A-1—4; IRS Publication No. 907, "Tax Highlights for Persons with Disabilities," CCH IRS PUBLICATIONS.

.10 Code Sec. 21(c)(2)(B).

.15 IRS Letter Ruling 8210023, 11-30-81, CCH IRS LETTER RULINGS REPORTS.

.20 Rev. Rul. 83-1, 1983-1 CB 9.

.25 Code Sec. 21(b)(1), as amended by the Working Families Tax Relief Act of 2004 (P.L. 108-311).

Credits for Aiding Handicapped and Disabled Individuals

¶25,696 In General. A taxpayer who aids a handicapped or disabled individual is rewarded under the federal income tax laws for helping to make it possible for such handicapped or disabled person to become a productive member of society. The following paragraphs explain how a taxpayer who incurs expenses to aid the handicapped or disabled or affords opportunities to such individuals can benefit from certain deductions and credits regarding his income tax.

¶25,697 Expenditures to Remove Architectural and Transportation Barriers to Handicapped and Elderly Persons. A taxpayer can elect to deduct the costs of removing architectural and transportation barriers for the year in which such expenses are paid or incurred, rather than amortizing those costs over the life of the asset (.05). Qualified costs include those paid to make any facility or public transportation vehicle owned or leased by the taxpayer in his trade or business more accessible to and usable by handicapped or elderly individuals. Barrier removal also must meet standards set by the Architectural and Transportation Barriers Compliance Board.

Deduction limitations

The maximum deduction for each tax year for such expenses is $15,000. Expenses incurred above this $15,000 limit must be treated as capital expenditures.

The $15,000 limitation applies both to a partnership and to each partner. In applying the $15,000 limit, a partner must combine his distributive share of the partnership's deductible barrier-removal expenditures (after application of the $15,000 limit at the partnership level) with his distributive share of any such deductible expenses distributed to him from any other partnerships and with any other barrier-removal expenditures that he has incurred.

A credit is also available for expenditures paid or incurred by eligible small businesses (those that had, for the preceding tax year, either gross receipts of up to $1 million or up to 30 full-time employees) to make a business accessible to disabled individuals. The amount of the credit for any tax year is 50 percent of the year's eligible access expenditures for the year that exceed $250 but do not exceed $10,250. The maximum credit is $5,000 per year. No deduction, including the deduction for expenditures to remove architectural and transportation barriers to handicapped and elderly persons, is allowed for any amount for which the disabled access credit is also allowed (.10).

Recapture of deductions

If the personal property for which the deduction is claimed is subsequently sold at a gain, the amount of the previously taken deduction is recaptured as ordinary income (.15). If similar real property is sold, the amount of this deduction is not subject to recapture.

Election procedures

An election to deduct such expenditures is made by claiming a separate deduction for barrier-removal expenditures on a timely filed income tax return (taking into account any extensions of time granted). In the case of a partnership, such an election is made by the partnership on the partnership's information return.

.05 Code Sec. 190; Reg. §§1.190-1—1.190-3; IRS Publication No. 907, "Tax Highlights for Persons with Disabilities", CCH IRS PUBLICATIONS.

.10 Code Sec. 44.

.15 Code Sec. 1245(a)(3)(C).

¶25,698 Work Opportunity Credit. Employers who hire individuals from certain designated target groups may be eligible for a credit with respect to wages and salaries paid to these individuals who begin work after September 30, 1996, and before January 1, 2006 (.05). One of these targeted groups includes handicapped individuals undergoing vocational rehabilitation. Individuals in this group are those who have a disability that is a substantial handicap to employment. Such an individual must be designated as a member of such a target group by a local agency qualified to do so as determined by either the Secretary of Labor or the Secretary of the Treasury and may not be a relative or dependent of the employer claiming the credit. The individual generally must obtain such designation on or before the day on which he begins employment in order for the employer to take the work opportunity credit.

The work opportunity credit applies to 40 percent of the first $6,000 of wages paid to each eligible employee during the first year of employment, assuming the employee performs at least 400 hours of service during that year, for a maximum of $2,400. The credit drops to 25 percent of wages if the hours of service during the first year are at least 120 but less than 400 hours. The employer's deduction for wages and salaries paid or incurred must be reduced by the amount of the credit determined for the tax year.

.05 Code Sec. 51, as amended by the Working Families Tax Relief Act of 2004 (P.L. 108-311); IRS Publication No. 907, "Tax Highlights for Persons with Disabilities", CCH IRS PUBLICATIONS.

¶25,699 Housing for the Handicapped and Disabled. A nonprofit organization that provides specially designed housing to physically handicapped individuals at the lowest feasible cost and maintains in residence those handicapped tenants who subsequently become unable to pay their monthly fees is treated for tax purposes as operated exclusively for charitable purposes and, therefore, is eligible for treatment as a charitable organization under the federal income tax laws (.05). The IRS has determined that such an organization is operated to relieve the major forms of distress to which physically handicapped individuals are susceptible (.10).

.05 Code Sec. 501(c)(3).

.10 Rev. Rul. 79-19, 1979-1 CB 195.

WORKING FAMILIES

Introduction

¶25,700 The working family—that is, the two-earner married couple or the employed taxpayer (single or married) with one or more dependents—has been the focus of many tax relief measures designed to alleviate some of the special economic problems faced by these taxpayers. Among these measures are:

(1) lower tax rates applicable to joint returns for married couples and heads of households (¶25,701 and ¶25,702);

(2) the earned income credit for low-income workers with or without dependents (¶25,706);

(3) the credit for dependent care expenses (¶25,710); and

(4) the exclusion for dependent care services that are provided by an employer (¶25,721).

Working families are also able to take advantage of tax laws that benefit taxpayers in general, such as the deductions for contributions to an individual retirement account (IRA) (¶25,725) or a Keogh plan (¶25,726). In addition, the use of income-splitting devices, such as the assignment of income-producing property (¶25,728), family partnerships (¶25,734) and the employment of one's spouse (¶25,731), may also benefit working families.

The following paragraphs—¶25,701 through ¶25,737—provide a guide for working families in making decisions that will avoid the pitfalls and maximize the tax advantages associated with these provisions.

Tax Status Factors in Preparing Return

¶25,701 Filing Status and Tax Rates. A six-tiered schedule of tax rates has been devised for the income taxation of individuals, including (in 2004) a 10-percent rate for the first level of income, a 15-percent rate for the second level of income, a 25-percent rate for the third level of income, a 28-percent rate for the fourth level of income, a 33-percent rate for the fifth level of income, and a 35-percent rate for all remaining income (.05). For example, in 2004, the first $7,150 of an unmarried individual's taxable income is subject to the 10-percent rate, income over $7,150 but not over $29,050 is taxed at the 15-percent rate, income over $29,050 but not over $70,350 is taxed at the 25-percent rate, income over $70,350 but not over $146,750 is taxed at the 28-percent rate, income over $146,750 but not over $319,100 is taxed at the 33-percent rate, and all income over $319,100 is taxed at the 35-percent rate (.10).

In computing how much income is actually subject to taxation (i.e., in determining *taxable* income, individuals automatically are entitled to two tax deductions, a personal exemption and the standard deduction (.15). A personal exemption is granted simply as a tax favor to ease the tax bite on all individuals. In 2004, the exemption is $3,100 (.20). An additional exemption of $3,100 may be claimed by an individual for each person who is dependent upon him for support (.25).

The standard deduction provides individuals with a tax savings for expenses they may have during a tax year without requiring them to specifically account for the expenses. Thus, for unmarried persons, the standard deduction in 2004 is $4,850, which means, for example, that someone who has income of $30,000 automatically is able to reduce taxable income to $25,150 even though actual tax deductible expenses for the year fall short of the standard deduction. If an individual's itemized deductions exceed the standard deduction, the itemized deductions should be deducted in lieu of the standard deduction. Itemized deductions are claimed on Form 1040 Schedule A. (For the limit on the amount of itemized deductions that may be claimed by high-income taxpayers, see Code Sec. 68, discussed at ¶6040). A wide range of trade or business expenses may be claimed in addition to the standard deduction or the itemized deductions claimed on Schedule A (.30).

A taxpayer's tax burden also depends on his income tax return filing status, leaving a single taxpayer who claims single filing status with a higher tax bill than a married couple filing a joint return and reporting the same amount of income. Four tax rate schedules have been devised, including one for married individuals filing joint returns and surviving spouses, one for heads of household, one for unmarried individuals other than surviving spouses or heads of households, and one for married individuals filing separate returns.

.05 Code Sec. 1(a)-1(e).

.10 Code Sec. 1(h) and Code Sec. 1222(11); Rev. Proc. 2003-85, I.R.B. 2003-49.

.15 Code Sec. 63(c) and Code Sec. 151.

.20 Rev. Proc. 2003-85, I.R.B. 2003-49.

.25 Code Sec. 152.

.30 Code Sec. 62(a).

¶25,702 Determination of Marital and Head-of-Household Filing Status. A working family's marital and head-of-household filing status is a critical factor in the determination of the tax rate that may be applied to its taxable income. Generally, an individual's marital status is determined on the last day of his tax year (.05). If he is married on that day (December 31, for a calendar-year taxpayer), then he is treated as having been married for the entire year and qualifies to file a joint return. If divorced on that day, then the taxpayer is treated as if single for the entire year and may not file a joint return.

Death of spouse

An exception to this general rule is triggered upon the death of a spouse. In such a case, the marital status of the couple is determined as of the date of the decedent's death. However, the effect of the exception is simply to treat both spouses as if married so that the survivor may still file a joint return for the tax year in which the death occurred and may still claim an exemption for the decedent (.10). In addition, the survivor may use joint return tax rates to determine his tax liability in the following two tax years if he remains unmarried, had been entitled to file a joint return with his spouse during the year of death, and maintains as his home a household that is the principal place of residence of a child or stepchild for whom he may claim a dependency exemption.

Divorce

A person is considered to be married until a decree of divorce or legal separation takes effect. Even taxpayers who live apart and have obtained an interlocutory (interim), but not final, decree of divorce are treated as married for tax purposes (.15).

Head-of-household status

An unmarried taxpayer may qualify for the head-of-household tax rates, which fall between the rates payable by single individuals and those payable by married individuals filing jointly, provided that the taxpayer is not a nonresident alien and cannot qualify as a surviving spouse (see "Death of spouse," above).

The qualified head of household must also maintain his own principal place of abode and have as a member of such household, for over half of the tax year, one or more of the following persons (.20):

(1) A son or daughter, including a legally adopted child, or their descendants, or a stepchild of the taxpayer, but, if married at the close of the taxpayer's tax year, that person must be one for whom the taxpayer is entitled to a dependency exemption (that is, such person must have less than $3,100 gross income for 2004, unless he is under age 19 or a student under age 24, must receive more than one-half of his support from the taxpayer, and must not file a joint return (.25)).

(2) Any other "dependent" of the taxpayer, *other than a nonrelative* (.30), for whom a dependency exemption would otherwise be allowable under the tax law's relationship test (.35).

As noted above, the taxpayer must maintain as his home a household that is also the principal place of abode of the person(s) described in (1) or (2), above, and such "dependent(s)" must be a member(s) of the household and live there for over half of the taxpayer's tax year (.40). Temporary absences, such as vacation, time spent in college, and the like, are permissible (.45). Also, if the child or other person is born or dies during the taxable year, the taxpayer is still entitled to head-of-household treatment. To be considered as maintaining a household, the taxpayer must pay more than half the cost of upkeep (see ¶25,712).

Head-of-household status may also be extended to certain married individuals living apart from their spouses, whether voluntarily or involuntarily (e.g., an abandoned spouse) (.50). To so qualify, an individual must:

(1) file a separate return (.55),

(2) maintain as his home a household that, for over half of the tax year, is the principal place of abode of a dependent son or daughter (including stepson or stepdaughter) for whom the individual is entitled to a dependency deduction,

(3) furnish more than half of the cost of maintaining the household (see ¶25,712), and

(4) live apart from his spouse during the last six months of a tax year.

Custodial parent not entitled to dependency exemption

If a custodial parent is not entitled to a dependency exemption for a child because of (1) a waiver of the right to the exemption or (2) a pre-1985 divorce or separation instrument (¶6150), he or she still qualifies for head-of-household status for tax filing purposes (.60). The individual's spouse must not be a member of the household at any time during the last six months of the tax year (.65).

.05 Code Sec. 7703.
.10 Code Sec. 2(a) and 151; Reg. §1.2-2.
.15 Rev. Rul. 57-368, 1957-2 CB 896.
.20 Code Secs. 1 and 2(b) and (c); Reg. §1.2-2.
.25 Code Sec. 151(c)(1) and Code Sec. 152(a). However, see *I. Hilliard*, CA-6, 63-1 USTC ¶9126, 310

F2d 631, in which a father who maintained a home for his daughter was permitted to claim head-of-household status, even though the daughter, who was widowed during the course of the tax year, filed a joint return for herself and her deceased husband.

.30 *J. Whalen,* 35 TCM 611, CCH Dec. 33,900(M), TC Memo. 1976-137. See, also, Code Sec. 151.

.35 Code Sec. 151 and Code Sec. 152.

.40 Code Sec. 2(b); Reg. §1.2-2(c); *J. Prendergast,* CA-9, 73-2 USTC ¶9608, 483 F2d 970, aff'g TC, 57 TC 475, CCH Dec. 31,201; *R.M. Manning,* 72 TC 838, CCH Dec. 36,232; *A.J. Johnson,* 39 TCM 868, CCH Dec. 36,724(M), TC Memo. 1980-9. However, see *C. Smith,* CA-9, 64-2 USTC ¶9534, 332 F2d 671.

.45 *W. Petlow,* 34 TCM 51, CCH Dec. 33,017(M), TC Memo. 1975-13.

.50 Code Sec. 2(c) and 7703(b).

.55 In *F.V. Habersham-Bey,* 78 TC 304, CCH Dec. 38,826, the Tax Court stated that this provision should be read ". . . as a requirement that the taxpayer be treated as filing separately for income tax purposes because a joint return was not filed with the taxpayer's spouse, rather than as a strict requirement that the taxpayer in fact file a separate return."

.60 Code Sec. 152(e).

.65 Code Sec. 1(a)-1(e).

¶25,703 Decision to File Separately. Married couples must decide whether to file a joint return or separate returns. If a spouse files separately, he or she must report only his or her own income, exemptions and deductions on his or her return. Historically, married couples who file joint returns have had much lower income tax bills than couples who earn the same amount of income but file separate returns. Joint filing can also reduce a couple's minimum tax liability. This occurs, in part, because married joint filers are allowed a $58,000 alternative minimum tax exemption amount (for tax years 2003-2004) while separate married filers are entitled to only a $29,000 alternative minmum tax exemption amount for the same tax years (.05).

Deductions subject to adjusted gross income floor

Medical expenses are deductible only to the extent that they exceed 7.5 percent of the taxpayer's adjusted gross income. Because a husband and wife filing a joint return are treated as one taxpayer, if the taxpayers file separate returns, each may be able to claim a greater medical expense deduction (.10).

Miscellaneous itemized deductions are deductible only to the extent that the total of such deductions exceeds two percent of adjusted gross income. If one spouse has more of the miscellaneous deductions and less income than the other spouse does, a tax saving can result from filing separate returns. It is also important to consider how separate filing alters the impact of the limitation on itemized deductions faced by high-income taxpayers (Code Sec. 68).

Nonbusiness casualty and theft losses are deductible only to the extent that they exceed 10 percent of adjusted gross income. The filing of separate returns may result in a tax saving if the casualty is suffered by one spouse.

Deficiency liability

Filing a separate return will limit both the taxpayer's personal liability for reporting obligations and his tax deficiency.

Prohibition against joint returns

Married taxpayers have no choice and *must* file separate returns if:

(1) either the husband or wife at any time during the tax year is a nonresident alien and the couple choose not to treat the nonresident alien spouse as a U.S. resident (see ¶25,704);

(2) the husband and wife have different tax years not due to the death of either spouse; or

(3) after the death of a spouse, the estate (assuming the decedent's estate is probated and a personal representative is appointed) elects to file separate returns (.15).

The best recommendation for married couples who are not sure whether to file a joint return or separate returns is to figure their tax under both methods and to use the method that will result in the lower tax.

.05 Code Sec. 55(d).
.10 Code Sec. 213(a).
.15 Code Sec. 6013.

¶25,704 Nonresident Alien Spouses. As a general rule, a married couple may file income tax returns jointly or separately. However, a joint return is preferable, in most cases, due to the substantially lower tax rate imposed on joint income (.05). However, if a U.S. citizen or resident alien is married to a nonresident alien, a joint return may not be filed unless both spouses file an election with the IRS to treat the nonresident alien as a resident alien (.10). If an election is made, a joint return must be filed by the couple in the year of the election, though separate returns may be filed in later years. While it may appear that a nonresident alien who has no income from U.S. sources need not be concerned with filing status since he or she is not subject to U.S. taxation, the filing of a joint return may, at least, reduce his or her spouse's U.S. tax bill on income subject to U.S. taxation. If the nonresident alien has U.S. source income, an election for a joint return is doubly beneficial, since he or she may be taxed on the U.S. income.

Nonresident aliens, who are not treated as resident aliens, generally are taxed only on their income from U.S. sources (.15). Income that is from U.S. sources but that is not effectively connected with a U.S. trade or business, such as gross investment income, is taxed at a flat 30-percent rate. Regular U.S. income tax rates, for a married person filing separately, are imposed on most income that is effectively connected with a U.S. trade or business, such as income from the performance of personal services in the U.S. This income may be offset by deductions.

When a nonresident alien is treated as a resident alien, he is subject to U.S. taxation on worldwide income (i.e., income from foreign sources as well as from U.S. sources). However, as with any other U.S. citizen or resident alien, he is eligible for a foreign tax credit or itemized deductions for taxes paid to foreign governments on income earned in those countries (.20). He may also exclude up to $80,000, of foreign earned income from U.S. taxation (for tax years 2002 and beyond) and may be eligible to exclude or deduct some of the cost of foreign housing (.25).

An election to treat a nonresident alien spouse as a resident alien is made by attaching a statement, signed by both spouses, to the joint return for the first tax year of the election (.30). The statement must: (1) declare that one spouse is a nonresident alien on the last day of the tax year while the other spouse is a U.S. citizen or resident alien, (2) declare that the spouses choose to have the nonresident alien treated as a resident alien for the entire tax year, and (3) provide the name, address, and social security number of each spouse. An election is effective for all following tax years unless it is revoked by the spouses or the IRS, one spouse dies, or the spouses are legally separated (.35). It is also revoked as of any year in which neither spouse is a U.S. citizen or resident alien.

Head-of-household tax rate. If a married couple decides against treating the nonresident alien spouse as a resident alien, the spouse who is the U.S. citizen or resident alien cannot avoid the return filing status of married filing separately by treating the nonresident alien spouse as a dependent and thereby claiming the filing status of head of household, a status that provides a lower rate of taxation than that of married filing separately. A head-of-household rate may be elected by the spouse only if he or she has a qualifying dependent and meets the other head-of-household requirements discussed at ¶25,702 (.40).

.05 Code Sec. 6013.
.10 Code Sec. 6013(a)(1), (g), and (h) and Reg. §§1.6013-1(b) and 1.6013-6.
.15 Code Sec. 871.
.20 Code Sec. 901.
.25 Code Sec. 911.
.30 Reg. §1.6013-6(a)(4).
.35 Reg. §1.6013-6(a)(3) and (b).
.40 Rev. Rul. 74-370, 1974-2 CB 7, amplifying Rev. Rul. 55-711, 1955-2 CB 13.

Earned Income Credit

¶25,706 Credit for Low-Income Workers. Individuals, whether married or unmarried, with low levels of income may claim the earned income tax credit to reduce some or all of their income tax bill regardless of whether they have a qualifying child. They may claim the credit only if their income is from their job as opposed to their investments. The goal behind the credit is to provide these individuals with an incentive to work rather than to turn to government-sponsored welfare programs for the unemployed. In an extraordinary measure, the credit may be claimed even if a person does not have an income tax liability for the year and is not required to file an income tax return. He is entitled to a payment from the government in the amount of the credit simply for having earned a low amount of income. If a person has an income tax liability but his earned income credit exceeds the liability, he is entitled to a payment in the amount of the excess. In this sense, the credit is not like a credit at all, since no income taxes have been paid against which to offset the credit. Nor is it like a tax refund. It amounts to a flat payment from the government. The goal, in part, is to offset the social security taxes paid by low-income individuals.

Eligible individuals. The earned income tax credit is available to both individuals with qualifying children and individuals without children if:

(1) the individual has a principal residence in the United States for more than one-half of the taxable year;

(2) the individual (or, if married, either the individual or the individual's spouse) is at least 25 years old and not more than 64 years old at the end of the taxable year; and

(3) the individual cannot be claimed as a dependent for any taxable year beginning in the same calendar year as the taxable year for which the credit is claimed.

An individual is considered married for purposes of the earned income tax credit if he or she is married at the end of the year (.05). If the individual's spouse dies during the year, the individual is considered married up to the date of death. An individual legally separated from his or her spouse is not considered to be married.

The earned income tax credit is determined by multiplying an individual's earned income amount by the appropriate credit percentage.

Different credit percentages and phaseout percentages are provided for low-income workers who have no qualifying children, one qualifying child, and more than one qualifying child (.10).

For 2004, the maximum credit is as follows:

One qualifying child: $2,604 (34% x $7,660). The maximum credit is reduced by 15.98% of adjusted gross income (or earned income, if greater) over $14,040. The phaseout is completed at $30,338.

Two or more qualifying children: $4,300 (40% x $10,750). The maximum credit is reduced by 21.06% of adjusted gross income (or earned income, if greater) over $14,040. The phaseout is completed at $34,458.

No qualifying children: $390 (7.65% x $5,100). The maximum credit is reduced by 7.65% of adjusted gross income (or earned income, if greater) over $6,390. The phaseout is completed at $11,490.

The earned income amount and the phaseout amount are adjusted for inflation. The credit percentage and phaseout percentage to be used in calculating the earned income credit are based on the tax year involved and the number of qualifying children claimed by the taxpayer. The appropriate percentages are listed in the following chart.

Tax Year Beginning	*Number of Qualifying Children*	*Credit Percentage*	*Phaseout Percentage*
In 1994	One	26.3	15.98
	Two or more	30.0	17.68
	None	7.65	7.65
In 1995	One	34.0	15.98
	Two or more	36.0	20.22
	None	7.65	7.65
After 1995	One	34.0	15.98
	Two or more	40.0	21.06
	None	7.65	7.65

The earned income amount and the phaseout amount to be used in calculating the earned income credit are based on the tax year involved and the number of qualifying children claimed by the taxpayer. The appropriate amounts are listed in the following chart.

Tax Year Beginning	*Number of Qualifying Children*	*Earned Income Amount*	*Phaseout Amount*
In 1995	One	$ 6,160	$ 11,290
	Two or more	8,640	11,290
	None	4,100	5,130
In 1996	One	$ 6,330	$ 11,610
	Two or more	8,890	11,610
	None	4,220	5,280
In 1997	One	$ 6,500	$ 11,930
	Two or more	9,140	11,930
	None	4,340	5,430
In 1998	One	$ 6,680	$ 12,260
	Two or more	9,390	12,260
	None	4,460	5,570
In 1999	One	$ 6,800	$ 12,460
	Two or more	9,540	12,460
	None	4,530	5,670
In 2000	One	$ 6,920	$ 12,690
	Two or more	9,720	12,690
	None	4,610	5,770
In 2001	One	$ 7,130	$ 13,090
	Two or more	10,020	13,090
	None	4,760	5,950

For tax years beginning in 2002, 2003, and 2004 the phaseout amount is increased an extra $1,000 for taxpayers who file a joint return. The increase is $2,000 for 2005, 2006, and 2007 and $3,000 after 2007. The following charts show the earned income amounts and phaseout amounts for 2004 for single filers and joint filers.

SINGLE FILERS

Tax Year Beginning	*Number of Qualifying Children*	*Earned Income Amount*	*Phaseout Amount*
In 2004	One	$ 7,660	$ 14,040
	Two or more	10,750	14,040
	None	5,100	6,390

JOINT FILERS

Tax Year Beginning	*Number of Qualifying Children*	*Earned Income Amount*	*Phaseout Amount*
In 2004	One	$ 7,660	$ 15,040
	Two or more	10,750	15,040
	None	5,100	7,390

.05 Code Sec. 7703.

.10 Code Sec. 32(b).

¶25,707 "Earned Income" —Basis for the Credit. As discussed at ¶25,706, the earned income credit is based on "earned income" (.05)—that is, on all wages, salaries, tips, union strike benefit payments (.10) and other employee compensation, plus the amount of the taxpayer's "net earnings from self-employment" (calculated without a deduction for self-employment taxes).

Pensions and annuity payments are specifically excluded from earned income for purposes of the earned income credit. The same is true for income received by nonresident aliens that is not connected with a U.S. trade or business (.15). Passive income in the form of interest, dividends, estate and trust distributions, alimony, and capital gains and losses is also not considered earned income. Nor do most rents qualify as earned income, except in those cases where the owner of the property renders services to occupants or aids materially in the production of farm products grown on rented land.

Prior to 2002, nontaxable employee compensation, such as parsonage allowances, elective deferrals to pension plans, employer contributions for nontaxable fringe benefits, salary reductions under a cafeteria plan, and meals and lodging provided for the convenience of the employer are treated as earned income for purposes of computing the credit. However, beginning in 2002 the definition of earned income was modified to exclude all forms of nontaxable employee compensation (.20).

For tax years beginning after December 31, 1997, earned income does not include certain workfare payments. These are cash payments certain families receive from a state or local agency that administers public assistance programs funded under the Federal Temporary Assistance for Needy Families program in return for (1) work experience activities (including remodeling or repairing public housing) if sufficient private sector employment is not available, or (2) community service program activities. The rule only applies to the extent the payments are subsidized by or received from the state (.25).

.05 Code Sec. 32(c)(2); Reg. §1.43-2(c)(2).

.10 Rev. Rul. 78-191, 1978-1 CB 8.

.15 Code Sec. 32(c)(2)(B)(iii).

.20 Code Sec. 32(c)(2)(A)(i), as amended by P.L. 107-16.

.25 Code Sec. 32(c)(2)(B)(v), as added by P.L. 105-34.

¶25,708 Claiming the Earned Income Credit. The earned income credit must be applied first against the taxpayer's tax liability. If the credit is greater than the tax liability, the excess is treated as an overpayment of taxes and is refundable.

There are procedures for the uniform treatment of adjustments that decrease the earned income credit. Specifically, when there is a deficiency, the notice of deficiency includes the earned income credit adjustment. In cases in which the taxpayer agrees with the findings of the IRS examining officer or in cases involving only the earned income credit adjustment, the correction is made in the same manner as an adjustment of a prepayment credit (.05).

Advance payment of the credit

An individual eligible for the earned income credit (¶25,706) may elect to receive advance payment of the credit from his employer through a reduction in withheld taxes (.10). The amount of the earned income credit that may be received as an advance payment is limited to 60 percent of the maximum credit available to an individual with one qualifying child. The advance payment is not available to an individual who does not have a qualifying child (.15). Farm workers, paid on a daily basis, are ineligible for the advance earned income credit payment arrangement (.20). Employees who qualify for advance payments may notify their employers of the election on Form W-5 (Earned Income Credit Advance Payment Certificate). Such person receiving advance earned income credit payments from his employer must file an income tax return regardless of income level (.25). Here, the advance earned income credit payments received are treated as an increase in tax in order to recapture any payments exceeding the amount of credit claimed on the income tax return, but are not considered a "tax" for purposes of computing other credits (.30).

It is important to remember that an employee who does not have amounts withheld from his wages and who would not normally file an income tax return because the amount of gross income is less than the amount required for filing a return should nevertheless file a return in order to claim the refundable earned income credit. In such a case, he receives a tax refund (in the amount of the credit) even though no income tax is due.

This refund may be claimed simply by filling out a brief written statement or form (such as the Form 1040A) and attaching to it a copy of his withholding statements, if any.

Notification

Employers must notify each employee who worked during the year and from whom no income tax was withheld that the employee may be eligible for a tax refund generated by the earned income credit. Notification requirements are met when an employer gives an employee: (1) a Form W-2 (Wage and Tax Statement), which has the required statement on the back of copy C, (2) a substitute Form W-2 with the same statement on the back of the employee's copy C, (3) a copy of IRS Notice 797, "Possible Federal Tax Refund Due to the Earned Income Credit (EIC)," or (4) a statement containing the exact same wording as IRS Notice 797 (.35).

Earned income credit table and worksheet

For those eligible taxpayers who do not elect to receive advance payment, the credit can be claimed on Form 1040A or Form 1040 using the earned income credit worksheet and earned income credit table to compute the credit amount.

Compliance. EIC compliance provisions deny EIC eligibility for prior acts of recklessness or fraud, require recertification for eligibility in future years when the credit is denied in a deficiency proceeding, and impose a due diligence requirement on return preparers (.40).

.05 Rev. Proc. 77-35, 1977-2 CB 568, as modified by Rev. Proc. 80-33, 1980-2 CB 768.

.10 Code Sec. 32(g) and 3507.

.15 Code Sec. 3507(c)(2)(B).

.20 IRS Publication 596, "Earned Income Credit" (Rev. 2003).

.25 Code Sec. 6012(a)(8).

.30 Code Sec. 32(g)(2).

.35 IRS Publication 15: Circular E, "Employers's Tax Guide," (Rev. Jan. 2004).

.40 Code Sec. 32(k), as added by P.L. 105-34.

Credit for Dependent Care Expenses

¶25,710 Qualification for the Credit. Many parents, or individuals who support disabled relatives, would be unable to look for work (much less hold a job) if they were not able to hire another person or organization to care for their dependents (.05). Caretaker costs can be especially burdensome to individuals with low-income jobs. In fact, the prospect of paying for a caretaker may be enough to dissuade someone from taking a job.

The tax credit for fees paid to caretakers provides some relief. In 2004, individuals who arrange care for one dependent may claim a credit of up to $1,050, while individuals who arrange care for two or more dependents may claim as much as $2,100.

One of the most attractive features of the credit is that it is one of those rare Code provisions that can be widely used by the taxpaying public. It is available, in varying degrees, to anyone who has children under the age of 13, who supports a disabled relative, or who has a disabled spouse.

The amount of the credit is keyed to the taxpayer's adjusted gross income. In 2004, the following computational rules apply.

(1) Taxpayers with adjusted gross incomes of $15,000 or less are entitled to a credit equal to 35 percent of employment-related expenses.

(2) Taxpayers with adjusted gross incomes over $15,000 and equal to or less than $43,000 may claim a credit that is reduced by one percentage point for each $2,000 of adjusted gross income, or fraction thereof, above $15,000.

(3) Taxpayers with adjusted gross incomes of over $43,000 are entitled to a credit equal to 20 percent of employment-related expenses.

Beginning in 2003, the maximum amount of employment-related expenses on which the credit is computed is $3,000 if the expenses relate to one qualifying child or dependent or $6,000 if the expenses relate to two or more children or dependents. However, expenses must be reduced by the amount of tax-exempt child and dependent care benefits an employee receives from an employer under a dependent care assistance program.

The following table outlines the *maximum* credit available at each adjusted gross income level in 2003 and later tax years.

Adjusted Gross Income		*Applicable Percentage*	*2004 Maximum Credit*	
Over	*But Not Over:*		*One Qualifying Individual*	*Two or More Qualifying Individuals*
$—0—	$ 15,000	35%	$ 1,050	$ 2,100
15,000	17,000	34%	1,020	2,040
17,000	19,000	33%	990	1,980
19,000	21,000	32%	960	1,920
21,000	23,000	31%	930	1,860
23,000	25,000	30%	900	1,800
25,000	27,000	29%	870	1,740
27,000	29,000	28%	840	1,680
29,000	31,000	27%	810	1,620
31,000	33,000	26%	780	1,560
33,000	35,000	25%	750	1,500
35,000	37,000	24%	720	1,440
37,000	39,000	23%	690	1,380
39,000	41,000	22%	660	1,320
41,000	43,000	21%	630	1,260
over 43,000		20%	600	1,200

.05 Code Sec. 21.

¶25,711 Persons Eligible for the Credit. Any taxpayer who maintains a household that includes a qualifying dependent (¶25,712) as a member for the entire tax year is eligible for the dependent care tax credit (.05). Thus, the credit is available to single individuals, widows, widowers, persons who are legally divorced or separated, and married persons alike.

On the other hand, with the exception of certain married persons living apart from their spouses (see "Married person living apart from spouse," below), married persons qualify only if they file a joint return. In addition, a married person with a nonworking spouse usually cannot claim the credit (unless the nonworking spouse is physically or mentally disabled or is a full-time student at an educational institution for at least five calendar months in the year) because expenses taken into account (¶25,712-¶25,716) may not exceed the earned income of the spouse whose income is lower.

Married person living apart from spouse

A special rule applies to a person who is married but is living apart from his or her spouse during the last six months of the tax year (e.g., an abandoned spouse). In such case, a married person is treated as "single" for purposes of the credit if that person:

(1) files a separate tax return for the year;

(2) maintains a household that for more than half of the year is the principal place of abode for a qualifying individual (¶25,712); and

(3) furnishes more than half the cost of maintaining the household (.10).

> ***Example 1:*** Denise Smith is a calendar-year taxpayer who supports her two children, ages four and seven. Her husband deserted the household in May. If Denise files a separate tax return (i.e., a separate return as a married person), she is treated as single for purposes of the child care expense credit because her husband had not lived in the household for the last six months of the taxable year. She can compute her credit without regard to what her spouse does on his return.

Divorced or separated spouses

Another special rule applies to a taxpayer who is divorced, legally separated, or separated under a written agreement and who has custody of a child who is either under age 13 or is physically or mentally incapable of caring for himself. In such case, the taxpayer may be eligible to claim a credit for his employment-related child-or-dependent-care expenses (see ¶25,712-¶25,716) only if:

(1) the child has received more than one-half of his support from either or both parents during the calendar year;

(2) either or both parents have had custody of the child for more than one-half of the year; and

(3) the taxpayer has had custody of the child for a greater portion of the year (.15).

> ***Example 2:*** Joey is a 10-year-old child whose parents are divorced. He spends one month out of each year with his mother, and one month with his father. The rest of the year is spent with his paternal grandparents, who provide over one-half of his support. Neither of his parents is entitled to a credit for employment-related child care expenses. The grandparents, however, may be entitled to the credit.

The custodial parent is granted the credit even though he has waived his right to a dependency exemption for the child or is not entitled to the exemption under the terms of a pre-1985 divorce or separation agreement.

For a discussion of the computation of "support," see ¶25,712.

Care provider's identity must be reported to IRS

An individual will be unable to claim a credit for payments he has made to someone who cares for his child or dependent unless he reveals the care provider's name, address, and taxpayer identification number on the return on which he claims the credit (.20). If the care provider is a tax-exempt charitable organization (under Code Sec. 501(c)(3)), the organization's name and address suffice. Form W-10 (Dependent Care Provider's Identification and Certification) may be used by the individual to obtain identifying information from the provider. If used, it does not have to be filed with the individual's tax return. An individual will be relieved of his reporting duty if he can demonstrate that he acted with "due diligence" in trying to provide the IRS with correct information.

.05 Code Sec. 21(e).

.10 Code Sec. 21(e)(4). This rule is similar to the "married person living apart" rules of Code Sec. 2(c), 32 and 7703(b) (see ¶25,702 and ¶25,711, supra). However, the dependent involved, for purposes of these Code sections, must be the taxpayer's child for whom a dependency exemption is available.

.15 Code Sec. 21(e)(5). See, also, Code Sec. 152(e).

.20 Code Sec. 21(e)(9).

¶25,712 Qualifying Dependents. There are three types of dependents, called "qualifying individuals," for whom deductible employment-related expenses may be incurred under the dependent-care-credit rules. As set forth below, the qualifying individual must usually receive more than half of his support from the taxpayer (or, if the taxpayer is married, from his spouse; this support requirement is eliminated for tax years after 2004), and fall within one of the following three categories (.05).

(1) *Any dependent under the age of 13 for whom the taxpayer is entitled to claim a dependency exemption:* A dependent in this category includes the following individuals who are under 13 years of age and receive more than half of their support from the taxpayer—the taxpayer's child, stepchild, or grandchild, his brother, sister, nephew, niece, brother-in-law, sister-in-law, and any other child who, for the tax year of the taxpayer, has as his principal place of abode the home of the taxpayer, including foster children. If the taxpayer is married, the above-mentioned relatives may be those of his spouse. Because of the dependency exemption requirement, the dependent (other than the taxpayer's child) must not have received $3,100 or more of gross income for the 2004 tax year (.10).

(2) *Any dependent, regardless of age, who is physically or mentally incapable of caring for himself:* "Dependent," in this context, means any disabled dependent, including the taxpayer's disabled relatives (and those of his or her spouse), who received more than half of his support from the taxpayer. But a dependency exemption is *not* required. Thus, even a dependent who has $3,100 or more of gross income for 2004 can fall into category (2).

(3) *Disabled spouse:* If the taxpayer's spouse is disabled (i.e., has a physical or mental condition rendering the individual incapable of dressing himself or providing for his hygienic or nutritional needs (.15)), the spouse automatically is a qualifying individual—that is, regardless of age, amount of support, or place of abode. The taxpayer must still file a joint return and must take into consideration the income that the spouse is deemed to have earned during the tax year for purposes of the earned income limitation (see ¶25,717). It is not necessary that the spouse be disabled for the entire tax year.

Support

Whenever it is necessary under the above rules to determine whether "over half" of the support of a dependent has been paid by the taxpayer for the tax year in which the credit is claimed, the amount of support contributed by the taxpayer is compared to the entire amount of support that the individual received from all sources, including any support that the individual himself supplied. It is immaterial whether amounts contributed are from taxable income or from exempt income (except for amounts received as scholarships (.20)). However, where the dependent does have an independent source of funds (including social security benefits), only the amount actually spent by him on his support is taken into account—not the total amount available for the support (.25).

"Support" includes food, shelter, clothing, medical and dental care (including premiums paid for medical insurance) (.30), education, and similar items (.35). However, support does not include life insurance covering a dependent or policies naming a dependent as beneficiary (.40).

The amount of an item of support is usually its cost—that is, the amount of expense incurred by the one furnishing the item. But, where property or lodging is furnished, the amount of support is the item's fair market value (.45).

For further information regarding the support requirement, see ¶6135. Also, note that where a dependent is supported by several persons, none of whom alone furnishes more than one-half of his support, these persons may enter into an agreement under which one of them may claim the dependency deduction.

Planning Note

CCH Analysts note that the requirement that the parent receiving the credit provide over one-half of the support for the dependent is eliminated for tax years beginning after 2004 (.50).

Determination of status

Generally, the status of a person as a qualifying individual is determined on a daily basis. For example, if a dependent or spouse of a taxpayer ceases to be a qualifying individual on September 16, the dependent or spouse is treated as a qualifying individual through September 15 only (.55).

.05 Code Sec. 21(b)(1).

.10 Code Sec. 151(d).

.15 IRS Publication 503, "Child and Dependent Care Expenses" (Rev. 2002).

.20 Code Sec. 152(d).

.25 *J. Dick*, DC Wis., 63-2 USTC ¶9594, 218 F.Supp. 839; *S.J. Ledman*, 29 TCM 301, CCH Dec. 30,017(M), TC Memo. 1970-69.

.30 *F. McGuire*, 77 TC 765, CCH Dec. 38,330.

.35 Reg. §1.152-1. See, e.g., *A.W. Peakes*, 24 TCM 757, CCH Dec. 27,405(M), TC Memo. 1965-146.

.40 *V.M. Cramer*, 55 TC 1125, CCH Dec. 30,697 (Acq.).

.45 Reg. §1.152-1; *E.P. Bielawa*, 20 TCM 13, CCH Dec. 24,601(M), TC Memo. 1961-1; *W.H. Stang*, 19 TCM 289, CCH Dec. 24,105(M), TC Memo. 1960-55.

.50 Code Sec. (21)(a)(1), as amended by the Working Families Tax Relief Act of 2004, §203(a) (P.L. 108-311).

.55 Reg. §1.44A-1(b)(3).

¶25,713 Employment-Related Expenses. As noted at ¶25,710 the dependent care credit is based upon the employment-related expenses incurred during a tax year or those household care expenses (¶25,715) and child care services incurred outside the household (¶25,716) to enable the taxpayer to be gainfully employed (¶25,714) during a time when the taxpayer's household contains one or more qualifying individuals (¶25,712). For example, if a child reaches age 13 in June, only those household care expenses incurred before the child's thirteenth birthday qualify (.05).

Payments to relatives

The credit is available for payments made to a relative, including a grandparent, unless such relative is a dependent for whom the taxpayer or spouse may claim a dependency exemption (¶25,712) or is the taxpayer's child and is under age 19 (.10).

> ***Example:*** Jane Chandler, a single parent, is also the legal guardian of her 17-year-old sister who lives with her. Jane's sister cares for Jane's three-year-old child during the day while Jane is employed. For her services, Jane pays her sister $75 per week. Jane will not be able to claim the dependent care credit for the amounts she pays to her sister because her sister is a dependent and Jane may claim a dependency exemption for her.

Reimbursement by state welfare program

Employment-related expenses that are reimbursed by a state welfare program are not qualified expenses for purposes of the credit (.15). The credit is allowable only to the extent that qualifying expenses exceed the amount of the reimbursement (.20).

Relationship to gainful employment

There must also be a direct relationship between the expenses and the employment. For example, the day-time child care expenses of a day-time worker are directly related, whereas his evening child care expenses are not. Thus, expenses that are incurred so that the taxpayer may be free to pursue personal or social activities do not qualify. Consequently, nursery charges incurred by an Air Force officer for the care of his child while he entertained guests were nondeductible (.25).

Although the taxpayer need not be gainfully employed for the entire year, only those expenses incurred *while* he is gainfully employed (see ¶25,714) are considered for purposes of the credit.

.05 Reg. §1.44A-1.

.10 Code Sec. 21(e)(6).

.15 IRS Letter Ruling 8210023, 11-30-81, CCH IRS LETTER RULINGS REPORTS.

.20 Rev. Rul. 83-1, 1983-1 CB 3.

.25 *W.D. Preston*, 20 TCM 1304, CCH Dec. 25,015(M), TC Memo. 1961-250.

¶25,714 Gainful Employment. For purposes of the dependent care credit, the taxpayer must be "gainfully employed while the child care expenses are incurred" (.05). Taxpayers who are actively looking for work, or who are employed part-time, also meet the gainful employment requirement (.10). In addition, gainful employment includes working for oneself, and may even consist of work within the taxpayer's home. On the other hand, gainful employment does not include unpaid volunteer work or work at a token salary (.15).

With the exception of the situation where certain married persons living apart from their spouses are treated as unmarried (see ¶25,711), *both* spouses must be gainfully employed in order to claim the credit because the earned income rules limit the available credit to the lesser of the spouses' earned income. Non-working spouses are considered to be gainfully employed if they are full-time students or disabled.

.05 Code Sec. 21(b)(2)(A).

.10 IRS Publication 503, "Child and Dependent Care Expenses" (Rev. 2003).

.15 Rev. Rul. 73-597, 1973-2 CB 69.

¶25,715 Household Services. In order for expenses to be considered as employment related (¶25,713), they must be qualified expenses for (1) household services or (2) child care services outside the household (see ¶25,716) incurred for the care of a qualifying dependent (¶25,712).

In general, the household services must be ordinary and usual services performed in and about the home that are necessary for the operation of the home and the well-being of one or more qualifying dependents. The services of a housekeeper, maid, or cook are usually considered necessary to the operation of the household if performed at least partially for the benefit of such dependent. However, amounts paid for the services of an individual who is employed as a chauffeur, bartender or gardener are not considered to be expenses paid for household services (.05).

Expenses incurred in connection with employing the person who actually provides the child or dependent care services, including expenditures that are personal as well as business in nature, usually qualify. The portion of expenditures allocable to an employed nursemaid for meals and lodging may be employment related, for example, as is the taxpayer's share of the employee's FICA tax (see ¶25,718).

Example: A divorced taxpayer with a two-year-old child in her household is forced to move to a larger apartment because a housekeeper had to be employed on a full-time basis. The additional rent required for this extra bedroom, as well as additional utility expenses incurred, may be taken into account in determining the amount of the credit (.10).

Occasionally, the person employed to provide child and dependent care service may, during the course of providing that care, also render some incidental benefit to nonqualifying members of the household or perform some nonhousehold services. If the services are performed at least partially for the benefit of a qualifying individual, the incidental benefits received by a nonqualifying individual are irrelevant and the expense need not be apportioned. However, when the individual performing the child or dependent care service has other, nonrelated duties, expenses must be apportioned between household and nonhousehold expenses to exclude the payments made for nonhousehold services (.15). Thus, if a cook doubles as a gardener in the taxpayer's household, the expense for the gardening time should be excluded.

.05 Reg. §1.44A-1(c)(2).

.10 IRS Publication 503, "Child and Dependent Care Expenses" (Rev. 2003).

.15 IRS Publication 503, "Child and Dependent Care Expenses" (Rev. 2003).

¶25,716 Child Care Services Outside the Household. Employment-related expenses incurred for services provided outside a taxpayer's household by a dependent care center may be taken into account for purposes of the credit, so long as the center complies with all applicable state and local laws and regulations (.05). A dependent care center is any facility that provides care for more than six individuals (other than individuals who reside at the facility) and receives a fee, payment, or grant for providing services for any of the individuals, regardless of whether the center is operated for profit.

On the other hand, qualifying outside-the-household care expenses do not extend to expenses for a child's education. Normally, outside-the-household care expenses include the costs of nursery school or day care for *preschool* children. In such case, incidental educational benefits that are an inseparable part of the care need not be apportioned. However, if the expenses go toward education in the first or higher grade level, they must be apportioned between the cost of care for the child and the cost of education.

Transportation expenses incurred while taking a child to an outside-the-home care location are not child care expenses (.10). This confines qualifying expenses to those actually incurred for the care of the child and excludes the indirect expenses that are incurred to enable a child to receive that care.

The outside-the-household care provided need not be the least expensive method available.

.05 Code Sec. 21(b)(2)(C).

.10 IRS Publication 503, "Child and Dependent Care Expenses" (Rev. 2003).

¶25,717 "Earned Income" Limitation. As emphasized throughout the discussion of the dependent care credit rules (¶25,710 -¶25,719), the amount of employment-related expenses that may be taken into account may not exceed the taxpayer's earned income for the taxable year (.05). If the taxpayer is married and the taxpayer's spouse has less earned income, the lesser amount is applied for purposes of the earned income limitation (.10).

Example 1: Sam and Alice Ferguson annually earn $20,000 and $2,800, respectively. During the 2004 tax year, they incur employment-related expenses of $3,000 for two dependent children. Because of the earned income limitation, only $2,800 of the expenses may be taken into account and the amount of credit is $644 (23% of $2,800).

Disabled or student spouse

An exception to the earned income limitation occurs when a working taxpayer's spouse is either disabled or a student (that is, enrolled full time in an educational institution during the year) (.15). In this situation, an incapacitated or student spouse is deemed to have received monthly earned income of $200 with respect to one qualifying individual or $400 with respect to two or more qualifying individuals. This additional income is attributable to the disabled or student spouse only for purposes of the earned income limitation. It does not increase the couple's adjusted gross income for purposes of determining the percentage of employment-related expenses to which they are entitled.

> ***Example 2:*** Carl Eiger earns $22,000 in 2004. His wife, Martha, is a full-time student from January 1 through May 31. The couple, in the course of providing day care for their two children, incurs $2,000 of employment-related expenses during the year. Under the special rule, Martha is deemed to have $400 of earned income for each month she is a student. The credit would be calculated as follows:

Income of Carl (working spouse)	$ 22,000
Deemed income of Martha (student spouse) . . . . ($ 400 X 5 Months)	2,000
Amount of employment-related expenses that may be taken into account (earned income of the lesser-earning spouse or $ 4,800, whichever is less	2,000
Amount of credit (23% of $ 2,000)	460

> ***Example 3:*** Morgan Dobrir, who earns $16,500 in 2004, incurs $2,500 of employment-related expenses in caring for his permanently disabled spouse, Maureen. Maureen is deemed to have earned income of $2,400 during the year ($200 × 12 months), and a credit of $624 (26% of $2,400) would be available.

Earned income may be attributed to only one spouse for each month. In a situation where both spouses are disabled, no credit may be claimed because expenses are not incurred in order that one spouse may be gainfully employed (¶25,714).

The term "earned income" for purposes of the dependent care credit is similar to the term "earned income" for purposes of the earned income credit (¶25,707). It means net earnings from self-employment, wages, salaries, professional fees and other forms of payment received when one is gainfully employed (.20). Income from dividends, pensions, or annuities; an amount from a health or accident plan; or money received as a gift or as alimony is not considered to be earned income.

.05 Code Sec. 21(d)(1)(A); Reg. §1.44A-2(b)(2).
.10 Code Sec. 21(d)(1)(B).
.15 Code Sec. 21(d)(2); Reg. §1.44A-2(b)(3).
.20 Reg. §1.44A-2(b)(2).

¶25,718 Special Points to Watch. Practically speaking, the dependent care credit directly affects, and is directly affected by, several other tax rules that may allow the taxpayer to claim employment-related expenses and deductions. These rules should be kept in mind when planning to claim the credit.

Special taxes for taxpayer-employers

When a taxpayer who has a qualifying dependent (see ¶25,712) in his household hires someone to care for that individual, the taxpayer becomes an employer and must consider additional tax consequences associated with that status.

> (1) *Social security taxes:* A taxpayer who hires someone to perform the care services must also be aware of the Social Security employment (FICA) tax that must be paid. If, during 2004, a taxpayer pays an employee $1,400 or more in wages for care services, the taxpayer must pay the employment tax and must withhold from the employee's wages additional employment tax (.05). In such case, however, the amounts

contributed by the employer are treated as employment-related expenses (¶25,713 - ¶25,716).

(2) *Federal unemployment (insurance) tax (FUTA):* Also, a taxpayer who pays cash wages of $1,000 or more to household employees in any calendar quarter is liable for federal unemployment (FUTA) tax for such employees (.10). Again, payment of such tax is considered an employment-related expense for purposes of the credit (¶25,713 - ¶25,716).

Effect of the medical expense deduction

Some expense amounts, such as the cost of at-home nursing care, have a dual income tax character: they qualify as a medical expense, and, if the amounts were paid to enable the taxpayer to be gainfully employed (¶25,714), they also qualify as an employment- related expense (¶25,713). However, the same expense amount cannot be used in computing both the taxpayer's medical expense deduction and his employment-related expense.

An exception to this general rule applies when the taxpayer, because of the earned income limitation (¶25,717) or dollar limitation (¶25,710), cannot utilize all the employment-related expenses he actually incurred (.15). However, if the taxpayer includes the expenses first as a medical expense, the amount that cannot be included in the medical expense deduction may not be included in the employment-related expense computation, because the entire amount has already been used in the medical expense computation.

Thus, it is advantageous for any taxpayer who has sufficient itemized deductions that are both employment related and medical to consider the expense under both the credit and the deduction methods before deciding which one creates the greater tax advantage.

> ***Example:*** During 2004, John Davis paid $5,000 of work-related expenses for the care of his physically handicapped dependent daughter. The work-related expenses were for services performed in Davis's home and qualified as medical expenses. Davis's adjusted gross income for 2004 is $18,000. If he takes $3,000 of these expenses into account for the purpose of applying the child care credit, he may treat the balance, or $2,000, as medical expenses. As Davis had no other medical expenses, he may deduct $650 ($2,000 minus 7.5 percent of $18,000, or $1,350) as a medical-expense deduction.

.05 Code Sec. 3121(a)(7)(B) and Code Sec. 3510. Also, see IRS Publication 926, "Employment Taxes for Household Employers" (Rev. Nov. 2003).

.10 Code Sec. 3306(a)(3).

.15 IRS Publication 503, "Child and Dependent Care Expenses" (Rev. 2003).

¶25,719 Year-of-Expense Payment. The employment-related expenses incurred can be utilized for credit purposes only in the tax year in which the taxpayer pays them. For example, if a calendar-year taxpayer incurs employment-related expenses in December and pays them in January of the following year, he may not include the expenses on his return for the year in which they were incurred. Instead, they should be included on his return for the following year (.05).

> ***Example:*** In 2003, John and Martha Anders, a married couple, had child care expenses of $3,200 for their 12-year-old child. The credit for child care expenses is limited to $3,000 for one child. Of the $3,200, they paid $2,000 in 2003 and $1,200 in 2004. John and Martha's adjusted gross income during 2004 was $50,000, with Martha's earned income of $5,000 being less than John's earned income. The Anders are allowed to include an increased credit of $200 in 2004, figured as follows:

(1)	2003 child care expenses paid in 2003		$ 2,000
(2)	2003 child care expenses paid in 2004		1,200
(3)	Total	$ 3,200	
(4)	Limit for one qualifying dependent		$ 3,000
(5)	Smaller of John's earned income or Martha's earned income in 2002	$ 5,000	
(6)	Smallest of lines 3, 4, or 5		$ 3,000
(7)	Minus: Child care expenses on which the Anders figured the credit in 2003		2,000
(8)	2003 child care expenses carried over for credit in 2004		$ 1,000
(9)	Increase in 2004 credit. Multiply line 8 by 20%		$ 200

Claiming the credit

The credit for child care expenses may be claimed on Forms 1040 and 1040A. The credit is computed on Form 2441 for taxpayers who file Form 1040 and on Schedule 2 for taxpayers who file Form 1040A. A filled-in Form 2441 is reproduced at ¶2187.

.05 IRS Publication 503, "Child and Dependent Care Expenses" (Rev. 2002).

Exclusion for Employer-Provided Services

¶25,721 Dependent Care Services. The value of child or dependent care provided under an employer's written nondiscriminatory plan generally is not includible in the gross income of employees (including self-employed individuals). The total amount excluded from gross income may not exceed $5,000 ($2,500 in the case of a separate return filed by a married individual) (.05).

Employer-provided dependent care assistance may be delivered in a number of ways, including employee reimbursement for work-related expenses, direct payment to providers of dependent care assistance, and establishment of on-site day care services.

The kinds of dependent care assistance that the employer may make available for the employee are the same as those that would be considered employment-related expenses under the dependent-care-expense credit rules (see ¶25,713). Therefore, the rules relating to gainful employment (¶25,714), household services (¶25,715), and child care services outside the household (¶25,716) are also applicable for purposes of the exclusion for employer-provided services and should be consulted and followed.

Assistance provided by an employer may not be excluded from an employee's gross income unless the employee's return reports the name, address, and taxpayer identification number of the person or organization providing dependent care (.10). If the organization is tax exempt, only the name and address need to be provided. Form W-10 (Dependent Care Provider's Identification and Certification) may be used to record this information, although the form does not have to accompany an employee's return.

.05 Code Sec. 129(d)(2).

.10 Code Sec. 129(e)(9).

¶25,722 Earned Income Limitations. The earned income limitation for the dependent care credit (see ¶25,717) applies to deny the exclusion of any expenditures on behalf of an unmarried employee that exceed his earned income for the tax year (.05). In the case of married employees, this limitation is based on the earned income of the lower-earning spouse for the tax year; a spouse who is incapacitated or who is a student is deemed to have received monthly earned income of $250 if one qualifying individual is involved or $500 if two or more qualifying individuals are involved.

Any amounts that are excluded under the exclusion rules may not be used for purposes of any credit (including the dependent care credit) (.10) or deduction. On the other hand, however, should the employee need to spend more money on dependent care services than the employer provides, the excess work-related expenditures apparently can be used in computing the employee's dependent care credit, assuming they are otherwise eligible for the credit (see ¶25,710-¶25,719).

Also, an employer's payment of child care expenses to an individual related to the employee or to an employee's child who is under the age of 19 and for whom the employee claims a dependency exemption may not be excluded from gross income.

.05 Code Sec. 129.

.10 Code Sec. 129(e)(7).

Retirement Income Planning

¶25,724 Introduction. Working families that are concerned about their retirement income should be aware of individual retirement accounts (IRAs) and Keogh plans (for self-employed individuals). These programs are unique in that their sole purpose is to permit eligible individuals to accumulate funds for their own retirement, without relying completely upon employer- or government-sponsored retirement programs. The basic advantages offered by these programs are that the individual's contributions, within certain limits, may be currently deductible on the individual's tax return, and that the income earned on the funds in these programs is generally not taxed so long as it remains in the retirement account or plan.

¶25,725 Individual Retirement Accounts. In 2004, a $3,000 deduction from gross income is permitted for contributions made by taxpayers with adjusted gross incomes of $40,000 or less ($60,000 or less for joint returns) or for those taxpayers not covered by an employer plan (.05). An individual who reaches age 50 by the end of 2004 is also entitled to make an additional $500 *catch-up* contribution.

Unemployed spouses may contribute up to $3,000 to an IRA in 2004. An individual is not considered an active participant in an employer-sponsored plan merely because the individual's spouse is an active participant for any part of a plan year. However, the maximum deductible IRA contribution for an individual who is not an active participant, but whose spouse is, is phased out at adjusted gross income between $150,000 and $160,000 (jointly computed). See ¶11,425 for details.

Individuals who are divorced or legally separated before the end of the year cannot deduct payments they make to their ex-spouse's IRAs (.10). Deductions are permitted only for payments made to the taxpayer's own IRA following the divorce.

For purposes of determining the deductible limits, "compensation" includes wages or earnings in the case of an employee, and earnings from a trade or business in the case of a self-employed person, but does not include income received from investments, any amount received as a pension or annuity or any amount received as deferred compensation (.15). In regard to divorce or separation instruments executed after 1984, compensation also includes any amount includible in the individual's gross income with respect to such instruments.

Time for contributions

Deductible contributions to an individual retirement arrangement may be made no later than the due date (excluding extensions) of the taxpayer's return for the tax year (.20). In addition, an individual may establish an IRA on the same date that he made the contribution. Individuals may claim deductions on their tax returns even though the contributions have not yet been made, so long as the claimed contributions are made no later than the due date of the tax return (.25).

Community property states

Community property laws do not apply to IRAs (.30). Therefore, each spouse may contribute up to $3,000 to his or her own plan in 2004 but may not take deductions for IRA contributions based on the earnings of his or her spouse. However, a spousal IRA may still be set up for an unemployed spouse.

Roth IRAs

Deductions to a Roth IRA are not deductible; however, the return on the contributions, unlike a regular IRA, is generally not taxed upon distribution (.35). The maximum yearly contribution to a Roth IRA is $3,000 (in 2004) assuming that no contribution is made to a regular IRA (the contribution limits on regular and Roth IRAs are coordinated). The maximum yearly contribution to a Roth IRA is phased out for single individual's with AGI between $95,000 and $110,000, for joint filers with AGI between $150,000 and $160,000, and for married individual's filing a separate return with AGI between $0 and $10,000. An individual may contribute to a Roth IRA whether or not the individual participates in an employer's pension plan. See ¶11,460 for details.

.05 Code Sec. 219.

.10 IRS Publication 590, "Individual Retirement Arrangements (IRAs)," (Rev. 2002).

.15 Code Sec. 219(f)(1).

.20 Code Sec. 219(f)(3).

.25 Rev. Rul. 84-18, 1984-1 CB 88.

.30 Code Sec. 219(f)(2).

.35 Code Sec. 408A.

¶25,726 Keogh Plans. A Keogh plan is a special retirement program for self-employed individuals (including partners). It may be opened instead of, or in addition to, an IRA (.05). However, as a general rule, the amount that may be contributed to a Keogh plan is more than that which may be contributed to an IRA (see ¶11,340). In addition, lump-sum distributions from a Keogh plan are taxed more favorably than lump-sum distributions from an IRA.

Contributions made to a Keogh plan are deductible if made during the particular tax year or if made by the due date, including extensions, of the tax return for that year (.10). However, only if a plan is in existence before the end of the tax year can contributions made during the following tax year be deductible.

☐ See ¶11,300-¶11,350 for a more detailed discussion of Keogh plans.

.05 Code Secs. 401-415.

.10 Code Sec. 404(a)(6) and Rev. Rul. 76-28, 1976-1 CB 106, as modified by Rev. Rul. 76-77, 1976-1 CB 107.

Assignment of Income

¶25,728 Advantages for Working Families. An important tax savings device of which working families should be aware is income assignment. Because of the graduated tax rate system that is imposed on taxable income (see ¶25,701), the ability to assign a portion of the income of a high-income earner to another family member with little or no income may result in tax savings to a working family.

Assignment of income v. assignment of income-producing property

In reality, it is a misnomer to speak of the advantages of "income assignment." That is because income may not be split merely by assigning the income itself. A person who assigns his right to income is still taxable on that income because, as its owner, he has a legal, enforceable right to it (.05). For example, a taxpayer may not escape tax on part of his salary even though he assigns a part of it to a family member under a legally enforceable contract.

However, a person who assigns his right to the property that produces the income may be relieved of income tax liability on the income from such property after assignment, so long as the use of the property is not restricted in any way.

By relinquishing ownership of the property itself, he has also given up the right to the income from the property. Thus, although an individual may not escape tax on bond interest despite having made a valid gift of the bond coupons to his or her spouse, he or she can shift the tax to the spouse by making a bona fide gift or assignment of the property itself. Similarly, where a parent places money in a savings account as trustee for his children or where the money is placed in a joint account for the parent and child, the parent will ordinarily remain taxable on the interest earned on the savings. Only if the parent can show that he has given up all control of the funds will the interest be taxed to the child (.10).

However, assignment of income by the transfer of income-producing property to a child under age 14 will not have the desired effect. The amount of the child's unearned income generally in excess of $1,400 is taxed at the top marginal rate of the parent. See ¶1010-¶1070.

.05 *E.R. Porter*, SCt, 1931 CCH ¶9609, 72 CtCls 680, 52 F2d 1056.

.10 *Jolly's Motor Livery Co.*, 16 TCM 1048, CCH Dec. 22,698(M), TC Memo. 1957-231; Rev. Rul. 58-65, 1958-1 CB 13.

¶25,729 Family Trusts. A taxpayer may desire to split income with a minor child or with one to whom he does not wish to entrust property at the time. In such a case, he may convey the property in trust for the child and, thereby, split his income between himself and the trust. But there are several limitations designed to prevent the taxpayer from escaping tax on the income from property where he in effect remains the owner of the property because of the control he retains over the trust (.05). The question is not whether the taxpayer has transferred the income, rather than the income-producing property, but whether he has in fact transferred anything at all.

Taxpayers should be aware, however, that tax benefits often associated with what are known as "family estate trusts" may be illusory. By transferring their property and lifetime services to a trust and having the trust pay their personal expenses, some taxpayers have attempted to avoid personal income tax liability. But the tax benefits claimed for these devices in so-called tax kits by their promoters have been successfully attacked by the IRS in the courts. The IRS has used two general approaches in its successful attempts to tax trust income to the grantors. The first is consistently ruling that such trusts are nullities for tax purposes, and the second is a combination of the assignment of income and grantor trust rules (.10).

Another, and potentially more serious, problem with family estate trusts is that improper use of them can render a taxpayer liable for civil (.15), and possibly criminal, tax penalties because the IRS views these trusts as a type of illegal tax protest (.20).

.05 *G.B. Clifford*, SCt, 40-1 USTC ¶9265, 309 U.S. 331.

.10 See, e.g., *D.H. McKenzie Family Estate*, 47 TCM 834, CCH Dec. 40,910(M), TC Memo. 1984-9; *L. Markosian*, 73 TC 98, CCH Dec. 36,858; *W.M. Raemer*, 41 TCM 1149, CCH Dec. 37,776(M), TC Memo. 1981-138; and *J.L. Landphier*, 41 TCM 1172, CCH Dec. 37,786(M), TC Memo. 1981-145.

.15 *E.G. Bass, Jr.*, 41 TCM 1177, CCH Dec. 37,789(M), TC Memo. 1981-146.

.20 Rev. Rul. 75-257, 1975-2 CB 251.

Employing One's Spouse

¶25,731 Qualifying as an Employee. An individual who owns a business may virtually create his own "working family" by employing his or her spouse and paying the spouse a salary. As with the proper use of income assignment (or rather, the assigning of income-producing property) (see ¶25,728), employing one's spouse can be an effective way of splitting the family's income so as to take advantage of the graduated tax rate system.

Handled properly, the employer gets a tax deduction for compensation paid (.05) and the spouse gets taxable cash income and, in some cases, other economic benefits with no or low tax cost, such as insurance coverage, IRA participation, etc. (see ¶25,732).

The employer cannot take a legitimate tax deduction if the spouse does not actually perform services for the company, or if the services rendered bear no reasonable relationship to the compensation paid. If the compensation paid is to be deductible in full by the employer, it must be reasonable. To be considered as "reasonable," the compensation paid to the spouse must be in accord with the prevailing rate of compensation for comparable positions with comparable employers. In the event that the compensation paid is determined to be excessive, the employer's deduction will be lost to the extent that the amounts paid exceed reasonable compensation. In addition, the excessive compensation received by the employed spouse may be subject to income tax.

Further, there must be an employer-employee relationship between the employer spouse and the employee spouse. Thus, this relationship did not exist and a husband could not deduct as a business expense compensation attributable to services performed by his wife where he deposited all income from the business into the couple's joint checking account (.10).

.05 Code Sec. 162(a)(1).

.10 IRS Letter Ruling 8707004, 11-6-86, CCH IRS LETTER RULINGS REPORTS.

¶25,732 Other Benefits. There are other benefits to employing one's spouse besides the income-splitting advantages:

(1) *Pension benefits:* If the business is in corporate form, is prospering, and has a defined benefit plan, the owner may wish to take advantage of the rules that permit a minimum pension of $10,000 a year, even though that amount is in excess of the participant's average compensation for his or her three best years (.05). Where the business is in the form of a partnership or sole proprietorship, Keogh plan benefits may be available (see ¶25,726).

(2) *IRA benefits:* In 2004, an employed spouse can contribute the lesser of $3,000 or 100% of compensation to his or her individual retirement account (IRA). However, in 2004, for an individual who is covered by an employer's pension plan, the deduction is phased out between adjusted gross income of $60,000 and $70,000 on a joint return and $40,000 and $50,000 for single individuals. An unemployed spouse may generally make a $3,000 (in 2004) contribution. See ¶25,725)

(3) *Other employee benefits:* Other employee benefits may be made available to an employed spouse. These include life insurance, accident and health coverage, paid tuition, and meals and lodging provided for the convenience of the employer.

(4) *FUTA tax savings:* Although social security tax (FICA) must be paid on an employed spouse's wages, the Federal Unemployment Tax (FUTA) is not imposed on such wages (.10).

.05 Code Sec. 415(b)(4).

.10 Code Sec. 3306(c)(5).

Family Partnerships

¶25,734 Two Types of Partnerships. A common device for splitting income among family members and thereby avoiding the high tax brackets (see ¶25,728) is the family partnership. Although most family partnerships are recognized for tax purposes (.05), different rules apply depending upon whether the family partnership is one in which capital is a material income-producing factor.

In family partnerships in which capital is *not* a material income-producing factor (e.g., a law practice), a family member is generally recognized as a partner if he performs substantial or vital services. Where capital is a material income-producing factor to the partnership (e.g., a business that requires a substantial inventory or a substantial investment in plant, machinery, or other equipment), the validity of the partnership depends upon whether there has been a bona fide transfer of the partnership interest so that the family member has dominion and control over the interest. This rule applies when such an interest is acquired by purchase or gift from another family member (.10).

.05 Code Sec. 704(e).

.10 Code Sec. 704(e); Reg. §1.704-1(e).

¶25,735 Control over Partnership Interest. The mere fact that the formalities of a gift have been complied with does not mean that the family partnership will be recognized in every case. The family member-donee must have control over the partnership that is consistent with partner status. This means that the donee must have reasonable authority as to management, control over distributions, authority to liquidate the interest, etc (.05). In addition, the partnership must not be a "sham". The partners must have acted in good faith in joining together to conduct the partnership business. Although there is no separate requirement that the partnership was created with a business purpose, it is a relevant factor to be considered in determining whether the partners joined together in good faith (.10).

If the family member partner is a minor lacking the maturity and understanding to manage his own affairs, he cannot be recognized as a partner unless control is exercised on his behalf by a fiduciary (.15). In other words, the partnership interest must be held by a trust. However, a minor, as well as any other family member, may be a limited partner, provided the limited partnership is organized in accordance with state law (.20).

.05 Reg. §1.704-1(e)(2)(ii).

.10 *J.A. Cirelli*, 82 TC 335, CCH Dec. 41,019.

.15 Reg. §1.704-1(e)(2)(viii); *E.M. Gammelgard Virgil*, 47 TCM 692, CCH Dec. 40,686(M), TC Memo. 1983-757.

.20 Reg. §1.704-1(e)(2)(ix).

¶25,736 Capital Interest Through Gift. Where a family member acquires a capital interest through gift or by purchase from another family member in a family partnership in which capital is a material income-producing factor, the donee is taxable on his share of the partnership income, subject to the following conditions (.05):

(1) the *donor* must be allowed an amount of partnership income which represents reasonable compensation for his services to the partnership, and

(2) the *donee's* share of the partnership income (after the allowance to the donor) must not be proportionately greater (on the basis of their capital interests) than the share allocated to the donor.

Example: The net profits of a partnership in which a husband has given a one-half interest to his wife are $100,000. The wife performs no duties for the partnership. The reasonable value of the husband's services is $20,000. Under the above conditions, there must be allocated to the husband $60,000 ($20,000 salary plus 50% of the other $80,000), and to the wife, $40,000.

.05 Code Sec. 704(e)(2).

¶25,737 Husband-and-Wife Partnerships. A bona fide partnership between a husband and wife is recognized for federal income tax purposes, even though they cannot legally be partners under state law. On the other hand, the fact that an asserted husband-and-wife partnership would be valid under state law does not necessarily mean that the partnership will be recognized for federal income tax purposes (.05).

From the standpoint of income taxation, the operation of a business as a husband-and-wife partnership may accomplish little that cannot be accomplished just by filing a joint return (see ¶25,701). However, such a partnership may benefit from the sheltering of more retirement income (see ¶25,725 and ¶25,726), and the separate entitlement of each spouse to social security benefits. Such benefits, of course, must be weighed against self-employment tax that such an arrangement can generate.

.05 Rev. Rul. 58-248, 1958-1 CB 255.

OLDER TAXPAYERS

Introduction

¶25,739 Although the federal income tax laws generally apply equally to all taxpayers, sometimes age does play a special role. For example, individuals age 65 or over are permitted to claim an additional standard deduction (see ¶25,741).

In addition, the medical expense deduction (see ¶25,764), as well as the rules on annuities (see ¶25,767), pensions (see ¶25,774), and self-employment retirement plans (see ¶25,786), are also of special interest to older taxpayers, to those who are retired or approaching retirement, and to those who advise them.

Tax Return Filing Provisions

¶25,741 Income Levels for Filing Returns. The following filing levels will apply to a taxpayer who is 65 years of age or older (the amounts for 2005 are unofficial projections):

	2004	*2005*
Joint return, one spouse age 65 or older	$16,850	$17,400
Joint return, both spouses age 65 or older	17,800	18,400
Married filing separately, age 65 or older	3,100	3,200
Single, age 65 or older	9,150	9,450
Head of household, age 65 or older	11,450	11,500
Qualifying widow(er), age 65 or older	13,750	14,200

The return-filing requirement levels are higher for the elderly than for other taxpayers because of the additional standard deduction amount available to them (see "Additional standard deduction," below). Although an additional standard deduction is available to blind persons, that amount is not taken into account in determining the filing levels listed above.

Personal exemption

Every taxpayer who files an income tax return may be entitled to deduct from taxable income a personal and a dependency exemption. Each individual, who does not qualify as a dependent on another person's tax return, may claim a personal exemption. In addition, a taxpayer is entitled to a dependency exemption for each person claimed as a dependent. Unless limited by the phaseout rules for certain high-income individuals, the exemption amount for 2004 is $3,100 (to increase to $3,200 in 2005) (.05).

An individual must satisfy five tests to entitle a taxpayer to claim a dependency exemption. The five tests are relationship or member-of-household, citizenship, gross income, support and joint return. Taxpayers cannot take an exemption for a person (even themselves) who can be claimed as a dependent on someone else's tax return, even if the exemption is not actually claimed (.10).

The exemption amount is reduced by two percent for each $2,500 or fraction thereof by which a taxpayer's adjusted gross income exceeds the appropriate threshold amount (for married, filing separately filing status, the reduction amount is two percent for each $1,250 or fraction thereof) (.15). The 2004 threshold amounts are: joint returns or surviving spouse, $214,050; head-of-household, $178,350; single, $142,700; and married, filing separately, $107,025 (to increase to $218,050, $182,450, $145,950 and $109,475 respectively in 2005) (.20).

Basic standard deduction

The basic standard deduction available to *all* taxpayers is as follows (.25):

	Basic standard deduction amount	
Filing status	*2004*	*2005*
Married filing jointly and Qualifying widow(er)s	$ 9,700	$ 10,000
Married filing separately	4,850	5,000
Single filers	4,850	5,000
Head-of-household filers	7,150	7,300

Additional standard deduction

To the basic standard deduction noted above, an elderly or blind *married* individual or a surviving spouse adds $950, or $1,900 if the individual was both elderly and blind in 2004 (to increase to $1,000 or $2,000 respectively in 2005). The increase for an elderly or blind *unmarried* individual is $1,200, or $2,400 if the individual was both elderly and blind in 2004 (to increase to $1,250, or $2,500 respectively in 2005). Thus, for elderly individuals the standard deduction amount is as follows:

	Standard deduction	
Filing status	*2004*	*2005*
Joint return filers, one spouse age 65 or older	$ 10,650	$ 11,000
Joint return filers, both spouses age 65 or older	11,600	12,000
Married filing separately, age 65 or older	5,800	6,000
Qualifying widow(er), age 65 or older	10,650	11,000
Head-of-household filer, age 65 or older	8,350	8,550
Single filer, age 65 or older	6,050	6,250

Determination of age 65

The determination of whether an individual is age 65 or older is made as of the close of the tax year for which the return is filed. An individual is considered to be age 65, for income tax purposes, on the day before his 65th birthday (.30).

Blindness defined

To qualify, a person need not be totally blind. Partial blindness can qualify the taxpayer for the blindness exemption. An individual is blind if his central visual acuity does not exceed 20/200 in the *better eye with corrective lenses* or the field of vision is not more than 20 degrees (.35). An individual is also considered blind under the law when eyesight can be corrected beyond the statutory limits only by special contact lenses that produce severe pain and infection when used for longer than brief periods (.40).

The exemption for blindness is allowable for the entire year if the taxpayer is blind at the end of the year, regardless of when blindness occurred. If a taxpayer's spouse dies during the year, the higher standard deduction for blindness is allowable if the spouse was blind at the date of death.

Self-employed taxpayers

A special return-filing rule applies if the older taxpayer is a self-employed professional, such as a doctor or accountant, or if he operates his own business. A self-employed person must file a return and pay self-employment tax if his annual net earnings from self-employment total $400 or more, regardless of his age and the amount of his income (.45). Net earnings from self-employment may be considered the net profit (total income from sales of services or goods minus allowable deductions attributable to earning such income) from his professional practice or business. The self-employment tax has two components: social security and hospital insurance. For 2004, the social security component of the tax is 12.4% of self-employment income up to a maximum of $87,900 ($90,000 for 2005), and the hospital insurance component is 2.9% of self-employment income with no limit on the amount of earnings that is subject to the tax. However, a deduction is allowed that is equal to one-half of the self-employment tax liability for the year (.50).

Income for return-filing purposes

Gross income is used to determine whether an individual must file a tax return. If a person is an employee, his total salary or wages, unreduced by any expenses incurred doing the job, is included in gross income. If he receives rental income, gross income is the total rentals received unreduced by any expenses incurred on the rental property. If the taxpayer has a merchandising business, gross income is the gross profit, which is the total sales receipts minus the cost of goods sold. Gross income from a business that renders a service is generally the total amount of fees or commissions received reduced by any expenses incurred in earning those fees or commissions.

> ***Example:*** Harry Eckert, age 66 and single, owns rental property that yields total rents of $6,500 in 2004. His expenses on the rental property (repairs, depreciation, janitor services, taxes, insurance, etc.) amount to $1,000, leaving a net rental income of $5,500. He also operates a small gift shop that, during the year, had total sales of $6,700. The cost of the merchandise sold was $3,300, and his adjusted gross profit was $3,400. Other business expenses of operating the shop, such as the cost of heat, light, telephone, depreciation, etc., were $1,500; thus, he had a net profit of $1,900.
>
> His gross income for return-filing purposes is $9,900—the $6,500 total rents and the $3,400 gross profit from the gift shop. Because his gross income is over $9,150, Eckert must file an income tax return for 2004.

Exempt income

Income that is exempt from tax is generally not included in gross income for filing purposes. Therefore, such items as amounts paid on a life insurance contract by reason of the death of the insured, most municipal bond interest, gifts, bequests, or inheritances are not includible in the gross income figure. However, the amount of foreign earned income excluded by U.S. citizens and residents living abroad (see ¶25,590 and following) is included in the gross income figure in determining whether a return must be filed.

.05 Code Sec. 151(d); Rev. Proc. 2003-85, I.R.B. 2003-49.

.10 Code Secs. 151(c) and 152.

.15 Code Sec. 151(d)(3).

.20 Rev. Proc. 2003-85, I.R.B. 2003-49.

.25 Rev. Proc. 2003-85, I.R.B. 2003-49.

.30 Reg. §1.151-1(c)(2).

.35 Code Sec. 63(f)(4).

.40 *E. Hollman,* 38 TC 251, CCH Dec. 25,495 (Acq.); Code Sec. 63(f)(4).

.45 Code Sec. 1402 and Code Sec. 6017; Reg. §1.1402(a)-1–Reg. §1.1402(a)-3 and Reg. §1.6017-1.

.50 Code Sec. 164(f).

¶25,742 Return-Filing Strategies. In addition to benefiting from the special income level filing requirements discussed at ¶25,741 taxpayers age 65 and older may benefit from special filing rules (.05).

Refund claims for tax withheld—Withholding exemptions

Even though an individual is 65 years old and may not have had enough gross income to require the filing of a return, a return should nevertheless be filed to obtain a refund of any tax withheld if that individual had wages, salary, or other income from which income tax was withheld. If a return is not filed or a separate claim for refund is not made, the withheld taxes will not be refunded.

Alternatively, the older taxpayer may claim an exemption from withholding taxes. An employee who certifies to an employer that the employee had no income tax liability for the preceding year and anticipates none for the current year may be exempt from withholding. An older taxpayer can use this technique to avoid a current reduction in pay for taxes that will not be owed. Form W-4, "Employee's Withholding Allowance Certificate" is used to claim the withholding exemption.

Joint or separate returns

Married couples have the option of filing either separate income tax returns or a joint income tax return. A joint return may be filed even though one spouse has no income. Generally, filing a joint return results in a lower tax liability than filing separate returns. Thus, for example, if a husband and wife are both 65 years of age or older and they file a joint return, for 2004 the first $17,800 of their combined income is not subject to tax. If only one spouse is age 65 or older, $16,850 of their combined income is not subject to tax.

If a married couple elects to file separate returns, each spouse generally reports his or her own income and claims his or her own deductions and exemptions. However, if a taxpayer's spouse had no gross income and was not the dependent of another taxpayer, the taxpayer may claim an exemption for his or her spouse on the taxpayer's separate return.

If one spouse files a separate return and itemizes deductions, the other spouse must do so also. However, in a recent letter ruling, the Service determined that a spouse who is entitled to claim head-of-household filing status is not considered married for income tax purposes. Thus, even if the other spouse, filing under the married, filing separately status, itemizes their deductions, the spouse claiming head-of-household status is still entitled to a full standard deduction (.10). See ¶25,743, "Head-of-household tax rates."

☐ See ¶25,546 and following for a discussion on the effects on residents of community property states.

Filing tax returns for the sick or disabled

An older person who becomes sick or disabled or remains in that condition for a long period of time may not be able to conduct his or her own affairs. In such situations, the individual's return must be filed by a duly authorized agent, committee, guardian, fiduciary, or other person charged with the care of the individual or the individual's property (.15).

A person who has a duty to file a return for a sick or disabled taxpayer generally must sign the return. When the return is filed and signed by an authorized agent, a completed power of attorney (Form 2848, "Power of Attorney and Declaration of Representative" or equivalent) form must be submitted with the return.

When joint returns are filed, Form 2848 may be used to authorize one spouse to sign the joint return as agent for the other spouse. In addition, however, when the signature of either spouse cannot be obtained because of disability, the return may be signed by the other if he or she is orally authorized to do so. It is sufficient if the signing spouse merely signs the other's name and adds the words "By . . . .. Husband (or Wife)." A statement explaining the reason for the inability of the incapacitated spouse to sign the return must be attached to the return (.20).

.05 Code Sec. 6012–Code Sec. 6013.

.10 IRS Chief Counsel Advice 200030023, 6-27-2000.

.15 Reg. §1.6012-1(a)(5); Rev. Rul. 67-191, 1967-1 CB 318.

.20 Rev. Rul. 70-216, 1970-1 CB 265.

¶25,743 Tax-Saving Computations. Generally, the tax rates and computations apply equally to all persons. However, special rates and methods of tax computation may be beneficial to older individuals and to persons who are responsible for elderly individuals (.05).

Widows and widowers—Joint return rates

A joint return may be filed by an executor or administrator on behalf of a decedent and his or her surviving spouse for the year in which death occurred, provided that such executor or administrator has been appointed. When death occurs before the close of a tax year, marital status is determined as of the date of death, rather than as of the last day of the tax year.

Also, a surviving spouse with a dependent child, a qualifying widow(er), may use the joint return rates on returns filed for each of the two years following the year of the death of his or her spouse. This tax advantage applies only if the a qualifying widow(er) was entitled to file a joint return for the year of death, remained unmarried, and maintained as his or her home a household that was the principal place of abode during the entire year of a child or stepchild for whom a dependency exemption was allowed. This benefit only entitles the qualifying widow(er) to use the joint return tax rates and does not authorize the qualifying widow(er) to file a joint return or to claim any personal exemptions other than his/her own and those dependency exemptions to which he/she is entitled.

Head-of-household tax rates

An individual who qualifies as a head of household is taxed at rates that fall between those applicable to joint returns and those applicable to single persons. These reduced rates may significantly benefit an unmarried person who has assumed the support of an elderly parent or parents, as well as an older taxpayer who maintains a household for a child or a grandchild.

A person qualifies as a head of household if he is unmarried at the end of the tax year and furnishes over one-half of the cost of maintaining for the entire year a household that is the principal abode for more than half of the tax year of a dependent child or stepchild, a descendant of a son or daughter, or any other dependent of the taxpayer. When a married child, stepchild, or descendant of a child resides with a parent, the parent can qualify as the head of household, even though he is not entitled to claim the child or his descendant as a dependent, provided that such ineligibility is due to a dependency waiver or to the provisions of a pre-1985 divorce or separation agreement.

Dependent parent

A person can also qualify as a head of household if he maintains a separate household for a dependent parent. The parent does not have to live in the taxpayer's house, provided the taxpayer furnishes more than one-half of the cost of maintaining the parent's principal abode. Costs associated with maintaining a household include such items as property taxes, mortgage interest, rent, utilities, upkeep and repairs, property insurance, and food consumed in the home. The payment of over one-half the cost of maintaining a parent in a home for the aged or a rest home qualifies a taxpayer for head-of-household status (.10).

☐ See, further, ¶25,745 for a discussion of parents as dependents.

Head-of-household v. joint return rates

The head-of-household rates are not as favorable to widows and widowers as are the joint return rates. Thus, if the taxpayer qualifies as a qualifying widow(er), joint return rates should be used.

> ***Example:*** Sam Caputo's wife, Mary, age 63, died on September 10, 2004, and Sam continued to live in their home with their two dependent children for the remainder of the year. Sam did not remarry in 2004. Sam's adjusted gross income in 2004 is $62,000. Sam, who is age 65, does not itemize his deductions. If Sam files as a head of household, his tax is $6,687.50 on taxable income of $44,350 ($62,000 – $7,150 basic standard deduction for head of household – $1,200 additional standard deduction for a head of household age 65 – (3 × $3,100 personal and dependency exemptions)). If Sam files as a qualifying widower, his tax is $5,592.50 on taxable income of $42,050 ($62,000 – $9,700 basic standard deduction for a qualifying widower – $950 additional standard deduction for a married taxpayer age 65 – (3 × $3,100 personal and dependency exemptions)). Sam should file as a qualifying widower and realize a tax savings of $1,095.

☐ See, also, ¶6070 for a discussion of persons eligible to use these rates.

.05 Code Sec. 2 and Code Sec. 6013.

.10 Rev. Rul. 70-279, 1970-1 CB 1; *J. Robinson*, 51 TC 520, CCH Dec. 29,400 (Acq.), aff'd, vac'd & rem'd on another issue, CA-9, 70-1 USTC ¶9269 and 70-1 USTC ¶9,310, 422 F2d 873; *W.C. Jewell*, 69 TC 791, CCH Dec. 34,997 (Acq.).

Older Individual as Dependents

¶25,745 Claiming Older Individuals as Dependents. When a person approaches age 65 and his income is derived primarily from nontaxable sources (¶25,750), it may be a wise tax strategy to allow one of his children or another close relative to claim him as a dependent (.05).

Dependency requirements

In order to be entitled to a dependency exemption for an older person, the following requirements must be met:

(1) the claimed dependent must have less than the exemption amount ($3,100 in 2004) in gross income for the calendar year in which the tax year of the taxpayer begins;

(2) over half the dependent's support for that calendar year must have been furnished by the taxpayer; and

(3) the dependent must be in one of the specified classes of individuals described below.

To qualify as a dependent, an individual must be a citizen, national, or resident of the United States, or a resident of Canada or Mexico, at some time during the calendar year in which the tax year of the taxpayer begins. The dependent must be the taxpayer's father, mother, or an ancestor of either; his stepfather or stepmother; or a brother or sister of his mother or father. Thus, although an older individual claimed as a dependent will usually be the taxpayer's parent, a taxpayer can claim as dependents his grandparents, aunts and uncles, or stepparents. Also, a person who is not a relative but who resides with the taxpayer may be claimed as a dependent if the relationship is not illegal under local law.

Support test

In order to claim an older individual as a dependent, a taxpayer must have furnished more than one-half of the total support of the individual for the tax year. Support includes the cost of food, shelter, clothing, medical and dental care, church contributions, transportation, recreation, etc. Moreover, if a parent or other older dependent lives in quarters for which the taxpayer is paying the rent or if the parent or other older dependent lives in a house that the taxpayer owns, a proportionate part of the fair rental value may be included in computing support (.10).

When an individual has an independent source of funds, including social security benefits, only the amounts actually spent by him for his own upkeep are matched against the amount spent by the taxpayer in determining who contributed more than one-half of the individual's support. Basic (Part A) and supplementary (Part B) Medicare benefits (.15) received and Medicaid payments (.20) made by or on behalf of an individual are disregarded in computing support for purposes of determining dependency. However, premiums paid for health insurance, but not proceeds received as the result of such coverage, are includible in computing the amount of support provided to an individual (.25).

Example: Tom Evans owns a house in which he lives with his wife, their two children, and his mother. His mother received social security benefits of $1,200, of which she spent $500 for her clothing, entertainment, and transportation. The remaining $700 was deposited in a savings account. Evans's expenditures for food for the household totaled $5,200. The fair rental value of the room that was used by his mother, based upon the cost of comparable rooming facilities, was $350.

Total support of Evans' mother is computed as follows:

Fair rental value of lodging	$ 350
Direct expenses paid by mother	500
Pro rata expenses for food (1/5 of $5,200)	1,040
Total support	$ 1,890

Because the amount of support furnished by Evans was $1,390 ($350 for lodging and $1,040 for food), which is over one-half of the $1,890 total support, Evans can claim his mother as a dependent.

.05 Code Sec. 151(e); Code Sec. 152; Reg. §1.152-1; Reg. §1.152-2.

.10 Rev. Rul. 58-302, 1958-1 CB 62.

.15 Rev. Rul. 79-173, 1979-1 CB 86.

.20 *M.E. Archer*, 73 TC 963, CCH Dec. 36,798.

.25 *F. McGuire*, 77 TC 765, CCH Dec. 38,330.

¶25,746 Multiple Support Agreements. Generally, more than one-half of the support of a dependent must be contributed by the taxpayer before a dependency exemption may be claimed. However, there is an exception if more than one-half of the support during the calendar year was furnished by two or more persons, each of whom would be entitled to claim the exemption but for the fact that he did not alone furnish more than one-half of the support (.05). Thus, an older individual who is supported by several of his children, no one of whom provides more than one-half of his support, may still be claimed as a dependent by one of them.

In such a case, the dependency exemption may be claimed by a taxpayer who furnishes more than 10 percent of the support, if everyone else who contributed more than 10 percent of the support files a declaration that he will not claim the individual as a dependent for any tax year beginning in such calendar year. The written declaration or waiver may be made on Form 2120, "Multiple Support Declaration."

Example: The four Smith brothers contributed the entire amount of support for their mother for the tax year in the following percentages: Alex, 30%; Ben, 20%; Charles, 29%; and Dan, 21%. Any one of them can claim the exemption for his mother by attaching to his return written declarations from the other three that waive the claim for exemption. The brothers can take turns, each claiming the exemption in a different tax year, if they wish.

The person who is entitled to the dependency exemption under the multiple support agreement may also deduct any of the dependent's unreimbursed medical expenses that he actually pays (see ¶25,764).

.05 Code Sec. 152(c); Reg. §1.152-3.

Income of the Older Taxpayer

¶25,750 Social Security and Railroad Retirement Benefits. Up to 85% of an individual's social security benefits or tier 1 railroad retirement benefits (generally, benefits that are paid as retirement, disability, or survivor benefits) may be includible in gross income and subject to tax (.05).

Reduction for benefits repaid

If a taxpayer is required to repay a portion of his social security or railroad retirement benefits to the government (for example, if he was made ineligible for benefits for a portion of the year), his annual benefits should be reduced by the amount of the benefits repaid. This reduction is to be made in the current tax year whether the repayment pertains to benefits received in the current or the previous tax year. If the repayment exceeds benefits for the current year, the excess repayment amount may be claimed as an itemized deduction for federal income tax purposes.

Reporting requirements

In order to facilitate the payment of tax on social security/railroad retirement benefits, the Secretary of Health and Human Services or the Railroad Retirement Board is required to report to the IRS the:

(1) aggregate amount of benefits paid with respect to any individual during the calendar year;

(2) aggregate amount of benefits repaid by the individual during the calendar year;

(3) aggregate reductions in benefits otherwise payable due to the receipt of workers' compensation benefits; and

(4) name and address of the individual with respect to whom benefits are paid (.10). Each individual receiving social security or railroad retirement benefits will be furnished with a written statement showing the aggregate amount of payments, repayments, and reductions made by the agency.

.05 Code Sec. 86.

.10 Code Sec. 6050F.

¶25,751 Welfare Benefits. Welfare assistance payments, such as aid to the blind or aid to dependent children, are not taxable as income, nor are state awards to crime victims, their surviving spouses, or dependents (.05).

However, state payments made to citizens meeting certain age and residency requirements that are not based on need are not welfare benefits and must be included in income.

Food benefits received under the Nutrition Program for the Elderly are not included in income, but payments received for providing services *to* the program are includible in income (.10).

.05 Rev. Rul. 74-74, 1974-1 CB 18; IRS Letter Ruling 8352025, 9-26-83.

.10 IRS Publication No. 554, "Older Americans' Tax Guide."

¶25,752 Veterans' Benefits. Often older citizens derive income as a result of their prior military service. Benefits paid by the Veterans Administration to veterans or their families are exempt from tax (.10). See ¶25,537. However, nondisability retirement pay is generally taxable. See ¶25,534.

.10 Rev. Rul. 72-605, 1972-2 CB 35.

¶25,753 Life Insurance Proceeds. It is common for older taxpayers to receive insurance proceeds upon the death of their spouses. Special rules govern the taxability of such proceeds (.05).

Proceeds of a life insurance contract that are paid by reason of the death of the insured older individual are exempt from tax. The exemption applies to proceeds of life insurance purchased for employees by employers, whether under group or individual employee policies, as well as to proceeds of life insurance policies purchased by the older individual for himself. It also applies to death benefits payments having the characteristics of life insurance proceeds payable by reason of death, such as workers' compensation insurance contracts, endowment contracts, or accident and health insurance contracts.

However, where the life insurance proceeds are held by the insurance company under an agreement to pay interest thereon, the interest payments received must be included in income (.10).

Installment payments of insurance proceeds receive special tax treatment. If life insurance proceeds payable by reason of the death of the insured are received by his beneficiary in installments, any part of the installment payment that in effect represents interest on the insurance proceeds must be included in the beneficiary's income (.15).

Estate tax consequences

Proceeds of life insurance on a decedent's life that were received by his executor or his estate are includible in his gross estate for estate tax purposes (.20). Whether proceeds payable to third-party beneficiaries are includible in the gross estate depends on whether the decedent possessed incidents of ownership in the policy at the time of his death. If the decedent had an incident of ownership, the value of the proceeds will be included in the gross estate (.25). Proceeds of group-term life insurance, whether paid by the employee or his employer, or both, are treated in the same manner as proceeds of ordinary life insurance.

Group-term life insurance

Retired employees must include in income the cost of group-term life insurance continued to be provided directly or indirectly by their former employer to the extent such cost exceeds the sum of the cost of $50,000 of coverage for such insurance and the amount (if any) paid by the retired employee toward the purchase of such insurance (.30). The cost of group-term life insurance is determined under the uniform premium table method detailed at Reg. §1.79-3.

> ***Example:*** Henry Bricker, a retiree, age 65, receives $100,000 of group-term life insurance coverage for 2004. He makes no contribution toward the plan. The rate per $1,000 of protection for 1-month period for 2004 is $1.27. Bricker must include $762 in income (($100,000 minus $50,000) divided by $1,000 times $1.27 times 12).

Key employees, including retired key employees, must include the cost of all group-term life insurance in income, such cost being the greater of actual cost or cost under the IRS's uniform tables.

.05 Code Sec. 101(a)(1); Reg. §1.101-1.

.10 Code Sec. 101(c).

.15 Code Sec. 101(d).

.20 Reg. §20.2042-1.

.25 *Old Colony Trust Co. Exr.*, 39 BTA 871, CCH Dec. 10,687 (Acq. and Nonacq.).

.30 Code Sec. 79(a).

¶25,755 Compensation for Sickness or Injury. Generally, payments received because of illness or injury are not taxable (.05). Typical payments take the form of workers' compensation or health or accident insurance payments.

Amounts received under a workers' compensation law as compensation for personal injuries or sickness or damages received (whether by suit or agreement) are not taxable. However, workers' compensation benefits that cause a reduction in social security or railroad retirement benefits may be taxable. See ¶25,750.

Amounts received through health or accident insurance or through an employees' health and accident plan as reimbursement for medical expenses or for permanent injury are also excludable, except to the extent that they are paid for by an employer or are attributable to contributions made by an employer that were not includible in the employee's gross income.

However, payments received by an employee from an employer-financed accident or health plan for expenses incurred by the employee for medical care are not includible in income. The excludable amount of such payments is limited to those expenses that would otherwise be deductible by the employee as medical expenses (see ¶25,764). The exclusion applies not only to payments for medical care received by the employee but also to such payments for his or her spouse and dependents.

In addition, payments received under an employer-financed accident and health plan for permanent loss or loss of use of a member or function, or for permanent disfiguration of the employee or of his spouse or dependents are excludable from income. In order for the exclusion to be applicable, the payments must be computed with reference to the nature of the injury without regard to the period of the absence.

.05 Code Sec. 104; Code Sec. 105.

Sales of Residence

¶25,757 Sales of Principal Residence. The once-in-a lifetime exclusion of up to $125,000 of gain from the sale of a principal residence for taxpayers over 55 years of age has been repealed and replaced with the a general exclusion of gain on the sale of a principal residence of up to $250,000 for single filers and $500,000 for joint filers. See ¶4426. Generally, the property must be owned and occupied for two out of the five years prior to the sale. The exclusion may be claimed every two years. If the sale occurs prior to the satisfying the two year requirement, the exclusion may be prorated if specific conditions are met. There are special rules for taxpayers in specific unique situations.(.05). See ¶4427.

.05 Code Sec. 121; IRS Publication 523, "Selling Your Home."

Tax Credit for Elderly or Disabled

¶25,761 Credit for the Elderly or the Permanently and Totally Disabled. The most important credit for older taxpayers is the credit for the elderly or the disabled. Qualified individuals age 65 or older, or those under age 65 who have retired with a permanent and total disability and who have disability income from a public or private employer because of such disability, may claim a credit against tax equal to 15 percent of an initial base amount—with certain reductions. The amount of the credit cannot exceed the individual's tax liability. Credits against tax are amounts that are subtracted from an individual's income tax liability in a given year. Unlike a deduction that is subtracted from gross income or adjusted gross income, resulting in a reduction of the amount of income subject to tax, the credit is subtracted from the tax itself, resulting in a dollar-for-dollar reduction in tax liability. The maximum credit available is $1,125. The credit is determined on Schedule R (Form 1040) or Schedule 3 (Form 1040A). Taxpayers may not claim the credit on a Form 1040EZ (.05).

Eligible individuals

The credit for the elderly or disabled is available to (1) individuals who are 65 years of age before the close of the tax year or (2) those under age 65 who have retired with a permanent and total disability and who have disability income from a private or public employer because of such disability. To qualify for the credit, an individual must be a citizen or resident of the United States.

For purposes of the credit, an individual is considered permanently and totally disabled if he can prove to the IRS that he is unable to engage in any "substantial gainful activity" by reason of a medically determinable impairment, physical or mental, that has lasted or can be expected to last for a continuous period of at least 12 months or can be expected to result in death.

Married couples

Individuals who are married at the close of their tax year must file a joint return in order to claim the credit for the elderly or disabled. However, the credit may be claimed by a married person filing a separate return if he has lived apart from his spouse at all times during the tax year.

.05 Code Sec. 22 and IRS Publication 524, "Credit for the Elderly or the Disabled."

¶25,762 Amount Subject to Credit. The credit for the elderly or disabled is designed primarily to benefit individuals who receive moderate amounts of social security, railroad retirement, and other pension, annuity, or disability benefits, or who have moderate amounts of income from other sources. To this end, the tax law allocates to each individual an initial amount to determine the credit and then reduces such amount for those who receive nontaxable social security, railroad retirement, or veterans' benefits and other pension, annuity, or disability benefits, or whose adjusted gross income exceeds a certain level (.05).

Initial amount

The tax credit is an amount equal to 15 percent of a specified maximum amount (called "initial amount").

The initial amount subject to the credit varies according to filing status, as follows:

Single individuals, head of household, or qualifying widow or widower	$ 5,000
Married individuals, joint return, one spouse eligible	$ 5,000
Married individuals, joint return, both spouses eligible	$ 7,500
Married individual, separate return	$ 3,750

Reduction of initial amount

With respect to eligible individuals under age 65, the initial amount that is subject to the credit is limited to the amount of disability income, if the amount of such income is less than the applicable base amount.

Disability income is the aggregate amount that is paid under any employer's accident and health or pension plan and that is includible in the disabled individual's gross income to the extent that it constitutes wages or payments in lieu of wages for the period during which the individual is absent from work because of his disability.

Special rules limit this initial amount where two qualified individuals file a joint return and at least one spouse is under age 65 at the end of the tax year. If one spouse is age 65 or older at the end of the tax year, the maximum amount cannot exceed the sum of $5,000 plus the disability income of the spouse who has not reached age 65 before the end of the tax year (up to

$2,500). If both spouses are under age 65, the maximum amount cannot exceed the sum of the spouses' disability income (up to $7,500).

The initial amount must be reduced dollar for dollar by nontaxable social security, railroad retirement, or veterans' benefits and by other pensions, annuities, and disability benefits that are excludable from gross income. Any workers' compensation benefits that reduce the amount of disability benefits must be treated the same as social security for reduction purposes. In the case of a joint return, the combined benefits of both spouses must be taken into account in making the reduction.

Because of the statutorily mandated reductions, no credit is available to the following:

(1) *Single individual:* No credit is available to a single individual who has adjusted gross income of $17,500 or more *or* receives $5,000 or more in nontaxable social security, railroad retirement, or veterans' benefits, or pension, annuity, or disability benefits that are excluded from gross income;

(2) *Married couple, joint return, both spouses eligible for credit:* No credit is available to a married couple who have an adjusted gross income of $25,000 or more *or* receive $7,500 or more in social security, railroad retirement, or veterans' benefits, or pension, annuity, or disability benefits that are excluded from gross income;

(3) *Married couple, joint return, one spouse eligible for credit:* No credit is available to a married couple who have an adjusted gross income of $20,000 or more *or* receive $5,000 or more in social security, railroad retirement, veterans' benefits, or pension, annuity, or disability benefits that are excluded from gross income; and

(4) *Married individual filing separate return:* A married individual filing a separate return is not entitled to any credit unless he is living apart from his spouse for the entire tax year. If the individual is living apart, no credit is available if he has an adjusted gross income of $12,500 or more *or* receives $3,750 or more in nontaxable social security, railroad retirement, or veterans' benefits or pension, annuity, or disability benefits that are excluded from gross income.

If the eligible individual's adjusted gross income level exceeds a specific amount, a further reduction is required. To the extent that such individual's adjusted gross income exceeds the applicable adjusted gross income level, the initial dollar amount must be further reduced by one-half of such excess. The adjusted gross income levels are as follows:

Single individual, head of household, or qualifying widow or widower	$ 7,500
Married individuals filing joint returns	$ 10,000
Married individual filing separate return	$ 5,000

Example 1: Tom Bullock, age 66 and single, has adjusted gross income of $10,500 for 2004 and receives $2,000 of nontaxable social security benefits for the year. The amount of his credit is computed as follows:

Initial amount	$ 5,000
Less: Social security benefits	2,000
Reduced initial amount	$ 3,000
Less: One-half of adjusted gross income over $7,500	1,500
Amount subject to credit	$ 1,500
Credit (15% of $1,500)	$ 225

Example 2: Jack and Martha James are both over 65 and file a joint return for 2004. Jack and Martha have an adjusted gross income of $15,000 and receive combined nontaxable social security benefits of $5,000. They are not entitled to the credit.

Initial amount	$ 7,500
Less: Social security benefits	5,000
Reduced initial amount	$ 2,500
Less: One-half of AGI over $10,000	2,500
Amount subject to credit	$ 0

Example 3: Matt Powers, age 68, receives $2,000 in nontaxable social security benefits. His wife, Maggie, age 63, receives $1,500 in disability benefits. Maggie is permanently and totally disabled. Matt and Maggie file a joint return for 2004 showing adjusted gross income of $14,000. The credit for the elderly or the disabled is determined as follows:

Initial amount ($5000 + Maggie's disability income)	$ 6,500
Less: Social security benefits	2,000
Reduced initial amount	$ 4,500
Less: One-half of adjusted gross income over $10,000	2,000
Amount subject to credit	$ 2,500
Credit (15% of $2,500)	$ 375

.05 Code Sec. 22.

Medical Expense Deduction

¶ 25,764 Medical Expenses Can Be Deductible. Medical expenses are deductible only to the extent that they are not compensated for by insurance or otherwise and exceed 7.5 percent of adjusted gross income (.05). The medical expense deduction is important not only to older taxpayers but also to those who may be providing support for them. The rules for determining a deductible medical expense and the limitations on the deduction are discussed below and at ¶ 25,765.

Deductible medical expenses include amounts paid for the diagnosis, cure, mitigation, treatment, or prevention of disease, or for the purpose of affecting any structure or function of the body, including amounts paid for therapy treatments and similar services for the taxpayer, his spouse, or dependents.

Included are amounts spent for medical care insurance (but see below), medicines and drugs, contact lenses (.10), artificial teeth and limbs, hearing aids, crutches, wheelchairs (.15), elastic stockings, and seeing-eye dogs and other service animals (.20). Transportation expenses that are primarily for and essential to medical care are also deductible, as well as hospital and nursing service costs. Expenditures to improve or preserve the general health of an individual, such as the costs of a vacation trip or of nonprescription vitamins, do not qualify as deductible medical expenses. Funeral expenses are not medical expenses (.25).

Medical care insurance

The cost of medical care insurance, including supplementary medical insurance for the aged under Medicare, is deductible as medical expenses subject to the 7.5-percent-of-adjusted-gross-income limitation (¶ 25,765). However, special rules apply depending on the type of medical insurance involved.

The premium cost of accident or health insurance is a deductible medical expense. However, where multipurpose accident and health insurance is involved—that is, a policy providing indemnity for loss of earnings when illness or accident causes absence from work, or for loss of limbs, life, or sight, as well as medical care expenses—the deductible medical expense is limited to that portion of the premium paid for medical care expenses. The portion paid for indemnification for loss of earnings, limbs, life, or sight is not a deductible medical expense.

If part of the premium cost of accident or health insurance is allocable to items other than medical care expenses, no amount is deductible unless the portion allocable to medical care expenses either is separately stated in the insurance contract or is furnished to the policyholder by the insurance company in a separate statement.

Premiums paid by a taxpayer before he reaches age 65 for medical care insurance for himself, his spouse, or a dependent after he reaches age 65 are deductible in the year paid if the premiums are payable in equal yearly payments or more often. The payments must be made under a contract over a period of 10 years or more, or until the taxpayer reaches age 65 (but in no case for a period of less than five years) (.30).

The monthly Medicare payments paid by older taxpayers for supplementary medical insurance (Medicare B) are deductible as medical care insurance. However, the part of the social security tax that covers basic Medicare (Medicare A) is not deductible except by an individual who is not entitled to social security benefits and who voluntarily pays premiums to obtain basic Medicare coverage (.35).

Meals and lodging

Amounts incurred for lodging, but not meals, while away from home primarily for and essential to medical care provided by a physician in a licensed hospital are deductible as medical expenses (.40). Lodging expenses will not be deductible if there is any significant element of personal pleasure, recreation, or vacation in the away-from-home travel. The lodging cannot be "lavish or extravagant under the circumstances" and no more than $50 per night per individual may be taken into account as a medical expense. For purposes of this rule, a licensed hospital includes a medical care facility that is related to or is equivalent to a licensed hospital. Such facilities would include outpatient clinics like the Mayo Clinic. See, also, "Nursing care and domestic care" below.

Medicines and drugs

Only drug expenditures for insulin or for medicines and drugs that legally require a prescription are deductible as amounts spent for medical care (.45).

Amounts spent for the preservation of general health or for the alleviation of physical or mental discomfort that is unrelated to some particular disease or defect are not deductible medical expenses. Thus, expenditures for toiletries, such as lotions or toothpaste, or for maternity clothes are not deductible (.50). However, the cost of a wig is deductible where hair is lost as a result of a disease and the wig is prescribed as essential to mental health (.55).

Nursing care and domestic care

The cost of hiring a trained nurse to look after the medical welfare of a patient qualifies as a deductible medical expense, whether the nurse's services are rendered in a hospital or other institution, at home, or on a trip that the patient may take.

In many instances, however, domestic help is employed to care for a patient who is at home recuperating from an illness. The portion of the cost of employing the domestic that is attributable to services required in caring for the home and any children who may be present is not a deductible medical expense (.60). But the portion of the cost of the domestic attributable to the services rendered directly to the sick person, where such services would otherwise be rendered by a nurse, does qualify as a deductible medical expense (.65).

If a person other than a trained nurse is employed as a traveling companion for one who is too ill to travel alone, and the trip is for the sole purpose of alleviating a specific chronic ailment, the travel expenses of the companion qualify as a deductible medical expense. This is also true if the sick person's spouse is the traveling companion.

Travel expenses

The out-of-pocket travel expense for trips that are primarily for and essential to medical care is a deductible medical expense (.70). However, if the travel is undertaken merely for the general improvement of the patient's health or morale, the travel costs are *not* deductible, even if the trip is made on the advice of a doctor.

Transportation expenses, such as bus, taxi, train, or plane fares, incurred primarily for and essential to medical care qualify as a medical expense. If an older taxpayer uses his car in traveling to get medical care, he may include amounts paid for gas, oil, parking fees, and other related items. However, in 2004, an older taxpayer may deduct 14 cents for each mile he uses his car for medical purposes (.75), plus tolls and parking fees, instead of deducting the actual operating expenses. Depreciation and car insurance, however, never qualify as medical expenses.

Therapeutic devices and treatments

Very often, the nature of an illness dictates the need for special treatments or the use of special therapeutic devices. No matter how marginal these treatments or devices may seem, a medical expense deduction may be available.

Therefore, amounts spent for psychiatric therapy, remedial reading, or the use of special therapeutic devices such as motorized wheelchairs or autoettes (.80), self-propelled wheelchairs, special controls on automobiles (.85), reclining chairs for cardiac patients (.90), and special mattresses and beds (.95) can qualify as medical expense deductions, provided that: (1) the special treatment or use of the special device is prescribed by a doctor and (2) the patient can show that the extra expense was incurred primarily for the prevention or alleviation of a physical or mental defect or illness.

Home additions and improvements

The cost of home additions and improvements can be a deductible medical expense if the addition or improvement is primarily for the medical care of the sick person (.100). Thus, medical expense deductions have been allowed for the cost of installing elevators or inclinators in the homes of persons suffering from heart disease (.105), air conditioning devices for persons suffering from an allergy or from difficulty in breathing caused by a heart condition (.110), and specially built swimming pools for persons suffering from polio (.115).

If the addition or improvement does not increase the value of the home, the entire cost of the addition or improvement is deductible as a medical expense. However, if the value of the home is increased, then the amount of the medical expense deduction is limited to the excess of the cost of the addition or improvement over the increase in the value of the home (.120).

Capital expenditures that are incurred by a physically handicapped individual for the removal of structural barriers in his personal residence qualify as a deductible medical expense where the expenditure is necessary to accommodate the handicapped condition.

Sanitariums and rest homes

The cost of caring for a patient in a hospital, including the cost of meals and lodging, is a deductible medical expense. However, there is no flat rule for determining the extent to which expenses for care in an institution other than a hospital, such as a sanitarium or a rest home, are deductible as medical expenses. Each situation involving institutional care has to be considered in light of its own facts. Basically, the determinative factors will be the condition of the patient and the nature of the services he receives. In general, these rules can be followed:

(1) Medical care is principal reason. If a principal reason for the presence of a person in an institution is to receive the medical care available at the institution, and if

meals and lodging are furnished as a necessary part of such care, the entire cost of the medical care and the meals and lodging is a deductible medical expense (.125).

(2) Medical care is not principal reason. If the receipt of medical care available at the institution is not a principal reason for the presence of a person in an institution, then only the actual cost of the medical care received in the institution is deductible as a medical expense. In such a case, the cost of meals and lodging at the institution is not a deductible medical expense (.130).

(3) Education or rehabilitation is principal reason. The cost of ordinary education is not a deductible medical expense. However, if a person is mentally or physically handicapped and he attends an institution principally to utilize the resources of the institution to alleviate the mental or physical handicap, the cost of attending the institution, including the costs of meals and lodging and of ordinary education, if furnished, is a deductible medical expense (.135).

Thus, deductible medical expenses include the cost of attending a special school designed to compensate for or overcome a physical handicap, such as a school for the teaching of Braille or lip reading. Also, the cost of care and supervision, or of treatment and training, of a mentally retarded or physically handicapped person at an institution is a deductible medical expense.

Life-care fees

Also includible in deductible medical expenses is the portion of a life-care fee or founder's fee paid to a retirement home under an agreement whereby the home agrees to provide lifetime care, including medical care. The portion of the fee allowed as a medical expense deduction must be set aside for medical care (.140).

.05 Code Sec. 213; Reg. §1.213-1(e).
.10 Rev. Rul. 74-429, 1974-2 CB 83.
.15 Rev. Rul. 67-76, 1967-1 CB 70.
.20 Rev. Rul. 57-461, 1957-2 CB 116; Rev. Rul. 68-295, 1968-1 CB 92.
.25 Code Sec. 2053(a); Reg. §1.642(g)-1.
.30 Reg. §1.213-1(e)(4)(i)(*b*).
.35 Rev. Rul. 79-175, 1979-1 CB 117.
.40 Code Sec. 213(d)(2).
.45 Code Sec. 213(b).
.50 Rev. Rul. 2002-19, I.R.B. 2002-16.
.55 Rev. Rul. 62-189, 1962-2 CB 88.
.60 *R.F. Borgmann*, CA-9, 71-1 USTC ¶9251, 438 F2d 1121.
.65 Rev. Rul. 58-339, 1958-2 CB 106.
.70 Reg. §1.213-1(e)(1).
.75 Rev. Proc. 2003-76, I.R.B. 2003-43.
.80 Rev. Rul. 74-429, 1974-2 CB 83.
.85 *S.H. Weinzimer*, 17 TCM 712, CCH Dec. 23,100(M), TC Memo. 1958-137; Rev. Rul. 70-606, 1970-2 CB 66; IRS Letter Ruling 8024169, 3-24-80.
.90 Rev. Rul. 58-155, 1958-1 CB 156.
.95 Rev. Rul. 68-212, 1968-1 CB 91; Rev. Rul. 2002-19, I.R.B. 2002-16.
.100 Reg. §1.213-1(e)(1).
.105 *J.E. Berry*, DC Okla., 58-2 USTC ¶9870, 174 FSupp 748; Rev. Rul. 83-33, 1983-1 CB 70.
.110 *R.F. Borgmann*, CA-9, 71-1 USTC ¶9251, 438 F2d 1211.
.115 *C.B. Mason*, DC Hawaii, 57-2 USTC ¶10,012; IRS Letter Ruling 8208128, 11-27-81.
.120 IRS Publication No. 502, "Medical and Dental Expenses."
.125 Reg. §1.213-1(e)(1)(v) (*a*).
.130 Reg. §1.213-1(e)(1)(v) (*b*).
.135 Reg. §1.213-1(e)(1)(v)(*a*).
.140 *H.W. Smith Est.*, 79 TC 313, CCH Dec. 39,273.

¶25,765 Computing the Deduction. Medical and dental expenses, including the cost of medical care insurance, are deductible only to the extent that they exceed 7.5 percent of the taxpayer's adjusted gross income. Expenditures for prescribed medicines and drugs are included as medical and dental expenses. The term "adjusted gross income" means the taxpayer's total income less his business expense deductions and certain other deductions (.05).

Example: In 2004, Herb and Dolores Ryan, both of whom are over age 65, filed a joint return on which they reported an adjusted gross income of $22,000. During the year, they paid doctor and dental bills totaling $1,900, of which $1,000 was reimbursed by medical care insurance. The Ryans also spent $300 for prescribed medicines and drugs not compensated by insurance and paid medical care insurance premiums of $780 for the year.

The Ryans' medical expense deduction would be $330, computed as follows:

Doctor and dental bills (not compensated by insurance)	$ 900
Medical care insurance premiums	780
Drug expenses (not compensated by insurance)	300
Total medical expenses subject to 7.5% limit	$1,980
Less: 7.5% of $22,000	1,650
Allowable medical expense deduction	$ 330

Claiming the deduction

The medical expense deduction can be claimed only as an itemized deduction on Schedule A, Form 1040. Taxpayers planning to itemize their deductions cannot file Form 1040A or Form 1040EZ.

.05 Code Sec. 213(a).

Rules for Taxing Annuities

¶25,767 Annuity and Pension Income. Individuals often provide for a source of retirement income prior to their retirement. A typical source of retirement income is a pension or annuity. An older individual may have purchased an annuity contract from a life insurance company or he may receive annuity payments as part of an employer's pension, profit sharing, or stock bonus plan. (Generally, pension or annuity income from an employer's pension, profit sharing, or stock bonus plan is taxed under the annuity rules set forth at ¶25,767.)

The pension or annuity usually will be in the form of a life insurance endowment or annuity contract that provides that the taxpayer be paid a certain amount of money for life or for a fixed term of years. Income from an annuity or pension may be fully taxable or only partially taxable, depending upon how much of the annuity or pension cost was paid by the taxpayer.

☐ The rules for taxing pensions are discussed at ¶25,773 and following.

¶25,768 Excludable Amounts. Amounts received from annuity contracts are includible in the recipient's gross income except to the extent that they are deemed to represent a reduction or return of premiums or other consideration paid (.05). Under the annuity-exclusion-ratio rule, the exclusion of a portion of each annuity payment cannot be continued indefinitely. Once the total of all exclusions that the individual has taken for payments under the annuity contract equals his investment in the contract, all subsequent payments will be fully taxed. On the other hand, if the annuitant dies before his investment in the contract is fully recovered tax free through the annuity exclusion, a deduction is provided for his last tax year in an amount equal to the unrecovered portion of the investment.

The exclusion-ratio rule is used to determine what portion of an individual's pension or annuity payments is excludable from income and what portion is taxable.

.05 Code Sec. 72; Reg. §1.72-1–1.72-6.

¶25,769 Lump-Sum Settlements from Annuities. A lump-sum payment of the proceeds of an annuity contract on surrender, redemption, or maturity is taxable as ordinary income to the extent that it exceeds the investment in the contract (premiums plus any other consideration paid) less any amounts previously recovered tax free (.05). This ordinary income part may be taxed under the special five-or 10-year averaging method. See ¶25,775.

.05 Code Sec. 72(e); Reg. §1.72-11(d).

¶25,770 Beneficial Three-Year Rule. The three-year basis recovery rule for annuity distributions was eliminated for individuals whose annuity starting date was after July 1, 1986 (.05).

.05 Code Sec. 72(d); Reg. §1.72-13.

¶25,771 Early Withdrawals. Penalties are imposed for premature distributions from an annuity contract. The penalty is equal to 10 percent of the taxable part of the distribution (.05).

The penalty will not apply to a distribution that is:

(1) made on or after the date the annuitant reaches age 59½;

(2) made on or after the death of an annuitant;

(3) attributable to the annuitant's becoming totally and permanently disabled;

(4) one of a series of substantially equal periodic payments made for the life of the annuitant or the joint lives of the annuitant and his beneficiary;

(5) allocable to an investment in the contract made before August 14, 1982;

(6) made from an annuity contract (i.e., a qualified funding asset) under a qualified personal injury settlement;

(7) made under an immediate annuity contract; or

(8) made under a contract purchased by an employer upon the termination of a qualified plan and held by the employer until the employee separates from service.

.05 Code Sec. 72(q).

Taxation of Pension and Employer Retirement Distribution

¶25,773 Additional Tax on Early Withdrawals. An additional tax of 10 percent is imposed on early withdrawals from qualified retirement plans (.05).

Among the distributions to which the penalty does not apply are:

(1) made on or after the date the employee attains age 59½;

(2) made to a beneficiary or estate on or after the date of the employee's death;

(3) attributable to the employee's becoming totally and permanently disabled;

(4) one of a series of substantially equal periodic payments made for the life of the employee or the joint lives of the employee and his beneficiary;

(5) made to an employee who separated from service with his employer in or after the year in which he attained age 55;

(6) paid to an employee to the extent that he has deductible medical care expenses, whether or not deductions are itemized for the tax year;

(7) made to an alternate payee under a qualified domestic relations order; or

(8) dividends paid with respect to corporate stock described in Code Sec. 404(k).

.05 Code Sec. 72(t).

¶25,774 Lump-Sum Distributions from Employee Trusts. Lump-sum distributions from a tax-qualified employee benefit plan receive special tax treatment. A "lump-sum distribution" is a distribution, within one tax year of the recipient, of the balance to the employee's credit from all of the employer's qualified pension plans, qualified stock-bonus plans, or qualified profit-sharing plans. A taxpayer who receives a lump-sum distribution may elect to have it taxed currently at favorable rates (¶25,775) or treat it as a rollover or partial rollover and defer taxation until a later time (¶25,776) (.05).

To qualify for the election of the special tax treatment accorded a lump-sum distribution, an employee (or his beneficiary) must receive the balance to his credit in one tax year and the distribution must become payable to the beneficiary on account of the following:

(1) the employee's death;

(2) the employee's separation from the service of his employer;

(3) the employee's permanent disability; or

(4) the employee's attainment of age 59½. (However, the IRS takes the position that a pension plan (as distinguished from a profit-sharing plan) cannot make a lump-sum distribution to an active employee who has not reached normal retirement age, even though he has reached age 59½ (.10)).

In the case of a self-employed person, such as a sole proprietor or partner, the distribution must be made because of one of the following:

(1) the self-employed person's death;

(2) the self-employed person's permanent disability; or

(3) the self-employed person's attainment of age 59½.

The rules for taxing distributions from a traditional Individual Retirement Arrangement (IRA) or from a Keogh plan for the self-employed are discussed at ¶25,781 and ¶25,786, respectively.

Taxable amount

The entire amount of a lump-sum distribution may not be taxable. The taxable amount for a lump-sum distribution is the sum of (1) the employer's contribution and (2) the income earned on the amount distributed.

Part of a lump-sum distribution to an employee who was a plan participant before 1974 is treated as long-term capital gain unless he elects to have the total taxable portion of the distribution treated as ordinary income. The portion of the taxable lump-sum distribution that is not allocated to capital gain receives ordinary income treatment.

.05 Code Sec. 402(d). **.10** IRS Letter Ruling 7748053, 9-2-77.

¶25,775 Averaging Methods. A lump-sum distribution from an employer's pension plan may qualify its recipient to elect five-year or 10-year averaging for the ordinary income from the lump-sum distribution. However, the five-year averaging method has been repealed for tax years beginning after December 31, 1999. Under transitional rules, 10-year averaging is still available for those who qualify (.05).

In order to qualify for use of the special five-year averaging rule, the recipient of the lump-sum distribution must have been a plan participant for five or more tax years before the tax year in which he received the lump-sum distribution. Further, the recipient must elect to combine all amounts that might qualify for the five-year averaging rule. This election can be made only once after age 59½.

If the five-year averaging rule is used, the portion of the lump-sum distribution allocated to ordinary income is subject to a totally separate tax. (Form 4972 "Tax on Lump-Sum Distributions" is attached to the recipient's tax return to take advantage of the five-year rule.) In all instances, the rate table for a single individual is used to figure the separate tax.

Pursuant to a special transitional rule, an individual who attained age 50 by January 1, 1986, is permitted to make one election to use five-year averaging using current tax rates for the year of distribution or 10-year averaging under the 1986 tax rates (.10).

.05 Code Sec. 402(d)(1)-(2).

.10 IRS Publication No. 575, "Pension and Annuity Income."

¶25,776 Rollover Treatment of Distributions. It is possible for an older employee who receives a distribution, including a partial distribution (see below), from a qualified pension, profit-sharing, stock bonus, or annuity plan to contribute on a tax-free basis (i.e., "rollover") to another such qualified plan or to a traditional IRA part or all of the portion of the distribution not consisting of employee contributions (.05). (See ¶25,780 for a discussion of IRA plans.) The surviving spouse of a participant in a qualified retirement plan may roll over to an IRA, but not to another qualified plan, part or all of the distribution he or she received on account of the death of the participant.

The investment of the amount distributed from the qualified plan into the new qualified plan or IRA must occur within 60 days after receipt by the individual (.10). Two other rules should also be noted: (1) the amount transferred to the new qualified plan or IRA must not include the individual's contributions to the original qualified plan, and (2) the property other than cash received from the qualified plan must itself be transferred to the new qualified plan or IRA.

The full amount (less the amount of employee contributions) of a lump-sum distribution or a plan termination distribution need not be transferred to an IRA or another qualified retirement plan in order to be treated as a tax-free rollover. Any amount not in excess of the value of all of the property received in the distribution may be rolled over. However, the portion of the distribution retained by the recipient is not eligible for five-year averaging of ordinary income from a lump-sum distribution as discussed at ¶25,775.

Direct rollover option

Qualified plans and tax-sheltered annuities (TSAs) must provide recipients with the option of having eligible rollover distributions paid in a direct rollover to an eligible retirement plan (.15). A direct rollover is distinguished from an ordinary rollover in that the funds are paid *directly* from the plan to an IRA or another plan that accepts such rollovers, rather than being paid to the recipient who then transfers the funds to another plan. An eligible rollover distribution paid in a direct rollover to an eligible retirement plan is not included in the recipient's gross income. If a recipient does not elect to have the eligible rollover distribution paid directly to an eligible retirement plan, the distribution is subject to 20 percent income tax withholding.

Rollovers of partial distributions

A distribution that is less than the balance to the employee's credit (a partial distribution) may be eligible for tax-free rollover treatment (.20). The amount of the distribution is *not* required to equal 50 percent of an employee's balance, as was the case for pre-1993 distributions. Moreover, a partial distribution may now be rolled over into a qualified plan or an IRA, not just to an IRA as was the case under the pre-1993 rules. Of course, like any other rollover, the rollover of a partial distribution must be made within 60 days after the date of distribution.

If an individual makes a rollover of less than the full distribution, the amount retained is taxed in the year of receipt and is not eligible for special tax treatment for lump-sum distributions (¶25,774).

.05 Code Sec. 402(c); Code Sec. 403(a)(4); Code Sec. 403(b)(8); Code Sec. 408(d).

.10 Code Sec. 402(c).

.15 Code Sec. 401(a)(31); Reg. §1.401(a)(31)-1.

.20 Code Sec. 402(c)(8); Code Sec. 402(d)(4)(k).

¶25,777 Qualified Plan Loans Treated as Distributions. A loan from a qualified employee benefit plan, a government plan, or a tax-sheltered annuity arrangement to an employee is treated as a distribution to the extent that it exceeds prescribed limits. However, a loan that is required to be repaid within five years is treated as a distribution only to the extent that the amount of the loan, when added to the outstanding loan balance of the employee under all other loans from such plan, exceeds the lesser of (1) one-half of the present value (but not less than $10,000) of the employee's nonforfeitable accrued benefit under the plan or (2) $50,000 reduced by the excess of the highest outstanding balance of loans from the plan during the one-year period ending on the day before the date on which the loan is made over the outstanding balance of the loans from the plan on the date the loan is made (.05). The five-year repayment requirement does not apply to any loan used to acquire a dwelling that will be used as the principal residence of the participant or a member of his family.

> ***Example:*** John Brown's nonforfeitable accrued benefit under his employer's qualified profit-sharing plan is $9,000. He obtained a $7,500 loan from the plan, which was payable within five years. This was the only loan that he had received from the plan. Even though the amount of the loan ($7,500) exceeded 50 percent of his nonforfeitable accrued benefit under the plan ($4,500), the loan is not treated as a distribution because his outstanding loan balance was less than $10,000.

Loan transactions subject to the distribution rule include:

(1) the receipt of a loan by a participant or beneficiary from a qualified plan, government plan, or tax-sheltered annuity program, or

(2) the assignment or the pledging of any portion of a participant's or beneficiary's interest in a qualified plan, etc.

The outstanding balance of any loan that is renegotiated, extended, renewed, or revised is treated as an amount received as a loan on the date of such renegotiation, etc. Any amount received as a loan under a contract purchased under a qualified plan (and any assignment or pledge with respect to such a contract) will also be treated as a loan under the plan.

.05 Code Sec. 72(p).

Individual Retirement Arrangements

¶25,780 Overview. Employees or self-employed persons receiving compensation can plan for their retirement by establishing their own individual retirement plans, even if they are already covered under another tax-qualified plan, such as an employee's pension plan. In addition, an individual retirement plan can be established for a nonemployed spouse (.05).

An individual retirement account is commonly spoken of as an IRA. However, an IRA also encompasses individual retirement annuities, simplified employee pensions, and employer or employee association trust accounts. For purposes of this discussion, individual retirement accounts and annuities are referred to as traditional IRAs. After 1997, an individual may be eligible to open a Roth IRA.

Investment in an IRA

IRAs are sponsored by banks, savings and loan associations, insurance companies, mutual funds, brokerage firms, and other financial institutions. Investment choices range widely and, although a taxpayer cannot be the trustee of his own IRA, he can establish a plan under which he is entitled to direct the trustee as to investments.

Contributions

Prior to 2002, an individual could make a deductible contribution to a traditional IRA up to the lesser of $2,000 or 100 percent of compensation that is includible in their gross income for that year if the individual was not an active participant in an employer-maintained retirement plan for any part of the plan year ending within the individual's tax year. After 2001, the maximum contribution amount increases. For tax years beginning in 2004, the amount is $3,000 (.10).

If an individual is an active participant in an employer plan, then the deductibility of IRA contributions depends on the individual's adjusted gross income. When adjusted gross income exceeds a specific amount, the maximum deduction is reduced and may be eliminated.

Rollover of IRAs

The selection of one of the above investment types does not mean that it cannot be changed later. Special "tax-free rollover" rules permit an individual retirement plan to switch from one type of investment to another (.15). For example, an individual can transfer assets from his individual retirement account to another account or to an individual retirement annuity (other than an endowment contract) on a tax-free basis. Only one such transfer can be made per year (.20).

Certain conditions, however, must be met in order to take advantage of the tax-free rollover provisions applicable to IRAs. First, the amount distributed from the old plan must be transferred to the new plan not later than the 60th day after it is received. Second, if property other than money is distributed from the old plan, the recipient must transfer the same property to the new plan.

It is not necessary to rollover the entire amount received from the IRA in order to receive tax-free rollover treatment. Tax-free rollover treatment, however, is denied for any amount received by an individual from an inherited IRA. However, this rule does not apply to an IRA inherited by a surviving spouse of the original IRA owner.

Under limited circumstances, the rollover rules also permit the transfer of funds from a qualified retirement plan, a tax-sheltered annuity, or a retirement bond to an IRA (.15). Thus, an individual who receives a distribution from a qualified retirement plan or tax-sheltered annuity plan upon retirement may postpone taxation until the year in which he reaches age 70½. See, also, ¶25,776.

.05 Code Sec. 219; Code Sec. 408; Code Sec. 409.

.10 Code Sec. 219(b)(5)(A).

.15 Code Sec. 402(c), (d)(4)(K), (e)(1)(B), Code Sec. 403(a)(4); Code Sec. 408(d)(3).

.20 Code Sec. 408(d)(3)(B).

¶25,781 Taxation of Distributions. The taxation-of-distribution rules for traditional IRAs are of immediate concern to older taxpayers because these rules control the amount of available income for their retirement years. Amounts paid or distributed from an IRA are includible in gross income in the tax year of receipt. The distributions are taxable as ordinary income; capital gain treatment is inapplicable. The lump-sum distribution rules (¶25,774) do not apply (.05).

Payments received under an individual retirement annuity are taxable under the annuity rules (¶25,767) and are includible in gross income in the tax year of receipt. Since the cost of the annuity would have been deducted in a previous year, the contract has a basis of zero when received by the individual and he is therefore required to include the entire amount of each annuity payment in his income.

.05 Code Sec. 402(d)(5); Code Sec. 408(d).

¶25,782 When Distributions Can Begin. In order to encourage the use of traditional IRAs for retirement purposes, the law requires an individual to begin drawing on his retirement fund no later than the tax year in which he reaches age 70½. (This rule does not apply to Roth IRAs). However, an employee may receive payments beginning no later than the required commencement date over (1) his life, (2) the combined lives of himself and his beneficiary, (3) a period not extending beyond his life expectancy, or (4) a period not extending beyond the joint life and last survivor expectancies of himself and his beneficiary (.05).

Distribution upon death

If the individual dies before receiving his entire interest in the traditional IRA, the remainder must generally be distributed to the beneficiaries within five years. The five-year rule does not apply, however, if the distribution to the participant has already begun and is payable over a term certain that does not exceed his life expectancy or the joint life expectancy of the couple. In addition, under a special rule a spouse may elect to treat the inherited IRA as his or her own.

When an employee begins to receive distributions before death and subsequently dies, the remaining portion of his interest must be distributed at least as rapidly as under the pre-death method of distribution.

When distributions to an employee have not commenced before death, the entire interest of the employee must be distributed within five years after his death. However, there are two exceptions to this five-year distribution rule.

> (1) The five-year rule does not apply if (a) any portion of the employee's interest is payable to (or for the benefit of) a designated beneficiary, (b) the portion of the employee's interest to which the beneficiary is entitled will be distributed over the life of the beneficiary (or over a period not extending beyond the life expectancy of the beneficiary), and (c) the distributions commence no later than one year after the date of the employee's death (or such later date that the IRS may, under regulations, prescribe).
>
> (2) The five-year rule does not apply if (a) the portion of the employee's interest to which the surviving spouse is entitled will be distributed over the life of the surviving spouse (or over a period not extending beyond the life expectancy of the surviving spouse) and (b) the distributions commence no later than the date on which the employee would have attained age 70½.

Similar rules are provided for after-death distributions from or under both an individual retirement account or an annuity. In addition, present rules applicable to after-death distributions under an annuity contract are to apply to a custodial account that is treated as a tax-sheltered annuity contract.

.05 Code Sec. 401(a)(9); Code Sec. 408(a)(6); Code Sec. 408(b)(3); Code Sec. 408(b)(4).

¶25,783 IRA Penalties. Because the purpose of an individual retirement plan is to build up funds to be used during retirement, it is not surprising that an individual who receives his benefits at an early age or at a very late one may be penalized. Moreover, an individual who contributed to his IRA an amount exceeding his allowable IRA deduction may be subject to a penalty tax.

Premature distributions

Prior to 1997, unless an individual has reached age 59½ or is disabled, any IRA distribution made to him is subject to a penalty tax equal to 10 percent of the distribution (.05). After 1996, in some limited circumstances, individuals may withdraw amounts, without penalty, to pay for medical expenses or health insurance. After 1997, distributions may also be made for certain educational and homebuying expenses. This penalty is in addition to any income tax that may result from including the distribution in the individual's gross income. Moreover, the penalty tax is imposed on a constructive distribution (¶25,784) resulting from an IRA disqualification.

Insufficient distributions

To encourage use of the IRA for retirement purposes, the law requires an older individual to begin drawing on his retirement fund no later than the close of the tax year in which he attains age 70½. (This rule does not pertain to Roth IRAs). Failure to distribute the required minimum amount subjects the individual to a 50-percent excise tax on the excess of the minimum required distribution over the amount actually distributed (.10), unless there is a good reason for the excess accumulation. Funds distributed from an IRA before an individual attains age 70 cannot be taken into account in determining the minimum amount that must be distributed after age 70 in order to avoid the excise tax (.15).

Planning Note

CCH Analysts note that the IRS has issued regulations, effective January 1, 2003, that simply the minimum distribution rules for separate accounts, including the calculation of the required minimum distribution during the individual's lifetime using a uniform table.(.20).

Excess contributions

If contributions to an IRA exceed the maximum deduction allowed, the excess is subject to a cumulative six-percent excise tax that is not deductible (.25).

An older taxpayer can avoid this tax by withdrawing the excess contribution and the earnings attributable to that contribution on or before the due date, including extensions, of his tax return for the year of the excess contribution (.30). The withdrawn excess contribution is not taxable and the excise tax is not imposed provided that no deduction was allowed for the excess contribution and the interest or other income earned on the excess (which *is* includible in gross income and may be subject to an additional 10-percent tax on early withdrawals) was also withdrawn.

An individual who owes penalty taxes must file Form 5329, "Additional Taxes Attributable to IRAs, Other Qualified Retirement Plans, Annuities, Modified Endowment Contracts, and MSAs," with his income tax return for the year.

.05 Code Sec. 408(f) - Repealed.
.10 Code Sec. 4974.
.15 IRS Letter Ruling 8151076, 9-24-81.
.20 Reg. §1.401(a)(9)-0.
.25 Code Sec. 4973.
.30 Code Sec. 408(d)(4).

¶25,784 Constructive Distributions. An individual (or his beneficiary) must not participate in a transaction with his individual retirement account that is prohibited by the tax laws. For example, if an individual borrows money from his account, it will cease to be an individual retirement account as of the first day of the tax year in which the loan was made. Disqualification of the account triggers a constructive distribution to the individual equal to the fair market value of all of the assets of the account (including amounts constituting excess contributions that could be returned tax free) as of the first day of such tax year (.05). This amount is taxed as ordinary income. In addition, a 10-percent penalty tax will be imposed on early distributions if the individual is not disabled or is not 59½ years of age on the first day of such tax year. Also, after the first day of the tax year in which the prohibited transaction occurred, all income earned by the account is taxed currently to the individual.

Borrowing against a retirement annuity or endowment contract, or using the contract to obtain money (including, but not limited to, pledging the contract as security for any loan), is also prohibited. Such a prohibited transaction will cause the fair market value of the annuity or endowment contract (including amounts that are excess contributions which could be returned tax-free) to be taxed to the individual as ordinary income as of the first day of the tax year in which the prohibited transaction occurred. The 10-percent penalty tax on premature distributions may also be imposed (see ¶25,783).

.05 Code Sec. 408(e)(2); Code Sec. 4975.

Self-Employment Retirement Plans

¶25,786 Retirement Plans for Self-Employed Persons. In planning for retirement, older self-employed individuals, such as doctors, dentists, lawyers, accountants, sole proprietors of a business, or partners of a partnership, may have provided for their retirement by establishing for themselves a retirement plan commonly called a Keogh plan. Contributions to such plans may be deducted from gross income and the income earned by such plans will be tax free until distributed (.05).

The general discussion at ¶25,787–¶25,790 highlights the special rules applicable to distributions of benefits from a self-employed plan. Such rules have a direct bearing on the amount of income available for retirement.

.05 Code Sec. 401-Code Sec. 404; Code Sec. 416.

¶25,787 Contributions to Self-Employed Plans. The maximum amount that can be contributed to a Keogh plan depends on the type of plan to which the contributions are made. Contributions may be made to either a defined contribution plan or a defined benefit plan (.05).

Defined contribution plans

Under a defined contribution plan, the amount that may be contributed each year to the plan is based upon a percentage of net self-employment income.

The maximum contribution allowed is limited for 2004 to the lesser of:

(1) $41,000, or

(2) 100% of net earned income from self-employment.

Defined benefit plans

A defined benefit plan is structured to provide self-employed persons with a specific amount of retirement benefits. Allowable contributions are based upon actuarial assumptions and cannot exceed the amount necessary to produce the maximum legal retirement benefits. Contributions may vary from year to year.

The annual defined benefit that may be received from a defined benefit Keogh plan for 2004 is the lesser of:

(1) $165,000, or

(2) 100% of the participant's average high-three years of compensation.

.05 Code Sec. 401(c)(2); Code Sec. 415.

¶25,788 When Benefit Payments Begin. The time period during which distributions from a self-employment retirement plan can be made is limited (.05). See ¶25,782.

In the case of a key employee who is a five-percent owner in a plan, a 10-percent penalty for premature distributions before age 59½ is generally imposed, unless the distribution is made on account of death or disability (.10).

.05 Code Sec. 401(a)(9).

.10 Code Sec. 72(m)(5).

¶25,789 Distributions in Case of Death. If an employee (including owner-employees) dies before his entire interest has been distributed to him or if the distribution to a surviving spouse commenced and the spouse died before the interest was entirely distributed, the remaining interest must be distributed within five years of the employee's death or the death of the surviving spouse (.05).

When an employee begins to receive distributions before death and subsequently dies, the remaining portion of his interest must be distributed at least as rapidly as under the pre-death method of distribution.

When distributions have not commenced to an employee before death, the entire interest of the employee is to be distributed within five years after the death of the employee. However, this five-year distribution rule does not apply if:

(1) any portion of the employee's interest is payable to (or for the benefit of) a designated beneficiary, (b) the portion of the employee's interest to which the beneficiary is entitled will be distributed over the life of the beneficiary (or over a period not extending beyond the life expectancy of the beneficiary), and (c) the distributions commence no later than one year after the date of the employee's death (or such later date that the IRS may, under regulations, prescribe); or

(2) the portion of the employee's interest to which the surviving spouse is entitled will be distributed over the life of the surviving spouse (or over a period not extending beyond the life expectancy of the surviving spouse), and (b) the distributions commence no later than the date on which the employee would have attained age 70½.

Similar rules are provided for after-death distributions from or under an individual retirement account or annuity (¶25,782).

Generally, distributions under all qualified defined benefit and defined contribution plans, IRAs, and tax-sheltered custodial accounts and annuities are required to commence no later than April 1 of the calendar year following the calendar year in which the participant attains age 70½ without regard to the actual date of retirement (.10).

.05 Code Sec. 401(a)(9).
.10 Code Sec. 401(a)(9)(C).

¶25,790 Taxation of Distributions. The method of taxing distributions from self-employment retirement plans is similar to that applicable to a corporate or other employer trust. The tax on the amounts contributed, to the extent deductible, is deferred until such time as the amounts are actually distributed under the terms of the retirement plan (.05).

If the retirement benefits are paid over a period of years in installments, the recipient is taxed according to the annuity rules beginning at ¶25,767. In applying the annuity rules, the self-employed individual's "investment in the contract" or cost cannot include his contributions to the plan to the extent he deducted them on returns for prior years.

Lump-sum distributions to a self-employed individual are taxed as explained at ¶25,774 and following. Basically, the total taxable amount of a lump-sum distribution is the sum of the employer's contribution and the income earned on the amount distributed (.10).

Rollovers from one qualified plan to another are not permitted if the employee is a five-percent owner at the time the distribution is made (.15).

.05 Code Sec. 402.
.10 Code Sec. 402(d)(4)(D).
.15 Code Sec. 402(c)(5).

Tax Help for Older Taxpayer

¶25,791 Taxpayer Assistance Programs. The IRS offers various taxpayer assistance programs ranging from computing tax liability to providing toll-free telephone assistance to encourage compliance with the tax laws. All taxpayers, regardless of age, can have their tax liability, including certain credits such as the earned income credit and the credit for the elderly, computed by the IRS. In order to receive such assistance, the instructions to the applicable form must be followed. In general, taxpayers must supply sufficient information to enable the IRS to compute the tax (.05).

Telephone assistance

The IRS offers tax assistance by telephone. The IRS answers specific tax questions. In addition, the IRS telephone service, Tele-Tax, provides recorded tax information tapes on approximately 140 tax topics, including the credit for the elderly. See Instructions to forms or IRS Publication 17 for the list of topics.

Volunteer assistance

In addition to direct help, IRS-trained volunteers assist taxpayers in completing their tax returns. The volunteer programs include the Tax Counseling for the Elderly (TCE) program and the Volunteer Income Tax Assistance (VITA) program.

The Tax Counseling for the Elderly program is designed to provide tax assistance to older individuals (age 60 or older) who cannot afford professional tax help. Nonprofit organizations administer the Tax Counseling programs. Generally, assistance is provided at community locations such as libraries, schools, senior citizens' centers, shopping malls, or at the sites of individuals who are unable to travel because of illness or handicap.

Under this program, two types of assistance are rendered. Taxpayers are taught to prepare their own returns under the direction of volunteers in the Self-Help TCE Assistance Program. Direct TCE Assistance volunteers can complete the tax returns for those individuals who are unable to complete their own returns. In addition, taxpayers may receive help regarding state and local taxes.

Under the VITA program, IRS-trained volunteers assist taxpayers who cannot afford professional tax help, particularly those who file simple forms such as Forms 1040EZ or 1040A, and who qualify for the earned income credit. Assistance is also given to low-income elderly, handicapped, and non-English-speaking individuals. Assistance is provided at local community sites.

.05 Internal Revenue Manual, 6560 (Toll-Free Telephone System Handbook) and 6570 (Taxpayer Education Handbook).

DAY-CARE PROVIDERS

Introduction

¶25,793 The past few decades have seen steady growth in the number of working couples with children, single parent households, and older individuals. This growth has brought a corresponding increase in the number of individuals who are in the business of providing day care for children and respite care for older individuals.

Although many of the tax concerns and problems faced by care providers parallel those faced by other business people, care providers are affected by some unique tax provisions. For example, if a day-care provider uses his or her personal residence in connection with providing the service, special computational methods must be used for determining the deductibility of certain expenses of the residence (see ¶25,800). In addition, day-care providers are generally required to provide their taxpayer identification number to individuals who use their services. Failure to provide the number may result in a penalty (see ¶25,801).

Initial Business Concerns

¶25,795 Form of Doing Business. Individuals who are giving serious thought to starting a day-care operation must give top priority to evaluating the various options they have concerning the form in which the operation will do business. Although there is seldom anything to prevent an individual from changing the form in which the individual does business, such a change may generate extra costs, a taxable event and/or increased taxes. Therefore, the decisions should be made only after all options have been considered.

Taxable organization

If the individual or individuals organizing the operation have a profit motive in starting the endeavor, then a choice must be made of doing business as a sole proprietorship, partnership, corporation or limited liability company (LLC). Because most day-care operations are conducted on a small scale, a sole proprietorship, partnership or LLC is typically the most advantageous form from both an economic and tax viewpoint. This is due to the fact that these forms of doing business may generally be started at a reasonable cost and avoid the possible double taxation imposed on doing business in the form of a C corporation. Double taxation may also be avoided by use of an S corporation, but the costs of organizing and maintaining the S corporation may tend to limit its attractiveness to small business operations. Of course, tax considerations are not always the deciding factor in business decisions. For example, the limited liability of doing business in the corporate form may tip the scale in favor of forming a corporation over a partnership or sole proprietorship.

Tax-exempt organization

An nonprofit organization that provides day-care to children away from their home may be recognized as a tax-exempt "educational" organization under Code Sec. 501(c)(3) (¶16,090) if: (1) substantially all of the care provided by the organization is provided to enable individuals (presumably the children's parents or custodians) to be gainfully employed; and (2) the organization's services are available to the general public (.05). A day-care center that meets these requirements, however, must file an application for exempt status on Form 1023, "Application for Recognition of Exemption," in order to be recognized as an exempt organization.

.05 Code Sec. 501(k); Rev. Rul. 70-533, 1970-2 CB 112.

¶25,796 Employment Tax Obligations. If a day-care center cares for only a few individuals it is possible for the owner to perform all the necessary tasks, and the assistance of others may not be needed. However, in most cases, due to the long hours of operation, the size of the facility and the responsibilities that are involved in caring for other persons, additional help is not only desirable, but may be a requirement of doing business. If the individual who helps in the operation of the day-care center is classified as an "employee," then the owner of the facility will be liable for the collection and/or payment of employment taxes (see ¶18,001 and following). Conversely, if the individual who helps in the operation of the day-care center is classified as an "independent contractor," then the owner has no employment tax obligations for that person.

Unfortunately, there are no hard-and-fast rules to determine whether an individual fits within the classification of an "employee" or an "independent contractor"—the determination is based on the facts and circumstances of each situation. For example, the IRS determined that a teacher of a day care center was an employee based upon a number of factors including the continuing relationship between the worker and the center, the worker made her services available to the public, and the center provided all of the material, equipment, and supplies (.05).

Further complicating matters, is that the definition of "employee" varies for each separate employment tax. For a discussion of the definition of employee for withholding income taxes see ¶18,009, for FICA taxes see ¶18,310, and for FUTA taxes see ¶18,320. There are costly consequences to the day-care operator if he or she does not comply with the employment tax obligations. If a day-care center owner is unclear whether one of its workers should be classified as an employee or independent contractor, a request may be made to the IRS to make the determination.

Employees of Exempt Organizations

Special rules apply to the payment of FICA and FUTA taxes if a day-care center qualifies as exempt from federal income taxes under Code Sec. 501(a). The day-care center is responsible for the payment of FICA taxes on wages paid to an employee unless: (1) it pays the employee less than $100 in a calendar year (.10); or (2) it makes a timely election on Form 8274 to be exempt from FICA taxes because it is operated by certain church or church organizations that oppose for religious reasons the payment of the tax (.15). On the other hand, all services performed by an employee for a day-care center which is a tax-exempt educational organization under Code Sec. 501(c)(3) are exempt from FUTA taxes (.20).

.05 IRS Letter Ruling 8921038, 2-23-89, CCH IRS LETTER RULINGS REPORTS.

.10 Code Sec. 3121(a)(16).

.15 Code Sec. 3121(w).

.20 Code Sec. 3306(c)(8).

Income Tax Consideration

¶25,798 Reporting Business Income. An individual who operates a day-care center must pay particular attention to the record-keeping that is necessary in order to accurately record the business' gross income. Accuracy is not only necessary from the standpoint of being a good business practice, but it is also necessary in order to verify reported gross income to the IRS should an item on the taxpayer's tax return be questioned. As a general rule, the reporting of gross income is the first item that is questioned on a business tax return during an IRS examination. If the taxpayer is able to verify the amount reported by means of a good record-keeping system, this will help establish the credibility of other items on the tax return. The following material presents some of the basic considerations that go into the establishment of a system for reporting the income from a day-care center operation.

Cash method of accounting

Due to the fact that operators of day-care centers are primarily involved in providing a service to their clients and they are not required to maintain inventories in order to account for their income, they are generally free to use the cash method of accounting to record their income and expenses. Although some types of business are prohibited from using the cash method and are thus required to use the accrual method, it is highly unlikely that many day-care centers would come within this prohibition.

Under the cash method of accounting, a day-care operator includes in business income all items of income that are actually or constructively received during the tax year. Constructive receipt occurs when an amount is credited to the day-care operator's account or made available without restriction as to the time and manner of payment.

> ***Example 1:*** Happy Kids Day Care is a calendar-year taxpayer that received a check from one of its clients on December 31, 2003. Because of an oversight, the check was not deposited in its business account until February 1, 2004. Under the cash method of accounting, the amount of the check must be included in business income for the 2003 tax year and may not be delayed until the 2004 tax year.

> ***Example 2:*** On January 3, 2004, Happy Kids Day Care received a check from one of its clients. The check was dated December 26, 2003, and was in payment of child care services that the business had provided during 2003. If the business is a calendar-year taxpayer, then the amount of the check must be included in gross income for 2004, the year in which the check was received.

Record-keeping system

Day-care operators, along with other business taxpayers, are required to keep accurate, permanent books and records so they can determine the various costs, expenses, and other amounts that affect their income tax liability for a tax year (.05). This is true, even if the day-care center is a tax-exempt organization. The IRS does not mandate that the record-keeping system take any particular form, but it does require that the system reflect current income on the basis of an annual accounting period (.10). At a minimum, the record-keeping system for a day-care center operation, as for any small business, should probably include the following: business checkbook; daily or weekly summary of cash receipts; monthly summary of cash receipts; check disbursements journal; depreciation record; and employee compensation record. The books and records must be kept available at all times for inspection by IRS employees, usually for a period of four years (.15).

Choosing a tax year

A taxpayer must compute his taxable income based upon an annual period called a tax year (.20). A tax year must be a calendar year, fiscal year, or in certain cases, a short tax year (¶15,025). Like most businesses, however, a day-care center is not free to chose its tax year. At a minimum, the tax year chosen must correspond to the accounting period upon which the business keeps its books and records. Moreover, there are numerous statutory limitations requiring the use of certain tax years. For example, a day-care center run as a sole proprietorship must use the tax year of the individual owner. Similarly if the business is organized as a partnership or S corporation, than an owner-based tax year must also be adopted. For this purpose, individuals and entities without books and records must adopt a calendar tax year.

.05 Code Sec. 6001; Reg. §1.6001-1(a).
.10 Reg. §31.6001-1(a).
.15 Reg. §31.6001-1(e).
.20 Code Sec. 441(a).

¶25,799 Business Expenses. If a day-care center is operated as a business, then like any business, it may claim a deduction for ordinary and necessary expenses incurred during the tax year in carrying out the business. For example, a day-care center may deduct the cost to purchase any toys or sporting equipment if they are used in the day-to-day operation of the business (and if they have useful lives of one year of less). Certain expenses such as illegal payments, fines or penalties are not deductible. For a detailed discussion of the requirements for business deductions, including the requirement to keep accurate records of any business expense, see ¶7101 and following.

If a day-care center has an expense for an asset that is used partly for business and partly for personal purposes, the total cost must be divided between the business part and the personal part. Only that part of the cost that pertains to business use may be claimed as a business expense. However, the determination of what part of an expense is use for personal or business use is not always easy to calculate. For example, the IRS ruled that the entire cost of basic telephone service a nondeductible personal expense, even where state law required the day-care operator to have a telephone in order to be licensed as a day-care provider (.05). In addition, if the day-care operator uses a portion of his home for business purposes, special rules must be applied in determining the allowable deduction (see ¶25,800).

Special rules for meal expenses. In general, a business may only deduct 50 percent of the costs that are incurred for meals (see ¶8250). However, there are a number of exceptions that may apply to day-care centers. First, the cost of meals furnished by a day-care operator is fully-deductible so long as the operator charges for the meal (.10). The business must generally keep detailed records and receipts of food purchased in order to claim the deduction. However, for tax years beginning after 2002, family day care providers may choose to use a standardize rate to claim any deduction for furnished meals instead of maintaining detailed records. The rates follow the USDA Child and Adult Food Care Program, Tier I rate in effect each December 31 of the year preceding the current calendar year (see tables below) (.15). For this purpose, family day care is day care provided to eligible children in the home of the provider that is non-medical, does not involve a transfer of legal custody, and generally lasts for less than 24 hours each day. No portion of the cost of food provided to the family day care provider's family, including food consumed by the provider or the provider's own children, is deductible.

2003 Rates

	Contiguous States	Alaska	Hawaii
Breakfast	0.98	1.55	1.13
Lunch/Supper	1.80	2.93	2.11
Snacks	0.53	0.87	0.63

2004 Rates

	Contiguous States	Alaska	Hawaii
Breakfast	0.99	1.57	1.15
Lunch/Supper	1.83	2.97	2.14
Snacks	0.54	0.88	0.63

2005 Rates

	Contiguous States	Alaska	Hawaii
Breakfast	1.04	1.64	1.20
Lunch/Supper	1.92	3.11	2.25
Snacks	0.57	0.92	0.67

Planning Note

CCH Analysts note that if taxpayers used the standard meal rates (United States Department of Agriculture (USDA) Tier I rates) for tax years prior to 2003 to claim their deductible food costs, then the IRS will not raise the issue of the amount of any deduction claimed in the prior tax years.

Another exception to the general 50 percent rule for business meals is that a day-care center may fully deduct the cost of meals provided to its employees if: (1) such meals would be excluded from the employee's wages as a *de minimis* fringe benefit (.20); or (2) the meals are furnished on the business premises to more than one-half of the employees for the convenience of the employer (.25). The term "*de minimis* fringe benefit" means any property or service the value of which is, after taking into account the frequency with which similar benefits are provided to the employers employees, so small as to make accounting for it unreasonable or administratively impracticable (.30). For example, the *de minimis* exception would apply to situations when the day-care operator provides such items as coffee and rolls to its employees. Meals are considered to be furnished for the convenience of the employer if there is a substantial business reason other than providing additional pay. In the case of a day-care center, the argument could be made that the employees are required to eat at the business location in order to be readily available should an emergency arise.

Capital expenditures

The purchase of some business assets must be capitalized and deducted over a period of time rather than deducted in full in the year of purchase. In general, assets which have been purchased for use in the day-care business and that have a useful life of more than one year are considered to be capital assets. Examples of capital assets include buildings, furniture and cars. Such assets depreciate over time, thus the cost to purchase the assets must be deducted over a period of a number of years. The exact amount of time over which a tangible asset is deducted in determined under the Modified Accelerated Cost Recovery System (MACRS). For example, a van or computer purchased for use in a day-care business is classified as five-year property, while the cost of a building placed in service on or after May 13, 1993, is deducted over 39 years. Intangible assets may be depreciable under Code Sec. 197. For a detailed discussion of the depreciation of capital assets and the MACRS, see ¶9001 and following.

Like regular business expenses, it is fairly common practice for day-care center operators to convert capital assets from personal to business use. For example, a day-care operator may use a car for business purposes instead of personal purposes. When this occurs, the basis of the asset for purposes of determining the depreciable amount each year must be adjusted to the lesser of: (1) the fair market value of the asset at the date of change; or (2) the original cost or other basis of the property, plus the cost of any permanent improvements or additions, less any losses on the property that have been claimed for tax purposes (.35).

Code Sec. 179 expense election. Day-care operators may deduct the cost of depreciable assets faster than normal if they elect to expense the cost to purchase the asset under Code Sec. 179. Under this section, a taxpayer may depreciate a certain amount of expense each year, regardless of the yearly depreciable amount under MACRS or Code Sec. 197. The amount that may be deducted is limited by an annual dollar limitation ($100,000 for 2003, $102,000 for 2004, and $105,000 for 2005, as projected by CCH). This limitation will be reduced by the amount by which the cost of all qualifying property placed in service during the tax year exceeds a certain investment limitation ($400,000 for 2003, $410,000 for 2004, and $420,000 for 2005, as projected by CCH). In addition, the expense may not exceed the total amount of taxable income the taxpayer derives from the active conduct of the day-care business (see ¶9130).

.05 Rev. Rul. 92-3, 1992-1 CB 291.
.10 Code Sec. 274(e)(8).
.15 Rev. Proc. 2003-22, I.R.B. 2003-10, 577.
.20 Code Sec. 274(n)(2)(B).
.25 Code Sec. 119(b)(4).
.30 Reg. §1.132-6(a).
.35 Reg. §1.167(g)-1.

¶25,800 Home Office Expenses. Generally, expenses incurred in the use of a taxpayer's home for business purposes are deducible if they are attributable to a portion of the home used exclusively and regularly as the taxpayer's principle place of business (see ¶7336 and following). The exclusive use rule does not apply to a taxpayer who uses his personal residence to provide qualified day care services for children, for persons age 65 or older, or for individuals who are physically or mentally incapable of caring for themselves (.05). This exception, however, will only apply if the operator has applied for, has been granted, or is exempt from having a license, certification, registration or approval as a day-care center under applicable state law.

Allocation of business use

If a portion of the taxpayer's home is used on an *exclusive* basis for providing day-care, then business expenses are fully deductible. Any indirect expenses must be allocated between business and personal use on the basis of the residential space actually used for furnishing day-care services. For this purpose, indirect expenses include items such as real estate taxes, insurance, maintenance, or utilities. However, basic telephone service will not be treated as a deductible expense, even if state law requires the day-care provider to have telephone service as a condition of receiving a license (.10).

The taxpayer can use any reasonable method to determine the business percentage of their home. However, the two most common methods are: (1) by dividing the area used for business by the total area of the home; or (2) if all of the rooms in the home are roughly the same size, dividing the number of rooms used for business by the total number of rooms in the home.

> ***Example 1:*** Zelda Marcos uses a portion of her home to operate a day-care center for children. The home is 1,600 square feet, of which 1,200 square feet is used exclusively for day-care purposes. Zelda's business percentage of her home is 75 percent. Thus, Zelda may deduct 75 percent of any indirect expenses incurred in maintaining the home as business expenses.

If a portion of the taxpayer's home is used on a *nonexclusive* basis for providing day-care, then any direct and indirect expenses are deductible only to the extent that the space in question was actually used for business purposes. To determine the amount of time the home was actually used for business purposes, the total number of hours that the business is operated must be divided by the total number of hours in a year (.15). The day-care operator does not have to record the exact amount of time a portion of his or her home is used for business purposes (.20). However, adequate records should be kept including the average amount of time a portion of the home is used for business purposes. For this purpose, day-care use includes the preparation and cleaning time related to providing the day care services (.25).

> ***Example 2:*** Assume the same facts as in Example 1 above, except that Zelda uses 1,200 square feet of her home 12 hours a day, five days a week, 50 weeks a year for the day-care business (3,000 hours a year). During the remainder of the year, including the other 12 hours of the each day, Zelda and her family uses this portion of the home. Thus, the percentage of hours during the year to which the home is available for business use is 34.25 percent (3,000 divided by the total number of hours in a year or 8,760).

Example 3: Assume the same facts as in Example 2 above, except that during the tax year Zelda incurs $2,000 in expenses related to her day-care business and $10,000 of other expenses arising from the general use of her home (i.e., utilities, insurance, real estate taxes). Zelda may only deduct $685 of her direct business expenses ($2,000 x 34.25%) as she did not use any portion of her home exclusively for day care. She may deduct $2,569 of the other expenses as business expenses ($10,000 x 34.25% x 75%) because this represents the portion of her indirect expenses attributable to the business use of her home. Thus, the total business deductions Zelda is eligible to take with respect to the business use of her home is $3,254.

Regular use

Business use of a portion of a day-care operator's home must be continuous, ongoing or recurring in order for indirect expenses to be deductible (.30). For example, the occasional use of a room that is ordinarily not available as part of the day-care service means the portion of indirect expenses for that room would not be deductible as home office expenses. On the other hand, if a room is available for day-care use throughout each business day and is so regularly used, it will be considered as used for the entire day. The occasional non-use of the room will not disqualify it from being considered regularly used.

Deduction limits

There is a limit on the amount that may be claimed as a deduction allocable to the use of a day-care operator's home for business purposes. The limit is the gross income derived by the operator from the use of his or her home for the business purpose, reduced by: (1) the business part of the amounts that would normally be deductible whether or not the operator's home is used for business purposes (i.e., itemized deductions such as real estate taxes or casualty losses); and (2) any business expenses that relate to business activity in the home (i.e., business phone, supplies, depreciation on equipment), but not the use of the home itself. Any amount which is not deductible because of this limit may be carried forward to be taken into account in the succeeding year (.35). The carryover, however, will be subject to any deduction limitation in that year, whether or not the taxpayer lives in the same home during that year.

Example 4: Assume the same facts as in Examples 2 and 3 above, except that during the tax year Zelda's gross income from her day-care business was $8,500, the amount of real estate taxes she paid on her home was $4,800, and $900 of her direct business expenses could only be used for the day care business and not personally by Zelda and her family. Zelda's deduction limit for the tax year is $2,800 ($8,500 less $5,700). The remaining $454 of eligible business expenses ($3,254 less $2,800) must be carried over to the next tax year.

.05 Code Sec. 280A(c)(4)(A) and (c)(4)(B).
.10 Rev. Rul. 92-3, 1992-1 CB 141.
.15 Code Sec. 280A(c)(4)(C).
.20 Prop Reg. §1.280A-2(i)(4).
.25 *R.B. Neilson*, 94 TC 1, CCH Dec. 46,301.
.30 *B. Uphus*, 67 TCM 2229, CCH Dec. 49,680(M).
.35 Code Sec. 280A(c)(5).

Reporting Requirements

¶ 25,801 Reporting Income and Expenses If a day-care center is operated as a sole proprietorship or a single member LLC, the owner must report all business income and expenses on Schedule C (Profit or Loss From Business) or Schedule C-EZ (Net Profit From Business) of Form 1040. In addition, if the day-care center shows a net profit of at least $400 for the tax year, the owner will have to file Schedule SE (Self-Employment Tax). Form 8829 is used to figure and report business expenses incurred in the use of the taxpayer's home, including any carryover. A separate Form 8829 must be used for each home used for the business during the tax year.

Day-care centers operated as a partnership, C corporation or S corporation must report all income and expenses on Form 1065 (U.S. Partnership Return of Income), Form 1120 (U.S. Corporation Income Tax Return), Form 1120-A (U.S. Corporation Short-Form Income Tax Return) or Form 1120S (U.S. Income Tax Return for an S corporation). A tax-exempt organization that owns a day-care center is generally required to report its income and expenses on Form 990-T (Exempt Organization Business Income Tax Return).

¶25,802 Form W-10. Many of the clients of a day-care operator are individuals who are interested in claiming a tax credit based upon the amount that they pay in child and dependent care expenses. In order to qualify for this credit, individuals must provide the IRS with the name, address, and taxpayer identification number of the individual or organization whom the taxpayer paid to provide child or dependent care services (.05). If the day-care provider is a tax-exempt organization, the taxpayer identification number need not be provided, but the name and address of the organization must be provided.

In order to secure the required information, individuals must obtain Form W-10, "Dependent Care Provider's Identification and Certification," and give it to their day-care providers. The day-care providers are required to complete the Form W-10 and return it to the client. If the day-care provider is a tax-exempt organization, the words "tax-exempt" should be written in the space in which the tax identification number would generally be written. The client does not file the Form W-10 with the IRS, but it is to be retained with their tax records. The information listed on the Form W-10 must also be entered on the client's tax return (.10).

In situations where the day-care provider refuses to provide a client with all the necessary information, the clients are instructed to provide as much information as they can to the IRS, including letterheads or invoices verifying the provider's name and address (.15). A day-care provider who fails to comply with a client's request for information is subject to penalty of $50 for each such failure unless the failure is due to reasonable cause and not willful neglect (.20).

.05 Code Sec. 21(e)(9).
.10 Code Sec. 6109(a)(2).
.15 Notice 89-71, 1989-1 CB 738.
.20 Code Secs. 6723 and 6724.

STUDENTS

Introduction

¶25,803 Students are faced with a variety of unique tax issues arising from the combination of three common factors of a student's life: (1) summer and part-time jobs (see ¶25,804); (2) financial dependence on, or independence from, parents (see ¶25,805 and ¶25,807); and (3) financial aid (see ¶25,808).

Who Must File?

¶25,803A Who Must File? Various limitations, ranging from the types and amounts of income to the amount of parental support determine whether a student must file a tax return. One possible limitation, age, play no part in this determination. A student who is a minor is treated like any other taxpayer. If sufficient income is earned, a tax return must be filed regardless of age. A minor student may file his own return or it may be filed by a parent of guardian. A parent may be held liable for a tax assessed against a minor's income.

Whether a student must file an income tax return depends on:

(1) whether he can be claimed as a dependent on someone else's tax return (it does not matter whether or not that person actually claims the student as a dependent),

(2) how much income the student earns for the year, and

(3) what kind of income is received.

If the student can be claimed as a dependent, he must file a tax return for the year if *any* of the following apply:

(1) the student's unearned income in 2004 is more than $800,

(2) the student's earned income in 2004 is over $4,850, or

(3) the total of unearned and earned income is more than the larger of (a) $800 (for 2004) or (b) the student's earned income up to $4,850 (for 2004) plus $250.

If a single student cannot be claimed as a dependent, he must file a return if he earns more than $7,950 for 2004 (the sum of the standard deduction ($4,850) and the personal exemption (3,100). The minimum filing level for married students filing joint returns in 2004 is $15,900 (the $9,700 standard deduction plus two personal exemptions of $3,100 each). For 2005, as projected by CCH, the filing level for joint filers will be $16,400, reflecting the standard deduction for joint filers of $10,000, plus two personal exemptions of $3,200 each.

Form W-4

Employees must fill out a Form W-4 which gives the employer information from which to determine the amount of income taxes to withhold from each paycheck. By claiming all the withholding allowances that a student is entitled to, the amount of taxes withheld will come close to the student's actual tax liability. In some instances, a student may not earn enough to be required to file a tax return. The student may claim an exemption from withholding if the student:

(1) had no tax liability in the previous year,

(2) expects no tax liability in the present year, and

(3) cannot be claimed as a dependent if income will be more than $800, including nonwage income.

The basic rule is that a student who is not claimed as a dependent can claim exempt status if the present year's income is expected to be less than the sum of the standard deduction and personal exemption amounts, and the student had no liability in the previous year.

A student needs to have enough taxes withheld from wages to cover all his income for the year including investment income or.estimated tax payments may have to be made. Estimated tax payments are required if taxes of more than $1,000 are expected to be owed for the year. Furthermore, a student working at two or more jobs should not claim the same number of allowances at each job or insufficient taxes will be withheld.

Form W-2

Every employee receives a Form W-2 which summarizes the wages or salary earned for the year, federal and state income taxes withheld, FICA and FUTA withholding and any additional employer withholding. Some payments and services are exempt from FICA and FUTA taxes. For example, services performed by a child under age 18 while employed by a parent in a trade or business are exempt from FICA taxes. Such services are exempt from FUTA taxes for a child under age 21.

Forms 1040EZ, 1040A and 1040

Form 1040EZ. In most situations, Form 1040EZ is sufficient for a student filing a tax return. This form is the shortest and simplest. However, not all students can use this form. Her is a list of items that would prevent a filer from using Form 1040EZ;

(1) interest income of more than $400,

(2) income other than wages, salaries, tips and taxable scholarships or fellowship grants,

(3) itemized deductions, or

(4) filing status other than single or married filing jointly with no dependents.

Form 1040A. This form is slightly longer than Form 1040EZ. It has no restrictions on filing status and allows the reporting of interest income over $400 and dividend income. Itemized deductions are not allowed.

Form 1040. This form is the longest and most complex tax return. It contains various schedules for students who need to report itemized deductions (Schedule A), interest income or gross dividend income, each totaling over $00 (Schedule B), self employment income (Schedule C) or self-employment tax (Schedule SE).

¶25,804 Types of Income. As with all taxpayers, income received by a student is subject to taxes. A student's income could include wages, tips, self-employment income (for example, from part-time work during the school year or from summer employment), investment income, or scholarship funds. Various recordkeeping requirements and dollar limitations apply so that these sources of income are properly reflected on the student's tax return.

Wages and salaries

The most typical source of student income is wages or salary. The paycheck received by the student represents the income earned for that pay period. The employer withholds taxes based on the number of withholding allowances claimed on the student's Form W-4 (see ¶25,807). The total amount of wages and withheld taxes for the tax year is contained on Form W-2 (see ¶25,807), which the employer distributes at the end of the year for tax-filing purposes.

Tips

All tips are subject to tax. This includes cash tips given by customers, or charged on credit cards or an employee's share of tips split with other employees ("allocated tips". A daily record should be kept as proof of tips received. If $20 or more of tips are received in one month, the monthly total must be reported to the employer. IRS Form 4070 "Employee's Report of Tips to Employer" can be used to report tip income if the employer has not done it for you. The employer must withhold taxes on such tips (.05). The tip and tax amounts are then included on Form W-2. Forms 4070 and 4070-A are available from the IRS to assist in recording and reporting tips. If tips are not reported, a penalty may be charged in addition to the tax owed.

Self-employment income

Earnings received from self-employment are taxable (.10). Self-employment income could come from mowing lawns, baby-sitting or any other service performed where the student is not an employee. Reasonable business expenses may be deducted when determining net earnings, so accurate records need to be kept to reflect the student's net self-employment income. The annual income and expense amounts are reported on Schedule C or C-EZ, Form 1040.

If a student has net earnings of $400 or more, self-employment 4,taxes must be paid. The tax is calculated on Schedule SE, Form 1040. A special exception from the payment of self-employment taxes exists for newspaper carriers under 18 years of age, regardless of the amount of their earnings (.15).

☐ For a discussion of the self-employment tax, see ¶7701 and following.

Investment income

A student's income may also include interest earned from checking or savings accounts, interest earned on U.S. savings bonds or other government instruments, or dividends distributed by a partnership, corporation or trust. Generally, interest and dividends are taxable forms of income. However, interest on debt instruments issued by state and local governments may be tax-exempt. The student should receive Form 1099-INT or Form 1099-DIV from the interest or dividend payor stating the total amount received for the year. Interest or gross dividend income each totaling over $400 must be listed on Schedule B, Form 1040, or Schedule 1, Form 1040A.

Financial aid

Numerous forms of financial aid are available and the income tax treatment differs with each type. For a discussion of the various types and their taxability, see ¶25,808.

.05 Code Sec. 3401(a)(16).
.10 Code Sec. 1401 and Code Sec. 1402.
.15 Reg. §1.1402(c)-3(b).

Deductions

¶25,805 Deductions. Once all of the student's income that is subject to tax has been calculated, certain subtractions need to be made in order to arrive at taxable income. The student's entitlement to the standard deduction and personal exemption is based on the status of financial dependence on parents or independence from parents.

Support test

A student under the age of 24 may be claimed as a dependent provided that the person paying for the support furnishes more than one-half of that person's total support (.05). In this context, the term "student" means an individual who during each of five calendar months during the calendar year in which the tax year of the taxpayer begins is a full-time student at an educational organization, or is pursuing a full-time course of institutional on-farm training under the supervision of an accredited agent of an educational organization, or of a state or political subdivision of a state (.10).

Total support includes the fair rental value of lodging furnished to the dependent, all items of expense spent directly by or upon the dependent and a proportionate share of the expenses incurred in supporting the entire household.

Standard deduction v. itemized deductions

If the student may be claimed as a dependent on someone else's return based on the support test (see above), the student's allowable standard deduction for 2004 is the greater of $800 or the sum of $250 plus the student's earned income. If no one can claim the student as a dependent, the allowable standard deduction amount is $4,850 (for 2004). This amount is subtracted from adjusted gross income when determining taxable income. For 2004, the dollar amounts are the $4,850 standard deduction and the $3,100 personal exemption for a total of $7,950.

An alternative for the non-dependent student is to itemize deductions. Every taxpayer is entitled to either the greater of the standard deduction amount or the itemized deduction amount. Schedule A, Form 1040, contains a list of deductible expenses such as local taxes, mortgage interest, medical expenses and charitable contributions that may be claimed if the sum of the itemized deductions exceeds the standard deduction amount. The typical student will probably not have these kinds of expenses, but in certain circumstances, a student may be able to itemize expenses. The itemized amount would be subtracted from adjusted gross income.

Personal exemption

In addition to the dependency deductions, taxpayers are also allowed a personal exemption from income for themselves. A student who is claimed as a dependent is not entitled to the personal exemption. However, for a student not claimed as a dependent, the personal exemption amount for 2004 is $3,100. This amount is also subtracted from adjusted gross income to determine the taxable income of the student.

Self-employment taxes

A taxpayer is allowed to deduct one-half of federal self-employment taxes paid during the year (.15). A student who pays self-employment taxes would make the deduction on Form 1040 as part of the determination of adjusted gross income.

Tuition and fees deduction

Taxpayers may be able to deduct up to $3,000 for qualified tuition and related expenses (.20). The deduction is "above the line" which directly reduces the payor's taxable income dollar-for-dollar up to $3,000. These provisions are effective for payments made in tax years beginning after 2001 and before 2006.

Normally, if a student pays the tuition and fees, the student gets the deduction. However, the payor cannot take this deduction if (1) the filing status is married filing separately (.25), (2) another person *can claim* an exemption for a payor student as a dependent whether the exemption actually was claimed or not (.30), (3) the student's modified adjusted gross income is more than $65,000 ($130,000 for joint filers) (.35), (4) the student was a nonresident alien for any part of the year and did not elect to be treated as a resident alien, (.40), and (5) the student or anyone else claims a Hope or lifetime learning credit during the tax year with respect to the student's tuition and related expenses (.45)

Someone who pays qualified tuition and related expenses with borrowed funds can deduct the amounts paid in the year the expenses are paid, not the year(s) in which the loan is paid back (.50)

Qualified tuition and related expenses include payments made to a college, university, vocational school, or other postsecondary educational institution eligible to participate in a student paid program administered by the U.S. Department of Education. Related expenses include student-activity fees and fees for course-related books, supplies and equipment, but only if the fees are paid to the institution as a condition of enrollment or attendance ((.55)

A payor cannot deduct higher education tuition and fees if these expenses are deducted under any other provision: for example, as a business expense. No deduction is allowed for qualified tuition and related expenses that have been paid with tax-free distributions of earnings from a qualified tuition plan or a Coverdell education savings account (.60)

Generally, there is no deduction for qualified expenses paid for with tax-free funds such as tax-free scholarships. Pell grants, employer-provided educational expenses, veterans' educational assistance and other nontaxable payment other than gifts, bequests or inheritances. The total of qualified expenses is *not* reduced for amounts paid with the student's earnings, loans, gifts, inheritances and personal savings. Also, there is no reduction for scholarships reported as income on the student's return or any scholarship which by its terms cannot be applied to qualified tuition and related expenses.

Certain expenses are excluded from "related expenses." These include room and board, insurance, medical expenses (including student health fees), transportation or similar personal living or family expenses. This is true even if the fee must be paid to the institution as a condition of enrollment or attendance (.65)

Special rules cover the treatment of expenses paid by persons other than the student, his or her parents or those who can claim the student as a dependent.

Student loan interest

All student loan interest on a qualified education loan is deductible. Further, there is no limit on the period during which the interest deduction may be taken. (.70). A qualified education loan is any debt incurred to pay the qualified higher education expenses of the taxpayer, the taxpayer's spouse, or an individual who was the taxpayer's dependent at the time that the debt was incurred. The expenses must be paid or incurred within a reasonable period of time before or after the debt is incurred and must be attributable to education furnished during a period during which the recipient was an eligible student.

In order to qualify, the education expenses must be attributable to a period during which the student was attending an eligible educational institution at least half-time, meaning one-half of the normal full-time work load for the course of study that the student is pursuing. For purposes of the deduction, a qualified education loan also encompasses debt used to refinance the qualified education loan.

.05 Code Sec. 152.
.10 Code Sec. 170(b)(1)(A)(ii).
.15 Code Sec. 164(f).
.20 Code Sec. 222.
.25 Code Sec. 222(d)(4).
.30 Code Sec. 222(c)(3).
.35 Code Sec. 222(b)(2).
.40 Code Sec. 222(d)(5).
.45 Code Sec. Code Sec. 222(c)..
.50 Notice 97-60, I.R.B. 1997-46, 8.
.55 Code Sec. 222(d)(1).
.60 Code Sec. 222(c).
.65 Code Sec. 222(d)(1), Code Sec. 25A(f)(1)(C).
.70 Code Sec. 221.

Credits

¶25,806 Credits. Certain amounts or credits may be subtracted from a student's taxable income. Credits reduce tax on income "dollar for dollar." The credit typically available to students is the earned income tax credit (.05).

Earned income tax credit. If a student is employed and has a child, the student may be eligible for the child and dependent care credit (¶25,710). The earned income tax credit is available to individuals with or without children (¶25,706).

☐ For a discussion of the education credits, see ¶25,810.

☐See ¶25,810 for information on the Hope and Lifetime Learning Credits.

.05 Code Sec. 32.

Financial Aid

¶25,808 Financial Aid. Most colleges and university students receive some form of financial aid. A some kinds of financial aid are taxable income, other kind of aid are not. The following is a discussion of the tax treatment of various forms of financial aid.

Scholarships and fellowship grants

The entire amount of a scholarship or fellowship grant is tax free if the student is a candidate for a degree at an educational organization ((.05)). For such a student, the portion of the funds used for tuition is excludable from income. In addition, amounts received for student fees, books, supplies and equipment are not includible in a student's income if these are required of all students in the course. However, funds used for room and board or personal items are not excludable. Additionally, payments received for research or teaching services required to be performed as a condition of receiving the scholarship or grant are not excludable. Nevertheless, athletic scholarships are excludable from income it they otherwise meet the requirements. The entire amount of a scholarship or fellowship is included in gross income if the student is not a candidate for a degree. If a grant does not specify that it be used for tuition or other course-related expenses, it still can be tax free if the proceeds are in fact used for such purposes.

Fulbright scholarships and Pell grants are excludable as scholarships. However, a Fulbright grant that is to be used for lecturing or teaching, it is treated as being received in exchange for services and it is taxable. Pell grants are excludable if they are used for qualifying tuition and course-related expenses during the grant period. Payments received for education, training or subsistence under any law administered by the Department of Veterans Affairs are tax free. However, a recipient of a VA grant may have to reduce the deduction for educational expenses by the amount of these tax-free payments.

An educational institution is one that maintains a regular faculty and curriculum and has a regularly enrolled student body in attendance at the place where it carries on its educational activities.

☐ For a complete discussion of scholarships and fellowship grants, see ¶25,505 -¶25,510.

Student loans

The student loan is a popular and frequently the sole source of obtaining the necessary funds. Due to its unique character, the student loan receives special treatment apart from other forms of indebtedness.

Cancellation of debt. The cancellation or discharge of debt is treated as income (.10)). However, recipients of various student loans do not have to include in income the discharge of such loans if the discharge was pursuant to a provision under which any part of the loan would be discharged if the recipient worked for a certain period of time in certain professions for any of a broad class of employers ((.15)). For example, the discharge of a percentage of a medical education loan based on each year of practice at a nonprofit state hospital does not result in income.

This provision applies to loans made by the United States, a possession of the United States, a state or any political subdivision, the District of Columbia, a public benefit corporation or tax-exempt charitable corporations.

Interest paid. Interest paid on a student loan is an "above-the-line" deduction (see ¶25,805) (.20).

Disclosure of return information. Certain return information may be disclosed to the Department of Education in order to implement the direct student loan program. Also, the Department of Education is permitted access to mailing addresses of taxpayers who owe an overpayment on a federal Pell grant or who have defaulted on student loans (.25).

Savings bonds

Parents may plan for their child's educational expenses by investing in U.S. savings bonds. The interest on Series EE savings bonds issued after 1989 is tax exempt if used for educational purposes (.30). Various limitations apply as to amounts, redemptions and uses of the proceeds (see ¶4725).

Students or their families are entitled to redeem U.S. savings bonds and exclude the earnings if the redemption proceeds are contributed to a qualified tuition program on behalf of the taxpayer, the taxpayer's spouse or a dependent.

The savings bond exclusion is phased out in 1993 for taxpayers with modified adjusted gross incomes above $87,750 for joint returns and $58,500 for other returns. This exclusion completely phases out for modified adjusted gross income of $117,750 or more for joint returns and $73,500 or more for other returns. For 2004, the phase-out begins at $89,750 for joint filers and $59,850 for other qualifying taxpayers.

State tuition programs

A tuition guaranty program allows parents to put money away for a child's college education. The parents pay a lump sum to a trust and name the student as the beneficiary. The trust guarantees that the student will receive four years of educational services at no cost. A state agency usually establishes the trust. The student is not taxed on the amount made as a gift, but is taxed on the amount by which the value of the educational services received exceeds the original gift. The deemed income amount is prorated over the four years that the student is in college.

Higher education expenses include tuition, books, lab fees, and room and board. Room and board expenses may be considered qualified higher education expenses only to the extent of the minimum room and board allowance applicable to the student as determined by the institution in calculating costs of attendance for federal financial aid programs.

Qualified tuition reduction

Employees of educational institutions are allowed to exclude the amount of a qualified tuition reduction from income (.35). The tuition reduction is a fringe benefit given to employees and is available to the employee's spouse and dependents. The student does not report the reduction as income. The exclusion is available for education at the elementary, secondary or undergraduate level. Restrictions as to graduate education and exceptions regarding certain types of employees apply (see ¶25,510).

Educational assistance programs

A form of financial aid that may be supplied by any employer is the educational assistance program (.40). The Code generally excludes benefits under such a plan from the gross income of the student/employee. For tax years beginning *after* 2001, graduate-level courses are included.

Taxable and nontaxable income

The chart below shows which types of income are taxable to a student and which are not.

Tax Treatment of Scholarship and Fellowship Payments

Payment for	Degree candidate	Not a degree candidate
Tuition	Tax free	Taxable
Fees	Tax free*	Taxable
Books	Tax free*	Taxable
Supplies	Tax free*	Taxable
Equipment	Tax free*	Taxable
Room	Taxable	Taxable
Board	Taxable	Taxable
Travel	Taxable	Taxable
Teaching	Taxable	Taxable
Research services	Taxable	Taxable
Other services	Taxable	Taxable

* If required of all students in the course

.05 Code Sec. 117(a).

.10 (Code Sec. 108.

.15 Code Sec. 108(f).

.20 Code Sec. 221.

.25 Code Sec. 6103(l)(13), Code Sec. 6103(m)(4) and Code Sec. 6103(p)

.30 Code Sec. 135.

.35 Code Sec. 117(d).

.40 Code Sec. 127(d).

Foreign and Exchange Students

¶25,809 Foreign and Exchange Students. Alien individuals are classified as either resident or nonresident aliens for U.S. tax purposes. The classification is important because resident aliens, like U.S. citizens, are taxed on their worldwide income. The U.S. tax on a nonresident alien's income depends upon the source of the income and whether it is effectively connected with a U.S. trade or business (¶25,813). Individuals who are temporarily in the United States as students or exchange visitors with an F, J or M visa under the Immigration and Nationality Act (.05) may qualify as exempt persons for purposes of determining residency under the substantial presence test (.10) (¶25,815).

Special rules exempt from U.S. income tax compensation paid by a foreign employer to a nonresident alien student or exchange visitor admitted to the United States with an F or J visa (.15) (¶25,823).

The rules for taxing scholarships and fellowship grants discussed above generally apply to both resident aliens and nonresident aliens admitted to the United States with an F, J or M visa. However, nonresident aliens are taxed only on the nonexcludable portion of a scholarship or grant that is U.S. source income, as determined by the residence of the payor. The taxable amount is subject to a lower 14 percent withholding rate (.20). Treaty provisions may also reduce the tax on a nonresident alien student's income (¶25,827).

.05 Sec. 101(a)(15)(F), (J) and (M) of the Immigration and Nationality Act (8 U.S.C. 1101(a)(15)(F), (J) and (M)).

.10 Code Sec. 7701(b)(3) and Code Sec. 7701(b)(5); Reg. §301.7701(b)-3.

.15 Code Sec. 872(b)(3).

.20 Code Sec. 871(c) and Code Sec. 1441(b); Reg. §1.871-9 and Reg. §1.1441-2(c).

Hope and Lifetime Learning Credits

¶25,810 Hope and Lifetime Learning Credits. Taxpayers may claim a Hope scholarship credit in the same year in which they receive a distribution from either a Coverdell education savings account (ESA) (formerly known as an "education IRA") or a qualified tuition program (QTP). However, expenses paid from either a Coverdale ESA (see ¶16,235) or a QTP (see ¶16,230) cannot be used as the basis for a Hope credit. For each student, a taxpayer can elect for any year only one of the credits—either the Hope scholarship credit or the lifetime learning credit. However, a taxpayer may claim the Hope credit for the first two years of an eligible student's post-secondary education and claim the lifetime learning credit for that same student in later academic years. If a taxpayer pays qualified expenses for more than one student in the same year, he can choose to take credits on a per-student, per-year basis. This means that he can claim the Hope credit for one student and the lifetime learning credit for another student in the same year.

Hope Scholarship Credit

The Hope scholarship credit offers a credit of up to $1,500 to "qualified tuition expenses" for *each* "eligible student" (.05). The credit for each year is the sum of:

(1) 100 percent of the first $1,000

(2) 50 percent of the next $1,000

of qualified tuition and related expenses paid for each eligible student. The maximum Hope scholarship credit that can be claimed in any given year is $1,500 times the number of eligible students.

> ***Example 1:*** John and Karen are married and file a joint return. They claim an exemption for their dependent daughter on their 2004 tax return. Their modified adjusted gross income is $70,000. Their daughter is in her sophomore year at the state university. John and Karen pay qualified tuition and related expenses of $4,000 for the year.
>
> Assuming that John and Karen, their daughter, and the state university meet all the requirements for the Hope credit, John and Karen can claim a $1,500 Hope Education credit for the year. This is 100 percent of the first $1,000 and 50 percent of the next $1,000.

The term "qualified tuition expenses" includes tuition and related expenses and fees required for enrollment at an "eligible educational institution." Student-activity fees and the cost of course-related books, supplies, and equipment are included as qualified tuition and related expenses only if the fees must be paid to the institution as a condition of enrollment or attendance.

An "eligible educational institution" is any college university, vocational school or other post-secondary educational institution eligible to participate in a student aid program administered by the U. S. Department of Education. This includes virtually all accredited, public, nonprofit, and privately owned, profit-making post-secondary schools.

An "eligible student" for purposes of the Hope scholarship credit is one who meets *all* the following requirements:

(1) did not have expenses that were used to figure a Hope credit in any two earlier years,

(2) had not completed the first two years of post-secondary education (basically, the freshman and sophomore years of college),

(3) was enrolled at least half-time in a program that leads to a degree, certificate, or other recognized educational credential for at least one academic period beginning during the academic year falling within the tax year for which the return is being filed

(4) was free of any federal or state felony conviction for possessing or distributing a controlled substance.

The standard for what is half of the normal full-time work load is determined by each educational institution.

Prepaid tuition and related expenses for an academic period that begins in the first three months of the year for which the credit is claimed can be used in determining the Hope Scholarship Credit. A student may claim a Hope credit for qualified tuition and related expenses paid with borrowed funds.

The credit cannot be claimed to the extent that the payments were made with certain tax-free funds. Such funds could include scholarships, Pell grants, employer-provided educational assistance, veterans' education assistance and any other nontaxable payments other than gifts, bequests or inheritances.

The Hope scholarship credit is reduced for taxpayers with modified adjusted gross incomes in 2004 of $42,000 or more ($85,000 for joint filers). The credit is completely phased out for single files with modified adjusted gross incomes of $52,000 ($105,000 for joint filers). The phaseout is computed on IRS Form 8863, "Education Credits Hope and Lifetime Learning Credits" which is attached to the taxpayers' returns.

Lifetime Learning Credit

A taxpayer may claim a lifetime learning credit of up to $1,000 for qualified tuition and related expenses paid for all students enrolled in an eligible education institution (see under "Hope scholarship credit", above) (.10). There is no limit on the number of years for which the lifetime learning credit can be claimed for each student.

A taxpayer who pays the education expenses (for example, a parent) *cannot* claim the lifetime learning credit if *any* of the following apply:

(1) his filing status is married, filing separately,

(2) he is listed as a dependent on another person's tax return,

(3) his modified adjusted gross income in 2004 is $52,000 or more ($105,000 for joint filers,

(4) the taxpayer or his/her spouse is a nonresident alien for any part of the year and the nonresident alien does not elect to be treated as a resident alien,

(5) the eligible student receives a tax-free withdrawal from a Coverdell ESA during 2004 and did not waive the tax-free treatment.

(6) the Hope credit is claimed for the same student in the same tax year.

If a taxpayer, such as a parent, claims the student as a dependent on his tax return, then only he can claim the lifetime learning credit based on that student's expenses. If the student has paid any of these expenses himself, the parent can still treat these expenses as if the parent had paid them. However, if the taxpayer does not claim the student as a dependent, then the student can claim the lifetime learning credit. Qualified tuition and related expenses paid directly to an eligible educational institution for a dependent by another person than the taxpayer are treated as paid by the dependent. This also applies to court-approved support arrangement.

> ***Example 2:*** Joanne Allen makes a payment directly to an eligible education institution in 2004 for her grandson Todd's tuition and related expenses. For purposes of claiming a lifetime learning credit, Todd is treated as receiving the money as a gift from his grandmother and, in turn, paying his tuition and related expenses himself. Unless an exemption for Todd is claimed on someone else's return, only Todd can use the payment to claim a lifetime learning credit. If anyone else, such as his parents, claims an exemption for him on his or her tax return, whoever claims the exemption may be able to use the expenses to claim a lifetime learning credit. In such a case, Todd could not claim a lifetime learning credit.

The definition of an "eligible educational institution" and "qualified tuition and related expenses" are the same as for the Hope scholarship credit.

The amount of the credit is 20 percent of the first $10,000 or qualified tuition and related expenses. This amount had been 20 percent of $5,000 for 2002. However, that amount may be reduced based on the taxpayer's modified adjusted gross income. As with the Hope scholarship credit, the lifetime learning credit is phased out in 2004 for persons with modified adjusted gross incomes between $42,000 and $52,000 ($85,000 and $105,000 for joint filers). A lifetime learning credit cannot be claimed for those with incomes in excess of the phase-out range. The phaseout is computed on IRS Form 8863, "Education Credits Hope and Lifetime Learning Credits" which is attached to the taxpayer's income tax return.

For tax years beginning in 2004 and thereafter, the amount of qualified tuition and related expenses that may be taken into account in figuring the lifetime learning credit increases from $5,000 to $10,000. The credit equals 20 percent of these qualified expenses, with the maximum credit being $2,000.

.05 Code Sec. 25A.

.10 Code Sec. 25A(c).

Education Savings Accounts

¶25,810A Education Savings Accounts. Coverdell education savings accounts (ESAs) are trusts or custodial accounts created in the United States only for paying the "qualified education expenses" of the designated beneficiary of the account (.05). The account must be designated as a Coverdell ESA at the time it is created (.10). When the account is created, the beneficiary must be under aged 18, unless he or she is a "special needs beneficiary" (see below). The person for whom the account is being set up need not be a relative of the person who sets up the account. The written agreement creating the account must meet the following requirements:

(1) the trustee or custodian must be a bank or an entity approved by the IRS;

(2) the document must provide that the trustee or custodian can accept only a contribution that (a) is in cash, (b) is made before the beneficiary reaches 18 years of

age unless he or she is a special needs beneficiary for tax years beginning after December 31, 2001, and (c) would not result in total contributions for the year of more than $2,000 for tax years beginning after 2001.The total contributions limit does not include rollover distributions.

(3) money in the account cannot be invested in life insurance contracts;

(4) money in the account cannot be combined with other property except in a common trust fund or common investment fund;

(5) the balance in the account generally must be withdrawn within 30 days after the earlier of the time the beneficiary reaches 30 years old (unless a special needs beneficiary) or the time of the beneficiary's death.

Contributions

Any individual, including the designated beneficiary of the account, can contribute to a Coverdell ESA if the individual's modified adjusted gross income is less than $110,000 ($220,000 for joint filers) (.15). Further, organizations such as corporations also my contribute to ESAs. There is no requirement that an organization's income be below a certain level. Contributions can be made after the beneficiary reaches 18 years old only if the beneficiary is a special needs beneficiary, and the contributions must be made by the due date of the return, not including extensions. All contributions to a Coverdell ESA must be in cash (.20).

Contributions to a Coverdell ESA are not deductible by the donor and are not included in the income of the beneficiary.

Modified adjusted gross income is adjusted gross income as shown on an individual's income tax return, with an add-back of certain foreign exclusion for taxpayers with income or deduction items (.25).

There are two annual limits on contributions to a Coverdell ESA. The first is the total amount that can be contributed for each designated beneficiary in any year, and the other is on the amount that any individual con contribute for any one designated beneficiary in one year.

Limit for each designated beneficiary. The total of all contributions to all Coverdell ESAs set up for the benefit of any one designated beneficiary cannot be more than $3,000. This amount was increased for the 2003 tax year. Prior to 2003, the limit was $2,000. This amount includes contributions, other than rollovers, to all the beneficiary's Coverdell ESA from all sources (.30).

Limit for each contributor. A person can contribute up to $3,000 for each designated beneficiary. This is the most any person can contribute to one beneficiary regardless of the number of Coverdell ESAs set up for the beneficiary. However, this limit is reduced for joint filers with modified adjusted gross incomes between $95,000 and $110,000 ($190,000 and $220,000 for joint filers. (.35).

Tax on excess contributions. The beneficiary must pay a six percent excise tax each year on excess contributions (any contribution above the maximum allowed) that are in a Coverdell ESA at the end of the year. However, corrective withdrawals of excess contributions may be made by the 15th day of the sixth month following the close of the taxpayer's tax year (June 15 for most individuals). Prior to 2003, the corrective action had to be taken before the fourth month of the close of the year during which the excess contributions were made(.40).

Rollovers and other transfers. Assets can be rolled over from one Coverdell ESA to another (.45). The designated beneficiary can be changed and the beneficiary's interest can be transferred to a spouse or former spouse because of divorce. Any amount withdrawn form a Coverdell ESA and rolled over to another Coverdell ESA for the benefit of the same beneficiary or a member of the beneficiary's family who is under age 30 is not taxable. An amount is rolled over if it is paid to another Coverdell ESA within 60 days after the withdrawal. A member of the beneficiary's family includes the beneficiary's spouse and the following individuals and their spouses:

(1) the beneficiary's child, grandchild or stepchild,

(2) a brother, sister half brother, half sister, stepbrother, or stepsister of the beneficiary,

(3) a brother or sister of the beneficiary's father or mother,

(4) a son or daughter of the beneficiary's brother or sister,

(5) the beneficiary's son-in-law, daughter-in-law, father-in-law, mother-in-law, brother-in-law or sister-in-law.

Qualified education expenses

The money from the Coverdell account must be used to pay "qualified education expenses" (.50) This includes:

(1) tuition and fees

(2) the cost of books, supplies and equipment

(3) amounts contributed to a qualified state tuition program

(4) in some situations, the cost of room and board.

The cost of room and board is a qualified education expense if the designated beneficiary is at least a half-time student at an eligible educational institution. A student is enrolled "at least half-time" if he or she is enrolled for at least half the full-time academic work load for the course of study the student is pursuing as determined under the standards of the school where the student is enrolled. The expense is limited to

Beginning in 2002, withdrawals can be used for certain elementary and secondary education expenses. Qualified primary and secondary education expenses include:

(1) tuition fees, academic tutoring, special needs services in the case of a special needs beneficiary, books, supplies and other equipment incurred in connection with enrollment or attendance as an elementary or secondary school student at a public, private or religious school;

(2) room and board, uniforms, transportation and supplementary items and services (including extended day programs) which are required or provided by a public, private or religious school in connection with such enrollment or attendance, and

(3) the purchase of computer technology or equipment or Internet access and related services, if such technology equipment or services are to be used by the beneficiary and the beneficiary's family during any of the years the beneficiary is in school (not including expenses for computer software designed for sports, games or hobbies unless the software is predominantly educational in nature.

Eligible educational institutions

An eligible educational institution is any college, university, vocational school or other post-secondary educational institution eligible to participate in a student aid program administered by the U. S. Department of Education. It includes almost all accredited, public, nonprofit and privately owned, profit-making post-secondary institutions (.55).

Special needs beneficiaries

The 18-year-old age limitation does not apply to "special needs beneficiaries." The IRS is authorized to issue regulations regarding contributions to an education IRA that would allow the account to continue past the date when a special needs beneficiary reaches age 18. Similarly, the regulations may disregard the 30-year age limit used to determine when the remaining balances in an education IRA must be distributed, and if rollover contributions can be received and beneficiaries changed (.60). According to the Conference Committee Report for the Economic Growth and Tax Relief Reconciliation Act of 2001, it is intended that the regulations will define a special needs beneficiary as an individual who, due to a physical, mental, or emotional condition (including learning disability), requires additional time to complete his or her education. The regulations have not yet been issued.

Distributions

The designated beneficiary of a Coverdell ESA can take distributions at any time. Whether the withdrawals are tax free depends in part on whether the distributions are more than the amount of beneficiary's qualified education expenses for the year. A beneficiary dies not have to be enrolled for a minimum number of courses to take a tax-free distribution. Any taxable withdrawals must be reported on line 16b of IRS Form 1040 or on line 11b of IRS Form 1040A.

Withdrawals normally are tax free if they are not more than the beneficiary's qualified education expenses for the tax year. However, a portion of the withdrawals is taxed to the beneficiary if the distributions are more than the beneficiary's qualified education expenses for the year (.65). Further, if a beneficiary receives a taxable withdrawal, he must pay an additional tax of 10 percent on the amount included in income (.70). The 10-percent additional tax does not apply to withdrawals:

(1) paid to a beneficiary, or to the estate of the designated beneficiary on or after the death of the designated beneficiary;

(2) made because the designated beneficiary is unable to do any substantial gainful activity because of a physical or mental condition over a long or indefinite time;

(3) made because the designated beneficiary received (a) a qualified scholarship excludable from gross income, (b) an educational assistance allowance, or (c) payment for the designated beneficiary's education expenses that is excludable from gross income under any U. S. laws;

(4) included in income only because the beneficiary waived the tax-free treatment of the withdrawal;

(5) a return of an excess contribution, and any earnings on it, made before the due date of the beneficiary's tax return, including extensions.

If the designated beneficiary dies before reaching age 30, the remaining assets generally must be withdrawn within 30 days after the date of death (.75). However, if a Coverdell ESA is transferred to a surviving spouse or other family member as the result of death of the beneficiary, the Coverdell ESA retains its status. This means that the spouse or other family member can treat the Coverdell ESA as his or her own and does not need to withdraw the assets until he or she reaches age 30. There are no tax consequences as the result of the transfer.

.05 Code Sec. 530.
.10 Code Sec. 530(b)(1).
.15 Code Sec. 530(c).
.20 Code Sec. 530(b)(1)(A)(i).
.25 Code Sec. 530(c)(2).
.30 Code Sec. 530(b)(1)(A)(iii).
.35 Code Sec. 530(c)(1); Reg. §1.79-3.
.40 Code Sec. 4673(a)(4).
.45 Code Sec. 530(d)(5).
.50 Code Sec. 530(b)(2).
.55 Code Sec. 530(b)(3).
.60 Code Sec. 530(b)(1).
.65 Code Sec. 530(d).
.70 Code Sec. 530(d)(4).
.75 Code Sec. 530(b)(1)(E).

ALIENS

Introduction

¶25,811 Introduction. Income derived from anywhere in the world by an individual who is a U.S. citizen is subject to U.S. taxation. Individuals who are citizens of other countries, however, are subject to special rules. An alien must first be classified as a resident alien or a nonresident alien (¶25,813). A resident alien is taxed in the same manner as a U.S. citizen (¶25,819). A nonresident alien is taxed only on U.S.-source income (¶25,821). Any U.S.-source income which is "effectively connected" with a U.S. trade or business is taxed at the graduated rates that U.S. citizens pay. Any remaining U.S. source income is generally classified as fixed and determinable income and is taxed at a flat 30 percent rate. For certain years, an alien may have dual status, that is, the alien will be a resident alien for part of the year and a nonresident alien for the remainder of the year (see ¶25,829). The rules with respect to nonresident aliens from any particular foreign country may be altered by a tax treaty with that country (see ¶25,827).

Schematic presentation of alien status

The following chart was devised by the IRS to provide a schematic presentation of the steps that must be followed in the determination of whether an alien is a resident or a nonresident of the United States for purposes of calculating the alien's U.S. income taxes (.05).

Figure 1-A. **Nonresident Alien or Resident Alien?**

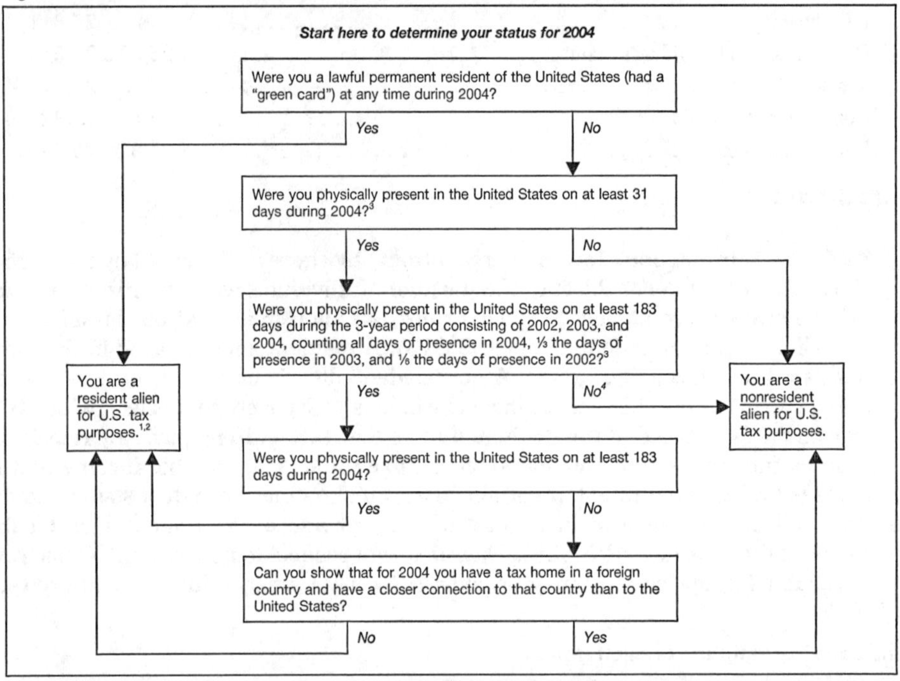

[1] If this is your first or last year of residency, you may have a dual status for the year. See *Dual-Status Aliens* in chapter 1.

[2] In some circumstances you may still be considered a nonresident alien under an income tax treaty between the U.S. and your country. Check the provisions of the treaty carefully.

[3] See *Days of Presence in the United States* in this chapter for days that do not count as days of presence in the United States.

[4] If you meet the substantial presence test for 2005, you may be able to choose treatment as a U.S. resident alien for part of 2004. For details, see *Substantial Presence Test* under *Resident Aliens* and *First-Year Choice* under *Dual-Status Aliens* in chapter 1.

.05 IRS Publication 519, "U.S. Tax Guide for Aliens", CCH IRS PUBLICATIONS.

Determining an Individual's Status

¶25,813 Resident v. Nonresident Alien. Whether an individual other than a U.S. citizen is liable for any U.S. income tax, a determination must be made whether the individual is a resident or nonresident alien (.05). An individual qualifies as a resident alien under one of two tests: the lawful permanent resident test (¶25,814) or the substantial presence test (¶25,815). Any alien who does not qualify as a resident under either one of these tests will be treated as a nonresident alien for federal income tax purposes (unless treated as a resident under a tax treaty). However, some individuals can elect resident status if they do not otherwise qualify as a resident alien under the substantial presence test.

.05 Code Sec. 7701(b).

¶25,814 Lawful Permanent Resident. An alien who is a lawful permanent resident of the United States under immigration laws (i.e., receives a "green card") will be considered a resident alien for federal income tax purposes (.05). Resident status begins in the first calendar year in which the alien is a lawful resident and is physically present in the United States for at least one day. Resident status continues until such status is revoked, or administratively or judicially determined to be abandoned.

.05 Code Sec. 7701(b)(1)(A)(i) and (6).

¶25,815 Substantial Presence. An alien will be considered to be a resident of the United States if the individual is present in the United States for at least 31 days during the calendar year, and at least 183 days during the current and two preceding calendar years (.05). For purposes of the 183-day requirement, each day present in the United States during the current calendar year counts as one full day, while each day in the first preceding calendar year counts as ⅓ of a day, and each day in the second preceding calendar year counts as ⅙ of day. Fractional days of presence are treated as whole days for purposes of counting these days (.10).

> ***Example:*** Ivan is physically present in the United States for 52 days in 2004, 300 days in 2003, and 186 days in 2002. Ivan meets the 31 days requirement for the current year. He also meets the 183-day requirement ((186/6) + (300/3) + 52 = 183). Thus, Ivan qualifies as a resident alien.

An alien is considered "present in the United States" only if the individual is physically present within the United States at any time during the day (.15). However, there are a number of exceptions as to what days an alien is considered to be present in the United States:

- Commuters who live in Canada or Mexico and who regularly commute to the United States for employment or self-employment are not considered to be present in the United States on any commuting days.
- An alien who is physically present in the United States for less than 24 hours while in transit between two foreign points is not treated as being present in the United States.
- An alien is not considered to be present in the United States on any day that the alien is prevented from leaving the United States due to a medical condition that developed during the U.S. visit.
- An exempt individual is not considered to be present in the United States despite physical presence.
- An alien who has a closer connection to a foreign country than to the United States and who is in the United States for less than half the year is not considered to be present in the United States.

Exempt individuals

A individual will not be considered "present in the United States" if he or she falls into one of the following categories: (.20):

(1) *A foreign government-related individual.* This includes an alien who has diplomatic status or a visa that represents full-time diplomatic or consular status, a full-time employee of an international organization, or a member of the immediate family of such individuals.

(2) *Teacher or trainee.* An individual alien who is a teacher or trainee and who is temporarily present in the United States under a "J" visa (other than a student) and who substantially complies with the requirements of the visa. This does not include any alien who, for any two calendar years during the preceding six calendar years, was an exempt teacher, trainee or student. However, the teacher or trainee will lose the exempt status only after four calendar years (out of the preceding six) as an exempt teacher, trainee or student if the alien was on an "F," "J" or "M" visa and was paid by a foreign employer. A

foreign employer can include an office or place of business that is located in a foreign country or a U.S. possession, but that is owned and operated by an American entity.

(3) *Student.* A student alien who is temporarily present in the United States under an "F," "J" or "M" visa and who substantially complies with the requirements of the visa. This does not include any alien who, for the past five calendar years, has been either an exempt teacher or trainee or an exempt student unless the IRS is satisfied that the conditions of the visa are being met and that the alien has no intention of permanently residing in the United States.

(4) *Professional athlete.* A professional athlete is exempt if the athlete is temporarily in the United States to compete in a charitable sports event. The charitable sports event must be organized to benefit a qualified charitable organization, the entire proceeds must go to the charity, and volunteers must be used to perform substantially all the event's work.

Closer connection to foreign country

The substantial presence test is not met by an alien who is present in the United States for fewer than 183 days during the current year if the alien has established a tax home in a foreign country with which the alien has a closer connection with than the United States (.25). This exception does not apply to any year during which the alien has an application for adjustment of status pending or has taken steps to apply for status as a lawful permanent resident of the United States. Nonresident aliens who meet the closer connection exception are required to file a statement with the IRS to explain the basis of the claim that they satisfy the exception. For example, a Canadian citizen who spends each winter at her condominium in Florida would be required to file such a statement. The IRS has provided Form 8840, Closer Connection Exception Statement for Aliens, to meet this requirement.

.05 Code Sec. 7701(b)(1)(A)(ii) and (3).
.10 Reg. §301.7701(b)-1(c).
.15 Code Sec. 7701(b)(7).
.20 Code Sec. 7701(b)(5); Reg. §301.7701(b)-3.
.25 Code Sec. 7701(b)(3)(B).

¶25,816 First and Last Year of Residency. An alien who was not a resident alien at any time during the preceding year, but who becomes a resident alien during the current year, is considered to be a resident alien only during that portion of the year that begins with the alien's residency starting date (.05). For an alien who qualifies as a resident under the lawful permanent resident test (¶25,814), the residency starting date is first day in the calendar year on which the alien is present in the United States as a lawful permanent resident. For an alien who qualifies as a resident under the substantial presence test (¶25,815), the residency starting date is first day of the calendar year that the alien was present in the United States. For this purpose, an alien can disregard up to 10 days of any period for which a closer connection to a foreign country than to the United States can be established. Unless the alien arrives in the United States on January 1st, he or she therefore will have a dual status year (¶25,829–¶25,830), whereby part of the year the individual will be taxed as a nonresident alien and the remainder of the year as a resident alien.

First-year election

An alien who moves to the United States too late in the year to meet the substantial presence test and does not otherwise qualify as a resident, may nonetheless elect to be a resident for part of that calendar year (.10). To qualify for the election, the alien must:

- not have qualified as a resident alien for the prior calendar year;
- meet the substantial presence test in the next calendar year;
- be present in the United States are at least 31 consecutive days during the current tax year; and

- be present in the United States are at least 75 percent of the days during the period from the first day of the 31-day presence period through the end of the year.

The election is made on the alien's tax return for the election year and is effective for that portion of the calendar year beginning with the first day that both the 31-day and 75 percent requirements are met. The election, however, cannot be made until after the alien qualifies as a resident alien under the substantial presence test in the following year. If the substantial presence test is not met before the alien's income tax return is filed, then the election will have to be made on an amended return. For purposes of the election-year return, the residency starting date is the first day of the 31-consecutive-day period under the first criteria for making the election. If more than one such period can be used, then the earliest one is used for purposes of the residency starting date.

> ***Example:*** Megan Pegeen, a citizen of Ireland, arrived in the United States on November 15, 2004, and remained through the rest of the year. In 2005, she will meet the substantial presence test for that year. Megan can elect to be treated as a resident alien as of November 15, 2004, because she was not a U.S. resident during 2003, she was in the United States for 31 consecutive days during 2004 (and will be in 2005), and she will be in the United States for 75 percent of the days from November 15, 2004, through December 31 of 2005. Megan, however, cannot make the election to be treated as a resident alien by April 15, 2004. This is because by April 15, 2004, Megan will only be credited with being present in the United States for 120 days (105 in 2004 + 15 (45/3) in 2004). Consequently, she would have to file her 2004 return as a nonresident alien and later file an amended return as a resident alien.

One-time joint return election

An alien is permitted to elect resident alien (and thereby file a joint return) if the individual is married to a U.S. citizen or resident alien at the end of the tax year (.15). The taxpayer may be either a resident or nonresident alien at the end of the tax year. However, both spouses must join in the election and it is effective for the entire tax year and all subsequent tax years unless neither spouse is a U.S. citizen or resident. The election may also be jointly revoked by the couple or terminated by reason of death, separation, divorce, or by the IRS for failure to keep adequate records. Once terminated, the election may not be made again by the couple. If the election is made, the taxpayer will be treated as a resident alien for the entire tax year for federal income tax and withholding purposes.

Last year of residency

An alien ceases to be treated as a resident alien during the calendar year: (1) after the last day that the alien was present in, or a lawful permanent resident of, the United States; (2) at the time that the individual has a closer connection to a foreign country than the United States; and (3) if the individual is not a resident of the United States, then at any time during the next calendar year (nominal presence of 10 days or less is to be disregarded) (.20).

.05 Code Sec. 7701(b)(2)(A).

.10 Code Sec. 7701(b)(4); Reg. §301.7701(b)-4(a).

.15 Code Sec. 6013(g) and (h).

.20 Code Sec. 7701(b)(2)(B); Reg. §301.7701(b)-4(b).

¶25,818 Interrupted Residency. Just as U.S. citizens who renounce their citizenship and go abroad are taxed as expatriates so are resident aliens who give up their resident alien status only to return to it within three years (.05). To qualify for expatriate treatment, an alien must:

(1) be treated as a resident alien for a minimum of three consecutive years (*the initial residency period*); and

(2) cease to be a resident alien and then become a resident alien again before the close of three calendar years following the close of the initial residency period.

The IRS does not need to show an intent to evade taxes to hold the alien liable for taxes as it does in the case of an expatriate.

An alien who is subject to this rule is subject to the graduated income tax, the alternative minimum tax, and the tax on lump-sum distributions from an employees' trust applied only to the alien's gross income that is effectively connected with a U.S. trade or business and U.S.-source income not effectively connected gross income. For this purpose, U.S.-source gross income includes gains from the sale or exchange of:

(1) property (other than stock or debt obligations) located in the United States; and

(2) stock issued by a U.S. domestic corporation or debt obligations of U.S. persons or of the United States, a state or political subdivision thereof, or the District of Columbia.

.05 Code Sec. 7701(b)(10).

Resident Aliens

¶25,819 Taxation of Resident Aliens. Generally, a resident alien is taxed in the same manner as a U.S. citizen. The individual's worldwide income is subject to taxation without regard to whether the income arose from a transaction or activity originating outside its geographic borders (.05). Income that is generally excludable by U.S. taxpayers is generally excludable by the resident alien. This would include up to $80,000 of income earned in a foreign country provided that the resident alien meets the exclusion's physical presence test (¶25,592). To mitigate the potential for double taxation of foreign-source income, the alien is allowed a credit or deduction for certain foreign tax credits (¶25,601).

Filing status

The resident alien's tax filing status is determined in the same manner as the tax filing status of any U.S. citizen. However, the alien cannot file a joint return unless the alien's spouse is also a citizen or resident alien for the entire tax year, or the spouse elects to be treated as a resident alien for the entire year (¶25,816). Of course, this election subjects the worldwide income of the partial-year, resident-alien spouse to taxation. If this election is not made and the couple has a dependent, the resident alien may qualify to be taxed as a head of household.

Personal exemptions

The personal exemption rules for a resident alien are the same as for a U.S. citizen. Regardless of whether the alien files a joint return, the alien can claim a personal exemption for their spouse if he or she has no gross income for U.S. tax purposes and is not a dependent of another taxpayer. This exemption can be taken even if the spouse is an alien who has not come to the United States. In addition to the exemption for dependents who are citizens or nationals of the United States, an exemption can also be taken for dependents who are residents of the United States, Canada or Mexico for some part of the calendar year in which the alien's tax year began.

.05 Code Secs. 876 and 877; Reg. §§1.871-1 and 1.876-1.

Nonresident Aliens

¶25,821 Taxation of Nonresident Aliens. A nonresident alien is taxed in the same manner as a U.S. citizen or resident alien on all income which is "effectively connected" with a U.S. trade or business. For this purpose, a nonresident alien who is married to a U.S. citizen or resident alien must use the tax rate schedule for married individuals filing separately unless the election to be treated as a resident alien has been elected to file a joint return (¶25,816). If the individual receives any U.S.-source income that is *not* effectively connected with a U.S. trade or business, then such income will be taxed at a flat 30-percent rate (unless a lower tax rate applies due to a tax treaty) (¶25,825). Such non-connected income generally includes fixed or determinable periodic income or capital gains (.05).

.05 Code Sec. 872(a).

¶25,822 U.S. Source Income. Nonresident aliens are subject to U.S. taxation only on income derived from U.S. sources (¶25,821). Income (other than personal service income, ¶25,823) is will be considered as derived from U.S. sources for the following categories of income.

- *Interest* on bonds, notes or other interest-bearing obligations of U.S. residents or domestic corporations (.05). It does not include:

  (i) Interest payments by an unrelated person from a domestic corporation or resident alien if at least 80 percent of the payor's gross income from all sources for the three tax years preceding the payment is active foreign business income. This means that the income is derived, directly or indirectly, from sources outside the United States from the active conduct of a trade or business in a foreign country or U.S. possession. If the payee is a related person, the income can be excluded in the same ratio that the payor's foreign-source gross income bears to its total gross income.

  (ii) Interest on deposits with foreign branch banks of a domestic corporation or domestic partnership engaged in the commercial banking business and interest on deposits or withdrawable accounts with savings institutions paid by a foreign branch of a domestic corporation or partnership.

  (iii) In the case of a partnership which is predominantly engaged in the active conduct of a trade or business outside the United States, interest paid by a trade or business of the partnership in the United States.

- *Dividends* paid by domestic corporations unless the corporation has made an election in effect to claim the possession tax credit (.10). A corporation is eligible to claim the credit if: (1) 80 percent or more of its gross income is from sources within the U.S. possession for the three-year period ending with the close of the tax year preceding the declaration of a dividend; and (2) 75 percent or more of its gross income during the three-year period is from the active conduct of a trade or business within a possession of the United States. Dividends from foreign corporations are generally not considered U.S.-source income unless during a three-year test period at least 25 percent of the foreign corporation's gross income is effectively connected with a U.S. trade or business. To the extent dividends paid by a foreign corporation are paid from the accumulated earnings and profits that a foreign corporation succeeded to from a domestic corporation, such dividends will be considered U.S.-source income.

• *Rents and royalties* from property located within the United States are considered U.S.-source income (.15). This would include intangible property such as patents, copyrights, secret processes and formulas, goodwill, trademarks, franchises and similar property.

• *Gains, loss or income from dispositions of real property* or property interests located in the United States are considered U.S.-source income (.20).

• *Insurance underwriting income* (premiums earned on insurance contracts less expenses and losses) derived from the insurance of U.S. risks is U.S.-source income (.25).

• *Income from the sale of personal property* is generally treated as originating in the seller's tax home and therefore may or may not be U.S.-source income (.30). However, the following types of personal property may be considered U.S.-source income:

(i) The source of income from the sale of inventory property depends upon where the sale was made (inside the United States or outside), not upon where the inventory was purchased or the location of the tax home of the nonresident alien (.35). If the inventory was purchased in a U.S. possession, or if it was produced by the nonresident alien either in the United States or outside and sold in the alternate location, then an allocation must be made between U.S.-source income and non-U.S. source income.

(ii) To the extent that gain on the sale or exchange of depreciable personal property represents the recapture of depreciation taken on the property, the gain is treated as U.S.-source income (.40). However, if the depreciation claimed on U.S. tax returns is less than the total depreciation claimed on the property, then the percentage that the U.S. depreciation bears to the total depreciation taken is the percentage of the depreciation recapture that is U.S.-source income. Any gain in excess of depreciation taken is treated as U.S.-source income in the same manner as gain on the sale of inventory property.

• While income from the sale of intangibles is generally classified on the basis of the location of the alien's tax home, any portion of the income that is contingent on the productivity, use, or disposition of an intangible must be treated as coming from the country in which the property is used (.45). Income from the sale of goodwill is treated as coming from the country in which the goodwill was generated.

• If the property is sold through a business office or other fixed place of business maintained by the alien in the United States, then the gain is U.S.-source income (.50). This rule applies to inventory property unless the inventory is sold for use, disposition, or consumption outside the United States and a material part of the sale is performed by the alien's office or other fixed place of business located in a foreign country.

.05 Code Sec. 861(a)(1), as amended by the American Jobs Creation Act of 2004 (P.L. 108-357).
.10 Code Sec. 861(a)(2).
.15 Code Sec. 861(a)(4).
.20 Code Sec. 861(a)(5).
.25 Code Sec. 861(a)(7).
.30 Code Sec. 865(a).
.35 Code Sec. 861(a)(6).
.40 Code Sec. 865(c).
.45 Code Sec. 865(d).
.50 Code Sec. 865(e).

¶25,823 Personal Service Income. Any income from wages, tips, remuneration, or other compensation for performing work or services in the United States is considered U.S.-source income that is derived from a U.S. trade or business (.05). If compensation is paid for work performed inside and outside the United States, then an allocation must be made, usually on the basis of time, in order to determine what portion of the compensation is for work performed in the United States (.10). A time allocation is made by multiplying the amount of compensation by a fraction, the numerator of which is the days spent working in the United States, and the denominator of which is the total number of days worked.

> ***Example:*** A Mexican citizen works for a Mexican computer service company, performing maintenance and repair at customers' work sites on both sides of the U.S.-Mexican border. He was paid $30,000 for working 225 days during the year, and he spent 45 of those days working on computers that were located in the United States. The Mexican citizen's U.S.-source income would be $6,000 ($30,000 × 45/225).

Transportation income

Income that is derived from providing international transportation that begins or ends in the United States creates an allocation problem. If the transportation begins and ends in the United States, it is 100 percent U.S.-source income (.15). However, round-trip transportation from a point in the United States to a foreign location is not considered to begin and end in the United States. If the United States is only the beginning or the end of the journey, then 50 percent of the income is U.S.-source income. This rule does not cover wages derived from working on a ship or aircraft. If the transportation is between the United States and a possession of the United States, 50 percent of the income is U.S.-source income and 50 percent is possession income.

Income from personal services provided on a ship or aircraft that is engaged in transportation between the United States and a foreign port is not considered transportation income unless the foreign port is a U.S. possession. Compensation for labor or services performed in the United States is not income from U.S. sources if the labor or services are performed by a nonresident alien in connection with the individual's temporary presence in the United States as a regular member of the crew of a foreign vessel engaged in transportation between the United States and a foreign country or a possession of the United States.

For this purpose, transportation income is income derived from, or in connection with the use (or hiring or leasing for use) of a vessel or aircraft, or the performance of services directly relating to the use of a vessel or aircraft. The term "vessel or aircraft" includes any container used in connection with a vessel or aircraft.

Pension payments

Payments from a pension fund must be identified as interest and principal (original contributions) before the payments can be classified as U.S.-source income. If the fund is a domestic fund, then all of the interest is U.S.-source income. The portion of the payment that represents return of principal is U.S.-source income to the extent that the time spent working to accumulate the fund was spent working in the United States (.20). This rule applies whether the distribution is made under a qualified or nonqualified stock bonus, pension, profit-sharing, or annuity plan (whether or not funded).

Foreign employer exclusion

Certain compensation paid to a nonresident alien by a foreign employer for work performed in the United States is excluded from U.S.-source income provided three conditions are met:

- the nonresident alien who performs the services must be temporarily present in the United States, but for no more than 90 days during the tax year;
- the compensation paid for the services cannot exceed $3,000; and

• the work must be performed as an employee or under contract with (a) a nonresident alien, foreign partnership, or foreign corporation not engaged in a trade or business within the United States, or (b) a citizen or resident of the United States, a domestic partnership, or a domestic corporation, provided that the labor or services are performed for an office or place of business maintained in a foreign country or in a U.S. possession by the employer or contractor (.25).

Students and exchange visitors

A nonresident alien who is in the United States as a student on an "F" visa or as a teacher, trainee or specialist on a "J" visa may exclude from gross income any compensation paid by the alien's foreign employer (.30). The term foreign employer means a nonresident alien individual, a foreign partnership, a foreign corporation, or an office or place of business maintained in a foreign country or in a possession of the United States by a domestic corporation, a domestic partnership, or an individual who is a citizen or resident of the United States.

.05 Code Secs. 861(a)(3) and 864(b); Reg. §1.864-2.

.10 Code Sec. 863(b).

.15 Code Sec. 863(c).

.20 Rev. Rul. 79-388, 1979-2 CB 270.

.25 Code Secs. 861(a)(3) and 864(b).

.30 Code Sec. 872(b)(3).

¶25,824 U.S. Trade or Business. A nonresident alien who is engaged in a U.S. trade or business is taxed, after allowable deductions, on income from that business and on any other U.S.-source income that is effectively connected with the business at the same graduated tax rates (including the alternative minimum tax) as other taxpayers (.05). To the extent that the alien's U.S.-source income is not effectively connected to the trade or business, it may be subject to a flat 30-percent tax to the extent that it qualifies as fixed or determinable income.

Trade or business in the U.S.

A U.S. trade or business includes any activity conducted in the United States that would be considered a trade or business if it were undertaken by a U.S. citizen or resident alien. For a nonresident alien, this includes most compensation for personal services. It does not include most passive investment activities.

Personal services. A nonresident alien who provides personal services for wages, salaries, fees, tips, bonuses, honoraria, commissions, etc., is considered to be engaged in a trade or business. Certain types of employment income are exempt from U.S. taxation (¶25,823).

Business operations. A nonresident alien who owns and operates a business in the United States that provides services, products or merchandise is engaged in a U.S. trade or business.

Partnerships. If a partnership is, at any time during the tax year, engaged in a trade or business in the United States, any of its nonresident alien partners are considered to be engaged in that business. The nonresident alien's presence in the United States is not required.

Estates and trusts. If an estate or trust is, at any time during the tax year, engaged in a trade or business in the United States, any of its nonresident alien beneficiaries are considered to be engaged in that business.

Stock, securities and commodities transactions. The act of buying or selling stock, securities or commodities in the United States through a U.S. resident broker or agent on the taxpayer's own behalf does not constitute a U.S. trade or business (.10). This rule is not altered by the fact that the trades are hedging transactions. This exception from the definition of U.S. trade or business does not apply to dealers, however.

Effectively connected income

A nonresident alien is allowed to take certain deductions and to apply the graduated tax rates to income that is effectively connected with a U.S. trade or business. If a nonresident alien has a U.S. trade or business, then all U.S.-source income is treated as effectively connected income, with the exception of certain investment income that is subject to the flat 30-percent tax (.15).

Deferred payments. If a nonresident alien receives payment in one year for a sale or exchange, or for personal services, that occurred in a prior year, then the compensation received is treated as if it were received in the year when the sale or exchange occurred or when the personal services were provided (.20). However, if property is sold within 10 years after it ceases to be used, or held for use, in connection with the conduct of a U.S. trade or business, then the sale is treated as if it occurred prior to the cessation of business use.

Wages. Wages and other compensation for personal services are always considered to be effectively connected with a U.S. trade or business.

Effectively connected investment income. U.S. source investment income (including gain or loss from the sale) is generally taxed at the flat 30-percent rate (¶25,825) unless it is effectively connected with the U.S. trade or business. If the income passes one of two tests, it is generally considered to be effectively connected with the U.S. trade or business (.25).

(1) The *asset-use test* turns on whether the income, gain, or loss is derived from assets used in or held for use in the conduct of the trade or business. This test is usually applied when the alien manufactures or sells goods in the United States and receives certain income, such as interest or dividends.

(2) The *business-activities test* turns on whether the activities of the trade or business were a material factor in the realization of the income, gain or loss.

Foreign income. Generally, income, gain or loss from sources outside the United States cannot be treated as effectively connected income. However, if the income is attributable to the nonresident alien's office or other fixed place of business located within the United States, certain types of income may be considered effectively connected. The office or place of business must be a material factor in the production of the income, and the income must be produced in the ordinary course of the trade or business carried on through the U.S. facilities. Foreign-source income which may be considered U.S.-source income includes the following (as well as their economic equivalent) (.30):

- *rental and royalty income* received from the active conduct of a business (or from any interest in such property) that leases or licenses intangible personal property and is located outside the United States;

- *dividend, interest, gain or loss* from the sale or exchange of stocks or bonds or debt obligations derived from the active conduct of a banking, financing, or similar business in the United States; and

- *income from foreign insurance companies* doing business in the United States that is attributable to U.S. business.

Real property

A nonresident alien must treat the gain or loss from the dispositions of a U.S. real property interest as though it was effectively connected with a U.S. trade or business (.35). A U.S. real property interest is:

- any interest in real property located in the United States or the Virgin Islands; and

- any interest (other than that of a creditor) in any domestic corporation, unless the alien establishes that the corporation was at no time a U.S. real property holding corporation during the shorter of (a) the period during which the alien held the interest, or (b) the five-year period ending on the date of disposition.

For this purpose, a U.S. real property holding corporation is a corporation that has real property with a fair market value that equals or exceeds 50 percent of the fair market value of its real property plus its other assets held for use in a trade or business.

A nonresident alien may elect to treat the income from real property as income that is effectively connected with the conduct of a U.S. trade or business, provided the property is located in the United States and held for the production of income (.40). This provision places the nonresident alien in the same financial position as a U.S. resident with respect to real property ownership in that it permits the deduction of related expenses. However, the election does not result in the nonresident alien's being treated as having a U.S. trade or business during the year for purposes of tax issues that are unrelated to the real property. The election is made by attaching a statement to the tax return or amended return that includes:

- a complete list of all real property, or interest in real property, located in the United States;
- the extent of the taxpayer's interest in the property;
- the location of the property;
- a description of major improvements to the property; and
- details of any previous elections and revocations of the real property income election.

Once made, the election covers all types of income from real property, including rents and royalties from mines, oil and gas wells, or other natural resources, and gain on the disposal of timber, coal, or iron ore with a retained economic interest. However, the election may not be made with respect to only one class of income. Also, the election remains in effect for all later tax years unless it is revoked with the consent of the IRS. Once an election has been revoked, a new election may not be made for five years.

.05 Code Sec. 871(b).
.10 Code Sec. 864(b)(2).
.15 Code Sec. 864(c).
.20 Code Sec. 864(c)(6).
.25 Code Sec. 864(c)(2).
.30 Code Sec. 864(c)(4), as amended by the American Jobs Creation Act of 2004, P.L. 108-357).
.35 Code Sec. 897.
.40 Code Sec. 871(d); Reg. §1.871-10.

¶25,825 Income Not Effectively Connected. Fixed and determinable income is subject to a flat 30-percent tax regardless of whether the nonresident alien who receives it is engaged in a U.S. trade or business (.05). Of course, this flat tax does not apply to fixed and determinable income that is effectively connected to a U.S. trade or business. Fixed or determinable income includes:

- interest (except portfolio investment interest, or interest on certain bank accounts, see below), contingent portfolio interest, dividends, rents, salaries, wages, premiums, annuities, compensations, remunerations, and emoluments;
- lump-sum distributions from exempt employees' trusts;
- amounts paid to beneficiaries under qualified annuity plans;
- timber, coal, and iron ore royalties;
- gains from the sale or exchange of patents, copyrights, goodwill, trademarks, and other intangible property to the extent that the gains are contingent on the productivity, use or disposition of the property;
- prizes, awards and gambling winnings with no offset for gambling losses (blackjack, baccarat, craps, roulette, and the big-6 wheel are exempt (.10)); and
- royalties paid by a foreign corporation to a nonresident alien for the right to use a patent in the United States.

Exceptions

Exceptions to the fixed or determinable income rule apply to the following specific situations:

Portfolio interest. For a nonresident alien, portfolio interest is not fixed or determinable income (.15). Portfolio interest means any interest (including original issue discount but excluding contingent interest) paid on an obligation that was issued after July 18, 1984, and that falls within one of two portfolio investment categories:

- Any obligation that is not in registered form but that meets the following requirements: (a) arrangements that are reasonably designed to ensure that such obligations will be sold or resold only to non-U.S. persons, (b) the interest is payable only outside of the United States, and (c) on the face of the obligation, there is a statement that any U.S. person who holds it will be subject to limitations under the U.S. tax law.

- Any registered obligation with respect to which the U.S. person who would otherwise be required to withhold tax from interest paid on the obligation has received a statement averring that the beneficial owner is not a U.S. person.

The portfolio interest exemption available to a nonresident alien individual has been restricted to exclude contingent interest received after 1994 (.20). Interest is contingent if the amount of the interest is determined by reference to: (1) receipts, sales or other cash flow of the debtor or a related person (.25); (2) any income or profits of the debtor or a related person; (3) any change in value of any property of the debtor or a related person; or (4) any dividend, partnership distributions or similar payments made by the debtor or a related person.

Interest is not contingent for purposes of the portfolio interest exemption solely by reason of the fact that: (1) the timing of the interest or principal payment is subject to a contingency; (2) the interest is paid with respect to nonrecourse or limited recourse indebtedness; (3) all or substantially all of the interest is determined by reference to non-contingent interest, or the principal amount of the debt on which such interest is paid; (4) the interest is related to currency or interest rate hedging transactions; or (5) the interest is determined by reference to changes in the value or yield on actively traded property other than U.S. real property interests, or on the index of the value or yield on such property.

The 30-percent tax remains applicable to portfolio interest that is paid to a 10-percent shareholder. If an obligation is issued by a corporation, a 10-percent shareholder is any person who owns 10 percent of the total combined voting power of all classes of voting stock. If it is issued by a partnership, it is anyone who owns 10 percent of the capital or profits interest in the partnership.

Bank accounts. Provided the interest is not effectively connected with the conduct of a U.S. trade or business, a nonresident alien does not include in fixed and determinable income interest received on the following:

(1) deposits (including certificates of deposit) with persons in the banking business; or

(2) deposits or withdrawable accounts with mutual savings banks, cooperative banks, credit unions, domestic building and loan associations, and other savings institutions chartered and supervised as savings and loan or similar associations under federal or state law (if the interest paid or credited can be deducted by the association); and

(3) interest-bearing deposits held by an insurance company (.30).

Dividend income. A portion of the dividends paid by a domestic corporation to a nonresident alien may be excluded from his fixed and determinable income. If at least 80 percent of the domestic corporation's gross income is active foreign business income, then the nonresident alien can exclude that percentage of the dividends paid by the corporation that the corporation's active foreign business income bears to its gross international income. If a nonresident alien receives dividends from a foreign corporation, then that portion of the income which is treated as U.S.-source income will also be excluded from being taxed at the 30-percent rate (.35).

Original issue discount. Original issue discount notes held by a nonresident alien are subject to the tax on fixed and determinable income when interest is paid on the note and when the note is sold (.40). Interest actually paid on the note is subject to the 30-percent flat tax to the extent that the interest actually accrued while the note was held by the alien. If the note is sold by the alien, the 30-percent tax is applied to the selling price to the extent that the interest on the note accrued during the period that the alien held the note, excluding interest on which the 30-percent tax has been previously paid. For this purpose, original issue discount notes do not include obligations payable within 183 days or less from the date of original issue, nor do they include tax exempt state or local bonds.

Social security benefits. A nonresident alien treats half of any social security benefits received as fixed and determinable income (.45). Included in this treatment is the social security equivalent of tier-one railroad retirement benefits. Social security benefits may be exempt from tax under some treaties. Under the treaties with Canada, Egypt, Italy, Japan, Malta, Romania, and the United Kingdom, U.S. Social Security benefits received by residents of those countries are exempt from U.S. tax (¶25,827).

Capital assets. The net gains from a nonresident alien's sale or exchange of capital assets (other than real property, see ¶25,824) are subject to the 30-percent flat tax, provided the assets are not effectively connected to the alien's U.S. trade or business and the alien spent a minimum of 183 days in the United States during the calendar year. The gain must be computed without regard to the 50-percent exclusion for gain from certain small business stock (.50). These rules apply regardless of whether the alien maintains a U.S. trade or business. However, if some of the capital assets are effectively connected to the U.S. trade or business and some are not, a separate calculation of the net gain must be determined for each category. The gains and losses from the business-related assets are reported on Schedule D (Form 1040), which is attached to Form 1040NR, and the gains and losses that constitute fixed and determinable income are reported on page 4 of Form 1040NR.

Unlike other forms of fixed and determinable income, capital losses for the year may be deducted from capital gains. However, no capital loss carryover from a prior year is permitted. If a nonresident alien is in the United States for less than 183 days during the year, then any gain from the sale or exchange of a capital asset is tax free. If the alien is in the United States for an aggregate of 183 days or more, then the net capital gain from the sale or exchange of capital assets is taxed at 30 percent. There are certain exceptions where gain will be taxed even though the alien was present in the United States for less than 183 days. Among these exceptions are:

- gains on lump-sum distributions from exempt employees' pension, profit-sharing or stock bonus trusts;
- gains on lump-sum payments under certain qualified employee annuity plans;
- gains on the disposal of certain natural resources;
- gains on contingent payments from the sale of patents, copyrights, and similar property; and
- gain on the sale of original issue discount notes (see above).

.05 Code Sec. 871(a)(1).

.10 Code Sec. 871(j).

.15 Code Sec. 871(h).

.20 Code Sec. 871(h)(4).

.25 Code Secs. 267(b) and 707(b)(1).

.30 Code Sec. 871(i).

.35 Code Sec. 871(i)(2)(D), as added by the American Jobs Creation Act of 2004 (P.L. 108-357).

.40 Code Sec. 871(a)(1)(C) and (g).

.45 Code Sec. 871(a)(3).

.50 Code Secs. 871(a)(2) and 1202.

¶25,826 The Nonresident Alien Return. A nonresident alien files an income tax return on Form 1040NR, U.S. Nonresident Alien Income Tax Return. This return is used for reporting effectively connected income from a U.S. trade or business and fixed and determinable income.

Filing status

A nonresident alien is limited as to the status under which a Form 1040NR can be filed. A married nonresident alien cannot file a joint return unless the spouse is a U.S. citizen or resident alien and the nonresident alien elects to be treated as a resident alien (see also ¶25,816). A nonresident alien who is a resident of Canada, Mexico, Japan, or the Republic of Korea can file as a qualifying widow(er) if the other standard requirements are met. Nonresident aliens are also precluded from filing as a head of household.

Income

The nonresident alien reports income that is effectively connected to a U.S. trade or business on Form 1040NR. The income that is fixed and determinable is also reported on Form 1040NR.

Deductions

With the exception of a deduction for personal exemptions and some itemized deductions (see below), a nonresident alien can only take deductions that are effectively connected with a U.S. trade or business. Deductions that can be taken as an adjustment to gross income that is effectively connected to a U.S. trade or business are: (1) the IRA deduction; (2) the self-employment health insurance deduction; (3) the Keogh retirement plan and self-employed SEP deduction; (4) the penalty on early withdrawal of savings deduction; and (5) the deduction for excluded scholarship and fellowship grants.

Itemized deductions

A nonresident alien can deduct itemized deductions, but this is generally limited to deductions that are effectively connected to a U.S. trade or business. Two exceptions to this rule are charitable contributions and casualty and theft losses, which can be deducted regardless of whether the deductions are connected with income that is effectively connected with a U.S. trade or business (.05). If the nonresident alien has no itemized deductions, the standard deduction cannot be taken in the alternative.

Charitable contributions. Contributions to U.S. charitable organizations are deductible without a showing that the contributions are effectively connected to the alien's U.S. trade or business. Although contributions to foreign organizations are not deductible, contributions to U.S. organizations that do charitable work overseas are deductible. Contributions to a Canadian charitable organization are deductible under a treaty with Canada. Special rules apply to the contribution of appreciated property.

Casualty and theft losses. A deduction can be taken for a loss from fire, storm, shipwreck, or other casualty, or a theft of property even though the loss was not connected with a U.S. trade or business. However, the property must have been located in the United States at the time of the casualty or theft.

Moving expenses. Moving expenses can be taken as an itemized deduction for the alien's move to the United States provided the standard requirements for a moving deduction are met (see also ¶25,596). However, the cost of moving back to the alien's native country cannot be taken as a moving expense deduction. A deduction for travel expenses while away from the alien's residence in a foreign country is lost if the moving expense deduction is taken.

Miscellaneous deductions. Miscellaneous deductions can be taken provided they are related to income that is effectively connected to a U.S. trade or business. These deductions are reduced by two percent of the alien's adjusted gross income. Related expenses include travel expenses, union dues, safety equipment and small tools, dues to professional organizations, subscriptions to professional journals, and tax return preparation.

Personal exemptions

Generally, a nonresident alien is only allowed a personal exemption. A nonresident alien who is a resident of Canada or Mexico or a national of the United States can take a spousal exemption if the spouse had no income taxable in the United States and the spouse was not the dependent of another taxpayer. Residents of Japan and the Republic of Korea can take additional exemptions for their spouses and children subject to two conditions:

- the spouse and children must live with the alien in the United States at some time during the tax year; and

- the exemptions for the spouse and children are allowed only to the same percent that the alien's U.S.-source income that is effectively connected with a U.S. trade and business bears to the alien's gross worldwide income.

Credits

Credits for taxes paid, taxes withheld, excess Social Security tax withheld, the regulated investment company credit, tax withheld at the source, and the tax withheld on partnership income can be taken regardless of whether the alien's income is effectively connected to the U.S. trade or business. Other credits, however, can only be taken to the extent that they relate to income that is effectively connected with a U.S. trade or business. Such credits would include the child care credit, the credit for prior-year minimum tax, and the earned income credit. The foreign tax credit is available, but a tax imposed by a foreign country or U.S. possession because the alien is a resident of that country or possession is not available as a foreign tax credit.

.05 Code Sec. 873(b).

¶25,827 Tax Treaties. The United States has entered into tax treaties with a large number of foreign governments, and these treaties make the impact of U.S. taxes more tolerable. Most of the treaties require that the alien be a resident of the foreign country, but some of them require that the beneficiary of the treaty be a citizen of the foreign country. A foreign person is not entitled to a reduced rate of withholding tax under a tax treaty on an item of income derived through a partnership (or other fiscally transparent entity) under certain circumstances (.05).

Withholding

If a nonresident alien's taxes would be reduced by a tax treaty, the alien can have the withholding from U.S.-source income reduced to reflect the lower treaty tax rate.

Treaty income

Treaty income is the nonresident alien's U.S.-source income that is subject to a reduced tax rate under the terms of a treaty. The remainder of the alien's U.S.-source income is called nontreaty income. The alien's tax is the sum of the tax on the treaty income, determined at the treaty rate, plus the tax on the nontreaty income that is effectively connected to a U.S. trade or business, determined at the graduated rates, plus the tax on fixed and determinable income taxed at the 30-percent rate. The total tax cannot exceed the tax that would be due on the U.S.-source income determined as if there had been no treaty.

Disclosure of treaty position

A taxpayer who takes the position that any U.S. tax is overruled or otherwise reduced by a U.S. treaty (a treaty-based position), must usually disclose that position on Form 8833, (Treaty-Based Return Position Disclosure Under Section 6114 or 7701(b)), and attach the form to the tax return. A taxpayer who is not required to file a return because of the treaty-based position, must file a return anyway to report the position. The filing of Form 8833 does not apply to a reduced rate of withholding tax on noneffectively connected income, such as dividends, interest, rents or royalties, or to a reduced rate of tax on pay received for services performed as an employee, including pensions, annuities, and social security. A failure to file Form 8833, may result in a $1,000 penalty. Corporations are subject to a $10,000 penalty for each failure.

Typical treaty benefits

Each treaty is unique, having been negotiated with representatives of the foreign country. However, certain types of provisions appear in many treaties. Listed below are common provisions found in many treaties, followed by a chart indicating which provisions appear in each country's tax treaty with the United States. This discussion is meant as a reference only, and the text of the treaty should be checked before deciding what action to take.

(1) *Visitors on a short stay.* Compensation for personal service in the United States during a short stay may be treated as tax exempt. Most treaties require that the nonresident alien be in the United States for no more than 183 days, but others specify limits of 180 days or 90 days. A fraction of a day counts as a whole day. Many treaties also require that the compensation be below a specific amount (frequently $3,000) and that the alien have a foreign employer.

(2) *Teachers and professors.* The academic income of nonresident alien teachers and professors may be tax exempt. They must be residents of the treaty country and must be temporarily visiting the United States for the purpose of teaching at a university or other accredited educational institution. This exclusion is often limited to the first two or three years after the alien's arrival.

(3) *Employees of foreign governments.* All treaties have provisions for the exemption of income earned by specified employees of foreign governments. The treaties vary as to who qualifies for this benefit, often limiting the exemption to temporary residents of the United States and nationals of the treaty country.

(4) *Trainees, students, and apprentices.* Students, apprentices, and trainees generally are exempt from tax on remittances (including scholarship and fellowship grants) received from abroad for study and living expenses. Sometimes a limited amount of compensation may also be exempt.

(5) *Capital gains.* Many treaties provide for the exemption of gains from the sale or exchange of certain capital assets by a nonresident alien.

.05 Code Sec. 894(c).

Dual-Status Aliens

¶ 25,829 Taxation of Dual-Status Aliens. An alien who is a resident alien for only part of the tax year and a nonresident alien for the other part of the year is considered a dual-status alien during that tax year. This usually occurs either in the year that the alien comes to the United States or in the year of departure. A resident alien who leaves the United States temporarily and with the intention of returning retains the status of resident alien.

Taxable income

A dual-status alien not filing a joint return is taxed on income from all sources during the part of the year that the alien is a resident. During that portion of the year that the alien is a nonresident alien, only the alien's income from U.S.-source income is taxable. The income that is taxed at the graduated rates (the income that is other than fixed and determinable) should be combined regardless of whether it was received during the alien's residency or nonresidency period.

Income from sources outside the United States that is not effectively connected with a trade or business in the United States is taxable if the alien received it while a resident alien. The income is taxable even if the alien earned it while a nonresident alien or if the alien became a nonresident alien after receiving it and before the end of the year.

Income from sources outside the United States that is not effectively connected with a U.S. trade or business is not taxable if the alien received it while a nonresident alien. The income is not taxable even if the alien earned it while a resident alien or if the alien became a resident alien or a U.S. citizen after receiving it and before the end of the year.

Restrictions

Filing status. A dual-status alien cannot elect head-of-household filing status. The joint return filing status is also not available to the dual-status alien, but an election may be made to be taxed as a resident alien for the entire year (¶25,816).

Standard deduction. A dual-status alien may not use the standard deduction. Only the allowed itemized deductions may be used, and if the alien has none, then a zero must be entered.

Exemptions. A dual-status alien's exemptions for spouse and dependents cannot exceed the alien's taxable income (determined without deducting personal exemptions) for the period during which the dual-status alien is a resident alien. Only the alien's personal exemption can be used to reduce below zero the U.S.-source income for the residency portion of the year. Special rules apply to residents of Canada, Mexico, Japan, Korea, or U.S. nationals.

Tax rates. A married nonresident alien for all or part of the tax year must use the married-filing-separately tax rate schedules unless the alien elects to file jointly with a spouse who is a U.S. citizen or resident (¶25,816).

Tax computation

All the income from the alien's period of residence and the income from the alien's period of nonresidence that is effectively connected with a U.S. trade or business is combined to determine the alien's gross income. After allowable deductions, this income is taxed at rates that apply to U.S. citizens and residents. The income and deductions are not annualized.

Income that is fixed and determinable and received while the alien is a nonresident is taxed at the flat 30-percent rate. No deductions are allowed against this income, except that capital gains and losses are netted.

Social security. Eighty-five percent of the social security payments that are received by the alien during the nonresidency portion of the year are included in income. This income is subject to the 30 percent tax, unless exempt by treaty(.05).

Credits and exclusions

Dual-status aliens are generally entitled to the same credits as U.S. citizens, including the credit for withholding tax. The credit for the elderly or the disabled is not available to a dual-status alien unless the alien is married to a U.S. citizen or resident alien and elects to be taxed as a resident alien for the entire year. The foreign earned income exclusion is only available to aliens who elect to be taxed as resident aliens for the entire year and who meet the exclusion's physical presence test.

Return forms

A dual-status alien who is a resident alien on the last day of the year must file a Form 1040. If the individual is a nonresident alien on the last day of the tax year, then he or she must file Form 1040NR. Across the top of the return, the alien should write, "Dual-status return." A separate schedule should be attached to the return that reflects the income received and expenses incurred during the nonresidency period of the year. For resident aliens, Form 1040NR can be attached as the schedule so long as "Dual-status statement" is written across the top of the return. For nonresident aliens, Form 1040 can be attached as the schedule so long as "Dual-status statement" is written across the top of the return.

Filing deadline

The return of an alien who is a resident alien on the last day of the tax year is due on April 15, or the 15th day of the fourth month following the close of the tax year. The return of an alien who is a nonresident alien on the last day of the tax year is due on June 15, or the 15th day of the sixth month following the close of the tax year. However, if the nonresident alien has wages that are subject to the same withholding as those of a U.S. citizen, the return is due on April 15 or the 15th day of the fourth month following the close of the tax year.

.05 Code Sec. 871(a)(3)(A).

¶25,830 Sailing or Departure Permit. With certain exceptions, all aliens must obtain a certificate of compliance, also known as a sailing permit or departure permit, before leaving the United States (.05). This rule applies to resident and nonresident aliens. The purpose of the departure permit is to ensure that the alien pays all taxes due for past years and for the current year up to the time of departure. Under certain circumstances, discussed below, the requirement of the departure permit may be waived.

Exempt aliens

An alien who qualifies under one of the following categories does not have to obtain a departure permit, provided proper identification and documentation can be produced.

- *Diplomats, their household and servants.* This group covers a representative of a foreign government with a diplomatic passport, regardless of whether the diplomat is accredited to the United States. This group also includes the diplomat's household members and servants.

- *Employees of foreign governments and international organizations.* An employee of a foreign government or international organization who received income only from U.S. sources that is exempt from U.S. taxation is exempt from filing a departure permit.

- *Students.* An alien student in the United States on an "F" visa is exempt, provided the student receives no taxable income while in the United States other than an allowance covering expenses incidental to study in the United States

- *Industrial trainees.* An alien industrial trainee visiting the United States on an "H-3" visa is exempt provided the trainee receives no income that is subject to U.S. tax other than an allowance covering the expense for the training.

- *Temporary visitors.* Aliens who visit the United States on a temporary basis and receive no U.S.-source income are exempt. This would include: alien military trainees, business people, tourists, and aliens in transit through the United States on a "C-1" visa.

- *Commuters.* A resident of Canada or Mexico who commutes to the United States for work is exempt, provided the compensation is subject to U.S. withholding.

Procedure

The departure permit should be obtained at least two weeks prior to departure, but it cannot be applied for more than 30 days prior to the departure date. Essentially, filing for the departure permit means filing the alien's last tax returns (for the prior year if it has not been filed, and for the current year) and paying any tax that is due. In order to facilitate an efficient processing of the form, the following documents should be available to the alien when the application is made:

- passport, alien registration card or visa;
- copies of any U.S. income tax returns filed during the two preceding years;
- receipts for any income taxes or estimated taxes paid;
- documentation as to any deductions or dependents claimed;
- employer statements showing wages paid and taxes withheld from January 1 of the current year to the date of departure;
- a profit-and-loss statement from January 1 of the current year to the date of departure if the alien is self-employed;
- documents showing any gain or loss from any sale or exchange;
- documents relating to scholarship or fellowship grants; and
- documents establishing that the alien qualifies for any special tax treaty benefits claimed (¶25,827).

Forms

The departure permit is obtained by filing either Form 1040C (U.S. Departing Alien Income Tax Return) or Form 2063 (U.S. Departing Alien Income Tax Statement). Both forms have a "certificate of compliance" section.

Form 2063. Form 2063 is the short form, and does not include a calculation of the tax due. This form is generally used by:

- aliens who have had no taxable income for the current tax year, up to and including the date of departure, and for the preceding year; and
- resident aliens who have received taxable income during the current tax year or preceding year and who intend to continue their status as resident aliens.

Form 1040C. Form 1040C is an income tax return wherein the alien reports all income received or expected to be received during the final tax year up to and including the date of departure. A departure permit is issued when the alien establishes that taxes for the prior years have been paid, and that the tax for the current year is reflected in Form 1040C and is paid. The IRS may accept a bond or employer letter that guarantees payment of the tax in lieu of the tax itself, but this can be done only for the current year or for the preceding year if the time for filing the return has not yet elapsed.

Form 1040C is not an annual income tax return; it is simply a calculation and payment of tax due through the date of departure. The alien is still obligated to file an annual return after the close of the year, and in completing that return, a credit would be taken for any tax paid with the submission of Form 1040C.

.05 Code Sec. 6851(d); Reg. §1.6851-2.

STATUTORY EMPLOYEES

Introduction

¶25,832 Introduction. Individuals who come within the definition of "statutory employees" can take advantage of a unique tax break when they claim deductions for their unreimbursed employee business expenses. This special tax break allows statutory employees to deduct their unreimbursed employee business expenses directly from gross income (.05). Thus, these individuals are able to bypass the general rule that requires employees to deduct their unreimbursed business expenses as miscellaneous itemized deductions to the extent that such expenses exceed 2% of the individual's adjusted gross income (.10).

Example 1: During 2004, Sandra Lovell was employed as a sales representative. Because of the nature of her employment, Lovell could not be classified as a statutory employee. She spent $5,000 on employee business expenses and was not reimbursed. Her adjusted gross income for the year was $60,000. Lovell must claim her $5,000 in business expenses as a miscellaneous itemized deduction on Schedule A of her Form 1040. Assuming that she has no other miscellaneous itemized deductions and that she is otherwise able to itemize deductions, she will only be able to deduct $3,800 of her expenses after application of the 2% floor ($5,000 – $1,200 ($60,000 × 2%) = $3,800). Because of the application of the 2% rule, Lovell has lost any tax benefit from $1,200 of her expenses. Assuming that she is in the 25% tax bracket, the loss of $1,200 in deductions will have increased her federal tax by $300.

Example 2: Assume the same facts as in Example (1), above, except that Lovell is classified as a statutory employee. In this situation, she may claim her $5,000 in unreimbursed business expenses as a direct deduction from her gross income. Because she is able to bypass the 2% rule imposed on miscellaneous itemized deductions, Lovell is able to increase her deductions by $1,200 and achieve a tax reduction of $300 when compared to the scenario in Example (1).

Narrow application

The unique tax benefit that applies to statutory employees is narrowly applied. This is due to the fact that the term "statutory employees" only encompasses individuals who cannot be classified as employees under the common-law rules (discussed at ¶25,833) and whose occupations fall within certain types of work (.15):

(1) traveling or city salesperson (see ¶25,834);

(2) life insurance salesperson (see ¶25,835);

(3) agent or commission driver (see ¶25,836); or

(4) homeworker (see ¶25,837).

A detailed discussion of the general definition of "statutory employee" is presented at ¶25,833.

Special rules apply to qualified real estate agents and direct sellers. The Internal Revenue Code specifically exempts real estate agents and direct sellers, if they met certain criteria, of being either an employee or a statutory employee (.20). For an explanation of these two special groups of workers, see ¶25,428, "Direct sellers and real estate agents."

☐ See, also, ¶18,360 for a complete discussion of the special rules effecting these two types of workers.

.05 Rev. Rul. 90-93, 1990-2 CB 33.
.10 Code Sec. 67(a).
.15 Code Sec. 3121(d)(3).
.20 Code Sec. 3508(a).

Statutory Employee Defined

¶25,833 Statutory Employee Defined. The determination of whether an individual worker is an employee or an independent contractor for federal tax purposes is important for several reasons. Wages paid to an employee are generally subject to income tax withholding and to payroll taxes imposed by the Federal Insurance Contributions Act (FICA) and the Federal Unemployment Tax Act (FUTA). It is the obligation of the employer to withhold the employee's share of these taxes from the employee's wages, as well as paying its own share, and to deposit these taxes with the IRS. On the other hand, compensation paid to independent contractors imposes no withholding or deposit requirements on the person paying the compensation. If an employer treats an *employee* as an independent contractor, the employer generally becomes liable for the income tax and the employee's share of FICA tax that was not withheld. Thus, it is vital that a business make an accurate determination concerning whether a worker is its employee or an independent contractor.

Statutory employee

Generally, the correct status of a worker is determined by applying what are called the "common-law rules" (see "Common-law rules," following) (.05). However, if a worker does not come within the common-law rules *and* the worker falls within one of four specific occupational groups, the worker is classified as a "statutory employee." For a statutory employee, an employer must generally withhold and pay Federal Insurance Contribution Act (FICA) taxes based upon the statutory employee's compensation. There is no obligation to withhold income tax and, generally, no obligation to pay Federal Unemployment Tax Act (FUTA) assessment based upon such compensation.

Thus, the term "statutory employee" can be defined as a worker who cannot be classified as an employee under the common-law rules but is classified as an employee for some payroll tax purposes because of a specific statutory requirement.

Common-law rules

A worker is an "employee" under the common-law rules if the person for whom the individual works has the right to direct and control the individual's work, both as to the final results and as to the details of when, where, and how the work is to be done.

Whether an employer-employee relationship exists under the common-law rules is determined by the facts of the particular situation. As part of this decision making process, a number of factors will be taken into consideration. No single or small group of these factors will necessarily control the determination. The factors are weighed against those that indicate an independent contractor status. The relative importance of any one factor may vary depending upon the occupation of the worker under consideration. Among the factors that will be considered are (.10):

(1) A person who is required to comply with instructions about when, where, and how the work is to be performed is ordinarily classified as an employee. It is the employer's right to instruct that is important, not whether the right is exercised. Instructions may be oral or in writing.

(2) Training of an individual by an experienced person who works with the individual is considered a factor of control that indicates that the employer wants the work to be performed in a particular method or manner.

(3) The establishment of set hours of work by the employer is a factor of control because such a condition bars the worker from being in control of his or her own time. Usually, independent contractors have control over their own work hours.

There are a total of 20 factors that the IRS usually considers when it determines if a worker is an employee under the common-law rules. For example, it was ruled that a commission salesman was an employee under the common-law rules because he received such typical employee benefits as paid vacations and participation in an employees' benefits plan (.15).

The IRS has also indicated that when making its determination whether an individual is an employee or an independent contractor, it will group all evidence into the following categories:

(1) behavioral control,

(2) financial control, and

(3) the relationship of the parties.

It seems logical that even when the IRS uses this "category method" to make its determination, it still would have to develop its evidence by using the traditional 20 questions (.20).

Special occupations

If a worker does not qualify as an employee under the common-law rules, it cannot be automatically assumed that the payor of the compensation would be correct in treating the worker as an independent contractor. Before this conclusion can be reached, the payor must determine if the worker performs work within one of the four occupations that apply to statutory employees (.25). If the worker is considered a statutory employee, then the payor does have certain payroll tax obligations concerning the compensation paid to the worker (see ¶25,841). However, if the worker is not a common-law employee and does not perform in one of the special occupations, the payor is generally safe in treating the worker as an independent contractor.

☐ See ¶18,001 for details concerning the income tax withholding obligations of an employer.

☐ See ¶18,201 for details concerning FICA and FUTA obligations of an employer.

.05 Code Sec. 3121(d)(2).

.10 Rev. Rul. 87-41, 1987-1 CB 296.

.15 *R.W. Lickliss*, 67 TCM 2382, CCH Dec. 49,718(M), TC Memo. 1994-103.

.20 Rev. Rul. 87-41, 1987 CB 296.

.25 Code Sec. 3121(d)(3).

Traveling or City Salesperson

¶25,834 Traveling or City Salesperson. Individuals who cannot be classified as employees under the common-law rules will be treated as a statutory employees if they are full-time traveling or city salespersons, and (.05):

(1) have as their entire or principal activity the solicitation of orders for merchandise on behalf of their principal and transmit the orders to their principal;

(2) obtain their orders from wholesalers, retailers, contractors, operators of hotels or restaurants or other businesses whose primary function is the furnishing of food and/or lodging; and

(3) sell merchandise that is bought for resale or for use as supplies in their customer's business operations.

Full-time basis

Generally, a traveling or city salesperson will be presumed to meet the "principal business activity" test in any calendar quarter in which the individual devotes 80% or more of working time to the solicitation of orders for one principal from wholesalers or other specified customers. The orders must be for merchandise for resale or supplies of the requisite character (.10).

One principal

In order for a city or traveling salesperson to be treated as a statutory employee, the salesperson's entire or principal business activity must be devoted to the solicitation of orders for one principal. A multiple-line salesperson is generally not within this occupational group. However, if the salesperson solicits orders primarily for one principal, the salesperson will not be excluded from being classified as a statutory employee solely because of side-line activities on behalf of one or more persons. In this situation, the salesperson is treated as a statutory employee with regard to the services rendered on behalf of the principal and not a statutory employee with respect to the other services (.15).

> ***Example 1:*** Sam Jordan's principal business activity is the solicitation of orders from retail pharmacies on behalf of Zetmet Wholesale Drug Company. Jordan also occasionally solicits orders for drugs on behalf of two other drug companies, Alpha Inc. and Beta Inc. Assuming the other requirements are met, Jordan would be treated as a statutory employee with regard to his employment with Zetmet but not with respect to services for Alpha and Beta.

> ***Example 2:*** Assume the same facts as Example (1), except that Jordan's principal business activity is the solicitation of orders on the behalf of Zetmet, Alpha and Beta. Because he has more than one principal, Jordan cannot be considered as a statutory employee.

General requirements

In addition to the tests that are unique to traveling or city salespersons, these individuals are subject to the requirements that are generally imposed on all types of statutory employees (see ¶25,838).

.05 Code Sec. 3121(d)(3)(D).
.10 Rev. Rul. 55-31, 1955-1 CB 476.
.15 Reg. §31.3121(d)-1(d)(3)(iv)(b).

Life Insurance Salesperson

¶25,835 Life Insurance Salesperson. Full-time life insurance salespersons are statutory employees if they cannot be classified as employees under the common-law rules and if solicitation of life insurance or annuity contracts for one life insurance company is their entire or principal business activity (.05).

Full-time basis

Generally, the contract of employment reflects the intention of the salesperson and the company with regard to "full-time" activity. The intention of the salesperson and the company as shown by the contract and their mutual performance govern in determining whether or not an individual is a full-time or part-time salesperson. An "entire or principal business activity" may or may not be full time. Therefore, an individual may regularly work only a few hours each day and still qualify as a full-time life insurance salesperson.

Life insurance or annuity contracts

The salesperson's efforts must be devoted to the solicitation of life insurance or annuity contracts, or of such contracts and accident and health contracts. Occasional or incidental sales of other types of insurance will not have any effect on this requirement. However, the salesperson who is required to devote substantial efforts to selling applications for insurance contracts other than life insurance and annuity contracts (e.g., health and accident, fire, car, etc.) does not meet this requirement (.10).

General requirements

In addition to the tests that are unique to life insurance salespersons, such individuals are also subject to the requirements that are generally imposed on all types of statutory employees (see ¶25,838) (.15).

.05 Rev. Rul. 54-312, 1954-2 CB 327.
.10 Reg. §31.3121(d)-1(d)(3)(ii).
.15 Code Sec. 3121(d)(2)(B).

Agent or Commission Driver

¶25,836 Agent or Commission Driver. Agent drivers and commission drivers that are not employees under the common-law rules will be treated as statutory employees if such drivers distribute meat or meat products, vegetables or vegetable products, fruit or fruit products, bakery products, beverages (other than milk), or laundry or dry-cleaning services for the principal (.05).

Specific requirements

The driver may sell at wholesale or retail. The driver may operate from the driver's own truck or a truck belonging to the company for whom the driver works. The customers may be designated by the company or solicited by the driver (.10).

The driver may distribute other products if such additional products are incidental to the handling of the items specified above.

The driver must perform the services for the person who engages the services of the driver. If the driver buys and sells merchandise and sells it or furnishes services to the public as part of an independent business, the driver is not a statutory employee (.15).

General requirements

In addition to the requirements that are unique to agent-drivers and commission drivers, such individuals must have the general requirements that are applicable to all job classifications in order to be classified as statutory employees (see ¶25,838).

.05 Code Sec. 3121(d)(3)(A).
.10 Reg. §31.3121(d)-1(d)(3)(i).
.15 Rev. Rul. 75-269, 1975-2 CB 401.

Homeworkers

¶25,837 Homeworkers. Homeworkers who cannot be classified as employees under the common-law rules (see ¶25,833) will be classified as statutory employees if they (.05):

(1) work in accordance to specifications furnished by the person for whom the services are performed;

(2) work on material or goods furnished by the person for whom the work is performed; and

(3) return the finished product to the person for whom the services were performed or to another person designated by such person.

Included workers

Homeworkers include individuals who make quilts, gloves, clothing, or needle craft products. However, the term also was ruled to include an individual who did typing in her home under an oral agreement with a corporation (.10). The individual was contacted when work was available and was furnished with materials and specifications. Each assignment was a separate transaction and she was not guaranteed a minimum quota of work or compensation. She was not restricted from hiring helpers. Under these facts, she was held not to be an employee under the common-law rules but was a statutory employee for FICA purposes.

General requirements

If a homeworker is to be treated as a statutory employee, the individual must meet the general requirements that are imposed on all statutory employees (see ¶25,838).

.05 Code Sec. 3121(d)(3)(C). **.10** Rev. Rul. 64-280, 1964-2 CB 384.

General Requirements

¶25,838 General Requirements. Workers that are not employees under the common-law rules and that come within one of the four specified occupational groups (i.e., traveling or city salespersons, life insurance salespersons, agent or commission drivers, and homeworkers) will be treated as statutory employees, if such individuals satisfy the specific requirements that are discussed at the indicated paragraphs.

A worker may qualify as a statutory employee if, in addition to meeting the specific requirements for the particular occupation, all of the following general requirements are met (.05):

(1) the worker is a member of one of the designated occupational groups;

(2) it is understood from a service contract that the services will be substantially performed by the worker;

(3) the worker has no substantial investment in facilities for doing the work; and

(4) the services must be performed in a continuing relationship.

Service contract

The service contract under which the work is done may be oral or written. The contract must contemplate that the worker perform substantially all the work. The important thing is not whether the worker delegates part of the work to another but whether the worker has the authority under the contract to do so. Mutual intent of the parties governs (.10).

Substantial investment

Whether a substantial investment is made by the worker depends on the value of the worker's investment compared to the total investment, whether the facilities furnished are essential for the work or for the convenience of the worker, whether the worker purchasing or leasing space from the person for whom the work is performed, and on whether the facilities furnished by the worker are considerably more extensive than those usually furnished by other workers performing comparable services.

The term "facilities" includes such items as office furniture, fixtures, tools and machinery. The term does *not* include education, training or the worker's own vehicle (.15).

Continuing work relationship

A continuing work relationship exists if the work is regular or frequently recurring. A single job transaction, even though it covers a considerable period of time, is not generally considered as being performed in a continuing relationship (.20).

.05 Code Sec. 3121(d)(3).

.10 Reg. §31.3121(d)-1(d)(4)(ii).

.15 Reg. §31.3121(d)-1(d)(4)(iii).

.20 Reg. §31.3121(d)-1(d)(4)(iv).

Reporting of Income

¶25,839 Reporting of Income. Amounts paid to statutory employees must be reported on Form W-2. For 2004, payments made to the statutory employee are shown in Box 1 as "other compensation." Box 2, which normally would show the amount of income tax withheld, is left blank. In addition, the box labeled "statutory employee" in Box 13 must be checked.

In completing Form W-2, social security wages paid and social security tax withheld, and medicare wages paid and medicare tax withheld are shown in Box 3, Box 4, Box 5 and Box 6, respectively.

Employee's reporting of income

For 2004, statutory employees report their income on Line 7 of Form 1040 if they do not claim any business-related expenses. If a deduction for business-related expenses is claimed, statutory employees generally file Schedule C, "Profit or Loss From Business." The compensation shown in Box 1 of Form W-2 is reported on Line 1 of Schedule C, and the box labeled "statutory employee" is checked. If certain conditions are met, a statutory employee may use Schedule C-EZ, "Net Profit From Business" (see "Proper form," in ¶25,840, **Claiming Business Deductions**).

If an individual had self-employment income and statutory employee income, the separate incomes are not combined. Instead, two Schedules C or C-EZ are filed.

Claiming Business Deductions

¶25,840 Claiming Business Deductions. Statutory employees, unlike common-law employees are permitted to deduct their allowable business expenses directly from gross income (.05). Thus, these individuals are able to bypass the restriction that generally only permits employees to deduct their unreimbursed business expenses as miscellaneous itemized deductions on Schedule A of Form 1040, and then only to the extent the expenses exceed 2% of the employee's adjusted gross income.

> ***Example 1:*** Betty Winslow, a single individual, is employed as a salesperson. Because of the nature of her employment, she cannot be classified as a statutory employee. During 2004, her gross wages were $30,000 and she incurred $2,000 in unreimbursed employee business expenses. Assume the total of her itemized deductions, not including the unreimbursed business expenses, was $500. If Winslow filed on Schedule A, she would only be able to deduct $1,400 of her business expenses ($2,000 – $600 (2% of her adjusted gross income)). Thus her maximum total itemized deductions for 2004 would be $1,900 ($500 + $1,400). Because the standard deduction allowed to a single individual for 2004 is $4,850, it would not pay Winslow to itemize her deductions. As a result, she would not derive any tax benefit from her business expenses.

> ***Example 2:*** Assume the same facts as in Example (1), except that Winslow can be classified as a statutory employee. As a result, she is able to claim her $2,000 in business deductions as a direct offset to her wage income on either Schedule C

or C-EZ. In addition, she would still be able to claim the standard deduction of $4,750. If Winslow is in the 15% tax bracket, she will obtain a tax reduction of $300 ($2,000 × 15%) because she was able to claim her business expenses as a deduction from her gross income.

Proper form

Statutory employees generally use Schedule C to report their income and expenses. Alternatively, a statutory employee may use Schedule C-EZ to report business income and expenses. The following requirements must be satisfied for an individual to use Schedule C-EZ;

(1) business expenses must be $2,500 or less,

(2) the cash method of accounting must be used,

(3) the business did not have any inventory during the year,

(4) the business did not suffer a net loss for the year,

(5) the taxpayer has only one business as a sole proprietor,

(6) there were no employees during the year,

(7) there is no depreciation (amortization) amount to be claimed,

(8) there is no home office deduction to be claimed, and

(9) the business has no prior year unallowed passive activity losses (.05).

.05 Rev. Rul. 90-93, 1990-2 CB 33.

.05 Form 1040, Schedule C-EZ.

Employment Tax Obligation

¶25,841 Employment Tax Obligation. After making the determination that compensation has been paid to a statutory employee, the payor must determine its employment tax obligations. The following material is a summary of the payor's obligations.

Income tax withholding

The payor has no obligation to withhold income tax on wages paid to a statutory employee (.05).

Federal Insurance Contribution Act (FICA) taxes

Social security and Medicare taxes, however, must be withheld from the compensation paid to the statutory employee. The payor also has the obligation to pay its share of such taxes (.10).

Federal Unemployment Tax Act (FUTA) tax

Taxes under the Federal Unemployment Tax Act (FUTA) must be paid on compensation paid to (.15):

(1) traveling or city salespersons; and

(2) agent or commission drivers.

There is no FUTA obligation for compensation paid to:

(1) life insurance salespersons, and

(2) homeworkers.

.05 Code Sec. 3401(a).

.10 Code Sec. 3121(d).

.15 Code Sec. 3306(i).

Determining a Worker's Status

¶25,842 Determining a Worker's Status. In situations when the payor cannot determine the exact status of a worker (i.e., employee, statutory employee, or independent contractor), the IRS can be asked to make the determination. Workers can also ask the IRS to make a determination if they believe that they have not been classified correctly by a payor (.05).

Form SS-8

Form SS-8, "Determination of Employee Work Status for Purposes of Federal Employment Taxes and Income Tax Withholding," is used to request a determination from the IRS concerning the exact status of any individual. A determination made in the case of any one worker is applicable to the status of other workers of the same class, provided that the work situations of the other workers do not differ materially from the situation of the worker.

A Form SS-8 determination may be requested only in order to resolve a tax matter. The taxpayer requesting a determination must file an income tax return for the year, or years, under consideration before the IRS will issue a determination. Determination letters are not issued for proposed transactions or for hypothetical situations. The Form SS-8 determination process does not constitute an IRS examination of any federal income tax return.

.05 Rev. Proc. 2004-1, 2004-1 I.R.B. 1.

TIP RECIPIENTS AND PAYORS

Introduction

¶25,844 The obligation to make sure that tip income is correctly reported to the IRS and that the proper federal taxes are paid on such income falls on both the tipped employee and the employer. The tipped employee must report tip income to the employer who will in turn withhold the proper amount of federal income and employment taxes from the wages and other funds under the employer's control. The employer must also pay certain employment taxes on such income and must report such income and pay the withheld taxes to the government. After the year's end, the employer will provide the employee with an Form W-2 that reflects the tip income reported by the employee to the employer during the year, as well as other wages. The employee will then report the tip income to the government on the Form 1040 or other federal income tax form the employee files and may be required to pay any shortfall in taxes.

Both the tipped employee and the employer must take their obligations seriously, since they both may be subject to penalties imposed by the federal government for failing to meet their tip income reporting, withholding, or taxpaying obligations. The obligations imposed on employers and their employees as it relates to tip income are discussed separately.

Overview

¶25,845 Obligations of the tipped employee. Tipped employees have three main obligations for federal tax purposes. They must keep daily records of their tips, report their tips to their employer and the IRS, and pay taxes on the tips.

Tipped employees must pay income taxes on all tips, whether paid in cash or property. Tipped employees must pay Federal Insurance Contributions Act (FICA) taxes on their "cash" tips.

¶25,846 Obligations of the employer. All restaurants have three main obligations for federal tax purposes: withholding, reporting, and recordkeeping. Large food and beverage establishments have another obligation. They must often compute a hypothetical tip amount based on a percentage of their gross receipts and allocate this hypothetical tip amount among certain tipped employees.

A restaurant is obligated to withhold income and FICA taxes on the tip income reported by an employee. The restaurant must also pay Federal Unemployment Tax Act (FUTA) taxes and the employer's share of FICA taxes on reported tips. Although a large food and beverage restaurant will report a hypothetical tip amount to its employees and to the IRS, the restaurant will not withhold or pay taxes on this amount.

A restaurant must report to the IRS the amount of tips and wages paid to or allocated to its employees and must give the IRS the withheld taxes. The restaurant also must report such amounts to the employees individually.

A restaurant must keep records of the tips and wages reported by or allocated to its employees.

¶25,847 Tips and other terms defined. Traditionally, tips have been sums of money given for good service. The basic characteristic of a tip is that it is freely given by a customer in recognition of some service performed for him. Thus, mandatory service charges imposed by a restaurant are not tips, even though the charges are paid over to a server or other employees and are counted as wages by the employer and the receiving employees (.10). On the other hand, tips freely determined by a customer, added to a customer's credit card bill, and later paid over to the server are considered to be tips.

Tips may be paid by a customer in cash or by check, in the form of property, such as tickets to a show, or in the form of a "tip" determined by a customer and charged to a credit card. Furthermore, a tip received by a server directly may be shared with other "indirectly tipped" employees who help the server, such as busboys and bartenders, in a tip pool or similar arrangement. Finally, a portion of a large food and beverage restaurant's gross receipts may be allocated to the waitstaff and other employees as a tip on that employee's tax forms, even though the restaurant does not actually pay such amount to the employee.

Not all tips are alike for tax purposes. All tips are subject to income taxes, that is, the taxes that are reported on an Form 1040 or similar income tax return. Most tips are also subject to FICA taxes, that is, the taxes that fund Social Security and similar governmental benefits. For example, the value of a tip given to an employee in the form of "property," such as tickets to a show, are includible in the employee's income and subject to income taxes on the Form 1040, but the value of the tickets are not subject to FICA taxes for either the employer or the tipped employee.

Other tip-related terms

The IRS places tipped employees into one of two categories for certain purposes, directly tipped employees or indirectly tipped employees (.20). A directly tipped employee is defined by the IRS as an employee who receive tips from the customer directly, such as waiters. According to the IRS, an indirectly tipped employee is an employee who receives tips from directly tipped employees through either tip pooling or tip splitting. For example, the bartender of a service bar is only indirectly tipped.

Other examples of indirectly tipped employees include employees who bus tables, service bartenders, and cooks. Employees, such as maître d's, who receive tips directly from customers and indirectly through tip splitting or pooling, are treated as directly tipped employees.

.10 IRS Publication 531, Reporting Tip Income.

.20 Audit Technique Guide For Bars And Restaurants, November, 2002, CCH IRS Positions, ¶201,900.

Employee Obligations

¶25,849 Recording tips on a daily basis. A tipped employee must keep a daily record or other documentation to prove the amount of tip income reported on the income tax return (.10).

The daily record must show the following: (1) name and address, (2) employer's name, and (3) the establishment's name.

A tipped employee must also show for each workday: (1) the amount of cash tips received directly from customers or from other employees, (2) tips from credit card charge customers when paid to the tipped employee by the employer, (3) the amount of tips the tipped employee paid out to other employees through tip splitting, tip sharing, or similar arrangements, and (4) the names of the other employees to whom the tips were paid.

Entries must be made in the daily record on or near the date the tips are received. The records should also show the date each entry is made.

Daily records

A tipped employee can use Form 4070A, Employee's Daily Record of Tips, to record tips. If a tipped employee does not keep a daily record of tips, then other documentation of the tip income must be maintained. This other documentation must be as credible and reliable as a daily record. The records must show: (1) tips added to checks by customers and paid over to the tipped employee, or (2) amounts paid for food or beverages on which the tipped employee generally would receive a tip.

Examples of other documentary records are copies of: (1) restaurant bills, (2) credit card charges, or (3) charges under any other arrangement containing amounts added by customers as tips.

.10 Reg. §31.6053-4.

¶25,850 Reporting tip income to an employer. For each calendar month during which an employee receives $20 or more in tips, the employee must give the employer a statement (or statements) of cash and charge tips by the tenth day of the month after the month in which the tips are received (.10). The employee may give the employer a written statement or may transmit a statement to the employer electronically (.11). If the tenth day is a Saturday, Sunday, or legal holiday, the employee can report the tips by the next business day. Form 4070, "Employee's Report of Tips to Employer," is available for this purpose.

Tips totaling less than $20 received by an employee during a single calendar month while working for any one employer are not required to be reported to the employer. If an employee works for more than one employer during a month and receives less than $20 in tips while working for each employer, no tips are required to be reported to any of the employers. Although these tips are not wages subject to FICA taxes, they do represent income subject to federal income taxes on the employee's tax return.

Reported tips should include only tips received by the employee for himself and should be based on the daily record of tips the employee maintains. Thus, a directly tipped employee, such as a server, does not have to include any tips paid out to other "indirectly tipped" employees, such as a service bartender. The "indirectly tipped" employee must report the tips received from the directly tipped employee on his or her own report to the employer. Similarly, where employees practice tip-splitting among themselves, each employee in a tip pool is required to report his share to his employer.

The value of tips received in the form of property, such as tickets to a show, are not reported to the employer. However, the value of tips paid in property must be included by the employee on the employee's Form 1040 or other federal income tax return.

.10 Rev. Rul. 95-7, 1995-1 CB 185.

.11 Reg. §1.6053-1(b).

¶25,851 Penalty for failure to report tips. Tipped employees who fail to properly report tips to their employers are subject to a penalty for this failure (.12). An employee who fails to properly report tips to an employer is subject to a penalty equal to 50 percent of the employee portion of the FICA taxes on those tips, unless the employee attaches to the employee's Form 1040 a satisfactory explanation showing that the failure was due to reasonable cause and not due to willful neglect. The explanation must be made in the form of a written statement containing a declaration that it is made under the penalties of perjury and setting forth all the facts alleged as a reasonable cause.

.12 Code Sec. 6053(a), Code Sec. 6652(b) and Rev. Rul. 95-7, 1995-1 CB 185.

¶25,852 Payment of income and other taxes on tips. All tips, in whatever form, earned and kept by the tipped employee are subject to federal income taxes, but only "cash tips" are subject to employment taxes (.13). "Cash tips" include checks and other monetary media of exchange. Cash tips also include amounts added to a charged check by the customer which are then paid over to the employee by the management.

Income taxes

All tips received by any tipped employee are taxable income and are subject to federal income tax. The tipped employee must include in gross income all tips received directly from customers, tips from charge customers that are paid by the employer, and the employee's share of any tips received under a tip-splitting arrangement. The value of tips received in the form of property, such as tickets to a show, is also included in taxable income.

Tips that the employee reported to the employer will be included on his or her Form W-2 that is used to compute income taxes on Form 1040 or a similar form. Unreported tips will not be included on the Form W-2, but must be included with other wage, tip, and similar income reported on Form 1040 or an equivalent form filed with the IRS. Unreported tips could include any tips that the tipped employee forgot to include in the tip report submitted to the employer, as well as tips that were not required to be reported to the employer, such as tips paid in cash or its equivalent where the total tips for the month were less than $20, or tips paid in the form of property, such as the value of tickets to a show left as a tip.

Employment taxes

Cash tips of $20 or more that are received in a month while working for any one employer are subject to withholding of income tax, social security or railroad retirement tax, and Medicare tax (.20).

Tips paid in a medium other than cash or cash equivalent (e.g., checks and tips charged on a credit card) and tips amounting to less than $20 in a month are not considered wages for employment tax purposes, so they are not subject to employment taxes (.30). Consequently, the value of noncash tips, such as tickets to a show, are not counted as tips or wages for social security tax purposes, even though they are counted as income subject to federal income tax.

How taxes are paid to the IRS

Income, social security or railroad retirement tax, and Medicare tax on the cash tips should be withheld from the employee's paycheck if the tipped employee makes a timely report to the employer of his or her cash tips and the employer has sufficient funds from which to withhold the taxes (.40). Funds include the employee's regular wages and funds that the employee pays over to the employer to cover the taxes that are to be withheld. The employer deposits the taxes on the reported tip income with the IRS in the same manner as the taxes on the employee's regular wages are deposited. The employer will also reflect all taxes withheld from the employee on the Form W-2 that it the employer provides to the employee.

Effects of underreporting or underwithholding. If an employee fails to properly report tips to his or her employer, the proper amount of FICA tax will not be withheld from his or her paycheck (.50). In certain cases where the tip income is properly reported, the proper amount of FICA taxes will not have been withheld from the tipped employee's paycheck because the tipped employee did not have a sufficient amount of other wages to cover the total amount of all taxes to be withheld from the paycheck and did not contribute funds to the employer to cover this shortfall. In either case, the employee will have to pay his share of FICA taxes on such tip income himself.

The employee pays his portion of the FICA taxes on unreported tip income by completing Form 4137, "Social Security Tax on Unreported Tip Income," and filing it with Form 1040. Because unreported tips received by the employee are deemed to be paid to the employee when actually received by the employee, the employee must use the social security and Medicare rates and contribution bases applicable to the year in which the tips were actually received. In contrast, reported tips received by the employee are deemed to be paid to the employee when they are reported to the employer, assuming that they are timely reported to the employer by the tenth of the month following receipt.

In the case of income taxes, even the tipped employee who properly reports tip income to an employer and pays sufficient funds to the employer to cover a tax shortfall may face an unexpected income tax liability at the year's end, if tip income for any given month did not total $20 or if the employee received tips in the form of property. This is because the $20 tip amount triggers the reporting of tip income to the employer and also the employer's withholding of income tax on those tips. When less than $20 in tips are earned in a particular month or tips of property have been received, income taxes will still be owed on those tips, but the income taxes will not have been withheld from the tipped employee's paycheck. Also, tipped employees who filed Form W-4, "Employee's Withholding Allowance Certificate," with their employer claiming an exemption from income tax withholding will have to pay tax on wages and tips from which no income tax was withheld. When insufficient taxes are withheld from an employee and the employee does not pay estimated taxes, the employee will not only have to pay the tax deficiency, but may also be liable for an estimated tax penalty.

Allocated tips

Every large food or beverage establishment must report to the IRS any tips allocated to its employees (.60). Generally, tips must be allocated to directly tipped employees when the total tips reported to an employer by employees are less than 8 percent of the establishment's food and beverage sales. The employer will report tips allocated to each directly tipped employee on the employee's Form W-2, Box 8, separately from wages and reported tips.

A directly tipped employee that does not have adequate records of actual tips will have to include the allocated tips shown on Forms W-2 as additional tip income on the income tax return Form 1040 or the equivalent form. Also, where adequate tip income records are not kept, the allocated tips will be subject to FICA taxes and will have to be reported on Form 4137. The employer will not have withheld income or FICA taxes on allocated tips. If the employee maintains adequate records, tip income is reported in accordance with those records, and the employer's allocation of tips will have no effect on the employee's taxes.

Social security or railroad retirement benefits

Tips and other pay are used to determine the amount of social security or railroad retirement benefits a tipped employee or the tipped employee's family may receive if the tipped employee retires, becomes disabled, or dies (.70). Also, tip income will be considered in determining eligibility for Medicare benefits at age 65 or if the tipped employee becomes disabled. Future benefits can be figured correctly only if the Social Security Administration (SSA) has correct information.

.13 Code Sec. 61, Code Sec. 3121(a)(12)(A), and Code Sec. 3401(a).

.20 Code Sec. 3121(a)(12)(A), and Code Sec. 3401(a).

.30 Reg. §31.3401(a)(16)-1.

.40 Rev. Rul. 95-7, 1995-1 CB 185.

.50 Rev. Rul. 95-7, 1995-1 CB 185.

.60 Code Sec. 6053(c), Reg. §31.6053-3.

.70 IRS Pub. 531, Reporting Tip Income.

Employer Obligations

¶25,854 General tip reporting rules. Employers are required to submit certain employment tax information returns and statements for employees each year. For example, Form W-2, Wage and Tax Statement, is required to be filed annually (.10). Tip income reported to the employer by the employee will be reflected on the Form W-2.

In addition to the above statements to employees, an employer must file quarterly and annual wage information statements with the IRS. Form 941, "Employer's Quarterly Federal Tax Return," is filed to report the quarterly total of wages, tips, and other compensation paid, tax deposits made, and income and FICA taxes withheld (.15). Form 940, "Employer's Annual Federal Unemployment (FUTA) Tax Return," or Form 940-EZ, must also be filed to report FUTA liabilities. In general, most non-agricultural and non-household employers must file Form 940 if wages of $1,500 or more were paid in any calendar quarter, or the employer had one or more employees for some part of a day in any 20 different weeks (.30).

.10 Reg. §31.6051-1.

.15 Reg. §31.6011(a)-4.

.30 Reg. §31.6011(a)-3, and Instructions to Form 940, Employer's Annual Federal Unemployment (FUTA) Tax Return.

¶25,855 Special TEFRA reporting rules for large food and beverage establishments Employers at large food and beverage establishments are required to file Form 8027, "Employer's Annual Information Return of Tip Income and Allocated Tips," with the IRS indicating the amount of gross receipts from food and beverage operations, total charge tips, total charge receipts on which there were charged tips, total amount of service charges of less than 10 percent paid as wages to employees, total tips reported by employees, and gross receipts from food or beverage operations (.10). Also, in those establishments where employees report to their employer aggregate tips of less than 8 percent of gross receipts, the employer must allocate to the directly tipped employees the difference between 8 percent of gross receipts and the reported tips and must report the total allocated tips to the IRS on Form 8027. A directly tipped employee's allocation will appear in Box 8 on the employee's Form W-2. The employer need not withhold taxes on the amount allocated or pay FICA or FUTA taxes on such amount.

Affected establishments

A large food or beverage establishment is one that provides food or beverages for consumption on the premises, where tipping is customary, and where there are normally more than 10 employees on a typical business day during the preceding year. Generally, tipping is not customary if 95 percent of the total sales are carryout sales or sales with a service charge of 10 percent or more. Also, tipping is generally not considered customary for a cafeteria style operation; however, if in fact, tipping is customary in a particular cafeteria style operation, then such operation may be a "large food and beverage establishment" (.30).

An employer that owns more than one establishment must file Form 8027 for each one. Also, an employer that is required to report for more than one establishment must complete and attach Form 8027-T, "Transmittal of Employer's Annual Information Return of Tip Income and Allocated Tips," to the Forms 8027. An employer that files 250 or more Forms 8027 must file the returns on magnetic media.

A person who owns 50 percent or more in value of the stock of a corporation that runs the establishment is not considered an employee when determining whether the establishment normally employs more than 10 individuals. Also, the "more than 10 employees" filing trigger is based on the total of all employees at the establishment, not just the number of directly tipped employees.

A new large food and beverage establishment must file Form 8027 if, during any two consecutive calendar months, the average number of hours worked each business day by all employees is more than 80 hours. To figure the average number of employee hours worked each business day during a month, divide the total hours all employees worked during the month by the number of days the establishment was open for business. After the test is met for two consecutive months, a return covering the rest of the year must be filed, beginning with the next payroll period.

Allocating tips

If the total tips reported to the employer during any payroll period are less than 8 percent (or the approved lower rate, as discussed below) of the establishment's gross receipts for that period, then the employer must allocate the difference between the total tips reported by employees and 8 percent (or the lower rate) of the gross receipts, other than nonallocable receipts, to the directly tipped employees.

Gross receipts include all receipts other than "nonallocable receipts." It may include receipts from cash sales, charge receipts, charges to a hotel room, and the retail value of complimentary food or beverages served to customers. State or local taxes are not included in gross receipts. Also excluded from gross receipts are charged tips shown on charge receipts unless cash sales are reduced by the amount of those tips paid in cash to employees.

Nonallocable receipts are receipts for carryout sales and receipts with a service charge added of 10 percent or more.

Lowering the allocation rate. An establishment, or a majority of the employees, may request a lower allocation rate, but not lower than 2 percent. A petition for a lower rate must clearly demonstrate that a rate less than 8 percent should apply and must include certain required information.

The request for a lower allocation rate must contain a statement indicating that the petition is signed under penalty of perjury and it must be signed by a responsible person who is authorized to make and sign a return, statement, or other document. The IRS charges a user fee to process this request.

Allocation methods. The tips may be allocated by one of three methods: (1) hours worked; (2) gross receipts; or (3) good-faith agreement. A good-faith agreement is a written agreement between the establishment and at least two-thirds of the employees of each occupational category of employees who receive tips (e.g., waiters, waitresses, employees who bus tables, and maître d's) working in the establishment when the agreement is adopted. The agreement must:

(1) provide for an allocation of the difference between total tips reported and 8 percent of gross receipts among employees who receive tips that approximates the actual distribution of tip income among the employees;

(2) be effective the first day of a payroll period that begins after the date the agreement is adopted, but no later than January 1 of the next year;

(3) be adopted when there are employees in each occupational category who would be affected by the agreement; and

(4) allow for revocation by a written agreement adopted by at least two-thirds of the employees in occupational categories affected by the agreement when it is revoked. The revocation is effective only at the beginning of a payroll period.

If no good-faith agreement applies to the payroll period, in most cases the establishment must allocate the difference between total tips reported and 8 percent of gross receipts by using the following steps of the "gross receipts method":

(1) Multiply the establishment's gross receipts (other than nonallocable receipts) for the payroll period by 8 percent, or the lower rate accepted by the IRS;

(2) Subtract from the amount figured in step (1), the total amount of tips reported by employees who were tipped indirectly for the payroll period to determine the directly tipped employees' total share of 8 percent (or the lower rate) of the gross receipts of the establishment. Indirectly tipped employees do not receive tips directly from customers;

(3) For each employee who is tipped directly, multiply the result in step (2) by a fraction, the numerator (top number) of which is the amount of the establishment's gross receipts attributable to the employee, and the denominator (bottom number) of which is the gross receipts attributable to all directly tipped employees so as to determine each directly tipped employee's share of 8 percent (or the lower rate) of the gross receipts for the payroll period;

(4) From each directly tipped employee's share of 8 percent or the lower rate of the gross receipts figured in step (3), subtract the tips the employee reported for the payroll period to determine each directly tipped employee's shortfall (if any) for the period;

(5) From the amount figured in step (1), subtract the total tips reported by both directly and indirectly tipped employees to determine the amount that has to be allocated among the directly tipped employees who had a shortfall for the payroll period as figured in step (4); and

(6) For each directly tipped employee who had a shortfall for the period as figured in step (4), multiply the amount in step (5) by a fraction, the numerator of which is the employee's shortfall (figured in step (4)), and the denominator of which is the total shortfall of all directly tipped employees, in order to determine the amount of allocated tips for each directly tipped employee.

Under the "hours worked" method of allocation, which establishments that employ fewer than the equivalent of 25 full-time employees (both tipped and nontipped employees) during a payroll period may use to allocate tips, the establishment must follow the steps described above for the gross receipts method except that for the fraction in step (3) of the gross receipts method, substitute one in which the numerator (top number) is the number of hours worked by each employee who is tipped directly, and the denominator (bottom number) is the total number of hours worked by all employees who are directly tipped for the payroll period.

Reporting allocated amounts

In addition to reporting allocated tip amounts to the IRS on Form 8027, an employer must give each employee who has been allocated tips a Form W-2 that shows the allocated amount in Box 8. The form must be furnished to the employee by January 31 of the following year. If employment ends before the end of the year and the employee asks for the Form W-2, a tip allocation is not required on the early Form W-2. However, the employer may include on the early Form W-2 the employee's actual tip allocation or a good-faith estimate of the allocation. A good-faith estimate is signified by writing "estimate" next to the allocated amount in Box 8 of the Form W-2.

If no allocation was shown on the early Form W-2 or if the estimated allocation on the early form differs from the actual amount by more than 5 percent, the employer must give the employee Form W-2c, "Statement of Corrected Income and Tax Amounts," during January of the next year.

If the employer allocates tips among employees by the methods described above, it will not be liable to any employee if any amount is improperly allocated. However, if the allocation shown on the employee's Form W-2 differs from the correct allocation by more than 5 percent, the employer must adjust that employee's allocation and must review the allocable amount of all other employees in the same establishment to assure that the error did not distort any other employee's share by more than 5 percent. Form W-2c is used to report the corrected allocation.

Higher penalty for incorrect Form 8027

Penalties apply to a failure to file correct information returns, and higher penalties apply to an intentional failure (.50).

> ***Example 1:*** Form 8027 requires certain large food and beverage establishments to report certain information with respect to tips. The form requires (among other things) that the establishment report its gross receipts from food and beverage operations. Adam's Apple Restaurant, in intentional disregard of the information reporting requirement, reported gross receipts of $1,000,000, when the correct amount was $1,500,000. The significance of the gross receipts reporting requirement is that Code Sec. 6053(c)(3)(A) requires an establishment to allocate as tips among its employees the excess of 8 percent of its gross receipts over the aggregate amount reported by employees to the establishment as tips under Code Sec. 6053(a). Adam's Apple Restaurant's misstatement of its gross receipts caused Adam's Apple Restaurant to show $80,000 on the Form 8027 as 8 percent of its gross receipts, rather than the correct amount of $120,000. Adam's Apple Restaurant correctly reported the amount of tips reported to it by employees under section 6053(a) as $80,000. Thus Adam's Apple Restaurant reported the excess of 8 percent of its gross receipts over tips reported to it as zero, rather than as the correct amount of $40,000. The requirement of reporting gross receipts is considered merely a step in the computation of the excess of 8 percent of gross receipts over tips reported to Adam's Apple Restaurant under section 6053(a), so that the penalty for intentional disregard will be $4,000 (i.e., 10 percent of the difference between the $40,000 required to be reported as the excess of 8 percent of gross receipts over tips reported under Code Sec. 6053(a), and the zero amount actually reported).

A failure is due to intentional disregard if it is a knowing or willful: (1) failure to timely file, or (2) failure to include correct information. Whether a person knowingly or willfully fails to file timely or fails to include correct information is determined on the basis of all the facts and circumstances in the particular case. The facts and circumstances that are considered in determining whether a failure is due to intentional disregard include, but are not limited to (1) whether the failure to file timely or the failure to include correct information is part of a pattern of conduct by the person who filed the return of repeatedly failing to file timely or repeatedly failing to include correct information; (2) whether correction was promptly made upon discovery of the failure; (3) whether the filer corrects a failure to file or a failure to include correct information within 30 days after the date of any written request from the Internal Revenue Service to file or to correct; and (4) whether the amount of the information reporting penalties is less than the cost of complying with the requirement to file timely or to include correct information on an information return.

.10 Code Sec. 6053 and Reg. §31.6053-3.

.30 IRS Technical Advice Memorandum 9834001, 3-19-98, CCH IRS Letter Rulings Reports.

.50 Reg. §301.6721-1; Rev. Proc. 2000-49, 2000-2 CB 491.

¶25,856 Recordkeeping obligations. All employers who withhold federal income tax must keep records of all remuneration paid to, including tips reported by, such employees. Non-cash tips and cash tips of less than $20 for any calendar month do not have to be reflected in the employer's records (.10). There is no particular form required for keeping the records. However, the records must be kept in a manner that will enable the IRS to ascertain whether any tax liability has been incurred and, if so, the extent of that liability.

Current regulations allow employers to establish electronic systems for their tipped employees to use in reporting tips to the employer (.50). The regulations also allow current employee substantiation requirements to be satisfied when using electronic tip reporting.

The regulations do not prescribe a particular form for employees to use in reporting tips, although the employee can use Form 4070, Employee's Report of Tips to Employer. Under the rules, an employer could adopt a system under which some or all of its tipped employees would furnish their tip statements electronically. The employer may select the type or types of electronic systems, such as telephone or computer, to be used by its employees. The system must, however, ensure that the information received is the information the employee transmitted and document all occasions of access that result in the transmission. Upon request, the employer must provide the IRS with a hard copy of the electronic statement if there is an examination. An electronic tip statement must contain exactly the same information required on a paper tip statement and must contain the employee's electronic signature.

An employee must maintain sufficient evidence to establish the amount of tip income received during a tax year, such as a daily record or other evidence, such as documentary evidence, that is as credible and reliable as a daily record. Form 4070A, Employee's Daily Record of Tips, is sufficient evidence of tip income under the substantiation requirements. The regulations provide that an electronic system maintained by the employer that collects substantially similar information as Form 4070A may be used to maintain the daily record if the employee receives and maintains a paper copy of the daily record.

Records are to be retained as long as they may become material in the determination of tax and must be available for inspection by the IRS. As a practical rule, however, employment tax records must be kept for at least four years after the due date of the tax for the return period or the date the tax is paid, whichever is later. Records relating to large food and beverage establishment tip allocations must be kept for at least three years from the due date of the return or statement to which they pertain.

.10 Reg. §31.6001-5.

.50 Reg. §31.6053-1 and Reg. §31.6053-4, as amended by Treasury Decision 8910, 12-12-2000.

¶25,857 Penalties for recordkeeping failures. There are no specific penalties for the failure to maintain adequate employment tax records for the period required. However, the burden of proof is on the taxpayer in disputes with the IRS. Thus, an employer may lose the dispute if its records are not adequate to support its position.

¶25,858 Withholding and payment of employment taxes. An employer is required to withhold income and the employee's share of FICA taxes on tips reported to the employer by tipped employees from wages and other employee funds under the employer's control. The employer is also subject to FUTA taxes and the employer's share of FICA taxes on reported tips. As for unreported or underreported tips, the employer is required to pay its share of FICA taxes on such tips after it receives an IRS "notice and demand" for its share of FICA taxes on such tip income. This notice and demand is also known as a "notice and demand under Sec. 3121(q)."

Tips as wages

For income, FICA, and FUTA tax purposes, wages are generally defined as all remuneration for services performed by an employee for an employer, with certain exceptions (.10). Tips received by an employee in the course of the employee's employment are considered remuneration for employment, or wages, for income, FICA, and FUTA tax purposes and are deemed to have been paid by the employer for purposes of computing the employer portion of the FICA taxes. However, tips paid in any medium other than cash or its equivalent are not subject to employment taxes or income tax withholding. Also excluded from employment tax liability and income tax withholding are tips where the employee receives less than $20 in cash tips in a calendar month.

When deemed paid. Tip remuneration is deemed to be paid by the employer when a written statement including the tips is furnished to the employer by the employee (.20). However, if the employee either did not furnish the statement or if the statement furnished was inaccurate or incomplete, in determining the employer's liability for FICA on those tips, the remuneration is deemed to be paid on the date on which notice and demand for the taxes is made to the employer by the IRS. In situations in which the employer requires all tips to be turned over to the employer by the employees, and the employer, in turn, distributes the tips among all the employees, the tips are wages when paid by the employer.

Employee's tip report

Every employee who, in the course of the employee's employment by an employer, receives in any calendar month tips that are wages must report all those tips in one or more written statements furnished to the employer on or before the tenth day of the following month (.30). The employee may usually furnish the statement on a Form 4070.

The employer withholds and deposits income and FICA taxes on tips reported to the employer by the employee from the employee's regular wages when the tips are reported and pays both employer and employee portions of the FICA tax and the withheld income tax to the IRS in the same manner as the tax on the employee's regular wages.

Withholding on reported tips

An employer must collect income tax, employee social security tax, and employee Medicare tax on the amount of tips reported by the employee (.40). The employer can collect these taxes from the employee's wages and other funds the employee makes available. The employer must stop collecting the employee social security tax when the employee's wages and tips reach $90,000 in 2005, $87,900 in 2004, $87,000 in 2003 and $84,900 in 2002 but must continue to collect the income and employee Medicare taxes for the whole year on all wages and tips.

Priorities have been established for the application of the employee's wages to the taxes that must be withheld on reported tip income (.50). From the employee's regular wages, exclusive of tip income, the employer must first satisfy the social security/Medicare tax and then the Federal income tax withholding imposed on this regular wage. Then, the social security/Medicare tax imposed on the amount of reported tip income must be satisfied. Next, the Federal income tax withholding on the amount of the reported tip income must be satisfied. After this, any state or local taxes, union dues, garnishments, and similar deductions are to be satisfied, in that order, if possible. Finally, the remainder of the wage, if any, is to be paid to the employee.

An employer is responsible for the employer social security tax on wages and tips until the wages (including tips) reach the limit. The employer is responsible for the employer Medicare tax for the whole year on all wages and tips.

Form 941, "Employer's Quarterly Federal Tax Return," is filed to report withholding on tips. Generally, if, by the tenth of the month after the month an employer received an employee's report on tips, the employer doesn't have enough employee funds available to deduct the employee tax, it no longer has to collect it. The period is extended to 30 days after the end of the calendar year, if the employer withholds employee FICA based on an estimate of the amount of employee tips. Any uncollected social security and Medicare taxes are shown on Form W-2, on Form 941, and as an adjustment on Form 941.

A special rule allows employers at their discretion to withhold employee FICA tax, based on an estimate of the amount of employee tips (.60). Such tax would be deducted from the employee's wages other than tips, but including any amounts paid by the tipped employee to the employer within the year for payment of the employee's share of the FICA tax.

Tax on unreported tips

If an employee fails to report tips to his employer, the employer is liable for only the employer portion of the FICA taxes, and the employee is liable for only the employee portion of the FICA taxes on the tips. The employer is not liable for its portion of the FICA taxes on those unreported tips until notice and demand for the taxes is made to the employer by the IRS.

No specific form or procedure is prescribed for a notice and demand made for purposes of collecting the employer's share of FICA taxes on unreported tips. Notice and demand is made by the IRS when it advises the employer in writing of the amount of tips received by an employee (or employees) who failed to report or underreported tips to the employer. Although no specific form is prescribed, a document will constitute notice and demand if it: (1) includes the words "notice and demand" and "Section 3121(q)," (2) states the amount of tips received by the employee (or employees), and (3) states the period to which the tips relate. However, such a document will not constitute notice and demand if it states that it is not a notice and demand.

After notice and demand is made, the employer reports the liability by making an adjustment for FICA taxes on the employer's Form 941, "Employer's Quarterly Federal Tax Return," for the calendar quarter in which notice and demand is made, and writing "3121(q)" next to the line for adjustments of social security and Medicare taxes.

To compute its liability on unreported tips after notice and demand is made, the employer must use the social security and Medicare rates and contribution bases applicable to the year in which the tips were actually received by the employee.

The IRS generally must assess the employer FICA taxes on the unreported tips within three years after April 15 of the calendar year following the year in which the notice and demand is made. Also, the employer is not subject to interest on the tax liability if the employer pays the tax on or before the due date of the Form 941 for the quarter during which notice and demand is made.

The employer is required to deposit tax due on the unreported tips after receipt of notice and demand referring to Section 3121(q). For purposes of applying the deposit rules, the amount of employer FICA taxes attributable to the amount of tips received by the employee (or employees), as shown on the Section 3121(q) notice and demand, is treated as employment taxes accumulated by the employer on the date of the Section 3121(q) notice and demand.

Notice and demand based on employer examination

The IRS asserts that it is entitled to base a "Section 3121(q) notice and demand" on the employment tax deficiency that it determines as a result of an examination of only the employer's tax returns. A few recent U.S. District court cases had indicated that the IRS must instead examine the returns of all affected employee's and determine their tax deficiencies before it prepares a "Section 3121(q) notice and demand" that is directed to the employer (.70). Nevertheless, the IRS position was vindicated by the U.S. Court of Appeals for the Eleventh Circuit, by the Federal Claims Court, an Illinois District Court, and finally by the United States

Supreme Court, each of which held that the IRS may assess a restaurant for an employment tax deficiency on unreported tips without first auditing or assessing its workers (.80).

.10 Rev. Rul. 95-7, 1995-1 CB 185.

.20 Rev. Rul. 95-7, 1995-1 CB 185.

.30 Code Sec. 6053.

.40 IRS Publication 15, Circular E, Employer's Tax Guide.

.50 Reg. §31.3402(k)-1(c), and IRS Publication 531, Reporting Tip Income.

.60 Code Sec. 3102(c)(3).

.70 *The Bubble Room, Inc.*, CtClm, 96-2 USTC ¶50,550; *Morrison Restaurants, Inc.*, DC-Ala., 96-1 USTC ¶50,202.

.80 *Morrison Restaurants, Inc.*, CA-11, 97-2 USTC ¶50,598, vac'g and rem'g DC Ala., 96-1 USTC ¶50,202. *The Bubble Room, Inc,*, CA-FC, 98-2 USTC ¶50,799; rev'g FedCl, 96-2 USTC ¶50,550; *330 West Hubbard Restaurant Corporation*, CA-7, 2000-1 USTC ¶50,225, aff'g DC-Il., 99-1 USTC ¶50,107; *Quietwater Entertainment*, unpublished opinion, CA-11, 2000-2 USTC ¶50,540, rev'g and rem'g DC-Fla., 99-2 USTC ¶50,695; *Fior D'Italia, Inc.*, SCt., 2002-1 USTC ¶50,459.

¶25,859 Credits for employers. An employer can claim a credit against the amount of the minimum wage that is required to be paid to a tipped employee, based on a portion of the tips received by the employee (.10). Also, the employer can claim a credit against its income tax liability, based on a portion of its share of FICA tax liability that results from reported tips (.20).

Minimum wage credit

Tipped employees are subject to the same minimum wage rates as non-tipped employees. However, their employers are singled out for special treatment that permits them to take a wage rate credit for tips received by tipped employees from customers (.20).

Under the Small Business Job Protection Act, the cash wage paid by an employer to a tipped employee must total at least $2.13 per hour. The remainder of the minimum wage of $5.15 per hour may be treated as coming from tips. Thus, now more than half of the minimum wage obligation can be treated as satisfied though tip income earned by the employee.

If a tipped employee's hourly tip earnings (averaged weekly) added to the hourly wage do not equal the minimum wage, the employer is responsible for paying the balance.

For purposes of this "minimum wage" tip credit, a tipped employee is one who regularly receives more than $30 a month in tips.

Any tips received by the employee in excess of the permissible tip credit are not considered remuneration for employment for purposes of the minimum wage laws, and need not be included in computing the employee's regular rate for overtime pay purposes. A tip credit may be taken only for hours worked by the employee in an occupation in which he qualifies as a "tipped employee."

In general, only tips actually received by employees as money that belongs to them that they may use as they choose, free of any control by the employer, may be counted in determining whether the employees qualify as "tipped employees" and in applying the statutory provisions that govern wage credits for tips. Required payments for services rendered or mandatory service charges imposed on customers by the employer under a contract are not tips for purposes of this "minimum wage" tip credit, but cash tips and amounts transferred by the employer to the employee pursuant to directions from credit customers who designate amounts to be added to their bills as tips, such as when paying by credit card, are tips for this purpose. Special gifts in forms other than money or its equivalent as described above, such as theater tickets, passes, or merchandise, are not counted as tips.

Although the tip credit may not be used unless the tips received are retained by the employee, this requirement is not intended to bar the pooling of tips among employees who "customarily and regularly" receive tips, such as waiters, waitresses, countermen, busboys, service bartenders, and the like. Both the amounts retained by the waiters and those given the busboys are considered the tips of the individuals who retain them. Employees who share in tips are tipped employees for this "minimum wage" credit if they receive more than $30 a month in tips from the pool.

Distinguishable from pooling arrangements under which all tips are merely split or redistributed among employees are arrangements where employees must credit or turn over their tips to the employer as part of the employer's gross receipts. The "minimum wage" tip credit does not apply to these arrangements and the employer must pay such employees the full minimum hourly wage. However, the pooled sums may, after receipt by the employer, be used by him in their entirety to satisfy the full minimum hourly wage requirement.

Income tax credit for FICA tax payment

Food or beverage establishments may take a business tax credit against their income tax liability for the employer's share of the FICA tax obligation attributable to certain tips in excess of those treated as employer-provided wages (tip credit) under the Fair Labor Standards Act (FLSA).

The employer social security and Medicare taxes on those tips that are used to meet the federal minimum wage rate are not taken into account in computing this credit (.30). For example, an employee worked 100 hours and reported $300 in tips for January 2004. The worker received $415 in wages (excluding tips) at the rate of $3.25 an hour. Because the Federal minimum wage rate at that time was $5.15 an hour, the employee would have received wages, excluding tips, of $515 had the employee been paid at the Federal minimum wage rate. Thus, $100 of the employee's tips were treated as employer-provided wages under the "minimum wage" credit. Consequently, only $200 of the employee's tips for January is taken into account in computing this income tax credit.

To prevent "double dipping," no business expense deduction is allowed for any amount taken into account in determining this credit against income taxes. An establishment can elect not to apply this credit and instead claim an income tax deduction for the FICA payments (.40).

This credit against income taxes is effective for the employer's share of FICA taxes on tips received by employees from customers in connection with the provision of food or beverages for consumption on the premises of an establishment where the tipping of employees is customary, regardless of when the tipped employee performed the services that generated the employer's credit. The credit also applies to the employer's FICA taxes paid on tip income received by a delivery person for the delivery of food or beverages for consumption off the premises of the restaurant (.50). The credit is reported on Form 8846, "Credit for Employer Social Security and Medicare Taxes Paid on Certain Employee Tips."

This credit is generated not only when tip income is properly reported by the tipped employee, but also when the employer is required to pay its share of FICA taxes on unreported tip income after the IRS issues a notice and demand for such taxes to the employer.

.10 CCH Payroll Management Guide, ¶ 2971.

.20 Code Sec. 45B;.

.20 Fair Labor Standards Act Sec 6(m); See also, CCH Payroll Management Guide ¶ 1360 and ¶ 2857.

.30 Instructions to Form 8846, Credit for Employer Social Security and Medicare Taxes Paid on Certain Employee Tips.

.40 Code Sec. 45B(d).

.50 P.L. 104-188, Act Sec. 1112.

¶ 25,860 Penalties for failure to withhold or pay tax. For each whole or part month that an Form 941 return is not filed when required (disregarding any extensions of the filing deadline), there is a penalty of 5 percent of the unpaid tax due with that return (.10). The maximum penalty is 25 percent. Also, for each whole or part month the tax is paid late (disregarding any extensions of the payment deadline), a penalty of 0.5 percent of the amount of tax generally applies. The maximum for this penalty is also 25 percent. The penalties will not be charged if there is an acceptable reason for failing to file or pay. Also, penalties may apply if the employer fails to make timely deposits of employment taxes.

.10 IRS Publication 15, Circular E, Employer's Tax Guide.

¶25,861 Avoiding audits on tip issues. The IRS has indicated that it will conduct an employment tax examination of a bar or restaurant otherwise selected for an income tax examination and all of their tipped employees if the establishment will not enter into a Tip Rate Determination Agreement (TRDA) or a Tip Rate Alternative Commitment (TRAC) (.10).

The foundation for the IRS tip examination is the "McQuatters formula," which is a formula that the IRS uses to determine the unreported tips of the tipped employees. According to the IRS, the McQuatters formula is a statistically valid computation of unreported tips based on a 28-day sample of the restaurant's charge tip receipts. First, the charge tip rate is established. Through interviews of restaurant management and tipped employees, the cash tip rate is established, typically 0.5 percent to 2 percent less than the charge tip rate.

A detailed IRS employment tax examination can be avoided when a bar or restaurant enters into a Tip Rate Determination Agreement or a Tip Rate Alternative Commitment.

Planning Note

The IRS has announced that it is simplifying its voluntary tip income compliance agreements and expanding them to all industries where tipping is customary (.20). Also, the IRS will now allow employers in the food and beverage industry to design their own agreements. Moreover, the IRS has now developed a TRDA and a TRAC for other industries where tipping is customary. Finally, the IRS announced that, effective October 1, 2000, when there are flagrant violations of the tip reporting rules, the IRS will resume tip examinations and assessments for FICA taxes on employers only, without first determining the tip income of individual employees. The IRS has simplified and shortened the TRDA and TRAC for the food and beverage industry and the TRAC for the cosmetology and barber industry. In addition, the latter agreement will now allow business owners with booth renters or independent contractors to participate. In another new development, the IRS has now created a TRDA and a TRAC for other industries where tipping is customary. Employers that can participate include taxicab and limousine companies, airport skycap companies and car wash operations.

Tip Rate Determination Agreement

Under a "Tip Rate Determination Agreement," an accurate tip rate is determined by the establishment, validated by the IRS, and used in subsequent periods by the tipped employees of the establishment. The employer's FICA tax liability for underreported tips of tipped employees who participate in the agreement may be limited to the FICA tax on underreported tips discovered during the six-month period in which the proper tip rate is established. Also, participating employees' audit exposure on a tip income issue is limited.

A six-month calendar period is used to establish the tip rate(s) used in the agreement. The tip rates will be determined, based on information available to the employer, historical information provided by the District, and generally accepted accounting principles using the McQuatters formula. In order for the establishment to participate in the program, 75 percent of the tipped employees must sign a "Tipped Employee Participation Agreement (TEPA)" with the restaurant owner.

To participate in the program, the employees must be current in filing and payment of tax on their individual income tax returns, continue to keep records of tips received and report at least the tip rate determined per the agreement. Employees are also required to maintain tip records, income tax returns and related information for at least four years after the later of: (1) the payment due date of applicable income and FICA tax for the return period to which the records relate; or (2) the date those taxes were paid.

The IRS will not examine a participating employee's tip income from the employer for the year at issue or for any subsequent year in which he or she is employed by this employer and receives tip income. However, the IRS may examine the tip records of a participating employee for compliance with this agreement.

A nonparticipating employee or an employee who revokes his or her TEPA may be subject to the full range of compliance and enforcement procedures of the IRS.

The participating employer is sent a Notice and Demand Letter for the employer's share of FICA tax on the unreported tips determined for the six-month period used to establish the tip rate(s). If a TRDA is not in effect, the IRS could base the Notice and Demand for the employer's share of FICA taxes on underreported tips earned earlier in time. Also, the IRS may still assert liability against the employer for the employer's share of FICA tax on unreported tip income of nonparticipating employees if such asserted liability is based upon the final results of an audit of a nonparticipating employee.

The employer must agree to encourage all of its tipped employees to participate in the program, establish tip rates with the IRS, make withholding based on tips reported, and include reported tips on Form W-2. Also, unless the employer reports tip rates on subsequent years' Forms 8027, "Employer's Annual Information Return of Tip Income and Allocated Tips" at or above the tip rates established for the Tip Rate Determination Agreement, the employer will have to provide the IRS with the name, social security number, wages, shifts, hours and/or sales, job categories, reported tips, charged tips paid out, and other information for each nonparticipating employee so that the IRS can determine the nonparticipating employees' tip rate.

Tip Rate Alternative Commitment for Food Industry

The TRDA, which was developed unilaterally by the IRS, proved to be unpopular with the food and beverage industry. The TRDA proved disadvantageous because it required tips to be reported at a predetermined rate and required the approval of the tipped employees. Consequently, the IRS began meeting with representatives of large restaurant chains in order to hammer out a new tip reporting agreement. The Tip Reporting Alternative Commitment (TRAC) agreement is the result of those discussions (.30). It has the advantage of not forcing tipped employees to report tips at a predetermined rate and allowing tipped employees to modify incorrect reports of tips earned.

Where a TRAC is in effect, the IRS will agree to issue a Section 3121(q) notice and demand for the employer's share of FICA taxes based solely on amounts reflected on Form 4137 or Form 885-T in the usual case. Unlike a TRDA, a TRAC agreement does not require employees to report a specific amount of tips, but instead focuses on implementing procedures that will encourage accurate reporting.

TRAC embodies three principal commitments on the part of the employer: employee education, employer reporting to the IRS, and employee tip reporting procedures. First, the employer agrees to maintain a quarterly educational program that trains newly hired employees and periodically updates existing employees as to their reporting obligations with respect to tips. Second, the employer agrees to comply with all Federal tax requirements regarding the filing of returns, payment and deposit of taxes, and maintenance of records. Third, the employer agrees to establish procedures to ensure accurate tip reporting by its employees.

Employee education. The employer must institute and maintain for each calendar quarter an educational program which trains newly hired employees and periodically updates existing employees as to their reporting obligations with respect to tip income received as either cash tips or charged tips. This educational program must emphasize that, in addition to charged tips attributable to employees, all cash tips paid to and retained by the employees must be reported to their employing establishment.

As part of this program, the employer must explain to its employees their obligation to maintain for their records the information required in daily tip record of Form 4070A. This educational program also should advise all participants of the benefits of proper tip reporting (e.g., Social Security wage credit history, increased retirement plan contributions, and creation of adequate records of tip income).

Requirements regarding returns, taxes, and records. Each calendar quarter, the employer must comply with the requirements for filing Form 941, "Employer's Quarterly Federal Tax Return." Form 941 must include all charged and cash tips reported by the employees to the employer.

For each establishment that is a "large food or beverage establishment," the employer must comply with the requirements for filing Form 8027, "Employer's Annual Information Return of Tip Income and Allocated Tips," send an additional copy of each Form 8027 to the IRS, and follow the proper tip allocation procedures.

The employer (or employing establishment) must comply with the requirements for filing an Form W-2 for every employee and include all reported charged and cash tips on the employees' Forms W-2, including tips verified or corrected by the employee. The employer must comply with the requirements for filing all other required federal tax returns, for paying the amount of any undisputed federal tax that is due, and for depositing federal taxes.

Each establishment must maintain records of gross receipts, subject to food or beverage tipping, and charge receipts showing charged tips for four years after the April 15 following the calendar year to which the records relate.

Upon request by the IRS, the employer will make the following quarterly totals available, by establishment, for statistical samplings of its establishments: (a) gross receipts subject to food or beverage tipping, (b) charge receipts showing charged tips, (c) total charged tips, and (d) total tips reported.

Tip reporting procedures. Each establishment must establish a procedure under which a written statement is prepared for tipped employees and processed on a regular basis (no less frequently than monthly), reflecting all charged tips for sales attributable to each directly tipped employee. The establishment must implement reasonable procedures under which each directly tipped employee is given the opportunity to verify or correct any statement of proposed attribution of charged tips, in order to reflect tip outs, tip sharing, tip pooling, and other adjustments. For example, the establishment would satisfy this paragraph if it provided a written statement that contained the following information: employee's charged sales, employee's total charged tips, and the ratio, as a percentage, of charged tips to charged sales.

The establishment must also adopt a reasonable method for reporting of charged tips received by indirectly tipped employees. For example, the employee may report to the establishment the amount and with whom tips were shared. Alternatively, the directly tipped employee may provide to the establishment a copy of Form 4070A indicating the shared tips. Based on the preceding information, the establishment could furnish the indirectly tipped employee with a written statement, which that employee would verify or correct in a manner similar to the procedure for directly tipped employees.

The employing establishment's procedures must enable employees to meet their reporting requirements. The employer may satisfy this requirement in most cases if it remits charged tips to the employees through the payroll system under a method that ensures reporting of tips by employees and is consistent with employment tax rules.

Each establishment must set up a procedure under which a written statement is prepared and processed on a regular basis (no less frequently than monthly), reflecting all cash tips for sales attributable to each directly tipped employee. For example, if the employee signs for charged tips on a daily basis, the employee may record the amount of cash tips received at the same time.

Revocation. The employer has the ability to prospectively revoke the TRAC agreement in writing. The IRS can prospectively revoke a TRAC agreement if the employer fails to meet its TRAC requirements pertaining to filing returns, paying and depositing taxes, maintaining records, and making the records available. It will also prospectively revoke the agreement if employees collectively and substantially underreport tip income for at least two continuous calendar quarters, even though the employer has substantially complied with employee tip reporting procedures. The IRS can also retroactively revoke a TRAC agreement if the employer fails to adequately educate tipped employees about their reporting responsibilities or to establish proper tip reporting procedures.

The IRS may terminate the TRAC agreement at any time following a significant statutory change in the FICA taxation of tips and may prospectively terminate the Tip Rate Determination Education Program or TRAC agreements after May 31, 2005.

Employer designed agreements. In addition to TRDA and TRAC, the IRS will now permit employers in the food and beverage industry to design their own program through an Employer's Tip Reporting Alternative Commitment (EmTRAC) (.40). This is in lieu of the IRS developed TRAC. EmTRAC will include the same employer commitments and protections as afforded under the TRAC agreement.

Tip Rate Alternative Commitment for Other Industries

The IRS has begun developing and offering TRACs to other industry. For example, it has developed TRACs for the hairstyling industry and gaming industry (.50).

The IRS has simplified and shortened the TRDA and TRAC for the food and beverage industry and the TRAC for the cosmetology and barber industry (.60). In addition, the latter agreement will now allow business owners with booth renters or independent contractors to participate. In another new development, the IRS has now created a TRDA and a TRAC for other industries where tipping is customary. Employers that can participate include taxicab and limousine companies, airport skycap companies and car wash operations.

.10 Audit Technique Guide For Bars And Restaurants, November 2002,, CCH IRS POSITIONS, ¶ 201,900.

.20 CCH IRS News Release 2000-26; Announcement 2000-19, I.R.B. 2000-19, 973; Announcement 2000-20, I.R.B. 2000-19, 977; Announcement 2002-21, I.R.B. 2000-19, 983; Announcement 2000-22, I.R.B. 2000-19, 987; Announcement 2000-23, I.R.B. 2000-19, 992.

.30 IRS Market Segment Understanding Guidelines With the Food Service Industry–Tip Reporting Alternative Commitment, 12-12-00, CCH IRS Positions ¶ 230,001.

.40 IRS News Release 2000-26, 4-26-00

.50 IRS Market Segment Understanding Program: Hairstyling Industry–Tip Reporting Alternative Commitment, 10-25-99, CCH IRS Positions Reports ¶ 230,200; IRS Market Segment Understanding Program: Gaming Industry–Tip Reporting Alternative Commitment, July 1, 1997, CCH IRS Positions Reports ¶ 230,100.

.60 CCH IRS News Release 2000-26; Announcement 2000-19, I.R.B. 2000-19, 973; Announcement 2000-20, I.R.B. 2000-19, 977; Announcement 2002-21, I.R.B. 2000-19, 983; Announcement 2000-22, I.R.B. 2000-19, 987; Announcement 2000-23, I.R.B. 2000-19, 992.